BIRD
HABITATS
IN IRELAND

*This book is dedicated to the memory of
Clive D. Hutchinson (1949–1998),
ornithologist, mentor and friend.*

Great Cormorants roosting (Richie Lort).

BIRD
HABITATS
IN IRELAND

EDITORS

RICHARD NAIRN & JOHN O'HALLORAN

The Collins Press

First published in Ireland in 2012 by
The Collins Press
West Link Park
Doughcloyne
Wilton
Cork

British Library Cataloguing in Publication Data

Bird habitats of Ireland.
1. Birds—Habitat—Ireland. 2. Birds—Ireland.
I. Nairn, Richard, 1952– II. O'Halloran, J. (John)
598'.09415-dc23

ISBN-13: 9781848891388

Design and typesetting by Fairways Design
Typeset in Minion Pro

Printed in Slovenia by Almarose d.o.o.

This publication has received support from
An Chomhairle Oidhreachta/the Heritage Council.

Photo on p. i: Eurasian Curlew with lugworm (Karl Partridge)

Supported by BirdWatch Ireland, British Trust for Ornithology,
Royal Society for the Protection of Birds and University College Cork.

Contents

Contributing Authors   vii

Acknowledgements   xi

A note on bird names   xii

Foreword   xiii

1.   Introduction   1

2.   Habitat Classification and Birds   6

3.   Bird Habitats: structure and complexity   14

4.   Rivers and Canals   24

5.   Lakes, Reservoirs and Turloughs   44

6.   Wet Grasslands, Marshes and Callows   60

7.   Lowland Bogs, Fens and Reedswamps   73

8.   Upland Heath and Blanket Bog   90

9.   Woodlands, Forest and Scrub   105

10. Lowland Farmland   124

11. Sea Cliffs, Islands and Rocky Coasts   138

12. Beaches and Dunes   152

13. Estuaries and Coastal Lagoons   166

14. Open Sea   181

15. Urban Habitats   196

16. Habitat Management for Birds   213

17. Climate Change, Habitats and Birds   233

18. Bird Habitats – A synthesis and future perspectives   247

Appendix 1: Names of Irish Birds   269

Appendix 2: Names of other species of animals and plants   275

Bibliography   278

Index   300

Razorbill with sand eels (John Fox).

Contributing Authors

Dr Lorraine Benson holds a PhD in European Regional Policy from the European University Institute in Florence, Italy and a Masters in Applied Environmental Science from University College Dublin (2009). Her MSc thesis was on the use of inland feeding sites by Brent Geese in Dublin. She is currently working for the Irish government in Brussels.

Dr Fintan Bracken is an environmental consultant with particular expertise in birds. His research interests include biodiversity and the effects of land-use change on the diversity of birds and butterflies. He has written several papers on bird diversity of peatland and farmland habitats. Fintan's research for this chapter was funded by the Environmental Protection Agency through the project 'BOGLAND: Protocol for Sustainable Peatland Management in Ireland' (see Renou-Wilson *et al.* (2010) for more details).

Dr Alex Copland is a Senior Conservation Officer with BirdWatch Ireland, specialising in farmland related projects. He has managed research and conservation projects on key species, including Corncrakes, breeding waders and Barn Owls, and studied impacts of agricultural policies and practices on bird populations on Irish farmland. He has published several papers on this work, presented at conferences in Ireland and internationally and is a collaborating researcher with UCC and UCD.

Dr Olivia Crowe is a Conservation Officer with BirdWatch Ireland with experience in the design and analysis of data from large national surveys of wild birds. She currently manages a range of long-term monitoring projects including the Irish Wetland Bird Survey, the Countryside Bird Survey and the Garden Bird Survey. Olivia has written extensively on Irish birds and published a major analysis of wintering waterbirds (*Irelands Wetlands and their Waterbirds* 2005).

Dr Sinéad Cummins is an environmental scientist working on the conservation team at BirdWatch Ireland for several years. With a primary focus on upland birds, her involvement includes surveys of breeding European Golden Plover, Ring Ouzel and Chough and coordination of the national Red Grouse Survey. Relevant publications include an Irish Wildlife Manual on Red Grouse and papers on Stonechat breeding ecology. More recently she has been coordinating the collection of baseline waterbird data for coastal Special Protection Areas.

Dr Alison Donnelly is currently a Research Lecturer in the Centre for the Environment at Trinity College Dublin where she leads the phenology research group. Her main research interests are in determining the impact of climate warming on the timing of life-cycle events of tree, insect and bird species in Ireland. In addition, she is investigating the potential for climate warming to result in a mismatch in the timing between interdependent species, which may negatively impact on biodiversity.

Roger Goodwillie is a botanist and birdwatcher with a special interest in turloughs. He worked for An Foras Forbartha (the Planning Institute which evolved into the EPA) before becoming an independent consultant in 1988. He was instrumental in setting up the Lavistown Study Centre in Kilkenny where he now lives. He has contributed to several books about wildlife, the most recent being the *Wetlands of Ireland* (Otte 2003).

Dr Sandra Irwin graduated with a PhD in aquaculture from UCC in 1998. Since then she has worked as a postdoctoral researcher on a variety of national and EU-funded projects in both Scotland and Ireland. Since her first research publication on swans in 1995, Sandra has more than 20 publications in international peer-reviewed journals. Sandra is programme manager on the multidisciplinary PLANFORBIO research programme, and also manages a number of other forest biodiversity research projects at UCC.

Dr Mark Jessopp is a marine ecologist at the Coastal and Marine Research Centre, and adjunct lecturer at University College Cork. He has worked on a variety of marine species ranging from plankton to top predators, with experience working on seabirds in both Ireland and the Antarctic. His current research focuses on the role of seabirds in the marine environment, and their interactions with fisheries through a combination of diet, telemetry and population-monitoring studies. He is also involved in research investigating the effects of large-scale offshore windfarm development on seabird populations.

Dr Tom Kelly is a Lecturer in Zoology at the School of Biology, Earth and Environmental Sciences, University College Cork where he teaches various aspects of Evolution, Epidemiology, Immunology, Animal Behaviour and Population Dynamics. He has published numerous papers in the international peer-reviewed literature as well as book chapters and reports. His main research areas are wildlife hazards to aviation, forest ecology (including birds and arthropods), the biology of gulls, epidemiology of tick- and mosquito-borne diseases to wildlife and man, and the origin of the avifauna of Ireland.

Alan Lauder is the Chief Executive and former Head of Conservation of BirdWatch Ireland. He previously led the management of the RSPB's reserves in the west and south of Scotland, prior to that heading up the BTO in Scotland. He has a wide range of ornithological interests. In particular, he has worked extensively on waterbirds, seabirds, wetland and grassland habitats, publishing work on breeding wildfowl, Great Cormorants and grey geese and advising on habitat management at sites across Europe.

John Lusby is Raptor Conservation Officer with BirdWatch Ireland. He has experience surveying and monitoring a range of Irish raptor species, and has focused much attention on improving the conservation of these species. One of his primary research interests is Barn Owl and Common Kestrel ecology, in particular predator–prey interactions, the effects of toxins and the impact of introduced small mammals on both species. He has established several raptor research and monitoring projects and has employed techniques such as radio telemetry, dietary analysis, nest camera technology and toxicology analysis.

Clive Mellon is an environmental consultant with a particular interest in birds and Lepidoptera. He has published papers in both ornithological and entomological journals such as *Irish Birds* and *Atropos*. Prior to becoming a consultant in 2004, he was the Conservation Manager of the RSPB in Northern Ireland where he was responsible for managing conservation projects for priority bird species. He holds a degree in law and continues to work on environmental legislation and policy issues.

Dr Allan Mee is currently managing the Irish White-tailed Sea Eagle reintroduction programme in Co. Kerry for the Golden Eagle Trust. He has been working on birds for over 25 years including survey and research work for RSPB and Scottish Natural Heritage on upland birds such as Golden Eagle and Eurasian Dotterel in the Scottish Highlands. He has led expeditions to Bolivia, Peru and Seychelles to survey and study threatened bird species. He carried out a postdoctoral fellowship on the endangered California Condor in California and Arizona for the Zoological Society of San Diego. He is currently chairman of the Irish Raptor Study Group.

Oscar Merne has been involved professionally in bird research and conservation for over 45 years, with 35 years in the Bird Research Unit of the National Parks and Wildlife Service, and, since retirement, as an environmental consultant. He has specialised in colonial breeding seabirds and migratory wetland birds. He has published over 250 scientific papers and other articles and has written and contributed to several books. He was the first warden of the Wexford Wildfowl Reserve.

Richard Nairn is an environmental scientist and writer. He was Director of the Irish Wildbird Conservancy (now BirdWatch Ireland) during the 1980s and currently heads Natura Environmental Consultants. He is a Chartered Environmentalist and Fellow of the Institute of Ecology and Environmental Management. He has published extensively on Irish birds and their habitats and he has written two books, *Wild Wicklow* (1998) and *Ireland's Coastline* (2005). He is one of the two joint editors of this book.

Dr Stephen Newton coordinates BirdWatch Ireland's research and monitoring programme on seabirds. This includes the management of long-term projects on Roseate Terns, Little Terns, cliff-nesting seabirds and petrel and shearwater colonies of islands in Dublin, Kerry, Mayo and Donegal. He coordinated the Irish input to the Seabird 2000 survey and was an editor of the resulting book: *Seabird Populations of Britain and Ireland* (2004). He has also led the joint NPWS-BWI Chough project for the last 10 years which resulted in the designation of 14 Chough SPAs. Stephen edited the journal *Irish Birds* from 2001 to 2009.

Éanna Ní Lamhna is an independent environmentalist. She was formerly president of An Taisce, the Irish National Trust, and is a regular broadcaster on radio and television. A botanist by training, she was responsible for Ireland's first Biological Records Centre in the 1980s. She has published several popular books on wildlife including *Wild Dublin* (2008). She is a lecturer on sustainability in the Dublin Institute of Technology.

Peadar O'Connell is the Species Policy Officer with BirdWatch Ireland. He wrote and compiled BirdWatch Ireland's Group Action Plans for Ireland's Birds in consultation with relevant stakeholders and experts. He has also worked on various aspects of environmental policy within the BirdWatch Ireland policy team. Prior to this, he worked on the Breeding Wader Management project on the Shannon Callows and on the national badger survey of Northern Ireland.

Professor John O'Halloran is Professor of Zoology and Ecology at University College Cork where he is Head of the School of Biological, Earth and Environmental Sciences. He has published over 180 research papers and articles and was awarded a Doctorate of Science for his published works by the NUI in 2009. He was former Editor of *Bird Study*, a Board Member of BirdWatch Ireland, Vice-President of British Trust for Ornithology and Council member of European Ornithologists' Union. John's main interests are in aquatic birds, forest ecology and ecotoxicology: the pathways of pollutants through ecosystems. He is one of the two joint editors of this book.

Dr Karl Partridge is an environmental scientist and has been an independent ecological consultant since 1991. He was formerly Regional Officer and Research Biologist with the RSPB in Northern Ireland. His key experience is in ornithology and environmental impact assessment but he has also wide experience of marine resource development, having worked in the field of aquaculture and fisheries for a number of years, both in Ireland and abroad. He acted as Picture Editor for this book.

Dr James Robinson is the Director of the RSPB in Northern Ireland. He was Conservation Manager for the RSPB in Northern Ireland and, before that, Head of Wetland Biodiversity at the Wildfowl and Wetlands Trust. He graduated with a PhD in seabird ecology at the University of Durham in 1999 and has produced over 50 publications on ecology and nature conservation. He is a member of the Irish Brent Goose Study Group.

Patrick Smiddy is an independent naturalist and editor of the journal *Irish Birds*. He was formerly a Conservation Ranger with the National Parks and Wildlife Service. His main bird interests include river birds, involving especially a long-term study of the Dipper, and the birds of estuaries and other wetlands. He has published his work in a wide range of scientific journals, and was awarded an Honorary Master of Science degree by the National University of Ireland in September 2000.

Dr Oisin Sweeney studied forest bird diversity for his doctorate at UCC where he was a member of the PLANFORBIO research team. He holds an honours degree in Zoology from the University of Glasgow and a Master's from the University of Pretoria, South Africa. Following this he worked for a UK-based NGO in Tanzania where he was part of a team carrying out rapid biodiversity surveys of forest patches. Oisín then worked for 15 months in Quercus, Queen's University Belfast, where he held the position of Research Technician.

Dr Mark Wilson is a postdoctoral bird researcher at UCC working on the PLANFORBIO research programme. He has broad interests in animal behaviour, bird biology, forest ecology and conservation. He previously worked for the Royal Society for the Protection of Birds as a researcher in Scotland. He is currently continuing his work on both forest biodiversity and habitat requirements of Hen Harriers. Mark has extensive experience and expertise in bird surveying and remote observation/tracking, as well as in experimental design, GIS and statistical analysis. He teaches on a wide variety of under-graduate and postgraduate courses.

Acknowledgements

The last few decades have brought a huge leap forward in Irish ornithology with the publishing of much research work and the realisation of many national surveys. From this body of knowledge we felt that it should be possible to examine the ecology of the bird species and communities one would find in each of the main habitat types. For example, we know that Meadow Pipit is virtually ubiquitous on blanket bogs and that Red Grouse only occurs where there is sufficient heather cover. But could this approach be applied to other species and habitats? If it could be done for plants, it should also be possible for birds, which are among the best studied of animal groups. This was the genesis of a book, conceived in 2009, but with a long incubation period.

Few scientific books are the work of a single author. Instead, science progresses by the combined efforts of many workers building on the research of those who have published their results in the past. This book is no exception. Firstly it would not have been possible without the dedicated efforts of a team of talented ornithologists. Most of them were talked into writing their chapters by a combination of flattery and persuasion. We consider the authors of the main chapters to be the leading experts on their topics in Ireland today and we acknowledge their efforts in completing this collaborative work.

We must also pay tribute to all those ornithologists, both living and dead, who have committed their work to print. From William Thompson in the nineteenth century, to the top bird researchers of today, each paper and book has contributed one more piece in the jigsaw of our combined knowledge of bird ecology. From this long list, we would single out one name above the rest. The late Clive D. Hutchinson, one of the most productive of modern Irish ornithologists, was the founder, in 1977, of the journal *Irish Birds*. Now in its ninth volume, this annual periodical has been the vehicle for a wealth of information and facts on the birds of Ireland.

Many of the data presented in the chapters that follow were collected by both volunteers and professional researchers. We acknowledge both, but wish to recognise the significant contributions made by volunteer birdwatchers, who have collected data in a very professional manner. Without their efforts the gaps in our knowledge would be many. From the outset, we were clear that the book would cover the whole island of Ireland as a biogeographic unit, including both the North and the Republic. In this regard, we thank Karl Partridge for his sound advice in selecting suitable authors on both sides of the border.

We are extremely grateful to several colleagues, with whom we discussed the overall concept and how it might be achieved. They are David Cabot, Rob Fuller, Ian Herbert, Oscar Merne, Stephen Newton and Pat Smiddy. Each of these scientists gave generously of their time and advice. Alan Lauder, Chief Executive of BirdWatch Ireland, James Robinson, Director of the RSPB in Northern Ireland, and Andy Clements, Director of the BTO, gave the book their enthusiastic support, which opened the way for their colleagues to contribute from their extensive knowledge and data.

We would like to acknowledge those who have peer-reviewed each of the chapters and suggested improvements. They are Malcolm Ausden, Colin Barton, Niall Burton, Don Cotton, Olivia Crowe, Anita Donaghy, Peter Ferns, Julie Fossitt, Rob Fuller, Esa Lehikoinen, Clive Mellon, James Pearce-Higgins, Ken Perry, Claire Pollock, John Quinn, Robert Scott, Ralph Sheppard, Pat Smiddy, Juliet Vickery and Derek Yalden.

We were fortunate to have the professional skills of Shark Design and the personal interest and commitment of its director, Mark Hackett. We thank Glen McArdle of Fairways Design for the design and layout of the pages.

In choosing pictures for this book, we were looking for a different approach to the usual close-cropped portraits of birds. We wanted to show the birds *in* their habitats with more of a context for each species. Karl Partridge again lent his support by compiling a picture list and by checking the quality of pictures submitted for the book. We were very fortunate to have a large number of high-quality photographs provided courtesy of Richard T. Mills, John Fox, Richie Lort, John Coveney, Karl Partridge, Darío Fernández-Bellon, Andrew Kelly, John Lusby, Conor Nolan and Mark Carmody. The photographers are acknowledged within the caption to each picture. Andrew Speer of Natura prepared the maps. Figure 3.1 was expertly drawn by Holly Pereira.

The launch of this book was marked by a symposium hosted by the Royal Dublin Society. For their prestigious facilities we thank the Society and its librarian Gerard Whelan. Organisation of the symposium was greatly assisted by Niall Hatch (BirdWatch Ireland), James Robinson (RSPB) and Shane Wolsey (BTO).

We are grateful to David Cabot who wrote a foreword for the book in his own inimitable style. Pat Smiddy helped in numerous ways, not least by reading and editing the Bibliography and advising on bird names.

Finally, we would like to thank our families and especially our long-suffering partners, Wendy Nairn and Deirdre Murray, who put up with numerous distractions from the more important things in life.

Richard Nairn and John O'Halloran
October 2011

A note on bird names

The use of scientific names for bird species is essential as one species may have several different vernacular (common) names. To avoid repetition in the text, we have given all the scientific names, with their appropriate common names, in Appendix 1 at the end of the book. The common names, as used in the text, generally follow those of the latest version of the British Ornithologists' Union (the primary English language bird taxonomy authority within Europe). However, there are some exceptions. In a number of cases, where only one member of a species group has occurred in Ireland, then a simpler name is preferred. There are a few cases (for example, Bewick's Swan, Red Grouse, Goosander, Hen Harrier and Common Guillemot) where the BOU names (Tundra Swan, Willow Ptarmigan, Common Merganser, Northern Harrier and Common Murre) would lead to confusion for both ornithologists and the general reader. For these we have used the familiar common names that are in general use in Ireland. However, for completeness, the BOU common names are also given in Appendix 1.

Foreword

David Cabot

Every now and then a seminal book appears about Irish natural history. First out of the trap was *Topographia Hiberniae (1185)* by Giraldus Cambrensis, a grandson of Henry I. His book stretches the credulity of the scientist but was an intriguing account of Ireland in Norman days. Part bestiary and part description of Ireland's natural history, it opened the account of Ireland's natural resources. Robert Lloyd Praeger concluded that 'Cambrensis was a careful recorder but credulous; and from his statements it often requires care and ingenuity to extract the truth.' Next off the block was Gerard Boate's *Ireland's Naturall History* (1652), the first regional natural history in the English language written essentially for adventurers and planters eager to secure a slice of the Irish landscape. There was a habitat approach to the landscape with Boate discussing different types of bogs, woodlands, coastal areas, lakes and rivers as well as mountains and uplands. He provided the first relationship between habitats and their flora and fauna, making specific comments about the various birds he observed in Ireland.

Birds then became the darlings of the natural historians, as the Victorians shot and plundered their way through them. With no binoculars or telescopes, this was the only way of getting close enough for identification. Birds took centre stage during the nineteenth century, championed particularly by the middle class Protestants, especially in Northern Ireland. Much of the information garnered by this happy band of hunters, watchers and collectors percolated into the four volumes of *The Natural History of Ireland* (1850) by William Thompson. Thompson took a much broader approach than just parroting lists of species, noting occurrences, locations, dates and so on. He understood, as well as making it clear, the strong relationship between birds and their habitats. This more enlightened vision diminished somewhat in *The Birds of Ireland* (1900) by Ussher and Warren and declined further in *The Birds of Ireland* (1954) by Kennedy, Ruttledge and Scroope, assisted by Humphreys. This criticism does not detract from the acuteness of these books, which arranged birds in their taxonomic order with comments on numbers, dates and distribution. Clive Hutchinson in his *Birds in Ireland* (1989) rekindled the relationships between birds and their habitats and saw value in relating habitats to the distribution and abundance of birds.

The remarkable feature of this earlier literature was that it was mainly generated by non-scientists or amateurs in accordance with the noble tradition long established in Britain, less so in Ireland. But today the balance has been tipped firmly in favour of the professional scientist who now dominates the literature. And so here we are now with this magnificent book. One has to gasp in awe of how quickly a diverse corpus of highly qualified scientists has emerged in the past 30 or so years, as if they were field mushrooms sprouting overnight, after some wetness and warmth. We are now, thankfully, up to speed with other European countries. Moreover the context in which we work is particularly interesting – a small island, perched on the jaws of western Europe, special wetlands of which some are rare within Europe, a magnificent coastline populated by many sea birds, a few endemic species and others of European scarcity, set in a landscape lacking the range and breadth of habitats found elsewhere in Europe.

Within this framework 25 skilled authors have shared their considerable knowledge on the major habitat types of Ireland, which range from rivers and canals through bogland and mountain to the open sea and urban areas. Each habitat, based on a standard classification adopted for Ireland, is described and discussed by these well-qualified ornithologists. Then follow accounts of birds that depend, in many different ways, upon each specific habitat. The amount of qualitative and quantitative information presented is stunning when compared with what was available only a few years ago. And therein lies some of the strength of this book – a virtual compendium of basic research on birds, related to their habitats, with an impressive common bibliography. Moreover, each chapter has been peer-reviewed, ensuring the highest scientific standards.

The book provides an unrivalled Irish text on the importance of our habitats for various bird species and groups of species, whether breeding or wintering. The logical next step forward would be a book about the management of habitats for the benefit of birds, especially those of European significance. If sufficient management case studies were available – and there already exist some fine success stories – then we would have moved from the descriptive analysis towards securing our cherished conservation objectives, which embody looking after habitats – their management, creation and modification – which in turn, will provide the continuance of our bird species.

1. Introduction

Richard Nairn and John O'Halloran

William Thompson (1805–1852) was one of the first Irish ornithologists to write about the links between birds and their habitats.

One of Ireland's earliest ornithologists, William Thompson, wrote in the preface to his *Natural History of Ireland* (1850): *The whole economy of the species will often be fully illustrated from original observation.*

The word *economy* was used here because, in the mid-nineteenth century, the science of ecology was unknown. Taxonomy was the leading branch of zoology as early scientists grappled with the complex interrelationships between species, genera and families of animals. Darwin was still almost a decade away from publishing his seminal work *On the Origin of Species* (1859).

Nevertheless, Thompson well understood the importance of habitat and diet in determining the bird fauna of an island like Ireland. He wrote:

The plants which appear on particular soils attract such land birds as feed on their seeds. The submarine rocks and grounds on which sea-weeds grow plentifully so as to afford shelter to the minute fishes, and the molluscus and crustaceous animals on which the wading and swimming birds feed, tempt them in greater number to the neighbouring shores. The oozy, the sandy, the gravelly, the stony, the rocky beach has each its favourite species as has every peculiar natural or artificial feature of a country from the level of the sea to the most lofty mountain summit.

Thompson was making the connection between birds and their habitats and then linking the species to their particular type of food, which itself is dependent on physical components of the habitat such as sediment type, wetness and altitude. Today, the sciences of ornithology and ecology have merged and most birdwatchers, whether amateur or professional, understand that habitat type is a key factor in defining the species of birds found in any one place.

Even so, from Thompson (1850) onwards, most books on Ireland's birds (Ussher and Warren 1900; Kennedy *et al.* 1954; Ruttledge 1966; Hutchinson 1989; Gibbons *et al.* 1993; Crowe 2005a) have focused on species, numbers, status and distribution while the ecology of the birds is sometimes given little space. This book takes a different tack. Instead of asking the questions what, where, how many, it tries to address the more complex question of why?

Most modern bird books are organised in a taxonomic style, with systematic accounts of each

Research on the Corncrake has shown the importance of early vegetation cover (Richard T. Mills).

Northern Lapwing (foreground) and European Golden Plover (centre) roosting on mudflats in an estuary (Richard T. Mills).

species or groups of species such as raptors, seabirds or wildfowl. In contrast, this book is organised by habitat type. Each chapter gives a brief account of what the habitat, or group of habitats, comprises before going on to describe the bird species and communities that are found there. In some cases, where the research is available, the reasons why these habitats are important for species or communities of birds are explored. For example, we know that the numbers and distribution of the Dipper are related to the structure and quality of its river habitat. Research on the Corncrake has shown the importance of the early vegetation cover in wet meadows on arrival in Ireland and the key requirement of long grass for the survival of the chicks. For estuarine bird communities, the type of sediment, degree of exposure and hence the invertebrate fauna are all key determinants.

Charles Elton was one of the pioneers of animal ecology. In his classic book *The Pattern of Animal Communities* (1966), he explained that patterns in nature are not regular, like the repeated designs on wallpaper. 'In natural ecological systems', he says, 'it is unusual for exact regularity to occur. We find the repetition of component parts but not a replication of identical ones, nor at exact intervals. Each is a little or even a good deal different from the rest'.

This inherent variability is evident in the habitats themselves – no two woodlands have exactly the same mix of soil types, aspect, annual rainfall or tree species. This variability is also reflected in the bird communities that occupy these habitats. In native woodlands there are many ecological niches that are occupied by particular species. For example, dense undergrowth encourages the nesting of species like Wren that need cover while tall mature trees are critical to birds such as Chiffchaff and Song Thrush that require prominent song posts. Older trees with cavities are important for breeding of the hole-nesting species such as Blue Tit, Great Tit and Eurasian Treecreeper. Each woodland has a unique mix of these features so that, while the basic components of a woodland bird community are known, the exact balance of species can vary greatly depending on local habitat features and on management.

Each estuary around the coastline has a similar spectrum of non-breeding wildfowl and wader flocks but the actual species making up these flocks are quite variable from place to place. Certain generalist species like Eurasian Curlew are widespread, whether on rock, sand or mud, while the specialists such as Common Shelduck and Black-tailed Godwit favour the extremely sheltered, muddy shores where their main prey live.

The book *Bird Habitats in Britain* (Fuller 1982) is a standard reference work on the subject for our neighbouring island. Fuller wrote that:

Bird communities cannot be thought of as fixed assemblages of species, each occurring at a characteristic population level. Within any habitat type there may be much variation in the nature of bird communities according to geographical position, vegetation, soil fertility, altitude, extent of the habitat, etc.

Much progress has been made in the last decade in describing and classifying Ireland's habitats. The publication of *A Guide to Habitats in Ireland* (Fossitt 2000) marked a major step forward in the logical classification and survey of habitats and this scheme is now widely used in all branches of ecology in Ireland (see Chapter 2). Significant advances have been made in describing and documenting the bird communities of Ireland, both breeding and non-breeding, of many habitat types and in understanding the regional variations and differences with other parts of Europe. A significant step change in the studies of birds and their habitats has happened in the last number of decades with detailed research projects now being undertaken by universities, institutes and the voluntary bodies. Since 1985 all those involved in research on birds and their habitats have gathered to meet about every five years to summarise their research and share experiences. At each of these meetings a summary of the research was collated and published (O'Halloran *et al.* 2008). Many of these research projects have been published in specialist journals but are often inaccessible to a wider audience.

So the time is right to bring this information together in one book, which we hope will attract interest from all walks of life. Its purpose is to review all of the relevant work on bird communities of each habitat in Ireland, to compile a comprehensive bibliography and to lay the foundation for future research work on the subject. Each chapter covers a group of similar habitats and is written by acknowledged experts on the subject, using both original observation and review of the published literature. Each chapter has also been peer-reviewed by at least one independent specialist to ensure that it is as comprehensive as possible.

The selection of habitat groups for description in this book was largely a pragmatic decision. Certain habitat types are frequently intermixed in mosaics – heath and mountain bog or beach and dune or woodland and scrub. Similarly, their bird communities are often overlapping or at least share some similar species. For example, terns may nest on sand or shingle or even on artificial structures, depending on the amount of vegetation cover and the degree of disturbance present. The structure and complexity of the habitat is often more important to birds than the plant species of which it is comprised. This concept is explored more fully in Chapter 3.

The reasons why certain habitats are addressed in a particular chapter owe more to the similarities in their bird communities rather than to common origins of the habitat itself. For example, lakes, reservoirs and turloughs are all formed by different processes, both natural and artificial, but the birds are attracted to them for quite similar reasons – water depth, aquatic vegetation types and the absence of disturbance being among the more important. Certain broad categories – such as lowland farmland or urban habitats – encompass a wide spectrum of habitat types, sometimes unrelated. But again, the bird communities that they support show similarities from one region to the next.

Mountain, woodland and river habitats in the Erriff Valley, Co. Mayo (Richard Nairn).

Eurasian Curlews feed on lugworms among other prey (Karl Partridge).

Many birds do not stick rigidly to particular habitat types. Some are wide-ranging and mobile. For example, Eurasian Curlew nest in mountain bog and lowland wet grassland. In winter most of them move to the coast to feed but some flocks roam around inland farmed areas in search of food. They can even be found on urban grassland such as sports pitches and public parks – wherever they can find suitable soil invertebrate prey. Other species are found in a very limited habitat range. Garden Warbler, for example, appears to be limited in Ireland to broadleaved woodland close to lake edges (Herbert 1991; Lovatt 1997).

Garden Warbler also illustrates a particular biogeographic puzzle. In England, Wales and southern Scotland, this is a common species in woodland, conifer plantations and farm copses (Gibbons *et al.* 1993). In Ireland, however, the species is relatively rare and seems to be confined to a few suitable areas in the northern midlands where a particular type of scrubby woodland is associated with the larger lakes (Herbert 1991; Lovatt 1997). Despite the large increase in afforrestation in the twentieth century, the breeding range in Ireland does not appear to have changed much since the end of the nineteenth century (Hutchinson 1989). Why should a migrant that winters in southern Africa, returning to Ireland each spring, choose a narrow habitat niche in Ireland while it appears to be less selective in Britain?

Perhaps some of the answers lie in the history of our woodlands, which is significantly different from that of British woods. Many common woodland species in the neighbouring island – Eurasian Nuthatch and Tawny Owl for example – are missing altogether from Ireland and this is usually attributed to the wholesale clearance of native woodland from Ireland from about 1600 to the mid-nineteenth century (McCracken 1971). It may also be that the woods of Ireland were not generally managed sustainably by coppicing and wood pasture in the same ways as British woods, leading to less diverse bird communities here. The changes that have occurred in the Irish landscape in just the last century are well illustrated by the following passage written by Ussher and Warren (1900): 'Roughly speaking, half the country is under grass, one quarter under tillage and woods, and nearly one quarter is unreclaimed wilderness. It is little wonder that in 1900 the Corncrake was "fairly numerous in every part of Ireland" and "Curlews nested in numbers on the great red bogs".'

Bird conservation is largely about protecting and managing the habitats in which the birds live. There is a difference between managing a habitat for birds and managing it for biodiversity generally. This depends on the objectives of management. For example, where a globally threatened species such as the Corncrake is present, there may be justification for managing a site primarily for one species. However, in practice, much habitat management is a mixture of managing for particular species and managing to maintain communities (Sutherland and Hill 1995).

In Europe there are clear priorities and strategies in habitat conservation for birds (Tucker and Evans 1997). These are based largely on the status of species listed in the European Union Directive on the Conservation of Wild Birds (The Birds Directive) and other species of conservation value (Tucker and Heath 1994). In Ireland, we are fortunate that the listing of Birds of Conservation Concern is well established and regularly updated (Newton *et al.* 1999; Lynas *et al.* 2007). This gives us a set of priorities in an all-island context, which can be nested within the international responsibilities.

In Chapters 4 to 15, each of the habitat groups is characterised in broad terms and their bird communities – both breeding and non-breeding – are described in so far as they have been studied. Any quantitative information on community structure and densities of particular species is summarised, although it should be remembered that these parameters are dynamic and constantly changing. A single census may give a snapshot but this may not be representative of the average situation. Any broad differences in the bird species associated with each habitat type in Ireland and the equivalent habitat in neighbouring parts of Europe, are discussed. Chapter 16 considers management of the various habitats for birds and conservation issues are fully addressed in Chapter 17 in the context of climate change.

Climate change is already proving to have significant impacts on the range and numbers of birds in Ireland. A series of mild winters in northern Europe makes Ireland less attractive for some of the wintering waterbirds, such as Bewick's Swan and Eurasian Wigeon, whose numbers here have declined (Crowe 2005). Equally, the absence of severe winter conditions and increasing summer temperatures have allowed certain continental species – Little Egret, Mediterranean Gull, Great Spotted Woodpecker, to name just a few – to gain a foothold in Ireland. How this phenomenon will impact on bird conservation, and particularly the protection of their habitats, remains to be seen.

In Chapter 18 we attempt a synthesis of all other chapters. The overall question is what makes Ireland's avifauna different from other countries. Whatever the effects of climate change on birds, it will be critically important to establish a baseline of the type of bird communities found in each habitat type at the start of the twenty-first century. Then, in a few decades we will be able to compare this with the changes that have occurred due to climate change and the responses of the habitats.

William Thompson (1850) was clearly a bird ecologist. In Volume I of his famous *Natural History of Ireland* he goes into great detail about the birds that colonised a new farm pond near Belfast, when this was created from *'marshy ground, the abode of little else than Snipe'*. In total, he recorded 70 species at this place and compared his results with similar studies in Kensington Gardens in London and Selbourne parish in southern England. His understanding of the links between habitat change and the impacts on bird species was remarkable for his time. In concluding, he hopes *'that sufficient has been said to denote the desirableness of our possessing full and accurate ornithological statistics of Ireland'*. This desire is still as strong in the ornithologists of today and it is the object of this book to present a comprehensive account of the bird communities of habitats in Ireland and to explore their ecology.

The Little Egret is a recent colonist in Ireland (Richie Lort).

2. Habitat Classification and Birds

Richard Nairn

Introduction

Classifying species and their interrelationships was one of the abiding preoccupations of the early naturalists, such as Charles Darwin. Modern ecologists are just as interested in the classification of communities of plants and animals and their habitats, seeing these as the essential background to our understanding of the ecology and distribution of species.

A habitat is described as the area in which an organism or group of organisms lives, and is defined by the living (biotic) and non-living (abiotic) components of the environment (Fossitt 2000). Habitats are the building blocks of the environment that are inhabited by animals and plants, and which are important as units for site description and conservation management. While classifications of habitat are very useful ways for humans to conceptualise the environment, organisms (such as birds) will perceive the environment in an entirely different way because they will be cueing into specific aspects of environmental variation that we do not usually measure in our classifications (e.g. microclimate, microhabitat, competitors). If one takes an individual bird view of habitat then the whole concept becomes a continuum of factors that are almost impossible to classify into units or groups because individuals and species arrange themselves across gradients in vegetation structure, soil type, climate, etc.

Birds use their habitats in a variety of different ways. Firstly, they depend on habitats for their food and water. This implies that their energy intake and hence survival is dependent on the habitat quality. Reproduction and survival, in turn, depend on good physical condition of individuals and this is directly connected with the food supply for both breeding adults and juveniles on hatching. Birds generally time their nesting season to coincide with the maximum availability of food for the juveniles thus ensuring the optimum breeding success. So population levels of the species are intimately connected with the availability of good quality habitat, providing adequate food resources. However, habitat quality for birds is also determined by other essential features such as shelter, nest sites, freedom from predation, and many other elements of which we are probably unaware.

Many of the bird species that occur in Ireland are migratory, so they not only depend on habitats here but also in other countries and even other continents. A Sanderling, which nested in the tundra of East Greenland, may spend a few weeks in August on a sandy beach along the Irish coast, ultimately moving to feed in coastal wetlands in West Africa for the winter months. Each of these regions has habitats that provide the birds with food, shelter and safety from predators to ensure that they survive until the following breeding season. Only those

Sanderlings nest in Greenland. Some pass through Ireland in autumn while others winter here (Richard T. Mills).

individuals best suited to their habitats will survive to pass on their genes to the next generation.

Why do we need to classify habitats?

An ornithologist studying a community of birds in an area of land will want to make sense of their distribution by relating it to the habitats present. Some species are restricted to woodland, scrub or hedgerows, others to watercourses and wet grassland. Certain species like Hooded Crow have a wider usage of almost all habitat types, while others such as breeding waders are quite generally selective, preferring open, wet grassland sites. Having made the study, our ornithologist will probably want to compare the results with those of other similar studies elsewhere. But, were the habitats similar or different? What type of wet grassland was included in each study? Was the grassland dependent on surface water or groundwater or a combination of the two? Was there any surface water present and was the vegetation long or short? One person's wet grassland might be another person's marsh or fen. Habitat classifications are especially valuable in long-term surveys because they allow us to assess whether broad habitat associations recorded at different times are changing. Comparing habitat-based studies makes it essential that we have some common system of description and classification of the habitats themselves so that everyone knows what is being described. For many detailed studies of bird–habitat relationships it is necessary to record much more detailed information on habitat and in ways that are tailored to the habitat cues and resources that a species uses. In many scientific studies, habitat classifications are not used but direct measurements of habitat variables are.

History of habitat classification

There have been many attempts in the past to make some sense of the 'untidy ways' of nature. Habitats do not lend themselves easily to being classified. They often occur in mosaics rather than pure stands. For example, a typical Irish mountainside is likely to comprise a complex patchwork of blanket bog, wet heath and acid grassland. Within the blanket bog there are often small wet areas known as flushes which may be treated as separate habitats. Often, the divisions between all these habitats can be indistinct and there are many intermediates between the main habitat types. Superimposed on this mosaic

Upland habitats often form a mosaic of blanket bog, acid grassland and heath (Richard Nairn).

are the effects of land use. So the hillside may be grazed or regularly burnt, which can radically affect the vegetation and hence the bird community. These land uses can change over time so that habitat classifications may need to be adjusted to reflect new emerging land uses.

For many years the description of habitats in Europe was left to the botanists. In Britain, plant scientists such as Tansley (1949) made great strides in this direction but it was not until the publication of the National Vegetation Classification (NVC) (Rodwell 1991–2000) that one consistent and reliable system was adopted for all plant communities on the island. The NVC relies on phyto-sociological characteristics – the type and abundance of individual plant species and communities. However, habitats also need to be described where there is little or no vegetation, for example, on sandy beaches, cliff faces and rocky mountain scree. Marine habitats (below low-water mark) are largely described by reference to their animal communities. In Britain, the Nature Conservancy Council developed a system for classifying all habitats as part of the Phase 1 Habitat classification (Joint Nature Conservation Committee 1993). This scheme was also widely used in Ireland and is still the predominant system in Northern Ireland. One of the difficulties in devising habitat classifications is how best to reconcile land use with semi-natural vegetation.

In the Republic of Ireland, however, it was clear that there were a number of habitat types that did not fit easily into the British Phase 1 Habitat classification. Peatlands, for example, are quite localised in lowland Britain, but originally covered approximately 17% of the land surface of Ireland. Conversely, grassland types have received more attention in Britain. It was felt by a number of ecologists that there was a need for a standardised Irish classification that could be used by ecologists and naturalists, even those without specialised botanical training. In the 1990s the Heritage Council convened a group of interested ecologists chaired by John O'Halloran and a new hierarchical classification of Irish habitats was developed (Fossitt 2000). This covers both land and marine habitats, although the marine component is largely based on a previously published system (Connor *et al.* 1997). It is based on physical characteristics and animal communities to allow grouping or subdivision at various levels. This is sensible, as the seas of Britain and Ireland are a continuum and the habitats concerned are really those of the north-east Atlantic Ocean.

The Irish classification of habitats is hierarchical using three different levels, which descend with increasing complexity (the two higher levels are shown in Table 2.1). It also has a series of alphanumeric codes which themselves become longer and more complex as one descends the hierarchy. For example, Peatlands (P) are divided into Bogs (PB) and Fens and flushes (PF). Bogs in turn are divided into five categories (PB1 to PB5) including Raised bog, Upland blanket bog, Lowland blanket bog, Cutover bog and Eroding blanket bog. In principle, these categories could be further divided in a fourth level, if the information was available to support this level of category splitting. Table 2.1 gives just the first two levels of this system.

Table 2.1 A habitat classification system for Ireland (after Fossitt 2000)			
Code	Level 1 Habitat	Code	Level 2 Habitat
NON-MARINE			
F	Freshwater	FL	Lakes and ponds
		FW	Watercourses
		FP	Springs
		FS	Swamps
G	Grassland	GA	Improved grassland
		GS	Semi-natural grassland
		GM	Freshwater marsh
H	Heath and dense bracken	HH	Heath
		HD	Dense bracken

Table 2.1 A habitat classification system for Ireland (after Fossitt 2000)

Code	Level 1 Habitat	Code	Level 2 Habitat
P	Peatlands	PB	Bogs
		PF	Fens and flushes
W	Woodland and scrub	WN	Semi-natural woodland
		WD	Highly modified/non-native woodland
		WS	Scrub/transitional woodland
		WL	Linear woodland/scrub
E	Exposed rock and disturbed ground	ER	Exposed rock
		EU	Underground rock and caves
		ED	Disturbed ground
B	Cultivated and built land	BC	Cultivated land
		BL	Built land
C	Coastland	CS	Sea cliffs and islets
		CW	Brackish waters
		CM	Salt marshes
		CB	Shingle and gravel banks
		CD	Sand dune systems
		CC	Coastal constructions
MARINE			
L	Littoral (intertidal)	LR	Littoral rock
		LS	Littoral sediment
S	Sublittoral (subtidal)	SR	Sublittoral rock
		SS	Sublittoral sediment
M	Marine water body	MW	Marine water

With the introduction of the EU Habitats Directive in 1992 a different listing of habitats has become the predominant issue in nature conservation. An *Interpretation Manual of European Union Habitats* (European Commission 2007) gives the broad descriptions of these habitat categories that are all threatened at European level. The status of those 'Annex I habitats' occurring in Ireland is reviewed by the National Parks and Wildlife Service (NPWS) (2008). Most of the habitats concerned are considered to have bad overall conservation status in this country.

Habitats for fauna

As early as the 1930s, in his book *The Ecology of Animals,* the ecologist C.S. Elton was already discussing the importance of habitats in the explanation of animal distribution and numbers (Elton 1933). Later, with R.S. Miller, he developed 'a practical system of classifying habitats by structural characters' (Elton and Miller 1954). Elton was very conscious that habitats are dynamic and constantly changing. He showed how vegetation also affects animal habitats through ecological succession. He used the examples of a river eroding its banks and laying down sediment elsewhere, of a sand dune advancing to replace intertidal areas or of the lime being leached out of soil (Elton 1933).

Elton used the example of a sand dune advancing down a beach to illustrate ecological succession (Richard Nairn).

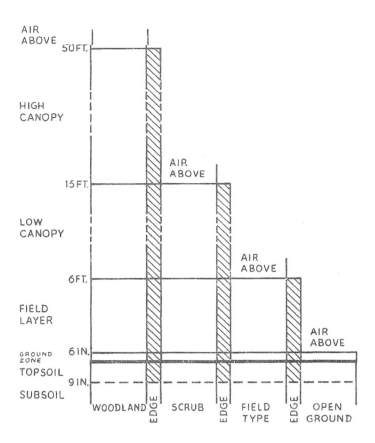

Elton's (1966) concept of terrestrial animal habitat classification.

In his comprehensive work, *The Pattern of Animal Communities,* Elton (1966) devoted a whole chapter to the classification of habitats. He acknowledged at the start that 'Definition of habitats, or rather lack of it, is one of the blind spots of zoology'. He went on to write:

> It is often held that the job of classifying habitats has already been done by plant ecologists, in so far as they have set up a whole series of plant associations, based on plant succession, relation to soils and so on, and since the food-chains of the animal community ultimately depend on these plants. But experience has been that, although vegetation is a highly important element in defining where animals live and in what their resources consist, the details of plant associations are frequently difficult to apply in a relevant way; and at the same time many aspects of habitat structure and in particular some of the forms of dead organic matter (not to mention many human artefacts) are largely omitted or given slight attention by plant ecologists, though they become essential in studying animal habitats.

From this premise, Elton constructed a model ecosystem that looked at animal habitats from a structural perspective. Elton's *Terrestrial System* used the concept of ecological succession from bare ground up to climax woodland, the latter term as adopted by Tansley (1949) for the ultimate natural vegetation of Britain and Ireland.

Bird habitat classification

Despite all the previous attempts at classifying habitats from different perspectives, the British Trust for Ornithology felt it was necessary to classify habitats in a different way for bird studies. Crick (1992) constructed 'a bird-habitat coding system for use in Britain and Ireland, incorporating aspects of land-management and human activity'. Crick's system is hierarchical and has four levels. This turned out to be quite complex and the lower levels are not mutually exclusive. Crick acknowledged that 'Any attempt to classify habitats into discrete categories is a potential minefield because, in reality, so many categories can intergrade with another. Most boundaries drawn are necessarily arbitrary and artificial'. In practice, Crick proposed so many habitat codes that these are very difficult to remember when in the field and complex to interpret on the final map.

The scheme proposed by Crick (1992) has been used for reporting coverage in the Countryside Bird Survey (CBS) in Ireland (Coombes *et al.* 2009, Crowe *et al.* 2011a). However, for this survey, farmland was the dominant habitat (68% of sections covered) followed by peatland (15%). More complex habitats such as woodland, freshwater or coastal habitats were generally not covered in this survey. This is because, relative to farmland, they are quite scarce and could only be sampled using a stratified approach. In the first ten years of the CBS, habitat categories appear to have been described quite well, though there were some potential areas of confusion. An analysis of the habitat levels completed in CBS forms shows that there was little recording of lower levels. This, in many cases, is simply an indication that the observer felt there was no relevant second or sub-level category in the 200m section they were covering (R. Coombes, pers. comm.).

For most practical purposes, it is sensible for studies of Irish birds to adopt the most widely used habitat classification in Ireland (Fossitt 2000) to help integration with other ecological studies and mapping. This allows an option to add further subdivisions where necessary to reflect the different uses or management regimes. For example, a uniquely Irish habitat is the turlough, classified under Fossitt's system in freshwater lakes and ponds (FL6). However, for much of the year, these habitats consist of wet grassland that floods only in periods of high groundwater levels. So we might envisage that a bird survey of these areas could classify the habitat as either flooded or unflooded (i.e. FL61 Flooded turlough or FL62 Non-flooded turlough).

No habitat classification can satisfy the needs of all ecological surveys and research. The types of habitat data that are collected depend on exactly what questions are being asked by the researcher. Sometimes, microhabitats can be important for birds. In woodland, for example, the presence of standing dead wood is a key component for those birds like Coal Tits that nest in cavities in old trees. In bird surveys of woodland it might therefore be worth subdividing some of Fossitt's categories further. Oak-ash-hazel woodland (WN2), for

The Coal Tit nests in cavities in old trees (Richard T. Mills).

An ancient oak at Charleville Castle, Co. Offaly provides plenty of cavities for nesting birds (Oscar Merne).

example, could be subdivided into pure hazel woodland (WN21) or hazel woodland with mature standards of ash or oak (WN22).

In a recent study of the influence of habitat heterogeneity on bird diversity in Irish farmland McMahon *et al.* (2008) used the Fossitt (2000) habitat classification. However, where opportunity existed to describe seasonal changes within the agricultural landscape in finer detail, such as the change from winter stubble to spring cereals, these changes were also recorded. McMahon *et al.* (2008) concluded that the Fossitt system is limited in its usefulness for the classification of significant habitats within Irish farmland. They suggested a more detailed classification of farmland habitat types based on considerations of ecological discreteness and value to help understand the relationships between agricultural management practice and farmland biodiversity. Gillings *et al.* (2008) considered the distribution and abundance of birds in relation to their habitats within lowland farmland in Britain in winter. Overall, they found that farmland bird species occurred at low densities and were highly aggregated in a small proportion of available pastures, stubble fields and farmyards.

Chapter 3 of this book explores the importance of structure and structural complexity of habitats as a key factor in the determination of bird communities. For the purposes of the book as a whole, we have subdivided the habitats at a high level, based largely on the similarities of their bird communities and the structure of the vegetation (Table 2.2). So, for example, reedswamp and fen are treated together as they are both wet habitats with tall vegetation and have rather similar bird communities. From an ecological perspective, some of these habitat categories are quite broad and others fairly narrow. For example, reedswamp can occur in lakes, canals, rivers and even in the tidal waters of estuaries. Fen, on the other hand, is specifically dependent on groundwater. Even so, the birds that occur in reedswamp and fen show much similarity, being dominated by species that exploit wet ground and need the shelter of tall grasses and herbs.

Table 2.2 Broad habitat categories used in this book

No.	Chapter	Subsection	Nearest Fossitt categories
4	Rivers and canals	Rivers	FW1/FW2 Rivers
		Canals	FW3 Canals
5	Lakes, reservoirs and turloughs	Lakes and reservoirs	FL1–5,7–8 Lakes and reservoirs
		Turloughs	FL6 Turloughs
6	Wet grasslands, marshes and callows	Wet grassland and Callow	GS2/4 Dry meadows/wet grassland GM1 Freshwater marsh
7	Lowland bogs, fens and reedswamps	Raised bog Fen Reedswamp	PB1 Raised bog PF1/2 Fen FS1/2 Reed, sedge and tall herb swamps
8	Upland heath and blanket bog	Upland heath and rock	HH1–4 Heaths
		Blanket bogs	PB2–5 Blanket bogs
9	Woodlands, forest and scrub	Woodland and forestry	WN–WD Woodlands
		Scrub	WS1–5 Scrub/immature woodland
10	Lowland farmland	Hedgerow	WL1/2 Hedgerow and treeline.
		Agricultural grassland	GA1 Improved grassland
		Arable land	BC1–3 Arable land
		Buildings	BL3 Buildings

Table 2.2 Broad habitat categories used in this book

No.	Chapter	Subsection	Nearest Fossitt categories
11	Sea cliffs, islands and rocky coasts	Cliffs	CS1–3 Rocky and sedimentary cliffs and islets
		Low rocky shore	LR1–4 Littoral rock
12	Beaches and dunes	Shingle beach	CB1 Shingle and gravel banks
		Sandy beach	LS 1–3 Littoral sand
		Sand dune	CD 1–6 Dune and machair
13	Estuaries and coastal lagoons	Sandflat and mudflat	LS2–5 Sand to mud shores
		Salt marsh	CM1/2 lower and upper salt marsh
		Coastal lagoon	CW 1 Lagoons and saline lakes
14	Open sea	Shallow marine areas	MW2–4 Inlets, bays, straits, estuaries
		Offshore marine areas	MW1 Open marine water
15	Urban habitats	Parks and gardens	BC4 Flower beds and borders
		Buildings	BL3 Buildings
		Quarries, sea walls, sewage works, airports, etc	Various

Conclusions

Clearly, no one system of habitat classification fits all situations and direct measures of habitat variables of particular interest may be more appropriate in some studies. In any case, many bird species have a tendency to ignore the divisions erected by scientists and select nest sites or feeding areas that provide them with the optimum chances of survival and reproduction. Birds will often exploit quite artificial habitats very successfully. For example, European Herring Gulls regularly feed on refuse tips and nest on rooftops in our coastal towns and cities. Parks and gardens are examples of habitats that mimic the conditions found on the edge of woodland and scrub with the addition of copious food supplies from the human residents nearby.

From an ornithological perspective, a knowledge of habitats and how birds use them helps us to understand why bird communities and populations are changing. This theme is explored further in Chapter 17. For consistency between studies, it is important that ornithologists use a standard terminology to describe the habitats used by their subjects. It makes practical sense to use the most widely applied habitat classification (Fossitt 2000) allowing integration with surveys of other organisms. In many cases, more fine-grain measurements or subdivisions may be needed for the study of detailed bird–habitat relationships. Using this system as a basis means that it can be tailored to suit the exact purpose of a particular study.

3. Bird Habitats: structure and complexity

John O'Halloran and Thomas C. Kelly

Introduction

Chapter 2 examined the broad definitions of habitats and here some common patterns of structure and complexity both within and between habitats are explored. In this chapter we explore how these patterns might influence the bird communities that use and occupy them. Birds, like most animals, use habitats to feed, roost and nest. The number of bird species – often collectively referred to as the 'community' that occupies a habitat – is the product of a variety of factors including climate, biogeography and the structure and complexity of the habitat itself. Let us briefly consider climate and biogeography and how they might influence habitats and birds in Ireland, before devoting the remainder of this chapter to the influence of habitat structure and complexity.

The climate of Ireland is often described as relatively aseasonal (Kelly 2008) largely due to our position in a temperate climatic zone, proximity to the Gulf Stream and exposure to predominantly south-westerly winds. The relatively mild moist conditions in both summer and winter provide an opportunity for year-round plant growth and the supply of food for many birds. The levels of rainfall, based on a 30-year average (Met Éireann www.met.ie), ranges from 1400mm in the west to just over 730mm in the east. The excess of input over evapotranspiration is sufficient to provide for a rich

European Golden Plover flock on a West Cork estuary (Richard T. Mills).

variety of standing, or lentic water habitats, and to contribute to variable flow rates in lotic or flowing water habitats, which is important in summer for breeding and in winter for feeding birds. The mild climatic conditions also mean that many Irish habitats are generally ice-free in winter and thus become a refuge for thrushes, such as Redwing and Fieldfare, finches and less frequently the exotically coloured Waxwing. In the same way, ice-free inter-tidal mudflats and adjacent fields are a rich habitat for shorebirds such as Black-tailed Godwit, Eurasian Curlew and Oystercatcher in the winter in Ireland.

The island nature and position of Ireland also exerts a strong influence on both the range of habitats and the number of species, when compared to adjacent nearby larger islands or mainland Europe. Ireland has a less diverse avifauna compared to Britain, which in turn is less species rich than the mainland of Europe. Kelly (2008) recently reviewed many elements of the avifauna of Ireland and demonstrated that Ireland's fauna is represented by 65–67% of the species present in Britain. This pattern is not unique to birds, but also occurs among

Oystercatcher is one of the shorebird species that feeds in coastal fields (Richard T. Mills).

a variety of invertebrate groups (McCarthy 1986). These patterns are typical of islands near large land masses and are explained, at least in part, by the size of the island, which is generally correlated with the number and complexity of habitats, i.e., larger islands possessing a richer variety of habitats (e.g. MacArthur and Wilson 1967, Hutchinson 1989).

Why are birds linked to habitats?

Birds, like all organisms, use habitats to live, feed and breed. Ecologists describe the composite of all these properties as the animal's niche. So put another way, the niche represents all the properties of a habitat that a species requires in order to survive. The 'breadth' of this niche will vary depending on the resources available and the number and type of other species in the habitat. When resources are limiting birds will compete with each other and this will lead to partitioning of their niches or resources in some way. The idea here is that instead of competing for a single resource, birds either divide the resource in the habitat into different niches or use the same habitats at different times (e.g. nocturnal species) or if neither of these options are possible, they shift to use different habitats.

Therefore, the more habitats the more species. In this book, for example, you will see birds using river, or riparian, habitats (Chapter 4), others using woodland (Chapter 9) and some species may share habitats where resources are not limited. Other species avoid competition by using different habitats. Within a habitat, however, there can also be partitioning as birds space themselves out along a particular resource within a habitat. A good example of this type of partitioning is the use of mudflats by shorebirds (Figure 3.1). Here we see the species of birds feeding in the same habitat, estuaries and coastal lagoons (see Chapter 13), but avoiding competition by using different parts of the resource. The long-billed species, e.g Eurasian Curlew and godwits, reach deeper into the mud to find lugworms and ragworms, whilst the smaller species, such as Dunlin and Common Redshank, feed on smaller prey items such as *Corophium* and the mud snail *Hydrobia ulvae*.

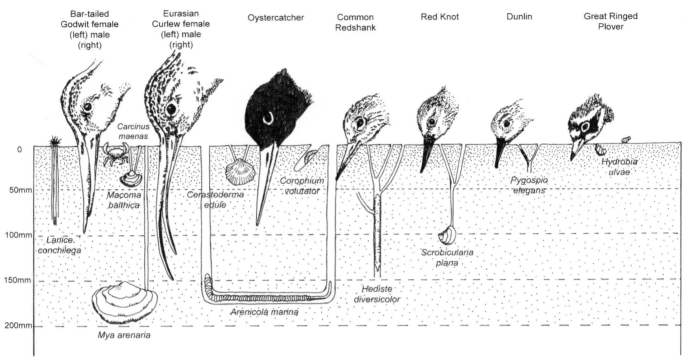

Figure 3.1 Wader bill lengths and availability of prey species showing depth of burrows. Invertebrates are not drawn to scale (Holly Pereira).

European Robin is one of the generalist species that can be found in almost any habitat (Richard T. Mills).

In these examples we can see that the birds are avoiding competition in the same habitat. They are specialising on particular prey types and avoiding competition which could lead to decline or extinction of the species. The shorebirds themselves could also be classified as habitat specialists in that they mostly feed on mudflats. Other species are much less specialist and not surprisingly are referred to as generalists. These are species that use a range of habitats e.g. upland and lowland farms, urban habitats and parks and gardens. Species such as Wren, Chaffinch and European Robin might be seen as generalist, as they are widely distributed across a range of habitats in Ireland (Coombes *et al.* 2009).

Structure and complexity within a habitat

Before looking at the intricate ways in which habitats are arranged or connected, let us first describe the complexity that exists within a habitat. In areas where there is little or no

Common Redshanks find their preferred prey in soft sediments (Richard T. Mills).

complexity there are few species. Rock outcrops and dry sandy areas are examples where complexity is low and the number of bird species is low. As complexity increases, so does the number of species. This will vary across habitats and scale within a habitat. In many ways the complexity usually means a greater number of habitats and microhabitats for the plants and animals on which the birds forage.

In mudflats and other shoreline habitats there appears to be little or no complexity at the macro level, but, at the scale at which the prey lives, there is considerable 'structure' or heterogeneity (Figure 3.1). Many prey items within these habitats, at the micro scale, will be influenced by *inter alia* salinity, sediment particle size and the degree of inundation by water. Ragworms for example, prefer very soft (i.e. minute particle size) sediment, *Corophium* prefer some standing water and lugworms prefer more sandy sediments. Thus, when we investigate habitats at this scale we see that subtle changes in structure influence the prey types and clearly influence the distribution of birds that feed on them within a habitat. Black-tailed Godwit, Common Redshank and Dunlin will typically prefer to feed in soft sediments on their preferred prey, while Bar-tailed Godwit will focus on the more sandy sediments where their preferred prey, such as lugworm, is found. Thus small changes in particle size and subtle changes in complexity will influence habitat use by birds.

For truly aquatic species, such as seabirds, ducks, swans, geese or other wildfowl, the complexity of the below-water-level habitat structure will also influence the use of this zone by birds. The water depth, presence or absence of surface and below-water vegetation will provide the niches and microhabitats for prey and food on which birds feed. Much research has been undertaken on the limitations and challenges for birds in these habitats, including the depth to which they can dive, the risk of heat loss and the ability to upend or surface-feed (see Figure 3.2 for some examples of different types of feeding in Whooper Swans). Much less research has been undertaken on how the aquatic (lentic) habitat complexity influences bird usage. In running or lotic waters we have greater knowledge. There has been much research on Dippers in Ireland and how they exploit the riverine habitat for breeding (Smiddy *et al.* 2004), feeding (Taylor and O'Halloran 1997) and roosting (Davenport *et al.* 2004) and all have been shown to be influenced by the properties of running water and the stream architecture.

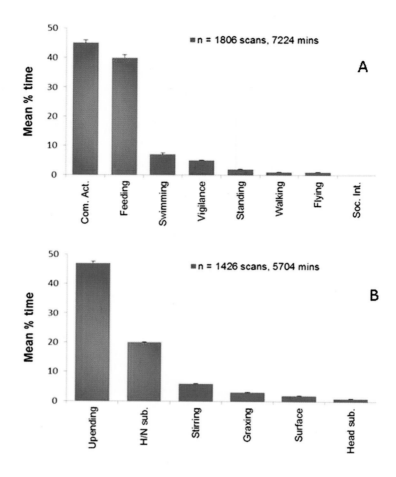

Figure 3.2 A: Daily activity budgets expressed as the mean percentage time (± s.e.) spent in different activities by Whooper Swans (Com. act. = comfort activities; Soc. Int = social interactions). B: The mean percentage feeding time (± s.e.) spent using different feeding methods by Whooper Swans (H/N sub. = head and neck submerged feeding; Head sub. Head submerged feeding) (redrawn after O'Donoghue and O'Halloran 1994).

Spatial distribution of habitats and their size

All habitats have structure when viewed at the macro scale and even more complexity when investigated in greater detail. For example, in the case of estuaries there is variation in structure from head to mouth (e.g. salinity, oxygen, sediment, temperature and current flow). In addition there will be adjacent salt marshes and lagoons adding to the complexity and variety of feeding habitats for birds. Comparable structure and complexity can be found in moorlands, uplands, sea cliffs, urban habitats and so forth, which are considered in the individual chapters. Some well known examples, e.g. grasslands, hedgerows and woodland, are considered in more detail here.

Grassland

Ireland is dominated by grassland – some 91% of the farmland area in the country is grass (DAF 2007). Grassland is generally of low complexity and is not very rich in bird life. Despite this, grassland species such as the Meadow Pipit are common and widespread where such habitats are available, though others, such as the Skylark and the Corncrake, have undergone steep declines which, in the case of Corncrake, has been catastrophic (Donaghy 2007). The decline in breeding bird species diversity in grasslands in Ireland appears to be associated with major changes in the management of this habitat which commenced in the 1960s when the virtually ubiquitous hay crop was replaced with the making of silage – a development enabled by the widening usage of mechanical grass cutters.

In other situations grasslands have been abandoned and the process of secondary succession commences leading to, for example, large areas covered by bramble and gorse. Of course these regenerating thicket habitats have a greater foliage height diversity and with this a correspondingly richer variety of bird species including Stonechat (e.g. Cummins and O'Halloran 2003), Linnet and Common Whitethroat as well as the commoner generalist species including Wren, European Robin, Dunnock, Blackbird and Song Thrush. Reed Bunting and Sedge Warbler can also be found in such emergent thicket habitats adjacent to wetlands. Much of the grassland in Ireland is grazed and the stock is often contained in the field by semi-natural boundaries, such as hedgerows, which provide both complexity in themselves and connectivity between habitats within the landscape.

Hedgerows form a network of corridors for small birds to move across open farmland (Richard T. Mills).

Hedgerows

Hedgerows are among the most diverse habitats in an intensively farmed landscape and in Ireland have been shown to be particularly important for birds (Lysaght 1989; Flynn 2002; Pithon *et al.* 2005; Fennessy and Kelly 2006; Kelleher and O'Halloran 2007). Enclosures of commonage on the lowlands in the sixteenth and seventeenth centuries led to the construction of field margins and the emergence of hedgerows. 'In Ireland, we don't have very much woodland but if we shoved all our hedges together we would probably have a very sizeable deciduous woodland area because what we seem to have in effect is linear woodlands' (O'Sullivan 1973). Most of these hedges are planted with native trees and shrubs though they vary in plant species diversity and structure, depending on such factors as soil drainage and chemistry (O'Sullivan 1973).

The 'linear woodland' nature of hedgerows emphasises their importance as a network of habitat corridors which in turn may connect with larger areas of native, semi-natural and coniferous woodland. Although hedgerows are like linear woodlands in terms of their plant diversity, it is unlikely that they would ever replace woodlands, because specialist bird species such as owls, hawks, Eurasian Treecreeper, Jay, Common Redstart and Wood Warbler require extensive tracts of continuous woodland.

How does woodland habitat complexity influence birds?

In contrast to the relatively simple structure of hedgerows, woodland and forest habitats are often presented as examples of how habitat structural complexity has a major influence on bird

The Eurasian Treecreeper nests in cavities or under a flake of bark on a tree (Richie Lort).

community richness. It is the presence of vegetation layers including trees (structure), the diversity of species of trees (composition) and management which has the greatest influence on the number of birds using woodland and forest habitats. The details of the bird communities of woodland and forest habitats are considered in detail in Chapter 9 and here we focus on the trees themselves, their age and management and how they influence the structure and complexity of the habitat.

Tree species diversity is a key driver of forest biodiversity, influencing structural complexity at the stand and landscape scales and thus the availability of habitats and microhabitats for a range of species, including birds. In forest and woodland ecology, biologists focus their research and studies at two levels: the stand level and the landscape level. Here we will consider the stand level, which represents the forest sites or plots, typically 8–10 hectares in size for plantation forests, or smaller for native or semi-natural woodlands.

Species composition and forest age are two of the major influences on the diversity and richness of the bird communities that use woodland habitats. Different species of trees provide the variety of structure – height, foliage cover, density, and amount of light penetrating through the canopy – that together influence the availability of prey to birds feeding in these habitats. When ornithologists study forest and woodland plots we routinely take measures of habitat structure and/or complexity as follows: canopy cover, cover of lower vegetation layers, amount of dead wood and distances to forest edge and to broadleaved woodland. More recently, in our studies we have been investigating the use of a ground-based laser to characterise the structure of the habitat and derive data to relate to bird and other biodiversity measures (see Irwin 2009). Earlier work on forest and woodland birds in Ireland (O'Halloran *et al.* 1998) investigated the number of bird species in the dominant conifers in comparison with those found in oak woodland. The communities present were broadly similar except for the one major group of birds, the hole nesters. The oak differed from the plantation forests by having dead and rotten parts (known as snags of standing dead wood) with holes, which provided opportunities for cavity nesters such as Blue Tit, Coal Tit and Eurasian Treecreeper to nest. Although our initial research looked at the avian communities associated with only two species of trees, subsequent research investigated the relationship between bird species diversity and a wider range of tree species (Wilson *et al.* 2006, 2010).

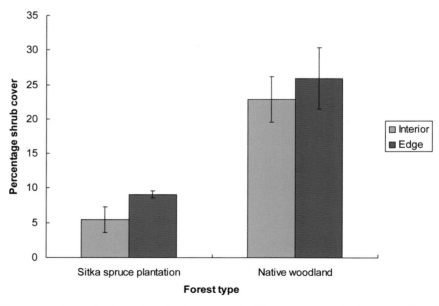

Figure 3.3 The percentage shrub and understory cover in Sitka spruce and native woodlands in Ireland. These have a significant influence on habitat diversity, habitat complexity and thus bird communities (data from PLANFORBIO http://www.ucc.ie/en/planforbio/).

During the BIOFOREST project (Wilson *et al.* 2006) we surveyed populations of birds in 44 plantation forests throughout Ireland in the summers of 2001 and 2002. Our study sites represented three combinations of tree species (pure Sitka Spruce, pure Ash, and Sitka Spruce/Ash mixed at inter-stand level) at five ages (4–8 years, 9–17 years, 23–29 years, 35–50 years and 50+ years). Bird species assemblages were found to be dependent on growth stage, which was driven in particular by the structure and management of the forest for timber production.

The changes in bird species composition over the commercial forest cycle were related to shrub layer and proximity to the forest edge. Figure 3.4 illustrates this clearly, where both the percentage shrub cover and percentage understorey cover at both interior and edge differs greatly between forest types. These differences in structure explain the differences in the bird communities found in these habitats. The bird assemblages of pre-canopy closure forests are typical of open (i.e. field) habitats. Some of the constituent bird species found at this stage including Stonechat, Whinchat and Skylark are of conservation concern in Ireland. As the forests mature, complexity decreases and these are replaced by the small number of forest specialist birds in Ireland, Common Crossbill and canopy feeders such as Coal Tit and Goldcrest (Wilson *et al.* 2006).

The Whinchat is one of the species that occurs in open habitats before the woodland canopy closes (Darío Fernández-Bellon).

Man-made structures and habitats

While much of the biological complexity discussed thus far is set in a natural or semi-natural context, here we consider that many birds have adapted to the unnatural habitat complexity provided by human construction and structures. We introduce how human structures are exploited by birds, many of which are covered in more detail in other chapters, especially in the chapter on urban habitats.

Managed grasslands

Playing fields, golf courses and urban parklands are actively managed where habitat 'structure' is reduced to a compact sward by repeated mowing, and are a major attraction for a diverse assemblage of birds. For example, flocks of Brent Geese and waders such as Oystercatcher can be seen on over 60 amenity grassland sites in Dublin (Benson 2009). All resident and migrant thrush species also exploit these areas. Areas of short grass are used by Black-headed, Common and European Herring Gulls, as well as Rook, Jackdaw, Hooded Crow and Common Starling. Wading birds, particularly Northern Lapwing and Oystercatcher, also exploit managed grasslands, especially in winter. In their study of the numbers of Oystercatcher using grasslands at the UCD Campus in Belfield, Quinn and Kirby (1993) showed that a higher proportion of immature birds occurred there than on the adjacent mudflats at Sandymount Strand. Overall, rainfall in the preceding 48 hours correlated with the numbers of Oystercatcher counted on the campus grasslands. This was explained by the fact that the flocks were feeding on earthworms which are closer to the surface and easier to get when the soil is wet. Wind speed on the mudflats also influenced the numbers using the grassland as Oystercatchers sought to avoid wind chill on the open mudflats. Finally Oystercatchers were also more likely to use the campus when high tide occurred in the middle of the day, as

Playing fields provide additional foraging habitat for waterbirds such as Oystercatchers (Richard T. Mills).

Black Guillemots nest in holes in pier walls as here at Bangor, Co. Down (Richard Nairn).

opposed to early or late in the day, because this led to a major loss of important daylight foraging time (Quinn and Kirby 1993). Black-tailed Godwit also exploit fields and Hutchinson and O'Halloran (1993) have shown the importance of such grass swards as supplementary feeding sites for godwits in winter.

The attraction created by mown grasslands for ground-feeding birds began to pose a major problem for airports where collisions with aircraft – known as bird strikes – were becoming an increasing hazard to both civil and military aviation. Part of the solution was to reverse-engineer the habitats adjoining the manoeuvering areas (i.e. runways and taxiways) by the cultivation of long grass (Brough and Bridgman 1980; CAA 1990; Kelly *et al.* 2000) which proved remarkably successful in reducing the numbers of the most hazardous species, e.g. gulls, plovers, Common Starling, pigeons and crows, while increasing the numbers of Skylark and Meadow Pipit. A worrying development, however, has been the post-myxomatosis recovery of the rabbit population which can graze down the long grass to a compact sward as well as attracting predatory species, including increasing numbers of Common Buzzard (Kelly *et al.* 2005).

Human structures providing habitats and complexity

River bridges provide a very important habitat for a range of bird species, including Dipper, Grey Wagtail, Barn Swallow, Wren and Blue Tit (Smiddy and O'Halloran 2004). These structures provide safe roosting sites and also tend to be warmer (by about 1 °C) than the surrounding landscape at night (Davenport *et al.* 2004). Pier walls can also provide important habitats. The pier and associated marina at Bangor, Co. Down, Northern Ireland is the breeding site for at least 23 pairs of Black Guillemot and the numbers increased over the 1985 to 1997 interval through the provision of artificial nest holes (Greenwood 1998). Most of the pairs breeding on the old north pier had the highest clutch size and fledging rates, while clutch sizes and fledging rates were lower on the central and south piers, possibly because the pairs breeding there were younger (Greenwood 1998). Black Guillemot also breed on and in the walls of Rockabill. Seabirds, including Black Guillemot and Shag have also colonised the pier at the abandoned Gulf Oil terminal at Whiddy Island, Bantry Bay Co.Cork (Kelly T. and Berrow S.D. unpublished observations) which was severely damaged as a result of the fire and explosion on the tanker *Betelguese* in 1979.

Although aquaculture may have some negative impact on estuarine and coastal habitats such as the bays of west Cork, Kerry and Mayo, research also indicates that some species may benefit from the structures associated with aquaculture production (Hilgerloh 2001; Roycroft *et al.* 2007 ; 2008). Wading bird species appear to derive some benefit from the presence of trestles used to cultivate the Pacific oyster (*Crassostrea gigas*) (Hilgerloh 2001), though the overall negative impact of these structures on the carrying capacity of the receiving habitat for waterfowl generally has not been quantified. A range of seabirds including gulls, Shag, Black Guillemot and Great Northern Diver exploit suspended blue mussel lines in Bantry Bay, Co. Cork without any obvious ill effect (Roycroft *et al.* 2007; 2008).

Large flocks of wading birds may roost during high tides on embankments, many of which were constructed when large areas of some of Ireland's estuaries were claimed from the seas in the nineteenth century. In the winter months, Short-eared Owls may also roost in the dense grassy vegetation that covers the drier summits of these barriers against the sea. Finally, quarries can often provide ledges for Peregrine Falcon and Raven to nest.

Black-headed Gulls roosting on a footbridge in Wicklow town (Richard Nairn).

While, in most cases, these human structures provide extra opportunities for species to nest, this is not so in the case of the Common Swift. This species is completely reliant in Ireland on human structures, such as old buildings and churches. This is in contrast to their probable ancestral habit of breeding in snags (standing dead wood), for example, at Białowieża forest, Poland. Dead wood generally is an important habitat resource for hole-nesting woodland species such as the Common Redstart. The retention of dead wood (Sweeney *et al.* 2010) as a breeding and feeding resource in Irish woodlands (Chapter 9) may be crucial in ensuring the long-term establishment of recolonising Great Spotted Woodpeckers.

4. Rivers and Canals

Patrick Smiddy and Richard Nairn

Introduction

Rivers, streams and canals are among the most obvious features of the Irish landscape. They range in size from the main arteries, such as the Shannon, Lagan, Boyne, Liffey, Slaney, Suir and Blackwater (Munster), all of which drain vast tracts of land, to tiny streams less than 1m in width. Their characteristics are equally variable, and range from the almost static canals to the slow-flowing meandering rivers of the lowlands to fast-flowing mountain rivulets rushing over rocky beds.

Ireland has a large and flat central plain with a rim of mountains around the coast. Many rivers that rise at the seaward side of these mountains flow more or less directly to the sea. Such rivers are often swift and turbulent, while those rising at the inland side of the mountains meander across lower ground in a much more leisurely way. Some of these lowland rivers also expand into large lakes along part of their course, for example the Shannon and Corrib. Several rivers have been harnessed for electricity generation by the building of dams, and artificial lakes have been formed behind them, the River Lee in County Cork being one such example (Twomey and McGettigan 2009). There are more than 13,500km of main river channel in Ireland (Cabot 1999). Rivers flowing over acidic rock formations are nutrient-poor, while those that flow over limestone and other base-rich rocks are rich in nutrients. Rivers in the latter category support a much higher density and diversity of invertebrate life, and this in turn supports a greater diversity of species at the top of the food chain, such as fish, birds and mammals.

Waterfall at Maghara, near Ardara, Co. Donegal (Richard Nairn).

Lowland section of the River Liffey in Dublin with much aquatic vegetation (Richard Nairn).

A section of the Grand Canal near Tullamore, Co. Offaly (Conor Nolan).

Ecologically, rivers are classified as eroding, or upland, and depositing, or lowland (Fossitt 2000). Upland rivers include natural watercourses that are actively eroding, and where there is little or no deposition of the finer sediments. Such conditions are nearly always associated with the upstream parts of river systems where gradients are steep and where there is a fast and turbulent water flow. Some rivers flowing directly off mountains and into the sea, such as in the west of Ireland, remain as eroding rivers for their entire length because of steep gradients and high rainfall. Waterfalls, cascades and rapids may occur commonly in this type of river. Upland rivers generally support little in the way of aquatic vegetation, apart from algae, lichens and mosses.

Depositing rivers are typically found in lowland areas where gradients are low and water flow is sluggish. As the name implies, fine sediments such as sand, silt and mud are deposited on the riverbed, and the river may meander across the countryside and change course considerably over time. Such rivers may vary in size from quite small to very large, but are generally larger and deeper than those in the upland category. Many such rivers have been modified quite significantly by drainage, canalisation, damming and the building of weirs in order to facilitate navigation and fisheries and to prevent flooding. Such rivers are also the most affected by pollution from industrial, urban and farming sources. Depositing rivers often host a luxuriant growth of terrestrial, emergent and submerged plant species. Many such rivers also become tidal for varying distances, depending on gradient, before entering estuaries or the sea.

There are two main canals in the Republic of Ireland, the Royal and the Grand, both of which cross the country from east to west and which, in the nineteenth century, made navigation possible between Dublin and the River Shannon. Other large canals occur in Northern Ireland, for example the Ulster, Lagan and Newry systems. In addition, many rivers, such as the Barrow, had canal sections build parallel to them in order to allow navigation past certain areas too dangerous for boats. These allowed cargo access to inland areas before the rail and road systems were built in Ireland. Canals require maintenance and dredging from time to time in order to keep them open. Since cargo is not transported by this method any more, many canals are now derelict, or are used only for recreational purposes, and some of them have become important bird habitats. Water flow in canals is minimal and the level is controlled by a system of locks. Because of the infrequent water movement, disused canals are quickly colonised by a range of submerged, floating and emergent aquatic plants.

Humans have exploited rivers for many thousands of years. Early settlers built weirs and fish traps, and watermills were constructed for grinding corn. Watermills increased both in size and number in the seventeenth and eighteenth centuries. Following the discovery of electricity, some water wheels were adapted for the provision of power for local lighting schemes. Hydroelectric schemes have changed the shape and appearance of many rivers, and led to the creation of artificial lakes. On the River Lee, County Cork, much of the unique riparian woodland of the Gearagh was lost due to flooding following the building of dams for electricity generation (de Buitléar 1985).

Early crossing points of rivers for humans and their domestic animals were simply at narrow and shallow points, but these were dangerous during flood conditions, and many must have drowned attempting crossings. The first bridges were probably rough wooden constructions. It is estimated that there are about 25,000 masonry arch road bridges with a span of over 1.83m in Ireland, most of which have been built since 1775 (O'Keeffe and Simington 1991).

Rivers have for thousands of years been used for the transport of products to and from inland parts, and many sections of rivers were canalised to enable larger boats to travel along them. Rivers were also joined up by the construction of canals. Most rivers in lowland Ireland have been drained at some stage in their history. Such works of drainage were undertaken in order to improve the adjoining lands for agriculture, and to facilitate development and exploitation of the bogs. The origin of many major drainage schemes dates to the early nineteenth century, but severe drainage of some systems continued in the twentieth century, and right up to the 1970s (Buckley and McCarthy 1987). Arterial drainage is the severest form of interference as its aim is to speed the flow of water by deepening, widening and straightening the river channel. Riverbank trees are also removed during such drainage, and the ecology of the river and its immediate surroundings is changed radically (de Buitléar 1985). Most river systems and their associated surrounding habitats of fen, marsh and turlough are only shadows of what they were pre-drainage, resulting in a severe reduction in the area of all of these habitats.

Many of the major river systems and their tributaries now have protective designations in place (under the EU Birds Directive and Habitats Directive) in an effort to conserve what remains of Ireland's natural heritage. The Office of Public Works (OPW) (the statutory agency with responsibility for drainage (Ryan 1986)) now takes a much more enlightened approach to conservation issues, with pre- and post-drainage assessments regularly undertaken. Indeed, most works are now more in the form of maintenance of existing systems, and flood-relief projects around towns (Fermoy, Co. Cork and Clonmel, Co. Tipperary being current examples of the latter). This changed attitude has considerably reduced the potential for further damage to river systems as natural habitats for birds and other wildlife. Waterways Ireland manages canals and other navigable waterways while the National Parks and Wildlife Service (NPWS) is responsible for nature conservation.

High water quality is also important in maintaining properly functioning aquatic systems. The Environmental Protection Agency (EPA) monitors the quality of river waters, and frequent reports are published. The EPA regularly monitors 1,080 rivers and streams for biological conditions along some 13,200km of channel length at about 3,200 locations. A less extensive chemical monitoring programme also takes place (EPA 2004). Traditionally, rivers were used as dumping grounds for waste from industries and sewage from towns. However, this is no longer acceptable or legal. Pollution of rivers from industrial sources is now happily a rare event. Nevertheless, many rivers are under stress from a number of sources, none more so than from poorly functioning town sewage systems. In many small towns local authority sewage works are struggling to treat the increased sewage input from the unsustainable building boom of the last 20 years. Modern agriculture has also had, in the recent past, a severe effect on river water quality, especially at times of low water flow during summer. Nutrient input through run-off from farmyards and from the spreading of slurry was the chief culprit. However, new regulations regarding the storage and spreading of slurry, and the construction of storage facilities on most farms has led to a considerable improvement in the situation.

The EPA monitoring programme shows that most rivers have unpolluted (Class A) waters (EPA 2004). However, there are considerable regional variations, with the cleanest waters being in the Donegal/Sligo, Western and Southern regions. The Cavan/Monaghan, Eastern and South Eastern regions have the greatest proportion of polluted river channel. Since the early 1970s, there has been a steady decline in the amount of seriously polluted waters (Class D), but there has been a corresponding rise in lesser levels of pollution (Class B and C). Most pollution is now believed to emanate from farming and municipal sources.

Increased volumes of water are being taken from rivers (and lakes) for human consumption and to meet industrial needs. Over most of Ireland there is a surplus of water available locally per person. However, in the east of the country, where most of the human population lives, there is (or there will be in the future) a shortage, and local authorities in the Eastern Region are currently assessing a proposal to pipe water from the River Shannon to the Dublin area.

Rivers and canals are also used for a wide range of recreational activities ranging from angling, shooting, sailing and rowing to swimming. All of these human activities have an impact, whether major or slight, on the quality of the river as a habitat for birds. Despite the fact that rivers and canals form such a significant part of the bird habitats of Ireland, there is a paucity of published studies dealing with the bird communities of such habitats, and only one riparian species, the Dipper, has been studied in any depth in Ireland. Few published studies (Bailey 1982; Carruthers 1986; Williams *et al.* 1988) deal comprehensively with the breeding species of rivers. However, a number of unpublished reports also exist, and some of these have been incorporated here to give an overview for the island of Ireland as a whole. A previous review (Hutchinson *et al.* 1998) covers riparian species as well as those of nearby wet grassland and bogs, habitats generally outside the scope of this review (see Chapter 6). However, there are many publications dealing with river ecology (*e.g.* Healy *et al.* 1988; Mollan 1993; Moriarty 1991, 1998; Reynolds 1996, 1998; Steer 1991), but most give either a very brief account of the birds of these areas or they refer to unpublished reports.

Birds of rivers: a general account

Across the world rather few bird species exclusively use the river channel as a habitat, although a large number use rivers for a particular purpose (breeding or feeding), for part of the year (migration or wintering), or they use the associated habitats (woodland, marsh or open country). There are relatively few specialists, and Buckton and Ormerod (2002) list only 60 species globally, divided equally between the passerines and non-passerines. Most of these specialists occur in Asia (28) and only four occur in Europe, with three of these occurring in Ireland, Common Kingfisher, Grey Wagtail and Dipper. Despite this, only the Dipper is totally dependant on the river corridor throughout the year, many Common Kingfishers (perhaps the young) dispersing to the coast for the winter, with Grey Wagtails inhabiting farmyards and other habitats outside the breeding season.

The specialist riparian species
Common Kingfisher: The Common Kingfisher is currently widely, but thinly, distributed throughout Ireland as a breeding species in rivers and streams. Some birds also breed in gravel workings. They generally favour slow-flowing lowland fresh waters with exposed vertical earthen banks in which they can excavate their nest holes. At least two broods are produced per breeding season. Their food requirements are a plentiful supply of small fish, such as sticklebacks and minnows.

Ruttledge (1968) reported a good population in many counties in the 1960s, with only very local declines recorded. He suggested that the severe winter of 1962/63 had little effect here, unlike

The Common Kingfisher is a widespread species on rivers and streams (Richard T. Mills).

in Britain and Europe where severe mortality took place due to the freezing of waterways (Dobinson and Richards 1964). However, the recent published evidence suggests that a considerable decline took place in the breeding range between the late 1960s and the early 1990s (Gibbons *et al.* 1993) with breeding birds apparently disappearing from many peripheral areas in the west and elsewhere. The densest population was shown to be in the north-east. While the species remained widespread, with breeding apparently continuing in all counties, there was an obvious thinning of the population, with many areas devoid of records by the early 1990s.

However, this may not be a true representation of the actual position during the period under discussion. Common Kingfisher is undoubtedly thinly spread (probably always has been), and the methodology for the *New Breeding Atlas* (Gibbons *et al.* 1993) probably militated against accurate recording of this scarce and easy-to-overlook species. A public appeal for records of Common Kingfishers by BirdWatch Ireland in 2007 revealed a much healthier situation than the published record suggested, with the species being shown to be widespread in lowland rivers (Crowe *et al.* 2010).

Some cold winters occurred in the period under review, and the British population declined following two of them, in 1979 and 1982 (Marchant *et al.* 1990). However, these winters were much less severe than that of 1962/63, therefore they are even less likely to have been the cause of any decline in Ireland. Therefore, the cause of the decline, if indeed it took place at all, must be sought elsewhere. Their fish prey is susceptible to pollution, and river pollution was a significant problem in the early 1970s. However, there has been a steady decline in the amount of seriously polluted waters since then (EPA 2004). Insensitive riverbank management practices may also be a factor. Today, rock armouring on lowland rivers in order to prevent erosion is a common practice, and this may also have destroyed some nest sites.

Land drainage is also a threat. Eight pairs of Common Kingfishers bred on 21.5km of river within the Blackwater catchment in Northern Ireland in 1984. This river was then drained and the meanders removed, reducing the study length to 19.5km. In 1987 only two pairs bred (Williams *et al.* 1988). In any case, Common Kingfishers are quickly able to make up for losses suffered during severe winters by their prolific breeding strategy, but loss of nest sites and food resources may make declines more permanent. Mammal predation, especially by the introduced American mink, is often cited as a possible cause of decline in many riparian species, but the evidence available at this point falls short of proof. However, some other mammals are also known to predate the nests of riparian birds, and one nest of a Common Kingfisher was dug out by a badger on the River Licky in Co. Waterford (Smiddy 1996). In the early 1990s the total Irish breeding population of Common Kingfisher was estimated at 1,300 to 2,100 pairs (Gibbons *et al.* 1993).

The density at which Common Kingfishers occur in the breeding season has been published for some rivers (Table 4.1). Densities are highest in Northern Ireland where up to 5.4 pairs per 10km of slow-flowing river have been recorded (Marchant and Hyde 1980; Bailey 1982). In the Republic of Ireland breeding densities are much lower with the highest recorded being 2.5 pairs per 10km on the lowland River Maigue, County Limerick (Buckley 1992). On two major rivers in the Republic surveyed in 2008, the Boyne and Blackwater (Munster), the highest density recorded was 1.03 pairs per 10km on the Boyne (Crowe *et al.* 2008, 2010). In 2010 the density on the River Nore was 1.4 pairs per 10km, while the density reached 1.2 pairs per 10km on the Rivers Boyne and Moy (Crowe *et al.* 2010). These figures are comparable with studies in Britain where peaks of up to 8 pairs per 10km have been recorded on slow-flowing rivers in England (Marchant and Hyde 1980) and Wales (Round and Moss 1984).

Common Kingfishers do best on slow-flowing rivers, and their absence from the 'fast' Flesk (Carruthers 1986) and the upland section of the Mulkear (Buckley 1992) is notable. Apart from these few estimates of breeding density there appears to be almost nothing known about many aspects of the ecology of the Common Kingfisher in Ireland. Nothing is known about diet, apart from the fact that they feed extensively on small fish, which are caught by diving from a perch on the riverbank.

It is known from elsewhere that there is a considerable dispersal in the autumn away from the natal rivers towards the coast, where some birds remain for the winter. Many birds also winter on the coast in Ireland in sheltered estuaries, but the exact status of these is unknown in terms of their age and origin. It is known that at least some adult birds remain on their breeding territories during the winter, but few authors have studied the species at that season. Bailey (1982) commented that only occasional birds were seen during the winter in his study area on the River Lagan. It is likely that because of the territorial nature of the adults that birds arriving on the coast, some as early as August, are in fact juveniles.

Table 4.1 Common Kingfisher densities (pairs/10km) at some Irish rivers during the breeding and winter seasons. P = present.

River	Breeding	Winter
Northern Ireland (slow) (Marchant and Hyde 1980)	0.0–5.4	–
Northern Ireland (fast) (Marchant and Hyde 1980)	2.0	–
Lagan (Bailey 1982)	4.0–5.0	P
Blackwater (Northern Ireland) (Watson 1984)	3.7	–
Maigue (lowland) (Buckley 1992)	2.5	–
Nore (Crowe *et al.* 2010)	1.0–1.4	–
Boyne and tributaries (Crowe *et al.* 2008, 2010)	0.9–1.2	–
Moy (Buckley 1993; Crowe *et al.* 2010)	0.0–1.2	–
Owenmore (Buckley 1993)	1.16	0.2
Mulkear (lowland) (Buckley 1992)	1.0	–
Mulkear (upland) (Buckley 1992)	0.0	–
Mulkear (all sections) (Buckley 1992)	0.6	–
Clare (Crowe *et al.* 2010)	0.7–0.8	–
Barrow (Crowe *et al.* 2010)	0.4–0.8	–
Blackwater (Munster) and tributaries (Crowe *et al.* 2008, 2010)	0.50–0.71	–
Dunkellin/Lavally (Buckley and McCarthy 1987)	0.16	0.0
Flesk (Carruthers 1986)	0.0	–

Grey Wagtail: The Grey Wagtail is widely distributed throughout Ireland as a breeding species. It occurs in all types of freshwater habitats at elevations ranging from sea level to the uplands, but especially in fast-flowing streams lined with broadleaved trees. A number of estimates of breeding density have been made, and these are shown in Table 4.2. In Northern Ireland densities peak at up to 10.7

The Grey Wagtail occurs in all types of freshwater habitats (John Fox).

pairs per 10km on the River Lagan (Bailey 1982), while in the Republic highest densities are on the Blackwater (Munster) and Boyne where the peak may reach 11.1 and 13.4 pairs per 10km respectively (Crowe *et al.* 2008). Other Irish studies reveal somewhat lower densities. This compares with peak densities of 13 pairs in Scotland, 14 pairs in England and 16 pairs in Wales, respectively, per 10km of river (Marchant and Hyde 1980).

Two broods are typically produced per breeding season. Grey Wagtails feed on invertebrate prey, many of terrestrial origin, which enables them to exploit the widest possible range of freshwater habitats. Although susceptible to severe winter weather (Dobinson and Richards 1964), there was little change in the range of the breeding population between the late 1960s and the early 1990s. The total Irish breeding population in the early 1990s was estimated at 22,000 pairs (Gibbons *et al.* 1993).

Most Grey Wagtails leave their river breeding habitats for the winter, especially in upland areas, and during that season many occur in places such as farmyards in lowland areas where cattle are housed and even on coastal beaches, presumably areas where invertebrate prey remains plentiful. However, there is evidence that at some lowland river sites, numbers can actually increase in winter (Table 4.2). Bailey (1982) saw Grey Wagtails at his River Lagan study site only occasionally in winter.

There is a strong autumn migration in coastal districts, especially at Clear Island, Co. Cork (Sharrock 1969), but very few birds from northern Britain are known to winter in Ireland, with no evidence that continental birds do so (Tyler 1979).

In Ireland, apart from the few estimates of breeding density, only breeding biology of the Grey Wagtail has been studied in any detail (Smiddy and O'Halloran 1998). These authors collected data in Cos. Cork and Waterford during the 1980s and 1990s. Most of the 220 nests (97%) examined were located on structures of one kind or another, mainly on bridges, and apart from six nests, all were situated directly over water. Only one of these six nests (at 1km) was more than 25m from the nearest water. Most nests (63%) were built less than 2m above water or ground level. The date of laying the first egg varied from 29 March to 2 July, with the peak in the second week of April. There was evidence of a second peak later in the season, but the real incidence of second clutches was probably higher than recorded due to declining observer effort later in the season.

The mean clutch size was 4.79 eggs and the mean number of young fledged from successful nests was four. Most clutches (71%) consisted of five eggs. Overall, 64% of nesting attempts produced at least one fledged young. Reasons for nest failure varied, the most common being the loss of eggs from nests (44%), but the actual cause of these losses was unknown.

River	Breeding	Winter
Table 4.2 Grey Wagtail densities (pairs/10km) at some Irish rivers during the breeding and winter seasons. P = present.		
Northern Ireland (slow) (Marchant and Hyde 1980)	0.6–9.8	–
Northern Ireland (fast) (Marchant and Hyde 1980)	7.8	–
Blackwater (Northern Ireland) (Watson 1984)	6.0	–

River	Breeding	Winter
Table 4.2 Grey Wagtail densities (pairs/10km) at some Irish rivers during the breeding and winter seasons. P = present.		
Lagan (Bailey 1982)	2.3–10.7	P
Republic of Ireland (Marchant and Hyde 1980)	2.3	–
Boyne and tributaries (Crowe *et al.* 2008)	2.25-13.40	–
Blackwater (Munster) and tributaries (Crowe *et al.* 2008)	2.64–11.10	–
Flesk (Carruthers 1986)	6.6	–
Maigue (lowland) (Buckley 1992)	4.45	–
Owenmore (Buckley 1993)	3.85	1.75
Moy (Buckley 1993)	3.75	–
Mulkear (all sections) (Buckley 1992)	2.5	–
Mulkear (lowland) (Buckley 1992)	2.5	3.25
Mulkear (upland) (Buckley 1992)	2.5	–
Dunkellin/Lavally (Buckley and McCarthy 1987)	0.82	2.27

Some rivers and canals mentioned in the text.

Dipper feeding at a weir on the River Dodder, Co. Dublin (John Fox).

Dipper: The Dipper is one of the most intensively studied species in Ireland, especially in the south-west and north-west. It is generally regarded as a unique subspecies (Irish race *hibernicus*), although some doubt has recently been cast on this status (Lauga *et al.* 2005; Hourlay *et al.* 2008). These authors found no statistical difference in DNA sequences between the Irish race (*hibernicus*) and either *aquaticus* or *cinclus* (both races widespread in Europe), and suggested that the validity of some of the subspecies, including *hibernicus*, would benefit from a reassessment. However, it is unique as the only truly aquatic passerine occurring in Ireland. Although often referred to as an upland species, here it can be found

The Dipper can feed by swimming, diving and walking on the bed of fast-flowing streams (Richard T. Mills).

A typical Dipper nesting bridge on a fast-flowing river (Richard T. Mills).

breeding in streams right down to the coast. Typically, the habitat occupied by Dippers will be either a fast-flowing upland stream or a river with plenty of riffles in the lowlands. It is sedentary and widely distributed, and is absent only from areas where its preferred habitat of fast-flowing streams is absent (Gibbons *et al.* 1993).

The Dipper was the only waterbird species that did not decline following drainage at the River Blackwater system in Northern Ireland (Watson 1984; Williams *et al.* 1988). Presumably this was because the nesting sites, which are mainly on man-made structures such as bridges, remained intact after drainage, and the food supply quickly recovered as well. Densities per 10km of river (Table 4.3) in Northern Ireland vary from about two to six pairs, but in very good habitat on small rivers reaches 12 pairs (Perry 1986). On the River Flesk in County Kerry densities reach about nine pairs per 10km of river (Carruthers 1986). In County Cork, densities can reach ten pairs per 10km in good habitat on small rivers (Pat Smiddy). However, densities on some of the major rivers and their tributaries are low at between about one and two pairs per 10km on the Rivers Boyne and Blackwater (Munster) (Table 4.3). This is probably, at least partly, because the surveys concerned were concentrated on habitats suitable for Common Kingfishers rather than Dippers (Crowe *et al.* 2008b). Peak densities on suitable Dipper rivers in Ireland are only marginally lower than those found in similar habitats in Britain, where over 16 pairs per 10km have been recorded in Wales (Marchant and Hyde 1980, Tyler and Ormerod 1994).

The Irish population of the Dipper has been estimated at 1,750 to 5,000 pairs (Gibbons *et al.* 1993). The Dipper certainly seems to be doing well and population estimates at the higher end of the scale are probably normal in ideal habitat. Dippers generally occur at their highest density in base-rich, productive streams. Dipper populations have been depleted by stream acidification in some areas in Britain, but there is little evidence that this has occurred in Ireland. Acidified streams generally have poor invertebrate and fish communities, although there is no evidence that the Irish Dipper feeds on fish of any kind.

Its method of feeding on aquatic invertebrates is not matched by any other species. It is not web-footed, but is capable of swimming, diving and walking on the bed of fast-flowing streams while facing the current. Having completed a feeding search it usually hops onto a projecting rock. It bobs and blinks in a peculiar way and quickly shakes the water from its black and white plumage before contemplating the next dive.

How do Dippers maintain dry plumage and remain warm and insulated during dives in cold water? The plumage of a Co. Waterford Dipper was studied and compared with that of Blackbirds in an effort to answer this question (Davenport *et al.* 2009). It has frequently been stated in the literature that Dippers have denser plumage than other passerines of similar size. This was found not to be the case, and this Dipper had a plumage density almost exactly the same as that of a Blackbird. However, Dipper plumage differs in that they have almost twice as many feathers, especially down and contour feathers, compared to a Blackbird – thus enhanced insulation stems from the fact that the Dipper has a far more extensive plumage with the apterylae (bare areas) between feather tracts being fully feathered. Such areas are naked in Blackbirds and other passerines. Dippers also have extensive down cover on the head and wings. It was also found that Dipper down feathers were structurally more complex and substantially finer than similar feathers on a Blackbird. Dippers also have a large uropygial (preen) gland that is about ten times the size of that of other similar-sized passerine species (Tyler and Ormerod 1994). The abundant oil from this preen gland is used to insulate the feathers from saturation when diving.

Dippers roost communally, often beneath bridges, but never actually in bodily contact with their nearest neighbour, unlike some other communal roosting species such as Wrens and Long-tailed Tits. Up to ten individuals may occur at favoured bridges with suitable roosting niches. Dippers are territorial both during the breeding season and in the winter, yet the owner of the territory in which the roost is situated will tolerate strangers for the duration of the night roost. The question of energy expenditure in the Dipper during roosting has been examined by recording the plumage surface temperature of the sleeping bird (Davenport et al. 2004). The hypothesis being tested was that the plumage surface temperature should be nearly identical with environmental temperature in order to minimise energy expenditure during the night. It was found that there was a slight, but statistically significant, loss of heat to the environment. Many bridge roost sites are simply open ledges, although others are apparently snug niches. Bridge roost sites are sheltered from the elements, and they are also a few degrees warmer than outside the bridge (Smiddy and O'Halloran 2004). Therefore, even allowing for some heat loss to the environment, birds roosting at bridges apparently have an advantage over those roosting away from bridges. Birds roosting at bridges may also be safer from predators than those roosting elsewhere as they are generally at a height of at least 2m with a smooth wall beneath that would be difficult for a mammalian predator to scale.

Dippers generally do not decline following severe winters, as do Common Kingfishers and Grey Wagtails. This may be because they occur only in fast-flowing waters which freeze over only in the most exceptional of circumstances, and which are very rare in Ireland. Their unique plumage characteristics described above, and wide tolerance of environmental variables seems to protect them against cold weather (Tyler and Ormerod 1994). In fact adult birds show a greater mortality during the period immediately after breeding than during the winter (Galbraith and Tyler 1982). During exceptionally cold winter conditions Dippers have occurred at the edge of lakes and at the head of estuaries. An exceptional sighting was of one seen on a tarmacadam road in Co. Cork during a rain shower when water was flowing down the road. A small stream running parallel with the road was probably its normal habitat (Berrow 1991).

Perry (1983) and Perry and Agnew (1993) studied the Dipper in the north-west, where they recorded a 64% population increase over the ten-year period 1972–1982, and a further 32% increase over the following ten-year period 1982–1992, amounting to an overall increase of 116% over 20 years. Most Dipper pairs nested in close association with bridges or other man-made objects along the river corridor. Perry (1983) noted that 83% of nests were at bridges in 1972 and 1982, with a further 2% at weirs, while in 1992 the number of nests associated with bridges was 94% (Perry and Agnew 1993). Only 6% of nests were at elevations greater than 150m, despite the fact that there was an abundance of apparently suitable upland habitat available (Perry and Agnew 1993).

The breeding biology of Dippers has been studied in south-west Ireland (Smiddy et al. 1995; O'Halloran et al. 1999). Data were collected in Cos. Cork and Waterford during the 1980s and 1990s. Most of the 501 nests examined (86%) were located on bridges or walls near bridges. Nests on natural sites were mostly on riverbanks or among tree roots. Most nests (85%) were built less than 2m above water level. The same nest site and nest is generally used each year, provided the nest has survived the floods of the previous winter. Irish Dippers start breeding earlier, lay fewer eggs, fledge fewer young and have fewer second broods than most other populations. The date of laying the first egg varied from 22 February to 17 May, with 62% of all clutches commenced by 7 April. The mean clutch size was

Caddis fly larvae are one of the preferred prey items of Dippers (Richard T. Mills).

4.16 eggs and the mean brood size at fledging was 3.48 young. Overall, only 8.2% of pairs were double brooded, and this was as low as less than 2% in some years. Reasons for nest failure varied and the most common was the desertion of eggs or young (11%). Predatory mammals and birds were believed responsible for just over 10% of losses, and human activity was believed to account for over 6% of losses. However, in over 63% of cases the cause of failure was unknown.

Adult Dippers are generally sedentary, and they remain in their breeding territory in most cases for their entire lives. However, there is a significant dispersal of young birds away from their natal rivers in the first autumn and winter of their lives (O'Halloran *et al.* 2000). Juvenile dispersal begins in June. Birds ringed as nestlings moved the greatest distances while those ringed as adults moved least. There was strong fidelity to the breeding site by both sexes. Females moved greater distances than males. Females ringed as nestlings accounted for 64% of movements over 5km, while only 31% of males ringed as nestlings travelled more than this distance. Females were more likely to cross over watersheds than males. Annual survival rates for full grown male and female Dippers combined were estimated at 68% (O'Halloran *et al.* 1999).

Dipper diet has been studied in the north-west (Ormerod and Perry 1985; Agnew and Perry 1993) and the south-west (Taylor and O'Halloran 1997, 2001). Agnew and Perry (1993) examined the diet of incubating Dippers in the north-west, and they found that during this period they were foraging selectively on larger prey items, such as caddis fly larvae, above their environmental representation and smaller prey items, such as mayfly nymphs, at about their environmental representation. As the nestlings grew following hatching, the adults switched to feeding them with the larger caddis flies and they themselves took more of the smaller mayflies (Ormerod and Perry 1985).

Taylor and O'Halloran (1997) compared the diet of Dippers using faecal and regurgitate pellets collected during summer, autumn and winter. They found that there was no significant difference in taxonomic composition of the diet as represented by the two pellet types. They also studied diet during an early winter spate, and examined the possible implications for Dipper populations subjected to climate change (Taylor and O'Halloran 2001). Diet differed significantly between base-flow and spate conditions. Diet during the spate period contained greater proportions of prey taxa of terrestrial origin. With greater precipitation predicted, although with regional variation expected, under climate change models, this could have a significant effect on the diet of Dippers, and on Dipper populations, in the future.

Organochlorine chemicals and mercury were widely used in agriculture and industry in Ireland in the past, but the use of these products is now banned. However, residues at low levels are still detectable in the eggs of birds, and they have been found in the eggs of Dippers in recent years here (O'Halloran *et al.* 1993, 2003). No apparent trend in mercury pollution was observed, but a decrease in contaminant levels was noted over the years. DDT occurred in only two eggs, but its derivatives (DDE and TDE) were found much more commonly. PCB contaminants were present consistently over the ten-year study period, and there was little change in the proportion of contaminated eggs collected over time. However, there has been no obvious significant effect on the birds within the study area and no major change in either population levels or breeding success has been observed.

Table 4.3 Dipper densities (pairs/10km) at some Irish rivers during the breeding and winter seasons. P = present.

River	Breeding	Winter
Northern Ireland (fast) (Marchant and Hyde 1980)	3.9	–
Northern Ireland (slow) (Marchant and Hyde 1980)	0.0–2.1	–
North-east Ireland (Perry 1986)	4.0–12.5	–
North-west Ireland (Perry 1983, 1986)	3.45–5.55	–
Blackwater (Northern Ireland) (Watson 1984)	4.17–4.61	–
Lagan (Bailey 1982)	0.0–1.8	1.0–2.0
County Cork (Smiddy, in Hutchinson 1989)	9.1	–
Flesk (Carruthers 1986)	6.6–8.8	–
Mulkear (all sections) (Buckley 1992)	2.05	–
Mulkear (lowland) (Buckley 1992)	0.25	1.75
Mulkear (upland) (Buckley 1992)	0.0	–
Blackwater (Munster) and tributaries (Crowe et al. 2008)	0.28–1.39	–
Owenmore (Buckley 1993)	1.16	0.6
Boyne and tributaries (Crowe et al. 2008)	0.30–0.66	–
Dunkellin/Lavally (Buckley and McCarthy 1987)	0.05	0.16
Moy (Buckley 1993)	0.0	–
Maigue (lowland) (Buckley 1992)	0.0	–

Studies on bird communities of Irish rivers
A brief outline of the various studies carried out on the bird communities of Irish rivers is given here before dealing with the species. Bailey (1982) studied the breeding birds on 9.9km of the River Lagan in Belfast between Drum Bridge and Stranmillis Weir, where the river becomes tidal. During the years 1974–1981 he recorded a total of 29 species, 18 of which were proved to breed in at least one of the years, in this rather sluggish part of the river, which included canal sections running parallel to the river. A decrease in the number of breeding pairs of some species was noted after the colonisation of the study area by American mink, but the severe winter of 1978/79 and pollution may also have been contributory factors. The most numerous species was the Moorhen, followed by the Little Grebe. Among the passerine species,

Moorhen is one of the more numerous species on the River Lagan near Belfast (John Fox).

The Reed Bunting nests in the marginal vegetation along many rivers and canals (Richie Lort).

Sand Martins use the eroded banks of rivers to make their nest burrows (Karl Partridge).

the Reed Bunting was the most numerous, followed by the Grey Wagtail.

The birds of 21.5km of the River Blackwater catchment in Northern Ireland were studied pre- and post-drainage in 1984 and 1987 respectively (Watson 1984; Williams *et al.* 1988). These authors found that all species, except the Dipper, declined markedly following drainage and the removal of meanders.

Carruthers (1986) studied the breeding birds on 4.5km of the River Flesk at Killarney during 1983 and 1984. The species range was low, and only five were proved to breed, with another six recorded without evidence of breeding. Additionally, the Common Sandpiper nested on the river upstream of the study site. The River Flesk was described as fast flowing, in contrast to the sluggish River Lagan. The Old Red Sandstone geology upstream (although the study site was on Lower Limestone) and the fast flow probably account for the paucity of species, although those that were present occurred in densities comparable to Northern Ireland and Britain. Carruthers (1986) also mentioned the mink as a recent colonist in the area, but whether this predator had an influence on the species present is unknown. The nearby River Laune, which is more low-lying was mentioned as having a much more diverse fauna, with Mute Swan, Tufted Duck, Little Grebe, Moorhen, Common Coot, Common Kingfisher and Reed Bunting, as well as the five species recorded on the River Flesk, all breeding (Carruthers 1986). However, no further details of the bird fauna of this river have been published.

Buckley and McCarthy (1987) carried out a survey of the bird communities on the Dunkellin and Lavally river catchments in Co. Galway. This survey covered all species within the catchment of the rivers concerned, and it was carried out in both the breeding and winter seasons. These rivers are situated at low altitude and some species, notably Common Kingfisher, Grey Wagtail and Dipper were present at very low densities, and the Common Sandpiper was absent. Buckley (1992) carried out a similar survey of the bird communities on the Mulkear river catchment in Cos. Limerick and Tipperary, where he studied the birds on both the lowland and upland sections of the river. Buckley (1992) also reported briefly on surveys of the River Maigue (Limerick) and the Rivers Moy and Owenmore (Mayo).

Two river systems were assessed in 2008, mainly for their Common Kingfisher populations, but all other riparian species were recorded (Crowe *et al.* 2008). The rivers, including tributaries, were the Boyne and Blackwater (Munster). Both rivers are designated as Special Areas of Conservation (SAC), although some of the tributaries are not. The surveys were extensive but covered just one breeding season. Totals of 214km and 282km were covered on the Boyne and Blackwater respectively by a team of surveyors. A total of 28 riparian species were recorded including 27 on the Boyne and 21 on the Blackwater, although breeding was not proved for all. The Sand Martin was the most abundant species on both river systems, and the Mallard was also abundant and widespread. Overall densities were rather similar on both rivers, although considerable variation was recorded for several species. The results are expressed as individual birds recorded, rather than territories (except for Common Kingfisher). For the purposes of this review, pair (or territory) densities have been calculated by dividing the number of individuals by two. There was little evidence that birds present within designated areas fared any better than those in undesignated areas. Drainage maintenance on the Boyne system does not appear to be impacting negatively on the bird populations there.

Other breeding and wintering birds of rivers

Almost all of the wildfowl use river habitats in one way or another. Probably the best-known species is the Mute Swan, which use these habitats throughout the year. Mute Swans breed on many rivers, favouring those that have a slow flow, and are of reasonably large size. On rivers where they are present, densities of up to three pairs per 10km of river are normal, but up to six pairs per 10km occur on the Boyne (Table 4.4). In Britain, densities of up to 13 pairs per 10km of river have been recorded, but most host lower numbers (Marchant and Hyde 1980). Smiddy and O'Halloran (1991) recorded breeding Mute Swans on a variety of habitats in east Cork, including small rivers. They found that although the number of cygnets fledged was lower at rivers than at other habitats, the difference was not significant, the river sample being quite small anyway. The Whooper Swan is a winter visitor, and its use of rivers is more for the grassy floodplain, where it feeds, although birds will visit the river channel to bathe and preen, and for safe roosting at night. Some geese, especially the Greater White-fronted and Greylag use river valleys in a similar way in winter.

Most of the duck species can be found in association with rivers in the winter, although the diving species are usually absent, or are present only during flood conditions. Floodplains are ideal winter feeding habitats for Eurasian Wigeon, Common Teal and Mallard, and very large flocks of the former two can be seen on almost every river. Northern Pintail and Northern Shoveler may occasionally occur also, but in much smaller numbers compared with the former three. In the breeding season the range of duck species is much lower than during the winter, and the commonest then is the Mallard, the most widespread of the Irish breeding ducks. The Mallard often occurs at densities ranging from about five to 20 pairs per 10km of river, but sometimes the numbers are even lower (Table 4.4). These figures are low by comparison with some British ones where exceptionally up to 139 pairs and 474 pairs per 10km of river have been recorded on fast- and slow-flowing rivers respectively (Marchant and Hyde 1980).

The Tufted Duck may occur (and breed) on some slow-flowing rivers such as the Lagan (Bailey 1982) and the Laune

Mute Swans prefer slow-flowing rivers of a reasonably large size (John Fox).

The introduced Mandarin Duck has established a breeding population on the Shimna River, Co. Down (Mark Carmody).

(Carruthers 1986). Common Pochard occasionally occurred on the Lagan, but did not breed. The scarce Red-breasted Merganser has been recorded breeding on the Flesk and the Laune (Carruthers 1986). The rare Goosander also occurs on rivers in the breeding season, but it and the Red-breasted Merganser are generally found only in those with a fast flow. The Red-breasted Merganser is mainly confined to the west, while the Goosander is a recent colonist and is found only in the north-west and the east. The Mandarin Duck has recently established a breeding population on the Shimna River, County Down (Mathers 1993). Two pinioned pairs were introduced to Tollymore Forest Park in 1978, and the young produced by these and succeeding pairs have flown free. They have now spread as far as Newcastle, and the estimated population in 2005/2006 was 20–30 pairs (NIBR 2008).

The Little Grebe occurs as a breeding bird in only the slowest-flowing rivers where there is an abundance of emergent vegetation to anchor their nests. On the River Lagan, presumably mostly on the canal sections, Bailey (1982) recorded up to 27 pairs per annum. However, they declined towards the end of the study period, and it was suggested the reason might be related to pollution levels causing a decrease in fish populations or to predation by mink. Numbers at this study site were maintained through the winter. No other river studied for this review held more than the occasional breeding pair. Densities in Britain ranged up to 13 and 17 pairs per 10km on fast and slow flowing rivers respectively (Marchant and Hyde 1980).

The Little Egret and Grey Heron both occur in rivers. The Little Egret is a recent colonist (Smiddy 2002), mainly to the south coast, but in the studies of the Boyne and Blackwater (Munster), egrets extended quite some distance inland, and even penetrated up quite small tributaries (Crowe *et al.* 2008). The Grey Heron is found throughout the country and few rivers are totally without them. The egret and heron both breed in woodland habitats beside rivers, but not exclusively so, and the river is used chiefly as a source for their fish prey.

The Moorhen is widespread but thinly distributed in rivers in both the breeding and winter seasons, but its close relative, the Common Coot, is found only on some slow flowing rivers in quite small numbers, and generally in lakes, both natural and those formed behind river dams. Bailey (1982) recorded high population levels of the Moorhen on the River Lagan (up to 66 pairs per 10km of river), but these declined towards the end of the study period, and he suggested the presence of mink as a cause. Away from the Lagan, Moorhens have not occurred in numbers greater than 15 pairs per 10km of river, and they often occur in numbers far lower than that (Table 4.4). Moorhens tend to shun rivers with a fast flow and, like some other species, can be badly affected by drainage works in their slow-flowing river habitat. Dredging and regrading of the bank on the River Ravernet (Antrim) caused a decline from five pairs to one pair between 1975 and 1976 (Marchant and Hyde 1980). In Britain, Moorhen densities commonly exceed 30 pairs per 10km of river, and have reached a peak of 58 pairs (Marchant and Hyde 1980). Clearly, the River Lagan population was exceptionally high by Irish standards. Water Rails are sometimes present beside rivers, but they are probably under-recorded to some extent because of their skulking nature.

There are a few inland colonies of Great Cormorants on the western lakes, but most of them breed in coastal waters. However, breeding and non-breeding birds visit rivers at some considerable distance from the nearest colony and from the coast. They are commonest in some rivers (*e.g.* Blackwater (Munster)) in the autumn, but some may be present throughout the year. They visit small as well as large rivers. Great Cormorants can be major predators of migrating salmon smolts on some rivers such as the River Bush, Northern Ireland (Kennedy and Greer 1988), and at Newport, Co. Mayo (Macdonald 1988), but at inland lakes the winter diet was composed mainly of roach and perch (Macdonald 1987).

Many wading birds use river valleys in a similar way to swans and ducks. European Golden Plover, Northern Lapwing and Black-tailed Godwit often occur in large flocks on floodplains in winter. Common Snipe and Eurasian Curlew flocks may also form, and these are occasionally joined by Dunlin, Common Redshank and the occasional Ruff. Some of the above species breed on the floodplains also, especially Northern Lapwing, Common Snipe, Eurasian Curlew and Common Redshank, but such species will not be discussed further here. The Common Sandpiper breeds on shingle banks along some rivers, especially in the west and north, and although Bailey (1982) recorded them regularly on the River Lagan, he had no proof of breeding, and the birds quickly moved on during their spring and autumn migration. Buckley (1992) recorded densities of six and three pairs respectively on the Rivers Moy and Owenmore, and Carruthers (1986) recorded breeding on the upstream part of the River Flesk. These densities compare with peaks of 27 pairs per 10km of river in north-east England (Marchant and Hyde 1980), and up to 16 pairs per 10km of river in Wales (Round and Moss 1984). Green Sandpipers occur throughout the year on some rivers in small numbers, especially the Blackwater (Munster) and Bride (north) in Co. Cork, while others have been recorded at the River Lagan both in summer and winter (Bailey 1982). Some gull species also occur in rivers, especially in winter, the most numerous being the Black-headed Gull.

The Common Sandpiper breeds on shingle banks along some rivers (Richie Lort).

Several passerine species are to varying extents associated with rivers also, but none exclusively so, apart from the specialist Grey Wagtail and Dipper. The Sand Martin nests in a range of habitats from coastal cliffs to sand and gravel pits, but sandy river-banks are also favoured. Only very small numbers (up to three pairs) bred in the study area of Bailey (1982) on the River Lagan. However, the Sand Martin was the most abundant species on both the Boyne and Blackwater (Munster) river systems with many small colonies present. The Pied Wagtail is also found in a variety of habitats, but many make their nests beside rivers, often on walls and bridges, and they frequently feed on the associated shingle banks. This wagtail was present on most rivers studied for this review in numbers ranging from two to five pairs per 10km of

The Sedge Warbler is a common summer visitor in the marginal vegetation along river banks (Richard T. Mills).

river (Table 4.4). These figures compare with densities of frequently in excess of ten pairs per 10km of river, and occasionally up to 84 pairs, in north-east England (Marchant and Hyde 1980). In Wales, Round and Moss (1984) showed Pied Wagtails to be two or three times more plentiful on rivers than Grey Wagtails, the opposite of the situation in Ireland.

The Sedge Warbler is a common summer inhabitant of riverside vegetation, and along the south coast it may be joined by the recent arrival, the Common Reed Warbler (Smiddy and O'Mahony 1997). A peak of seven pairs of Sedge Warblers per 10km of river has been recorded in Ireland (Table 4.4). They have not been reported from several studies, but whether this reflects a real absence or not remains unknown. In Britain, up to 39 pairs per 10km of river have been recorded, mostly in southern

England, with far lower densities further north (Marchant and Hyde 1980). The Reed Bunting represents a similar picture to the Sedge Warbler in that most studies do not report their presence (Table 4.4). Up to 19 pairs per 10km of river have been recorded on the River Lagan (Bailey 1982), but with far fewer on the Rivers Boyne and Blackwater (Munster) (Crowe *et al.* 2008). Densities in Britain are far greater with up to 76 pairs per 10km of river recorded in eastern England, with fewer further north and in Wales (Marchant and Hyde 1980). Many other warbler species occur by rivers, but are not strictly riparian in nature. Grasshopper Warblers and Common Whitethroats as well as Blackcaps, Willow Warblers and Chiffchaffs are common summer visitors to river valleys.

In general, little systematic work has been done on the non-breeding bird species of rivers (and canals), or on those species found in these habitats during the autumn and winter. Bailey (1982) made some observations on such birds, and he found that many of the resident breeding species remained throughout the winter, such as Little Grebe, Mallard, Moorhen, Common Snipe and Dipper. He found that most Common Kingfishers and Grey Wagtails deserted the River Lagan in winter, the former probably for estuarine areas, and the latter for coastal and farmland sites. Reed Buntings declined in winter, and these probably moved to farmland habitats. However, he noted many winter arrivals to his study area, especially Fieldfares, Redwings, Siskins and Lesser Redpolls, with many flocks of other finches also found along the bankside vegetation, as well as a party of Tree Sparrows. Finch flocks (among other species) are especially attracted to this type of habitat when alders grow there. Buckley (1992, 1993) and Buckley and McCarthy (1987) also made brief observations on the winter riparian birds of their study rivers. This is probably an approximate reflection of the status of species at a wider level in riparian habitats in winter.

Table 4.4 Densities (pairs/10km) of selected species recorded breeding on rivers in Ireland based on published studies (1 = 9.9km of Lagan, Bailey 1982; 2 = 21.5km of Blackwater (Northern Ireland), Watson 1984); 3 = 4.5km of Flesk, Carruthers 1986; 4 = Dunkellin/Lavally catchment, Buckley and McCarthy 1987; 5 = Mulkear catchment, Buckley 1992; 6 = Maigue, Buckley 1992; 7 = 214km of Boyne, (Crowe *et al.* 2008); 8 = 282km of Blackwater (Munster), (Crowe *et al.* 2008). P = present.

Species name	1	2	3	4	5	6	7	8
Mute Swan	1–3	–	–	1	0–1	3	2–6	1–3
Mallard	5–11	5	7–20	7	1–3	12	3–13	3–10
Tufted Duck	1–9	–	–	–	–	–	–	P
Little Grebe	5–27	–	–	–	–	–	P	P
Water Rail	0–1	–	–	–	–	–	P	–
Moorhen	32–66	15	–	3	1–3	4	1–7	1
Common Coot	0–2	–	–	–	–	–	0–1	P
Pied Wagtail	2–5	2	0–2	–	1–3	4	P	P
Sedge Warbler	1–7	–	–	–	–	–	1–3	0–1
Reed Bunting	7–19	–	–	–	–	–	1–3	0–1

Breeding birds of canals

Although Johnston and Dromey (undated) gave a general account of the typical birds of Irish canals, the Royal Canal is one of the few canals in Ireland that has been surveyed systematically for its bird populations. The main line of the canal is 145km in length. It was built during the years 1790 to 1830 to link the River Liffey in Dublin to the River Shannon in Co. Longford. During the 1950s the canal became disused and was officially closed to navigation in 1961. Restoration work on a large scale began in 1986 and, by the early 2000s, a complete navigation channel was open again. As part of the planning for this restoration a full survey of the ecology of the canal was undertaken in 1990 (Dromey *et al.* 1991). By this stage a major dredging programme was already under way on the eastern section of the canal between Dublin and Mullingar. Accordingly, the ecological survey was approached in three separate units as follows:

Mallards are common along rivers and canals (Richard T. Mills).

- Unit 1: Recently dredged and navigable channel;
- Unit 2: Watered canal but not recently dredged;
- Unit 3: De-watered or dry canal.

For the breeding bird surveys, two separate methods were used. Firstly, a sample section of each of the above units was selected to represent the habitats present in the entire canal. These study sections included a total of 25km of canal (approximately 17% of its entire length). Each of these study sections was visited six times during the breeding season from mid-April to early July. As the canal towpath was a grassy track in many parts, a mountain bicycle was the easiest form of transport. This allowed the observer to walk a section and cycle back to the starting point. All territorial birds seen or heard within the canal boundaries were plotted on visit maps and ultimately transferred to species maps. This allowed the estimation of population size and a comparison between the bird communities under different forms of management. Secondly, two complete censuses of riparian birds only was carried out on the entire 145km of the canal, one in May and the second in late June–early July 1990. A team of volunteer census observers undertook this survey.

Riparian species on the Royal Canal were found to be quite limited in diversity of species and density of breeding territories (Table 4.5). Certain riparian species, normally found breeding on lowland rivers in Ireland, were conspicuously absent. These include Common Sandpiper, Common Kingfisher and Sand Martin, all of which require bare earth, sand or gravel banks for nesting. The Dipper could nest under the many bridges on the canal but it requires fast-moving water in which to feed and the flow in the canal is generally minimal, so is unsuitable. Common Coot and Tufted Duck, which occasionally nest on rivers, were probably absent because of the limited area and depth for feeding in the canal.

Riparian species recorded breeding on the Royal Canal were present in very low numbers by comparison with similar sections of canal surveyed in Britain (Marchant and Hyde 1980; Briggs 1988). The highest densities for all species, with the exception of Grey Wagtail, were found in Unit 2 of the canal which, at that time, offered a combination of open water, dense marginal vegetation and undisturbed banks with overhanging trees (Table 4.5).

The overall density of Mute Swan territories at 0.5 per 10km of canal was low by comparison with populations in Britain, where an average of 1.5 territories per 10km was reported from regular

Mute Swan with a healthy brood (Richard T. Mills).

Grey Wagtails nest in the bridges and walls of the locks on canals (John Fox).

census-taking of 17 sample stretches of canal totalling 75km (Marchant and Hyde 1980). The Montgomery canal in Wales held eight breeding pairs (average 1.8 pairs per 10km) in 56km of channel. A lower density of pairs (1.2 per 10km) was found in a sample of eight disused canals in Britain (totalling 35.5km in length) (Marchant and Hyde 1980).

Of the seven pairs of Mute Swan that attempted to breed on the Royal Canal in 1990, five (71%) succeeded in hatching young. This is close to the average hatching success (76%) found by Collins (1991) for 34 canal nests of Mute Swan in the Dublin area. Collins (1991) found a higher rate of egg loss from nests in urban areas (41%) compared with rural locations (17%), but no other significant difference between breeding success. The distribution of breeding territories along the Royal Canal may also be influenced by the availability of food. Swans are entirely vegetarian, feeding mainly on the leaves and stems of submerged aquatic plants such as water crowfoot and pondweed. In areas such as Maynooth, Co. Kildare, where regular dredging has reduced the abundance of submerged aquatic plants, the swans were clearly supplementing their diet with artificial food supplied by local people. The density of Mallard territories (peak of 1.2 per 10km in Unit 2) was also very low compared with canals in Britain, where Marchant and Hyde (1980) reported up to 170 pairs per 10km in north-east England.

The total breeding population of Moorhen on the Royal Canal was estimated at 62 pairs in 1990. This gives an overall density of four pairs per 10km, which is extremely low by comparison with a sample of 17 canals in Britain which held an average of 30 pairs per 10km (Marchant and Hyde 1980). A lowland river and a disused canal in Northern Ireland held over 50 pairs per 10km (Bailey 1982). The only section of the Royal Canal that provided optimum conditions for Moorhen was Unit 2, where the 5km stretch west of Mullingar was not yet open to navigation and had not been recently dredged. It had abundant submerged aquatic plants and wide fringes (up to 2m) of emergent vegetation on both banks. This area had an average density of 30 pairs per 10km.

Grey Wagtail is a characteristic species of lowland rivers and it also occurred on the Royal Canal with an estimated 21 pairs in 1990. Breeding territories were commonly associated with bridges and locks where fast-flowing water occurred. Nests were often built in holes in the masonry or on tree roots growing out of the canal banks. The overall density of this species on the Royal Canal at 1.4 pairs per 10km is low by comparison with densities on lowland rivers in Britain (Marchant and Hyde 1980). On long level sections of the canal few territories occurred, while in the series of eight locks near Killucan, Co. Westmeath, five territories were concentrated in 4km of canal. The lowest density of territories was found on the western section of the canal (Unit 3) where there was little flowing water and where most of the locks were disused.

Other species associated with wetlands were found on some parts of the canal. The total of 34 Sedge Warbler territories recorded in May 1990 was considered to be a substantial underestimate of the true population compared with a more intensive study of three 25km sections of the canal. The highest Sedge Warbler territory density was 12 in 8km (15 per 10km) in a disused section of the canal between Ballynacarrigy and Abbeyshrule, Co. Longford. Marchant and Hyde (1980) also found a higher density of Sedge Warblers on disused canals (7.5 pairs per 10km) compared to active canals (5.4 pairs per 10km). A census was also taken of non-riparian species along the Royal Canal in 1990, and a total of 25 species was recorded. European Robin, Blackbird, Wren, Willow Warbler and Chaffinch dominated this community, which was rather similar to that found in field boundaries. The canal can be considered as a double line of hedgerows crossing the country, although in places there are sizeable gaps in cover, especially where the canal crosses areas of raised bog.

Table 4.5 Breeding populations of riparian bird species and territory density on the Royal Canal, 1990 (Dromey *et al.* 1991)

Species	Unit 1		Unit 2		Unit 3		All sections	
	Pairs	Pairs/10km	Pairs	Pairs/10km	Pairs	Pairs/10km	Pairs	Pairs/10km
Mute Swan	2	0.3	5	1.2	0	0.0	7	0.5
Mallard	3	0.4	5	1.2	3	0.8	11	0.7
Moorhen	22	3.0	32	7.4	8	2.0	62	4.0
Grey Wagtail	13	1.8	6	1.4	1	0.3	21	1.4
Sedge Warbler	16	2.2	16	3.7	2	0.5	34	2.2

Summary and Conclusions

It is clear the breeding bird communities of rivers and canals have been poorly studied in Ireland by comparison with other European countries. The few published studies available suggest that breeding densities of some of the key species may be at lower levels than in other comparable habitats elsewhere. However, there is no monitoring scheme in place specifically for riparian birds, as there is for birds of the wider countryside (Countryside Bird Survey). A monitoring scheme for wetlands concentrates mainly on ducks, geese, swans, wading birds and gulls (Irish Wetland Bird Survey). This scheme covers many river valleys, especially the important callows and floodplains. Of the truly specialist riparian species, Common Kingfisher, Grey Wagtail and Dipper, only the latter has been intensively studied in Ireland. The results suggest that bridges are the preferred nesting habitats and that populations are stable. In the Grey Wagtail only breeding biology has been studied in any detail, and again populations are considered satisfactory, but subject to fluctuations following severe winters. The Common Kingfisher has been little studied here, and research is urgently needed, although census work in recent years has shown a reasonably healthy population in the rivers studied to date. Other species found on rivers and canals are not exclusive to that habitat, although many of these are restricted to freshwater habitats for foraging and or nesting, i.e. rivers, canals, lakes. Nevertheless, more population studies in the breeding season, concentrating on breeding success, habitat and dietary requirements are needed in order to understand the situation in these habitats. Studies in the autumn and winter season are also required for all species.

5. Lakes, Reservoirs and Turloughs

Clive Mellon and Roger Goodwillie

Introduction

Ireland's lakes or loughs are a priceless resource for both humans and wildlife. They provide us with most of our drinking water and support important fisheries. They also offer many recreational opportunities of both economic and aesthetic value such as boating, angling, wildfowling, sightseeing and of course bird watching. Ireland's freshwater resource is substantial. It is estimated that there are more than 13,870 lakes in Ireland with 12,200 in the Republic amounting to 2.3% of land cover (Freshwater Ecology Group *et al.* 2007). In Northern Ireland there are 1,670 lakes or 4.4% of land cover, a figure which is assisted in no uncertain terms by Lough Neagh, an impressive inland sea which covers some 383km² (Gibson and Jordan 2002). These wetland riches are largely a legacy of recent glacial history, as many lakes were formed by the gouging action of glaciers or lie in hollows between drumlins left by the receding ice.

Most lakes in Ireland are located in the west and the central lowlands, with relatively few in the south-east. The vast majority are very small – some 8,500 are less than one hectare in area while fewer than 2% exceed 50 hectares (Freshwater Ecology Group *et al.* 2007). Yet our landscape is dominated by a small number of very large freshwater bodies, five lakes having a surface area of more than 10,000 hectares (Table 5.1).

Bunduff Lough, Co. Sligo (Richard Nairn).

Table 5.1 Ireland's largest lakes		
Lake	Location (County)	Size (hectares)
Lough Neagh	Antrim, Down, Armagh, Tyrone, Derry	38,300
Lough Corrib	Galway, Mayo	18,240
Lough Derg	Tipperary, Clare, Galway	11,800
Lower Lough Erne	Fermanagh	10,950
Lough Ree	Westmeath, Longford, Roscommon	10,500

In combination, the myriad of small lakes and the larger water bodies are a great resource for both breeding and non-breeding waterfowl. Birds are attracted to lakes for a variety of reasons, mainly food, shelter and breeding habitat. Various factors influence the use of lakes by birds including water quality and depth, abundance of aquatic organisms, vegetation and shelter, while freedom from human disturbance is also an important requirement. In a study at Lough Leane, Co. Kerry, it was found that waterfowl showed a clear preference for the shallow and sheltered sections of the lake and for areas with higher nutrient levels which supported the greatest food supply of macroinvertebrates and macrophytes (Ní Shuilleabháin 2000).

Classification of lakes

Lakes and ponds have been defined as all bodies of open and standing fresh water that lack a strong unidirectional flow of water. Lakes can be categorised according to size, altitude, catchment geology, water quality and their associated vegetation communities, although the most frequent classifications relate to the trophic (nutrient) or acid status of the waters. The Water Framework Directive (2000/60/EC) attaches greater emphasis on the ecological status of waters which involves assessments of lake biota including phytoplankton, macrophytes, invertebrates and fish. Further freshwater habitat classifications are used in the selection and designation of Special Areas of Conservation (SACs) under the Directive on the Conservation of Wild Fauna and Flora 92/43/EEC (Habitats Directive).

Although there is considerable overlap in the species of birds which frequent different types of lakes, there are some significant differences depending on the nature, size and location of the water body. For example, a small upland lake might support a very different bird assemblage to a large, nutrient-rich lake in the lowlands. This section therefore considers how birds use four broad categories of water bodies: lowland lakes (eutrophic and mesotrophic), oligotrophic or dystrophic lakes of bog and upland, turloughs (and marl lakes) and artificial reservoirs.

Lowland lakes – eutrophic and mesotrophic waters

Eutrophic lakes are nutrient-rich waters often discoloured by algae and other suspended material. While some water bodies are naturally eutrophic, many Irish lakes have become eutrophic through enrichment by human influence, especially waste water and agricultural run-off. Examples of naturally eutrophic systems are the lakes of the Upper Lough Erne and Lough Oughter complex in Cos. Fermanagh and Cavan. Some eutrophic lakes, such as Lough Neagh, have become hypertrophic due to the sheer volume of nutrients entering the waters. Nutrient-rich lakes often support abundant invertebrate fauna such as chironomid larvae which are an important source of food for both fish and birds (Winfield *et al.* 1989).

Upper Lough Erne at Crom Castle, Co. Fermanagh
(Richard Nairn).

Moorhens breed on the smallest farm ponds and the largest
of lakes (Richard T. Mills).

Mesotrophic lakes are moderately rich in nutrients. Some former oligotrophic lakes, such as Lough Mask, Co. Galway, are now classified as mesotrophic due to increased phytoplankton growth. Similarly a number of former mesotrophic lakes, such as Lower Lough Erne, Co. Fermanagh, have become more enriched over time and are now classed as eutrophic waters (NIEA 2005).

Breeding Birds

Many species of birds breed on or around the shores of these lowland lakes and are dependent both on the waters of the lake and on associated habitats for food and shelter. The presence of small islands or a fringe of emergent vegetation generally enhances the potential for breeding birds.

Common Coot and Moorhen are among the most familiar breeding species of our inland waterways. The Moorhen has a wider distribution in Ireland since it is more adaptable, being content to breed anywhere from the smallest farm pond to the largest of lakes. Common Coots prefer somewhat larger lakes and ponds, but the two species can be seen together on many waters. Both species are omnivorous and while Moorhens prefer to pick food from the surface or dip into shallow water, Common Coots are equally adept at surface feeding or diving for weed, invertebrates and small fish (Cramp and Simmons 1980).

Great Crested Grebe prefer large, shallow lakes with fringing vegetation where they can conceal their nests. This elegant waterbird is mostly associated with the lowland areas of north-eastern and central Ireland and is scarce or absent across much of southern Ireland. Lough Neagh supports by far the largest breeding concentration in the country (Hutchinson 1994). Here the combination of shallow, food-rich waters and areas of extensive reed fringe provide ideal conditions for the grebes. The development of a new census technique, which involves searching the shallows in a small boat or wading through emergent vegetation, showed that the population was even higher than previously thought (Perry 2000). In the late 1990s an estimated 2,017 pairs were recorded on Lough Neagh and its associated lakes. The birds breed colonially on the lough and 10 colonies of over 50 pairs were identified (Perry *et al.* 1998).

In some areas there is also evidence that a genuine increase has occurred. The Cavan lakes were first surveyed for Great Crested Grebe in 1976, and during a census in 1986–88 an estimated 813 birds were recorded, representing a 44% increase in their population (Lovatt 1988).

Little Grebe can be surprisingly secretive in the breeding season and often only betray their presence on lakes and ponds when their whinnying call is heard. Despite this, they are more widespread than the Great Crested Grebe across lowland Ireland, frequenting any still waters and even very small ponds where there is sufficient vegetation for their nests.

Great Crested Grebe in territorial display (Andrew Kelly Photography, www.akellyphoto.com).

Many different species of wildfowl nest on our lakes. The ubiquitous Mallard can be found in any wetland habitat from the smallest pond to the largest of lakes. After the Mallard, the most common and widespread breeding duck is the Tufted Duck. This species has a similar distribution pattern to the Great Crested Grebe, frequenting the larger lowland waters, with Lough Neagh and Lough Derg (Shannon) being among the most important sites.

The Gadwall is a rare and localised breeding duck but may be overlooked due to its superficial similarity to the female Mallard. It first bred in Ireland in 1933 and appears to be largely restricted to Lough Neagh and the wetlands of Co. Wexford. The Irish population in the early 1990s was estimated at just 30 pairs (Gibbons *et al.* 1993). However there is evidence of an increase in numbers, particularly around Lough Neagh. A recent survey of Ram's Island on Lough Neagh found that numbers increased from one pair in 2005 to 37 pairs in 2009, which is attributable to the removal of rats from the island (Allen 2010). The Irish population may have originated from birds released in England during the nineteenth century (Holloway 1996) and it also seems likely that released birds have augmented the population in some parts of Northern Ireland more recently (Gibbons *et al.* 1993).

The Northern Shoveler is a scarce breeding duck of marshes fringing shallow bays, with possibly fewer than 100 pairs, many of which are found around the bays and islands of Upper Lough Erne. Common Teal are often associated with upland lakes and pools, but also nest around the shallow fringes of our larger lakes. The Common Pochard is much better known as a winter visitor but is a locally common breeder around Lough Neagh. Elsewhere this is a scarce bird with breeding seldom confirmed, although a pair did nest successfully at Lough Ourna, Co. Tipperary in 2007 (Hillis 2008).

Gadwalls appear to be largely restricted to Lough Neagh and the wetlands of Co. Wexford (Richie Lort).

Mute Swans with family (John Fox).

Common Scoters are restricted to breeding in small numbers on some of the western lakes (Karl Partridge).

The elegant Mute Swan adorns most of our lowland lakes, with Ireland supporting a healthy population estimated at some 20,000 birds (Gibbons *et al.* 1993). Its northern cousin, the Whooper Swan, graces many Irish wetlands in winter with its evocative bugling. Some Whoopers, often injured birds, remain in Ireland every summer, and a few pairs breed each year mainly at Lough Neagh/Beg, although breeding has also occurred at lakes in Cos. Fermanagh and Donegal (Hillis 2010).

The Red-breasted Merganser is a characteristic species of the larger lakes in the west of Ireland, particularly in Cos. Mayo and Galway. This fish-eating sawbill species is equally at home breeding on coastal inlets and sea loughs. The Common Shelduck is another familiar coastal species which is still a rare breeding bird on inland waters away from Lough Neagh. It is well established around the lake's sandy shores, where rabbit burrows are frequently used as nesting holes.

One of the most enigmatic breeding birds of our large lakes is the Common Scoter. In Scotland it typically breeds on remote lochans, yet in Ireland the Common Scoter builds its nest in dense vegetation on the islands of some of our largest western lakes. Breeding was first recorded on Lower Lough Erne in 1905 (Ussher 1905) and the population there reached a peak of 137–167 pairs in 1967 (Ferguson 1967). Sadly, numbers declined rapidly during the 1980s until it had become extinct as a breeding bird by 1993 (Tierney *et al.* 2000). However Common Scoters became established on several other loughs and when the first full Irish census was carried out in 1985/86, Common Scoters were found to be breeding on Lough Conn/Cullin, Co. Mayo, Lough Corrib and Lough Ree (Ruttledge 1987).

In 1995 about 100 pairs were found between these three lakes (Underhill *et al.* 1995) and another full British and Irish survey was completed the following year in the aftermath of the *Sea Empress* oil pollution incident. By now the Lough Corrib population had increased to 40 pairs but Lough Conn/Cullin had declined to just 17 pairs, although a new breeding site was also discovered at Lough Arrow, Co. Sligo (Delany and Gittings 1996). This site continues to support breeding scoter, with an estimated 5–6 pairs in 2006 (David Tierney, pers. comm.).

All known sites were again surveyed in 1999 showing a continued decline at Lough Conn/Cullin to just five pairs. The study noted a significant increase in the ratio of males to females (Tierney *et al.* 2000) and this was emphasised by a further survey at Lough Conn/Cullin in 2004 when only 2/3 potential pairs were found. Part of the problem was that although the number of males had remained constant at 23–25 birds, the number of females had dropped to just three by 2004 (Heffernan and Hunt 2004).

Sadly, the Lough Conn/Cullin population seems to be following the pattern of Lower Lough Erne where the number of females also dwindled. It seems likely that this was at least partly caused by predation of the incubating females by American mink (Partridge 1989), although deterioration in water quality may also have contributed, since both Lower Lough Erne and Lough Conn/Cullin have experienced increased enrichment in recent years (Tierney *et al.* 2000).

Nesting Tufted Ducks have suffered from predation by introduced mink (Richard T. Mills).

Predation by mink has also been implicated in declines of breeding waterfowl at other lakes. At Lough Carra, Co. Mayo, surveys of nesting Mallard, Tufted Duck and Red-breasted Merganser on the islands in 2005/6 found significant declines in numbers of all species compared to 1968–74. Predation by mink is considered to have been a key factor in this decline and Tufted Duck are now restricted to nesting on a single island in association with Black-headed Gulls, which afford some protection from mink and other predators (Meehan *et al.* 2009).

One species which is not universally welcomed to our lakes is the Ruddy Duck. This North American bird is thought to have originally escaped from the wildfowl collection at Slimbridge in Gloucestershire around 1960, and quickly became established in the UK, France and Holland. It has contributed to the decline of the endangered White-headed Duck in Spain through hybridisation and is now the subject of a European-wide eradication programme (Hughes *et al.* 2006). The first recorded breeding in Ireland was at Lough Neagh , Co. Armagh in 1973 (Culbert and Furphy 1978), and a population soon became established in the Lough Neagh area, with 25–29 pairs recorded in 2003/4 (Allen *et al.* 2006). Elsewhere in Ireland Ruddy Ducks have been widely recorded, although there are very few confirmed breeding records (Perry *et al.* 1998b). More recently the Lough Neagh population has declined and breeding has not been proven since a brood was seen at Lurgan Park Lake , Co. Armagh in 2007 (Dave Allen, pers. comm.). This suggests that the current eradication programme in England and Wales is also having an effect on the Irish population, since it is thought that there are regular movements between Britain and Ireland outside the breeding season (Allen *et al.* 2006).

The Great Cormorant is another controversial resident of lowland lakes where it can sometimes come into conflict with fisheries interests. Although most Great Cormorant colonies are coastal, inland nesting has been on the increase since the 1970s

Great Cormorants may nest and roost on trees in lakes (Richie Lort).

and there are now a number of well-established inland colonies in Ireland, mostly on wooded islands in the midlands and west. The largest colonies are around Lough Derg (Shannon), Lough Scannive and Lough Cutra , Co. Galway and numbers at these sites increased through the 1980s, possibly assisted by the spread of roach into many lake systems (Macdonald 1987).

Gulls and terns

The Great Cormorant is not the only 'seabird' which breeds on our inland waters. The islands on some of our larger lakes make ideal nesting sites for colonies of noisy gulls, with Black-headed Gulls being the most widespread and numerous. Of all Ireland's regularly breeding gulls, only the pelagic Black-legged Kittiwake does not have any inland breeding stations.

The Black-headed Gull is primarily an inland gull, and the most recent inland population estimate of 7,880 apparently occupied nests represents well over half of the Irish total for the species (Mitchell *et al.* 2004). The largest colonies are on Lough Neagh, Lough Erne and Lough Corrib, but numbers have declined dramatically in recent years. At Lough Neagh between 1985–88 and 1998–2002 Black-headed Gull numbers declined from over 30,000 pairs to just under 3,000. A similar rate of decline was found at Lough Corrib where numbers fell from 4,300 to 430 pairs. However not all sites have fared badly and in the same period numbers on Lough Erne rose sharply from 800 to 2,800 pairs (Mitchell *et al.* 2004).

About half of our breeding Common Gulls are also located inland, although in much smaller numbers. The most important colonies are on Lough Corrib, Lower Lough Erne and Lough Mask , Co. Mayo, but very small colonies can also be found away from large lowland lakes around upland pools in the north and west.

Just over one third of our Lesser Black-backed Gulls breed inland around lakes, although there is no equivalent to the huge moorland breeding colonies in Britain such as Tarnbrook Fell in Lancashire. By contrast the largest inland colony in Ireland numbers about 500 nests at Inishgoosk, a small island on Lough Derg , Co. Donegal (Mitchell *et al.* 2004). European Herring Gulls nest at only a few inland sites, most notably Lough Derg (Donegal) and Lough Corrib, while a few pairs of the largely maritime Great Black-backed Gull can be found among the gull colonies of Loughs Neagh, Erne and Corrib.

The inland gull colonies in the west of Ireland have been relatively well studied in the past 30 years, with the first breeding survey of Cos. Mayo, Galway, Sligo and Donegal being undertaken in 1977/78 (Whilde 1978). A repeat survey in 1992/93 found an overall decline of 38% in breeding gull numbers (Whilde *et al.* 1993) and the decline continued until by 2000 Herring and Lesser Black-backed Gulls had virtually disappeared from Lough Corrib (Mitchell *et al.* 2004). More recently numbers have at least stabilised, although the reasons for the catastrophic declines at this site during the 1980s and 1990s are still not fully understood (Hunt and Heffernan 2007a).

Botulism is considered to be a key factor in the loss of the large gulls while it is suggested that predation by mink may have affected the colonies of Common and Black-headed Gulls, although movement between other colonies may also be a factor (Whilde *et al.* 1993). At Lough Mask poor productivity and evidence of predation by mink led to a trapping programme in an attempt to enhance breeding success – with cautiously encouraging results (Hunt and Heffernan 2006, 2007b).

Several species of terns also nest within our lakes, often in association with Black-headed Gulls – a relationship which affords them greater protection from predators. In 1995, there were 31 colonies on inland lakes, which represented 21% of the total number of Irish colonies (Hannon *et al.* 1997). Most nest close to the water on rocky shores, which can leave them vulnerable to flooding from fluctuating water levels or storm events. Artificial structures such as tern rafts can provide safer nesting sites and are often occupied very quickly after being installed. A new raft at Portmore Lough RSPB Reserve , Co. Antrim held a nesting pair of Common Terns within just two months of construction, numbers rising to 50 pairs within three years (John Scovell RSPB, pers. comm).

One of the most bizarre Irish tern colonies is the top of a disued torpedo-testing platform on Lough Neagh, Co. Antrim. This structure is hazardous to climb, provides a safe breeding place for both Common Terns and Black-headed Gulls and is now the most important colony on Lough Neagh (Stephen Foster NIEA, pers. comm).

The Common Tern is by far the most frequent inland breeding tern, the other species being almost exclusively coastal in Britain and Ireland. However small numbers of Arctic Tern do breed inland, mostly on Lough Corrib, which held 47–49 pairs in 2007 (Hunt and Heffernan 2007a). Ireland's only inland colony of Sandwich Tern is on a rocky islet on Lower Lough Erne, Co. Fermanagh. The terns do not fish in the lough but habitually fly overland and into Donegal Bay to catch food for their young. They nest

Breeding colony of Common Terns and Black-headed Gulls on an island in Lough Gill, Co. Sligo (Richard Nairn).

among Black-headed Gulls but in 2010 the terns inexplicably vanished from the lough when their gull hosts relocated to a nearby island. Happily, in 2011 the terns were able to find the gulls and 62 pairs settled themselves on the new island (Brad Robson RSPB, pers. comm.).

Wetland habitats around the fringes of lakes, such as inundation grasslands, are often important for breeding waders as described in Chapter 6. However, some waders do breed directly on the lakeshore, and small numbers of Oystercatcher, Great Ringed Plover and Common Sandpiper breed along the stony shores of some of our larger lakes. A pair of Little Ringed Plover bred in 2008 at a pond in Co. Tipperary (Collins 2008) and again in 2010 (Hillis 2010), which raises hopes that this species might become a more common feature around Irish ponds and gravel pits.

Non-breeding birds

Many of our large lakes support significant populations of passage and wintering waterfowl, mainly from northern and eastern Europe. The importance of Irish wetlands as an international resource for waterbirds has been comprehensively described (Sheppard 1993; Crowe 2005) and a significant number of our larger lakes have received statutory recognition as nationally or internationally important sites for birds. Some have been designated as Special Protection Areas (SPAs) under the Council Directive on the Conservation of Wild Birds (79/409/EEC) (the Birds Directive) or are Ramsar sites under the Convention on Wetlands. These lakes typically support internationally important numbers of birds and the main criteria for SPA and Ramsar classification are (JNCC 1999):

1. areas regularly holding 1% or more of the Irish population of species listed in Annex I of the Directive;
2. areas used regularly by 1% or more of the biogeographic population of any regularly occurring migratory species;
3. areas used regularly by 20,000 or more waterfowl in any season.

Many of these important sites are systematically monitored through the Irish Wetland Bird Survey (IWeBS) in the Republic of Ireland and Wetland Bird Survey (WeBS) in Northern Ireland. These schemes, which involve a combination of professional and volunteer effort, provide comprehensive data on the population and distribution of waterbirds throughout Ireland. The most recently published data (Boland *et al.* 2010 and Calbrade *et al.* 2010) demonstrate the current importance of our largest lakes for wintering and migratory waterbirds. Our most important lakes (excluding turloughs) are highlighted in Table 5.2.

Table 5.2 Top ten most important Irish lakes for non-breeding birds 2008/9		
Lake	County	Average peak counts of birds 2004/5 – 2008/9
Lough Neagh/Beg	Antrim, Down, Armagh, Tyrone, Derry	53,444
Lough Corrib	Galway, Mayo	25,596
Lough Ree	Westmeath, Longford, Roscommon	14,745
Southern Roscommon Lakes	Roscommon	12,354
Iniscarra Reservoirs	Cork	11,761
Upper Lough Erne	Fermanagh	8,213
Kiltullagh Lough	Galway	7,188
Lough Owel	Westmeath	6,145
Lough Derg (Shannon)	Tipperary, Clare, Galway	4,930
Lough Derravaragh	Westmeath	4,156

Pochard winter in large numbers at Lough Corrib, Co. Galway (John Fox).

Greater Scaup feed extensively on molluscs (Richard T. Mills).

Lough Neagh/Beg is by far the most important site for non-breeding waterbirds in Ireland, but although it still supports an impressive assemblage of species in the winter, numbers of some species have declined dramatically in recent years. Most alarming is the decline in numbers of wintering diving ducks – Common Pochard, Tufted Duck and Common Goldeneye – which was first detected in 2001/02. Only Greater Scaup numbers have not been affected, and indeed this species has increased significantly in recent years. A number of possible reasons for the decline has been suggested, including the short-stopping of wintering birds from Eastern Europe induced by climatic changes (Allen *et al.* 2004).

In support of this, Common Pochard numbers have also crashed across the UK (Calbrade *et al.* 2010), while numbers of both Common Pochard and Tufted Duck have also declined at their other main Irish station, Lough Corrib (Boland *et al.* 2009). In winter 2008/09 the total peak count of Common Pochard in the Republic of Ireland was just 3,731 birds (Boland *et al.* 2010). Greater Scaup, however, originate from Iceland, which may in part explain why they are unaffected by recent changes to the distribution of birds from further east.

Another possible factor for the declines at Lough Neagh could be deteriorating water quality within an already hypertrophic system (Maclean *et al.* 2007). All these species feed extensively on the larvae of chironomid midges and the progressive enrichment of the lough may be contributing to the decline. Greater Scaup have a slightly different diet from the other ducks, taking larger larvae and a higher proportion of molluscs and so may not be affected in the same way. However, there is currently no direct evidence of significant changes to the biomass or distribution of chironomid larvae in the lough (Allen *et al.* 2002). The recent changes in diving duck populations at Lough Neagh are summarised in Table 5.3.

Species	Maximum count 1990/91	Maximum count 2002/3	Maximum count 2008/9
Common Pochard	40,928	9,080	5,799
Tufted Duck	22,278	9,769	5,126
Common Goldeneye	13,591	3,661	3,684
Greater Scaup	1,539	2,565	6,335

Table 5.3 Changes in diving duck numbers at Lough Neagh

The reduction in Common Coot numbers is even more difficult to explain since little is known about the origin of the Common Coot which winter here although there is no doubt that our resident birds are clearly augmented by visitors from north-western Europe (Wernham *et al.* 2002). Numbers at Lough Neagh in 2008/09 were the lowest since monitoring began (Calbrade *et al.* 2010), while a 50% decline was recorded at Lough Corrib between 2006/07 and 2008/09.

Contraction of wintering range is also cited as the main reason behind the virtual disappearance of the Bewick's Swan as an Irish wintering bird (Calbrade *et al.* 2010). This species of the Russian tundra was once more numerous in Ireland than the Whooper Swan, and in 1975/6 over 2,000 birds were present in Ireland, mostly at coastal sites but also at Lough Neagh and the lakes and turloughs of central and western Ireland (Merne 1977). Nowadays finding a Bewick's Swan among the herds of Whoopers is quite a prize, and in 2010 just 80 were counted, most of them in Co. Wexford (Boland *et al.* 2010b).

The Icelandic Whooper Swan continues to prosper as a winter visitor both on lakes and at other key sites. Lough Neagh and Upper Lough Erne are two of the most important sites in Ireland for the species, supporting 1,803 and 799 birds respectively in January 2010. Other lakes which support internationally important numbers are the Lough Oughter complex in Co. Cavan and Lough Iron, Co. Westmeath. The swans are mainly attracted to the rich feeding in the farmland and wetlands surrounding these lakes, but will often utilise the open water as a safe roost or feed in the shallow margins. Their dependence on farmland is demonstrated by the fact that just 5.8% of birds were found on lakes during the 2010 swan census, with 58.4% using improved pasture (Boland *et al.* 2010b).

Whooper Swans take off from a lake (Richie Lort).

European Golden Plover in flight (Richard T. Mills).

Whilst there is evidence that Amercian mink can impact upon breeding bird populations, there is still little evidence of how another introduced species, the zebra mussel, might ultimately affect our waterfowl populations. The zebra mussel is now well established in several major waterways, including Lough Derg and Lough Erne, where its impacts on the Lough's ecology have been studied. Since its discovery in Lough Erne in 1996, phytoplankton and zooplankton abundance has declined along with nutrient concentrations (total phosphate), while water clarity has increased (Maguire and Gibson 2005). Some of these changes may be expected to have a detrimental effect on waterbirds. However, the introduction of zebra mussels into Lough Erne coincided with a significant increase in wintering Tufted Duck and Common Coot on the Erne system (Collier *et al.* 2005), both of which are known to feed on this species (Cramp and Simmons 1980).

Dabbling ducks such as Eurasian Wigeon, Common Teal and Mallard also flock to our winter wetlands, Common Teal mainly from Iceland, while Eurasian Wigeon arrive both from Iceland and European Russia/Fennoscandia (Wernham *et al.* 2002). The Eurasian Wigeon is our most numerous wintering waterfowl species, and while many winter in grazing marsh and coastal sites, significant numbers are also associated with our lakes and turloughs. Northern Shoveler also winter in important numbers and both Lough Rea , Co. Galway and the South Roscommon Lakes are of international importance for this species (Boland *et al.* 2010).

Flocks of waders such as European Golden Plover and Northern Lapwing can often be seen wheeling over our wetlands in winter. Mostly these birds feed and roost in farmland but some will also feed along the lakeshores and even roost on small islands such as the 'flats' of Lough Neagh, which held maxima of 8,486 European Golden Plover and 6,263 Northern Lapwing in 2008/09 (Calbrade *et al.* 2010). Lakes act like magnets for migratory birds, which often follow the courses of rivers or lakes on the way to breeding or wintering grounds. Waders such as the Eurasian Whimbrel often pass through in large numbers, pausing only to feed briefly along the shores. Birds of prey such as Osprey and Marsh Harrier are recorded annually, while the prospect of genuine rarities means that many lakes are well surveyed by birders in spring and autumn.

Whilst the larger lakes are systematically monitored, some small lakes are not currently counted under the WeBS or IWeBS schemes (Crowe 2005). The cumulative importance of these small lakes was illustrated by a series of counts at 115 small lakes in Co. Down between 1986/87 and 1990/91, with peak totals of between 4,400 and 5,100 birds, with especially high numbers of Common Coot and Mallard (McElwaine 1991). This amply demonstrates the richness and importance for waterfowl of all our lowland lakes – both large and small.

Turloughs and Marl Lakes

Turloughs are temporary lakes of limestone areas that appear when groundwater levels are high but which disappear when the water table falls. A turlough has to flood every year to fit into the category but does not have to dry out as often. Some examples always retain a lake in the centre (Coole Lough, Co.

Galway, Killaturly Lough, Co. Mayo) while others do not dry out every year (Lough Funshinagh, Co. Roscommon). In all about 300 turloughs have been documented (Sheehy Skeffington *et al.* 2006) though much fewer have had any analysis of their birdlife.

Cores cut into the bases of turloughs often reveal one or several layers of white calcareous sediment (marl) showing that the basin was a permanent lake for a period in the past (Coxon 1986). The change is caused by shifts in underground drainage patterns, either the opening or blockage of fissures. Some basins persist as marl lakes (for example, Lough Carra), their white muddy beds formed of stonewort fragments and precipitated lime. These lakes are generally poor in nutrients as the high alkalinity removes useable phosphate from the system. The water is crystal clear if unpolluted and the lakes are often fringed by fens and thin reedbeds. They generally support a typical, if small, waterbird assemblage which is not influenced by fluctuating water levels.

Turloughs because of their fleeting nature suit mobile organisms such as birds and insects, or those that can remain dormant in dry weather like water fleas. In winter there is little invertebrate food available other than snails and insect larvae, but in summer dense blooms of algae and crustaceans may occur, of benefit to young water-birds. Normally the flooding is a seasonal phenomenon, but even during the flooded period the water level fluctuates depending on the rainfall going through the system. Turloughs may appear occasionally in summer, given sufficient rain to raise the water table and there are apocryphal tales of people camping on a seemingly dry pasture, waking to find the tent flooded.

Non-breeding birds

Turloughs can be thought of as the floodplains of underground rivers appearing when there is too much water in the subterranean channel. They also share the wintering birds of these habitats, the dabbling duck, wild swans and inland waders that find floodwaters wherever they appear. The common birds of turloughs such as Eurasian Wigeon, European Golden Plover, Whooper Swan and Common Teal could equally well be seen on the Little Brosna Callows or along the Blackwater, but they may be easier to find in the enclosed basin of a turlough. Some diving duck occur, Tufted Duck, Common Pochard and occasionally Common Goldeneye, but in quite small numbers. Ruttledge (1989) comments on the preference for turloughs shown by Whooper Swan, Eurasian Wigeon, Common Teal, Northern Pintail and Greater White-fronted Goose, though the latter two have much declined since then. Whooper Swans still occur in large numbers and subjectively one associates the call of Whooper Swans with a frosty morning at a turlough. The proportion of the winter population recorded on turloughs is quite small at 3% of the total (Boland *et al.* 2010) though the small size of turlough habitat as opposed to intensive pastures conceals a higher relative density. Often the swans use the turlough for roosting but fly to a ryegrass field on a nearby hill for food. This has been a marked change since Ruttledge's time and the intensification of farmland may bring the birds into conflict with dairy farming.

Falling water levels in a turlough in County Clare (Richard Nairn).

Eurasian Wigeon are common winter visitors to western turloughs (John Fox).

Common Redshank are seen around many turloughs (John Fox).

Mobility is a feature of birds living on turloughs; there are constant changes in the shoreline, giving greater space for dabbling duck and swans when water levels rise and more habitat for waders when it falls. Added to this is disturbance which may cause birds to abandon one site and move to a neighbouring wetland. Madden and Heery (1997) studied groups of turloughs in South Galway and noted that changes in numbers were measured in hours rather than days. For this reason turlough complexes are often defined as the wintering site rather than individual turloughs.

Crowe (2005) lists two turloughs of international importance (Rahasane and the Coole/Garryland complex, Co. Galway) and five of national importance for their winter birds. Rahasane qualifies by having large enough numbers of Black-tailed Godwit as well as Whooper Swan, Greater White-fronted Geese, Eurasian Wigeon, Northern Pintail and Northern Shoveler. Coole/Garryland qualifies on Whooper Swan alone. Elsewhere the national sites support Whooper Swan (Lough Coy/Ballylee in Co. Galway), Greater White-fronted Geese and Northern Shoveler (Rostaff Turlough, Co. Mayo), Northern Shoveler (Doolough Turlough, Co. Galway) and European Golden Plover (Fortwilliam Turlough, Co. Longford).

By any reckoning, Rahasane Turlough must be seen as the premier turlough site in Ireland for waterbirds. It has greater numbers and more variety than any other site. Its size is one virtue as birds can find the security and conditions they need; also it has richer feeding than most by having a permanent river (the Dunkellin) flowing through it. The river brings in more nutrients than appear in the bare limestone turloughs of the Burren and can therefore support more animal life. Northern Lapwing, Eurasian Curlew, Common Redshank and Common Snipe are seen in turloughs generally but Rahasane adds Common Greenshank and Dunlin as well as Tufted Duck, Little Egret and Great Cormorant. Occasionally, Bar-tailed Godwit and Ruddy Turnstone may appear, while stray Pink-footed Geese have been recently reported. Passage movement in spring or autumn is often obvious by the sightings of a few Spotted Redshank, Curlew Sandpiper, Ruff or Eurasian Whimbrel. Even if one cannot cover the whole basin the visits of a Peregrine will often be sufficient to dislodge some hidden gems.

Numbers of waterfowl at Rahasane have declined in the last few decades and the site temporarily fell out of the top 20 wetlands in the country. All waterbirds combined declined by 63% between the two winter surveys (Sheppard 1993, Crowe 2005), the decline in Common Teal being the most significant (from 3,000 to 270). This may have been due to the impact of higher water levels caused by upstream drainage (Ruttledge and Ogilvie 1979; Buckley and McCarthy 1987). Subsequently the river exit was cleared, numbers are rising (including those of Common Teal and other dabbling duck) and the site made it back into the top 20 sites in Ireland in 2006–07 where it has remained (Boland *et al.* 2008, 2009, 2010).

Breeding birds

Most turloughs dry out to give a grassland habitat which is much grazed later in the year. Northern Lapwing, Common Snipe and small numbers of Common Redshank may nest soon after the sites are exposed when the vegetation gives enough cover but when the ground still remains soft for feeding. Occasionally pools are left in isolated places to dry out slowly by evaporation but sometimes a central lake is semi-permanent, in which case it becomes filled with water plants – and sometimes is attractive to Black-headed Gulls. Heery and Madden (1997) found high numbers of Little Grebe on one such site at Termon North (Co. Galway) in May, a maximum of 94 birds on a water body of 9ha, with up to ten nests.

This number of grebes compares with Lough Funshinagh (Roscommon) where 300 pairs of Black-necked Grebes were estimated in 1932 (Humphreys 1978). Breeding by the grebes was first proved in Roscommon from Brierfield Turlough in 1915 and though this site was subsequently drained the birds were found on Funshinagh in 1918 and especially in the years 1929–1951. Even in this period there were years when the water level was too high or too low and the birds did not nest. In some years the premature drying of the basin led to the disappearance of the adults and a lot of chick mortality. Other breeding wildfowl recorded by Humphreys from the Lough Funshinagh site over the years are Mallard, Common Teal, Gadwall, Northern Pintail, Northern Shoveler, Tufted Duck, Common Pochard and Red-breasted Merganser. Most of these species continue to nest sporadically (e.g. Hillis 2003, 2008, 2010) but in very small numbers. Indeed, one of the features that makes an early trip to any turlough exciting is the possibility of the unknown – the explosion of a Common Teal or even a Garganey from a reed bed, the swerving displays of nervous Northern Lapwing and the piping of a distant but unseen Common Redshank.

Another species that tantalises with occasional sightings in turloughs is the Red-necked Phalarope, lost as a regular breeding species in the early 1970s but present in some years in Mayo until 1986. Turloughcor (Doolough Headford) and Glenamaddy are mentioned by Hutchinson (1989) as sites where the species has occurred in spring. The presence of small pools for midge larvae and bogbean for cover creates the right type of habitat for this tiny planktonic feeder. Dunlin also nest occasionally in turloughs though they prefer the machairs of the west coast.

Turloughs are difficult habitats for plants, being flooded when they are trying to grow or being exposed when they need water. But such unpredictability suits migratory birds which may drop in for an hour or a week or sometimes stay to nest. We can identify with this itinerant approach and it is worth checking out any turlough when passing – just in case.

Lakes of bog and uplands – dystrophic and oligotrophic waters

Both of these nutrient-poor types of lake are typical of our uplands or blanket bogs, even down to sea level in the west of Ireland. Dystrophic lakes typically have peat-stained, acidic water and peaty margins, while oligotrophic waters are more often characterised by rocky shorelines (Fossitt 2000). While there is considerable overlap with many of the species found in lowland waters, these lakes also support a rather distinct bird community.

Breeding birds

Upland lakes and bog pools often support few breeding birds, although pools with dense vegetation around the margins may conceal a pair of Common Teal while those with stony shores or islands may well support a pair of Common Sandpipers or even a small colony of Common Gulls.

One of the most evocative breeding species of this habitat is the Red-throated Diver. A few pairs of this rare and secretive bird still breed on remote bog loughs in Co. Donegal, although its foothold remains tenuous indeed. In 2009, six pairs bred,

Altan Lough, Co. Donegal, with Errigal Mountain in the background (Richard Nairn).

The Red-throated Diver breeds on a few isolated lakes in Co. Donegal (Darío Fernández-Bellon).

Glendalough, Co. Wicklow, with ice on the water surface (Richard Nairn).

but only three were successful, producing a total of four young (Hillis 2010). Despite the large number of moorland lakes in Donegal very few satisfy all the divers' stringent breeding requirements. These divers prefer small lakes (<5 hectares), with suitable fresh water or marine feeding areas nearby. Nesting sites are equally important, the birds using islands, peninsulas or floating vegetation to conceal their nests. Gently sloping sides are crucial as the ungainly birds need to be able to slide easily to and from the nest, while freedom from disturbance is also important especially during incubation and fledging periods (Cromie 2002).

The Goosander is a recent addition as a breeding bird, with breeding first proven in Co. Donegal in 1969 (Sheppard 1978). Although particularly at home on fast-flowing rivers, this fish-eating species will also breed beside lakes, especially upland loughs with adjacent woodland where they will nest in tree cavities, or nest boxes if provided (Cramp and Simmons 1980). Recently a small population has become established at Glendalough in Co. Wicklow, breeding in most years since at least 2002 (Hillis 2010).

Non-breeding birds
Upland lakes can appear quite barren during the winter months, although some may be graced by parties of Whooper Swan especially during spring or autumn migration. Some of these loughs are also used by small groups of Greater White-fronted Geese which winter at traditional bogland sites in both upland and lowland areas. The geese mainly utilise the lakes for roosting while feeding on the adjacent bog. A recent study at Slieve Beagh, Cos. Monaghan and Tyrone, also found that the geese were feeding in the oligotrophic waters, eating aquatic vegetation such as broad-leaved pondweed– the first time this plant had been recorded as a food species (Mayes *et al.* 2009). Many of these traditional flocks have disappeared in the past few decades, with peat extraction, drainage and shooting disturbance among the reasons for the losses (Ruttledge and Ogilvie 1979).

Reservoirs

Many natural lakes which have been described in this section act as reservoirs for the supply of water to the human population. Lough Neagh, for example, is a major source of water for the people of Northern Ireland. Man-made reservoirs developed for the supply of water or hydroelectric power can over time develop into important bird habitats, particularly where there are shallow margins with emergent vegetation or gently sloping banks which allow easy access for grazing wildfowl. One such reservoir has even been classified as a Special Protection Area for its important bird populations. Poulaphouca Reservoir in Cos. Kildare and Wicklow was formed by the damming of the River Liffey in 1944 and supports an important winter flock of Greylag Geese, which use the reservoir for roosting along with a large winter roost of Lesser Black-backed Gulls (NPWS 2005).

The Iniscarra Reservoirs in Co. Cork were also developed as part of a hydroelectric scheme and have developed into one of the finest sites for wintering waterfowl in Ireland, with large populations of dabbling ducks, Tufted Duck and wintering waders (Boland 2010). This is in stark contrast to the aptly named Silent Valley Reservoir in Co. Down where the deep, steep-sided and nutrient-poor waters are rarely troubled by birds of any description.

Summary and conclusions

Our freshwater lakes, reservoirs and turloughs comprise an internationally important resource for breeding and non-breeding waterbirds.

Eutrophic lakes in the lowlands support the largest numbers and diversity of species often due to the nutrients contained in the water, which provide rich feeding for birds. Many of these lakes are also shallow with emergent vegetation or islands, which provide ideal habitats for breeding or wintering birds. Turloughs can also hold important numbers of birds and several have been recognised as being of national or international importance. Upland lakes and pools support a characteristic bird community including rare breeding birds such as Red-throated Diver and totemic bogland species such as wintering Greater White-fronted Geese.

Inniscarra dam and reservoir on the River Lee, Co. Cork (Richard T. Mills).

In recent years enormous efforts have been made to ensure that key wetlands are monitored systematically through the IWeBS and WeBS schemes. As a result we have been able to identify that many lakes merit designation as Special Protection Areas under the EU Birds Directive. In addition, we are now in a position to quickly detect changes to important non-breeding bird populations such as have been witnessed at Lough Corrib and Lough Neagh recently. We are perhaps less well informed about some of our breeding bird species, which can be subject to rapid changes in status and even extinctions, such as the Common Scoters on Lower Lough Erne.

The progressive eutrophication of our lakes through nutrient enrichment and the effects of alien species are among the most significant threats to our waterbirds, although the effects of climate change leading to changes in the distribution of some species could have an increasing impact on the status of non-breeding birds.

Acknowledgements

Thanks are due to David Tierney, Jackie Hunt and Ralph Sheppard for providing information on breeding Common Scoter and gulls, John Scovell, Brad Robson (both RSPB) and Stephen Foster (NIEA) for information on terns and to Dave Allen and Don Cotton for providing information on various aspects of the chapter.

6. Wet Grasslands, Marshes and Callows

Karl Partridge

Introduction

Grasslands dominate the Irish landscape making up 52% of the area in the Republic (EEA/EPA 2009) and 58% of Northern Ireland (Cooper *et al.* 2009). The 44,030km^2 of farmed grassland on the whole island represents 51.5% of the land area. Wet grassland (GS4 of Fossitt 2000) is an important habitat for breeding waders (Northern Lapwing, Eurasian Curlew, Common Redshank and Common Snipe), all of which are in decline, and for wintering waterbirds. Wet grassland is found mainly in low-lying areas: in drumlin hollows, around lakeshores and along the few remaining rivers that have not been subject to arterial drainage. It occurs within a habitat mosaic on upland margins where it is important for breeding Eurasian Curlew and Common Snipe.

Freshwater Marsh (GM1 of Fossitt 2000) is found on level ground near riverbanks, lakeshores and in other waterlogged situations. Characteristic species include rushes, sedges, meadowsweet, grasses and a range of other broadleaved herbs. Marsh differs from swamp in that the vegetation is more species-rich, standing water is absent for much of the year and reeds and other tall vegetation are not dominant. The distinction between wet grassland and marsh is not always clear and many wet grassland sites include a marshy component (Fossitt 2000).

Habitat Characteristics and Distribution

In general, wet grassland (and marsh) occurs on ground that has a high water table, is usually flooded in winter and where impeded drainage occurs throughout the year. It is often found on gleyed soils that are agriculturally unimproved or only semi-improved and grazed by cattle during the drier summer months. Lowland wet grassland includes both pastures and hay meadows. Such grassland retains its characteristic flora and associated insect and invertebrate populations which form a vital food resource for wintering and breeding birds. The variation in plant species composition, vegetation height and wetness depends on edaphic factors such as the hydrological regime, grazing management, topography, site drainage, etc. Appropriate grazing maintains a degree of control over vegetation structure and composition, providing both nesting cover and open areas where birds – especially

Wet meadows at Clonmacnoise on the River Shannon Callows (Richard T. Mills).

waders – can access soil-dwelling invertebrates by probing the soft ground. Wet grassland is of most value where the soil retains a high moisture content into the summer months and insect-rich pools are available for chick-rearing.

The abundance and distribution of wet grassland and marsh is well documented for Northern Ireland as a result of the Northern Ireland Countryside Survey (NICS) (Cooper and McCann 2002; Cooper et al. 2009) but no similar scheme exists for the Republic. The schematic vegetation map of Ireland produced by O'Sullivan (1982) and reproduced by Bourke et al. (2007) provides the best mapped representation of potentially wet grassland in Ireland. However, this was based on soil maps from the 1960s and a significant proportion of the 15,653km^2 of 'moderate to poor quality pasture and meadow on imperfectly to poorly drained soils' which then formed 19% of vegetation cover in Ireland has since been lost through drainage and agricultural improvement. The vegetation map shows a large block of this grassland type in north-central Ireland, occupying most of Fermanagh and Cavan, and large parts of south-west Tyrone, north Monaghan, south Leitrim and north Roscommon. The more recent CORINE land cover project identifies 16,389 hectares of inland marsh in the Republic of Ireland (0.23% of the land area) but this is probably an underestimate because of the 25 hectares minimum resolution of habitat parcels (EEA/EPA 2009).

Within the NICS, wet grassland falls mainly in the 'Fen, Marsh and Swamp (BH11)' category, which consists of rush-dominated vegetation of peaty soils, marshy grasslands and water-inundated vegetation. This currently covers 3.3% (47,255 hectares) of Northern Ireland. Between 1998 and 2007 there was a 10.7% decrease in area, mainly within lowland landscapes (Cooper et al. 2009). This followed a 19% decrease recorded between 1986 and 1998 (Cooper and McCann 2002).

Wet grassland was clearly once a widely distributed habitat in Ireland and prior to the development of arterial drainage would have occurred extensively as callows along rivers, around lakes and in a multiplicity of small wetlands. Originally undertaken by private landowners in a piecemeal fashion, state-funded arterial drainage commenced with the Drainage Act of 1842, with further Acts of 1863 and 1925 resulting in the drainage of 190,000 hectares by the 1940s (Kelly 1984). Thereafter, arterial drainage in the Republic developed rapidly with 240,000 hectares of land drained between 1950 and 1980. In Northern Ireland the 1930–1942 Lower Bann Scheme resulted in a 29% increase in river discharge capacity, a lowering of Lough Neagh and drainage of some 57,000 hectares of land. Over 6,000km of rivers and watercourses were damaged by arterial drainage before these schemes came to an end in the 1980s (Wilcock 1997). Williams et al. (1988) documented the impact of drainage on wetland birds (breeding waders, wintering wildfowl and riparian birds) and those such as Corncrake that require low-intensity grassland management.

Callows (from the Irish word *caladh* – river-meadow) is a term used in Ireland to denote true floodplain grassland – fields beside a river or large lake that regularly flood in winter and that dry out in summer for use as pasture and fodder conservation (pit silage is usually precluded due to poor spring conditions). In bird habitat terms, therefore, callows *at their best* change dramatically from winter through spring to summer. In winter, when the first floods have seeped across the fields, expanses of shallow water and their waterlogged margins provide feeding and refuge for wildfowl and waders. In spring, when the winter floods are draining off the fields, leaving truly wet grassland, the habitat is

Whooper Swans in flight over the River Blackwater Callows in Co. Waterford (Richard T. Mills).

attractive to breeding waders. In wet meadows, the grassland sward in the summer provides habitat for other ground nesting birds such as Corncrake and Meadow Pipit. This progression means that callowland can potentially provide habitat for a very significant diversity of bird species, possibly the most diverse of any habitat, especially if it is extensive.

Most rivers in Ireland have been affected by arterial drainage schemes which, as stated above, tend to reduce (or eliminate) the incidence of flooding in winter. This allows the land to dry out quicker and more completely in spring, which subsequently leads to a simplification of the grassland sward through intensification of agriculture. So, while callows large and small are widespread throughout Ireland there is great variation in the extent to which individual callows reach their potential as a habitat for birds. Three examples illustrate this.

The River Shannon/Little Brosna Callows, the largest and most intractable of floodplains, exhibits the most year-round bird species diversity and is the best studied. Heery (2003) provides an overview of callows in Ireland, and the Shannon/Little Brosna Callows are dealt with specifically by Heery (1993) and Hooijer (1996). The Blackwater Callows in Co. Waterford have a winter wetland bird community similar to the Shannon Callows (Sheppard 1993; Crowe 2005a), but a negligible summer community due to intensification and tillage. The floodplain of the River Moy around Foxford in Co. Mayo rarely floods (due to severe arterial drainage in the 1960s) but local conditions have meant that significant pockets of semi-natural grassland and unimproved hay meadows remain, giving a diversity of ground nesting birds a chance to survive.

Breeding Birds

Waders

Some of the most important sites in Ireland for breeding waders are found on wet and marshy grassland, occurring on callows around the shores of the larger lakes (Lough Neagh/Beg; Upper Lough Erne) and along the Shannon Callows. Baseline surveys of these important sites were carried out during the late 1980s and repeat surveys of a sample of sites have been carried out at intervals since then in Northern Ireland (Stanbury *et al.* 2000; RSPB unpublished) and on the Shannon Callows (Tierney *et al.* 2002, Finney *et al.* 2006, Finney and Warnock 2009, 2010). Breeding wader populations have declined at all of the main sites over the past two decades. However, the start of the decline probably pre-dates the 1986/87 baseline surveys, since 20 years prior to this Ruttledge (1966) noted that Northern Lapwing had decreased as a breeding species.

Grassland on Hare Island, Lower Lough Erne, Co. Fermanagh (Karl Partridge).

Lake islands can also hold significant numbers of breeding waders, e.g. Cruninish, Hare Island and Horse Island on Lower Lough Erne, Dernish Island on Upper Lough Erne, and the islands of Lough Corrib (Whilde 1990). Offshore islands can also hold large numbers of breeding birds. Cabot (1963) recorded 115 pairs of Northern Lapwing on Inishkea North and 15 pairs on Inishkea South in 1961. A more recent 2009 survey (Suddaby *et al.* 2010) has confirmed the importance for breeding waders of Inishkea North (253 wader pairs) and Inishkea South (124 pairs). The absence of mammalian predators such as foxes is an important

Northern Lapwings commonly breed on wet grasslands where the sward is kept short by grazing (Richard T. Mills).

factor, although gull predation is thought to be significant, especially for Dunlin.

Apart from the main site complexes, a sample survey of 146 tetrads (2km x 2km) in Northern Ireland in 1987 showed 51% of the total wader population (68% of Northern Lapwing, 42% of Eurasian Curlew, 95% of Common Redshank and 40% of Common Snipe) using damp grassland habitats in scattered pockets throughout the wider countryside and on hill margins (Partridge and Smith 1992). A repeat of the tetrad survey in 1999 (Henderson *et al.* 2002) indicated a decline of 66% in Northern Lapwing numbers, 58% in Eurasian Curlew and 30% in Common Snipe, with few breeding wader pairs left in the east of the province. Unfortunately, no similar sample surveys have been carried out in the Republic and the Countryside Bird Survey does not adequately monitor population trends in these species (Coombes *et al.* 2009).

Breeding Northern Lapwing nest in a wider range of habitats than other waders, such as spring cereals, cutover bogs, upland rough pasture, but breeding Common Redshank, Common Snipe and Eurasian Curlew are more closely tied to damp grassland sites. Northern Lapwing prefer cattle-grazed pasture with a relatively short sward and a proportion of bare soil exposed, often as a result of poaching. The ground is often broken and hummocky, with clumps of rushes, providing camouflage for nesting birds and chicks. On Upper Lough Erne, nests are often close to water (Partridge 1988a). On the Shannon Callows, aftergrazing of hay meadows in late summer is required if the sward is to be short enough for nesting Northern Lapwing the following spring (Herbert *et al.* 1990). Here, grazing by horses and sheep, rather than cattle, appears to produce a short sward attractive to Northern Lapwing (Nairn *et al.* 1988).

Twenty years ago breeding Eurasian Curlew were most abundant in west, central and northern Ireland in a broad band stretching from Clare to Antrim (Gibbons *et al.* 1993). Eurasian Curlew once bred widely on hill marginal land, lowland damp grassland and river and lake callows. They nest in very damp rush pasture in Fermanagh and Tyrone. Around Upper Lough Erne the typical Eurasian Curlew field contained scattered clumps of rushes rather than dense *Juncus* cover, with an open aspect and an absence of hedges or scrub close by (Gretton and Mellon 1986). However, many of these Eurasian Curlew sites are no longer occupied (Henderson *et al.* 2002) and the population on key sites in Northern Ireland fell by 33% between 1985–87 and 2000 (based on unpublished RSPB data). The more important islands on Lower Lough Erne are now managed as RSPB reserves. With

The Common Redshank prefers tussocky vegetation giving good cover for their nests (Richard T. Mills).

The Common Snipe prefers ground soft enough for them to probe (Richard T. Mills).

habitat management and predator control, wader numbers here have increased over the past decade. Vegetation analysis by Tickner (1990) showed the National Vegetation Classification M24 *Cirsium-Molinia* fen meadow (Rodwell 1992) and variants of this community hold most waders, with other tall grasslands (*Holcus-Agrostis* grassland and MG10a *Holcus-Juncus* rush pasture) also important. On the Shannon Callows, 11 pairs of Eurasian Curlew were counted in 2006 compared to 34 pairs in 1987 (Finney *et al.* 2006). During the 1987 survey the majority of pairs (62%) nested in hay meadows with the remainder using tussocky pasture (Nairn *et al.* 1988). Indications are that the population has declined by up to 80% in the last 25 years, with no more than 1,000 pairs left in Ireland (Lauder and Donaghy 2008), if that, and they are now on the IUCN 2010 *Red List of Threatened Species*, categorised as 'near threatened' (Birdlife International 2011).

Common Redshank are found mainly on wet grasslands with tussocky vegetation as they require good cover (*Juncus, Iris*, etc) for nesting. They also require wet features such as shallow ditches and small marshy pools where the edges are accessible to chicks for feeding (Partridge 1988b; Herbert *et al.* 1990). In Northern Ireland the bulk of the breeding population is restricted to Lough Neagh/ Lough Beg and Lough Erne, although in the 1980s they were also breeding in damp, unimproved river valleys such as Glenwhirry, Co. Antrim, from which they have since been lost (Neil Warnock, RSPB, pers. comm). Pastureland, close to water, is the preferred habitat along the Shannon Callows (Herbert *et al.* 1990) with nests concealed in tussocks or clumps of grass (Finney *et al.* 2006). The 1988–91 *Breeding Bird Atlas* (Gibbons *et al.* 1993) shows the loss of birds from central and eastern Ireland, due to drainage and agricultural intensification, with birds concentrated along the Shannon from Lough Ree to Lough Derg, in east Galway and south east Mayo. The number of breeding pairs on the Shannon Callows fell by 71% between 1987 and 2002 (Nairn *et al.* 1988; Tierney *et al.* 2002). A scoping survey carried out on a sample of sites in 2010 indicated that Common Redshank had declined further since 2002, with the cumulative 1987–2010 decline now put at 89% and the future of the Callows population is extremely vulnerable (Finney and Warnock 2010). Around Upper Lough Erne a similar decline has taken place (63% between 1985–87 and 2000; RSPB, unpublished).

Common Snipe is the most widely distributed and abundant breeding wader in Ireland occurring on wet grassland, blanket bog, raised bog, and fen (Gibbons *et al.* 1993; Partridge and Smith 1992). Green (1986, 1988) found that of all the lowland wet grassland waders Common Snipe is the most dependent on ground wetness and that a water table no deeper than 20–30cm below ground level keeps the ground soft enough for them to probe. On the Shannon Callows the extent and timing of flooding has a strong influence on the nesting distribution of breeding Common Snipe – as well as other ground-nesting birds – and ground wetness is maintained through May if relatively high rainfall occurs in April, after winter floodwaters recede (Herbert *et al.* 1990). Around Lough Erne, Common Snipe favour extensive areas of soft rush growing on saturated ground with open areas maintained by light grazing. Sometimes breeding pairs can be found on very small sites (<50m²) occupying the intersection of drainage ditches in the corner of a field (Partridge 1988b). The decline in breeding Common Snipe at key Irish sites, variously recorded at between 30% and 68%, with a 72% decline on Upper Lough Erne (RSPB data, 2000), mirrors the 62% decline at lowland wet grassland sites in England and Wales between 1982 and 2002 (Wilson *et al.* 2005).

Other breeding waders found on wet grassland in Ireland include Dunlin and Black-tailed Godwit. The majority of the Dunlin population (estimated 150 pairs, Lauder and Donaghy 2008) breeds on machair sites in the west and north-west, (Suddaby *et al.* 2010). Scattered pairs breed on inland sites on the Roscommon/Mayo border and in east Galway (Gibbons *et al.* 1993). About ten pairs now nest in Northern Ireland, mainly on Lower Lough Erne (NIBA 2002). Here, the preferred habitat is the damp, moss-dominated shoreline (Partridge 1988b). According to Hutchinson (1989) about 2–3 pairs of Black-tailed Godwit have bred annually in Ireland, since 1975. Nine breeding sites were identified during the last *Breeding Atlas*. Breeding birds feed on earthworms and favour a soft peaty substrate with a high water table. Two pairs nested on the Shannon Callows in 1987 on peaty soil where the vegetation was very short in June and was later cut for hay (Nairn *et al.* 1988) and one pair probably bred there in 2005 (Hillis 2007).

Floodplain grassland can, given certain rainfall conditions, become inundated during the summer, to the detriment of the breeding birds. The 2002 and 2006 breeding seasons on the Shannon Callows (and probably other callows) were characterised by extensive flooding during late May and June (Caffrey *et al.* 2006). Breeding success was severely disrupted for both Corncrake and waders. After both flooding events, the number of Corncrakes arriving back in the subsequent year was halved. Wader eggs were found floating and productivity was thought to be almost zero at key sites (Finney *et al.* 2006). It can be assumed that all ground-nesting birds were also severely affected. Deemed a 'once in 20–year' event, flooding on the Shannon Callows occurred during May and June in 2003 and 2009; and during July to August in 2007, 2008 and 2009. If climate change means a greater incidence of summer flooding on callows then the effect on their breeding birds could be severe.

Waterfowl

Unimproved wet grassland that is tussocky and lightly grazed often provides ideal nesting habitat for a range of duck species, provided it is close to water. Observations carried out during breeding wader surveys have shown that Mallard, Moorhen, Tufted Duck, Common Teal, Gadwall, Common Pochard and Northern Shoveler all use this habitat or adjacent areas of swamp or marsh, either for feeding or nesting. Due to the paucity of studies in Irish habitats, the data referred to below are based largely on work carried out in Britain or other parts of Europe (Cramp and Simmons 1977; Harrison and Castell 1998; Owen *et al.* 1986; Thomas 1980). Crowe (2005a) summarises breeding ecology and status from an Irish perspective.

Mallard (23,000 pairs) is the most abundant breeding duck species in Ireland found near any type of fresh water. It nests on the ground, in tall vegetation where cover is dense, but also sometimes in tree holes and on buildings. High breeding densities occur on Lough Neagh, in the north Midlands, in Connaught and in Clare (Gibbons *et al.* 1993). On damp grassland sites,

Mallard drake calling in flight (Richard T. Mills).

Tufted Duck with a young brood (Richard T. Mills).

Mallard often nest in drainage ditches and in the Shannon Callows they have used hay meadows (Heery 1993).

Moorhen (75,000 pairs) is also abundant and ubiquitous, but the 1988–91 *Atlas* showed a contraction in range due to drainage and mink predation. Nests are built on the ground, close to water, and they feed on a wide variety of plant and animal material, usually taken from the water.

Tufted Duck (1,750–2,000 pairs) also nest amongst thick vegetation, usually less than 20m from the water's edge. They are associated mainly with larger water bodies, Lough Neagh/Beg (433 pairs) being the main site (NIBA 1998), with Loughs Corrib, Mask, Conn, Ree and Derg also important. Tufted Duck feed by diving in open water and subsist largely on aquatic macroinvertebrates. On Lough Neagh the main winter food is chironomid larvae together with *Asellus*, *Gammarus* and molluscs (Evans 2000).

Although breeding Common Teal are usually associated with oligotrophic waters the species will also adapt to well-vegetated lowland wetlands where they usually nest close to the water in dense marginal vegetation. Food consists mainly of the seeds of aquatic plants (including knotgrass, spikerush, pondweed, branched bur-reed, and docks) which they take by feeding in shallow water. The Irish breeding population of Common Teal suffered a large range contraction between 1968–72 and 1988–91, the most recently estimated population being 400–675 pairs (Gibbons *et al.* 1993).

The remaining species all occur in low numbers (figures below from Lynas *et al.* 2007) and are restricted in distribution. Gadwall is a rare breeder whose Irish population (50 pairs) is concentrated at Lough Neagh; Common Pochard (<30 pairs) too are found mainly on Lough Neagh. Both nest in thick vegetation near the water or, in the case of Common Pochard, on vegetation growing in the water. Breeding Northern Shoveler (20 pairs) are found mainly around Lough Neagh and in the north Midlands. The Shannon Callows held 12 pairs in 1987 (Nairn *et al.* 1988) and 51 pairs were recorded on Lough Erne and Lough Neagh during breeding wader surveys in 1985–87 (Partridge 1988b). Numbers have clearly declined since then. On the Shannon Callows, Northern Shoveler nest in rough grassland near areas of water and wet mud where they find food and safety (Heery 1993). The bird filters food through a specially adapted spatulate edge to the bill, taking small invertebrates and seeds.

The diversity of breeding birds on callows will be greater if the grassland is agriculturally unimproved and the callows are extensive. An impressive diversity of ground-nesting birds was found breeding on 74 hectares of unimproved hay meadow on callowland at Clonmacnoise by the River Shannon in the mid-1980s (Tubridy 1987): Mallard, Common Teal, Northern Shoveler, Corncrake, Water Rail, Northern Lapwing, Common Snipe, Common Redshank, Meadow Pipit, Skylark, Whinchat, Sedge Warbler, Willow Warbler and Reed Bunting. The current list is still more or less the same and to this can be added, for the Callows as a whole: Common Quail, Eurasian Curlew, Common Grasshopper Warbler and Stonechat (Heery 1996–2009).

Other Breeding Birds

Wet grassland and associated habitats attracts a range of other breeding birds whose composition varies according to the wetness of the ground and the mix of habitats present (see above). For example, where scrub and small trees have invaded the site Reed Bunting is often present. This species is a typical inhabitant of marshes and often occurs where there are drainage ditches filled with emergent vegetation, waterlogged ground and low scrub. The 1988–91 *Breeding Atlas* showed that Reed Bunting occur at high densities in Ireland with the population then estimated at 130,000 pairs. Wren is one of the most widespread birds in Ireland and is common almost everywhere. On wet grassland sites where rushes are abundant it can be heard churring from denser clumps of vegetation. In Ireland the Grasshopper Warbler, a summer visitor, is patchily distributed with a distinct westerly distribution. It requires dense ground cover within its territory, several suitable song posts and a rich source of invertebrate food (Gibbons *et al.* 1993). Its habitat preferences include marshy fields, young conifer plantations and waste ground (Hutchinson 1989). In Northern Ireland it is particularly abundant in dense rush pasture and 38 calling birds were recorded in this habitat in Fermanagh during wader surveys in 1986–87 (Partridge, unpublished data). There is now concern about the status of this species following a decline in the population of 47% between 1998 and 2003 (Coombes *et al.* 2009). In 2008, Common Grasshopper Warblers were heard throughout the Shannon Callows from 29 April to 9 July (Heery 2009). The Sedge Warbler, also a summer visitor, is a characteristic bird of lowland marsh and waterside habitats where it utilises patches of dense vegetation and scrub. It is especially abundant in the north and west Irish Midlands, around Lough Neagh and in Co. Down. There was a 21% decline in the population between the first and second breeding atlases, with an estimated 110,000 pairs in Ireland in 1988–1991 (Gibbons *et al.* 1993).

Finally, any account of the wet grassland avifauna would be incomplete without mention of the Corncrake. The 1988 all-Ireland Corncrake survey found the majority of birds nested in hay meadows and silage fields and only 15.1% in rough grassland in the Republic and just 2% in Northern Ireland (Mayes and Stowe 1989). This once widespread bird has disappeared from most parts of the country with the population falling in recent years from 9,032 calling birds in 1982, to 903–930 birds in 1988, and just 128 birds in 2009 (Mayes and Stowe 1989; BirdWatch Ireland 2008; Lauder 2010). While hay meadows form the main nesting habitat, marshy and rushy fields are also important, especially early in the season. Corncrake habitat usage in Ireland is treated more comprehensively in Chapter 10.

Reed Buntings use rocks, trees and bushes as song posts in wet grassland (John Fox).

The Sedge Warbler is a typical summer visitor in dense vegetation on wet grassland (John Fox).

The Eurasian Whimbrel feeds on wet grassland sites during migration through Ireland in the spring and autumn (Richard T. Mills).

Grey Heron feeding on an eel (Karl Partridge).

Non-Breeding Birds

Passage Migrants

Eurasian Whimbrel is a widespread and regular passage migrant using wet grassland sites in spring and to a lesser extent on their return south in autumn. A study at Cork Harbour from 1977–79 revealed a substantial northward migration, mostly between 20–30 April (Pierce and Wilson 1980). Reports of over 1,000 birds were received in the past from west Cork and Roscommon (Hutchinson 1989). A substantial passage amounting to several hundred birds was recorded through Upper Lough Erne in 1985–87 and also through the Lough Neagh basin. The spring passage occurs from about 20 April but extends later than in Cork, to 19 May (Partridge 1988b). The autumn passage is in late August/ early September. Around Loughs Neagh/Beg there are recent records of 180 birds at Back Lower (NIBA 2002), 260 birds at Mullagh (NIBA 2004) and 500 birds at Kiltagh Point (NIBA 2006). Small flocks (25–55 birds) use the Shannon Callows in spring and cumulatively these may amount to thousands of birds (Nairn *et al.* 1988). Small flocks also occurred elsewhere in Central Ireland in spring and groups of less than six in autumn (Heery 2005). Eurasian Whimbrel were recorded as probably breeding in Ireland when for the first time in May/June 2005 birds were seen on several occasions on the same piece of blanket bog at an undisclosed locality in Connaught (Perry 2006).

Wintering Birds

Wintering waterbirds are comprehensively monitored through the Wetland Bird Survey (WeBS) in Northern Ireland and the Irish Wetland Bird Survey (I-WeBS) in the Republic. Together they provide an annually updated assessment of the status and distribution of waterbirds across the whole island. A total of 785 sites are counted, the majority of which are inland wetlands (lakes, turloughs, rivers, callows, marshes, grassland and flooded grassland). Data for the period 1994/95 – 2000/01 have been assessed and published (Crowe 2005a). Freshwater wetlands occur in profusion across Ireland. Despite the cumulative impact of drainage and agricultural improvement many of these still contain areas of wet grassland and marsh. Some of the most important Irish wintering sites for waterbirds comprise wet grassland, in particular the callows along the middle Shannon and associated tributaries (River Suck, Little Brosna River) and wetlands around the largest lakes in Northern Ireland. Many of the smaller sites occur in association with turloughs, lakes and rivers (Crowe 2005a). Most sites contain a range of other wetland habitats including swamp, marsh, rush pasture and, usually at a higher level, improved grassland. The mosaic of habitats, each component of which has its distinctive flora, provides a variety of ecological niches which are exploited by different waterbird species according to their particular food preferences and feeding ecology.

The most recently published data (Boland *et al.* 2010a) illustrate the large numbers of wintering waterbirds present on flooded grassland in the middle Shannon (Little Brosna Callows 29,393 birds; Shannon Callows 9,197 birds; River Suck 7,266 birds). The principal species using these areas are dabbling duck (Eurasian Wigeon, Gadwall, Common Teal, Northern Pintail and Northern Shoveler), waders (Black-tailed Godwit, European Golden Plover and Northern Lapwing) and Mute Swan, Whooper Swan and Greater White-fronted Geese. Different diets, body sizes and feeding strategies in water of varying depths allow such a diversity of waterbirds to co-exist – note the different bill shapes of Eurasian Curlew, Northern Shoveler and Eurasian Wigeon; and different neck lengths of Whooper Swan, Northern Pintail and Common Teal.

The availability of floodwater is critical in determining the number of birds using a site. Studies at the Ouse Washes show that shallow and gradual flooding is most favoured by waterbirds (Owen *et al.* 1986). The extent of flooding has a marked effect on bird numbers on the Shannon Callows and on the Blackwater Callows, Cos. Cork and Waterford (Crowe 2005a). The wildfowl frequenting the callows and other wet grassland sites feed largely on vegetation or seeds. A study of similar habitat, the Ouse Washes in England (Thomas 1982; Owen *et al.* 1986), has shown that plant species that are typically abundant on callows in Ireland provide productive feeding for wildfowl. Eurasian Wigeon were grazing the leaves of floating sweet grass, creeping bent grass and other 'soft-leaved' grasses. Other waterbirds were taking the seeds of curled dock, common spike rush and brown sedge. Floating sweet-grass is particularly abundant and widespread on the Little Brosna Callows (Heery 2003). The soft wet soils, particularly as the floods are receding, are prime habitat for vigorously probing waders, and the naturally rich floodplain soils are made richer by the dunging activity of the waterbird assemblage.

The feeding ecology and diet of wintering waders using inland wetlands has not been well studied. Data from Britain and Europe (Cramp and Simmons 1983) show that European Golden Plover consume mostly earthworms (Beaudoin and Cormier 1973), beetles and other invertebrates, preferring permanent pasture where prey densities are higher (Fuller and Youngman 1979); Northern Lapwing take a wide variety of prey, mostly insects and other small invertebrates as well as plant material; while one French study of Black-tailed Godwits on passage found that they took mainly earthworms. Many inland wetlands attract large numbers of Common Snipe in winter with resident birds being supplemented by a large influx of birds from Iceland, the Faeroes and northern Europe. Common Snipe forage across a wide range of wetland and damp habitats (Crowe 2005a). Up to 1,500 birds have been recorded on one day on Clear Island, Cork (Hutchinson 1989). Jack Snipe occupy similar winter habitats but are scarcer, accounting for only 10–20% of Common Snipe in shooters' bags (Crowe 2005a).

Black-tailed Godwits provide one of the Shannon/Little Brosna Callows' most spectacular sights, with up to one tenth of the world population of the Icelandic subspecies *islandica* congregating there at times. The dense wheeling flocks with white wing flashes are a memorable sight. Studies on the Cork Harbour population are beginning to show that the godwits fly from coastal grasslands to flooded inland callows, possibly because the open landscape of callows provides a safer environment on which to roost and loaf, as well as forage (Hayhow 2008; 2009). Wildfowl and waders on passage, such

Black-tailed Godwits are rare breeders in Ireland but winter here in significant numbers on wet grassland (Richard T. Mills).

as Eurasian Wigeon, Garganey, Ruff, Eurasian Whimbrel and Black-tailed Godwits, use the habitat as staging posts on their northward migration. This is illustrated by the presence of regular flocks of godwits on callows (and turloughs) throughout central Ireland from March to the end of May (Heery 1996–2009).

Greater White-fronted Geese utilise natural wetlands and seasonally inundated areas as wintering sites. Analysis of habitat use in 1994 (Table 6.1) showed eight flocks using wet grassland, marsh or callows as their main winter habitat (i.e. 24% of all flocks). Mayes (1991) found that the geese selected the bulbous bases and roots of jointed rush, stolons of creeping bent grass, roots of creeping buttercup and stolons of white clover on the Little Brosna callows as well as rye-grass.

Table 6.1 Foraging habitats used by Greater White-fronted Geese at 34 Irish sites, based on Fox *et al.* (1994b)	Number of Sites	
	Main Use	Minor Use
Improved Grassland	22	4
Wet Grassland and Marsh	8	4
Callows	6	6
Bog	5	2
Arable and Root Crops	2	0
Dry Grassland	2	1
Salt marsh	0	1

Note: several habitats may be used at a single site.

Use of these semi-natural grassland habitats has declined greatly in recent years as smaller Irish flocks become extinct (Mayes *et al.* 2009). While many flocks still exploit rushy pasture and low-intensity grassland the trend has increasingly been for geese to shift to intensively managed grassland which is of greater nutritional value (Fox *et al.* 2006).

According to the most recent census, 14,981 Whooper Swans and 80 Bewick's Swans wintered

Whooper Swans feed mostly on grassland in winter (Richard T. Mills).

in Ireland in 2009/10 (Boland *et al.* 2010b). Whooper Swans use 21 habitat types with 66% found on improved pasture and 9.6% on potato fields. The proportions using wet grassland and marsh habitats include 1.4% on freshwater marsh, 1.5% on flooded rough/unimproved pasture, and 2.2% on rough/unimproved turlough pasture. Thus, about 5% of the Irish wintering population was found in these habitats in January 2010 which is much lower than normal, due to frozen lakes and wetlands. Bewick's Swans feed mostly on grassland and on arable crops, with 84% of the 2010 population found in Wexford. The Irish Whooper Swan wintering population has increased by 45% since 1986 whereas Bewick's Swans have suffered a severe decline and they now winter further north and east in Europe.

Conservation of Wet Grasslands

While significant work has been carried out on the avifauna of Irish wet grasslands in recent years, large gaps remain in our knowledge of the extent, distribution and characteristics of this important habitat and its birds. Little information is available on the general avifauna of wet grassland and marshland sites in Ireland, and their environmental variables, especially for the passerine bird component (c.f. Fuller 1982 for Great Britain). The key species dependent on wet grassland and marsh during the breeding season – Eurasian Curlew, Common Redshank, Northern Lapwing, Common Snipe and the enigmatic Corncrake – have all recently experienced marked declines in population size and geographical range. This is not just an Irish phenomenon but has also been recorded in Britain (Wilson *et al.* 2005), in continental Europe (Thorup 2006) and indeed worldwide (Delany 2003).

Wet grassland habitat at Portmore Lough, Co. Antrim (Karl Partridge).

The primary reason for the decline of farmland birds is the intensification of land use by farmers, in particular through drainage and other changes in grassland management (Teunissen *et al.* 2008; Wilson *et al.* 2004). This leads to a deterioration and fragmentation of the habitat, which may in turn increase the extent of predation due to changes in the density of the breeding birds or predators, and in the amount of cover where nests or chicks can be concealed. Also, if food supply is reduced, breeding birds may have to spend more time foraging, leaving the nest unattended. Predation is now thought to be a very significant factor in the decline of breeding waders in Europe (Macdonald and Bolton 2008). A study of Eurasian Curlew in Northern Ireland showed that high levels of breeding failure due to nest predation could account for the general observed decline in the Northern Ireland Eurasian Curlew population (Grant *et al.* 1999). Studies on the Shannon Callows (Finney *et al.* 2006; Finney and Warnock 2009, 2010; Prosser *et al.* 2008) and on machair grassland (Troake and Suddaby 2008) indicate high levels of predation of nests and young of Northern Lapwing and Common Redshank. Predation mainly by Foxes and Hooded Crows resulted in a loss of 69% of Northern Lapwing clutches at three sites in north-west Mayo (Troake and Suddaby 2008).

Work at key sites shows that wader declines can be halted or even reversed if several limiting factors are tackled simultaneously, instead of focusing on mitigation of predation alone (Wilson *et al.* 2004). The Northern Ireland Northern Lapwing Recovery Project, implemented through the Countryside Management Scheme, showed that where sites were actively managed for breeding Northern Lapwing, numbers remained stable whereas those on unmanaged control sites declined. Positive management by farmers involved appropriate grazing, control of rushes and wetland management (Whiteside *et al.* 2008). At Inishee Island on the Shannon Callows a predator-proof fence has led to a significant increase in wader fledging success in 2009 and 2010 (Finney and Warnock 2009, 2010). Similar measures at the RSPB's Portmore Lough reserve, adjacent to Lough Neagh, have also been effective. However, while such fencing may be invaluable at key sites with a high density of nesting birds, it would be impractical to use it throughout the wider countryside. The protection and restoration of wetlands and their unique birds needs to be achieved through habitat protection and restoration, possibly at a landscape scale. Mechanisms such as agri-environment schemes, which are carefully targeted and include specialist management options, are required in the first instance.

Control and management of extensive wet grassland sites by conservation bodies is often the only way to maximise their full potential for wetland birds and many of the best sites in Europe are managed thus. For example, after 20 years of habitat enhancement work by the RSPB, the 485-hectare Berney Marshes reserve in Norfolk now supports about 270 pairs of breeding waders, as well as large numbers of wintering wildfowl (Gilbert and Ausden 2009). Although covering a much smaller area, some of the Lower Lough Erne islands have seen an increase in their breeding wader populations as a result of being managed as RSPB reserves (Claire Ferry, pers. comm.). While the Shannon Callows provide perhaps the largest area of semi-natural wet grassland in Ireland, the untamed nature of the site brings both benefits and drawbacks. The cost, complexity and likely environmental impact of providing a Shannon drainage scheme – which has been mooted for many years – has militated against such a scheme. At the same time, the inability to control flooding makes it difficult to control water levels and breeding bird habitats have, in recent years, been subject to unpredictable flooding, resulting in greatly reduced breeding success.

Acknowledgements

I would like to thank Stephen Heery for contributing to the text relating to the Shannon Callows, Claire Ferry (RSPB, Belfast), Kathryn Finney and Dave Suddaby (both BirdWatch Ireland) for providing access to data and reports and Dr Anita Donaghy (BirdWatch Ireland) for reviewing and commenting on the draft text .

7. Lowland Bogs, Fens and Reedswamps

Fintan Bracken and Patrick Smiddy

Introduction

Peatlands are one of the most characteristic landscape features in Ireland and everyone is familiar with the large raised bogs of the Irish midlands and the blanket bogs of our uplands and Atlantic coast. Peatlands cover between 17% and 20.6% of the total area of Ireland, a percentage exceeded in Europe only by Estonia (22%) and Finland (30%) (Hammond 1981; Lappalainen 1996; Aalen *et al.* 1997; Connolly and Holden 2008). This chapter will deal with two of the main types of bogs found in Ireland, raised bogs and fens, while blanket bogs are dealt with in Chapter 8. Reedswamps often occur in association with fens but they are not dependent on groundwater and can also occur in other situations, both freshwater and tidal.

Raised bogs cover approximately 314,000 hectares of the land surface of Ireland and are typical of the central plain of the country (Aalen *et al.* 1997). Raised bogs were formed where shallow lakes were overgrown by vegetation, which subsequently led to plant debris accumulating to form peat (Hammond 1981).

Bog cotton is a typical plant of raised bogs in the central plain of Ireland (Richard Nairn).

Reedswamps are found throughout the country, on the coast as well as inland (Richard Nairn).

Meadow Pipit is the commonest breeding bird on raised bogs (Richard T. Mills).

Fens are peat-forming systems that are fed by groundwater or moving surface waters (Fossitt 2000). Fens can be found nearby springs and seepages, on river flood plains, in flat basins and in glacial lake beds. True intact fens are rare in Ireland as they have mostly been claimed for agriculture.

Reedswamps are distributed throughout the country, on the coast as well as inland, often in association with other habitats such as rivers, lakes, estuaries and coastal lagoons. They are especially associated with the major rivers such as the Shannon, and the larger lakes such as Lough Neagh. Most reedswamps are dominated by one or two tall grasses or sedges. Common reed depends on regular flooding but it can tolerate occasional drying out in summer. It can survive in both fresh and brackish waters.

Many reedswamps begin as shallow lakes, and through natural succession develop into fens. This process occurs through a gradual build-up of peat from dead plant material, which raises the surface out of reach of ground water. While reedswamps are dominated by one species, the common reed, fens, in turn, develop shorter and more diverse vegetation, which may include typical species such as meadow sweet and ragged robin. Over longer periods of time fens further develop into woodland dominated by alder, willow and birch with a luxuriant ground flora (Anon 1974). The grazing of farm animals may alter and reduce the vegetation in some reedswamps and fens. Common reeds may also occur in drier habitats on the higher mudbanks of tidal rivers, such as the Blackwater (Munster).

Unfortunately, to the casual visitor these habitats often appear 'empty' as many of the bird species that live in them are skulking in nature. This perception makes them vulnerable to damage as they are often viewed as wastelands. Historically, these wetlands have been exploited, especially through drainage programmes in the nineteenth century, and the arterial drainage schemes of the twentieth century. Few such lowland wetlands remain untouched, and much of our present agricultural grassland is based on former fens and reedswamps. Over the last 20 years, during the economic boom, many of the remaining wetlands suffered further damage due to infilling with rubble and builder's waste. Sustainable exploitation of some wetlands takes place on a small scale, such as the harvesting of reeds for thatch, and rushes and willows for basket making.

A high proportion of Irish peatlands has been damaged in varying degrees during the last 60 years due to several factors. These include the introduction of large-scale, mechanised turf extraction schemes in the 1940s for fuel and horticultural peat, afforestation programmes commencing in the 1950s, intensification of agriculture following Ireland's entry to the EU and land reclamation (Feehan and O'Donovan 1996). The area of peatland suitable for conservation in Ireland has been seriously reduced in recent times leaving less than 15% of the original extent shown in Hammond's peatlands map of Ireland (Hammond 1981) in near-intact condition (Crushell 2002; Foss 2007; Douglas *et al.* 2008).

The importance of raised bogs and fens as habitats in an international and national context is illustrated by the inclusion of both in Annex I of the EU Habitats Directive. This affords special conservation status to peatland habitats including active raised bogs, degraded raised bogs still capable of natural regeneration, calcareous fens with saw sedge and species of the *Caricion davallianae*, and alkaline fens. Many important raised bog and fen sites in Ireland are allocated special protection through their designation as Nature Reserves, Special Areas of Conservation (SAC), Special Protection Areas (SPA), Natural Heritage Areas (NHA) and Areas of Special Scientific Interest (ASSI).

Raised Bogs

The numbers of bird species occurring on raised bogs during the breeding season is quite low and is often lower than blanket bogs (Madden 1987b; Hutchinson 1989; Feehan and O'Donovan 1996; Wilson 2002). Only eleven species were found during the breeding season at three midlands raised bogs (Sharavogue and Clara, Co. Offaly and Carrowbehy, Co. Roscommon) with Meadow Pipit and Skylark dominating the bird community of this habitat with 62% and 30% of the birds recorded respectively (Bracken *et al.* 2008, Table 7.1). Other common species of raised bogs in the spring and summer are Eurasian Curlew, Common Snipe, Mallard and Wren (Bracken *et al.* 2008, Table 7.1). Willow Ptarmigan (hereafter called Red Grouse) also occurs on raised bogs where its main food, heather, occurs in sufficient abundance but the species is more typical of blanket bogs (Bracken *et al.* 2008) (see Chapter 8). Several species of raptor including Peregrine, Common Kestrel and Merlin may hunt over raised bogs with Merlin often establishing breeding territories on raised bogs (Wilson 1990; Norriss *et al.* 2010).

Other surveys of breeding birds of raised bogs have also been conducted with 17 breeding species found within the Dunkellin/Lavally river catchments, Co. Galway (Buckley and McCarthy 1987). Four breeding species of wader, European Golden Plover, Northern Lapwing, Common Snipe and Eurasian Curlew were found by Partridge (1988a) during a survey of 95 raised bog sites mainly in Co. Tyrone as part of the Northern Ireland breeding waders survey. Only two breeding species, Meadow Pipit (20 territories) and Skylark (15 territories), were found to be wholly associated with the intact raised bog habitat during a survey of the intact dome of Dunloy Bog ASSI in County Antrim in 2004 (Allen and Mellon Environmental 2007). Another species, Eurasian Curlew, included the bog within its territory but nested and did most feeding in the lagg area and adjacent grasslands (Allen and Mellon Environmental 2007). Twenty-one breeding species were recorded at Finn Lough in Co. Offaly which is sandwiched between an esker ridge and a cutover bog (Rochford 1988). The bird community of an area of intact raised

Merlin often breed on raised bogs (Richard T. Mills).

bog in Mongan Bog, Co. Offaly, comprised 12 different species including Common Kestrel, Common Redshank and Linnet but only Mallard, Common Snipe, Skylark and Meadow Pipit were proven to have bred and Eurasian Curlew was suspected of nesting (Madden 1987a). Table 7.2 (modified from Wilson 1990) summarises some of the findings from these studies of the birds of raised bogs in Ireland during the breeding season and illustrates that both species diversity and densities are low in this habitat.

Table 7.1 Community proportion (%) of each bird species recorded in raised bog and fen habitat types from the study of Bracken *et al.* 2008		
Species	Raised Bog	Fen
Mute Swan	0	1.6
Mallard	1.0	1.2
Red Grouse	0.5	0
Moorhen	0	0.4
Common Snipe	1.3	9.1
Eurasian Curlew	3.7	0
Woodpigeon	0	1.2
Rook	0	0.4
Hooded Crow	0.3	0
Skylark	30.2	2.4
Willow Warbler	0.3	4.3
Common Grasshopper Warbler	0	2.0
Sedge Warbler	0.3	7.9
Wren	0.5	9.1
Stonechat	0.3	2.0
Meadow Pipit	61.7	40.2
Goldfinch	0	0.4
Greenfinch	0	0.4
Reed Bunting	0	17.7

Detailed studies were carried out on the dispersion patterns and habitat use of ground-nesting bird species on three raised bogs in Co. Offaly, All Saint's Bog, Clara Bog and Raheenmore Bog in the mid-1990s (Huvendiek 1996; Pohler 1996). A territory mapping study of 266 hectares of Clara Bog found 14 breeding species in the relatively intact western part, with Skylark being the most abundant with 82 territories followed by Meadow Pipit with 81 (Pohler 1996). The eastern part has been seriously disturbed by a network of surface drains and only had nine breeding species with Meadow Pipit being the most abundant with 72 territories and Skylark with 52. Pohler (1996) only regarded four of the recorded breeding bird species (Meadow Pipit, Skylark, Common Snipe and Eurasian Curlew) as typical breeders in open raised bog habitats. The study also examined the dispersion patterns of breeding birds and their habitat relationships in Clara Bog (Pohler 1996). Skylark and Meadow Pipit showed no distinct response to site-specific differences in habitat properties, indicating their unspecialised mode of habitat use in open raised bog habitats. However, occupied Meadow Pipit areas of the peatland had higher and denser grass/sedge-dwarf shrub vegetation that unpopulated parts. There was very little difference between

Table 7.2 Records of presence and densities of birds on raised bogs during the breeding season (x = presence; * = breeding species; densities given in individual/km²) (modified from Wilson 1990)

Species	Mongan Bog, Co. Offaly[1]	Co. Tyrone[2]	Dunkellin/ Lavally, Co. Galway[3]	Sharavogue, Co. Offaly[4]	Clara, Co. Offaly[4]	Carrowbehy, Co. Roscommon[4]
Mallard	X *	–	–	–	5.0	5.3
Red Grouse	–	–	X	–	–	5.3
Common Kestrel	X	–	–	–	–	–
Peregrine	X	–	–	–	–	–
European Golden Plover	–	X	–	–	–	–
Northern Lapwing	–	2.0	0.7	–	–	–
Common Snipe	X *	16.0	2.2	–	7.5	5.3
Eurasian Curlew	X *	6.0	0.7	3.3	10.0	23.7
Common Redshank	X	–	2.2	–	–	–
Rook	X	–	–	–	–	–
Hooded Crow	X	–	–	–	2.5	–
Raven	X	–	X	–	–	–
Great Tit	–	–	0.7	–	–	–
Skylark	X *	–	13.6	80.0	127.5	105.3
Willow Warbler	–	–	3.6	–	–	2.6
Sedge Warbler	–	–	4.3	–	–	2.6
Wren	–	–	3.6	–	–	5.3
Blackbird	–	–	2.8	–	–	–
Song Thrush	–	–	0.7	–	–	–
European Robin	–	–	1.4	–	–	–
Stonechat	–	–	5.0	–	–	2.6
Meadow Pipit	X *	–	43	210.0	275	163.2
Linnet	X	–	–	–	–	–
Lesser Redpoll	–	–	2.8	–	–	–
Reed Bunting	–	–	5.0	–	–	–
Total Densities	–	–	**101.9**	**293.3**	**427.5**	**321.1**

1 Recorded during 10 equally spaced visits between 29.1.85 and 9.1.86 (Madden 1987a)
2 Northern Ireland Breeding Wader Survey (Partridge 1988)
3 Dunkellin/Lavally 1985/86 (Buckley and McCarthy 1987)
4 Recorded during 2 visits in 2006 (Bracken et al. 2008)

Skylarks are plentiful on bogs in summer but leave in search of food during winter (Richard T. Mills).

Scragh Bog is a small fen site in Co. Westmeath (Richard Nairn).

occupied and unoccupied areas of the peatland in the case of Skylark. Eurasian Curlew seemed to prefer the wetter parts of Clara Bog and also areas with low and sparse grass/sedge-dwarf shrub vegetation. Common Snipe prefer higher cover of lawn-forming sedges and areas with a higher proportion of open water in Clara Bog (Pohler 1996). Common Redshank has recently been recorded breeding on bogs in Ireland with three recent occurrences of the species breeding on both blanket and raised bog. However, bogs are only suitable as marginal breeding habitats for Common Redshank due to their low productivity (Nairn *et al.* 2004).

Gulls may also be present on raised bogs and it has been noted that colonies of Black-headed Gulls are common in bogs with open bodies of water, especially if they have reedbeds or other safe nesting areas (Feehan and O'Donovan 1996). In the late 1800s, 100 pairs of the Lesser Black-backed Gull were recorded on a bog in Co. Kildare but this colony later disappeared due to turf developments and since then no Lesser Black-backed Gulls have been found breeding on bogs in the country (Creme *et al.* 1997).

During the winter period from late September to mid-February, numbers of species are usually lower than during the breeding season but densities vary (Wilson 1990). Many species including Meadow Pipit, Skylark and Reed Bunting form migratory flocks in winter and leave raised bogs in search of food in the neighbouring countryside. Meadow Pipit is usually scarce and Skylark often absent from raised bogs between late November and early February (Wilson 1990). Winter season surveys of birds of raised bogs within the Dunkellin/Lavally river catchments, Co. Galway and the Owenmore catchment, Co. Sligo found 7 and 17 species respectively (Buckley and McCarthy 1987; P. Buckley cited in Wilson 1990).

In winter, wildfowl are important visitors to raised bogs, with the Greater White-fronted Goose or 'bog' goose one such winter visitor with a traditional and specialised association with bogs (Wilson 2002). Blanket bogs and raised bogs were the species' traditional habitat before the exploitation of bogs by people began to change things (Wilson 1990; Wilson 2002). The species feeds by probing for the nutritionally rich underground storage organs of cotton grass and white-beaked sedge (Wilson 1990; Wilson 2002). As bogs and in particular raised bogs have gradually disappeared, the Greater White-fronted Goose has adapted and taken advantage of grasslands and other crops (Wilson 2002). Although the Greater White-fronted Goose may still utilise raised bogs for night-time roosts, there are few flocks that continue to feed exclusively on bogs throughout the winter (Fox *et al.* 1994b; Fox 2003).

Fens

Fens are much more species-rich habitats than raised bogs (Crushell 2000). In 2008, a study of the breeding season birds of fen found 16 bird species at three fens, Scragh Bog (Co. Westmeath),

Table 7.3 Densities of birds (individual/km²) recorded on fens during the breeding season (From Bracken *et al.* 2008)

Species	Scragh Bog, Co. Westmeath	Pollardstown Fen, Co. Kildare	Bellacorick flush, Co. Mayo
Mute Swan	–	20.0	–
Mallard	21.4	–	–
Moorhen	0.0	5.0	–
Common Snipe	100.0	35.0	33.3
Woodpigeon	7.1	10.0	–
Rook	–	5.0	–
Skylark	–	5.0	83.3
Willow Warbler	35.7	30.0	–
Common Grasshopper Warbler	–	25.0	–
Sedge Warbler	–	100.0	–
Wren	42.9	65.0	66.7
Stonechat	–	–	83.3
Meadow Pipit	321.4	205.0	266.7
Greenfinch	7.1	–	–
Goldfinch	–	5.0	–
Reed Bunting	192.9	90.0	–
Total Densities	**728.6**	**600.0**	**533.3**

Table 7.4 Densities (± S.E.) of each species (individual/km²), for selected species and all species combined for raised bog and fen habitat types (From Bracken *et al.* 2008)

Species	Raised Bog	Fen
All species	352.8 ± 17.5	635 ± 44
Mallard	3.7 ± 2.5	7.5 ± 5.5
Red Grouse	1.9 ± 1.5	0 ± 0
Common Snipe	4.6 ± 2	57.5 ± 13
Eurasian Curlew	13.0 ± 4	0 ± 0
Skylark	106.5 ± 9.5	15 ± 7.5
Willow Warbler	0.9 ± 1	27.5 ± 10
Common Grasshopper Warbler	0 ± 0	12.5 ± 5
Sedge Warbler	0.9 ± 1	50 ± 21
Wren	1.9 ± 2	57.5 ± 15
Stonechat	0.9 ± 1	12.5 ± 7
Meadow Pipit	217.6 ± 13.5	255 ± 34
Reed Bunting	0 ± 0	112.5 ± 24

Pollardstown Fen (Co. Kildare) and Bellacorrick flush (Co. Mayo) (Bracken *et al.* 2008, Table 7.1). Unlike raised bogs, the bird communities of fens are not dominated entirely by Meadow Pipit and Skylark although Meadow Pipit does comprise about 40% of the individuals sighted (Bracken *et al.* 2008, Tables 7.1 and 7.3). Reed Bunting (18%), Wren (9%), Common Snipe (9%) and Sedge Warbler (8%) also make up large proportions of the breeding season communities of fens (Bracken *et al.* 2008, Table 7.1 and 7.3). Fens also support higher densities of birds than raised bog with almost twice as many birds per square kilometre found on fen (635 birds/km^2) compared to raised bog (353 birds/km^2) (Bracken *et al.* 2008 and Table 7.4).

Fens provide breeding and feeding sites for a wide variety of bird species due to the presence of reedbeds and areas of tall sedge, wet marshy ground, areas of open water and fen carr (or fen woodland) (Crushell 2000). Twenty-seven different bird species have been found breeding on or in the immediate vicinity of Pollardstown Fen, including Little Grebe, Great Crested Grebe, Mute Swan, Common Teal, Water Rail, Moorhen, Sedge Warbler, Reed Bunting, Stonechat, Skylark and Meadow Pipit (Madden 1987c). Thirteen species were recorded at Kebble Fen, Rathlin Island, Co. Antrim, with six of these species associated with the core fen habitat: Sedge Warbler (24 territories), Reed Bunting (6), Water Rail (up to 3), Common Snipe (2), Common Teal (1), and Grasshopper Warbler (1) (Allen and Mellon Environmental 2007). In addition, other species were associated with bracken and bramble growth around the fen margins and included Stonechat (4 territories), Wren (3), Meadow Pipit (3), Blackbird (2), European Robin (1), Dunnock (1) and Common Whitethroat (1). A pair of Whinchat had been recorded at the fen in previous years (Allen and Mellon Environmental 2007).

During the autumn and winter season substantial numbers of wildfowl may occur on fens where an adequate area of open water occurs (Crushell 2000). Species such as Eurasian Wigeon, Shoveler, Tufted Duck and Common Pochard are frequent and Whooper Swans, Gadwall, Northern Pintail and Common Goldeneye may also occur (Crushell 2000). Grey Heron, Eurasian Curlew, Northern Lapwing, Common Redshank and Common Snipe are also common winter species on fens (Crushell 2000). Flocks of finches such as Chaffinch, Greenfinch, Linnet and Goldfinch are common in fen carr during the winter (Crushell 2000). Birds of prey such as Common Kestrel, Sparrowhawk and Hen Harrier may hunt over fens at any time of the year.

Cutover and Cutaway Peatlands

Cutover bog describes peatland, including fens and some areas of wet heath, where part of the original mass of peat has been removed through turf cutting or other forms of peat extraction (Fossitt 2000). Much of the recent research into the bird communities of peatlands has focused on cutover and cutaway peatlands. The bird communities of cutover/cutaway bogs have a much more diverse avifauna than many other peatland habitats (O'Connell and Foss 1999; Kavanagh 1998). The diversity of the bird communities of these peatlands is due to the fact that cutover/cutaway peatlands often contain a mosaic of land uses and habitat types including permanent wetland, seasonal wetland, grassland, birch/willow scrub, birch woodland, forestry, heather-topped bog and bare peat (Kavanagh 1998). This heterogeneity of habitat types has resulted in approximately 90 different species being recorded on cutover/cutaway bogs (O'Connell and Foss 1999). These species can be divided into seven groups: open ground species (e.g. Skylark, Meadow Pipit and Eurasian Curlew); open woodland generalist species (e.g. European Robin, Wren and Blackbird); open woodland specialist species (e.g. Chiffchaff, Common Whitethroat and Willow Warbler); reedbed specialists (e.g. Sedge Warbler); rush specialists (e.g. Reed Bunting); breeding Grey Partridge; and feeding visitors (e.g. Woodpigeon, Jackdaw and Common Starling) (Kavanagh 1990b; O'Connell and Foss 1999).

Thirty-six species were found on an area of cutaway bog in Mongan Bog, Co. Offaly, during ten visits in 1985/86, with 19 of these breeding (Madden 1987a). At Turraun Cutaway Bog in Co. Offaly, 43 species were recorded, of which 24 were either confirmed to be breeding or probably breeding

(Kavanagh 1990b). This shows the rich bird diversity that can be found in cutover/cutaway peatlands as this was a single area of 118 hectares that contained several habitats including grassland, areas of rushes, open woodland and a reedbed (Kavanagh 1990b). Turraun Cutaway Bog forms part of the Lough Boora Parklands which is comprised of about 2,000 hectares of cutaway bog on Bord na Móna lands, situated halfway between Tullamore, Co. Offaly and the River Shannon. Wetland creation and natural recolonisation were the land-use options used to claim cutaway peatlands (Heery 1998). Grey Partridge, Merlin and many species of waders and waterfowl including Northern Lapwing, Common Redshank, Common Sandpiper, Tufted Duck and Little Grebe have been recorded breeding in the Parklands (Heery 1998). Six species of breeding waders, Great Ringed Plover, Northern Lapwing, Common Snipe, Common Redshank, Eurasian Curlew and Common Sandpiper, were recorded on cutaway peatlands around the Boora area and also at Blackwater cutaway bog in Co. Offaly (Cooney 1998; Hudson *et al.* 2002). There appeared to be a decrease in wader numbers in 2002 at these peatlands compared to a previous survey in 1998 and this may be due to changes to the habitat as a result of natural succession and conversion of land to forestry and agricultural purposes (Hudson *et al.* 2002).

At Clonsast Bog in Co. Offaly, short rotation forest plantations were established on the cutover bog in the late 1980s. Thirty-four species were recorded over the survey period, with the bird assemblages of the mixed-tree, short-rotation deciduous plantation dominated by Willow Warbler (24% of the recorded territories), Chaffinch (11.5%), Reed Bunting, European Robin and Wren (10% each) (Kavanagh 1990a). The commonest species in the pure willow plantation were Sedge Warbler (18%), Willow Warbler (16%), Reed Bunting (14.5%), Chaffinch, Dunnock and Blackbird (8% each) (Kavanagh 1990a). The dominance of warblers and buntings was due to the presence of permanent, early successional stages due to a short rotation coppicing regime in these plantations (Kavanagh 1990a). (See also Chapter 9).

Reedswamps

During summer, reedswamps are important as breeding sites for a wide variety of birds, while in winter, following dieback of the vegetation, they may become an important roosting habitat for a smaller number of species. Reedswamps have been favourite sites for study by Irish bird ringers in the last 20 years, but much of this research remains unpublished. Indeed, very little has been published on any aspect of the habitats under discussion here (Nairn 2003).

Breeding birds

Ireland's former extensive reedswamps and fens were the breeding habitats of a number of species long since extinct. The Bittern was

Reed Bunting male perches on a reed stem (Richie Lort).

Cutover bogs are widespread as turf has been cut for fuel for thousands of years (Richard Nairn).

The Grey Partridge has recently been reintroduced to cutaway bogs in the Irish midlands (Richard T. Mills).

once widespread in such habitats, as was the Marsh Harrier (D'Arcy 1999). The Bittern has not bred since at least the mid-1800s, although stragglers turn up fairly regularly in reedbed habitats to the present day, and 'booming' has been recorded, indicating at least that birds occasionally establish a territory (Hutchinson 1989). There has also been a serious decline in Britain, but signs of a recovery have been evident there recently, and 'booming' birds occasionally turn up at sites away from their main East Anglian habitats (Parkin and Knox 2010). Such wandering individuals may be the source of recent records in Ireland. The Marsh Harrier was a widespread breeding species across Ireland up to the early nineteenth century, but by the middle of that century only a few pairs remained. By the early twentieth century breeding had ceased entirely (Hutchinson 1989). Records of migrants have increased in recent years, in line with an increase in breeding numbers in Europe and in Britain (Parkin and Knox 2010), and it may only be a matter of time before Irish wetland habitats are again colonised. A male Marsh Harrier constructed nest platforms at a site in Co. Clare in 1981, although among migrants, males are far rarer than females or immature birds. Summering birds are currently regularly recorded at a number of sites (Hillis 2007), but it remains to be seen if the unexpected breeding of a pair in Co. Down in 2009 (Scott et al. 2009) is the start of the recolonisation process. The main causes of decline in these two species were drainage of wetland habitats and persecution by shooting. The Common Crane was probably a widespread species in the extensive wetlands of prehistoric times. Bones of Cranes have been identified from peat deposits in Ireland, and Bronze Age people at Ballycotton (Cork) ate them (Boisseau and Yalden 1998). Nowadays, Cranes are merely stragglers to Ireland, but eastern Britain was recolonised in the 1980s and breeding continues (Parkin and Knox 2010).

At the present time reedswamps provide breeding habitats for several resident and migrant bird species. Typical of the residents is the Water Rail, and of the migrants, the Sedge Warbler. Many species that essentially occupy open freshwater areas build their nests within reedbeds. The Great Crested Grebe is one such species. In Northern Ireland, at least 660 adult birds were recorded in 1975, many of which had nests in extensive reedbeds (Furphy 1977). At Lough Neagh, where it was believed that an increase had taken place in the previous ten years, at least 288 birds were present in 1975. In the same survey 758 birds were estimated to be present in the Republic of Ireland, and many of these also nested in reedbeds (Preston 1976). Reedbeds, and the nests of any species breeding within them, are subject to damage during gales. Such was the case in Northern Ireland during the 1975 Great Crested Grebe census. One reedbed on the south shore of Lough Neagh held 130 adult birds in late May, but by mid-June following severe gales only 70 remained and no broods were raised (Furphy 1977). Rarer grebes also use reedbeds, and many of the Black-necked Grebes in the (now extinct) colony at Lough Funshinagh (Roscommon) in the early 1900s nested in such habitat (Humphreys 1978) (see Chapter 5).

More recent survey work at Lough Neagh has again shown the importance of that site to breeding Great Crested Grebes (Perry *et al.* 1998a). In 1998 the breeding population was counted at Lough Neagh where a total of 138km of lakeshore was surveyed. The lough held 1,827 breeding pairs, a significant increase on the previous survey, although a different survey technique was used where the observer waded into reedbeds in search of nests. The largest number of breeding pairs was found within beds of common reed, but at Lough Neagh the highest breeding density was within bulrushes. An increase of 44% in the population on lakes in County Cavan also took place between 1975 and 1986–88, and many of them were nesting within reedbeds (Lovatt 1988).

Many duck species and Mute Swans also utilise reedbeds for breeding. A reedbed at the former coastal lagoon at Ballycotton, Co. Cork, once had breeding Gadwall, Mallard, Northern Shoveler, Common Pochard and Mute Swan (Smiddy 2005). Hutchinson (1979) estimated that there were 120 pairs of Mallard breeding there in 1968. Reedbeds are also used for breeding by Water Rail, Moorhen and Common Coot, although these species breed widely in other habitats as well, and the rare Spotted Crake has also been recorded in recent times and probably breeds (Hillis 2004). Grey Herons generally nest in trees, but occasional nests have been recorded in reedbeds (Smiddy 2005). The invasive Ruddy Duck also uses reedbeds for nesting (Culbert and Furphy 1978; Perry *et al.* 1998b; Allen *et al.* 2006).

Many small passerine species, especially warblers, favour reedbeds as a nesting habitat, although some may not be exclusive to that habitat. The migrant Sedge Warbler is easily the commonest species, although densities do not appear to have been established for any Irish reedbed site. The Common Reed Warbler has been breeding regularly in reedbeds along the south and east coasts of Ireland only since 1980, although the first breeding record was of a pair in Co. Down in 1935. The total breeding population was estimated at less than 100 pairs in 1995–96 (Smiddy and O'Mahony 1997). The current situation is that breeding continues at many sites along the south and east coasts, although there is evidence of a recent decline at some, such as Ballyvergan Marsh (Cork). In Northern Ireland the Common Reed Warbler first became established as a regular breeding bird in 2004 (Northern Ireland Birdwatchers' Association 2005). It now breeds in suitable habitat throughout County Down. Another key

Great Crested Grebes nest in reedswamps around the shores of large lakes (Karl Partridge).

The Water Rail is perfectly adapted to life in reed-swamps where it slips between the reeds stems (Richard T. Mills).

Grey Herons feed on frogs and many other wetland prey species (Ian Herbert).

stronghold is the reedbeds at Portmore Lough (Antrim) where numbers continue to increase and 27 singing males were recorded in 2009 (John Scovell RSPB, pers. comm.). The results of the 2007–2011 atlas survey are awaited with interest. The Common Grasshopper Warbler has a wide distribution in Ireland, but it is much scarcer than the Sedge Warbler. They generally occur among rank wetland vegetation, but they will also nest in associated wetland habitats at the periphery of reedbeds.

That specialist reedbed bird, the Bearded Reedling, was first recorded in Ireland as recently as 1966. Rather surprisingly, a pair bred in Co. Wicklow in 1976 following occurrences in that county in 1974 and 1975. Breeding was again recorded there in 1982 to 1985, with up to 11 pairs present during the peak in 1983, but none have occurred since then (Hutchinson 1989). Birds were also recorded at reedbed sites in Counties Cork and Wexford during the 1970s and 1980s, but without definite evidence of breeding. Savi's Warbler has also been recorded singing in reedbeds in Ireland, but despite earlier optimism that breeding may be imminent (Hutchinson 1989) this has not happened, and the species remains a rare vagrant. It has also recently declined as a breeding species in Britain (Parkin and Knox 2010). There are only two records of Cetti's Warblers in Ireland, and both involved males recorded in song. Given the current strength and distribution of the British (including Welsh) population (Parkin and Knox 2010), this species now seems a more likely future colonist here than the Savi's warbler. Although sensitive to cold winters, Cetti's Warbler could do well in the mild climate of the south and south-east coasts of Ireland.

Mute Swan nesting in a reedswamp (John Coveney).

The Common Cuckoo, although much scarcer now than formerly, frequently occurs in reedbeds. At Ballyvergan Marsh they are regularly recorded in the breeding season. Elsewhere, Common Cuckoos are known to commonly parasitise the nests of Common Reed Warblers (Davies 2000). However, while Common Reed Warblers breed at Ballyvergan Marsh, it is unlikely that the 'Reed Warbler' Common Cuckoo gens occurs here, and it is more likely that they parasitise the nests of the Sedge Warbler and Reed Bunting. Both of these species are common breeders here, and both have also been recorded as hosts of the Common Cuckoo in Ireland (Sealy *et al.* 1996).

Non-breeding birds

Reedswamps are used by a wide variety of species outside the breeding season, although very little information about them has been published. Ridgway and Hutchinson (1990) and Smiddy (2001) gave general accounts of the birds of two fen habitats. Almost all bird of prey species utilise these habitats because of the large number of small prey species present during the course of the winter or the migration period. The migration of Barn Swallows and Sand Martins has been studied at Ballyvergan Marsh, and observations have been made on the birds of prey attending the roost site at dusk. Sparrowhawks regularly patrol the reedbed and on almost all occasions they interacted with (chased) the roosting hirundines (Smiddy *et al.* 2007a). Common Kestrels, Merlins and Peregrines occurred less frequently, and the first two often chased the hirundines. However, although the Hen Harrier was next to the Sparrowhawk in frequency of occurrence, no interaction

Sedge Warbler is the commonest migrant found breeding in reedbeds (Richie Lort).

took place between it and the hirundines, probably because of its mode of hunting which mainly involves flushing birds from dense cover.

Dawson (2005) studied the daily use by Hen Harriers of Kilcolman National Nature Reserve, a rich limestone fen situated in the north of Co. Cork. He found that 'ringtails' (females and immatures) made up significantly more of the observations there than adult males. Both sexes were recorded in every month of the year, but most observations for both sexes took place in the period between September and February. Between January and March 2005, ten male and 213 ringtail flights were recorded over the fen. Flights averaged 0.16 per day and 3.55 per day for males and ringtails respectively, with the majority of flights occurring in the morning. Flight duration for males averaged 3.67 minutes and for ringtails 2.74 minutes, but there was no significant difference between the sexes, or within or between days. Both sexes concentrated on areas of swamp and rich fen for hunting, but with males tending to be more restricted than ringtails in the variety of habitats used.

While most bird of prey species use reedswamp habitats as foraging areas, the Hen Harrier also uses these habitats as night roost sites. The harriers usually roost on clumps of common reed or sedge tussocks close to the ground, but small shrubby trees within the marsh may also be used. At Ballyvergan Marsh and Ballycotton up to five harriers have been observed flying to the marsh from the surrounding countryside (mainly farmland) at or near dusk. Most birds engage in some late hunting over the marsh before settling to roost. Ringtails have been observed much more frequently at such roost sites than males, which are rather rare. This is probably because males tend to stay at or near their breeding habitat in the uplands during the winter. Although Kilcolman National Nature Reserve is only just south of the breeding grounds of the Ballyhoura Mountains (Cork/Limerick), the same observation has been made, with males much scarcer there than females (Dawson 2005). In winter, at least at the coastal sites of Ballyvergan Marsh and Ballycotton, Short-eared Owls sometimes hunt alongside the harriers at dusk.

Hen Harriers often hunt in reedbeds in winter (Richard T. Mills).

Barn Swallows roost in large flocks at night in reedbeds (Richard T. Mills).

The use of the reedbed at Ballyvergan Marsh by Barn Swallows and Sand Martins has been studied from mid-April to early October (Smiddy *et al.* 2007a, Cullen and Smiddy 2008). Neither of these species breed within the marsh, but they utilise the habitat extensively for feeding, and especially for roosting purposes. Small numbers of both species used the reedbed during spring migration, and even right throughout the breeding season. This confirms observations made elsewhere for the Barn Swallow (Turner 2006). However, it was during the autumn migration that the most extensive use was made of this reedbed. Sand Martins migrated much earlier than Barn Swallows, and almost 90% of them had passed through the site by mid-July, and thereafter numbers were negligible. On the other hand, only about 50% of Barn Swallows had migrated through by mid-August, when numbers were highest. It was estimated that at least 36,000 Barn Swallows and 9,000 Sand Martins migrated through Ballyvergan Marsh during any one year.

The behaviour of Barn Swallows and Sand Martins at the Ballyvergan Marsh roost site follows a pattern of gathering into a flock high over the reedbed from at least one hour before it was time for roosting to take place. Small flocks continue to fly in from the surrounding countryside and join those already present. There is much twittering high in the air. The flock begins to descend lower as roosting time approaches and several low passes just over the reeds may be made. Eventually, when the light level is right they descend into the reedbed and quickly settle down on a reed stem. Suddenly, all is quiet within the roost. Birds rise rather early the following morning, and departure from the roost site takes place quickly.

The time that Barn Swallows roosted relative to sunset was measured (Smiddy *et al.* 2007b). Roosting time varied from between 11 and 35 minutes after sunset (mean of 22.2 minutes). The time interval between roosting of the earliest and latest birds usually spanned a period of about 10 to 15 minutes, but could be as long as 30 minutes whenever late stragglers arrived at the roost. The light intensity at the time of roosting varied between 41 and 6 lux (mean of 22.9 lux), although the earliest birds to roost did so at a light intensity of about 80 lux. Roosting took place a little earlier on overcast evenings compared with evenings with a clear sky.

Several other species have been recorded using reedbeds as roost sites. At Ballyvergan Marsh up to 50 Pied Wagtails sometimes roost there during the autumn months, and for many years in the 1980s an enormous flock of Common Starlings gathered there on winter evenings, but only a small flock has been using the site in recent years. Common Starlings probably are the most spectacular birds of all when gathered together in an enormous flock over a roost site on a cold winter afternoon. Observations at Ballyvergan Marsh and in the surrounding countryside indicate that the birds feed on farmland in relatively small numbers. At dusk each of these small flocks head towards the roost site,

Common Starlings perform spectacular aerobatics above reedbeds which they use as winter roosts (Richard T. Mills).

but they do not enter for some time, and they first join up with whatever flocks are already present. Eventually the flock may number tens of thousands of birds, and for a time before entering the roost they perform spectacular aerial manoeuvres involving gathering into a tight ball, swooping low and spreading out again into long and thin flocks. All of this is accompanied by a tremendous 'whoosh' of the wings, especially when they swoop low. Suddenly the entire flock descends into the reeds where a murmur of 'conversation' goes on between the birds for some time. Late arrivals at the roost go straight into the reeds. Departure from the roost the following morning is a much less spectacular affair, and birds simply depart quickly for the feeding grounds without ceremony.

The reasons for communal roosting in birds have been debated, and it is probably related to several factors. Individuals within flocks are probably much less prone to predation than lone individuals. The temperature within flock roosts may be a few degrees higher than if the same birds were roosting alone, therefore improving their chances of survival during cold nights. It has also been hypothesised that birds within a roost which failed to find sufficient food during any day may be assisted in doing so by following birds the next day that had returned to the roost the previous evening with full crops.

Water Rails and Moorhens are common inhabitants of reedbeds in winter, and wrens and other common resident passerines may also be present. Thrushes, especially Fieldfares, but also Redwings, Song Thrushes and Blackbirds may seek out reedbeds as winter roost sites. If small sallows and alders grow within the habitat it is all the more suited to them. Wintering Chiffchaffs and roving flocks of Long-tailed Tits may also occur within reedbeds in winter, and Lesser Redpolls will often be present if alders grow there. However, Reed Buntings, a common breeder in the habitat, may be largely absent in winter, and farmland may be a more favoured habitat at that season.

Moorhens are common inhabitants of reed-beds in winter (Karl Partridge).

The Common Snipe probes in the soft peaty soils on cutaway bogs (Richard T. Mills).

Summary and Conclusions

Irish raised bogs are dominated by two bird species, Meadow Pipit and Skylark, which account for over 90% of all birds recorded (Bracken *et al.* 2008). A similar situation exists in eastern Canadian peatlands with studies showing that four species made up the majority of the recorded birds despite the large numbers of birds found (Desrochers and Van Duinan 2006). Fens, on the other hand, hold a greater diversity of species including species such as Reed Bunting, Wren, Common Snipe and summer migrants such as Common Grasshopper Warbler and Sedge Warbler. Meadow Pipit occurs in high numbers in fens (45% of the population) but Skylark numbers are relatively low compared with raised bogs (2.5% of the community) (Bracken *et al.* 2008).

Peatlands, such as raised bogs and fens, are found in many areas in western Europe and temperate North America with over 100 species and several families of birds found on these peatlands but no bird species from Eurasia or North America are exclusive to peatlands (Desrochers and Van Duinan 2006). Much of the ornithological research on peatlands are from North America (Desrochers *et al.* 1998; Wilson *et al.* 1998) and Fennoscandinavia (Berg *et al.* 1992) which includes Finnish, Swedish, German and western Russian peatlands. The species occurring on Fennoscandinavian peatlands are similar to Irish raised bogs with species such as Mallard, Eurasian Curlew, Common Snipe, Common Redshank, European Golden Plover, Northern Lapwing, Skylark and Black-headed Gull common but also include species such as Eurasian Whimbrel and Wood Sandpiper. Species diversity has been shown to be somewhat greater in North American peatlands compared to Fennoscandinavia (Desrochers and Van Duinan 2006). Shorebirds dominate the bird communities in Eurasian peatlands (Hakala 1971; Väisänen and Järvinen 1977) while songbirds are dominant in North American peatlands (Calmé *et al.* 2002). In both North America and Europe, peatlands are often important staging areas for migrants outside the breeding season especially for shorebirds, ducks and geese (Desrochers and Van Duinan 2006). As in Irish raised bogs, a very small number of birds can be found on North American and Fennoscandinavian peatlands in winter (Desrochers and Van Duinan 2006).

The bird communities of raised bogs in Britain are very similar to Ireland with Meadow Pipit and Skylark characteristic species, and Mallard, Eurasian Curlew, Common Snipe and Common Cuckoo also typical species (Fuller 1982). British fens are also more species-rich than raised bogs with Reed Bunting, Sedge Warbler, Moorhen, Mallard and Common Reed Warbler being common (Fuller 1982). The communities of fens in both Ireland and Britain are similar with Wren, Willow Warbler, Greenfinch and Goldfinch being other common species. Many fens are important as pre-migratory feeding habitats for *Acrocephalus* warblers which in Britain and Ireland includes the Sedge Warbler (Fuller 1982). The winter bird community of fens in Britain is dominated by species associated with fen scrub and carr, such as flocks of Lesser Redpolls and Siskins, but wetland species such as Moorhen, Common Snipe, Mallard, Water Rail and Common Teal are widespread (Fuller 1982).

Despite the relatively low species diversity of raised bogs in Ireland several of the commonly recorded species in this habitat are of high conservation concern, including Eurasian Curlew and Red Grouse (Lynas *et al.* 2007). Raised bog and fen are also important habitats for species of high conservation concern (Red-listed species) such as European Golden Plover, Northern Lapwing and Common Redshank, and Amber-listed or species of medium conservation concern including Common Snipe, Skylark and Common Grasshopper Warbler (Lynas *et al.* 2007). The Grey Partridge is another Red-listed species and the vast majority of the remaining wild Grey Partridges in Ireland are found on cutaway peatlands in Offaly.

The bird communities of reedswamps are less well studied than either raised bogs or fens. They are important breeding habitats for some resident species such as Reed Bunting and Great Crested Grebe and migrants such as Sedge Warbler and Common Reed Warbler. In the non-breeding season, large communal roosts of Common Starlings and hirundines occur in reedswamps where they are safe from predators. Some now-extinct species in Ireland, such as the Bittern and Marsh Harrier, bred in reedswamps before there was extensive drainage of these habitats. Reedswamps are still widespread in the country but are now much reduced in area compared with previous centuries.

Raised bogs and fens are very important habitats in terms of both a national and international context and hence most of the remaining important areas of these habitats have been given formal conservation designations such as SACs and SPAs. All new draining of raised bogs, fens and reedswamps should cease and restoration of existing drained peatlands could be implemented in certain areas. It is important that the remaining intact raised bogs and fens of Ireland are protected, conserved and managed so the integrity of these important bird habitats is maintained.

The Common Grasshopper Warbler has a distinctive song that sounds like its insect namesake (John Fox).

8. Upland Heath and Blanket Bog

Sinéad Cummins, Peadar O'Connell and Allan Mee

Introduction

Upland heath and blanket bog are open semi-natural and natural habitats that characterise many large swathes of mountainous areas in Ireland. Uplands lie above 150m and cover almost 19% of the country (Perrin *et al.* 2009). In Ireland they tend to occur in the coastal counties surrounding the flatter midlands (Cabot 1999). Ireland's uplands and peatlands, along with the plant communities and fauna they support, are of international importance due to their limited distribution in Europe and further afield.

Both upland heath and blanket bog are considered peatlands, differing largely in terms of peat depths, altitude and plant species composition. Perhaps most important is that they often occur as a mosaic, creating a patchwork effect across upland landscapes. As a rule of thumb, heath is found on shallower soils (<50cm in depth) than blanket bog (>100cm in depth) and has more than 25% shrub cover and/or mosses (Fossitt 2000). Heath can be further divided into 'montane', 'dry' or 'wet' depending on topography, underlying soils and plant composition. Montane heath has substantial cover of dwarf shrubs and/or mosses and occurs at high altitudes on mountains (usually >350m) largely on areas of loose rock and coarse sediment on tops of mountains and ridges (Averis *et al.* 2004, Fossitt 2000). Dry heath can be found in calcareous (base-rich) or siliceous soils (acid and free draining) and both types are characterised by ling heather with the latter differing from wet heath in the absence of purple moor grass. Wet heath is found on peaty soils (acid rich) and along with ling heather and cross-leaved heath, purple moor grass and sedges are also common (Fossitt 2000). Above 200m, blanket bog is referred to as upland/mountain blanket bog and is generally composed of ling heather, crowberry and bilberry with natural drains, lakes and flushes being common features (Malone and O'Connell 2009). Lowland

Upland heath in Co. Waterford is dominated by ling heather (Richard T. Mills).

(Atlantic) blanket bog occurs in flatter low-lying areas (<150m) along the western seaboard and was formed due to the unique climatic conditions (high rainfall) of the region. Lowland blanket bog is similar in plant species composition to upland blanket bog in terms of habitat structure, albeit with fewer heather and more grass and sedges (Fossitt 2000) and offers similar opportunities for birds that are usually found in a more upland environment.

Exposed siliceous rock occurs in upland areas and forms an important component of the landscape with cliffs used by Peregrine and Raven for lookouts, and ledges and crevices for nesting. Scree and boulder fields are an important component of Ring Ouzel and Northern Wheatear territories. Exposed rock may have up to 50% cover of vegetation with plant communities of mosses, herbs and ferns on rocky ledges and crevices along with scattered patches of heather, scrub and grassland (Fossitt 2000). Cliffs and corries are also the primary sites for rare and relict Arctic–Alpine flora not generally found elsewhere either as a result of their topography and climatic conditions, or because of the difficulty of access for grazing herbivores (Galen 1990).

Upland blanket bog and heath are characteristic of large swathes of Ireland's mountainous landscape and hold important bird assemblages all year round. The benefits of peatlands, sometimes referred to as ecosystem services, include the supply of clean drinking water, alleviating the effects of flooding, and acting as a carbon store in their natural state. With careful peatland management and restoration they could play an important part in the national climate-change strategy (Malone and O'Connell 2009). Historically used in Ireland as grazing land, predominantly for sheep, uplands have been pivotal to the livelihoods of many rural communities.

A pool in upland blanket bog in Co. Sligo (Richard Nairn).

The main land-use changes that have impacted on upland heath and blanket bog habitats in Ireland are discussed below. Heather is known to be especially sensitive to grazing (particularly by sheep) and there has been a major decrease in heather cover over the past century in Ireland (Bleasdale 1998) and Britain. Such changes have been partially attributed to increases in sheep populations on these marginal habitats as a result of the EU grants to farmers in the 1980s and 1990s (Fuller and Gough 1999). Sheep prefer to graze patches of acid grassland with short dense swards, sometimes referred to as 'grazing lawns', and have been implicated in damage to uplands. Some acid grassland is desirable (i.e. species-rich plant communities) but the spread of grassland patches through grazing is threatening heathland communities (Annex I listed) (Williams *et al.* 2009). Much of the peatland in Ireland suitable for conservation has been dramatically reduced in size, with less than a quarter remaining in relatively intact condition (Foss *et al.* 2001). Inappropriate burning of heather (often outside the legal dates to do so) can lead to soil erosion, nest destruction, mortality and bracken encroachment (Hudson and Newborn 1995). The impact of burning can be even greater when combined with high levels of grazing, with frequent burning (every 3–4 years) shifting heather towards grass, sedge or rush (Turner 2004).

Peat cutting, usually in the form of turbary, is a common practice on much of Ireland's peatlands and had led to the destruction of 47% of Ireland's total area of peatlands (Malone

Cutover blanket bog in Co. Derry showing the effects of extensive drainage (Karl Partridge).

and O'Connell 2009). All commercial cutting and use of tractor-mounted extrusion cutters ('sausage' machines) is banned in protected areas, however, no accurate figures exist for the amount of peat extracted by domestic cutting (Douglas *et al.* 2008).

Over the last 50 years or so plantation forests have become a common sight particularly on upland blanket bog and heath, habitats of high conservation value. Extensive planting has been carried out on upland blanket bog and wet heaths and while the rate of planting has slowed there is still no prohibition against planting on deep peat (Douglas *et al.* 2008).

More recently, in the last 20 years, renewable energy projects, specifically wind farms, have been built on numerous upland sites across the country. Wind energy targets led by the government, to obtain 40% of our national energy needs from renewable sources by 2020 in response to EU targets (Directive 2009/28/EC), has led to many more wind turbines being located in the uplands. The effects of locating these windfarms (and associated infrastructures i.e. powerlines, roads) largely in upland areas important for many breeding bird communities are poorly understood, particularly within the Irish context. Impacts on such communities are likely to include displacement, disturbance, avoidance (Pearce-Higgins *et al.* 2008; 2009), collision risk and fragmentation of territories. The cumulative impacts on priority species of locating many windfarms in the uplands are not fully understood. Windfarms which are poorly sited can pose a threat to vulnerable species and habitats including those protected under the Habitats and Birds Directives (O'Briain 2011).

The cumulative impacts of the above land-use changes on upland bird populations in Ireland and in particular on their breeding productivity and long-term survival are not yet fully understood. So far, bird studies on such impacts in Ireland have been limited to single species or narrow time frames with few, as yet, looking at longer-term trends in population dynamics. More resources are needed to allow for research into the potential viability of these upland breeding bird populations.

Upland landscapes seem familiar and constant, yet we often take for granted the wealth of flora and fauna that exists there. This chapter provides an overview of nationally important birds of conservation concern, as identified in the Red and Amber lists of the birds of conservation concern in Ireland (Lynas *et al.* 2007). Upland bird assemblages in Ireland resemble those found in Britain, but are more limited, and except for rare breeding attempts by some species they lack the montane specialists such as Ptarmigan, Dotterel, and Snow Bunting. Britain in turn holds fewer upland breeding species than Europe.

Upland bird communities may be less diverse than in other habitats e.g. estuaries, but are nonetheless an important group, many are specialists uniquely adapted to their upland environment and depend on these habitats for all (Red Grouse) or part of their life cycle (Hen Harrier). Given that upland breeding birds can be difficult to census effectively (cryptic camouflage, low breeding density and reluctance to leave the nest) there is often a dearth of quantitative information regarding their population densities (Reed *et al.* 1985). Many upland birds are rare and/or threatened in Ireland (Lynas *et al.* 2007), as they are throughout much of Europe (BirdLife International 2004), and face many challenges including food, nest site availability and predation, in a inhospitable climate.

Amongst the most important birds that occur in upland peatland habitats are breeding waders (Stroud *et al.* 1987), including European Golden Plover, Eurasian Curlew, Dunlin and Common Snipe. Other key species recorded breeding on blanket bogs in Ireland are Red Grouse (Watson and O'Hare 1979a, 1979b) and Skylark (Bracken *et al.* 2008), while upland heath (and associated planted forest) holds important breeding populations of Hen Harrier (Norriss *et al.* 2002). Although some Annex I species are concentrated in Special Protection Areas (SPAs), most are widely dispersed and hence may not be well protected by current conservation planning regulations.

Montane heath

Breeding birds

European Golden Plover are Annex 1 listed (EU Birds Directive 79/409/EEC) and Red-listed in Ireland (Lynas *et al.* 2008) due to recent declines of over 50% of the breeding population. Most recent estimates show 150 breeding pairs remaining in the Republic of Ireland, mainly in the west and north-west counties (Cox *et al.* 2002, Cummins *et al.* 2003, 2004). Figures for Northern Ireland are more worrying with an estimated 10–20 pairs remaining (Allen and Mellon, unpublished data). Breeding European Golden Plover are associated with upland and lowland blanket bog and areas of eroded bog and heath during late spring and summer (Watson and O'Hare 1979a; Stroud *et al.* 1987). They prefer small patches of heather and mixed grasses as opposed to dense stands of heather, with areas of wet ground and rushes (Whittingham *et al.* 2001) providing an important source of insects for chicks, in particular tipulid larvae i.e. leatherjackets (Byrkjedal and Thompson 1998). European Golden Plover are known to be associated with flat peatlands and montane ridges (Brown and Stillman 1993; Stillman and Brown 1994; Pearce-Higgins and Grant 2006). With four eggs typical of a clutch, nests are built in a scrape usually lined with short vegetation e.g. grasses (Byrkjedal and Thompson 1998). *Cladonia* lichens appear to be particularly favoured for lining nests at upland sites (Mee 1997), possibly due to their insulation properties in reducing heat loss from unattended eggs (Reid *et al.* 2002). European Golden Plover eggs, nests and even adults are notoriously cryptic. Off-duty adults usually leave the nest territory following changeovers at the nest and forage in nearby grassland up to 10km from nest sites (Whittingham *et al.* 2001). Often

European Golden Plover arrive to breed on upland bogs in the late spring (Richard T. Mills).

these grasslands have short swards (<5cm) from grazing, and are poorly drained with some cover of rushes and an abundance of tipulid larvae. Increases in peat extraction in the uplands are thought to have contributed to the decline of an estimated 25–50% in breeding European Golden Plover populations (Donaghy and Murphy 2000; Gibbons *et al.* 1993). Climate-change models suggest that an advancement in egg-laying, due to higher mean temperatures in April, may result in significantly lower breeding success of European Golden Plover because of a mistiming between chick hatching and the emergence of adult tipulids, the main food source of plover chicks (Pearce-Higgins *et al.* 2005) (see Chapter 17).

Rare breeders/Passage birds

Although Ireland lacks the species largely confined to montane heaths found in sub-Arctic tundra and Alpine locations in Europe and Scotland, one montane specialist, the Dotterel has bred in Ireland and is recorded annually as a passage migrant. Dotterel nested at Nephin More, Co. Mayo, in 1975 (Hutchinson 1989) although spring and early summer records are of small groups of birds on passage to more northerly breeding grounds. In the Scottish Highlands Dotterel are largely confined to high montane plateaux dominated by woolly fringe moss. Such habitats are uncommon in Ireland where slopes are typically too steep to be attractive to breeding Dotterel, although good examples occur at some sites, i.e. the Slieve Mish Mountains in Co. Kerry. Dotterel has been lost as a breeding species in Wales and is very rare in northern England and the southern uplands of Scotland with most of the 630 breeding males recorded in 1999 found in central and northern Scotland (Whitfield 2002). Although long-term climatic factors may be involved, loss of woolly fringe moss and an increase in grassland cover resulting from severe overgrazing by sheep have been implicated as the most important factors in the decline of Dotterel in these areas (Fuller and Gough 1999; Thompson and Brown 1992; Thompson and Whitfield 1993; Galbraith *et al.* 1993; Scott *et al.* 2007). Long-term grazing by sheep and even cattle in montane areas in Ireland may have had similar effects from the early nineteenth century onwards.

Winter visitors

Red Grouse is one of a few species resident in the uplands all year round. Upland birds have not been systematically surveyed outside the breeding season but *Winter Atlas* fieldwork provides a good indication of the status and distribution of wintering species in the uplands (Lack 1986). Passage and wintering European Golden Plover also use upland heath although blanket bog is probably more favoured. Choughs use upland heath sites in the coastal mountains, especially in autumn and winter, although they primarily forage in adjacent improved and semi-improved grassland or dry acid grassland (Trewby *et al.* 2004). Snow Buntings are largely autumn passage migrants and winter visitors mainly on the north and west coasts but also venture inland where they are often recorded on exposed mountain tops (Hutchinson 1989).

Upland heath and blanket bog

Breeding bird communities

WADERS

European Golden Plover are also present in blanket bog where their habitat requirements are similar to those in montane heath (see above).

Dunlin: Although this species prefers low-lying coastal machair habitats in Ireland (Hutchinson 1989), small breeding populations (threatened status) are found in upland blanket bog areas in the north-west. The race of Dunlin breeding in Ireland *Calidris alpina schinzii* is on Annex I of the EU Birds Directive (79/409/EEC). Suddaby *et al.* (2008) located 15 breeding territories of Dunlin on upland blanket bog on the Slieve Fyagh plateau, Co. Mayo, the single largest remaining upland breeding population in

A breeding Dunlin calls to defend its upland territory (Richard T. Mills).

Ireland. The average clutch size was 3.8 eggs.

Eurasian Curlew: Considered to be a rare breeder in the uplands of Ireland, although distribution is poorly known, the breeding population has declined by around 88% in the past 20 years (Lauder and Donaghy 2008). In early spring, Eurasian Curlews move inland from coastal estuaries to breed in upland blanket bogs, lowland raised bogs and rough pasture. Clutches usually contain four eggs and the chicks hatch after about 28 days and rapidly become mobile, fledging in 32–38 days (Cramp and Simmons 1983). Studies of Eurasian Curlew breeding populations on the Antrim hills have shown that falling productivity levels are responsible for declines in breeding populations with increases in predator populations (foxes and hooded crows) largely blamed for these observed declines (Grant *et al.* 1999). The total breeding population in Northern Ireland was estimated at approximately 2,000 pairs in 1999, representing a 60% decline on previous estimates in 1987 (Henderson *et al.* 2002). A recent study of breeding Eurasian Curlew at upland sites in the west and north-west of the country has identified only a handful of breeding pairs in areas where Eurasian Curlew were breeding in the past (Anita Donaghy, pers. comm.).

Common Snipe: Common Snipe are probably the most widespread and numerous wader breeding in Ireland (Hutchinson 1989; Gibbons *et al.* 1993). However, they are very secretive, and little is known about their breeding habits: abundance and distribution estimates from atlas surveys are unlikely to reflect their true extent. Cummins *et al.* (2004) encountered Common Snipe on almost 20% of sites surveyed which probably represents an underestimate of such a secretive, ground-dwelling species. Field counts using methods targeted towards Common Snipe (i.e. using dogs to flush birds for better count accuracy or dusk counts of drumming or chipping birds) are needed to provide better information on densities in upland habitats.

Raptors

The uplands are of particular importance for populations of breeding raptors, principally Peregrine Falcon, Merlin, Hen Harrier, recently reintroduced Golden Eagle and the scarce Short-eared Owl.

Merlin: The national population is estimated at 250-plus pairs (IRSG 2006) and although closely associated with upland unenclosed habitat, in Ireland they tend to nest largely in upland conifer forest plantations (Norriss *et al.* 2010). They use the tree nests of other species (i.e. Hooded Crows), a shift from more traditional ground nesting in heather (Haworth and Thompson 1990; McElheron 2005). The population of Merlin in Northern Ireland was estimated at 34 breeding pairs and 49 occupied territories in 2008 (Ewing *et al.* 2011). Haworth (1985, 1987) surveyed the upland heath and bogs of west Galway for breeding birds. Nesting Merlins were located at 12 sites, 11 of which were on densely vegetated islands on large inland loughs, but were closely associated with extensive blanket bog. In Britain, Merlin nest primarily in heather moorland (Stillman and Brown 1994) where ground nesting predominates probably due to the low numbers of mammalian predators on heavily keepered moors. Ground-nesting Merlin in west Galway were found in dense heather or heather-fern (Haworth 1985, 1987), habitat that is very restricted on open moorland or bog due to grazing pressure and burning.

Merlins frequently nest in upland forest plantations and hunt across open hillsides (Darío Fernández-Bellon).

However, greater protection from predation afforded by island sites was also likely to be critical.

Habitat loss, especially the conversion of heather moorland to grass moorland, has been identified as the main reason for former areas of Merlin breeding range remaining unoccupied in Britain (Rebecca and Bainbridge 1998). In Wicklow traditional heather-nesting areas suffered from uncontrolled and indiscriminate burning to encourage grass growth for sheep grazing and birds switched

Hen Harriers traditionally nested in upland heather but are increasingly using young forest plantations (Richard T. Mills).

from ground sites to nesting in mixed woodland (McElheron 2005). Small passerines, particularly Meadow Pipit and Skylark, are the main prey item of Merlins (Clarke and Scott 1994; McElheron 2005). However, Fernández-Bellon and Lusby (2011) found that, although, these open-country passerines were predominant in Merlin pellets in Ireland, their importance in the diet (32% by number combined) was lower than previous studies had shown for Northern Ireland (Clarke and Scott 1994) and Britain. Woodland passerines also provide a significant proportion of prey items in spring, declining as the season progresses (Fernández-Bellon and Lusby 2011).

Hen Harrier: An Annex I species, this raptor breeds in the uplands and commonly nests in new and second rotation pre-thicket forestry, dispersing more widely in the autumn to coastal areas (Barton *et al.* 2006, Wilson *et al.* 2009, O'Donoghue 2010). Although Hen Harriers now primarily nest in commercial conifer plantations (see Chapter 9), the traditional nesting habitat for the species in Ireland is heather moorland and scrub. The breeding population has recently been estimated at 128–172 breeding pairs in the Republic of Ireland (Ruddock *et al.* 2011), and 63 territorial pairs in Northern Ireland (Sim *et al.* 2007). The two biggest factors affecting their population in recent years have been habitat loss and persecution. Ireland is legally obliged to take measures to protect this species, including designating Special Protection Areas that provide suitable habitats. The results of the second national survey of breeding Hen Harriers in Ireland (Barton *et al.* 2006) revealed that mean densities of territorial pairs were highest in the Ballyhoura Mountains in Cos. Cork and Limerick (13.3–14.8 pairs/100km^2), Slieve Beagh in Co. Monaghan (12.3 pairs/100km^2) and the Nagle Mountains (Co. Cork) (11.3/100km^2). Although populations currently appear to be either stable or increasing at some sites, breeding productivity varies widely between different areas (Irwin *et al.* 2008) and recent declines have been documented particularly in south-western areas, including the Stacks–Mullaghareirk Mountains and the Ballyhouras in Cos. Kerry, Cork and Limerick and the Slieve Aughty mountains, Co. Clare and west Clare (Ruddock *et al.* 2011).

Although there have been national surveys to estimate population size and distribution (Norriss *et al.* 2002, Barton *et al.* 2006, Sim *et al.* 2007, Ruddock *et al.* 2011) there has been no specific study of traditional heather-nesting harriers in Ireland. Just three pairs nested in heather in the Mullagha-reirks–Slieve Aughties in 2000 compared to 14 pairs in forests or scrub habitats (Norriss *et al.* 2002). Whether such differences reflect the availability of these habitats at the time is not stated. Loss of existing heather moorland due to afforestation has been extensive in many upland areas such as the Nagles in Co. Cork and the Ballyhouras on the Cork–Limerick border. Apart from nesting habitat, the density of small passerines, particularly Meadow Pipits, is important in determining harrier breeding density and breeding success (Redpath and Thirgood 1999). Until the recent introduction of the Bank Vole (first identified near Listowel, Co. Kerry by Classens and O'Gorman 1965), Ireland lacked voles, an important part of the diet of Hen Harrier in Britain and continental Europe (e.g. Redpath *et al.* 2002). Scrub habitat, such as gorse, and low-intensity grassland bordering upland heath also appear to be important foraging habitat for harriers, usually located between upland heath and improved grassland on lower slopes.

Like other species of harrier, Hen Harriers nest on the ground, though in Northern Ireland some have been found to nest in trees in such plantations (Scott 2000). Nests typically comprise a vegetation-lined scrape in tall, dense shrubs on flat to moderately sloping ground. Heather (especially *Calluna*) and bramble dominate the vegetation immediately around most nests, but many other plants may contribute to nest cover, including willow, gorse, purple moor grass, rushes and bog myrtle. In plantations, young conifer trees give good cover. As in Britain, many Hen Harriers in Ireland now nest in young commercial conifer plantations (Wilson *et al.* 2009), but do not make extensive use of older forests with closed canopies. However, nesting in second rotation pre-thicket forests seems to occur much more frequently in Ireland than in most parts of Britain (Petty and Anderson 1986; Madders 2000). This means that it may be possible to maintain Hen Harrier populations in heavily afforested areas by structuring the age of plantations in order to ensure continuity of nesting habitat availability. However, traditional open habitats such as moorland may be important both as nest sites and as foraging habitat, particularly as the success of Hen Harriers nesting and foraging in forest habitats is not well understood (Wilson *et al.* 2010).

The Short-eared Owl is mainly a winter visitor but occasionally nests in upland areas in Ireland (Richard T. Mills).

Short-eared Owl: In Ireland, the Short-eared Owl is largely a winter visitor along the coast (Hutchinson 1989). A rare breeder in uplands, it tends to prefer grass- and sedge-dominated moorland (Haworth and Thompson 1990). Short-eared Owls occupy similar nesting habitat to Hen Harriers, but are largely dependent on small rodents as prey. They are a rare but possibly regular breeder at a few upland sites in south-west Ireland where heather moorland is the principal nesting habitat although nests have been located in heather within young forestry plantations (Jones 1979). A small number of pairs (1–5) also breed in Northern Ireland (Scott 1999). Our current small population of nesting Short-eared Owls is likely to benefit from the presence of introduced voles but studies are needed to determine this.

PASSERINES

Twite: Red-listed in Ireland, the breeding population of Twite in Ireland is estimated at between 54–110 breeding pairs with strongholds in Cos. Mayo and Donegal (McLoughlin and Cotton 2008). They favour uplands dominated by heather and bracken in which to nest (Haworth and Thompson 1990) but winter largely in coastal areas (estuaries, salt marsh and coastal grasslands), again mostly in the north and west. The winter population was estimated at 650–1,100 birds for the period 2005–2008 (McLoughlin and Cotton 2008). The species has seriously declined in both range and abundance and appears to be extinct as an upland breeding species in Ireland presumably due to loss or degradation of heather moorland due to overgrazing, afforestation and burning (McLoughlin and Cotton 2008). The loss of hay meadows to silage harvesting along

Stonechats are often found in the uplands in summer (Karl Partridge).

with changes in tillage farming have added to their decline (Taylor and O'Halloran 1999).

Stonechat: Stonechats are small insectivorous passerines that are often found in upland bogs and heath in summer (Hagemeijer and Blair 1997), in particular in patches of gorse and heather (Magee 1965; Greig-Smith 1984). The Stonechat has a widespread distribution in Ireland albeit occurring in greater

Meadow Pipits are widespread and common on upland bogs and heaths (Richard T. Mills).

The Northern Wheatear is a summer migrant that breeds in rocky upland areas (Richie Lort).

densities in coastal areas particularly in winter (Lack 1986). This coastal bias is well documented, with birds moving to the coast or migrating further south (Wernham *et al.* 2002) to escape freezing ground temperatures in winter. Given their insectivorous diet (Cummins and O'Halloran 2002), Stonechats were one of the species to be hit hardest during recent cold winters (*BTO News* 2011). Although multi-brooded, breeding success of Stonechats in Ireland is relatively low with overall nest survival rates averaging 34% with most nest losses (50%) due to predation at the chick stage (Cummins and O'Halloran 2003). Recovery of populations here from recent harsh winters is possible providing their preferred habitats are available and are of sufficient quality. Recent large-scale scrub removal on farmland and inappropriate burning of scrub and heath during the nesting season could prove detrimental to any such recovery.

Skylark: Data in Ireland (Copland *et al.* in prep) indicate that upland habitats are favoured haunts during the breeding season where they prefer rough, open vegetated landscapes. Commonly encountered on upland breeding bird surveys, Skylark is also likely to have been affected by the most recent cold winters, although as yet no data have been published. The prevalence of Skylark in peatland habitats (84 indivduals/km^2) (Bracken *et al.* 2008) and its absence from farmland in Ireland during the breeding season is in contrast to Britain, although it does redistribute to farmland habitats in winter (Copland 2009). Bracken *et al.* (2008) surveyed the bird communities at 12 sites including three lowland and three montane blanket bog sites. Meadow Pipit (50–66%) and Skylark (24–45%) dominated the avifauna at both bogland types, accounting for almost 96% of all birds encountered on Atlantic lowland bogs and 90% on montane bogs.

Meadow Pipit: Meadow Pipits are widespread and abundant in upland bog and heath in summer months with estimates from an Irish study of 191 individuals per km^2 (Bracken *et al.* 2008). Meadow Pipits prefer tussocky vegetation (Pearce-Higgins and Grant 2006) with most wintering in more lowland areas to avoid freezing temperatures (Hutchinson 1989). In Ireland, Skylarks like peatlands with low dense vegetation, whereas Meadow Pipits are more generalist, not exhibiting any strong preferences for heather-dominated or grass-dominated moors (Bracken *et al.* 2008). By contrast, in Britain, Skylarks were more abundant in grass-dominated areas (Stroud *et al.* 1987). Meadow Pipit densities across these habitats in Britain are more variable. They were recorded as higher in heather-dominated areas of blanket bog in some studies (Stroud *et al.* 1987) and increasing with increasing grass cover in other studies (Smith *et al.* 2001). Studies in Britain have shown positive associations between numbers of Hen Harriers and numbers of Meadow Pipits (i.e. favoured prey species) (Redpath and Thirgood 1997; Smith *et al.* 2001).

SUMMER MIGRANTS

Concern has been expressed as to the current trends in populations of summer migrants in upland habitats, many of which are species of real conservation concern (Lynas *et al.* 2007). In summer, migrants such as the Ring Ouzel (winters in Morocco), Whinchat (winters in central and southern Africa) and Northern Wheatear (winters in central Africa) are characteristically found breeding in upland heath and bogs, although in the case of the former two species, numbers have drastically fallen in recent times. Ring Ouzel are Red-listed in Ireland and Britain and estimates for Ireland are at 35 pairs (BirdWatch Ireland 2010). In Britain, declines have been tentatively related to increases in afforestation (Wotton *et al.* 2002, Buchanan *et al.* 2003). Early indications from the most recent bird atlas survey (data unpublished) show worrying declines for Whinchat (BTO News 2011). They usually breed in either scrub or young plantation forests and are closely associated with bracken cover (Stillmann and Brown 1994). A summer migrant from sub-Saharan Africa, Northern Wheatear prefer tightly grazed grassier slopes produced by sheep and rabbits and where they nest in drystone walls, rocks, scree and rabbit burrows (Hutchinson 1989). Recent analyses of Countryside Bird Survey Data in Ireland (Crowe 2011b) have indicated that Northern Wheatears have a distinct preference for peatland habitats and avoidance of farmland habitats.

GAMEBIRDS

The Red Grouse (a subspecies of the Willow Grouse, which has a circumpolar distribution) is only found on peatland habitats that have reasonable heather cover (blanket bog, heath and raised bogs) as heather is integral to its life cycle for food, shelter and nesting habitat (Lance 1972; Watson and O'Hare 1979b). Generally single-brooded, the average clutch size (6.7) (Lance 1972) and brood sizes (2.9) in Ireland (Watson and O'Hare 1979b) is slightly lower than figures reported for Scotland and England. Recent surveys of the population in Ireland (Allen *et al.* 2005, Cummins *et al.* 2010) have highlighted worrying declines with a population now increasingly fragmented largely as a result of the many land-use changes and pressures in the uplands in the past 40 years. These changes have had a negative impact on the population which is currently on the *Red List* due to declines of over 50% in range in the past 30–40 years (Lynas *et al.* 2007; Gibbons *et al.* 1993). The population for Northern Ireland was estimated at 202–221 breeding pairs (Allen *et al.* 2005) while the estimated figure in the Republic of Ireland is over ten times that with an adult breeding population of approximately 4,200 individuals (Cummins *et al.* 2010). Average grouse densities in Ireland are low ($1.1/km^2$) with up to $9/km^2$ recorded pre breeding season in the best areas (Cummins *et al.* 2010). Densities of pairs ranged from $0.58–0.83/km^2$ on blanket bog and heath in the Owenduff–Nephin SPA, Mayo (Murray and O'Halloran 2003).

The Red Grouse prefers to nest in good cover of heather (Richard T. Mills).

Grouse were recorded in 23% of 1km squares visited in Northern Ireland with the highest densities of 3 pairs/km^2 in Co. Antrim (Allen *et al.* 2005). By contrast, in northern England in 2007, breeding densities of over 50 adults per km^2 (post breeding season densities of 200 grouse per km^2) were recorded, whereas in Scotland lower densities were recorded with 25 adults per km^2 (post breeding season densities 60 birds per km^2) (Game and Wildlife Conservation Trust Review 2008). Historically in Ireland, there would have been more lands managed for Red Grouse, particularly on private estates, in areas with suitable habitat (Ussher and Warren 1900). Almost 98% of the national population is now distributed across blanket bog and heath, most of which, is not specifically managed for Red Grouse (Cummins *et al.* 2010).

EU subsidies (1970s to 1990s) per head of ewes and cattle resulted in overstocking, particularly on marginal lands that were of little value to arable farming with numbers of sheep totalling 7.5 million in 2000 (Central Statistics Office). Approximately 60% of the estimated population of Red Grouse occupy commonages. Steps have been taken in the past few years to ensure appropriate levels of stocking on commonages (Single Farm Payment Scheme). It is important that these areas continue to be monitored regularly by government officials to ensure stocking densities are optimal and in line with the recovery of vegetation from over grazing damage.

The Greater White-fronted Goose uses upland bogs in small numbers in the west of Ireland (Karl Partridge).

The dramatic cliffs of Benwisken, Co. Sligo, offer good nest sites for the Peregrine (Richard Nairn).

RARE BREEDERS/PASSAGE BIRDS

A rare species that may occasionaly nest in blanket bog is the Eurasian Whimbrel, whose possible breeding was documented in an area of upland blanket bog at 300m (Perry 2006). A pair of Snowy Owls laid a clutch of eggs in Glenveagh National Park, Co. Donegal, in 2001. These are normally breeding birds of Arctic and sub-Arctic tundra, where populations track those of microtine rodents and small mammals (Watson 1957; Gilg *et al.* 2003). Although the nest was unsuccessful, further anecdotal evidence suggests that the species may have bred successfully in west Donegal in 1999 (L. O'Toole, pers. comm.).

WINTERING BIRDS

Though widespread across bogs in the nineteenth century, wintering Greater White-fronted Geese are scarce on former wintering bogland sites (Fox *et al.* 2006; Norriss and Walsh 2008). Changes in land use on bogs (drainage, mechanised turbary and afforestation), along with the claim of the Wexford Slobs from Wexford Harbour have seen numbers rapidly increase there with the majority of wintering flocks (about 75%) remaining at Wexford through the winter (Hutchinson 1989).

Cliffs, corries and boulder fields

Apart from the slopes and plateaux, the uplands hold substantial areas of cliff, boulder and scree, which provide important habitats in themselves, harbouring some characteristic vegetation and plants such as relict Arctic–Alpine flora. Upland crags and corries are important as nest sites for a small number of bird species including Peregrine, Golden Eagle, Raven, the scarce Ring Ouzel, and more rarely, inland-nesting Chough.

Peregrine: Although now more common and in higher densities on coastal cliffs and lowland quarries (Moore *et al.* 1997, Madden *et al.* 2009), upland crags are an important nesting habitat for Peregrines. Of an estimated population of 390 occupied breeding territories in the Republic of Ireland (Madden *et al.* 2009), approximately one third are in uplands. Unlike the Merlin, instances of tree nesting or ground nesting are very rare: most birds nest on cliffs, quarries or on other man-made structures. Irish Peregrines are not known to be migratory. Although most upland breeders appear to winter on coastal estuaries where prey densities are high, some individuals do remain in the upland during the winter. Numbers have increased in both the Republic and Northern Ireland since the banning of DDT in the 1970s (Crick and Ratcliffe 1995; Norriss 1995; Wells 2007; Madden *et al.* 2009). Densities are higher in the drier eastern uplands, such as the Wicklow Mountains, than in western uplands where rainfall is high. Cliff orientation, height and rainfall all appear to be important in determining occupancy rates (Norriss 1995). Survey work in 2002 (Madden *et al.* 2009) found further increases in the national Peregrine population with high levels of

Peregrine adult (below) and juvenile close to a cliff nest site (Richard T. Mills).

occupancy in upland sites, compared to surveys in 1981, such as the Derryveagh (88%) and Bluestack Mountains (120%) in Donegal, the Ox Mountains (80%), and the Nephin Beg Mountains (120%) in Mayo, and the Comeragh Mountains (133%) in Waterford. Breeding success of Peregrines in some upland areas in Ireland has probably been limited somewhat by contraction in the distribution of Red Grouse and by low grouse densities. While large-scale afforestation in the uplands has undoubtedly negatively impacted on traditional moorland prey such as Red Grouse and Meadow Pipit, alternative prey, such as Woodpigeons, associated with woodland, are likely to be important items in the diet of upland Peregrines (Redpath and Thirgood 1997).

Golden Eagle: Upland crags also provide suitable nest sites for the reintroduced population of Golden Eagles in Co. Donegal as well as extensive foraging areas of upland heath and bog. Nesting to date has primarily been on upland crags ranging from the Bluestacks in south Donegal to the hills further north, although birds have been reported in potential breeding habitat in upland areas of Mayo (Lorcan O'Toole unpublished data). Territorial occupancy has increased annually from 2004 to the present (seven in 2009–11) although not all known territories are occupied in all years. Low availability of upland prey species such as Red Grouse and hares may limit breeding success at some sites. However, mountain hares, rabbits, Red Grouse, badger and fox cubs have appeared in the diet of two successful pairs (L. O'Toole in litt). Fulmars were also important prey items at one nest near the coast. Annual survival of eagles in the uplands undoubtedly benefits from abundant sheep carrion especially in winter and spring but this may be negated by levels of deaths as a result of consuming carcasses with poison (Golden Eagle Trust unpublished data). Upland Donegal and Kerry have the highest densities of mountain ewes in Ireland but carrion levels were found to be lower than in most regions of Scotland (Bourke 2001). However, Bourke (2001) found that live prey biomass, principally mountain hares, in the uplands of Kerry was similar to levels found in those parts of Scotland with good eagle productivity at nests.

Raven: Raven is one of the few upland species thought to be on the increase, despite suffering from widespread persecution in the late nineteenth and early twentieth centuries (Holloway 1996). They construct wool-lined nests on high cliffs, crags, ravines, and trees and opportunistically feed on

A pair of Ravens circling above a mountain territory (Richard T. Mills).

Choughs are mainly coastal but a small number are found in the uplands, especially in Co. Kerry (Richard T. Mills).

Boulder slopes at Slieve Tooey, Co. Donegal, hold some of the last nesting pairs of Ring Ouzel in Ireland (Richard Nairn).

carrion, small mammals, young birds and eggs. Ravens utilise upland heath perhaps more than any other habitat, especially where high densities of sheep provide a constant source of carrion. Nesting in the uplands is usually on crags up to at least 450m (McGreal 2007) but up to 550m in the MacGillycuddy's Reeks in Kerry (A. Mee, pers. obs). Nesting at higher elevation is most likely limited by the severity of weather in the uplands (as Ravens begin nesting as early as late February) rather than nest site availability. Haworth (1985) located 17 occupied territories in west Galway, with all but one on cliffs.

Chough: The national population of Chough was last estimated at 838 breeding pairs following a survey during the breeding seasons of 2002/03 (Gray *et al.* 2003). Population strongholds in counties Cork, Kerry and Donegal account for three quarters of the population. While largely coastal in their distribution, 43 breeding pairs (5% of population) were found inland, some of which were recorded at inland upland sites. The Irish population contributes a significant portion of the north-west European population (BirdLife International/ EBCC 2000). The Chough is on Annex I of the EC Birds Directive (EU Birds Directive 79/409/ EEC). Breeding sites are on cliffs, abandoned buildings or inland quarries, but birds fly to forage on nearby grassland or heavily grazed and degraded heath. Pairs have been recorded at inland sites in the uplands all year round on both the Beara (Trewby *et al.* 2004a) and Dingle Peninsulas (Trewby *et al.* 2004b) although there is some movement by Choughs between coastal and inland sites. At some sites, such as on the Iveragh and Dingle Peninsulas, upland heath has been replaced by improved or semi-improved grassland and this short-cropped habitat is used by Choughs throughout the year, particularly in winter (Trewby *et al.* 2004b) (see Chapter 11).

Ring Ouzel: In some mountain areas the vertical and near vertical slopes of upland corries and cliffs hold some of the last refuges free from grazing. These mountain corries and associated boulder slopes provide nesting habitat for the few remaining pairs of migrant Ring Ouzels which arrive back as early as late March (Riddiford and Findley 1981). Irish, British and Fennoscandanavian breeders (nominate *Turdus t. torquatus*) winter in southern Spain and north-west Africa, but predominately in the Atlas Mountains of Morocco and Tunisia where they inhabit juniper woodland (Ryall and Briggs 2006). The ecology of Ring Ouzels in Ireland is little studied. Vegetative cover, such as heather or bilberry, appears to be an important component of nest site selection (Flegg and Glue 1975).

Once prevalent in all but five counties in Ireland (Ussher and Warren 1900) they have been in steep decline throughout the twentieth century (Sharrock 1976; Gibbons *et al.* 1993) and have been recently lost as a breeding species in Northern Ireland (A. McGeehan, pers. comm.). Several causes of these declines in Ireland and Britain have been suggested, including increased predation associated with nearby forest cover (Buchanan *et al.* 2003), loss of heather cover near nest sites (Sim *et al.* 2007), climate change (Beale *et al.* 2005) and low first year and adult survival (Sim *et al.* 2010). Local effects such as disturbance from human recreational activities have also be detrimental by excluding breeders from suitable habitat (Appleyard 1994; Jones 1996). Recent strongholds have been in the uplands of Donegal and Kerry (Cox *et al.* 2002; Gibbons *et al.* 1993). Cox *et al.* (2002) surveyed the uplands of Donegal and found pairs at 15 sites, eight on the Glencolumbkille Peninsula and four in the Derryveagh Mountains with breeding confirmed at ten sites. Carruthers (1998) found Ring Ouzels in eleven 10km squares in Kerry, and estimated a population on 10–15 pairs, although not all sites were apparently occupied in any one year. More recently studies in the MacGillycuddy's Reeks in Kerry have located a breeding population of 4–9 pairs in 2008–11 (A. Mee unpublished data). Pairs were located in typically suitable cliffs with some heather and woodrush cover. Pairs often forage in nearby wet flushes and upland heath for invertebrate prey to deliver to chicks. A mosaic of habitats that includes close cropped grass and wet flushes for foraging and heather (or bracken) for cover from potential predators is probably the ideal. Lack of cover due to overgrazing or burning of heather is likely to be detrimental by increasing predation risks.

Future for Irish Uplands

The protection of peatlands is required by the EU Habitats Directive and the Ramsar and Biodiversity Conventions. Active blanket bogs are priority EU Habitats that must be maintained at, or restored to, favourable conservation status. The conservation status of bog is defined as favourable when its natural range and the area it covers within that range are stable or increasing (Douglas *et al.* 2008). Blanket bog, is often closely linked with several other rare and threatened habitats including wet heath, dry heath and quaking bogs. One of the most important future considerations is to maintain physical connectivity, where possible, across these mosaics of habitats. The effects of changing land uses on this sensitive ecosystem, particularly cumulative impacts on extent and biodiversity, have been highlighted by several declines in key upland bird species including the Red Grouse, breeding waders and migrant passerines.

How birds interact and adapt to changes in the habitats they occupy has a very important impact on their conservation status. Factors such as land use changes, introduced alien species, and climate change all affect upland birds to some degree. Where some species may be able to adapt to change, others may be less successful and their populations decline. Upland birds are particularly sensitive to changes, as they have evolved to survive in specialised, low intensity, low disturbance habitats. Future climate changes may impact on upland birds. For example, Willow Grouse populations in Europe (including the subspecies 'scoticus' endemic to Britain and Ireland) have been studied and a north-westwards shift in their breeding range is predicted by the end of this century, resulting largely in their disappearance from Ireland with populations in Britain restricted to the most northerly parts of Scotland (Huntley *et al.* 2007). Likewise, climate change is predicted to result in a significant elevational shift

Glenade, Co. Leitrim (Richard Nairn).

in Ring Ouzels as their favoured habitat retreats upwards (von dem Bussche *et al.* 2008).

Policies and legislation are often the driving forces behind land management and conservation. There is a strong need to align land-use policies with conservation policies to achieve a more sustainable use of the uplands for the future.

Monitoring, in particular of those species with an unfavourable conservation status, needs to be carried out as a matter of priority. The Irish government needs to realise the importance of such monitoring to avoid further losses and to meet its obligations under current EU legislation. Uncertainties about the factors affecting a species status and the cumulative effects that may be at play need to be identified through research and monitoring, and appropriate management should be taken to counteract or lessen these factors. In protected sites, the easiest way to develop a strategic approach is to create management plans for the designating interests. This approach allows special measures to be put in place that will benefit the species in question. However, outside of protected areas it is more complex as other interests often outweigh species conservation in these areas. Environmental schemes, particularly agri-environmental schemes, are of particular importance in these areas, but resources are limited and funding should be provided for targeted measures based on conservation results for biodiversity or special interest species. On a local scale cross-community conservation projects can target a threatened species or its habitat to benefit a larger suite of species (e.g. Brennan *et al.* 2008). In an ideal scenario, farming in the uplands would be environmentally sustainable while also providing an economically viable option for rural communities, and past mistakes with regards to overgrazing and inappropriate burning would be an exception rather than commonplace.

Renewable energy is an important component of a programme of measures to combat further climate change. Strategic planning of windfarms to minimise their impacts on biodiversity and priority habitats should still allow Ireland to meet its energy targets. Lack of such planning, especially those resulting in habitat fragmentation and degradation within or near SPAs, is likely to result in further declines in upland bird populations. Post-construction monitoring and research is needed to evaluate such impacts and inform future planning. To date no overall assessment of collision risk or habitat displacement have been made in relation to Irish windfarms. Discovery of two dead White-tailed Eagles at upland windfarms in Kerry in 2011 suggests that such research, particularly cumulative impact effects, will be critical. Ideally, all those with an interest and stake in the uplands (farmers, state agencies, landowners, conservationists, wind energy companies, nature lovers, etc.) will learn from past mistakes and work together to build a better future for bird communities in the upland environment.

Current initiatives to strive to protect and monitor upland flora and fauna include BirdWatch Ireland's *Action Plan for Upland Birds in Ireland 2011–2020* (BirdWatch Ireland 2010), the Irish Peat Conservation Council's (IPCC) *Action Plan on halting the loss of peatland biodiversity* (Malone and O'Connell 2009) and the National Parks and Wildlife Service's guidelines for a national survey and conservation assessment of upland vegetation and habitats in Ireland (Perrin *et al.* 2010). All three provide a means to gather baseline data and to identify how best to proceed with the conservation effort for priority birds and habitats in the uplands.

Owenreagh Windfarm, Co. Tyrone (Karl Partridge).

9. Woodlands, Forest and Scrub

Oisín Sweeney, Thomas C. Kelly, Sandra Irwin, Mark Wilson and John O'Halloran

Irish forest habitats: semi-natural woodland, scrub and coniferous plantations

Throughout this chapter, 'woodland' will be used to refer specifically to semi-natural forests, most of which are either unmanaged or managed at low intensity. Ireland's mild and damp climate encourages rapid tree growth, and broadleaved woodland represents the natural climax vegetation type throughout much of the island (Cross 1998). Fossil evidence indicates that trees migrated to Ireland from the south during the early Holocene (*c.* 10,500–9,000 years ago) following rapid temperature increases that characterised the end of the last glacial cold stage (Mitchell 2006). Following this period, Ireland was almost completely covered in broadleaved and mixed woodland for around 3,000 years. However, clearance by man over the past 6,000 years, primarily for agriculture, drastically reduced natural forest cover (Cross 1998; Cole and Mitchell 2003). By around 1650, between 2 and 12% of Ireland remained forested (Rackham 1995; McCracken 1971). The current level of 1% native forest cover is one of the lowest levels of natural forest cover in any European Union (EU) member state.

Few, if any, patches of woodland exist in Ireland that have not been subject to modification by man. As a result, Ireland's native woodlands are best described as 'semi-natural.' Maps and historical texts can be used to identify areas of woodland that are relatively old. For example, in Northern Ireland, some maps are available from the 1600s, and areas that have been continuously wooded since the

Oakwood at Ballinacor, Co. Wicklow (Richard Nairn).

1600s to the present are termed 'ancient woodlands' (The Woodland Trust 2007). In the Republic of Ireland records date from much later and the earliest available maps are from the 1840s. Additionally, specific reference is sometimes made to individual woodlands in historical texts (Rackham 1995). It is therefore extremely difficult to determine whether (and to what extent) ancient woodland exists in the Republic of Ireland, and 'long-established woodland' is probably the most accurate term for forests present on the 1840s maps.

Many Irish woods have naturally regenerated on abandoned land. However, some (such as St John's Wood in Co. Roscommon and Tomnafinnogue in Co. Wicklow) were formerly managed as coppice with standards and now grow unmanaged. Oak and ash are the most common canopy species in most of Ireland's semi-natural woodlands, with birch, hazel, rowan and holly commonly found as understorey species. Other woodland types include riparian woodland, found along watercourses; carr woodland on lake margins and flushes, dominated by willow and alder; bog woodland, which forms on drained and cutover bog; and yew woodland, which is a rare habitat in Ireland and in Europe as a whole (Fossitt 2000). Muckross Wood in Killarney is the best known of the Irish yew woodlands and is thought to be at least 3,000 years old, making it the oldest stand of yew in Europe (Mitchell 1990; Rackham 1995).

Although Ireland does have some large woodlands, such as St John's Wood (110 hectares) and Dromore Wood in Co. Clare (120 hectares), both now Special Areas of Conservation, most woodland patches are small (between 10 and 50 hectares) and highly fragmented. Remaining woodlands are often located in marginal areas that were unsuitable for agriculture and therefore escaped historical clearance. In other cases they have been continuously managed for fuel or building materials such as hazel wattle (Budd 1998), which has ensured their long-term persistence. This continuous use by man means that, in Ireland as in Britain, ancient woods do not possess features associated with ancient woodland in other parts of Europe, such as veteran trees or large dead logs. This is illustrated by St John's Wood which was last cut over around 1920 (Rackham 1995), yet pollen analysis suggests that the area may have been continuously wooded for 3,000 years (Budd 1998).

In the context of Irish habitat types, scrub has been defined as any habitat 'dominated by at least 50% cover of shrubs, stunted trees or brambles' (Fossitt 2000). Many pre-thicket plantation forests (those under five years old) fit this definition and, as will become evident later in the chapter, many bird species are common to both broadleaved scrub and pre-thicket forest. Scrub is often a transitional habitat between open habitats (such as grassland) and closed-canopy woodland. It is likely that, in the absence of grazing, many familiar Irish habitats such as fens, heath, species-rich grassland and improved grassland would, over time, become scrub as a result of colonisation by plant species such as brambles, gorse, willow and alder. Resulting scrubland habitats would in most places be succeeded by closed-canopy woodland, the climax vegetation state for much of Ireland, as the pioneer trees and shrubs die or are outcompeted by more long-lived tree species. In areas dominated by agriculturally improved grassland, there is little doubt that such succession would significantly improve the biodiversity value of the land. From a bird perspective, an increase in scrub would allow breeding by many open-habitat

Hazel scrub in the Burren, Co. Clare (Richard Nairn).

Forest plantations near Mullaghanish, Co. Cork (Richard T. Mills).   Coal Tit collecting nesting material (Richard T. Mills).

specialist species that are absent from large areas of improved grassland. A similar situation would probably be true for a variety of taxa, as structural diversity and potential food sources increase with the appearance of scrub. However, succession is a concern for some conservation organisations when attempting to manage for biodiversity as scrub encroachment has the potential to threaten habitats of high conservation value. An Irish example of scrub encroachment in the absence of grazing is the case of hazel colonisation of the Burren which is thought to threaten the diverse flora of the region (BurrenLife 2005).

Coniferous plantations have been established in Ireland since the 1700s as a result of premiums from the Royal Dublin Society (O'Carroll 1984). State-sponsored afforestation schemes and EU grant schemes from the 1980s to the present encouraged the rapid expansion of commercial forestry. Alongside Spain, Portugal, Italy, Iceland and Bulgaria, Ireland has recently experienced one of the fastest rates of afforestation in the EU. The vast majority of Ireland's 'new' forest cover is composed of monocultures of non-native coniferous plantations, dominated by the North American Sitka spruce. This tree prefers moist, nutrient-rich soil but can also tolerate boggy conditions (Joyce and O'Carroll 2002). These habitat preferences make it ideally suited to growth in Ireland and help to explain its prevalence in the Irish forest estate. Plantations now cover almost 10% of the country and therefore comprise the vast majority of the existing forest habitat on the island. In fact, plantations account for almost 90% of Ireland's forest cover (only Malta has a higher proportion), compared with around 70% in Britain and a pan-European average of just 3% (MCPFE 2007). In the 1950s, when plantation forest cover began to dramatically increase in Ireland, the conservation of biodiversity was not a high policy priority and timber production and commercial interests were the primary concerns in forestry. Although by their nature plantations are commercial ventures, there is a growing global awareness of biodiversity and an understanding that plantations must have a broader role than just timber production. This resulted in the implementation of recent large-scale scientific programmes funded by the National Council for Forest Research and Development investigating the biodiversity of plantations (Iremonger *et al.* 2006; PLANFORBIO programme 2007–2012). Although planting of native broadleaved species has increased in Ireland, the vast majority of plantations are dominated by non-native conifers.

The Irish woodland avifauna

Characteristic species

Ireland possesses some notable woodland subspecies. Both the Jay and Coal Tit are considered to be Irish subspecies and Kelly (2008) suggests that these subspecies exist because they survived extensive historical woodland clearances. One of the distinguishing features of the Irish Coal Tit is that it shows greater sexual dimorphism, in the form of bill stoutness (bill depth/bill length), than the British race. This is explained as a consequence of competitive release from other species, such as Eurasian Nuthatch, Willow Tit and Marsh Tit which are found in Britain, resulting in greater competition between individual Coal Tits (intraspecific competition). The intraspecific competition results in different feeding niche partitioning between the sexes and the stouter bill possessed by females may aid in opening tough seeds, such as those of yew (Gosler and Carruthers 1994). Interestingly, the breeding distribution of many of Ireland's breeding woodland birds has remained relatively stable for the last century. In the late nineteenth century, Common Crossbill and Siskin were recorded as being widespread in summer, and Common Redstart and Wood Warbler were both rare and occasional breeders. Garden Warbler may have been more widely distributed, while Blackcap had a relatively restricted distribution at that time (Ussher and More 1894). The latter has steadily increased in abundance in Ireland (Ruttledge 1983) and is now referred to by BirdWatch Ireland as 'one of Ireland's top-20 widespread garden birds'. Ruttledge (1983) points out that this increase in breeding Blackcaps coincided with an increase in the numbers overwintering in Ireland.

Sparrowhawk is probably the most abundant bird of prey in Ireland, though it is not quite as widely distributed as Common Kestrel, being absent from areas with scant tree cover (Hutchinson 1989). Of all the Irish raptors, only the much rarer Goshawk is as closely associated with forest and woodland habitats. However, unlike some other woodland specialists, Sparrowhawks have benefited from the recent expansion of the Irish forest estate through plantation forestry. Although Sparrowhawks will nest in many types of tree, they prefer conifers when available, and many now live in plantation forests. Sparrowhawks take a broad range of avian prey, their diet being dominated by songbirds. Because their hunting techniques rely on agility and stealth rather than speed, they benefit greatly from the small-scale topographic variation in plantation forest landscapes provided by forest edges, clearings, and linear open spaces, as well as from features of adjacent open landscapes such as hedgerows, treelines and copses. Although Pithon *et al.* (2005) found no association between Sparrowhawks and either forests or farmland habitats, this may have been due, at least in part, to biases in detectability between open and wooded habitats, as well as to a low level of detection for this species.

The Sparrowhawk is a characteristic woodland predator (Richie Lort).

Ireland in a European context

For those interested in biogeography, the absence of certain species from Irish woodlands is striking. Forests in Ireland are relatively species-poor in a European context and represent the western edge of an east–west decrease in species richness of European woodland birds (Fuller *et al.* 2007), although the drivers behind this observed gradient are not well understood. In their study of the geographical patterns of woodland breeding birds in Europe, Fuller *et al.* (2007) identified a suite of forest species (birds that breed and forage in forest habitats of any age) and compared the number of such species in six blocks across Europe. Ireland possesses less than half the number of species found in Eastern Europe and 30% less than Britain (Table 9.1). Archaeological evidence suggests that Ireland did once possess some forest bird species, such as Capercaillie, Black Grouse and Great Spotted Woodpecker, that are currently found in Britain and mainland Europe (D'Arcy 1999; Yalden and Carthy 2004). To this list Kelly (2008) adds Crested Tit, a species that prefers coniferous woodland, which possibly may have occurred too. Their present-day absence from Ireland (notwithstanding the current recolonisation by the Great Spotted Woodpecker which will be discussed later) may be partially attributed to Ireland's history of woodland clearance, and such clearances are perhaps one explanation when attempting to account for the current impoverished woodland bird fauna of Ireland (Yalden and Carthy 2004; Kelly 2008).

Table 9.1. Number of forest bird species recorded in six 200 x 250km blocks across Europe. Data taken from the text of Fuller *et al.* (2007). See paper for definition and list of forest bird species and precise locations of sample blocks.

Geographical Region	Number of forest bird species recorded
Ireland	31
Britain	46
North France	60
West Europe	62
Central Europe	63
East Europe	66

In other parts of Europe, the suite of species that inhabits broadleaved woodland includes migrants such as Common Redstart, Pied Flycatcher and Wood Warbler, all of which are very rare breeders in Ireland and have been absent from the vast majority of Irish woodland habitat for the past 100 years (Ussher and More 1894). Resident woodland species such as Greater and Lesser Spotted Woodpeckers, Eurasian Nuthatch, Marsh Tit, Willow Tit and Firecrest also occur in many European countries including Britain (Fuller 1995), but are absent from Ireland. There are several possibile explanations as to why Irish woodlands lack so many species. Island biogeography predicts that small, isolated islands should possess fewer species than larger land masses (MacArthur and Wilson 1967). The historical clearance of woodlands may have caused the extinction of some species while most current woodland patches may not be large enough to support some species (Wilson 1977). Finally, habitat and climatic conditions

The Woodcock is very difficult to detect on its nest in the woodland undergrowth (Ian Herbert).

may not presently exist for colonisation and source populations may not be large enough for sufficient numbers of individuals to reach Ireland with sufficient regularity for a colonisation event to take place (Kelly 2008; Simberloff 2009). Ireland's position to the west of the most westerly African–Eurasian migratory flyway may also limit opportunities for the expansion of populations of migrant species such as Pied Flycatcher, Wood Warbler and Common Redstart from the western seaboard of Britain, where they breed abundantly (Robinson 2005), to apparently suitable breeding habitat in Ireland, just 80km to the west. Furthermore, migrant species arriving in spring may be at a disadvantage to residents. In Ireland where winters are typically mild, winter survival rates of resident birds should be high, resulting in a correspondingly high demand for nest sites and food sources come the breeding season, which may exclude the later arriving migrant species (O'Connor 1986).

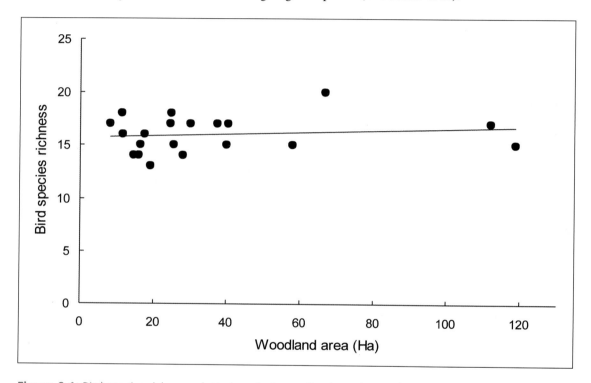

Figure 9.1: Bird species richness plotted against woodland patch area for 20 mature semi-natural broadleaved woodlands throughout Ireland. Bird data were collected in 2007 and 2008 using point counts, and ArcGIS was used to calculate the area of the woodlands. Source: Oisín Sweeney, unpublished PhD data.

Bird communities of Irish woodlands

Broadleaved woodland

Interestingly, although the species-area relationship dictates that larger woodland patches should contain more species, this pattern is not evident for birds in Irish semi-natural woodlands (Figure 9.1). The lack of such a relationship may be due to the absence from Ireland of forest bird specialists that are unable to utilise surrounding non-forest habitat, with the result that woodlands do not truly represent 'islands' as in classic species-area theory (Rosenzweig 1995). Many of the generalist birds found in Irish woodlands also use other habitats such as hedgerows, parks and gardens (see chapters 10 and 15), which helps to explain why many of these species can inhabit very small woodland patches.

A large portion of the bird community in Irish broadleaved woodland is comprised of a small number of common and widespread species such as Great Tit, Blue Tit, Blackbird, European Robin,

Wren and Chaffinch (Wilson 1977; Nairn and Farrelly 1991; Carruthers and Gosler 1995), although the relative abundance of these species may vary considerably between individual woodlands (Wilson 1977). In spring, the bird community is augmented by migrants such as Spotted Flycatcher, Blackcap and Chiffchaff. The Spotted Flycatcher is a particularly important member of the breeding bird community of Irish broadleaved woodland, as this species is on the *Amber List* of birds of conservation concern in Ireland. It is a species of European concern (Lynas *et al.* 2007) and has undergone a large decline in Britain over the last 30 years (Hewson *et al.* 2007). A notable aspect of the Irish woodland bird fauna is that Goldcrest and Coal Tit, species commonly associated with coniferous forests throughout Europe, also occur at relatively high abundance in Irish broadleaved woodlands (Batten 1976; Wilson 1977). This plasticity of habitat use is exhibited by many other species and is one of the most interesting aspects of the Irish bird fauna.

Studies in the tropics have shown that, for some birds, the carrying capacity of plantations may be lower than that of native forests and that some species found in native forests may be absent entirely from plantations (Farwig *et al.* 2008). The birds absent from plantations are mostly forest specialist species and their absence may be due, in part, to habitat requirements that are not met in uniform, monoculture plantations. However, in Ireland, most of the native woodland avifauna is comprised of generalist bird species common to many habitats, and so many species are found in both non-native plantations and broadleaved woodland. This is not to say that the bird communities of broadleaved woodland and plantations are identical, merely that similar sets of bird species can be found in either woodland type (Sweeney *et al.* 2010a). Although individuals of most common woodland bird species can be found in both semi-natural broadleaved woodlands and plantations, the relative abundance of each species differs between the woodland types. In semi-natural woodlands, the common species present tend to account for a similar portion of the total bird community, whereas bird populations in plantations tend to be dominated by a small number of abundant species. This is illustrated by Figure 9.2 which plots the abundance of each species against their rank and which shows the difference in community structure between native woodlands and plantations.

Scrubland

There are several bird species commonly associated with scrubland habitat, and this suite of species is distinct from that typically found in mature broadleaved woodlands or older plantations. Resident species such as Stonechat, Meadow Pipit, Reed Bunting, Lesser Redpoll and Linnet commonly breed in open, scrubby habitats. The Linnet is one of the only species of

Oakwoods at Glenveagh, Co. Donegal, have a characteristic mossy covering on rocks and tree trunks (Richard Nairn).

The Wren is one of the commonest species in the woodland undergrowth (Richard T. Mills).

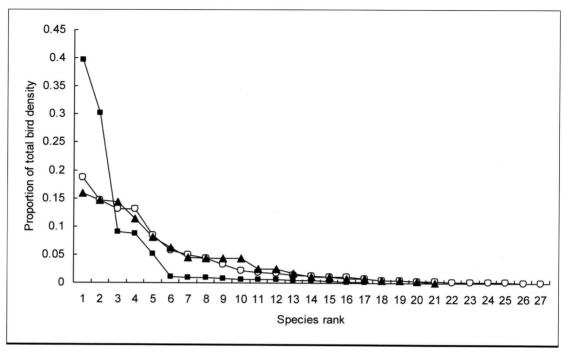

Figure 9.2: Rank-abundance curves showing the proportion of the total bird abundance accounted for by each constituent species in commercially mature Sitka spruce plantations (¢), Oak native woodlands (Á) and Ash native woodlands (p). Data were collected in 2007 and 2008 using point transects. Source: Oisín Sweeney, unpublished PhD data.

conservation concern (Lynas *et al.* 2007) to breed in scrub. The Stonechat is one of the most common and, thanks to its recognisable alarm calls and agitated behaviour in the presence of intruders, most obvious scrubland species. Stonechat numbers have increased in recent years (Coombes *et al.* 2009) but, because it occupies a variety of habitats as well as scrub, it is difficult to link population changes to changes in the extent of scrub. Several migrant warblers including Sedge Warbler, Willow Warbler, Common Grasshopper Warbler and Common Whitethroat breed in scrub, and of these the Common Grasshopper Warbler is on the *Amber List* of birds of conservation concern in Ireland (Lynas *et al.* 2007). In general, migrant species tend to be more vulnerable to population decline than are resident species (Heldbjerg and Fox 2008), and some have undergone recent population declines in Britain (Hewson and Noble 2009). This illustrates the importance of scrub in supporting breeding populations of Ireland's migrant birds. Another migrant species that is almost completely reliant on scrub for breeding is the Garden Warbler. This species is rare in Ireland and has its breeding stronghold here in the lakelands of the midlands and north-west. It has a strong preference for dense scrub dominated by brambles, and also breeds in failed coniferous plantations. The edges of woodland and the stunted vegetation associated with lakeshores are important in providing such habitat (Herbert 1991).

Plantation forests

The commercial cycle of a plantation forest can be viewed as a series of growth stages, through which the bird community

The Lesser Redpoll is typical of scrubland habitats (Richie Lort).

changes (Wilson *et al.* 2006). Pre-thicket plantations (<5 years old) are inhabited by species typical of open habitats, including breeding migrants, and their bird communities are distinct from those of older plantations (Figure 9.3). Many of these open habitat species may persist into the thicket stage (~15 years old) but, as canopy closure progresses, the open habitat specialists are lost. Common generalist species, such as European Robin and Chaffinch, make up a large proportion of the bird community of older plantations, along with the more coniferous forest adapted species such as Goldcrest and Coal Tit (Table 9.2). There is little change in the bird community from the mid-rotation stage at which the canopy closes (approximately 20 years), until commercial maturity (Figure 9.3). These older plantations are dominated by a handful of species whose abundances far exceed those of all other species present (Figure 9.2). This may be due to the low structural diversity that can be typical of older plantations, which may result in plantations having a low carrying capacity for most bird species. This is supported by the fact that many bird species present in Sitka spruce plantations are associated with non-crop broadleaf vegetation, rather than the crop trees themselves (Wilson *et al.* 2010). In this regard, native yew woodlands seem to be more akin to coniferous plantations than to broadleaved woodland. Birds breeding in yew, with the exception of Coal Tit, have been shown to actively select patches of broadleaves within the yew

The Chaffinch is common and widespread wherever there are trees or scrub (Richie Lort).

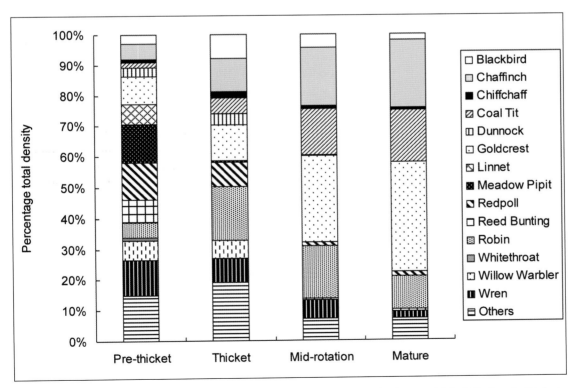

Figure 9.3: Proportion of bird population made up of different species in pre-thicket (0–5 yrs); thicket (5–15 yrs); mid-rotation (15–35 yrs) and commercially mature (35–50 yrs) Sitka spruce plantations. Species at low abundance are grouped as 'other' for clarity. Graph adapted from data from Iremonger *et. al.*, (2006).

woodland, tending to avoid those areas dominated by yew (Carruthers and Gosler 1994). Largely as a result of the high densities of Coal Tit and Goldcrest, species particularly well adapted to coniferous tree species, total bird density may be high in plantations of both Norway and Sitka spruce, although Norway spruce may support slightly more bird species than Sitka spruce (Batten 1976; Sweeney *et al.* 2010b).

Although commercially mature plantations are of limited utility to many species when compared with semi-natural broadleaved woodlands, they do provide an important habitat for some species. For example, Common Crossbills forage only in commercially mature plantations as they feed on the seeds in cones. Without such plantations this species would be absent from Ireland. Siskins breed in plantations and feed on cones, while Long-eared Owls have undergone population increases that have mirrored the expansion of coniferous plantations, suggesting that plantations are important to the life history of this species (Hutchinson 1989). Little Egrets locally use mature coniferous plantations for nesting (T.C. Kelly, pers. obs.), as does Ireland's rapidly increasing Common Buzzard population.

Common Buzzards have been recorded nesting in several tree species in Northern Ireland (Eimear Rooney, unpublished data), but prefer to nest in conifers when these are available (Cramp and Simmons 1980). This species used to be quite common in Ireland, but by the start of the twentieth century had been effectively wiped out by persecution (Sharrock 1976). However, Common Buzzards recolonised the North of Ireland in the 1950s (Kennedy *et al.* 1954), and by 1990 the total Irish population was estimated at 120 pairs (Norriss 1991). Since this time, aided by the banning of strychnine in 1991, Common Buzzards have undergone a remarkably rapid population increase and range expansion (Nagle 2004). By 2001 the population in the Republic of Ireland was estimated at between 160 and 200 pairs (O'Sullivan 2002), and Common Buzzards are now resident in most Irish counties (Damian Clarke, unpublished data). The current population size is not known, as raptor populations are not efficiently counted by general bird surveys, particularly in woodland habitats. During over ten years of research from 2001 to the present (a period when the Common Buzzard population in Ireland was rapidly increasing), in over 150 plantation forest and native woodland sites, Common Buzzards were recorded only once (J. O'Halloran *et al.* unpublished data).

The Common Buzzard has recently spread throughout the island of Ireland and is often found nesting in woodland (Richie Lort).

A national soaring survey was piloted in 2011 by members of the Irish Raptor Study Group and should, if carried out on a national scale, give much more accurate information about the current Common Buzzard population than is currently available. Although Common Buzzards hunt and scavenge in mixed and open habitats, their preference for nesting in trees gives rise to their association with woodland cover. The recent recolonisation of Ireland has been concentrated in relatively rich farmland in lowland landscapes (see Chapter 10), suggesting that the historical association of this species with upland areas in Ireland was more likely due to the effects of persecution than to a genuine habitat preference (Tony Nagle, pers. comm.). This is in keeping with the recorded use of habitat by Common Buzzards in Northern Ireland, where breeding has been recorded more frequently in landscapes dominated by lowland agriculture than in the peatlands and plantation forests of the uplands (Eimear Rooney, unpublished data).

A female Hen Harrier hunts over a young forest plantation (Richard T. Mills).

From a conservation perspective, pre-thicket plantations are the most important stage of the forest cycle in Ireland. At this stage, plantations more closely resemble scrubland than they do forests, and this is reflected in the composition of the species that use these stands. Many of Ireland's breeding warblers are species that breed on or close to the ground and require shrub cover and, in some cases, display perches. Young plantations, especially those in their second rotation where shrubs tend to be more common, provide suitable breeding habitat for all of these species. As a result, the densities of most migrant species are higher in pre-thicket than in commercially mature plantations or semi-natural broadleaved woodlands (Table 9.2). Because the bird community of pre-thicket is so distinct from that of older plantations, this age class is very important to the overall bird diversity of the plantation forest cycle (Fuller and Browne 2003). Young plantations therefore complement native scrub and provide important breeding habitat for Ireland's migrants, and also support resident species of conservation concern such as Linnet and Hen Harrier (Lynas *et al.* 2007).

Once widespread in Ireland, the Hen Harrier population was depleted by the middle of the last century through loss of suitable breeding habitat (O'Flynn 1983). The rapid expansion of Ireland's forest estate through the latter half of the twentieth century was associated with a recovery in Hen Harrier numbers. This species now breeds in forested landscapes in the uplands of the south and west of Ireland where it actively selects young second-rotation coniferous plantations for nesting (Wilson *et al.* 2009; see also Chapter 8) (Figure 9.4). Most recent estimates put the number of breeding pairs in Ireland at around 150 (Barton *et al.* 2006). Although they remain on the *Amber List* of species of conservation concern due to their continued vulnerability to persecution and habitat destruction (Lynas *et al.* 2007), their protection through the designation of Special Protection Areas that include habitats such as heath and bog as well as coniferous plantations will hopefully ensure the persistence of this large raptor in the Irish countryside.

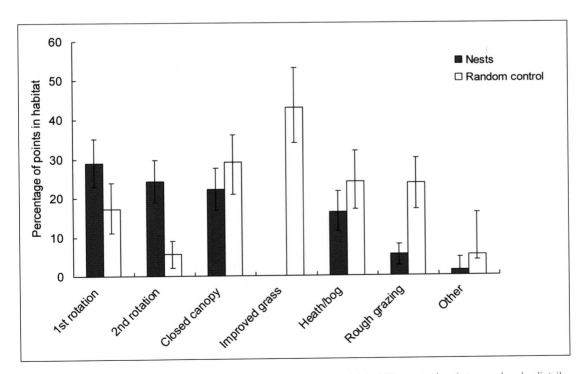

Figure 9.4: The distribution of 148 Hen Harrier nest sites and 14, 800 control points randomly distributed using ArcGIS in six common habitat types in Ireland. Data is combined from studies in 2000 and 2005 and the figure adapted from Wilson *et al.* (2009).

Rhododendron in Howth Deer Park, Co. Dublin (Oscar Merne).

Long-tailed Tits move around in flocks in the winter (Richie Lort).

Influence of vegetation on bird communities

Observed differences between the bird communities of native and plantation woodlands are primarily driven by understorey vegetation structure. Understorey structure may be influenced by the species of tree that comprises the canopy or, perhaps more importantly in the context of plantations, by forest management. The influence of habitat structure on bird communities is considered in Chapter 3, and it is well documented that understorey and shrub vegetation provides nest sites and food for many breeding birds (Fuller 1982). Grazing of shrub and understorey vegetation by deer can reduce the abundance of woodland birds in some British woods, mainly by removing preferred habitat structures (Gill and Fuller 2007). In Ireland, Wren abundance may be lower in woodlands which have been intensively grazed than in those with greater field cover (Wilson 1977), and bird diversity is positively associated with shrub cover in both native and plantation woodlands (Fig 9.5). This suggests that overgrazing has the potential to adversely affect woodland birds here too. Because of the association between bird diversity and vegetation structure, the poor understorey and shrub layers that are typical of many coniferous plantations probably contribute to their low carrying capacity for many species relative to semi-natural woodlands.

One potential threat to the understorey vegetation in semi-natural woodlands is the invasive *Rhododendron ponticum*, an evergreen shrub native to some countries of Europe and across much of Asia. Rhododendron has become well established in many parts of Ireland, notably in Killarney and Glenveagh national parks, the Vee in Co. Waterford and the Pettigo Bog Special Protection Area in Co. Donegal. In woodland, this species can establish itself in areas that have been disturbed by deer grazing and where the moss cover is thin (Cross 1981). Because it shades out native vegetation and it is unpalatable to grazers, selective grazing by deer may severely reduce the cover of native shrub species. The infestation of broadleaved woodlands with Rhododendron may therefore change the bird community structure and result in lower bird species richness than in areas that remain free of the shrub (Batten 1976). Due to its ability to invade, Rhododendron can also impact on the 'open space biodiversity areas' in plantation forests and may undermine the utility of such areas for biodiversity.

Winter bird communities

Most studies of woodland birds are undertaken during the breeding season as this is the period when population recruitment is taking place. However, because winter is an important time for survival (Carruthers and Gosler 1995; Newton 1998) studies on winter bird communities are of interest, although it may be more difficult to collect data on bird populations when they are not holding territories and singing. Because birds behave differently in winter than in the breeding season, the distinct structuring of bird communities that is evident between different woodland types in the breeding season may break down in winter and communities may be much less distinct. This is probably due to a decrease in food availability in the winter, requiring some species to use a variety of habitats and a diversity of food sources to meet their daily food requirements. Much of a bird's energy may be used in metabolism in winter, and Long-tailed Tits may feed for as much as 90% of the day in order to meet their energetic demands. Other tit species may store excess food when available in summer for use in hard times during winter (Perrins 1979). From the limited number of studies that have addressed winter bird communities, it appears that species vary in their response to changing seasons, with some species (e.g. Blue Tit) becoming more widespread and abundant across plantation forests in winter and some (e.g. Woodpigeon) less so. Differences in juvenile dispersal, nesting requirements and feeding requirements are all potential explanations as to why different species respond in different ways (O'Halloran *et al.* 1998). The departure of summer migrants lowers the number of species present in all Irish woodlands in winter and results in the bird communities of scrub and pre-thicket becoming less distinct from other forest habitats. Older Sitka spruce plantations may be particularly species-poor in winter and, as in the breeding season, bird species richness in winter tends to be highest in broadleaved woodland (Figure 6). In Britain, one study has shown that bird communities in winter differ between broadleaved and coniferous stands with species richness being higher in broadleaves, possibly due to differences in shrub cover (Donald *et al.* 1997). As well as the departure of long-distance migrant species in winter, resident species such as Meadow Pipit, Reed Bunting and Lesser Redpoll may show partial migration and move to lower altitudes in winter. As a result, the winter bird community of woodland and scrub in upland areas may be much less diverse than in summer, or indeed less diverse than in similar habitats in the lowlands (MacLochlainn 1984).

Flocks are common in woodlands in winter when birds do not hold breeding territories. Flocking has several benefits to birds, including reducing predation risk and increasing foraging efficiency (Newton 1998). Typical flocks in Irish broadleaved woodlands in winter are mostly tit species (Blue Tit, Great Tit, Coal Tit and Long-tailed Tit) which are often associated with Goldcrest and Eurasian Treecreeper. Such flocks move rapidly through a woodland gleaning the branches and trunks of arthropods and, in the case of Blue and Long-tailed Tits, feeding on catkins where available. Redwing, a winter visitor to Ireland, also commonly forms flocks in woodlands, as well as in open country. Redwing flocks are highly mobile and their presence in a particular area may be dependent on the availability of berry crops on trees such as rowan and hawthorn (MacLochlainn 1984).

Future patterns in Irish woodland habitat

In mainland Europe, the abandonment of farmland has led to an increase in scrub and forest cover in recent years (MCPFE 2007). Increasing levels of scrub in the landscape will benefit, at least in the short term, bird species that utilise shrubs and scrub for breeding (Sirami *et al.* 2008). However, as scrubland habitats gradually develop into closed canopy forests, this new habitat will be lost and woodland bird populations may begin to increase. In Ireland, the number of farms has declined since 2000, and it appears that this has not been compensated for by a corresponding increase in farm size (DG AGRI 2009). Therefore, land abandonment seems also to be occurring in Ireland, and we may expect an increase in the area of scrub cover in the coming years. Furthermore, the Forest Service aims to increase forest cover in Ireland by 300,000 hectares over the next 20 years which will result in an area of planted forest of 1 million hectares, or approximately 14% of land area, by 2030 (COFORD 2009). This will require the establishment of new plantations which will in turn periodically provide habitat (in the form of pre-thicket plantations at the start of each rotation) for scrubland birds. Finally, short-rotation willow coppice will increase in extent in the near future as the Irish government has set renewable energy targets for heat and electricity production from biomass (COFORD 2009). Such coppice provides suitable breeding habitat for many of the species that currently breed in scrub and young woodland (Kavanagh 1990). With careful management, the habitat requirements of scrubland birds should therefore be met in the Irish landscape in the medium to long term.

Much of the planned increase in Ireland's forest cover is likely to be in the form of non-native coniferous plantations. However, besides the establishment of such plantations, programmes such as

The Goldcrest often accompanies mixed feeding flocks of tits in woodland (Richard T. Mills).

Pre-thicket forest plantation is an attractive habitat for Hen Harriers and some passerines (Richard T. Mills).

the Native Woodland Scheme (Forest Service 2004), which is designed both to protect existing semi-natural woodland and to promote the establishment of new broadleaved woodland, should ensure that the area of broadleaved woodland increases also.

Typically, when a plantation has reached commercial maturity (approximately 40–50 years) all of the crop trees are harvested by clear-felling, and the area is replanted for another rotation (cycle of tree growth from planting to felling). Replanting after harvest is a requirement of forest regulations which states that all felled areas must be replanted for further rotations (Forest Service 2000a). This system is in contrast with many countries around the world where continuous cover forestry is practised. This approach involves felling small portions of stands (in some cases even individual trees) at different times so that a diversity of age classes is retained within a single stand. Frequently, natural gap regeneration replaces planting as the method of establishing the next crop of trees under a continuous cover forestry regime. Continuous cover forest is termed a 'low impact silvicultural system', which means that it has little impact on the forest environment (Ní Dhubháin 2003). In contrast to clearfelling, which removes most non-crop understorey vegetation as well as the crop trees, the selection of small groups of trees would allow long-term persistence of non-crop vegetation at the stand scale, thus maintaining structural diversity which, as has been discussed, benefits bird communities. Furthermore, the creation of many gaps in the canopy would allow more light penetration and therefore increase the potential for establishment of understorey vegetation over a large portion of a stand. Current forest biodiversity guidelines (Forest Service 2000b) encourage foresters to leave some trees when felling for the benefit of biodiversity, and to move towards a system of continuous cover forestry. Plantation forest management is therefore graduating towards a more biodiversity-orientated model, and it is hoped that future plantations will reflect this improved forest management system. One consequence of an expansion of continuous cover forestry is that areas of pre-thicket would become smaller and more patchily distributed. This would have potential implications for the breeding migrants, open habitat residents and Hen Harriers that currently use pre-thicket, and research is required to determine whether increasing continuous cover forestry is likely to negatively impact some bird species.

Old-growth woodland typically includes features such as large, hollow trees and large volumes of dead wood that are used by many animals and plants, including birds. As a consequence, old-growth features are desirable in woodlands so as to maximise the potential for biodiversity conservation. At present, Ireland's forest estate is relatively young and, because of the nature of forestry economics, developing old-growth woodland conditions into the future will be difficult. It is therefore important that policies such as the Forest Biodiversity Guidelines are adhered to and incentives devised to ensure the development of old-growth conditions. It is possible that, as the plantation forest estate increases in area and more long-lived broadleaved species are used in plantations, continuous cover forestry will become more common practice (Forest Service 2000a). Coupled with felling practices that encourage the retention of several trees throughout subsequent rotations (with the same trees retained in each rotation), and the protection of existing patches of semi-natural woodland, this will increase the likelihood that Irish forests, both semi-natural and plantation, develop old-growth conditions in the future.

Potential future changes in woodland bird communities

The coming years promise to be an exciting period for Irish ornithologists and woodland ecologists. Having bred for the first time in 2006, the Great Spotted Woodpecker appears to be recolonising Ireland, with 18 nesting pairs confirmed in 2010 (McDevitt *et al.* 2011). It is likely that the recent large population increases in Wales and Scotland (Risely *et al.* 2009) have resulted in increased propagule pressure from Britain to Ireland, resulting in the sudden rise in the number of breeding pairs. A route through Scotland to Co. Antrim, the shortest crossing point between the islands, is one possible entrance point to Ireland (Kelly 2008).

Woodpeckers are ecosystem engineers, which means that their modification of their habitat affects not just them, but also other species that share their habitat. Ireland does not have many hole-nesting species, a fact that may be partially explained by a lack of suitable nest sites. Should they successfully

Willow Warbler is one of the commonest summer migrants from Africa (Richie Lort).

The Great Spotted Woodpecker is a recent colonist in eastern Irish woodlands (Richard T. Mills).

recolonise, the excavation of nest cavities by Great Spotted Woodpeckers will eventually increase the availability of nest sites for secondary hole nesting species, populations of which may be limited at present by a lack of holes for nesting (Newton 1994). Species such as Blue Tit and Great Tit may therefore increase in density in Irish woodlands in future, which may in turn affect the populations of species that compete with, prey on or are preyed upon by these species. The Great Spotted Woodpecker may also affect species populations through direct interactions, for example through predation of tits breeding in nest boxes (Mainwaring and Hartley 2008).

Climate change is another potential driver of change in Irish woodland habitat and the bird communities that utilise it. Although current predictions are imprecise and largely speculative, climate change across Europe may result in some bird species changing their ranges either to colonise areas that were formerly climatically unsuitable, or to desert areas that are becoming climatically unsuitable. Ireland may therefore receive some species that have been absent up to this point. It is less likely that Ireland will loose resident bird species, however, as Ireland's generalist bird fauna contains species that are currently widespread around different climatic zones in continental Europe. A considerable number of woodland and scrub-associated species such as Lesser and Middle Spotted Woodpecker, Short-toed Treecreeper, Eurasian Nuthatch, Firecrest, Crested, Willow and Marsh Tit, Woodlark, Cetti's Warbler, Tree Pipit and Lesser Whitethroat may all potentially find Ireland a suitable breeding ground as the climate changes (Huntley *et al.* 2007). All are currently either very rare breeders or completely absent from Ireland. Predictions on future bird distributions are completely based on climatic projections however, and the ability of Ireland to absorb such species will also depend on the availability of suitable habitat, as well as other variables such as inter-specific competition and dispersal ability. The impact of climate change on bird communities in future is therefore difficult to predict with any degree of accuracy. The actions of ecosystem engineers such as the Great Spotted Woodpecker, coupled with an expansion in the area of land under coppice, plantation forest and, in particular, broadleaved woodland and a move towards a more biodiversity orientated style of forestry may help to ensure the future enrichment of Ireland's woodland bird fauna.

Acknowledgements
Thanks to Fraser Mitchell and Rob Fuller for invaluable input to this chapter.

Table 9.2 Species listed alphabetically according to their common names, their population densities (Number/hectare ± SE) in four first (data derived from Wilson *et al.* 2006) and second (data derived from Sweeney *et al.* 2010b) rotation Sitka spruce plantation forest age classes. (M) denotes a migrant species.

Species	Scientific name	Pre-thicket		Thicket		Mid-rotation		Mature	
		1st rotation	2nd rotation	1st rotation	2nd rotation	1st rotation	2nd rotation	1st rotation	2nd rotation
Blackbird	*Turdus merula*	0.48 (0.34)	0.53 (0.18)	2.45 (0.63)	1.31 (0.30)	1.46 (0.40)	1.17 (0.30)	0.49 (0.18)	0.40 (0.10)
Blackcap (M)	*Sylvia atricapilla*	0.04 (0.04)	0.06 (0.06)	0.32 (0.12)	0.35 (0.28)	0.46 (0.46)	0.89 (0.39)	0	0.32 (0.19)
Blue Tit	*Cyanistes caeruleus*	0.08 (0.08)	0	0.38 (0.38)	1.14 (0.76)	0.06 (0.06)	0.36 (0.36)	0	0.48 (0.48)
Bullfinch	*Pyrrhula pyrrhula*	0.17 (0.17)	0.11 (0.11)	0.73 (0.35)	0	0.08 (0.08)	0	0.08 (0.08)	0
Chaffinch	*Fringilla coelebs*	0.82 (0.48)	1.69 (0.33)	3.34 (0.96)	8.52 (1.26)	6.17 (1.80)	2.61 (0.67)	5.79 (0.67)	4.51 (0.92)
Chiffchaff (M)	*Phylloscopus collybita*	0.17 (0.17)	0.06 (0.06)	0.66 (0.55)	0.92 (0.38)	0.26 (0.11)	0.5 (0.14)	0.16 (0.07)	0.05 (0.05)
Coal Tit	*Periparus ater*	0.26 (0.26)	0.84 (0.42)	1.54 (0.53)	12.30 (2.78)	4.93 (1.21)	18.64 (2.96)	4.42 (0.27)	15.44 (3.18)
Common Cuckoo (M)	*Cuculus canorus*	0	0	0	0	0	0.12 (0.12)	0	0
Dunnock	*Prunella modularis*	0.46 (0.21)	1.61 (0.54)	1.17 (0.48)	3.47 (0.91)	0.13 (0.08)	0.95 (0.28)	0	0
Goldcrest	*Regulus regulus*	1.46 (0.85)	0.33 (0.22)	3.64 (1.05)	11.33 (2.02)	9.00 (0.73)	24.72 (3.15)	9.19 (2.04)	20.30 (3.81)
Goldfinch	*Carduelis carduelis*	0.23 (0.23)	0.09 (0.09)	0.10 (0.10)	0	0	0	0	0
Common Grasshopper Warbler (M)	*Locustella naevia*	0.03 (0.03)	0.11 (0.11)	0	0	0	0	0	0
Great Tit	*Parus major*	0.12 (0.12)	0.44 (0.13)	0.27 (0.27)	0.36 (0.15)	0.53 (0.18)	0.05 (0.05)	0.09 (0.09)	0.33 (0.17)
Greenfinch	*Carduelis chloris*	0	0	0.53 (0.53)	0	0	0	0	0
Jay	*Garrulus glandarius*	0	0	0	0.23 (0.22)	0	0.26 (0.16)	0	0.54 (0.26)
Lesser Redpoll	*Carduelis cabaret*	1.92 (0.37)	0.54 (0.17)	2.41 (0.84)	0	0.37 (0.22)	0	0.35 (0.20)	0
Linnet	*Carduelis cannabina*	1.07 (0.56)	0.80 (0.60)	0	0	0	0	0	0
Long-tailed Tit	*Aegithalos caudatus*	0	0	0.07 (0.07)	0.67 (0.67)	0.15 (0.15)	1.05 (0.68)	0	0

Table 9.2 Species listed alphabetically according to their common names, their population densities (Number/hectare ± SE) in four first (data derived from Wilson *et al.* 2006) and second (data derived from Sweeney *et al.* 2010b) rotation Sitka spruce plantation forest age classes. (M) denotes a migrant species.

Species	Scientific name	Pre-thicket		Thicket		Mid-rotation		Mature	
		1st rotation	2nd rotation	1st rotation	2nd rotation	1st rotation	2nd rotation	1st rotation	2nd rotation
Meadow Pipit	*Anthus pratensis*	2.02 (0.70)	1.49 (1.23)	0.16 (0.16)	0.45 (0.45)	0	0	0	0
Mistle Thrush	*Turdus viscivorus*	0	0.06 (0.06)	0.33 (0.21)	0.12 (0.07)	0.20 (0.14)	0.06	0.40 (0.33)	0.15 (0.10)
Common Pheasant	*Phasianus colchicus*	0	0.23 (0.23)	0	0.07 (0.07)	0	0	0.06 (0.06)	0
Reed Bunting	*Emberiza schoeniclus*	1.19 (0.91)	0.17 (0.17)	0	0	0	0	0	0
European Robin	*Erithacus rubecula*	0.80 (0.38)	5.18 (0.81)	5.30 (0.85)	11.31 (1.22)	5.57 (1.19)	7.26 (0.74)	2.77 (0.97)	4.64 (1.25)
Sedge Warbler (M)	*Acrocephalus schoenobaenus*	0.11 (0.11)	0	0	0	0	0	0	0
Siskin	*Carduelis spinus*	0.33 (0.27)	0	0.33 (0.23)	0.12 (0.11)	0.07 (0.07)	0.05 (0.05)	0.32 (0.18)	0
Skylark	*Alauda arvensis*	0.05 (0.05)	0	0	0	0	0	0	0
Song Thrush	*Turdus philomelos*	0.11 (0.11)	0.12 (0.07)	1.66 (0.68)	1.07 (0.43)	0.50 (0.43)	0.42 (0.21)	0.05 (0.05)	0.21 (0.21)
Sparrowhawk	*Accipiter nisus*	0	0.1 (0.10)	0	0	0.07 (0.07)	0	0.20 (0.15)	0
Stonechat	*Saxicola torquata*	0.12 (0.12)	0.43 (0.43)	0	0	0	0	0	0
Eurasian Treecreeper	*Certhia familaris*	0.10 (0.10)	0	0	0.23 (0.23)	0.13 (0.07)	0	0.12 (0.05)	0.35 (0.14)
Common White-throat (M)	*Sylvia communis*	0.16 (0.16)	3.36 (1.48)	0	0	0	0.13 (0.13)	0	0.27 (0.27)
Willow Warbler (M)	*Phylloscopus trochilus*	1.00 (0.12)	3.67 (0.55)	1.84 (0.65)	3.24 (0.58)	0.15 (0.09)	0.22 (0.22)	0.22 (0.09)	0.11 (0.07)
Woodpigeon	*Columba palumbus*	0	0	0.45 (0.27)	0.47 (0.18)	0.17 (0.06)	0.06 (0.06)	0.12 (0.07)	0.50 (0.21)
Wren	*Troglodytes troglodytes*	1.86 (0.46)	4.55 (0.37)	2.45 (0.61)	3.59 (0.40)	2.00 (0.65)	2.64 (0.91)	0.58 (0.16)	2.63 (0.79)

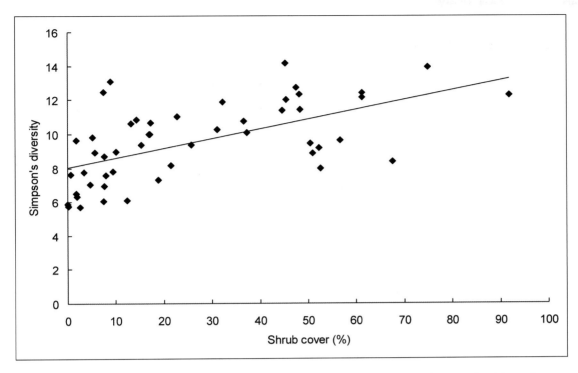

Figure 9.5: Bird diversity (Simpson's Diversity) plotted against percentage shrub cover for 20 semi-natural broadleaved woodlands and 30 mature coniferous plantations throughout Ireland. Source: Oisín Sweeney, unpublished PhD data.

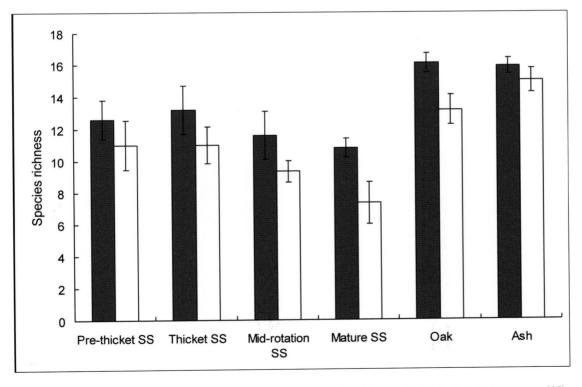

Figure 9.6: Breeding (dark bars) and winter (open bars) species richness (± SE) in four Sitka spruce (SS) age-classes, and in Oak and Ash semi-natural broadleaved woodland. Data were collected in 2007 and 2008 using point counts. Source: Oisín Sweeney, unpublished PhD data.

10. Lowland Farmland

Alex Copland and John Lusby

Introduction

Farming is the predominant land-use on the island of Ireland, accounting for nearly two-thirds of the land area. It is a habitat almost all are familiar with; it is, by and large, what we consider to be the 'countryside'. Farmland is a semi-natural habitat, managed by humans to provide food. However, it is also a landscape where people work and live. As a result, many farmland bird species have a special place not just in the natural heritage of Ireland, but also in its cultural heritage. Although few people living in Ireland have heard a Corncrake or seen a Barn Owl, many will 'know' of these birds (and probably 'see' a Barn Owl every week in the titles to RTÉ's *The Late, Late Show*).

Unfortunately, many of these iconic farmland bird species are under serious threat. A generation ago, Corncrakes were numbered in their thousands and could be heard in every county (Sharrock 1976). Today, about 150 singing males can be heard, restricted to a few late-cut hay meadows in the extreme north and west of Ireland (Donegal, Mayo, Connemara and Kerry (Alcorn 2009; Gallagher 2009; Gordon 2009)). The Irish Barn Owl population consists of a few hundred pairs, predominantly concentrated in the south-west and Midlands of the country (Lusby *et al.* 2009), with population declines estimated at over 50% in the last 25 years (Lynas *et al.* 2007). Other familiar farmland birds, including the Northern Lapwing, Skylark, Chough and Yellowhammer, have also experienced substantial declines in both range and population size (Lynas *et al.* 2007). Less familiar is the Corn Bunting, likely to be the most recent extinction among Ireland's avifauna, having not been recorded breeding in Ireland since the mid-1990s (Taylor and O'Halloran 2002).

Benbulben, Co. Sligo is set in a landscape of agricultural grassland (Richard Nairn).

Nevertheless, conservation initiatives and management intervention has assisted these populations – halting declines and stabilising numbers. Substantial conservation efforts in the remaining range of the Corncrake has stabilised its population over the past ten years (Donaghy 2007). The Grey Partridge, whose population was down to just six pairs in the late-1990s at one midlands site, now numbers over 90 pairs, with birds spreading out into its former farmland habitats (Copland and Buckley 2010). Recent and ongoing research into breeding waders (Lynch *et al.* 2007), Chough (Boylan 2011) and Barn Owl (Lusby *et al.* 2009) will help to inform future strategies to conserve and restore the populations of these species. Although the future for any of these species is not secure, targeted conservation offers the potential to restore populations and former haunts for many of these threatened species.

A Corncrake calls from deep vegetation in early summer (Richard T. Mills).

The reason for the decline (and, perhaps, the current recovery) of farmland birds in Ireland can be very closely linked to the various foci and developments of agricultural policies. The principal driver of these has been the EU and, in particular, the Common Agricultural Policy (CAP). Originally designed as a market support tool to encourage increased production, it led to increasingly intensive and specialised farming practices. The mechanisation and loss of small-scale, mixed farming (to make farming more 'efficient'), the drainage of wetlands and removal of trees and scrub (to 'reclaim' or 'improve' areas for agricultural production), the reseeding of grasslands (with faster-growing species), the huge inputs of fertiliser (to allow crops to grow faster) and pesticides (to get rid of anything that threatened these crops) all had substantial, negative impacts on the wildlife that was associated with farmed habitats. In recent years, however, there has been a substantial change in the focus of these agricultural policies. The public (i.e. the EU taxpayers who fund the CAP) are seeking increased environmental goods to be delivered by farming. This has resulted in the development of so-called *agri-environment schemes*, where farmers are paid to adopt farming methods that benefit wildlife occurring on their land. Properly targeted measures within these agri-environment schemes have the potential to deliver substantial benefits to threatened habitats and species in the wider countryside (Copland *et al.* 2011).

Compared to other countries in Europe (and especially Britain), there have been limited studies on farmland birds in Ireland (McMahon 2007). Nevertheless, in recent years, much research has been done. Many of these are focused on individual species, including Corncrake (Donaghy 2007), Barn Owl (Lusby *et al.* 2009), European Robin (Fennessey 2001), Song Thrush (Kelleher 2006) and Twite (McLoughlin 2009), although a few have studied farmland bird communities as a whole (Flynn 2002; McMahon 2005; Johnson 2008; Copland 2009).

This chapter focuses on what might be considered the areas of intensive food producing farmland – what we might term the dairy, meat-safe and bread-bin of Ireland. When considering lowland farmland as a habitat for birds, it is perhaps best seen in two categories: the cropped areas (the pastures, meadows and tillage areas) and the non-crop areas (the hedgerows, farmyards, farm woodlands and other such habitats). This chapter deals only with the habitats that are unique to farmland. Other habitats types that often occur on farmland (woods, ponds, etc.) are dealt with in other relevant chapters. In addition, the many highly specialised and rare farmland habitats, such as wet grasslands or machair, are also dealt with in other chapters.

Agricultural Grasslands

Covering a total of 3.9 million hectares, agricultural grassland habitats provide the largest single habitat type in Ireland (DAFF 2008). There is much variation in the type of grasslands, from intensively managed, heavily fertilised, reseeded rye-grass monocultures to extensively managed, species-rich permanent pastures. In this section, grasslands are grouped into those that are generally highly improved and those that are of a semi-natural type. This second group encompasses a large variety of habitats but, due to the drive for increasing productivity, are generally limited in extent.

Mixed flocks of Jackdaws and Rooks benefit from the abundance of soil invertebrates in a recently mown meadow (Karl Partridge).

Brent Geese graze the pastures on the Wexford Wildfowl Reserve, Co. Wexford (Richard Nairn).

Improved agricultural grasslands

Improved agricultural grasslands are, by and large, something of a desert for biodiversity, certainly given the scale of the habitat and the number of species associated with them (Copland and O'Halloran 2010a). Largely dominated by Italian or Perennial Rye Grass, which is heavily fertilised to encourage rapid, early growth to maximise yields, there are little opportunities for other plant species to successfully compete and grow. Furthermore the management of this habitat, usually cut two or even three times per annum for silage, or heavily grazed by cattle, suits very few species of plant or animal, particularly birds in the breeding season. This probably results in a limited range of insect and invertebrate prey species, both above and below ground, limiting the bird population associated with these habitats, making them suboptimal for farmland bird species (McMahon and Whelan 2005). However, for the species that find this habitat suitable, they can occur in large numbers. During the breeding season, opportunities exist for ground-feeding birds to access surface-dwelling invertebrates such as slugs, which may occur in high densities due to the high fertility of the soil (McMahon *et al.* 2010). Large flocks of species such as Common Starling, Jackdaw, Rook and Hooded Crow often appear on these fields immediately after silage harvesting (Copland 2009). Similarly, Barn Swallows often forage over improved grassland fields, particularly those with cattle, or during mowing operations, due to abundant flying insects often found with such management (Copland 2009). In winter, the relatively tall vegetation present can be used by Common Snipe, which can forage in the open sward structure often associated with this habitat (Copland 2009).

Wintering geese and swans are often found grazing on improved grassland (Crowe 2005a) although these are unlikely to have been their original preferred habitats. The best known site in Ireland is the Wexford Wildfowl Reserve where up to one third of the world population of Greater White-fronted Geese, together with flocks of Light-bellied Brent Geese and Whooper Swans graze the large open fields (see Chapter 16). In the nineteenth century, White-fronted Geese were widespread thoughout the boglands and marshes of Ireland (Ussher and Warren 1900) but extensive drainage forced the geese to concentrate in the recently reclaimed polderland in Wexford (Ruttledge and Ogilvie 1979). The geese traditionally fed on the rhizomes of the common cotton grass and deer sedge found in the peatlands but switched to feeding on reseeded grassland, especially in spring (Cabot 2009). When they arrive in

An unimproved hay meadow at Bunduff, Co. Sligo (Richard Nairn).

A wheat crop in Co. Wexford in June (Richard Nairn).

north-west Ireland from their Icelandic breeding grounds in autumn, Whooper Swans concentrate in large flocks on the improved agricultural land around Lough Foyle and Lough Swilly together with Greater White-fronted Geese and Greylag geese. As in Wexford, the fields here are large and flat with few fences, giving the wildfowl all-round visibility to watch for predators or disturbance (Speer 2011).

Semi-natural grasslands

Unlike wet grasslands (Chapter 6) and machair (Chapter 12), the utilisation of dry semi-natural agricultural grasslands by birds in Ireland is extremely restricted. Although Corncrakes occur in the flood meadows of the River Shannon Callows, their traditional haunt in Ireland was formerly in dry meadows throughout Ireland. The majority of the population still occurs in these habitats in the extreme north and west of Ireland, particularly Cos. Donegal, Sligo, Mayo and Galway (Alcorn 2009; Gordon 2009). Conservation work, aiming to protect breeding meadows by offering farmers payments to delay mowing, cut from the centre of the field towards the edges and establish areas of early and late cover, has been operating in these areas since the early 1990s (Copland 2002). Choughs use semi-improved and semi-natural grassland at coastal locations to forage throughout the year, with use peaking in winter (Trewby *et al.* 2006). Grazed pastures are typically more attractive to foraging Chough than ungrazed grasslands due to short swards.

Arable Crops

Although arable crop management is generally very intensive, the variety of different crop types being grown results in a diverse range of opportunities and challenges for birds. Due to the differing management processes behind the growing of arable crops, this habitat can best be considered as several different habitat types. The main two types are the growing crop of barley, wheat, potatoes, etc. and the non-growing habitat (usually stubbles, but might include bare, ploughed earth) that are often present through the winter after the crops have been harvested. Of course, the different types of crop are likely to provide different resources for a range of bird species. The majority of arable cropping is managed on an annual cycle, with sowing in spring (or autumn for winter wheat) and harvesting in late summer. However, added to this category are non-cropped habitats such as set-aside and wild-bird cover that may have longer management cycles.

Breeding birds of arable crops

Due to the relatively limited amount of tillage in Ireland, coupled with the generally intensive production methods now being used to grow these crops, few species specialised in utilising this habitat in the breeding season are represented within the Irish avifauna. Copland (2009) recorded just 19 species that were considered to be using the 466 hectares of this habitat that were surveyed (out of a total surveyed area of 6,180 hectares). Of these, only seven species had more than ten individuals present (Common Pheasant, Barn Swallow, Blackbird, Jackdaw, Rook, Chaffinch and Yellowhammer). However, excluding birds recorded on boundary habitats, these totals represent 16.4% of all Common Pheasants and 35.1% of all Yellowhammers recorded, suggesting that for a limited number of specialist (and in the case of Yellowhammer, seriously threatened) bird species, this is an important habitat. These data are supported by studies of Yellowhammers in Tipperary (Collins 2000) and west Limerick (Hunt and Kiely 2002), which showed that this species was regularly found in cereal-growing areas, albeit at very low densities when compared to those in the UK.

Although normally associated with lowland wet grasslands as a breeding habitat in Ireland, Northern Lapwing also use arable crops for nesting (Lynch *et al.* 2007). However, modern farming practices and in-field management may limit the nesting success of this species in these types of habitat (Lynch *et al.* 2007).

The Common Pheasant is one of the few species living in arable cropfields (Richard T. Mills).

Non-breeding birds of arable crops

Traditionally, arable crops would have been harvested in the autumn and the land left unused throughout the winter. The unused land would often be the crop stubbles, left untouched after the autumn harvest until the ground was ploughed and seeded the following spring. In areas where the soil is heavy or wet, ploughing may occur in autumn to allow the winter weather to break down the bare soil to ease spring sowing. Occasionally, cereal crops may be undersown with grass as part of a cropping rotation (i.e. cereal crop one year; grass the following year). To extend the growing season, resulting in larger crop yields, autumn sowing (particularly of wheat) has become a feature in more recent years. Unlike Britain and many other continental European countries, where autumn sowing of cereal crops has become the dominant arable cropping practice, spring sowing still dominates in Ireland (64.5% of all cereals are spring-sown) (DAF 2008). This compares to 23.5% in the UK which is spring sown (DEFRA 2008).

Bewick's Swans foraging on root crops in Co. Wexford (Richard T. Mills).

Ó'hUallacháin and Dunne (2007), studying the winter diet of Common Pheasants, identified that cereals were important, along with vegetables and cultivated crops. McMahon (2005), comparing bird populations on grassland and winter cereals, noted that Rook, Skylark, European Golden Plover, Common Pheasant and Mistle Thrush were positively associated with winter cereals. It is suggested that the open structure of the crop, which allows access for birds to invertebrates and plant seeds on the soil surface, is likely the reason for the selection of this habitat over grassland habitats. However, in comparing winter wheat to stubbles, set-aside and grassland, McMahon *et al.* (2003) demonstrated that only two species (Common Snipe and Chaffinch) were positively associated with this habitat, echoing studies in many other countries that have shown that winter cereals are not a favoured foraging habitat for birds during the winter, particularly when compared to stubbles (Wilson *et al.* 1996; Newton 2004).

Tilled land

Tilled land as defined here is land used for growing crops but has no crop growing in it. This includes both stubbles and bare soil. This habitat is most closely associated with arable cropping management, but will include areas that have been ploughed prior to reseeding of grasslands. Also, unless there have been unforeseen management problems on a farm, this habitat is typically only present during the non-breeding season.

McMahon *et al.* (2003), in comparing wintering bird populations on stubbles, set-aside, winter wheat and grassland, demonstrated that stubbles held the highest diversity of species. Seed-eating species, including Skylark, Yellowhammer and Rook (which forages on crop seeds left after harvesting), were particularly strongly associated with stubbles.

Copland (2009) recorded 30 species using these types of habitat from 82 farms in winter in Ireland. These habitats comprised a total of 370 hectares (10.2% of the total area surveyed). The number of individuals for each species recorded using these habitats, together with the percentage of the total population recorded on all farms during the winter for each species recorded are shown in Table 10.1. These habitats appear to be particularly important for several species, including Skylark (97.8% of all Skylarks recorded during the winter were in these habitats), along with European Golden Plover (95.9%), Northern Lapwing (64.3%), Linnet (44.5%), Common Snipe (26.6%), Pied Wagtail (17.3%), Rook (13.8%) and Meadow Pipit (10.9%). Also shown in Table 10.1 are the contribution to this habitat from stubbles and bare earth. Stubbles were used by 29 of

Yellowhammer in full song (Karl Partridge).

the 30 species, with just 11 of the 30 species present on bare, tilled earth. Nevertheless, the bare earth was important for European Golden Plover, Northern Lapwing, Common Snipe and Pied Wagtail (all typically insectivorous species). By contrast, and supporting the findings of McMahon *et al.* (2003) mentioned above, seed-eating birds such as Skylark, Linnet and Rook were more closely associated with stubbles.

Set-aside

Set-side was introduced as a market control measure by the EU to stop over-supply of tillage crops (typically cereals) onto the European market (the so-called grain mountains). Taking land out of commercial production offered an opportunity for this land to be managed for other objectives, of which biodiversity became the most important (Henderson *et al.* 2000). As a result, set-aside management measures were included in several agri-environment schemes, including REPS (DAFRD, 2000). However, following the decoupling of agricultural support from levels of production, set-aside

Table 10.1 Number of individuals and the proportion of the total farmland population for each species recorded in tilled habitats in winter (data from Copland 2009)				
Species	No. Birds	% of total	Stubble	Bare Earth
Common Pheasant	8	8.1	8	–
European Golden Plover	93	95.9	2	91
Northern Lapwing	148	64.3	3	145
Common Snipe	217	26.6	89	128
Black-headed Gull	7	0.8	–	7
Woodpigeon	54	5.0	54	–
Skylark	134	97.8	134	–
Meadow Pipit	130	10.9	122	8
Grey Wagtail	1	1.8	1	–
Pied Wagtail	51	17.3	5	46
Dunnock	3	0.4	3	–
European Robin	4	0.2	2	2
Blackbird	9	0.3	9	–
Fieldfare	20	0.7	20	–
Song Thrush	33	3.1	33	–
Redwing	20	0.5	20	–
Mistle Thrush	7	3.0	7	–
Coal Tit	1	0.2	1	–
Blue Tit	3	0.4	3	–
Magpie	13	3.9	13	–
Jackdaw	41	3.1	35	6
Rook	317	13.8	269	48
Hooded Crow	5	2.4	5	–
Common Starling	151	2.8	48	103
Chaffinch	183	5.9	138	45
Greenfinch	8	3.2	8	–
Goldfinch	2	1.1	2	–
Linnet	118	44.5	118	–
Lesser Redpoll	1	0.5	1	–
Yellowhammer	10	7.0	10	–
Species	**30**	**45.5**	**29**	**11**
Individuals	**1,792**	**4.6**	**1,163**	**629**

The Woodpigeon is the only bird species that prefers set-aside grasslands in winter (Richard T. Mills).

The Linnet prefers scrub with good vantage points over its territory (Richard T. Mills).

became redundant as a market control measures, and was abolished in 2009. Due to the value that set-aside was demonstrated to provide for environmental objectives, there have been calls for a replacement measure to be developed within European agricultural policies, and these are ongoing within current CAP reform negotiations.

Breeding birds

Due to the small proportion of land under tillage production in Ireland the area of set-aside was correspondingly low. Copland (2009) surveyed only two set-aside plots comprising 2.7 hectares. Nevertheless, Bracken and Bolger (2006), in a study of set-aside in Cos. Laois and Kildare demonstrated that set-aside held significantly higher species diversity and species richness than paired grass or tillage sites during the breeding season. Also, the abundance of Meadow Pipit, Skylark and Woodpigeon were all significantly greater in set-aside areas. Of the set-aside types studied, non-rotational set-aside (i.e. land that was set-aside from production for several years) was more closely associated with several species (Meadow Pipit, Skylark, Common Pheasant, House Sparrow, Magpie, Common Snipe and Common Starling).

Non-breeding birds

McMahon *et al.* (2003) compared set-aside plots during winter in Co. Kildare to fields of winter wheat, stubbles and grassland. The set-aside studied had been sown with clover and rye-grass, which might limit the suitability of this habitat for birds, resulting in only Woodpigeon (which feeds on clover during the winter) preferring this habitat. Studies on set-aside in Europe and North America have generally demonstrated that this habitat can offer substantial opportunities for the conservation of farmland birds (Van Bushkirk and Willi 2004).

Wild-bird cover

Although not a very widespread habitat (probably accounting for about 5,000 hectares in Ireland), wild-bird cover has the potential to deliver substantial benefits to (principally) seed-eating farmland birds, as has been shown in other countries (e.g. Stoate *et al.* 2003; Anderson 2009). Introduced as *LINNET* (Land Invested in Nature – National Eco-Tillage) in Ireland (Keleman 2009) and *Giant Bird Tables* in Northern Ireland (Mawhinney 2009), wild-bird cover aims to provide seed-rich habitats for seed-eating birds during the winter through the planting of seed-rich bearing crops, such as cereals (including oats and triticale), oilseeds (such as linseed and rape), kale or quinoa, that are not harvested but left for the seeds to be eaten by birds. These habitats have been provided by the national agri-environment schemes (the Rural Environment Protection Scheme (REPS) and, more recently, the Agri-Environment Options Scheme (AEOS) in Ireland and in Northern Ireland, the Countryside Management Scheme (CMS). Limited studies on these habitats prior to their introduction on a larger scale through REPS, coupled with studies in other countries, suggest that these habitats have the potential to offer real benefits for seed-eating farmland birds such as Grey Partridge (Kavanagh and Fattebert 2009), House Sparrow, Linnet and Yellowhammer (Stoate *et al.* 2003; Anderson 2009).

The case of the Grey Partridge in Ireland is worthy of specific comment. Despite being widely regarded as a farmland bird throughout its range, in Ireland it is restricted to just one site (Boora, Co. Offaly) that is a former industrial peatland (Buckley *et al.* 2011). Having undergone huge range contraction and population declines in Ireland, the population dropped to fewer than ten pairs in the mid-1990s (Copland and Buckley 2010) at Boora. Recent conservation action at the site, principally establishing wild bird cover crops on these cutaway peatland habitats, along with other conservation measures, has increased the population substantially. Such management has also had beneficial effects for other farmland species, including breeding Northern Lapwing and Skylark, and wintering Linnet, Reed Bunting and Stock Dove (Copland and Buckley 2010). However, Grey Partridge are still a farmland bird, and it is farmland management, especially of arable crops and associated field margins, that will dictate whether Grey Partridge will recolonise parts of its former range (Buckley *et al.* 2011).

A hedgerow landscape at Redcross, Co. Wicklow (Richard Nairn).

Hedgerows, boundaries and field margins

In the farmed landscape, hedgerow habitats contain the greatest number of birds, both in terms of individuals and species (Copland and O'Halloran 2010a). However, other field boundary habitats, in isolation or combined with the presence of hedgerows, are also important for bird populations, such as wet ditches, stone walls or grassy margins (Moles and Breen 1995; Copland and O'Halloran 2010b).

Breeding birds

Many birds associated with hedgerows are probably not specialised farmland birds but are generalists, utilising hedgerow habitats as a surrogate for woodland or woodland-edge habitats which are otherwise rather scarce in the Irish countryside (Pithon *et al.* 2005).

Several studies that have been conducted on birds on Irish farmland have focused on the interaction between hedgerows and breeding bird populations. Generalist species, such as Wren, European Robin, Dunnock, Blackbird and Chaffinch tend to dominate farmed landscapes (Lysaght 1989; Moles and Breen 1995; Flynn 2002; Fennessy and Kelly 2006; Copland 2009), often at higher densities than is seen in the UK (Lysaght 1989; Fennessy and Kelly 2006). Studies have shown that a high density in Ireland of tall, wide and unmanaged hedgerows, favoured breeding habitat for these species, is probably the reason (Lysaght 1989; Moles and Breen 1995; Flynn 2002; Fennessy and Kelly 2006). Hedgerow volume (expressed as a density, comprising elements of hedgerow height, width, length and gappiness) and the number of hedgerow trees were together shown to be the best positive predictor of bird occurrence in 122 farms surveyed throughout Ireland (Copland and O'Halloran 2010b). However, hedgerow trees were also a negative predictor for Meadow Pipit, Reed Bunting and Yellowhammer, indicating that not all farmland bird species prefer very enclosed landscapes. The area of bare soil along field boundaries was also shown to be a positive predictor for certain species, especially those that feed on the ground (such as Wren, Dunnock, European Robin, Blackbird, Song Thrush and Mistle Thrush) and also for Yellow-hammer, suggesting that such habitats provide useful foraging opportunities for such species. A similar result was shown for European Robin (Fennessy and Kelly 2006), which avoided hedgerows with dense basal vegetation.

Non-breeding birds

Studies have shown that other feeding habitats associated with boundaries, such as wet ditches (Moles and Breen 1995) and stone walls (Copland 2009), are important boundary habitat features during the winter. Although hedgerows

The Mistle Thrush is often found foraging on the ground but also benefits from a heavy berry crop (Richard T. Mills).

continue to provide roosting and feeding opportunities for birds during the winter (Copland 2009), their value is probably reduced compared to summer, when there would be more leaves and shelter. The drive to seek food at this time of the year often forces birds into richer foraging habitats that may be less affected by the weather (Moles and Breen 1995).

Farmyards and rural buildings

Farmyards, and other farm buildings, offer a unique habitat in the countryside. It is likely that the buildings provide shelter for many species choosing nest sites. Furthermore, many farmyards are likely to offer substantial feeding opportunities. The presence of livestock in farm buildings, especially over winter, is likely to be important, with many bird species taking advantage of spilt animal feeds. The storage of other material suitable for birds (e.g. bulk grain) may provide food for many species throughout the year. Also, some farmyard habitats, such as nutrient-rich effluent from silage pits, create insect-rich pockets that are utilised by insectivorous birds such as, Grey and Pied Wagtails. Unlike urban areas, where open areas may be limited to gardens and parks, farm buildings are usually adjacent to large areas of open countryside. Also, farmyards and surrounding open spaces are often less disturbed than those associated with other built habitats. As a result, the bird communities utilising farmyards and buildings differ from those in urban areas. Despite the likely value of this habitat type to many species, relatively little work has been undertaken assessing the value of this type of habitat.

Breeding birds

Copland (2009) recorded birds in farmyards and other farm buildings (along with all other farm habitats) in both winter and summer. These built habitats on farmland comprised 1.3% of the total study area. A total of 34 species were recorded during the breeding season (47.2% of all species recorded on farmland in summer). The most abundant species recorded were Barn Swallow, House Sparrow, Common Starling, Jackdaw and Rook (see Table 10.2). In summer, farm buildings are clearly important to several species that selectively nest in buildings such as Barn Swallows, House Martins, Pied Wagtails, House Sparrows and Common Starlings. Feeding opportunities within farmyards are probably also exploited by some of these species as noted below for winter.

It has been shown that older buildings may provide better nesting opportunities for Barn Swallows (Smiddy 2008), although further work is required to determine the exact preferences for this species.

	Table 10.2 Number of individuals and the proportion of the total farmland population for each species recorded in built habitats (data from Copland 2009)			
Species	Winter (No.)	Winter (%)	Summer (No.)	Summer (%)
Common Kestrel	0	–	4	26.7
Merlin	1	25.0	0	0
Common Pheasant	2	2.4	1	1.1
Stock Dove	0	–	1	5.3
Woodpigeon	3	0.4	14	1.7
Collared Dove	24	36.9	21	30.9
Common Swift	0	–	1	2.3
Sand Martin	0	–	4	6.3
Barn Swallow	0	–	579	46.2
House Martin	0	0	37	35.9
Meadow Pipit	20	2.3	6	0.8
Grey Wagtail	30	62.5	12	35.3
Pied Wagtail	108	48.4	89	55.3
Wren	49	4.5	42	2.1
Dunnock	16	2.0	19	2.7
European Robin	70	5.0	65	4.7
Stonechat	0	0	1	1.7
Blackbird	71	3.7	45	2.6
Fieldfare	2	0.1	0	–
Song Thrush	4	0.5	5	1.0
Mistle Thrush	1	0.5	0	–
Willow Warbler	0	–	1	0.1
Goldcrest	7	1.4	2	0.6
Spotted Flycatcher	0	–	2	1.6
Coal Tit	2	0.7	0	0
Blue Tit	11	2.0	24	3.5
Great Tit	9	3.0	8	2.2
Magpie	12	4.7	28	7.3
Jackdaw	386	39.1	327	35.5
Rook	175	9.7	119	5.5

Table 10.2 Number of individuals and the proportion of the total farmland population for each species recorded in built habitats (data from Copland 2009)				
Species	Winter (No.)	Winter (%)	Summer (No.)	Summer (%)
Hooded Crow	46	25.3	5	2.6
Common Starling	307	6.4	451	29.4
House Sparrow	293	50.2	474	70.3
Chaffinch	369	17.0	43	3.4
Greenfinch	34	17.0	5	1.7
Goldfinch	7	4.7	2	1.2
Linnet	7	2.8	5	2.0
Lesser Redpoll	4	2.3	0	0
Bullfinch	2	0.8	0	0
Yellowhammer	19	15.8	9	6.0
Reed Bunting	16	7.5	0	0
Species	**32**	**38.5**	**34**	**47.2**
Individuals	**2,107**	**9.6**	**2451**	**8.0**

Similarly, Chough often use derelict rural and farm buildings in coastal locations for nesting (Trewby *et al.* 2006).

Derelict buildings also provide important nesting and roosting opportunities for raptor populations including Barn Owls, Common Kestrels and Peregrine Falcons. The Barn Owl in particular is intrinsically linked with farmyards and ruined buildings in Ireland. Mature trees with hollow cavities and purpose built nest boxes are used, however comprehensive monitoring has shown that buildings, particularly ruined structures, are the dominant site type for the Irish Barn Owl population (Lusby *et al.* 2009). In 2009, a total of 119 active nest and roost sites were registered nationally, of which 95% were man-made structures. Ruined mansions, castles and ruined farmhouses were the most abundant sites, with a wide diversity of other structures including mills, churches, priories, abbeys, and even occupied dwellings also recorded as part of this study (Lusby *et al.* 2009; Lusby *et al.* 2010). Barn Owls generally require a dry and secluded area for nesting (Shawyer 1998). An assessment of specific nesting locations within a sample of 61 sites showed that chimneys were widely used, with wall cavities and roof spaces also serving as common nest site locations (Lusby *et al.* 2009).

Although the abundance of suitable structures available for Barn Owls varies throughout the country, in general the Irish countryside possesses a wealth of such buildings, ranging from small derelict cottages to impressive historic ruins. Nagle (2007) found that the loss of ruined buildings was important in the decline of Barn Owls in Co. Cork. Numerous studies in the

A Barn Owl brings a rat back to its nest in an old farm building (Richard T. Mills).

A small mixed farm in the Mourne Mountains, Co. Down (Richard Nairn).

Barn Swallows at the nest in a farm building (Karl Partridge).

UK and continental Europe have shown the lack or loss of potential nest sites to be a factor which has negatively impacted Barn Owl populations (Newton 2004; Shawyer 1998; Taylor 1994). Although the Barn Owl is in decline in Ireland (Lynas *et al.* 2007), recent survey work through the Barn Owl Research Project suggests that the availability of nest sites is not a significant contributing factor over large parts of the country. A detailed investigation of all suitable buildings within 17 randomly selected 10km squares in Cos. Cork and Kerry indicated high availability of sites which would provide nesting and roosting opportunities in comparison to the recorded Barn Owl density (Lusby *et al.* 2009).

Common Kestrels also readily use buildings for both nesting and roosting, often occupying the same sites as Barn Owls. Common Kestrel nesting requirements are less specific than those of Barn Owls, and they will use almost any structure as long as there is a suitable nesting area free from disturbance and which provides adequate protection from the elements and predators (Village 1990). A study by Lusby and Watson (2010) highlighted the diversity of nesting situations Common Kestrels can utilise, with nests located in ruined mansions, derelict farmhouses, farm buildings, churches, quarries, cliff faces, old corvid nests and hollow cavities in trees. Peregrine will also readily use man-made structures, and it is likely that this trend will increase with the current Peregrine population expansion. A Peregrine survey conducted in 2002 estimated the national population at 390 occupied territories, of which the majority were cliff nesting

A ruined abbey in Co. Tipperary, a typical nesting site of Barn Owl and Common Kestrel (John Lusby).

(74%), with only 2.8% recorded using man-made structures, the remaining pairs occupying quarry sites (23%)(Madden *et al.* 2009).

Non-breeding birds

In Co. Cork, observations of birds using cattle housing in winter noted a total of 18 species, of which Chaffinch, Pied Wagtail, Feral Pigeon and European Robin were the most commonly encountered (Sleeman *et al.* 2006; Roycroft and Sleeman 2008). In winter, Copland (2009) recorded 32 species (38.5% of all species recorded using farmland in winter – see Table 10.2). The most numerous species were Jackdaw, Chaffinch, Common Starling, House Sparrow, Rook and Pied Wagtail. From these data it is clear that the availability of food to granivorous species is important throughout the year, particularly in winter for finches (17.0% of all Chaffinches and Greenfinches recorded in the winter were in built habitats) and buntings (15.8% of all Yellowhammers were recorded in these habitats). These built habitats are also important for wintering wagtails, with both Grey Wagtail and Pied Wagtail occurring in good numbers compared to other farm habitats. It is likely that farmyards, particularly areas of nutrient-rich run-off from, for example, silage pits offer insect-rich habitats for these species.

Pied Wagtail is a common inhabitant of farmyards where it is attracted by insect prey (Richard T. Mills).

Conclusions

Irish farmland was traditionally characterised by small mixed farms scattered over a landscape that was subdivided into small fields with hedgerows and stone walls. This postcard image still persists in small areas of the country, particularly the west of Ireland, but elsewhere the farming landscape has changed drastically in the last few decades. Intensification of farming practices and the conversion of small farms into much larger holdings has occurred everywhere, and particularly in the east, south and midlands. By contrast, western parts of the country, where farming on poor land means low economic returns, has seen land abandonment – a return to rushy fields and scrub where once there were vibrant small farms. The effects of these changes on the bird populations of farmland are a mirror of what has happened across the rest of Europe. The decline of the Corncrake, the extinction of the Corn Bunting and threats to such species as Yellowhammer illustrate this perfectly. There are also positive changes, however. The reduction in the use of poisons has allowed the spread of the Buzzard and the reintroduction of other birds of prey. The spread of scrub and unmanaged field boundaries is providing additional habitat for many woodland edge species. EU-supported agri-environment schemes (such as REPS and AEOS) and other initiatives (such as the BurrenLife project) have been working with farmers to foster the most appropriate farming practices for conservation of habitats and whole landscapes. Allied to this is a growing awareness of the important role that lowland farmland plays in conservation of Ireland's birds and their habitats. We now know far more about the interaction between these species, their habitats and the crucial role that farming plays, However, with continuing population declines and range contractions for many species, the future for farmland birds in Ireland is not yet secured.

11. Sea Cliffs, Islands and Rocky Coasts

Stephen F. Newton

Introduction

Some of the most famous and dramatic landscapes in Ireland are sea cliffs – the Cliffs of Moher, Co. Clare, and Slieve League, Co. Donegal, to name but two. The former is also one of Ireland's most important seabird colonies; whilst the latter is certainly higher, the avifaunal interest is not so great. An array of rocky offshore islands are equally famous: in Co. Kerry, Skellig Michael, a World Heritage Site, is renowned for the archaeological remains of its monastic settlement – the most remote in Europe – and it is also nearly as well known for its Atlantic Puffin colony. A second Kerry island, Great Blasket, is renowned from its literary perspective, due to the writings of Tomás Ó Criomhthain, Peig Sayers and Maurice O'Sullivan.

Amongst coastal habitats, the separation of hard and soft shores is fairly clear cut: the former comprises sea cliffs and exposures of bedrock without any significant vertical component, whilst the latter, sandy and shingle beaches plus muddy or sandy estuaries, is covered by two other chapters in this book. Here, we look at the interface of bedrock and the sea; in terms of bird habitats, we are examining a major transition from the terrestrial landscape to the marine seascape and those species that exploit this world of rock are literally living on 'the edge'.

Flat bedded limestones and shales at Loop Head,
Co. Clare (Richard T. Mills).

The length of the Irish coastline has been estimated at 7,524km (Nairn 2005, Neilson and Costello 1999). These publications suggest the length of cliff-backed coast to be 828km plus another 250km of soft cliff comprising glacial till and boulder clay. However, there are no clear-cut estimates of non-cliff rocky shore but I estimate that up to 63% of the Irish coastline could be cliff and rocky coast. Overall, sea cliff and rocky shores dominate the coastline of Ireland and, although the number of bird species inhabiting these habitats is modest, the biodiversity value of the populations involved is high, most notably for breeding seabirds. Irish shores also support the largest resident maritime population of the charismatic Chough in Europe. Rocky coasts support the major bulk of the Irish population of some wintering and non-breeding waders, especially Purple Sandpiper, Ruddy Turnstone and a significant proportion of our Oystercatchers. It is also the principal core habitat for a single Irish passerine, the Rock Pipit, whereas other typical passerines can also be found in a wider range of habitats, including rocky and cliffed shores, e.g. the Wren.

The overall distribution of sea cliffs and rocky shores varies around the island of Ireland. The following estimates exclude narrower estuaries, which deeply incise the coast. Approximately 15% of the coast from Carlingford (Louth) to Carnsore Point (Wexford) is hard substrate, including the prominent cliffed headlands of Howth, Dalkey, Bray Head and Wicklow Head. The south coast, defined as Carnsore Point to Mizen Head (Cork), comprises approximately 75% hard shores. The west coast, from Mizen Head to Lough Foyle (Donegal), supports many wide but deeply incised bays, harbours and estuaries separated by, usually cliffed, long peninsulas e.g. Sheep's Head, Beara, Iveragh and Dingle. There are also long stretches of high cliff such as the Cliffs of Moher, the north Mayo coast from Benwee Head to Killala Bay and Slieve League. Hard rocky coasts comprise about 50% of the overall shore length. In Northern Ireland, Co. Antrim is dominated by cliffed coastline, while in Co. Down the outer shore of the Ards Peninsula is largely rocky; further south, hard substrate is present from Killard Point to St John's Point and along the Mourne coast from the south of Newcastle to Kilkeel.

Bedrock geology exerts a fundamental control on the suitability of sea cliffs and rocky shores as bird habitats, while the structural geology (faults, fracturing, bedding planes, joints, cleavage) determines the presence of cliffs or lower elevation rocky shores. Post-glacial uplift (isostatic) and various forces of erosion are also important agents in shaping the coastline. Geological and geomorphological factors will be returned to in the paragraphs below when dealing with the habitat requirements of different avian groupings and individual species.

In structuring this chapter, some rather arbitrary splits have to be made: coastal cliffs are highly variable mosaics of different habitat types, in which vertical or sub-vertical rocks are the principal component, though vegetated areas occur in steep or flat areas where soil is able to develop or accumulate. Such vegetation can be lush due to the fertilising effect of seabird guano in the vicinity of colonies. There is also usually a transitional zone at the top of most cliffs, where a cap of boulder clay or other subsoil occurs and likewise, at the base, talus slopes can also be partially vegetated. Sea stacks, whether attached to mainland cliffs or isolated and surrounded by water, provide isolated patches of terrestrial habitat in a coastal setting. Thus, within the coastal cliff zone, the following habitats can occur: flatter **ground** (both rocky and soily, with

Razorbills on the Great Saltee, Co. Wexford (Richard T. Mills).

The Rock Pipit is present on cliff habitats throughout the year (Richard T. Mills).

or without vegetation), the cliffs themselves with bare ledges and **crevices**, soily slopes, which provide opportunities for **burrowing** species, **scree** or talus slopes at the base or intermediate levels and, although rare in Ireland, **trees** can grow on some sea cliffs. Having mentioned sea stacks as, almost, integral parts of cliffs, rockier coastal islands can be viewed as cliff habitat with a higher proportion of flatter soily/vegetated ground in the interior. Further rocky habitats that are covered here include intertidal sloping rock or platforms, often at the base of cliffs and storm-worked supratidal boulder beaches.

Resident species, habitat restricted

Few Irish species are year-round resident and almost cliff-restricted; the Rock Pipit is one and perhaps another is island-restricted populations of the Wren. Both can, and do, nest and forage in this habitat. Wrens prefer broken rocky cliffs and steep well-vegetated slopes and gullies with talus in a coastal setting, where scrubby or taller vegetation occurs in clumps, patches or thickets. In most settings, plant species involved would be bramble, bracken and umbellifers, but sometimes ling heather can predominate. Although Wrens can eke out a living on cliffs, finding a sufficient arthropod and arachnid food resource there, the majority of Ireland's Wrens live in woodland, scrub, hedgerow and gardens. However, there is certainly an ecotype resident on steep, cliffy or rocky but isolated islands such as Skellig Michael, Inishtearaght and Inishtrahull. Wrens on Tory Island and the Inishkea islands in Mayo, for example, have a wider array of available habitats, including machair and farmland. In the more remote archipelagos of Scotland, Wrens have become sufficiently differentiated from their mainland cousins to form distinct subspecies, e.g. the St Kilda, Hebridean, Fair Isle and Shetland subspecies. Most of Ireland's remotest islands are probably too small to permit the evolution of differentiated forms.

Rock Pipits are the 'ultimate' Irish cliff passerine, and they rarely occur away from this narrow coastal zone. On some islands, e.g. Tory and Inishbofin, birds can be found foraging 'inland', albeit not far from the sea. However, such inland feeding is not regular. Their nests are usually in crevices, but vacated burrows could conceivably be used. If available, Rock Pipits can also forage on narrow pebbly beaches in coves and caves, where seaweed strandlines are present. Grassier cliff-top areas are well utilised as foraging habitat on both island and mainland situations. Amongst near passerines, Rock Doves nest and roost on sea cliffs and in caves; some clearly forage on more vegetated cliffs in both summer and winter. Although they have the potential to move to more inland habitat types to forage, whether they do so or not is not known. Now that populations of wild type or 'true' Rock Doves are difficult to find, the introgression of feral pigeons has no doubt increased the likelihood of using non-cliff habitats for foraging. For example, P. Smiddy (in litt.) has seen 'Rock Doves' several kilometres inland on cultivated ground. The islands of Inishbofin and Inishshark are one of the few places left with pure Rock Doves; their feeding zone and habitat preference is still very much 'beside-the-sea'. They spend most of their time along cliffed coast and also descend on to the shore. They feed by very rapid picking and have a slightly longer and slimmer bill than the Feral Pigeon. They have also been recorded feeding on heather, seed heads of Thrift and among seaweed (A. McGeehan, pers. comm.).

A third resident passerine, the Chough, is also a sea cliff specialist, with the capability to utilise cliffs for all its immediate needs. The vast majority of Irish breeding Choughs nest on sea cliffs (Cabot 1965, Bullock *et al.* 1983, Berrow *et al.* 1993, Gray *et al.* 2003). Choughs are also communal roosting species and utilise dramatic sea cliffs as winter and non-breeding roosts. Glen Head is a spectacular roost in south-west Donegal, as are several in Kerry: Brandon Creek (below Mount Brandon), Sybil Point, Slea Head, the red cliffs at Inch, Bray Head (Valentia) and so on. (Trewby *et al.* 2006).

Although some pairs of Choughs are probably reliant on their sea cliff-based territories year round, others will spend a larger proportion of time foraging on short sward, agricultural habitats and occasionally cereal stubbles. Also, in their first two years of life, Choughs live in flocks and most of the better known Irish flocks heavily utilise dune habitats for a significant part of the annual cycle, usually late summer to early winter.

Resident species, wider habitat tolerance

Until the recent reintroduction of Golden and White-tailed Eagles, only two raptors regularly nested on Irish sea cliffs: Peregrines and Common Kestrels. However, Common Buzzard, in its early colonising years, was a cliff-nester in north-east Antrim and the pair of Golden Eagles that nested at Fair Head in the 1950s also built on a sea cliff. For Peregrines, a much higher proportion of the national population nests on sea cliffs: 44% of pairs in the core areas in 2002 (Madden *et al.* 2009). Coastal Peregrines can be resident in their sea cliff territories year round and they will utilise cliff-breeding birds as prey in summer months when seabirds and Rock Doves are present. They undoubtedly prey on passing flocks of racing pigeons and these can be the most important prey item in the diet of those birds that breed on pigeon flight paths. On the west coast some pairs specialise in other locally breeding seabirds, even nocturnal species, e.g. Manx Sheawaters are taken on Inishbofin/Inishshark. Later in the summer and autumn, Peregrines can forage at sea, locating passing seabirds from cliff top vantage points – Leach's Storm Petrel, Grey Phalarope and Arctic Skua are amongst documented prey (A.McGeehan, pers. comm.).

Common Kestrels, on the other hand, mostly forage over agricultural land or low-lying coastal habitats such as dunes, machair and shingle beaches and only use cliff ledges for nesting. Some of the longer established Golden Eagle pairs have selected coastal home ranges that include large sections of sea cliff, e.g. Slieve Tooey in Donegal (Golden Eagle Trust website). However, exact locations of roost sites are not publicly known and could be either true sea cliffs or inland cliffs in the same general vicinity. White-tailed Eagles are being reintroduced from an inland release point in Kerry, but the question remains whether this will influence their eventual choice of cliff sites for nesting (inland versus coastal) when the population commences breeding.

In addition to Choughs, three other Irish corvids nest on sea cliffs: the Raven and, occasionally, the Hooded Crow and Jackdaw. In the case of the Raven, sea cliffs are used solely for nesting and most

Choughs are social birds that utilise cliffs for all their immediate needs (Richard T. Mills).

Common Kestrels use cliffs for nesting but forage elsewhere (Richard T. Mills).

coastal foraging in the breeding season is done on the actual shoreline for crustaceans, bivalves and gastropods (Berrow 1992). Some of the predominant large mammalian component of their diet could have been scavenged from cliff-fall victims. Small numbers of the other two species may nest on sea cliffs. The Stock Dove is a species mostly associated with farmland. It has become fairly scarce in Ireland and its typical nesting habitat would be tree holes or ivy-covered walls (pers. obs.); Hutchinson (1989) states that they have also been recorded nesting in cliff crevices and even rabbit burrows. Hutchinson did not specify whether the latter were in coastal locations or inland. However, since that time, I have recorded them nesting in a hole in a drystone granite wall on Rockabill Island (Dublin), a very marine location, about 3m up in a cavity regularly used by Black Guillemots (Hulsman *et al.* 2007). In June 2011, I observed one emerge from a cliff-top burrow (either rabbit or Atlantic Puffin) on the south side of Lambay Island; it flew a few metres and onto a spur and immediately a Feral Pigeon appeared and vigorously displayed to the 'uninterested' Stock Dove. The Rockabill bird had a 6km+ commute over sea to the nearest suitable foraging habitat, whereas small numbers of Stock Doves are present on Lambay most of the year. It has been suggested that Stock Dove first bred in Ireland on the Copeland Islands off Co. Down. Although they subsequently spread country-wide, recent massive decreases in Northern Ireland mean that the pendulum has gone nearly full circle and only the Copeland's population is still in 'good heart'. There, they mostly breed down rabbit holes but occasionally also in the undergrowth beneath dense stands of Soft Rush. At Copeland Bird Observatory, they regularly nest in Black Guillemot boxes. Some of the nesters on Big Copeland certainly commute to feed on the adjacent coast of Co. Down (A. McGeehan, pers. comm.).

Summer migrant species, wider habitat tolerance

Three passerine migrants that breed in Ireland and winter in Africa use sea cliffs for nesting during the spring and summer. House Martins principally nest under eaves of houses (Hutchinson 1989), though small colonies of birds continue to nest in natural habitat under sea cliff overhangs, for example near Dunmore East in Co. Waterford (pers. obs.) and at The Gobbins cliffs, Co. Antrim (on the cliffed coastline of Islandmagee). These birds certainly hunt for insects along the cliffs, but also will forage over adjacent farmland. Northern Wheatears are widely distributed on vegetated sea cliffs and rocky islands on the south and west coasts and also Donegal. They are relatively scarce elsewhere on the north coast, though a few nest on Rathlin Island in Co. Antrim. The broad distribution in Britain is very similar (Conder 1989) and in the study island of Skokholm off Pembrokeshire in Wales, 86% of nests were in burrows and 14% in holes in walls or under rocks. On Irish islands, nesting in burrows is also recorded, though on Puffin Island off Kerry the approximately 20 pairs probably nest equally under inland rocks, on very steep cliff-top, broken, rocky slopes (pers. obs.) and in screes and rockfall. Interestingly, there are no stone walls on this island. Northern Wheatears are very common on Inishbofin (Co. Galway); some nest down rabbit burrows but most use holes at or near ground level in stone walls. Finally, one of Ireland's rarest breeding birds, the Ring Ouzel, occasionally nests on maritime cliffs, particularly in south-west Donegal on the Glencolumbkille Peninsula where ling heather is present, such as on the Slieve League area and Slieve Tooey (Cox *et al.* 2002).

House Martins still nest in caves and under cliff overhangs although the majority are found on the eaves of houses (Richie Lort).

Breeding seabirds

In terms of numbers and population level importance for a particular avian group, sea cliffs and rocky coasts are vitally important for breeding seabirds. Virtually all of Ireland's 24 species of breeding seabird have been regularly reported as nesting on sea cliffs and rocky islands; the only full exceptions are Black-headed and Mediterranean Gulls. Two of the terns, Sandwich and Little, mostly nest on dunes, beaches and flat islands, though in the case of Little Terns, some nest on limestone pavement near the shoreline in the Aran Islands (Hannon *et al.* 1997). Amongst the other 20 species, all show a greater or lesser dependence on sea cliffs and rocky shores and islands for nesting and in this broad zone all microhabitats and structural settings are utilised by one or more of the twenty. Although the majority of seabirds do not utilise the rocky habitats for foraging, the large *Larus* gulls and Great Skua all take eggs and depredate chicks of other seabirds. They also eat shellfish on rocky shores (e.g. mussels) and in the case of Great Black-backed Gulls and Great Skuas, depredate other breeding seabirds such as Atlantic Puffins, Black-legged Kittiwakes, terns (e.g. Hudson 1982). The diet of most seabirds comprises fish, though smaller European Storm Petrels probably consume a significant proportion of zooplankton (D'Elbée and Hémery 1998). Given that seabirds are virtually all colonial, then one would expect the quality, i.e. abundance of suitable forage fish, of surrounding seas as important in determining the numbers that breed and the outcome of nesting attempts – i.e. breeding productivity. Returning to the geological theme, the type of rock and its structure (bedding, joints and cleavage) influence the species that nest on a cliff or island. On the east coast of Ireland, rocky headlands and islands are rather scarce and this spreads the population out to some degree and may limit the likelihood of over exploitation of fish resources. In the south and west, cliff habitats are more common, with the result that not all are used by nesting seabirds.

The Fulmar is a virtually ubiquitous species nesting in varying densities on all rocky coasts in Ireland. It was first discovered nesting in Mayo only 100 years ago (Fisher 1952) in 1911. It is able to utilise a wider variety of cliff types than any other seabird species. It can use vertical bare rock with small ledges and crevices as on Great Skellig, through to very low boulder clay cliffs as on Shenick Island in County Dublin, where it nests in the cavities left by boulders that have fallen out of the clay. On Clare Island (Mayo), one of Ireland's largest colonies, it nests on very steep grassy cliffs. Its ability to nest in these more accessible locations is no doubt related to its habit of defending itself and its offspring by ejecting or spitting a stream of hot and very pungent stomach oil at the intruder. Unguarded Fulmar chicks also have this

The Fulmar nests widely on cliffs and rocky shores (Richard T. Mills).

capability. However, relative to most other seabirds on cliffs, the Fulmar often occupies some of the most protected and enclosed niches and these sites are well defended throughout most of the year. This provides protection both from the elements and aerial predators. A clear day in January can see all sites at a potential colony occupied by bickering birds, almost five months before the first egg is laid. Fulmars also have one of the longest breeding seasons and they are often the last species to leave colonies at some point in late August when their young fledge. Fulmars begin to gather on cliffs as early as late October and come and go depending on weather. On windy days more materialise from out at sea as they appear to like to cavort in the updraughts. By mid-December they are scarce but a resurgence is evident on the cliffs from mid-January.

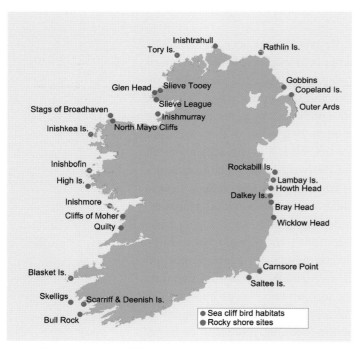

Map of the main sea cliffs, islands and rocky shore sites mentioned in the text

Great Cormorant (left) and Shag, showing the plumage differences (John Coveney).

Although seabird colonies on cliffs or rocky islands seem chaotic places, an often asked question is how each species finds its niche and each individual finds its place. Most have slightly different requirements and it is the interspecific timing of events that sorts out this 'land grab'. A typical Irish sea cliff colony usually includes Fulmars, Shags, Black-legged Kittiwakes, Common Guillemots and Razorbills, with a scattering of Great Black-backed and European Herring Gulls. As already covered above, the Fulmars have selected and occupied the most sheltered ledges and cavities very early in the year and one or both of the pair are available to defend that site when the other species return from their wintering grounds in the surrounding seas. Fulmars are very poor walkers, so they usually do not nest at the back of wide ledges and at most sites they can alight, more or less, on the lip of the eventual nest scrape.

Shags build a larger nest and on mainland sea cliffs this needs a secure foundation on a wider ledge, usually with some protection from the elements, with sites in caves or under overhangs often preferred. However, a few Shags have been recorded nesting in Elder trees growing on the north cliffs of Lambay (Merne 1993). Shags commence their nest cycle, nest-building and egg-laying, earlier in the spring than most other sea cliff inhabitants, which generally all lay eggs in May. Timing of laying varies by colony and can be significantly earlier in south and west coast colonies, such as Great Saltee and Inishbofin, where active nests are found in March and fledged young seen in April; elsewhere, laying usually commences in late April but active nests are still present at the end of July.

The next significant arrivals at our typical colony are the Razorbills in late April. Their eggs are laid in more sheltered niches on larger ledges, in crevices and under boulders at cliff bases. The last two species to return are Common Guillemots and Black-legged Kittiwakes, usually around the beginning of May. The Common Guillemots usually 'smother' the remaining horizontal or sub-horizontal ledges and rocky slopes, filling in around the well-established Shags and Razorbills. Numerically, Guillemots outnumber Razorbills at most Irish colonies by about 10–20:1. Their nest sites are simply a space measuring about 15cm by 20cm and breeders virtually touch each other. They have a distinct incubating pose and frequent bowing seems to be a means of placating incubating neighbours.

Black-legged Kittiwakes build their nests from seaweed and other coastal and terrestrial vegetation on the more sheer parts of cliffs, and they only require a small protrusion in the rock to act as a foundation. On the other hand, they will use much wider ledges if Common Guillemots are not present at a particular colony. When large *Larus* gulls nest on true sea cliffs they tend to nest rather solitarily, on vegetated ledges, spurs, tops of sea stacks and towers. If such habitats are unavailable, then they will occupy sites on the top of cliffs. Great Cormorant and Northern Gannet colonies are fewer in number, but most tend to be very large, particularly for the Northern Gannet. There are now six Irish Northern Gannet colonies, with five on the east and south coasts and a single, very small proto-colony on the west. All are on islands and in two cases, Little Skellig in Kerry and the Bull Rock in Cork, Northern Gannets dominante 90%+ of the available nesting space. Little Skellig is a dramatic sight, with 30,000 nesting pairs of Northern Gannets and many more non-breeders occupying every ledge, ridge, platform and slab on a pyramidal rocky bastion that is almost devoid of terrestrial vegetation. This island 'erupts' from the Atlantic between two more diverse islands, Skellig Michael and Puffin Island, with respect to bird habitats. Still, where ledges are too narrow for Northern Gannets, a handful of typical cliff nesters, Common Guillemots, Razorbills and Black-legged Kittiwakes find space to nest.

Clare Island (Mayo) has been recorded as an Irish Northern Gannet colony since 1978 (Preston 1979). Here the Northern Gannets nest on a small stack off the northern cliffs and for no obvious reason the colony has not developed; i.e. increased at a near constant rate, despite all other colonies doing so. This is unusual as there is a large gap in the geographic range with no other Atlantic colonies until St Kilda off the Outer Hebrides or Ailsa Craig in the Firth of Clyde are reached. The latter is really in the northern reaches of the Irish Sea. Northern Gannet colonies in the western Irish Sea and Celtic Sea are a far less dominant feature in each island's cliff-nesting avifauna, though in each Northern Gannets dominate in one particular part of the island. On Great Saltee, most breeding Northern Gannets occur on the highest point of the island in the south-west corner. The bulk of the birds occupy very steep slopes rather than vertical cliffs, with the uppermost birds extending onto soily ground on the interior plateau. Such ground was vegetated prior to occupation by Northern Gannets, but now is an area

Black-legged Kittiwakes at a cliff-nesting colony (Richard T. Mills).

Every space is occupied in a Northern Gannet colony (Richard T. Mills).

of bare soil. On Ireland's Eye, Dublin, the Northern Gannets originally colonised a sea stack off the north-east corner of the island. This presently supports about 300 pairs (O. Merne, pers. comm.), and a secondary area on the adjacent main island is now occupied. One presumes the original colonists of Ireland's Eye came from the Grassholm colony off Pembrokeshire or from Great Saltee. Although the Dublin colony continues to grow at a reduced rate a further group of recruiting Northern Gannets jumped to the neighbouring island of Lambay in 2006, approx 10–12km to the north. They initially occupied a spur off the north cliffs, displacing hundreds of Common Guillemots who usually nested on the sloping sides and top of the promontory. Nesting by Northern Gannets commenced the next year, 2007, and the colony has continued to grow to the east and west along the interface between the top of the sea cliffs and the steep vegetated slopes with rocky outcrops. The latter are the home to the

Great Cormorants space their nests evenly throughout the breeding colony (Richard T. Mills).

Introduced American Mink have been found in several important seabird colonies, representing a serious threat to ground-nesting birds (Richard T. Mills).

island's Great Cormorant population. There is almost unlimited grassy slope-type habitat available on Lambay and the Northern Gannet colony could well match the size of the Great Saltee colony in a few years. After a couple of years, Common Guillemots recolonised some of their former territory and now cohabit with the Northern Gannets on the original spur, filling the interstices between the larger, evenly spaced Northern Gannet nests.

Coastal nesting Great Cormorants utilise a wide variety of habitat types in Ireland. The majority are on islands, and most of them are long established, but even within a small geographical area there is a wide choice of habitats and settings. A significant part of the Irish population nests on the north County Dublin islands of St Patrick's (off Skerries), Lambay and Ireland's Eye (Merne and Madden 1999, 2000) with a combined total of *c.* 2,000 pairs present in recent years (Mitchell *et al.* 2004). These typify the wide choice of habitat settings. Thulla, a low-lying islet off the south-east corner of Ireland's Eye, composed of very crenulated rocky terrain, supports a dense sub-population, with the residue on the very steep north slopes, very similar to the setting of the Lambay colony, above the true sea cliffs. On St Patrick's, the Great Cormorant colony is on the vegetated boulder clay slopes and the interior plateau of the island – the vegetation is usually rapidly killed off by the seabirds' guano. Very few Great Cormorant colonies are found on the true sea cliffs but one of the most recently established on Bray Head (in 2010) is in such a setting. It is also one of the very few mainland colonies, though other small ones are present in Waterford and mid- and east Cork (Smiddy 1998).

Islands, by their very nature, even if only a few hundred metres from the mainland, provide a refuge from several typical predators of ground-nesting birds. These include Red Foxes, Stoats and Pine Martens, and the paucity of trees can result in reduced densities or an absence of Hooded Crows. Most of the large *Larus* gull colonies are in the interior of larger islands, but populations of European Herring Gulls in particular have declined in recent decades (Madden and Newton 2004), and the species is presently Red-listed (Lynas *et al.* 2007). Nesting habitat requirements of the three species are usually similar, with the two smaller species, Herring and Lesser Black-backed, usually more colonial. Great Black-backed Gulls often nest solitarily on cliff tops but they can also be colonial, e.g. on Lambay and Puffin Islands. The solitary nesting gulls in some settings (e.g. Great Saltee), have been shown to be more active predators of other birds. They either kill them directly for food (young auks, adult Atlantic Puffins and Manx Shear-waters) or act as kleptoparasites, harassing others to drop prey being brought in for their mates or chicks. Colonial birds tend to use other foraging behaviours, scavenging behind fishing boats or catching their own fish and shellfish along the shoreline (see Hudson 1982 for a discussion). Some inshore islands have recently been colonised by the non-native American Mink. These voracious carnivores can reach islands up to 2km from the mainland coast and can have a devastating effect on smaller gull (Common and Black-headed) and tern colonies (see Craik 1995 for their impact in Scotland). American Mink were first recorded on Puffin Island in summer 2007 (Lars Soerink, in litt.) and their impact on the internationally important Manx Shearwater, European Storm Petrel and Atlantic Puffin colonies has yet to be determined. The island was visited in late April 2011 and abundant evidence of Mink presence was located: several piles of Manx Shearwater feathers and a freshly killed European Storm Petrel and Common Gull. It would appear that these mustelids can survive the winter on a diet of Rabbit and then exploit the burrow and crevice nesting seabirds in the summer. A post Seabird 2000 reassessment of the breeding populations of Puffin Island is urgently needed. Irish islands support many mixed colonies of the two similar-sized burrow nesting species, Manx Shearwater and Atlantic Puffin. On the east coast (Lambay and Great Saltee) colony size and breeding success is probably severely limited by the presence of rats, both Black and Brown Rats on Lambay and Brown Rat only on Saltee. The presence of rats probably explains why European Storm Petrels are absent, despite the presence of suitable habitat, given that they are present on several rat-free Welsh islands on the opposite side of the Irish Sea.

Atlantic Puffin on the Great Skellig (Richard T Mills).

The key Irish islands for Manx Shearwaters, European Storm Petrels and Atlantic Puffins are the Kerry archipelagos comprising the Skellig and Puffin group, the Blasket Islands and, to a lesser extent, Scariff and Deenish. The cliff-nesting seabird avifauna of these is generally poor, with Common Guillemot, Razorbill and Black-legged Kittiwake colonies limited to the bedding plane ledges or faulted zones with inlets and caves. However, at nightfall the interior of the islands become alive with the sounds of shearwaters and petrels returning to nesting burrows and crevices to take over incubation duties or feed their young. Most Manx Shearwaters nest in burrows on the vegetated slopes, but a few also nest under piles of slabby rockfall debris that are a common product of weathering in the Devonian Old Red Sandstone rocks of the area. European Storm Petrels also utilise this habitat type, but old stone walls and the buildings and steps of the monastery on Skellig Michael form ideal nesting habitats. Indeed, on that island about 50% of the population of 10,000 pairs nest in man-made habitat (Mitchell and Newton 2004). Wherever a network of old walls is present on west coast islands, European Storm Petrels are invariably present, as long as rats are absent. The combination of walls and monastic settlements is also present on High Island (Galway), Inishglora (Mayo) and Inishmurray (Sligo). The largest colony of European Storm Petrels in Ireland is on Inishtooskert in the Blaskets. Most of the 27,000 pairs nest in natural habitat, with some even nesting under the basal stems of ling heather (Beatty *et al.* 1997). European Storm Petrels on Inish na Bro have been recorded nesting under heather in holes in the peaty soil (Smiddy 2003). Ireland has a single Leach's Storm Petrel colony, on the Stags of Broadhaven (Mayo). These dramatic stacks have a relatively thick skin of peat on their upper slopes and it is here that the Leach's Storm Petrels dig their burrows. At the other extreme, islands with boulder beaches extending above high-water mark can support nesting petrels, e.g. Inishglora (Mayo) and Beginish (Kerry; Smiddy *et al.* 2000).

One of the most recent colonists of west coast islands is the Great Skua. The first birds settled on several medium-sized islands off Connemara and south Mayo in 2000 (Newton *et al.* 2002). Birds are still nesting at these sites, but several others have settled in north-west Mayo and breeding is also quite likely on some Donegal islands. The national population is probably 10 (possibly 15) pairs in 2011. Great Skuas usually nest in better vegetated, inland and higher parts of islands where there is cover for nests, eggs and young.

Black Guillemots display on the pier at Bangor, Co. Down (Richard Nairn).

Common Terns form large nesting colonies (Richard T. Mills).

Although rarely perceived as a colonial bird, the Black Guillemot is very much a breeding bird of rocky coasts. In spring, April to early May, Black Guillemots congregate at favoured pre-breeding places in the early morning, where they presumably pair up. Birds disperse from these sites later in the morning to forage and select nest sites in cracks and fissures in caves, under boulders and in a variety of holes, often in man-made structures, such as quaysides, harbours, stone walls, piers and lighthouses. Rockabill, a small 0.9-hectare granite island off the north Dublin coast dominated by a lighthouse and associated buildings, supports a breeding population of about 75 pairs. Only about 15 pairs nest in natural habitat, a further 40 pairs in holes in lighthouse walls and the remainder have accepted custom-made wooden boxes placed in preferred nesting areas. Black Guillemots occur around all Irish coasts, where rocky habitat is available. Their distribution on south and west coasts is nearly continuous, but on east and north coasts the population is disjunct, though where rocky headlands occur, such as Bray Head and Wicklow Head, numbers can be high (see Madden *et al.* 2001).

The final group of breeding seabirds on Irish rocky islands is the terns; these have been systematically surveyed in 1984 and 1995 (Whilde 1985, Hannon *et al.* 1997) and there is annual monitoring on key east coast colonies in both Northern Ireland and the Republic. All terns, except the Little Tern, nest on islands; in the west, Arctic Tern colonies predominate, such as in the Slyne Head area, the islands of Blasket Sound, and Rock Island at the west end of the Aran Islands (Galway). Most west coast Sandwich and Little Tern colonies are in other habitats, e.g. machair, and are covered in other chapters. Arguably, one of the most important seabird colonies in Europe is the Dublin island of Rockabill (Casey *et al.* 1995, Newton 2004) In 2010, bare granite rock and limited earth-covered ground on this island supported 1,093 pairs of Roseate, 1,940 pairs of Common and 234 pairs of Arctic Terns, a grand total of 3,267 pairs of terns. For the Roseate Tern, this is the single most important colony in Europe, supporting 80%+ of the population, excluding the Portuguese Azorean islands. Roseate Terns usually lay eggs under boulders or vegetation, but on Rockabill at least half now nest in boxes laid out in terraces in more open areas. This permits much better viewing of the birds and their nesting attempts, and particularly their field-readable rings. By this means, key demographic information is recorded, such as survival rates, age at first breeding, colony of origin, nest site and partner faithfulness (Newton and Crowe 2000, Ratcliffe *et al.* 2004, Ratcliffe *et al.* 2008). A small number of Roseate Terns has also become established on granite islands at Dalkey, south Dublin, nesting in boxes deployed in a traditional Common and Arctic Tern colony.

Winter visitors, rocky shores

Waders and other waterbirds of rocky shores have not received the same attention as their estuarine counterparts. However, pioneering surveys of the former habitat type were made on the Northern Ireland coast during the Winter Shorebird Count in 1984–85 (Moser and Prys-Jones 1988) and on the west coast in 1987 by Green *et al.* (1988). Further analysis of the latter data set on habitat preferences was undertaken by Kirby *et al.* (1991). These studies identified the importance of boulder beaches and intertidal rock for Purple Sandpipers, Oystercatchers and more surprisingly, Grey Plovers. Purple Sandpipers are almost wholly restricted to this habitat type, although in County Clare they utilise sandy beaches covered with a thick deposit of wrack (Foster *et al.* 2010) alongside Ruddy Turnstones, Sanderlings and Dunlins.

Purple Sandpiper (in front) and Dunlin (behind) are common waders on rocky shores (Richard T. Mills).

The first comprehensive survey of non-estuarine habitat was undertaken in the winter of 1997–98 (named NEWS, Non-Estuarine Coastal Waterfowl Survey; Colhoun and Newton 2000, Colhoun *et al.* 2008) and was repeated nine years later in the 2006–07 winter. These were especially important for establishing the overall population sizes of coastal wintering waterbirds when combined with the number counted annually on estuaries and harbours by I-WeBS (Irish Wetland Bird Survey) and UK-WeBS (in Northern Ireland). A wide variety of waterbirds can be recorded on rocky shores but for many of these, such occurrences will often be short pauses on migration, e.g. Eurasian Whimbrel and Eurasian Curlew, or for roosting e.g. Northern Lapwing and European Golden Plover, or temporary refuge after disturbance on preferred muddy or sandy habitats. Regular surveys on Lambay Island (Madden *et al.* 2004) have shown that small numbers of Common Redshank and Eurasian Whimbrel regularly spend the winter on rocky habitats. Blue Mussels need a hard substrate upon which to anchor and flatter mussel beds are ideal foraging habitat for species such as Oystercatcher and Common Eider.

Having covered breeding terns on Rockabill in the previous section, the same island provides excellent intertidal rock covered in barnacles and mussels, ideal habitat for several non-breeding wader species including Purple Sandpiper and Ruddy Turnstone. This concentration of wintering waders on a small rocky island has attracted the attention of Merlins, who sometimes reside on the island for up to a week exploiting small passerine migrants, but in one January at least ten Ruddy Turnstones were depredated (Pierce and Roe 2006). Other waders occasionally forage on rocky shores, e.g. Dunlin and Red Knot and, in one recent year (2006), exceptional numbers of non-breeding, over-summering Red Knot utilised Rockabill extensively. Although they principally roosted on the island, some were noted foraging on barnacles, mussel spat and possibly more mobile fauna such as amphipods. The peak count of Red Knot on the island was 1,500 (Baer and Newton 2006), when in a typical summer only a handful would be recorded (Rockabill Tern Reports, BirdWatch Ireland).

One wintering species not previously mentioned, which principally occurs on west coast rocky islands is the Barnacle Goose. The majority of occupied islands are uninhabited, well vegetated and tend to be those at the flatter end of the range (Merne and Walsh 1994, Walsh and Crowe 2008). Islands are used for both grazing and roosting and those with the largest flocks often have machair or short-sward maritime grassland. Cabot and West (1983) have studied the population dynamics of the Barnacle Goose wintering on the Inishkea Islands, Co. Mayo, since 1961 and this study is

Barnacle geese winter on numerous offshore islands on the west coast of Ireland (Karl Partridge).

The European Storm Petrel nests in a burrow and only comes ashore under cover of darkness (Richard T. Mills).

continuing at present with satellite tagging of birds to follow their migrations from Ireland through Iceland to the breeding grounds in East Greenland. Cabot (2009) suggests that density-dependent factors may be limiting the population growth. He found that winter temperatures close to the Inishkea Islands were correlated with subsequent goose productivity on the breeding grounds. Mild weather allowed good growth of grasses, so that in winter the birds built up critical energy reserves for breeding. Cabot (2009) records that, on the Inishkea Islands, the geese feed mainly on white clover stolons during the autumn, switching to red fescue and smooth meadow grass as the stolons become depleted. While the overall population has continued to expand from 8,300 birds in 1959 to 70,501 in March 2008, the Irish wintering component of the population has increased at a much slower rate (Walsh and Crowe 2008).

Overview

In reviewing the bird-habitat associations on sea cliffs and rocky shores in Ireland, one recurring question comes to mind: do Ireland and its offshore islands differ in any significant way when compared to its north-east Atlantic neighbours – Britain, northern France, the Faeroes and Iceland? There are many similarities, the overall suite of cliff-nesting seabirds in the North Atlantic is much the same, though a few patterns are discernible under closer scrutiny. Great Skuas and Arctic Terns are most abundant in northern Scotland, the Faeroes and southern Iceland. The Great Skua is currently colonising Ireland but is absent from Wales, western England and northern France. The number and size of Leach's Storm Petrel colonies increases towards the north with the core of the population occupying the St Kilda archipelago and southern Iceland. On the other hand, Sandwich, Roseate and Common Tern colonies are more frequent in the southern parts, including Ireland. Ireland would appear to provide the optimum habitat for the European Storm Petrel and the small island of Inishtooskert currently supports the largest quantitatively documented colony in the world (27,000 pairs). The Faeroese islands reportedly hold some massive petrel colonies but to date, tape-playback has not been used to confirm the existing population estimates, which are really qualitative guesswork.

Ireland does appear to differ from adjacent areas in Wales and western Scotland in the prevalence of highly mixed colonies of Manx Shearwaters, Atlantic Puffins, European Storm Petrels together with ubiquitous rabbits in the Kerry islands (Skellig Michael, Puffin, Scariff-Deenish and the Blaskets). Through the tape-playback methodology (see Mitchell *et al.* 2004), we have robust estimates of the numbers of nesting petrels and shearwaters but we still lack an appropriate method for estimating the numbers of Atlantic Puffins nesting on these very steep and difficult to access islands. This situation contrasts with the Pembrokeshire islands, Rum and St Kilda where each species has a more discernible, almost monospecific, colony-nesting area.

From a conservation perspective, Ireland's sea cliffs and rocky islands support very significant parts of the world population of the following species (in descending order): European Storm Petrel (25%), Manx Shearwater (13%), *carbo* Great Cormorant (10%), Northern Gannet (9%), Razorbill (7%) and Shag (5%). The Kerry islands form a 'super-colony' of 30,000 pairs of Manx Shearwaters that ranks third in importance behind the Pembrokeshire islands and Rum in the Scottish Hebrides (Newton *et al.* 2004). The same group of Kerry islands is home to about 75,000 pairs of European Storm Petrels, about three quarters of the Irish population and between 10% and 40% of the world population – the imprecision due to the lack of census data from the Faeroes. The Irish south coast supports three significant Northern Gannet colonies with Little Skellig ranking fifth (in Britain and Ireland) behind St Kilda, Bass Rock, Ailsa Craig and Grassholm.

The fate of the European Roseate Tern population lies in Irish hands: Rockabill is the engine that drives this population and also supports a very large Common Tern colony (2,000 pairs), which must be one of the most aggressive in the world. All Irish coasts, north, east, south and west, support breeding Black Guillemots, and although the population is relatively small in a biogeographical sense, this is different to the situation in Britain where they are restricted to the north and west. Perhaps this is due to the older, highly folded Cambrian to Devonian rocks of much of eastern and southern Ireland, which offer better nesting cavities compared to the Jurassic–Cretaceous and younger rocks of eastern and southern England, which are often dominated by white chalk.

The south and west coasts of Ireland also support a large and thriving population of Choughs that has an almost continuous distribution. Elsewhere in north-west Europe, the Chough population is much more fragmentary with more threatened 'outposts' in the southern Scottish Hebrides and western Brittany. One species not covered in this review, so far, is *Homo sapiens*. The actions of man have had remarkably little impact on our rocky coastline, though in some cases it has been 'modified' and incorporated into harbours e.g. Dunmore East in Co. Waterford. At the latter, a thriving fishing port is also home to a significant cliff-nesting Black-legged Kittiwake colony (McGrath 2004). Human inputs, such as nest-box provision for Roseate Terns and Black Guillemots, island creation or modifi-

cation for Common and Arctic Tern at Belfast Harbour and Dublin Port; major construction by Blue Circle Cement of an entire island in Larne Lough, have boosted east coast seabird populations considerably. Finally, Irish sea cliffs are also well used vantage points for seawatching. Headlands such as at Galley Head, the Bridges of Ross and Kilcummin Head are regular haunts of seawatchers which can be found, from July through to November, staring at the stormy ocean seascape tracking the flux of Northern and Southern hemisphere seabirds on their amazing migrations.

Colony of Black-legged Kittiwakes in Dunmore East, Co. Waterford (Richard T. Mills).

12. Beaches and Dunes

Richard Nairn

Introduction

Beaches and dunes are among the most visited parts of Ireland's coastline. They are attractive to a wide range of visitors, including swimmers, sunbathers, walkers and birdwatchers. Most people are familiar with the sight of a flock of gulls or waders along the strandline or the sound of a Skylark above the sand dunes. However, few ornithologists have systematically surveyed these habitats and they remain a fertile ground for future research.

Sandy beaches and shingle are generally found in bays and estuaries where the sediment eroded from headlands and islands is deposited. Where a beach dries out at low tide the wind may lift the sand to form a line of sand dunes above high water mark. On the north-western coasts of Ireland a special type of sand dune, known as machair, occurs. This is a flat, windswept, sandy, vegetated plain formed from highly calcareous shell sand, which has been continuously grazed.

The total length of sandy coast in Ireland has been calculated at 2,382km (Neilson and Costello 1999). Much of this is backed by sand dune, shingle beach or machair. In practice, sand and shingle are often intermixed on beaches and the combination can change frequently in response to sediment dynamics and major storms. Sand dunes are found all around the Irish coast but the greatest length occurs in counties Donegal, Mayo and Wexford. Dunes are less frequent on the south coast of Ireland. Shingle beaches occur all around the coast but vary greatly in size and form. Some of the finest examples are on the east and south coasts. Storm beaches are a particularly western form of shingle beach, where rocks up to boulder-size can be lifted up the shore by high tides and Atlantic storms.

Sandy beach and dunes in Co. Mayo (Richard Nairn).

Sand and shingle are normally quite low in nutrients for vegetation growth, yet the plant communities that occur in these environments are distinctive and contain many rare species. The more mobile habitats such as shingle and sandy beaches are often quite dynamic, changing naturally from winter to summer and from year to year. The breeding birds found on beaches, dunes and machair are quite thinly spread. However, some species like Chough, gulls and waders, appear to prefer these open habitats in winter, being attracted to feed along the shore and strandline, as well as to roost there.

Bird communities of sand dunes are poorly studied in Ireland. There is only a single published census of breeding birds on east coast dunes (Nairn and Whatmough 1978) although Merne (1991) summarised a census on dunes at Carnsore Point, Wexford in the 1970s. West coast machair has received more attention with three major surveys of breeding waders (Nairn and Sheppard 1985; Madden *et al.* 1998; Suddaby *et al.* 2009). The non-breeding birds of shingle and sandy beaches are frequently covered by national surveys such as IWeBS and NEWS although those that occur at the mouths of estuaries (such as Lough Foyle or Dublin Bay) are better known than those of the more remote west coast (such as the Mullet Peninsula). Little Terns, which normally nest on shingle or shell sand beaches, have been well studied in one location in Co. Wicklow but have only been surveyed twice on a systematic, national basis over the last few decades. Sandy beaches also occur in estuaries and these are referred to in Chapter 13.

Dunlin, Sanderling and Turnstone on a shingle beach in Co. Donegal (Richard Nairn).

Breeding bird communities of sand or shingle beaches and sand dunes in Ireland differ less than those of most other habitats in Britain and the rest of Europe. Certain bird species are absent from Ireland, but the dominant species are much the same. For machair, there are significant differences between the bird communities in Ireland and Britain as the Irish machair is not cultivated and lacks the diversity of breeding waders found in Scotland. Non-breeding species of sand and shingle beaches are quite similar to those in Britain and may differ more in terms of the degree of exposure of the beaches and hence the density of prey species.

Shingle beaches

Shingle beaches occur widely around the Irish coast. However, they vary considerably in terms of their size and slope. Some fine examples can be found at the Murrough, Co. Wicklow; Dungarvan, Co. Waterford; Ballycotton, Co. Cork; Mutton Island, Galway Bay; Inishmore, Aran Islands; Clew Bay, Co. Mayo; Bloody Foreland, Co. Donegal; Strangford Lough and Dundrum Bay, Co. Down. An inventory of shingle beaches in Ireland found that the largest areas of this habitat are in Co. Mayo (Moore *et al.*, in press).

Breeding birds

A typical breeding bird of shingle beaches is the Great Ringed Plover. It lays its four eggs in a shallow scrape among the stones, relying on camouflage to ensure their safety. The nest is usually not far from the high spring tide mark as the birds must make a trade-off between bare stones with little vegetation cover and the risk of flooding by high spring tides with onshore winds. Within a few hours of hatching, the chicks move into the cover of whatever sparse vegetation is found on the beach. The main threat to the brood is disturbance

Great Ringed Plover with chicks on a stony beach (Richard T. Mills).

Oystercatchers often nest on stony beaches or on the grass which fringes them (Richard T. Mills).

or predation and the adult birds can frequently be seen feigning a 'broken wing' which serves to lure intruders away from the nest or chicks. Great Ringed Plovers are widespread on the coast but are nowhere abundant. Several pairs per kilometre of beach would be the maximum density though higher, local densities can occur in response to protection schemes for Little Terns (e.g. Kilcoole, Co. Wicklow and Baltray, Co. Louth).

The Oystercatcher is another typical breeding bird of shingle beaches although it rarely nests on the mainland, preferring the relative isolation of offshore islands. The shrill piping calls of the adults are a familiar sound for anyone who regularly lands on islands in the spring and summer. The eggs and chicks of the Oystercatcher are perfectly camouflaged among the stones and the juveniles quickly learn to feed themselves. Oystercatchers are widespread on the Irish coast but there is a curious gap in breeding distribution between west Cork and east Waterford (Gibbons *et al.* 1993).

Among the terns, three species in particular seem to favour shingle beaches for nesting (Mitchell *et al.* 2004). The Little Tern is the only one of the five species that regularly occurs on mainland coasts while Common and Sandwich Terns are usually found on islands, such as those in Strangford Lough (Brown 1990). All mainland Little Tern colonies in Co. Donegal, of which there were several in the 1960s, have died out. The Little Tern forms small colonies of nests from May to August. These are usually located on wide shingle beaches (sometimes sand with a scattering of shells is preferred). A nearby coastal lagoon is often a feature of the breeding colonies as this provides alternative feeding when the sea is perhaps too rough to fish efficiently.

Little Tern at a nest on a Co. Wexford beach covered in empty cockle shells (Oscar Merne).

Little Terns are concentrated in a few colonies with only four of these numbering more than 50 pairs. The largest groups are in Wicklow, Wexford, Kerry and Mayo. The total breeding population in Ireland was estimated at 206 apparently occupied nests during Seabird 2000 (1998–2002) although earlier surveys indicated a range of 282 to 315 nests (Mitchell *et al.* 2004). This suggests an overall decline of some 35% in the Irish population over three decades, although more local trends are masked in this estimate. The general trend is a reduction in the number of colonies. For example, in Co. Mayo, only three colonies were located in 1995 compared with 11 in 1984.

The best studied Little Tern colony is that on the Murrough, between Kilcoole and Newcastle, Co. Wicklow (O'Briain and Farrelly 1990). At this site, BirdWatch Ireland and the NPWS have mounted a wardening scheme each summer since the mid-1980s and the nests are carefully monitored and protected from disturbance. However, other more natural hazards seem to be the most significant factors in breeding success. High spring tides regularly wash away some of the clutches laid lower down the beach. The birds will re-lay if this occurs early in the season. Once the chicks hatch they become a target for some predators and scavengers such as Fox, Stoat, Hedgehog, Hooded Crow, Rook, Common Kestrel and Peregrine. Electric fences have been used to deter mammal predators and the wardens regularly light bonfires and patrol through the night to keep them away. Culling has been used to limit scavenging by corvids. Breeding success varies significantly from year to year with a total of 880 fledged in a 17-year period (1991–2007); the number of pairs ranged from 22 to 106 (mean 48) in this period with number of chicks fledged per pair in the range 0.05–2.30 (Keogh *et al.* 2010).

The Sandwich Tern is the largest of the five tern species nesting in Ireland. It appears to favour low-lying islands, sand and shingle substrates and remote beaches that are close to a steady source of sand eels and sprats which can be fed to the chicks. The total population of Sandwich Terns in Ireland in 1995 was 3,716 apparently occupied nests (Mitchell *et al.* 2004).

Boulder beaches are a particularly western type of shingle beach found on exposed Atlantic coasts and islands. Large boulders, formed either by scree eroded from local cliffs or by wave action on rocky shores, are piled up by storms against the land. The boulders typically have large cavities between them which shelter a variety of breeding birds. Of greatest importance are probably the European Storm Petrels which can nest in many thousands of cavities on a single beach. Typical examples of such large colonies are the islands of Inishglora, Inishkeeragh and Duvillaun Beg, Co. Mayo, which are estimated to hold, respectively, 1,788, 1,635 and 950 apparently occupied sites (AOS) for European Storm Petrels, mainly in boulder beaches. It is suggested that seawater may penetrate quite far into these beaches and that only the uppermost parts of the boulder cavities may be dry enough for nesting by European Storm Petrels (Mitchell *et al.* 2004). Boulder beaches are also occasionally used for nesting by Common Eider, Common Gull, Common Tern and Arctic Tern (S.F. Newton, pers. comm.)

A storm beach at Quilty, Co. Clare with Black-headed Gulls feeding in the surf (Richard T. Mills).

Non-breeding birds

Outside the breeding season shingle beaches are used by a variety of shorebirds including gulls, waders, herons and Great Cormorants. An extensive survey of non-estuarine coasts was carried out in the winter 1997/98 covering about 50% of the estimated non-estuarine habitat in the Republic of Ireland. This survey covered a range of habitats including shingle and sandy beaches, although the predominant habitat was probably rocky shores (Colhoun and Newton 2000, Colhoun *et al.* 2008). Over 65% of the birds counted in this survey were waders with the most abundant being Oystercatcher, European Golden Plover, Northern Lapwing, Eurasian Curlew, Dunlin, Great Ringed Plover, Ruddy Turnstone, Common Redshank and Sanderling. Gulls accounted for nearly one-fifth of the total birds counted with the most abundant being Common Gull, Black-headed Gull, European Herring Gull and Great Black-backed Gull.

Roosting waders, gulls, Great Cormorants and herons frequently use shingle beaches during the high tide period in winter. A study of one

Ruddy Turnstones are common winter visitors to shingle beaches (Richie Lort).

large roost site on a shingle beach at Mutton Island, Inner Galway Bay over a five-year period, demonstrated that numbers were relatively stable here, despite major engineering work on a nearby part of the island (Nairn 2005). A number of other high-tide roosts on shingle beaches on islands and on the mainland close to Galway city were also recorded in this study. The principal species using these high tide roosts were Oystercatcher, Great Ringed Plover, Eurasian Curlew, Common Redshank, Bar-tailed Godwit, Dunlin and Ruddy Turnstone.

Sandy beaches

Many sandy beaches or sand flats in Ireland are located at the mouths of estuaries where the rising and falling tides slow down and drop their sediment load. Large areas of sandflat are found in Dublin Bay, Wexford Harbour, Bannow Bay, Tramore Bay, Dungarvan Harbour, Youghal Harbour, Castlemaine Harbour, Tralee Bay, Sligo Bay, Inner Donegal Bay, Loughros Bay, Gweebarra Bay, Ballyness Bay, Sheephaven Bay and Lough Foyle. Other sand beaches are located on open coasts or bays, where they are exposed to the wave action of the sea. Good examples of this type of beach are those at Lettermacaward, Co. Donegal; the Mullet, Co. Mayo; Fanore, Co. Clare; Derrynane, Co. Kerry; Tramore, Co. Waterford; Brittas Bay, Co. Wicklow; Portmarnock, Co. Dublin; Dundrum Bay, Co. Down and White Park Bay, Co. Antrim.

Particle size of the sand is a key to its movement and the type of beach which develops. The larger grains of sand are deposited first while the finer sediment is held in suspension until the tide reaches more sheltered parts of bays and estuaries. Grain size and the amount of organic material washed down from rivers are the main physical parameters that dictate the type and density of invertebrate communities occurring in sandy beaches. Superimposed on this is the degree of exposure to wave action with the highest densities of fauna occurring in the most sheltered shores. The faunal diversity of sandy shores was reviewed by Wilson and Emblow (2002). Over 70 species of large invertebrates have been recorded from Dublin Bay which is one of the best studied sandy shores in Ireland (Wilson 1982).

Beach–dune dynamics are important factors in the management of these habitats. At its simplest, there is a natural movement of sand in summer from beach to the dunes, caused by wave action and onshore winds, and back again with winter trimming of the dunes. There can be significant conflict between nature conservation management, which encourages this natural dynamic, and land uses (such as golf courses) which require fixed, stable environments (Richie 2001).

Breeding birds

Breeding birds of sandy beaches are quite similar to those of shingle beaches. Both Little Tern and Great Ringed Plover will nest on sand beaches, especially where there is a scattering of shingle or mollusc shells.

Non-breeding birds

Gulls: One of the most familiar sights on a sandy beach is a flock of scavenging gulls, poking around in seaweed at low tide or roosting at the top of the beach at high tide. Among the most frequently encountered species are Black-headed Gulls and Common Gulls. The latter species are more often dominant on the west coast. Other species such as Herring, Lesser Black-backed and Great Black-backed Gulls are generally fewer in number but widely distributed. Some of the big sandy bays such as Lough Foyle, Dundalk Bay, Dublin Bay, Wexford Harbour, Castlemaine Harbour, Tralee Bay, Galway Bay, Sligo Bay and Donegal Bay, can hold several thousand individual gulls. These are often left uncounted in the regular wetland counts in favour of the wildfowl and waders. A focus on the non-breeding gulls in Dublin Bay has shown that the numbers and range of species is significant (Merne *et al.* 2009). The flocks of commoner gulls often hold some surprises. Increasingly, numbers of Mediterranean Gull,

Iceland Gull, Glaucous Gull and many other rarer species appear among the commoner gulls. Vagrant American gulls seem to be especially common in Ireland. No doubt this is because it is the first landfall they encounter on crossing the Atlantic. They are not, of course, restricted to sandy beaches and many are recorded in harbours and ports, such as Killybegs. However, a range of gulls has been recorded on a sandy beach at Sandymount Strand, Dublin Bay, including Laughing Gull, Sabine's Gull, Bonaparte's Gull and Yellow-legged Gull (Dempsey and O'Clery 2007).

Terns: One of the most remarkable features of Dublin Bay is a very large post-breeding roost of terns that occurs on the outer sandflats in late summer and early autumn (Merne *et al.* 2008, Merne 2010). The birds gather at dusk, probably after feeding in the shallow waters on the Kish Bank, and settle on the sand near the tide line. When high spring tide occurs at dusk the birds congregate on the supra-tidal sand spit at Booterstown–Merrion Strand. This roosting behaviour has been known since at least the 1950s and occasionally reaches massive proportions with 20,000 to 30,000 terns estimated in August 1996 (Newton and Crowe 1999). In 2006 and 2007 numbers of terns using the beach peaked at 11,700 in late August. The majority of the birds were Common Terns but Arctic, Roseate, Sandwich, Little and Black Terns were also present and the peak numbers present far exceeded the local breeding populations in the Dublin region. This suggests that Dublin Bay is a key post-breeding, staging area for terns from all around the Irish Sea coast and is one of the largest concentrations of terns in Ireland, Britain and possibly in Europe.

Waders: The results of a 1987 survey of wintering waders on a total of 563 non-estuarine sections of the west coast allowed analysis of the habitat preferences of these species (Kirby *et al.* 1991). Of the five habitat categories used in the analysis, three were bedrock, boulders and sand. Sandy beaches accounted for 40% of the total length surveyed but only 8% comprised boulders. The waders that showed a preference for sandy beaches were Sanderling (84% of the total count), Great Ringed Plover (72%), and Dunlin (64%).

Sanderlings are especially associated with the long sandy Atlantic beaches that occur right down the west coast from Donegal to Kerry. They gather here in small flocks in August, on return from their Arctic breeding grounds. Feeding in the wet sand at the advancing or retreating edge of the tide, they run up and down the beach ahead of the waves. They appear to pick their prey, small marine invertebrates, from the surface of the wet sand. Sanderlings are probably underestimated in the regular monthly counts undertaken each winter but their winter population in Ireland is considered to be in the order of 2,000 birds (Crowe *et al.* 2008a).

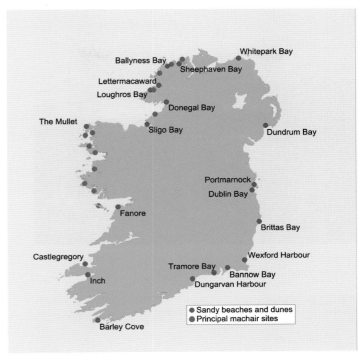

Some of the sandy beaches and dunes mentioned in the text.

Sanderlings forage on a sandy beach where the sand is wet (Richard T. Mills).

Oystercatchers on the shoreline at Quilty, Co. Clare (Richard Nairn).

Dunlins roosting on seaweed (Richard T. Mills).

A high-tide roost of Brent Goose, Oystercatcher and Bar-tailed Godwit at Dungarvan, Co. Waterford (Richard Nairn).

Oystercatchers favour the more exposed sandy beaches on open coasts and at the mouths of estuaries. Their main prey on the sandflats is probably the common cockle and large flocks of these waders can be found where the shellfish are at high densities. In south Dublin Bay, the highest density of the cockle correlated well with the preferred feeding areas of the Oystercatchers (Quinn and Kirby 1993). In Strangford Lough, Co. Down, a strong relationship was also found between Oystercatchers and cockle populations (Brown and O'Connor 1974).

On some parts of the Irish coast, annual winter accumulations of stranded seaweed on the driftline reach massive proportions. A good example of this is found at Quilty, Co. Clare. Here, on the north-east side of the pier, huge depths of rotting seaweed act as a magnet for large flocks of waders including Oystercatcher, Ruddy Turnstone, Dunlin, Purple Sandpiper and Sanderling. They feed intensively here on the high density of sandhoppers and other invertebrates in the kelp (Green *et al.* 1988; Colhoun and Newton 2000).

The site at Quilty supports the largest single flock of Purple Sandpipers in Ireland with nationally important numbers regularly occurring here (Crowe 2005, Foster *et al.* 2010). When a sample of these birds was caught in April 2010, the wing and bill lengths suggested that they belong to the same breeding population (possibly from the Canadian Arctic) as that wintering in north-west Scotland. It is suggested that the high proportion of first-year birds (35%) in the flock here may be due to habitat segregation by the age classes with young birds favouring muddy/sandy bays over rocky shores (Foster *et al.* 2010).

On a sandy beach called Nethertown, close to Carnsore Point at the south-east corner of Wexford, a variety of waders and gulls have been monitored feeding and roosting within 100m of operating wind turbines. This site is one of the few coastal windfarms in Ireland and the birds appear to have habituated to the new structures without being displaced by their movement (Nairn *et al.*, in press).

Waders often roost at high tide in tight flocks on the end of sand spits. The main attraction of these sites is usually their proximity to the intertidal mudflats and sandflats which are the principal low tide feeding areas. Being remote locations they tend to be less disturbed than the more accessible parts of the beach. Good examples of wader roosts on sand spits are found at North Bull Island, Dublin Bay; Raven Point, Co. Wexford; Cunnigar, Dungarvan, Co. Waterford; Inch Strand, Co. Kerry; Rosses Point, Co. Sligo and Streedagh, Co. Sligo (Merne 1991).

Geese: Geese also roost on sand spits. One of the best examples is probably the large night roost of Greater White-fronted Geese at the Raven in Wexford Harbour. The evening flight of these flocks in the winter sunset is a memorable sight. Large flocks of Barnacle Geese, which winter in the Lissadell area of Sligo Bay, often use the sand spit of Rosses Point in the south side of Drumcliff Bay when they are disturbed on their preferred grassland feeding areas. Brent Geese also use sand spits for high-tide roosting in Lough Foyle, Rogerstown Estuary, Malahide Bay, Baldoyle Bay, Dublin Bay (North Bull Island and Merrion Strand), Wexford Harbour and Tramore Inner Bay.

Sand dunes

Anyone who has walked along a sandy beach in strong winds will be familiar with the phenomenon of blowing sand. Sand dunes are formed by the wind picking up sand grains from the beach and building them above high-water mark. This process is aided by certain pioneer plant species, notably the dune grasses, which trap the moving sand around them and thus become buried. The pioneer vegetation at the top of the beach normally grows on the stranded seaweed from a previous winter. These small sand piles are known as embryo dunes. In some places they are part of an annual cycle and will be eroded away in the winter, recycling the sand onto the beach or even to offshore bars. Where sand is accreting, the embryo dunes coalesce into a first line of foredunes. This is usually a low ridge dominated by marram grass, but with a variety of other species such as sea bindweed, sea spurge and sea holly. If not eroded by storms and high tides, these foredunes will eventually accumulate enough sand to become a permanent ridge of high 'yellow' dunes. This ridge is termed yellow because of the prevalence of such plants as bird's-foot trefoil and stonecrop. Behind the first dune ridge lie the fixed dunes. These are so-called because the carpet of vegetation is virtually complete and the sand is now fixed and prevented from moving in the wind. Exceptions occur if there are blowouts or pathways where pedestrians, vehicles or burrowing rabbits have broken the thin skin of vegetation, exposing the sand to the wind.

Moving from the beach inland, one walks through a natural succession of vegetation types. Pioneer vegetation on the embryo dunes is followed by more variety in the foredunes and a complete cover of creeping vegetation, mosses and lichens on the fixed dunes. Woody species are typically absent on the front part of the dune system as the soil is low in nutrients and there is high wind exposure. On the back dunes there is often a dense cover of bracken (especially where grazing was formerly present) and burnet rose. Gorse and hawthorn scrub may be present here and occasional trees, such as sycamore, may colonise. The introduced shrub, sea buckthorn, is common on north and east coast dunes. It appears to thrive where there is mobile sand, often growing in quite exposed

Sand dunes and estuary at Trawbreaga Bay, Co. Donegal (Richard Nairn).

In the winter sea buckthorn has a huge berry crop that attracts flocks of migratory thrushes, such as Fieldfare (John Fox).

positions on the foredunes and fixed dunes. Dune heath is a rare habitat on the back dunes, where the calcium components of the sand have been leached by centuries of rainfall and heather can colonise. Finally, where the wind erodes a hollow in the dunes down to the winter water table, a damp habitat called dune slack may form with creeping willow one of the dominant plants.

The Skylark is one of the dominant breeding bird species on sand dunes (Richard T. Mills).

Breeding birds

Embryo dunes are relatively unsuitable for breeding birds due to the amount of bare sand and generally high disturbance levels at the top of the beach. Occasionally, Great Ringed Plovers will nest among embryo dunes if there are suitable patches of gravel. Terns may also nest among the pioneer vegetation. One of the best examples of this was a small island called Tern Island that once existed in Wexford Harbour. It was little more than a sandbank covered with a thin growth of lyme grass but, during the 1960s and early 1970s, it supported a colony of over 3,000 pairs of all five Irish species of terns. In the mid-1970s, winter storms dismembered the island and redistributed the sand around Wexford Harbour. At Malahide in north Dublin, a very large tern colony was located on sand dunes and adjacent salt marsh until it dispersed in the 1950s (Merne 1991). There is a most unusual record of a pair of Peregrine nesting successfully on a dune island in Wexford Harbour. There were four chicks approximately 2–3 weeks old present on 31 May 2002 (S. Newton pers. comm.).

Fixed dunes are more stable and generally fully vegetated, except where blowouts occur. The dominant species on these habitats are Skylark and Meadow Pipit, both of which nest in grassy tussocks on the ground. Nairn and Whatmough (1978) recorded breeding densities in dunes at Murlough, Co. Down, equivalent to about one pair of both Skylark and Meadow Pipit in every 1–2 hectares of fixed dunes (Table 12.1). Merne (1991) found that Meadow Pipit and Skylark were the most numerous in a three-year census at Carnsore, Co. Wexford. A more recent study estimated about 40–50 pairs of Skylark (less than one pair per hectare) and lesser numbers of Meadow Pipit in about 56 hectares of dunes at Tramore (McGrath 2001).

The main study plot at Murlough covered 38.5 hectares and included fixed dunes, sea buckthorn scrub, dense bracken/burnet rose and dune heath. In total, some 21 species of birds (all but four species were passerines) were breeding in this area. While Skylark and Meadow Pipit were the dominant species, Wren, Linnet, and Chaffinch were also members of this community. At Carnsore, the other significant breeding species were Stonechat, Wren, Linnet and Reed Bunting (Merne 1991).

Table 12.1 Densities of breeding birds recorded at various sand dune sites in Ireland (figures given in territories per hectare)

Site	Murlough, Co. Down	Carnsore, Co. Wexford	Tramore, Co. Waterford
Source	Nairn and What-mough 1978	Merne 1991	McGrath 2001
Area of census	38.5ha	24.0ha	56.0ha
Years of census	1976–1977	1978–1980	
Skylark	0.58	0.38	0.71–0.89
Meadow Pipit	0.47	0.43	
Wren	0.23	0.12	
Linnet	0.22	0.10	
Chaffinch	0.21	0.00	
Stonechat		0.13	
Reed Bunting		0.09	

Dune scrub and woodland is relatively common on the more stable, landward parts of sand dunes in Ireland. Typical vegetation is dominated by gorse, blackthorn, hawthorn and occasionally woodland with sycamore and conifers the most common tree species. In places scrub can be found close to the high-water mark especially when the invasive sea buckthorn is involved. Despite the fact that this introduced woody species can shade out other more diverse plant communities, the scrub provides a dense cover for nesting birds. A census was carried out over three years of a second smaller study plot at Murlough covering 9 hectares of sea buckthorn scrub. This habitat held 19 breeding bird species with the total density of territories over three times that on the surrounding open duneland. The bird community in the scrub was quite different, being dominated by Willow Warbler (2.00 territories per hectare), Chaffinch (1.55), Blackbird (1.00), European Robin (1.00), Dunnock (0.78) and Wren (0.78).

Dune slacks are absent at Murlough but they are found in some other dune systems such as those at North Bull Island, Dublin; the Raven, Co. Wexford; Inch, Co. Kerry and Sheskinmore, Co. Donegal. Usually, slacks are quite small features and they do not have distinctive bird communities. However, they provide surface water features in otherwise dry habitats and, as such, have significant benefits for many birds.

In some dune systems, especially those associated with estuaries, Common Shelduck nest in old rabbit burrows. At Tramore, Co. Waterford, Common Shelduck nests are more often found under brambles or small bushes (McGrath 2001). These large colourful ducks lead their ducklings out across

The Willow Warbler dominates the breeding bird community in dune scrub (Karl Partridge).

the dunes to reach the intertidal mudflats, where they feed by scything their bills through the mud to sieve out small invertebrates.

Non-breeding birds

Little is recorded in the literature of the non-breeding or wintering birds of sand dunes. One of the positive features of the sea buckthorn scrub is that it carries a heavy crop of orange berries in the autumn–winter period. This provides welcome food for flocks of migrant thrushes and finches arriving on the north and east coast and some large concentrations of these species have been recorded, mainly by bird ringers. The thrushes, especially Fieldfare, Redwing, Blackbird and Song Thrush, also use the scrub for night roosting in winter.

Sand dunes are important feeding areas for Chough both in the breeding season and during the winter, when they form large foraging flocks. Choughs were recorded in both dunes and machair during the national surveys in 1992 and 2002/03 (Berrow *et al.* 1993; Gray *et al.* 2003). In their first two years of life, Choughs live in flocks and the majority of well-established Irish flocks utilise dune habitats for a significant part of the annual cycle, usually late summer to early winter (Trewby *et al.* 2006).

Raptors such as Common Kestrels are common visitors to sand dunes and Short-eared Owls regularly hunt on dunes by daylight in winter. Short-eared Owls, Sparrowhawks and Long-eared Owls frequently hunt in dune scrub and woodland where they find high concentrations of bird prey, especially in winter. Short-eared Owls at Ballymacoda did not hunt by day, but a May migrant did (Smiddy 2000).

Short-eared Owls often hunt by daylight on sand dunes (John Fox).

Machair grassland and marsh in Co. Mayo (Richard T. Mills).

Machair

Machair is a habitat that is unique in Europe to western Scotland and north-west Ireland. It consists of a flat sandy plain with a dense sward of vegetation which is often tightly grazed. The main vegetation characteristics are described by Bassett and Curtis (1985), Curtis (1991b) and Gaynor (2006). Curtis (1991b) summarised the main geomorphological and ecological characteristics of these as follows:

- A mature coastal sand plain with a more or less level surface;
- Significant proportion of shell fragments in the sand producing a lime-rich soil (pH >7);
- Grassland vegetation with a low frequency of sand-binding species and with a core suite of characteristic herbaceous species;
- Significant modification, principally by grazing, during the recent historic period;
- A moist, cool, oceanic climate with high winds.

Breeding birds

Waders breeding on the Irish machair have been systematically surveyed in each decade since the 1980s (Nairn and Sheppard 1985; Madden *et al.* 1998; Suddaby *et al.* 2010). The first survey covered 51 machair sites and was based on a single visit to each in late May – early June 1985. Nine wader species, totalling 604 pairs, were found breeding at 38 of the sites (Table 12.2). Over half of the breeding waders recorded were Northern Lapwing (312 pairs) with Dunlin (121 pairs), Great Ringed Plover (64 pairs), Common Snipe (54 pairs) and Oystercatcher (21 pairs) also present at some sites where the habitat was suitable. In 1996 and 2009 the survey was extended to three visits between late April and mid-June. In 1996, breeding waders were found at 31 sites with a total of 697 pairs of eight species. Northern Lapwing still remained most numerous with 313 pairs but Oystercatcher had increased to 166 pairs. Numbers of breeding Dunlin had declined drastically after the 1980s to only 60 pairs in 1996 and 52 pairs in 2009. The decline in density of all breeding waders on the Irish machair

Northern Lapwing is a typical breeding bird on the machair of the north-west coasts (Karl Partridge).

has continued with an overall decline of 24% in a 24-year period (Table 12.2). The reasons for this dramatic decline are largely unknown but may include climate change (Dunlin is at the southern limit of its breeding range in Ireland) and increased predation (this has been shown to cause declines in Northern Lapwing populations in the Shannon Callows (Chapter 6)).

Table 12.2 Percentage changes in breeding wader populations since 1985 based on their densities at 35 sites surveyed in each of three surveys (after Suddaby et al. 2009)

Sites	Number of sites	Average density pairs/hectare			Percentage change	
		1985	1996	2009	1996–2009	1985–2009
Mainland sites	31	0.19	0.17	0.06	-63%	-68%
Island sites	4	0.21	0.55	0.82	+66%	+301%
All sites	35	0.19	0.21	0.15	-30%	-24%

Most Dunlin breeding on machair are now found on the Inishkea Islands, Co. Mayo (Richard T. Mills).

The average density for all breeding waders on the Irish machair was estimated in 1985 at 0.19 pairs per hectare. This was substantially less than the densities of breeding waders on Scottish machair where a range of 0.94 to 1.40 pairs per hectare was estimated around the same period (Fuller *et al.* 1986).

There are significant differences between the Irish and Scottish machair habitats. In the Scottish Hebrides, machair plains form continuous strips along the coast and the range of vegetation types is greater including cultivated land and transitional peatlands (or blackland) on the landward side. In Ireland the machair is divided into a number of small sites, often isolated from one another. Grazing is universal in the Irish sites and often this is a dominant factor with a short sward and significant trampling by domestic animals. Only Northern Lapwing seem to be able to survive in these conditions. Recreational use of the Irish machair is also widespread with sports pitches, golf courses and caravan parks an ever-present source of disturbance. Perhaps the only site in Ireland which represents 'undamaged' machair and is comparable to the Scottish habitat is on the Inishkea islands, off Co. Mayo. Here there are substantial populations of Oystercatcher, Northern Lapwing, Great Ringed Plover, Common Redshank, Common Snipe and Dunlin, which are all key species in the Scottish habitat. For example, of the 230 pairs of Northern Lapwing breeding on Irish machair in 2009, some 84 pairs were on the island of Inishkea North alone. Similarly, of the total of 52 pairs of Dunlin estimated to breed in machair in Ireland, 38 pairs were on the Inishkea Islands (Suddaby *et al.* 2009).

The breeding wader populations of the Scottish machair have also declined significantly between the first survey in 1983 (Fuller *et al.* 1986) and a repeat survey in 2000 (Jackson *et al.* 2004). Between these surveys the populations of Great Ringed Plover and Dunlin had declined by around 50% while Common Redshank, Northern Lapwing and Common Snipe populations had also declined on the islands of South Uist and Benbecula. One of the causes of these declines has been predation of eggs by hedgehogs which were released illegally on the islands (Jackson and Green 2000; Jackson *et al.* 2004).

Of the other species of breeding birds recorded on Irish machair sites during the 1985 survey, Meadow Pipit, Skylark and Northern Wheatear were the most numerous.

Non-breeding birds
Chough are regularly seen foraging in dunes and machair although there are no records of breeding in these habitats unless suitable nesting sites, such as abandoned buildings, are present (S.F. Newton, pers comm.)

At the Inishkea Islands, Co. Mayo, large flocks of wintering Barnacle Geese feed on the machair grasslands and on island fields that are striped with old cultivation ridges. On arrival in autumn they concentrate mainly on white clover stolons, switching to red fescue and smooth meadow grass as the winter progresses (Cabot 2009). Over 2,500 geese were present here in the aerial/ground surveys of March 2008. Smaller flocks are also found on machair on some of the nearby islands such as Duvillaun and on the nearby mainland around Termoncarragh Lake.

Summary

Beaches and sand dunes are important habitats for birds at certain times of year. Shingle beaches hold few breeding species but Little Tern is probably of highest conservation concern. European Storm Petrel colonies occur in western boulder beaches on some islands. In winter, shingle is an important habitat for roosting waders. Sandy beaches also hold few breeding species but they have enormous importance for wintering waders and, in some cases, as night roosts for post-breeding terns.

On sand dunes, the density and diversity of breeding birds increases with distance from the beaches and as the structure of the vegetation becomes more complex. Sea buckthorn scrub on dunes holds particularly high densities of breeding birds and is an important feeding and roosting habitat for migrant thrushes and finches. West coast machair holds a distinctive type of breeding bird community with waders as the key species of conservation concern. Both the density and diversity of waders on Irish machair are lower than on similar areas of machair in western Scotland. There have been dramatic declines in numbers and density of most wader species on the Irish mainland sites while offshore islands remain of key importance for these species.

The free movement of sediment is a key factor in the conservation of beaches and dunes, and by extension, of their bird communities. By their very nature, beaches are mobile systems, changing with every tide and often undergoing major changes during storms. The dynamic equilibrium that this involves has become a central concept in the enlightened management of beaches and dunes (Richie 2001). The need to allow the coastline some space to adjust naturally is even more necessary in the light of the predicted rise in sea levels due to climate change.

13. Estuaries and Coastal Lagoons

Oscar J. Merne and James A. Robinson

Introduction

The island of Ireland has a long and indented coastline (recently estimated at 7,524km; Nairn 2005), with many bays and estuaries. Of this, estuaries (including associated mudflats and salt marshes) occupy about 784km, or about 10% of the coastline. The length of the coast occupied by coastal lagoons has not been calculated, but even though about 133 lagoons have been identified, most are very small and together they occupy less than 1% of the coastline.

This chapter reviews the many Irish estuaries and coastal lagoons that support large numbers of a diverse range of migratory waterbirds. Some of the coastal lagoons not only provide habitat for these birds during the winter months and on passage migration in spring and autumn, but also breeding sites for colonial gulls and terns and a variety of other bird species.

The importance of estuaries and coastal lagoons for waterbirds

Ireland's estuaries and coastal lagoons are important for many hundreds of thousands of waterbirds, especially during the winter months. Waterbirds are defined as birds that are ecologically dependent on wetlands (Wetlands International 2006). Boland *et al.* (2010a) and Calbrade *et al.* (2010) identified 21 estuaries and coastal lagoons that regularly supported more than 10,000 waterbirds (Table 13.1). Numerically, these sites are among the most important bird habitats in Ireland during the winter. Many other coastal wetlands of these habitat types support internationally or nationally important concentrations of at least one waterbird species, i.e. they support regularly over 1% of the biogeographic population or all-Ireland population, respectively, during the non-breeding season.

Waders roost at sunset on the upper sandflats in Dublin Bay (Richard T. Mills).

Table 13.1 Estuaries and coastal lagoons in Ireland that have supported more than 10,000 wintering waterbirds in the period 2004/05–2008/09 and the species for which the site has supported at least 1% of the biogeographic population over the same period (data collated from Boland et al. (2010a) and Calbrade *et al.* (2010))

Site	Country	Five-year peak mean	Internationally important species
Strangford Lough	NI	80,931	Mute Swan, Whooper Swan, Light-bellied Brent Goose, Common Shelduck, Red Knot, Black-tailed Godwit, Common Redshank
Dundalk Bay	RoI	57,627	Light-bellied Brent Goose, Oystercatcher, European Golden Plover, Red Knot, Black-tailed Godwit, Bar-tailed Godwit
Wexford Harbour and Slobs	RoI	43,401	Whooper Swan, Greater White-fronted Goose, Light-bellied Brent Goose, European Golden Plover, Black-tailed Godwit, Bar-tailed Godwit
Lough Foyle	NI/RoI	35,913	Whooper Swan, Light-bellied Brent Goose, Bar-tailed Godwit
Dublin Bay	RoI	30,113	Light-bellied Brent Goose, Red Knot, Black-tailed Godwit, Bar-tailed Godwit
Lough Swilly	RoI	29,130	Whooper Swan, Greater White-fronted Goose, Greylag Goose, Light-bellied Brent Goose
Cork Harbour	RoI	27,665	Black-tailed Godwit
Rogerstown Estuary	RoI	23,731	Light-bellied Brent Goose, Black-tailed Godwit
Tralee Bay	RoI	22,650	Light-bellied Brent Goose
Inner Galway Bay	RoI	20,032	Light-bellied Brent Goose, Great Northern Diver
Belfast Lough	NI	19,411	Black-tailed Godwit
Shannon and Fergus Estuary	RoI	18,782	Whooper Swan
Ballymacoda	RoI	18,394	Black-tailed Godwit
Dungarvan Harbour	RoI	18,217	Light-bellied Brent Goose, Black-tailed Godwit
Tacumshin Lake	RoI	16,568	None
Bannow Bay	RoI	16,335	Light-bellied Brent Goose
The Cull and Killag	RoI	16,325	Light-bellied Brent Goose
Broadmeadow (Malahide) Estuary	RoI	11,805	Light-bellied Brent Goose
Boyne Estuary	RoI	11,463	Light-bellied Brent Goose
Carlingford Lough	NI/RoI	10,361	Light-bellied Brent Goose
Outer Ards	NI	10,240	Light-bellied Brent Goose

Black-tailed Godwits feed in the sheltered muddy sections of an estuary (Richard T. Mills).

The Common Redshank is often found feeding at the upper parts of estuaries close to the high tide mark (Karl Partridge).

Over 10% of the entire biogeographic populations of the following species occur in these Irish habitats (Crowe *et al.* 2008a). The Light-bellied Brent Goose breeds in the high Arctic islands of north-east Canada and migrates across Greenland and Iceland to reach the shores of Ireland in the winter (Merne *et al.* 1999, Robinson *et al.* 2006). Almost the entire population (currently numbering about 40,000 birds; Irish Brent Goose Research Group) spends the winter months in Irish estuaries and coastal lagoons. The Greater White-fronted Goose which breeds in western Greenland (current population about 24,000 birds; A. Walsh, pers. comm.) winters mainly in Scotland and Ireland, and about 39% of the population is found in Irish estuaries and coastal lagoons.

The Icelandic breeding population of Whooper Swans (numbering 20,900 birds; Wetlands International 2006) winters in Iceland, Ireland and Britain. Around 12,700 birds occur in Ireland and of these about 3,100 (14.8% of the biogeographic population) are found in our estuaries and coastal lagoons.

The Icelandic population of Black-tailed Godwit (numbering about 47,000 birds; Wetlands International 2006) winters on the Atlantic fringe of Europe from Ireland and Britain to Spain and Portugal (with some in Morocco). About 31% of this population is found on Irish estuaries and coastal lagoons. The Bar-tailed Godwit breeds in high Arctic Scandinavia and northern Russia and migrates to winter in coastal western Europe and north-west Africa. Of a total population of 120,000 (Wetlands International 2006), 18,060 are estimated to winter in Ireland (Crowe 2005) of which 16,520 (13.8% of the biogeographic population) are found on our estuaries and coastal lagoons.

The Common Redshanks which spend the winter in Ireland come from two populations breeding in Iceland, Faeroes, Britain and Ireland, with a combined population of 190,000 birds (Crowe 2005). About 33,000 of these occur in Ireland and the great majority (27,900; around 15% of the biogeographic population) are found in our estuaries and coastal lagoons. Most of the European Golden Plover wintering in Ireland are migrants from Iceland and Faeroes. This population numbers about 930,000 birds (Wetlands International 2006), of which about 150,000 occur in Ireland. The numbers found at estuaries and coastal lagoons are estimated at about 96,000, which is 10.3% of the biogeographic population.

A further eight waterbird species – Mute Swan, Common Teal, Oystercatcher, Great Ringed Plover, Northern Lapwing, Red Knot, Dunlin and Eurasian Curlew – also winter on Irish estuaries and coastal lagoons in numbers that represent between 4% and 7.5% of their respective biogeographic populations.

While most of these coastal wetlands are primarily important for migratory waterbirds during the winter months, some also support significant breeding seabird populations (Mitchell *et al.* 2004), waterbirds on passage migration (e.g. Calbrade *et al.* 2010), and flocks on non-breeding summering birds (especially waders).

The general ecology of estuaries and coastal lagoons in Ireland

The nutrient status of many of our larger estuaries is usually much more elevated than that of open rocky, sandy or shingle shores. This is because the rivers which flow into the estuaries carry with them natural nutrients that have been leached from often very large fertile catchment areas, often augmented by nutrients derived from artificial fertilisers, livestock slurry and silage effluent (Barnes and Green 1972; Barnes 1974; O'Higgins and Wilson 2005). In the estuaries, these nutrients mix with natural nutrients brought in from the sea by the twice-daily tides and are trapped in sheltered areas. Furthermore, many of our larger estuaries have towns and cities built around them, and these are the source of large volumes of sewage effluent, most of which does not receive tertiary treatment (i.e. not stripped of nutrients) before discharge. All these nutrients concentrated in the estuaries promote primary production of aquatic plants and algae on the mudflats and in the salt marshes, and this in turn leads to elevated productivity in the shellfish, crustaceans and worms and fish on which the estuarine waterbirds feast.

All the major Irish cities are located on large estuaries, and this places development pressures and threats on these habitats. Land-claim due to city expansion, port developments and industrialisation, pollution, the introduction of non-native invasive species, disturbance, and other pressures are ever present and impact on the naturalness of the estuaries and their rich communities of plants and animals, including the great abundance and variety of birdlife that depend on the estuarine systems. Other estuaries, not subject to these kinds of pressures, are often seen as sites for major aquacultural development. From the point of view of estuarine bird conservation, there may be a conflict between large-scale aquaculture and birds, as aquaculture may compete for significant space in the intertidal zone and result in disturbance to the birds (Hilgerloh *et al.* 2001b). By contrast, there is also evidence of positive effects of mussel longlines on the behaviour of some species (Roycroft *et al.* 2004b). In addition, the impacts of climate change on estuarine habitats will cause new problems for wintering waterbirds. 'Coastal squeeze' occurs when mudflats and salt marshes are prevented from moving inland because they become 'squeezed' against flood defences. The result is less habitat for waterbirds unless alternative habitat can be created.

Some of the estuaries and coastal lagoons mentioned in the text.

European Golden Plover roost on a Co. Cork estuary (Richard T. Mills).

Of the 133 coastal lagoons that have been identified around our shores (103 in the Republic of Ireland and 30 in Northern Ireland: Healy 2003), many are artificial or man-modified, but that does not necessarily mean they are of no value as bird habitats. Indeed, a number of such lagoons are internationally important bird sites. For example, the artificial lagoon at Inch, on the east side of Lough Swilly (Co. Donegal), formed by the building of sea walls/causeways between Inch Island and the mainland, is internationally important for wintering waterbirds, notably as a night roost and daytime bathing/drinking site for Whooper Swans and Greater White-fronted Geese (Speer 2011), as well as supporting an important breeding colony of Sandwich Terns in summer (Perry and Speer 2003, 2004). Other notable artificial lagoons are the main channels on the North and South Slobs in Wexford Harbour. The Slobs were claimed from the shallows of the Slaney Estuary in the middle of the nineteenth century and turned into empoldered farmland. The dykes creating the polders were built across the permanent deep-water tidal channels, cutting them off from the estuary and altering them to non-tidal brackish lagoons which soon developed distinctive communities of brackish plants and invertebrates (Merne 1974, Healy 2003). In Northern Ireland, of 30 lagoons identified (Bamber *et al.* 2001), only a brackish wetland at Rathgorman and a couple of areas in Strangford Lough are considered natural.

Some bays have been cut off from the sea to form coastal lagoons. In some cases this has been a natural process, as, for example, where longshore drift has gradually caused the build up of shingle barriers impeding the flow of water into and out of the bay. Lady's Island Lake and Tacumshin Lake, on the south Wexford coast, are fine examples of such lagoons (Healy 2003). In other cases, building dune systems and storm beaches have resulted in the formation of lagoons behind them (e.g. at Lough Gill on the Dingle Peninsula in Co. Kerry, Lough Donnell on the west coast of Co. Clare), while rocky shelves or reefs have also been responsible for lagoon formation (e.g. the Salt Lake near Clifden, in Connemara).

Lady's Island Lake, Co. Wexford, is one of the best examples of a coastal lagoon in Ireland (Richard Nairn).

Our estuaries and coastal lagoons usually enjoy an ice-free status during the winter months because of our (usually) temperate winter climate, which, in spite of our relatively northern latitude (*c.* 51°30'–55°30' N), is greatly ameliorated by the warm North Atlantic Drift washing our shores. This means that our coastal wetlands are able to provide food for the large numbers of swans, geese, ducks, waders, gulls and other waterbirds which use Ireland as the terminus of migratory flyways from Greenland, Canada, Iceland, Scandinavia, Siberia and eastern Europe (Wernham *et al.* 2002; Delany *et al.* 2009). With recent milder winters on the continent creating suitable conditions for 'short-stopping' by waterbirds (e.g. Austin and Rehfisch 2005, Maclean *et al.* 2008), shifts in the distribution of some species from eastern breeding grounds could lead to fewer birds spending the non-breeding season on our shores in the future.

Estuaries

River estuaries are among the most productive biotopes on the planet, especially where large rivers meandering through fertile lowlands transport nutrients from the land (from leaching and run-off) down to the sea (Barnes and Green 1972). The sea itself, with its twice-daily rising tides, is also a source of nutrients in the estuaries. Many cities and large towns are located around river estuaries, and they too are a source of additional nutrients – often in the form of human sewage which is discharged into the estuaries.

Although Ireland is a small island, it has a very long coastline, frequently intersected by large and small rivers, which drain both the central plain and the hills and mountains close to the coast. The fast-flowing and relatively short rivers which drain the uplands close to the coast tend to have small estuaries that are less important for waterbirds.

By far the largest estuary in Ireland is that of the River Shannon and its many tributaries, which drain *c.* 21,500 square km – approximately one quarter of the island. The Shannon Estuary, from Limerick city to the open sea between Loop Head (Co. Clare) and Kerry Head (Co. Kerry) is *c.* 90km long, and includes the estuaries of the Rivers Fergus, Maigue, Deel and Feale. Other major estuaries in Ireland are those of the River Foyle and its tributaries which flow into Lough Foyle; the Bann Estuary; the Glynn River that flows into Larne Lough; the River Lagan that flows into Belfast Lough; the Rivers Comber and Quoile that flow into Strangford Lough; the Rivers Blackstaff, Carrigs and Moneycarragh that flow into Dundrum Bay; the Newry River that flows into Carlingford Lough; the Rivers Castletown, Fane, Glyde and Dee which flow into Dundalk Bay; the Boyne Estuary; the Rivers Liffey, Tolka and Dodder which flow into Dublin Bay; the River Slaney and its tributaries which flow into Wexford Harbour; the Rivers Barrow, Nore and Suir which flow into Waterford Harbour; the River Blackwater which flows into Youghal Harbour; the River Lee which flows into Cork Harbour; the River Laune which flows into Castlemaine Harbour; the Rivers Corrib, Clare and Kinvarra which flow into Galway Bay; the River Moy which flows into Killala Bay.

Apart from the great Shannon estuary, those on the west coast, from Cork Harbour to Loughs Swilly and Foyle, are generally rather small, and their nutrient status is often low because the rivers which flow into them are relatively short and drain off poor-quality lands. Compared with the large nutrient-rich estuaries of the eastern side of Ireland, the western estuaries generally support relatively small numbers of waterbirds. However, there are a number of exceptions, notably Castlemaine Harbour and Tralee Bay (Co. Kerry), Inner Galway Bay (Co. Galway), Ballysadare Bay, Sligo Harbour and Drumcliff Bay (Co. Sligo), and Lough Swilly (Co. Donegal). Although the rivers that flow into these estuaries and bays originate from minor catchments, the estuarine mudflats and sandflats are sufficiently large and nutrient rich to support significant numbers and diversity of non-breeding waterbirds.

Mudflats in the inner part of Lough Swilly, Co. Donegal (Richard Nairn).

The most important estuaries in Ireland for non-breeding waterbirds are listed in Table 13.1. These are classified as internationally important for wetland birds according to criteria of the Ramsar Convention on Wetlands of International Importance. All or large parts of these have been designated as Special Protection Areas for birds under the EU Birds Directive (79/409/EEC updated to 2009/147/ EC; see Stroud *et al.* 2001, MacLochlainn 2002, and Merne 2005).

Our estuarine waterbird populations were first reviewed in the early 1970s (Hutchinson 1979; Prater 1981) and mid-1980s (Sheppard 1993), and have been monitored continuously in Northern Ireland since the mid-1980s by the UK Wetland Bird Survey (WeBS: Calbrade *et al.* 2010) and in the Republic of Ireland since 1994/95 by the Irish Wetland Bird Survey (I-WeBS: Boland *et al.* 2010). Additional surveys, such as the annual all-Ireland Brent Goose census and the WeBS Low Tide Counts schemes, have provided important supplementary information on the status, distribution and fortunes of our estuarine waterbirds.

The main habitats in Irish estuaries which are important for birds are mudflats and sandflats, salt marshes and the tidal channels which flow through the estuaries. The functions of these estuarine subdivisions are reviewed in the following sections of this chapter.

Estuarine mudflats and sandflats

The mudflats and sandflats which are such a major feature of most Irish estuaries are perceived by many as unattractive when exposed at low tide. This is the case particularly in the summer months when few waterbirds are present to lend colour and activity to an otherwise seemingly desolate and lifeless vista. However, the mudflats and sandflats are teeming with life, with sometimes huge numbers and densities of invertebrates burrowing in the substrate or living on the surface of the soft muds (Eltringham 1971). The estuarine invertebrate fauna is made up mainly by three groups of organisms, polychaete worms, crustaceans and molluscs, and these are the main food resource for hundreds of thousands of waterbirds which forage in the estuaries during the non-breeding season (Figure 3.1).

The most numerous waterbirds found in Irish estuaries during the non-breeding season are Light-bellied Brent Geese, Common Shelduck, Eurasian Wigeon, Common Teal, Mallard, Oystercatcher, European Golden Plover, Northern Lapwing, Red Knot, Dunlin, Black-tailed Godwit, Bar-tailed Godwit, Eurasian Curlew and Common Redshank. Indeed, for some of these, estuaries are their most important wintering habitat in Ireland (e.g. Brent Geese, Common Shelduck, Red Knot, Dunlin, Common Redshank), while others are equally at home and numerous at inland freshwater wetlands (e.g. Whooper Swan) (Boland *et al.* 2010; Calbrade *et al.* 2010). Other waterbirds regularly found in estuaries include divers, grebes, Great Cormorants, Grey Herons, swans, other goose species, other duck species, other wader species, gulls, and terns.

At high water, inundated mudflats and sandflats provide a habitat for diverse fish communities that can be important sources of food for birds during the breeding and non-breeding seasons. From bottom-dwellers, such as plaice, dab and flounder, to species that occupy the water column, such as herring, sprat, sand eel and mackerel, these fish are food

Common Shelduck feed by sieving tiny shellfish from the estuarine mud (Richard T. Mills).

Brent Geese graze on green seaweed and seagrasses in the intertidal area (Karl Partridge).

for piscivorous waterbirds such as divers, grebes, Great Cormorants, and diving ducks during the non-breeding season, and colonial seabirds such as terns during the summer months (e.g. Chivers 2007).

However, the invertebrates and fish are not the only food resource for waterbirds in the estuarine mudflats and sandflats: most of the Irish estuaries also have mats of green algae, and some of them have large beds of eelgrasses. This green matter is exploited by large numbers of grazing wildfowl, especially Light-bellied Brent Geese and Eurasian Wigeon, and is a major cause of redistribution during the winter (O'Briain and Healy 1991; Fox *et al.* 1994a; Mathers and Montgomery 1997; Mathers *et al.* 1998). More recent work has focused on food choice and resource depletion of this resource by Brent Geese (Inger *et al.* 2006a, 2006b, 2006c).

Eelgrasses are not seaweeds (which are algae), but are among the very few flowering plants that grow on muddy and muddy-sand substrates and are completely submerged by the sea. Three species occur in Ireland: narrow-leaved eelgrass, which grows mainly on the lower shore; dwarf eelgrass, which also grows on the lower shore; and marine eelgrass, which grows near or below the spring low water mark (Blamey *et al.* 2003). Extensive beds of eelgrasses are nowadays confined to four Irish bays and estuaries: Lough Foyle, Strangford Lough, Castlemaine Harbour and Tralee Bay (Nairn 2005). Before a 'wasting' disease wiped out or severely reduced eelgrass beds in the early 1930s, they were much more widespread than at present (Ó Briain 1991). Apart from the four main sites mentioned above, small beds of eelgrasses are now found mainly at Malahide Estuary, Merrion Strand (Dublin Bay), parts of the outer Shannon Estuary, parts of Sligo Bay and Lough Swilly (Nairn and Robinson 2003).

Eelgrass biomass is at its height when the Brent Geese arrive in Ireland from their breeding grounds in the north-east Canadian Arctic archipelago, and thousands congregate in Strangford Lough, Lough Foyle and the Kerry bays/estuaries where the main eelgrass beds are located. As the autumn progresses the eelgrass beds are gradually depleted by the Brent

Eurasian Wigeon are among the commonest estuarine ducks in winter (Richard T. Mills).

Dunlin roost at high tide in an estuary (Richard T. Mills).

Tern colony on a mooring dolphin in Dublin Port (Oscar Merne).

Geese (and by large flocks of Eurasian Wigeon), and natural die-back also occurs. The Brent Geese gradually disperse to other bays and estuaries to feed on what eelgrasses may be there, and also on green algae and salt marsh grasses (e.g. Ó Briain and Healy 1991). With growing numbers of Brent Geese in recent times (*c.* 37,000 wintered in Ireland in 2008/09; compared to 11,900 in 1960/61; Irish Brent Goose Research Group) the carrying capacity of these coastal food resources is stretched in some areas (notably Co. Dublin), and the geese are increasingly flighting to recreational grasslands (playing fields and parks) and other terrestrial grasslands for grazing in mid- to late winter (Benson 2009). Other arable crops, e.g. autumn stubbles, winter and spring cereals, and waste potatoes, in areas adjacent to estuaries are also occasionally used by these birds (Robinson *et al.* 2004).

Mats of green algae are often very extensive in Irish estuaries during the summer months (when temperatures are highest and there is more sunlight), especially in those estuaries which are nutrient rich. The two most common and widespread green algae are gutweed and sea lettuce, which thrive in estuarine and brackish waters. The former is most abundant on the upper shore, while the latter is found throughout the intertidal zone (Pitkin 1977; Hayward *et al.* 1996). Light-bellied Brent Geese and Eurasian Wigeon graze the algal mats in large numbers, especially after their preferred eelgrasses are depleted. In some Irish estuaries, the extent of these algal mats can act to reduce feeding opportunities and food abundance for waterbirds (Fahy *et al.* 1975; Jeffrey *et al.* 1992; Lewis and Kelly 2001; Lewis *et al.* 2003).

As natural die-back of eelgrasses and green algae occurs in autumn, invertebrates that feed on detritus benefit from the nutrients from these plants, and, in turn, the nutrients are passed on to the waterbirds which feed on the detritivores.

At low tide, the exposed mudflats and sandbanks not only provide rich feeding grounds for waders and other estuarine waterbirds, but also safe loafing or roosting sites, and their ecology has been the focus of research across the island (Jeffrey 1977; Smiddy 1977, 1992; Grant 1982; Pritchard 1982; Merne 1985; Quinn and Kirby 1993; Hutchinson and O'Halloran 1994; Nairn *et al.* 2000; Murphy *et al.* 2006; Smiddy and O'Halloran 2006a, 2006b, 2008). Large flocks of waders, notably Oystercatchers, European

Golden Plover and Northern Lapwing, may be seen motionless and packed tightly together on the flats while digesting their last meal. The last two may have been foraging inland and moved to the estuaries to roost. Mixed gull flocks also commonly loaf and roost on the estuarine banks. At high tide, estuaries often have sand and shingle spits or bars which function as safe and undisturbed roosting sites where thousands of birds congregate whilst awaiting the turn of the tide.

Estuarine mudflats and sandflats are covered twice each day by the tide, so it is not possible for any birds to nest on these flats. However, natural islands within estuarine sites such as Strangford Lough and Carlingford Lough provide safe nesting areas for many thousands of seabirds that take advantage of abundant fish species to rear their chicks. These islands occur in locations where they remain surrounded by deep water through the tidal cycle, ensuring ground predators have no access. Some estuaries have man-made piers, jetties, mooring dolphins and other artificial structures located within them, which provide suitable nesting places for certain species. Examples are derelict mooring dolphins in the Liffey Estuary in Dublin Port where nearly 500 pairs of Common Terns, and some Arctic Terns, are nesting, due to a conservation programme involving the provision of a shingle substrate, shelters for tern chicks, and barriers to prevent eggs and chicks falling over the side (Merne 2004). A large colony of Common and Arctic terns nests at a man-made lagoon adjacent to Belfast Lough (Chivers 2007). In the Lee Estuary, Cork Harbour, there was a colony of Common Terns on disused steel barges (Wilson et al. 2000). These have now mainly moved to the safety of the roof of one of the Martello towers nearby (P. Smiddy, pers. comm.). In the Liffey Estuary and in Belfast Lough, increasing numbers of Black Guillemots are nesting in cavities in harbour walls (Greenwood 2010). Some estuaries have shingle or sandy beaches on the upper shore, which are inundated only by the highest spring tides or by storm surges, and these are sometimes used by breeding waders such as Oystercatchers and Great Ringed Plovers.

While the great majority of the non-breeding waterbirds found in estuaries are winter visitors or passage migrants in spring and autumn, some estuaries regularly support significant numbers of non-breeding birds (particularly waders and gulls) through the summer months. Generally these are species which take two or more years to reach breeding age, and so have no need to move to breeding grounds outside Ireland. Why undertake the arduous and sometimes dangerous long-distance migrations to the Arctic tundra when you can enjoy the relatively benign Irish summer, feeding and resting in our estuaries, where there is an abundance of food and much less competition from other birds than in autumn, winter and spring? Unfortunately, the WeBS and I-WeBS counts cover only the September to March part of the year, so our information on non-breeding summering birds is incomplete. However, waterbird counts were carried out monthly throughout the year at five major estuarine sites in south Co. Wexford during the 1970s (O. J. Merne, unpublished) and these showed that significant numbers of waders (especially Oystercatchers, Dunlin, Black-tailed Godwits, Eurasian Curlews and Common Redshanks) were present between April and August. Some of these were late spring or early autumn passage migrants, but many were present through the summer. More recently, weekly counts of waders in Dublin Bay have been carried out throughout the year for several years (S. Holohan, unpublished), and these have revealed that large numbers of non-breeding waders spend the summer in the bay.

Salt marshes

Salt marshes tend to form in sheltered bays and estuaries, where fine sediments brought down by rivers accumulate on the upper shore and are colonised by the annual salt-tolerant common glasswort. This pioneering succulent plant in turn traps more sediments and accelerates the build up of muds, which are then often colonised by a slimy film of microscopic algae that help prevent the sediments from being eroded away by currents, tidal scour and wave action (Nairn 2005; Ranwell 1972). Once stabilised, the embryonic salt marsh is progressively colonised by other salt-tolerant vascular plants, such as common salt marsh grass and common sea lavender. Increasingly, these perennial plants bind the sediments

Salt marsh in Co. Donegal (Richard Nairn).

Little Egrets roosting at Timoleague, Co. Cork
(Richard T. Mills).

with their roots and stolons. Other plants commonly found in salt marshes are sea purslane, sea plantain, annual seablite, sea-spurry, sea aster and sea arrow grass. Further up the salt marsh, where tidal inundation is less frequent, sea milkwort and common scurvygrass tend to dominate, while further still red fescue, sea rush and salt-tolerant sedges are usually present (Moore and O'Reilly 1977).

In some estuaries, the invasive alien cord-grass (introduced to Ireland in the late 1920s) takes the place of common glasswort as the first vascular plant to colonise elevated mudflats, and, like glasswort, traps sediments, and its massive rhizome system stabilises the substrate. However, unlike the annual glasswort, cord-grass is so dense that other salt marsh plants find it difficult to establish in the cord-grass beds and it can affect numbers of feeding waterbirds by reducing the extent of feeding areas (Boyle 1977).

Curtis and Sheehy Skeffington (1998) published a comprehensive inventory of salt marshes in Ireland, and investigated their geographical variation. They listed about 250 salt marshes, of which just over half were formed on mud. Most of the remainder were located over sand, shingle and (mainly on the west coast) peat. Salt marshes within estuaries generally tend to form on mudflats because of the extensive deposition of fine particles in the estuaries. Compared to the rest of Ireland, salt marsh is a scarce habitat in Northern Ireland, covering only *c.* 250 hectares and restricted to a few sites. Tidal ranges in Northern Ireland tend to be smaller than elsewhere in Ireland, reducing the tidal area over which this habitat can establish, and this may explain its rarity.

Irish salt marshes do not generally support a large breeding bird community, possibly because many of the larger salt marshes are on major estuaries subject to very high spring tides. Any nesting attempts are likely to fail due to inundation by the spring tides occurring at fortnightly intervals. Only where the salt marsh remains dry at the highest spring tides is there a chance for nests of birds such as Oystercatchers and Common Redshanks (and ground-nesting passerines such as Skylarks and Meadow Pipits) to survive until the chicks fledge. However, there have been a couple of notable exceptions in the past. The salt marsh tip of Malahide 'Island' (in reality a sand dune peninsula) supported a major mixed colony of nesting Common and Arctic Terns (with small numbers of the rare Roseate Tern) for much of the first half of the twentieth century (Kennedy *et al.* 1954). Also, the salt marsh 'Patches' in Tacumshin Lake, on the south coast of Co. Wexford, were the breeding sites of large numbers of European Herring Gulls in the 1960s and 1970s, and, for several years, terns displaced temporarily from the nearby Lady's Island Lake. Oystercatchers, Great Ringed Plovers and Common Redshanks also nested on the 'Patches' at that time (Merne 1974).

Estuarine salt marshes are generally situated adjacent to extensive mudflats and sandflats, where non-breeding waterbirds feed in large numbers when their food resources are not covered by the tide.

As the rising tide advances, the feeding birds must retreat to safe roosting sites where they sit out the high tide until the flats are exposed again and the birds can recommence feeding. Most of the species found feeding on the estuarine mudflats move to the salt marshes during the high tide period.

Waders usually congregate in dense flocks on salt marshes for high-tide roosting – sometimes reaching tens of thousands on the larger estuaries. During the neap-tide phase there are usually extensive areas of uncovered salt marsh available to the roosting flocks, out on the salt marsh edge, away from terrestrial predators and disturbance. However, when extreme high spring tides occur (usually in January and July),

Brent Geese take off from the salt marsh on North Bull Island, Dublin Bay (John Fox).

most, if not all of the salt marsh is covered for a couple of hours and the waders have to seek safe roosting places elsewhere. Low-lying coastal fields are sometimes used as an alternative to the usual salt marsh roosting sites, while it is not uncommon for some species (e.g. European Golden Plover, Red Knot, Bar-tailed Godwit) to pass the high-tide period engaging in dramatic aerobatic twisting and turning above the salt marsh when roosting habitat is limited or they are disturbed. The salt marshes in Lough Foyle, Strangford Lough, Dundalk Bay and at the North Bull Island in Dublin Bay are notable for this kind of wader activity at high tide.

Where such large numbers of waders and other waterbirds concentrate to roost at high tide it is quite commonplace to find several birds of prey taking the opportunity to hunt the flocks for their next meal. Peregrines and Merlins are regularly seen, while Hen Harriers, Sparrowhawks and Short-eared Owls also hunt at roosts.

Although quite at home floating or swimming on the water, large flocks of gulls and wildfowl often move onto the salt marshes to rest, sleep, preen, socialise, etc., especially when the sea or estuarine channels are rough from strong winds.

Some waterbirds use salt marshes for feeding, notably wildfowl such as Light-bellied Brent Geese and Eurasian Wigeon. Common salt marsh grass forms swards which are grazed by these geese and ducks, especially when intertidal green algae and eelgrasses are covered by the tide. The large salt marsh at Lurgangreen, Dundalk Bay, is a daytime feeding site for hundreds of Greylag Geese, and also a night roost for geese that feed on inland fields during the day. Elsewhere, small numbers of Whooper Swans and Greater White-fronted Geese regularly feed on salt marsh vegetation, e.g. on the Fergus Estuary, Co. Clare. Estuarine salt marshes usually have drainage channels, creeks and runnels where Common Teal often feed on small surface invertebrates and plant seeds at all stages of the tide, while some waders (especially Common Redshanks) move into the channels as the flats are covered by the tide and continue to feed on invertebrates in the muddy substrate.

Many salt marsh plants produce an abundance of small seeds in late summer and autumn, and these are often washed up by high spring tides to form a tideline along with seaweeds and flotsam and jetsam. Seed-eating birds such as Greenfinches, Goldfinches, Linnets – sometimes scarce species such as Twite and Snow Bunting – often congregate in winter flocks to feed on these seeds.

While most of Ireland's salt marshes are used by waterbirds (and some other species) as high-tide roosting sites and foraging habitats, relatively few of the c. 250 salt marshes listed by Curtis and Sheehy Skeffington (1998) are particularly important for birds. Notable exceptions include the large salt marshes at Lough Foyle, Strangford Lough, Dundalk Bay, the Boyne Estuary, Baldoyle Bay, the North Bull Island in Dublin Bay, Kilcoole Marshes (Co. Wicklow), Bannow Bay (Co. Wexford), Cork Harbour, Castlemaine Harbour and Tralee Bay in Co. Kerry, parts of the Shannon/Fergus Estuary, and Lough Swilly (Co. Donegal). Smaller salt marshes in other Irish estuaries also have a locally important role as secure roosting sites for waders and other waterbirds.

A Grey Heron wades in the weedy shallows (Richie Lort).

Tidal channels (breeding/non-breeding birds)

Estuaries, by definition, have river channels coursing through them to the open sea. Thus, even at extreme low spring tides there is river water flowing through the estuaries. The volume of water will vary considerably in accordance with whether or not the river is in flood. The volume of water pushing up the estuary on the rising tide will also vary considerably between spring and neap tides, and is also amplified if there are very strong onshore winds. One way or another, there is always water present in estuaries and this allows the free movement of fish within them. Not surprisingly, piscivorous birds often concentrate in estuaries, where foraging is assisted by the relatively sheltered conditions and the concentration of the fish in restricted space. Thus estuaries sometimes support significant numbers of fish-eating bird species such as Great Crested Grebes, Great Cormorants, Grey Herons, Red-breasted Mergansers, gulls, and, between late March and early October, several tern species (e.g. Chivers 2007). Nowadays, increasing numbers of Little Egrets are also found in estuaries. The channels sometimes have beds of mussels and other bivalve shellfish, and diving ducks such as Common Eider, Greater Scaup, Common Scoter and Common Goldeneye feed on these during the winter months.

Coastal lagoons

The *Interpretation Manual for European Union Habitats* (European Commission 2007) defines lagoons as 'expanses of shallow coastal salt water, of varying salinity or water volume, wholly or partially separated from the sea by sandbanks or shingle, or, less frequently, by rocks. Salinity may vary from brackish water to hyper salinity depending on rainfall, evaporation and through the addition of fresh seawater from storms, temporary flooding by the sea in winter or tidal exchange. With or without vegetation of *Ruppietea maritimae*, *Potametea* or *Zosteretea charetea*'. Coastal lagoons are rare and threatened in Europe and are classified as Priority Habitats in Annex I of the EU Habitats Directive.

This definition was modified and simplified by Healy (2003) for surveys of Irish coastal lagoons carried out in 1996 and 1998. She defined a lagoon as 'an isolated, or partially enclosed, body of brackish water with a restricted tidal range, and containing elements of brackish flora and fauna, and one or more lagoonal specialist species'. The surveys identified a total of 103 coastal lagoons in the Republic of Ireland, of which 67 were classified as natural and 36 as artificial.

In general usage, the term 'lagoon' is somewhat loosely applied. For example, the areas of tidal mudflats lying between the North Bull Island and the mainland in north Dublin Bay are often referred to as the North and South Lagoons. However, they are fully saline and tidal and therefore do not fit the above definitions. In this section only true lagoons are considered.

A large number of these lagoons are of little value to waterbirds, often because of their small size and/or poor trophic status. Indeed, 71 are less than 10 hectares in extent, while only 15 are greater than 50 hectares. In Northern Ireland, *c.* 30 coastal lagoons have been identified, mainly around Lough Foyle, Larne Lough, Belfast Lough and Strangford Lough (Anon. 2003). Only three of these are considered

Inch Levels and lagoon with Lough Swilly, Co. Donegal, in background (Richard T. Mills).

to be natural or largely so (Bamber *et al.* 2001). As in the rest of Ireland, many of these lagoons are of little or any importance for birds, but some form small parts of very important coastal wetland sites, notably Strangford Lough, with lagoons at Castle Espie and Quoile Pondage.

Three of the most important coastal lagoons for waterbirds in Ireland are Inch Lough in Co. Donegal, and Lady's Island and Tacumshin Lakes in Co. Wexford (Crowe 2005). Lady's Island and Tacumshin Lakes, on the barrier coast of south Co. Wexford, have been well studied in relation to their geomorphology and hydrology (Carter and Orford 1982; Orford and Carter 1982; Hurley 1997, 1998), and their brackish water fauna and flora (Good and Butler 1998; Hatch and Healy 1998; Healy and Oliver 1998; Oliver and Healy 1998).

Inch Lough is a large (278 hectares), shallow, brackish, man-made lagoon, created in the nineteenth century when sea dykes/causeways were built between Inch Island and the mainland on the eastern side of Lough Swilly. In the summer, the site has supported between 73 and 286 pairs of Sandwich Terns since 1986, colonies of fewer than a hundred pairs each of Common Tern and Black-headed

Arctic Tern nest at Lady's Island Lake, Co. Wexford (Richard T. Mills).

Gull, breeding Mute Swans and a range of breeding ducks. The site supports large numbers of Whooper Swans and a variety of geese and other waterbirds during the non-breeding season (Speer 2011).

Lady's Island Lake, on the south coast of Co. Wexford, is one of the largest (360 hectares) and finest natural sedimentary and percolating lagoons in Ireland (Healy and Oliver 1998), and also the most important for waterbirds. Its scientific value is exceptional because of its rich and interesting fauna and flora, and it may be the best example in Europe of a percolating lagoon (Healy and Oliver 1998). Formerly a shallow tidal bay, it was cut off from the sea by a process of east–west longshore drift. The site supports large numbers of Light-bellied Brent Geese and Gadwall but only around 4,000 waterbirds in total during the non-breeding season. Numbers of waterbirds at the site have dropped due to the effects of pollution and saline intrusion. The site supports 2,000 pairs of Sandwich Terns, 140 pairs of Roseate Terns and 800 pairs of Common and Arctic Terns, most of which relocated following erosion of sandbanks in Wexford Harbour. Around 1,000 pairs of Black-headed Gulls nest at Inish together with small numbers of Mediterranean Gulls. Little Terns have deserted the site in recent decades.

Tacumshin Lake is a large (528 hectares), natural, shallow, sedimentary and percolating lagoon, separated from the sea by a dune barrier of sand and shingle (Healy and Oliver 1998). However, it is 'younger' than Lady's Island Lake with the barrier not closing permanently until the mid-1970s. Before this closure the lagoon was largely tidal, with impeded flow through a natural outlet at the west end of the barrier. During the non-breeding season the site supports regularly 16,500 waterbirds, including a range of species present in nationally important numbers (Boland *et al.* 2010). In the summer, several species of duck and wader also breed at the site, and it has supported rare breeding species for Ireland such as the Black-tailed Godwit, Garganey and Northern Pintail in the past. In the autumn, large flocks of migrating Sand Martins and Barn Swallows sometimes roost at night in the reeds, and up to 600 Lesser Black-backed Gulls loaf on the mudflats for several weeks before departing south for the winter.

Black-tailed Godwit, Eurasian Wigeon and Mute Swans (Richard T. Mills).

Summary

The estuaries and coastal lagoons around Ireland provide habitats that support an enormous number and diversity of waterbirds throughout the annual cycle. In the autumn, these birds arrive from breeding grounds in Canada, Greenland, Iceland, northern Europe, Scandinavia, Russia and Siberia whereas terns from wintering grounds in Africa travel to Ireland to nest here in the summer months. The importance of Ireland in the flyways of these birds places a responsibility on statutory agencies and conservation bodies across the island to look after them when they are here. The majority of the most important coastal sites for waterbirds now receive protection under national and European legislation and for many species, such as the Light-bellied Brent Goose and Black-tailed Godwit, their populations continue to flourish.

However, we must not be complacent because our estuaries and coastal lagoons, and the waterbirds they support, may face serious threats in the future. Land claim for urbanisation, industrial activity and new port facilities, pollution from nutrients from agriculture and domestic sewage, the spread of detrimental invasive species, aquaculture, human disturbance and wildfowling can all pose threats of damage or destruction to our estuaries and coastal lagoons should development not proceed sustainably (e.g. Nairn 1986; Fitzpatrick and Bouchez 1998; Hammond and Cooper 2002; Phalan and Nairn 2007). Economic and social pressures to continue to develop the island will bring some sensitive sites into conflict with those who wish to claim land for purposes that damage the integrity and quality of our estuarine sites. This, coupled with the impending impacts of a changing climate, means efforts will need to be redoubled to support the future protection of these coastal sites and the natural heritage they offer to the people of this island.

Although ongoing and regular surveys of waterbirds at estuaries and coastal lagoons have created an amazing data set that allows us to inform the designation of sites, monitor trends in the fortunes of our waterbird populations, and examine declines or increases at individual sites, the scale of research to underpin future conservation measures remains limited. For example, understanding the individual and cumulative impacts of proposed human development on the waterbirds at an estuary or coastal lagoon would help to inform decision making about the sustainability of planning decisions. New research on how climate change will affect the numbers and distribution of waterbirds in these habitats is also necessary to help those responsible to plan for effective conservation measures in the future.

14. Open Sea

Mark Jessopp and Thomas C. Kelly

Introduction

Situated at the edge of the European continental shelf, Ireland is surrounded by open sea, with the Atlantic Ocean to the west, the Celtic Sea to the South, and the Irish Sea to the east. Under the United Nations Convention on the Law of the Sea, nations can claim territorial waters to the outer edge of the continental margin, and consequently Ireland's marine jurisdictional zone is nearly ten times the size of its land area at approximately 900,000km^2 (see Figure 1, Marine Institute). Almost two thirds of this area is more than 100m deep. While bird habitats in coastal areas such as cliffs, beaches, and estuaries can be readily surveyed, the immense scale, expense of surveying, and other constraints such as bad weather, means that the open sea is probably the least understood of all Ireland's bird habitats. Most of us appreciate the changeable nature of the sea surface, from the rare glass-like flat calm, to raging storms with huge white-capped waves. Paradoxically, its vastness often leads people to view this habitat as a somewhat homogeneous environment. In Chapter 3, we discussed how in areas with little or no complexity, there are relatively few species, yet an estimated 1.4–1.6 million marine species inhabit the open sea (Bouchet 2006). Looking below the ocean surface we see a complex three-dimensional environment where many dynamic physical and biological processes interact to produce a remarkably heterogeneous habitat that numerous bird species have become highly adapted to exploit.

Habitat complexity in the marine environment occurs over very different scales to terrestrial systems. Relatively 'small-scale' local features such as tidal races and eddies, and 'large-scale' processes such as oceanic circulation patterns create a dynamic, ever-changing habitat; a patch of water rich in prey today may be severely diminished tomorrow. Ireland's marine area is greatly influenced by a north-easterly directed component of the Gulf Stream, which moves heat from the equator to the Arctic, known as the North Atlantic Drift. The meeting of this warm water with the Western Europe

European Storm Petrel at sea (John Fox).

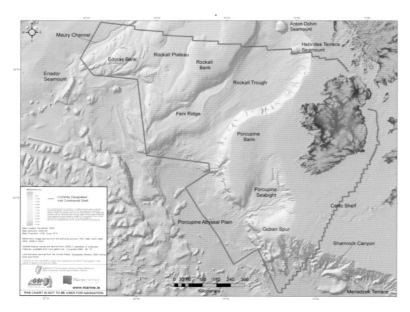

Ireland's sea area is many times the size of the land area (Marine Institute).

Arctic Terns on migration (Richard T. Mills).

continental shelf results in a complex hydrography, and much warmer conditions than would be expected for Ireland's northerly position. Areas of upwelling and frontal systems rich in nutrients are also biologically very productive. Seasonal increases in day length and temperature stimulate rapid phytoplankton growth that acts as the basis of a complex food chain, attracting high densities of zooplankton. Such an abundant food source is readily utilised by many birds and fish species, the latter also being fed on by larger predatory fish, marine mammals, and birds.

In Irish waters, a diverse group of bird species occurs; from species that are present throughout the year, such as Fulmars and Northern Gannets, to long-distance migrating species present only in the summer months like Arctic Terns and Manx Shearwaters. These examples represent the seabirds, a group of birds fundamentally different to the more familiar song birds, which have a number of unique adaptations enabling them to thrive in the marine environment. Seabirds spend much of their time great distances away from land, and many have developed longer, more tapered wings to aid soaring and sustain prolonged flight with little effort, or in the case of diving species, have evolved shorter wings to aid manoeuvrability underwater. Seabirds are generally darker and less colourful than other birds, but often have a light underbelly to mask them from prey below. Typically, seabirds have a greater number of feathers relative to body size to aid in waterproofing and insulation, and webbed feet to aid in diving or movement along the water surface during take-off. Specialised salt glands have also been developed to extract and excrete the high concentrations of salt from food and water to reduce dehydration. But probably the most striking, although not readily apparent difference between seabirds and their terrestrial counterparts is their increased longevity; Atlantic Puffins and Black-legged Kittiwakes can typically live 20–30 years, and a Manx Shearwater was recorded alive some 50 years after first being trapped and ringed, indicating an incredibly long lifespan. Balancing this longevity, seabirds tend to mature later and have lower clutch sizes, typically raising 1–2 young per season. This lower rate of reproduction makes their populations particularly vulnerable to losses associated with predation or fisheries bycatch.

At least 45 species of seabird have been recorded during ship-based surveys in Irish waters, with 24 of these species regularly breeding around the Irish coast (Pollock 1994; Pollock *et al.* 1997; Mackey *et al.* 2004).

History

Our earliest understanding of habitat use by seabirds in the open sea comes from the dedicated effort of land-based observers. The insights gained from these studies are largely dependent on highly developed field identification skills; seabirds passing off headlands often present very brief views, and only highly experienced observers can make reliable identifications. In North Donegal in the autumn of 1953, Gibbs *et al.* (1954) recorded large numbers of Sooty Shearwaters e.g. 'at least 137 birds off Malin Head during 5.5 hours observation on September 9th were of this species', and these authors also identified a small number of Great Shearwaters moving past Inishtrahull and Malin. Up to the late 1950s knowledge of oceanic birds in Irish waters was highly fragmentary and for the most part not based on systematic study. 'Wrecks' of Leach's Storm Petrels and Little Auks were known to occur following severe Atlantic storms (Sergeant 1952; Boyd 1954; Kennedy *et al.* 1954), with both of these species sometimes seen at inland localities. The first records of Wilson's Storm-petrels were two separate individuals shot in Fermanagh and Mossvale, Co. Down, respectively in early October 1891 (Hutchinson 1989), and Ireland's only accepted record of a Madeiran Storm Petrel was one that was killed at Blackrock Lighthouse in Co. Mayo on 11 October 1931 (Ruttledge 1966).

The founding of an observatory on Clear Island in 1959 changed everything as the comparatively new technique of 'sea-watching' (Sharrock 1973) revealed a major seabird migration route off the south-west coast on a scale that had not been suspected let alone detected before (see for example, Green 1965, Newell 1968; Bourne 1973a; Sharrock 1973; Hutchinson 1989; Enticott 1999). These and other discoveries stimulated even more systematic and coordinated sea-watching known as 'The Atlantic Sea-watch' from headlands around Ireland (see Pettitt 1965; Phillips 1965; Devlin 1966; Hayward 1967; Hounsome 1968). Jones and Tasker (1982)

Manx Shearwaters (John Covney).

Sea-watching enthusiasts at the Bridges of Ross, Co. Clare (John Coveney).

provide a relatively recent overview. These pioneering sea-watch studies raised fundamental questions regarding the ecological and oceanographic conditions in the deep-sea waters further offshore. Given the high abundances observed from headlands, the deep-sea was presumably capable of sustaining large aggregations of what were heretofore considered to be rare pelagic seabird species (e.g. Bourne 1966). This issue was highlighted by Pollock (1994) who points out that 'Land based studies have shown large numbers of seabirds to be present in the neritic (inshore) zone at times of peak migration during spring and especially autumn' and 'many of these movements are known to occur during well

Northern Gannet, Ireland's largest seabird (John Coveney).

defined weather conditions (Hutchinson 1989) leading to the reasonable assumption that the largest numbers of seabirds are in deeper waters – outside the range of inshore studies'.

One of the first attempts at answering these questions was undertaken in 1966 when a pelagic cruise on the *Richard* departed from Kinsale for the Labadie Bank to the south-west of Co. Cork (M.A. Hartnett, pers. comm.). At-sea surveys are financially costly and logistically difficult, and as a result, tend to be conducted from 'ships of opportunity' where survey effort is limited to where ships are going on their primary business. This results in high survey coverage along shipping routes, and otherwise seasonally and spatially patchy data that may fail to survey important areas for seabirds. Dedicated ship-based surveys were first conducted in Ireland's Atlantic region in 1978 (Tasker 2000), and off the south and west coasts in 1980 (Pollock *et al.* 1997), although survey coverage has been sporadic. There have been two main phases of ship-based research in Irish waters to date. The Seabirds at Sea Team (SAST) of the UK's Joint Nature Conservation Committee (JNCC) conducted dedicated surveys in Irish waters using ships of opportunity and occasional charter vessels between August 1994 and January 1997 (Pollock *et al.* 1997), with the aim of identifying and describing year-round dispersion patterns of seabirds. Building on this study, the Coastal and Marine Research Centre (CMRC) of University College Cork (UCC) used ship-based surveys between 1999 and 2003 to target the offshore seabird populations of Irelands Atlantic Margin, in the Porcupine–Rockall–Hatton region (Mackey *et al.* 2004). Much of the data in Irish waters have concentrated on inshore, coastal and continental shelf waters less than 200m deep and, as a result, our knowledge of species inhabiting the vast area further offshore is more limited. Nonetheless, the volume of data aggregated over the years has shown that the distribution of seabirds in the open sea is anything but uniform, with birds often occurring in high densities over relatively small areas (Pollock *et al.* 1997; Cronin and Mackey 2002; Mackey *et al.* 2004). However, even with this increased range of observations, our knowledge of the ecology of seabirds at sea is still extremely limited. A review of European Seabirds At Sea (ESAS) survey coverage in Irish waters was recently conducted for National Parks and Wildlife Service to highlight gaps in survey effort and seasonal and temporal coverage, as well as discussing the age of existing data (Pollock and Barton 2008). While these data are acknowledged to be patchy in their coverage, available at a fairly coarse spatial resolution, and now mostly in excess of ten years old, they represent the most comprehensive data set available on the distribution and relative abundance of seabirds given that there is currently no seabirds-at-sea monitoring programme operating in Irish waters.

While there is no dedicated monitoring in offshore waters, seabird research is progressing in Ireland. The Beaufort-funded Ecosystem Approach to Fisheries Management aims to address the role of top predators, including seabirds, in the marine environment, focusing on diet and critical foraging areas, determining population-level food and energy requirements, and investigating interactions with commercial fisheries. The Future of the Atlantic Marine Environment (FAME) project brings together partners in France, Ireland, Spain, Portugal and Britain to monitor and track seabirds throughout the Atlantic area and, by combining these data with oceanographic information, inform the designation of Marine Protected Areas.

Seabird Diet

Seabirds utilise the open sea and its plentiful food resources, but are constrained by the need to return to land to breed, incubate eggs, and rear their offspring, usually in large colonies, and often restricted to offshore islands free from terrestrial predators. With large numbers of birds occupying such limited space, the potential for intense local competition for food resources is great, particularly considering that seabirds often have partially overlapping diets (e.g. Cherel *et al.* 2002, Forero *et al.* 2004). The distribution of prey in relation to nesting sites is therefore considered to be one of the most important factors determining seabird abundance and distribution (Ollason *et al.* 1997, Ford *et al.* 2007). Outside the breeding season, it is debatable whether this competition is reduced. Although no longer constrained by the need to return regularly to land to feed chicks, the potential for competition remains high, as food abundance and availability in winter may be limited or more dispersed (as in the case of fish spawning aggregations). Diet studies, mainly consisting of analysis of regurgitates from birds returning to the colonies to feed their young (Barrett *et al.* 2007), show that the main prey items of seabirds foraging out at sea include small schooling pelagic fish (e.g. lesser sand eel, herring and sprat), and moderately sized pelagic crustaceans and squid; most of which are found in the upper- to mid-water column (Bourne 1986; Shealer 2002). However, very little information is available on the diet of seabirds in Ireland, which represents a critical gap in our knowledge of seabird ecology. Feeding aggregations of seabirds are known to occur around productive ocean areas high in zooplankton prey, and many seabirds have evolved sensitivity to dimethyl sulfide (DMS), a pungent chemical given off by phytoplankton, particularly when being grazed by zooplankton, which they use to home in on these temporary prey-rich areas.

Haddock, herring and whiting all form large spawning aggregations in Irish nearshore coastal waters. In other temperate waters, such demersal bottom-feeding fish feature regularly in the diet of seabirds (Barrett *et al.* 2007), but as relatively few diet studies have been conducted in Irish waters, the relative importance of these species to seabirds is currently unknown. Likewise, large offshore spawning aggregations of blue whiting, hake and mackerel off the west coast of Ireland may provide a good source of food for foraging seabirds. These species are pelagic, living and feeding in the water column, and are likely to come towards surface waters in the search for food, particularly when their zooplankton prey migrate up through the water column. When near the surface, these fish become accessible to plunging and pursuit diving seabirds such as Northern Gannets, Atlantic Puffins and shearwaters, while smaller species such as terns and Black-legged Kittiwakes may forage preferentially on zooplankton in the surface waters. The diet of seabirds during the non-breeding period and in areas further offshore is very poorly studied; coupled with the inaccessibility of the offshore area for direct observations, ingested prey may be largely digested by the time birds return to colonies, making the identification of prey remains in regurgitates

Fulmar (left) and Great Black-backed Gull compete for food (John Coveney).

The Black-legged Kittiwake may feed on plankton in the surface of the sea (Richard Nairn).

even more difficult. Molecular techniques such as genetic identification of remains, or stable isotope analysis of tissues such as blood and feathers will prove to be invaluable in gaining a better understanding of seabird diet both during the non-breeding period, and in offshore areas.

Seabird habitats

Northern Gannets can dive up to 20m deep (John Fox).

It should be noted that seabirds can only access a tiny fraction of the total open sea habitat. While the waters to the east of Ireland are relatively shallow, rarely reaching depths greater than 100m, the large marine area to the west of Ireland quickly drops to depths far below the ability of even the deepest-diving seabirds to reach. For example, Northern Gannets have a typical dive depth of up to 20m (Brierley and Fernandes 2001; Garthe *et al.* 2007), while Atlantic Puffins and Sooty Shearwaters have been recorded at maximum depths of approximately 60–70m (Piatt and Nettleship 1985; Burger and Simpson 1986; Shaffer *et al.* 2006). This 'top layer' of the ocean where light penetrates with enough intensity to support prolific phytoplankton growth, makes these waters incredibly rich in prey biomass. For the purposes of this chapter, we will divide the 'open sea' into two distinct large-scale habitats reflecting differences in hydrodynamic processes and associated productivity. These are 'shelf waters', extending from the coast to the edge of the continental shelf (identified as the 200m depth contour); and deep-sea 'oceanic' waters, extending from the continental shelf 200m contour outwards.

Since this book focuses on bird habitats, it should also be noted that seabirds spend a significant portion of the year at colonies. As mentioned in Chapter 11, sea cliffs and rocky coasts are vitally important for breeding seabirds, and the location of these habitats is a key factor determining seabird distribution at sea. Chapter 11 gives a very good description of the distribution of seabird colonies around Ireland, and the relative abundance of seabirds occupying these areas to go with the following account of the open sea habitat.

Shelf waters

The vast majority of this habitat occurs to the east and south of Ireland. The Irish Sea to the east is mostly less than 100m deep, although there are some deeper areas up to 200m. To the south of Ireland there is an extensive shelf area extending some 300km into the Celtic sea. Sediments within the central Irish Sea area are generally muddy and sandy, becoming more gravelly southwards, and sand, shelly sand and gravel predominate within the Celtic Sea. The south-west and north-west coasts have a much narrower shallow water zone, with depths dropping beyond the 200m contour within 60km of the coast, while the shelf extends out as far as 170km to the west of Galway Bay. Large areas of bedrock occur, generally in the vicinity of headlands, where the seafloor is swept clear by wind-wave and tidal current action, with sand and gravel more common further offshore.

Surface currents in shelf waters predominately run clockwise around the Irish coastline, although there is a northward surface current in the Irish Sea from St George's Channel to the North Channel, and a counterclockwise gyre to the north-east of Dublin. A large frontal system runs along the 200m contour on the west coast (Irish Shelf front) with a further three tidal fronts located to the north-east of Co. Derry (Islay front), east of Dublin (Irish Sea front), and south-east of Co. Wexford (Celtic Sea front). The shelf waters are an important habitat for many seabirds, particularly during the breeding season when foraging is constrained to nearshore waters by the need to return to colonies on a regular basis to feed chicks. As a result, the density of many seabird species is positively related to distance from the nearest coast (Roycroft *et al.* 2006).

High densities of Manx Shearwaters are recorded in inshore waters (John Coveney).

A Great Northern Diver in winter (Richard T. Mills).

Breeding season

Fulmars, Manx Shearwaters, Northern Gannets, Shags, Great Cormorants, Black-legged Kittiwakes, Great Black-Backed Gulls, terns, Common Guillemots, Razorbills and Atlantic Puffins all commonly occur in Irish shelf waters. Other more inshore species such as Red-throated Diver and Great Northern Diver are often seen in shallow coastal waters, while waders (Dunlin, Oystercatcher, Ruddy Turnstone, Eurasian Whimbrel) are often seen on passage over nearshore coastal waters. However, these birds are more often associated with beaches, dunes, bays, and estuaries, which are the focus of previous chapters.

Of the auks, Common Guillemots and Razorbills are regularly sighted over shelf waters, with few records in deeper waters further offshore, while Black Guillemots were all encountered inshore along the west and north coasts of Ireland (Stone *et al.* 1995; Mackey *et al.* 2004). Atlantic Puffins occur in greatest densities during the late spring/summer period when they are constrained by the need to make repeat foraging trips to and from the breeding colonies. These birds specialise in pursuit diving where the wings have been modified for propulsion underwater, resulting in a large area in which to feed. Manx Shearwaters are also often found over the continental shelf (Stone *et al.* 1995), and occur in high abundances in the vicinity of the Irish Sea frontal system (Begg and Reid 1997; Guilford *et al.* 2008). Off the west coast of Ireland, Manx Shearwaters have a wide distribution, and high densities have been recorded in the shallower shelf waters within foraging range of breeding colonies such as the Blasket islands, particularly in spring and summer.

European Shags, Great Cormorants, Black Guillemots, Lesser Black-backed Gulls, Razorbills and Common Terns all have relatively restricted foraging distributions, with mean foraging ranges of around 40km or less (Wanless *et al.* 1991; Monaghan *et al.* 1994; Hamer *et al.* 1997; Grémillet *et al.* 1999; Daunt *et*

Great Cormorants are excellent divers in pursuit of their prey (John Coveney).

al. 2002; Grémillet *et al.* 2004; Enstipp *et al.* 2006). While Common Guillemot, Atlantic Puffin and Black-legged Kittiwake have been recorded undertaking foraging trips of up to 200km, mean foraging range is also less than 40km (Langston 2010; Roos *et al.* 2010), making these birds common in the coastal shelf waters during the breeding season. Within these waters, a range of foraging strategies enable seabirds to exploit different components of the ecosystem, reducing inter-species competition. European Shag, Great Cormorants, and Common Guillemots are all excellent pursuit divers, reaching depths that are inaccessible to birds such as Common Terns, Black-legged Kittiwakes and Lesser Black-backed Gulls which excel at surface feeding and shallow plunge diving. Black-legged Kittiwakes are found in moderate to high densities all around the Irish coast, and a correlation between their distribution and that of Manx Shearwaters suggests a high degree of ecological overlap (Begg and Reid 1997).

Manx Shearwaters, Fulmars and Northern Gannets have much larger foraging ranges than many other seabirds, with mean foraging range of 70km for Fulmar, 140km for Northern Gannet, and 170km for Manx Shearwater. Maximum foraging range for these birds is in excess of 400km (Langston 2010; Roos *et al.* 2010). With the majority of breeding populations concentrated along the west coast of Ireland, Fulmars are more commonly recorded in deeper waters to the west of Ireland, although they are appear widely distributed in low to moderate density over shelf waters. Northern Gannets are generally found in low to moderate density over Irish shelf waters throughout the year, with highest densities in coastal areas close to the main breeding colonies in the south-west during summer months. Large flocks of Northern Gannets plunge-diving in coastal waters provide a visually stunning spectacle as they dive from height and fold back their wings just before hitting the surface. This highly specialised method uses less energy than pursuit diving and enables Northern Gannets to dive to depths of over 20m (Garthe *et al.* 2000, Lewis *et al.* 2002), and take widely distributed prey.

Non-breeding season

During the spring/summer breeding period, shelf waters are dominated by breeding birds undertaking provisioning trips, and as a result, there is intense local competition for prey. Immature, and non-breeding birds are likely to forage further offshore and over deeper waters where possible to take advantage of abundant prey and reduce competition in coastal shelf waters. However, all seabird species disperse towards the end of the summer to take advantage of seasonally and spatially patchy prey in other waters. Manx Shearwaters winter off the east coast of South America (Guilford *et al.* 2009), European Storm Petrels winter as far south as South Africa, and Razorbills generally move south to the Bay of Biscay and Iberia (Cramp *et al.* 1974). As a result, some migratory bird species are recorded only rarely in Irish coastal shelf waters during winter months. A number of seabirds also disperse throughout home waters throughout the non-breeding period. High densities of Black-legged Kittiwakes are common in the shelf waters and the shelf break to the south-west, and while immature Northern Gannets tend to winter off the west coast of Africa, the Mediterranean, and the Bay of Biscay, adults tend to disperse throughout home waters during the winter months, and they are seen frequently in shelf waters year-round (Cramp *et al.* 1974).

European Storm Petrels winter as far south as South Africa (John Coveney).

Oceanic waters

The deep-sea oceanic waters constitute a vast area of habitat, primarily along the west coast where the bathymetry drops away quickly from the 200m contour giving rise to extensive abyssal plains, while waters to the east, and largely along the south of Ireland do not fall below the 200m depth contour. The deep-sea waters to the west of Ireland also experience some of the harshest ocean conditions in the world, being exposed to the full force of Atlantic storms with predominant winds from the west and south-west. Both deep-water and surface currents tend to run north to north-easterly along the shelf break past the west coast, and run in a south-westerly direction along the eastern side of the Rockall Bank. Large areas of seafloor sediment to the west and south of the Irish coast remain uncharacterised; however, the relationship between sediment and demersal fish species is probably less important in terms of seabird diet in deep-sea waters than it is in shallower coastal and shelf waters where this component of the ecosystem is more readily accessed. A large upwelling is known to occur periodically around south-west Ireland, with an area of a few thousand square kilometres being affected (Raine *et al.* 1990).

Breeding Season

The oceanic waters of Ireland represent an area accessible only to far-ranging birds during the breeding season. Of the breeding seabirds commonly found in Irish waters, Manx Shearwater, Fulmar and Northern Gannet have the greatest potential to forage far offshore. Hamer *et al.* (2001) reported an average foraging distance of 160km from colonies, while Votier *et al.* (2010) recorded an average foraging round-trip of 370km with a maximum of 1,121km for Northern Gannets, while Fulmars have been recorded undertaking foraging trips of up to 184km from their colonies (Hamer *et al.* 1997). As such, these birds can exploit productive waters further offshore during regular provisioning trips. Data suggests that the majority of Northern Gannets remain close to colonies during the breeding season, but individuals have been recorded in low to medium densities along the shelf break and deep waters to the west of Ireland from February to May, and in low densities during the June to August breeding season (Pollock *et al.* 1997), suggesting that these offshore birds are non-breeders.

Few auks are recorded in the deeper oceanic waters during the breeding season; Razorbills are rarely sighted in the offshore oceanic zone while Common Guillemots are recorded in low densities during spring months, particularly over the Hatton–Rockall Bank (Mackey *et al.* 2004). The presence of important breeding colonies of Atlantic Puffins on the Great Skellig and Puffin Island, Co. Kerry, and the Saltee Islands, Co. Wexford, is reflected in the wide distribution (albeit in low densities) over oceanic waters to the west of Ireland during the spring and summer (Pollock *et al.* 1997; Cronin and Mackey 2002; Mackey *et al.* 2004). Great Black-backed Gulls are rarely sighted in oceanic waters during the breeding season, but Lesser Black-backed Gulls have been recorded across a wide offshore distribution, particularly in spring (Mackey *et al.* 2004).

Fulmars have been recorded undertaking foraging trips of up to 184km from their colonies (John Coveney).

Lesser Black-backed Gulls are widely distributed at sea in spring (Richard T. Mills).

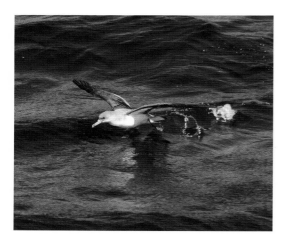

Cory's Shearwater pass through Irish waters each year (Karl Partridge).

Great Shearwaters migrate west of the Porcupine Seabight (John Coveney).

Atlantic Puffins are relatively scarce in winter (John Coveney).

While five species of shearwater are regularly recorded in Irish waters (Sooty Shearwater, Cory's Shearwater, Great Shearwater, Balearic Shearwater and Manx Shearwater), only Manx Shearwater actually breeds here (although a Cory's Shearwater has occupied a burrow for several years on Great Skellig). In addition to the high concentrations associated with the Irish Sea frontal system in shelf waters, Manx Shearwaters have been recorded in relatively high densities in the deep-water regions north and north-west of the Porcupine Bank in spring and summer (Mackey *et al.* 2004). This area falls within the foraging range of the western and south-western Irish breeding populations (Coulson 2002).

Leach's Storm Petrels are predominantly found over deeper water from July to September (Mackey *et al.* 2004). A small breeding population exists in Co. Mayo on the Stags of Broadhaven, with a much larger population breeding on the Scottish island of St Kilda (Mitchell *et al.* 2004), however, it is not known whether observations at sea are of breeding adults foraging over oceanic waters. Leach's Storm Petrels are known to form 'wrecks'; large concentrations of birds that have been blown off course and stray into the nearshore waters where they have been observed from headlands to the north such as Kilcummin and Brandon Head during strong north-westerly winds.

Non-breeding season

Numerous seabirds make far-ranging excursions into the deep oceanic waters outside of the breeding season. However, survey coverage of these waters over the winter months is extremely limited, so seabird abundances in this vast offshore area may be higher than current data suggests. Medium densities of Fulmar, Great Shearwater, Northern Gannet, Great Skua, Black-legged Kittiwake and Atlantic Puffin have all been recorded beyond the 200m contour over winter months, primarily to the south-west in the Porcupine Seabight, and to the north-west at the Rockall Bank. While the majority of adult Northern Gannets are located within shelf waters during the breeding season, adult birds tend to disperse throughout their coastal home waters over winter. These birds are rarely recorded in deep-sea waters to the west of Ireland between September and January, but as previously mentioned, survey effort is low, so they may be more common. Fulmars on the other hand, have been recorded in medium to high densities in deep-sea waters, particularly along the north-west coast where survey coverage over the winter months is greater (Pollock *et al.* 1997).

Atlantic Puffins are relatively scarce in Ireland's Atlantic margin during the overwintering period. Where these Atlantic Puffins disperse to at the end of the breeding season is the focus of ongoing studies, with geolocator tags being recently recovered from instrumented birds upon their return to breeding colonies on Great Skellig during the summer of 2011. Analysis of the data will provide insights into the overwintering distribution of these charismatic seabirds. Similar tagging studies on Atlantic Puffins from north-east UK demonstrated that the nearby North Sea was the most intensively used region, but that many birds also made excursions into the north-east Atlantic in the early winter, a relatively recent phenomenon that possibly reflects worsening conditions in the North Sea (Harris *et al.* 2010). Prey type and availability is probably very different between the relatively shallow North Sea and the deep offshore waters of the Atlantic, and how this distributional change relates to prey availability is an interesting avenue of future research.

Migratory species

Arctic Terns are recognised as a common seasonal component of seabird assemblages in the offshore waters of Ireland, occurring in medium densities during their migration between the high Arctic and Antarctic. In addition to their presence in a number of offshore deep-water surveys (Pollock *et al.* 1997; Cronin and Mackey 2002; Mackey *et al.* 2004), recent telemetry studies have given us an unprecedented insight into the vast scale of this migration. Using light-sensitive geolocation loggers, Egevang *et al.* (2010) illustrated the migration route of Arctic Terns from Greenland as they head south along the east Atlantic, returning northward along the west Atlantic. High abundances in the oceanic waters of Ireland occur in April–June, with relative scarcity at other times of the year, suggesting that the Arctic Terns observed in offshore surveys may be from another population that migrates northward along the east Atlantic.

The Sooty Shearwater breeds on islands in the southern Pacific and Atlantic (John Coveney).

Wilson's Storm Petrel is a rare but regular visitor to Irish waters, with the majority of sightings occurring over the shelf edge between June and August (Pollock *et al.* 1997; Mackey *et al.* 2004). While this is a predominantly pelagic species in Irish waters, there are occasional sightings of Wilson's Storm Petrel from headlands such as Clear Island, the Old Head of Kinsale, Galley Head, Brandon Head, the Bridges of Ross, and Kilcummin Head associated with strong onshore winds. Land-based sea-watches have also recorded strong westward migration of Great Skuas in the coastal waters to the north (Gibbs *et al.* 1954), and a spectacular movement of Great Shearwaters off Clear Island in September 1965 involving over 10,000 individuals was the largest of its kind ever detected in British and Irish waters (Newell 1968). Sooty Shearwater is a long-range migrant, breeding on islands in the southern Pacific and Atlantic. Sea-watch data show a seasonal trend in abundance, peaking in August–September (Hutchinson 1989), which is consistent with peaks in abundance during offshore surveys.

High densities of the smaller skua species (Pomarine, Arctic and Long-tailed Skuas) have been noted in the oceanic of the Hatton–Rockall basin in spring, over 70% of which were recorded heading north or north-east. This suggests an important offshore migratory route for these species to their feeding/breeding grounds in the Arctic tundra. Interestingly, the majority of Arctic Skua sightings were made during kleptoparasitic (pirate) attacks on Black-legged Kittiwakes, the presence of which during this time of year must provide a valuable food resource for migrating Arctic Skuas (Cronin and Mackey 2002).

Three species of divers occur regularly off the Irish coast: Red-throated Diver, Black-throated Diver and Great Northern Diver. All three prefer shallow coastal waters associated with sandy or rocky bottoms (Pollock *et al.* 1997; Mackey *et al.* 2004). Great Northern Divers have been observed migrating westwards across the Hatton–Rockall basin towards their summer grounds in Canada or Greenland. The Rockall Trough also appears to be an important area for migration of Lesser Black-backed Gulls, Pomarine Skuas and Long-Tailed Skuas during the spring and autumn migration between southern wintering and northern breeding grounds (Mackey *et al.* 2004). While much of the survey effort around the Porcupine Seabight and Porcupine Bank, and the north-eastern margins of the Rockall and Hatton Banks was under the auspices of petroleum exploration, with limited survey coverage in surrounding areas for comparison, it is hypothesised that 'hot spots' of species richness occur around these regions. This is unsurprising as these areas represent comparatively shallow waters with a steep drop-off, which are commonly associated with highly productive upwelling areas.

Overview of seabird distribution

As mentioned in the earlier section on the history of seabird research, one of the early findings from data on bird abundance in the open sea was that the flocks of seabirds counted from headlands during sea-watch surveys are rarely encountered in ship-based 'seabirds at sea' surveys. Given the high abundances of some species observed from headlands, waters further offshore were thought to sustain large concentrations of otherwise rarely observed pelagic seabirds, yet birds are recorded in relatively low densities during ship-based surveys, rarely exceeding five individuals per km surveyed (Mackey *et al.* 2004). It should be noted however, that these at-sea surveys follow strict procedures which omit birds 'associating' with the survey ship, and specifically avoid fishing vessels which often have large numbers of birds following them to forage on their discards. The Sabine's Gull is a good example as numerous 'seabirds at sea' studies (e.g. Pollock (1994) Pollock *et al.* (1997), Mackey *et al.* (2004)), observed relatively few individuals of this species during lengthy cruises off the south, west and north-west coasts of Ireland, but 346 individuals have been counted on one day (29 August 1997) during sea-watches off Brandon Head Co. Kerry (Ed Carty pers. comm. and in prep; see also Elkins and Yésou 1998).

Pomarine Skuas migrate through the Rockall Trough in spring and autumn (John Fox).

Trawler working off Wicklow Head Lighthouse, Co. Wicklow (John Coveney).

It is generally agreed that the large aggregations of pelagic seabirds observed from headlands during stormy weather involve birds either moving towards favourable feeding grounds or attempting to return to foraging grounds from which they had been displaced by inclement conditions (e.g. Bourne 1973b, Elkins 2004). Obvious questions are raised about the combination of meteorological conditions that 'drive' seabird species from the deep pelagic zone towards the coastline. It is likely that different species with different aerodynamic properties will respond in different ways to ambient meteorological conditions, and this is just one of the factors that needs to be taken into account when attempting to explain the patterns of movements detected by sea-watching from headlands (e.g. Sharrock 1973, Hutchinson 1989, Elkins 2004 and references therein). Birds often move ahead of advancing depressions, and are therefore concentrated as they approach land (Elkins 2004). Colm Moore's (1975) excellent but little cited paper on movements of seabirds in the Irish Sea showed this effect very clearly.

High concentrations of specific seabirds during inclement weather can give us valuable information on the general distribution of species further from the coast. From a sea-watching perspective, onshore winds are best for observing seabirds blown inshore from their usual offshore areas. Aggregations of Sabine's Gull, skuas (especially Pomarine and Long-tailed Skua), Grey Phalarope, and Leach's Storm Petrel have been recorded from headlands at the Bridges of Ross, Kilcummin and Brandon Head during strong north-westerly winds. While some movements have also been recorded off south coasts, it is generally agreed that these species all have a more northerly offshore distribution, having rarely been recorded in any significant numbers from headlands further south along the west coast. Along the more southerly headlands along the west coast, in particular Cape Clear where many hours of sea-watching data are available, Balearic, Cory's, and Great Shearwaters have all been recorded during strong south-west to westerly winds (e.g. Sharrock 1973), but are less frequently recorded at more northerly headlands.

Analysis of seabird distribution data from at-sea surveys, coupled with environmental information gathered from remotely gathered satellite data is leading to an increased understanding of the distribution of many seagoing species. Sea surface temperature can be used to identify areas of upwelling of cold, nutrient-rich waters, while measuring chlorophyll-a gives a direct measurement of ocean primary productivity, which in turn correlates well with zooplankton abundance. Sea surface height anomalies can be used to identify large-scale eddies that contain high concentrations of prey, while wind field may affect the foraging dynamics of seabirds. All of these variables have previously been correlated with the distribution of marine predators, and their relationship with seabird abundance in Irish waters will enable us to use predictive models to estimate distribution and fill in the gaps of survey coverage. Existing seabird distribution and environmental covariate data is currently being collated to do just such an analysis, with results expected to provide valuable information to support seabird conservation.

Future trends

One of the most exciting advances in seabird research is the growing use of telemetry technology to remotely monitor individual birds when they leave breeding colonies and head out to sea. Technological advances mean that satellite relay and global positioning system (GPS) loggers are continually decreasing in cost and size, and are now miniaturised to the extent that we can attach these to foraging seabirds to collect information on foraging hot spots and areas of high risk in relation to fisheries bycatch. Light level loggers, or geolocation devices, use the time of local sunrise and sunset to estimate broadscale position, and have become so small that they can be attached to even the smallest seabirds (e.g. Arctic Terns; Egevang *et al.* 2010) to follow individual birds across migration routes and overwintering areas that would be prohibitively expensive to survey by traditional means. Relatively few studies of this kind have been conducted in Irish waters, but this is a growing area of scientific research here, and will lead to a great increase in our understanding of seabird ecology. Coupled with

Common Guillemot (John Coveney).

Windfarm on Arklow Bank off Co. Wicklow
(John Coveney).

this, Stable Isotope Analysis (SIA) has become an invaluable tool for ecologists to investigate diet and habitat selection (Hobson *et al.* 2002, Cherel *et al.* 2006). Survival, breeding success and chick growth are all closely related to food availability, so knowledge of diet and prey distribution is fundamental to our understanding of how seabirds utilise the open sea habitat. The ratios of stable carbon and nitrogen isotopes in tissues reflect prey composition during tissue formation, and can provide both spatial information, and the relative contribution of inshore versus offshore, and benthic versus pelagic organisms in seabird diet (Michener and Schell 1994, Cherel *et al.* 2006).

Ireland has a legal obligation to designate a network of marine Special Protected Areas (SPAs) for seabird conservation under the EU Birds and Habitats Directives, and information on the distribution and habitat use of seabirds is essential for their effective designation. However, while it is relatively easy to identify and designate breeding colonies and their nearshore waters that are used for activities such as rafting on the surface before returning to colonies at dusk, difficulties arise in identifying and designating protected areas in regions that cover the foraging range or critical foraging habitats of seabirds away from their breeding colonies. The dynamic nature of the open sea habitat means that small, static SPAs are unlikely to meet long-term conservation objectives, particularly considering the competing interests of marine fisheries, aquaculture, tourism, recreation and other uses of the marine environment that will impact on seabirds ranging outside designated areas. How this issue is addressed is a source of continuing research and discussion across Europe, and given its large territorial waters, Ireland has a unique opportunity to be at the forefront of marine conservation.

A recent Strategic Environmental Assessment currently undergoing public consultation has identified the east coast of Ireland as having high wind resource, with the west coast having high wave resource for potential development of large-scale offshore renewable energy installations (Anon 2010). While wave energy is still in its infancy, wind generation is envisaged to be the best option for meeting targets of generating 20–30% of Ireland's energy from renewable resources by 2020. Adverse effects of offshore wind farms have previously been reported for some seabird species, with the main potential risks being collision (Hüppop *et al.* 2006), habitat exclusion (Larsen and Guillemette 2007), barriers to movement of migrating birds or between feeding and breeding areas (Masden *et al.* 2010), and changes in food availability (Kaiser *et al.* 2006), with cumulative effects of these across multiple wind farms. Langston (2010) provides a useful review of current knowledge. It is clear that such installations will become a relatively common feature of the marine landscape, and how seabirds adapt to these structures will be a source of important future research.

Finally, reform of the European Common Fisheries Policy is currently under way, and will probably include an undertaking to significantly reduce the amount of fishery discards at sea. Scavenging on fisheries discards has become a common foraging tactic for many seabirds such as northern Fulmars and Northern Gannets, as much of the discards are incredibly abundant, and can be obtained without the energetic cost of diving. Many discards are also from demersal fisheries, providing access to a food source usually beyond the normal diving ability of most seabirds. Numerous observations of seabirds scavenging around fishing vessels in Irish waters have been made previously (Hillis 1971; Watson 1978, 1981; Pollock 1994), with Fulmars, Northern Gannets, gulls, Great Cormorants and Black-legged Kittiwakes all recorded feeding on discards. This discarding activity is believed to have made some seabird species over-reliant on fisheries discards, and a recent review suggests that decreasing the amount of discards can result in increased mortality, reduced body condition and reduced breeding success in species such as Fulmar, which are reliant on discards. Additional knock-on ecosystem effects can occur as birds such as skuas previously reliant on discards turn to predation on smaller seabirds in order to supply their food needs (Furness 2003). How seabirds in Irish waters will be affected by changes in fishing and discarding practices remains to be seen, and represents a priority research area.

Fulmars scavenge on fisheries discards (John Coveney).

15. Urban Habitats

Éanna Ní Lamhna, Richard Nairn, Lorraine Benson and Thomas C. Kelly

Introduction

The urban environment is probably the fastest-growing habitat on Earth and it is expected that 60% of the world's human population will be living in cities by 2025 (Wheater 1999). While the construction of urban landscapes may have a massive negative impact on the pre-existing natural habitat including forests and wetlands, the long-term effects may not be wholly destructive. For example, Cannon *et al.* (2005) suggest that as much as 500,000 hectares of England and Wales may be covered by gardens. Nevertheless, it is generally agreed that bird species diversity is reduced in urban habitats for a variety of reasons including disturbance, atmospheric and noise pollution, and the presence of predators such as cats (e.g. Cannon *et al.* 2005).

Sixty per cent of the human population of Ireland lives in urban areas, which are defined as cities and towns having a population of 1,500 or more. Dublin – our largest city – has a population of over 1 million inhabitants. Table 1 below shows the population of our cities according to the most recent Census figures in 2006.

Gardens provide abundant bird habitats in urban areas such as Cork city (Richard T. Mills).

Table 15.1 Human Population of Irish cities (2006 Census Figures)	
Dublin	1,187,000
Belfast	600,000
Cork	120,000
Derry	90,000
Galway	74,000
Limerick	53,000
Waterford	46,000
Kilkenny	22,000

Even in such densely populated areas, there are distinct habitats for wildlife. Birds in particular have adapted to life in urban areas. Some are commensal species that depend on humans and their lifestyles in order to survive. Other species see cities as an adaptation of natural habitat such as cliffs. Birds that live in urban areas can be observed by the many inhabitants as they go about their daily lives. But whether it is a case of familiarity breeding contempt, cities are not generally thought of as places outstanding for variety and numbers of birds. Yet, of the total 450 species or so on the Irish Bird list, 214 have been recorded in the Dublin city area (Ní Lamhna 2008), 200 species in Belfast (Scott 2004), while at least 126 species have been recorded for Waterford city (McGrath 2006).

With the exception of Kilkenny, all the cities in Table 1 are on river estuaries on the coast, so some of the habitats that contribute to the biodiversity of birdlife in urban areas have been described elsewhere in this volume. The habitats that are described in this chapter are primarily those of urban areas – the hard surfaced areas of inner cities with their high density of buildings, parks and urban open spaces, suburban gardens and city watercourses such as canals, ponds and rivers and streams in urban areas. Fossitt (2000) categorises these habitats as cultivated land, built land, and in the case of lawns and parks, as amenity grassland. These are all considered to be highly modified habitats. In addition, we have added a number of other artificial habitats – sewage treatment works, quarries, landfills, harbours and airports – that are all connected with the urban way of life.

There is now an extensive literature on the topic of urban avifaunas (e.g. Marzluff et al. 2001; Kelcey and Rheinwald 2005). It seems to be generally agreed that there are three major but broadly defined habitats within the urbanised landscape (e.g. Wheater 1999; Clergeau et al. 2001). Firstly, there is the urban core – where the built, i.e. inert, environment overwhelmingly dominates and green areas are at a minimum. Consequently, there is relatively little primary production so most of the food that is available to birds and other animals is either decomposing and mostly inedible waste. The core merges into the suburban that will be composed of a more equal ratio of built to green environments and which will contain domestic gardens with a wide variety of plants (many of which will have been introduced) capable of sustaining herbivores, pollinators and more 'natural' net primary producer (NPP)-based food chains. In addition to private gardens this habitat type may include public parks, playing fields, golf courses and natural and man-made wetlands, all of which potentially enhance avian biodiversity. Finally there is the peri-urban fringe where the suburban merges into the countryside and the landscape is overwhelmingly dominated by green habitats. It has been shown that there is a gradient in bird species richness from the urban core to the peri-urban fringe (e.g. Clergeau et al.2001). Taking censuses of birds in urban habitats presents many challenges and the various methodologies are being continually evaluated and modified (e.g. Rowe 2008; Fennessy and Kelly 2008; De Laet et al. 2011; Clifford 2011).

Hard Surfaces – Streets, Pavements and Buildings

Hard surfaces define urban areas, and include pavements, streets, walls, bridges and quaysides. Yet, for some birds, this is the preferred habitat, providing them with the necessary food, shelter and breeding sites. One example is the Common Swift, a breeding summer migrant and indeed the quintessential city bird. In 2009 the first Common Swifts were recorded in Dublin on 10 April and in Armagh on 16 April. They were gone by the beginning of September (Birdtrack). They are totally dependent on aerial insects. Cool wet summers, when there is reduced aerial insect life, impact badly on the growth rate of young Common Swifts. Fledging takes up to 56 days in cold, wet, summers, as opposed to 35 days during warm dry summers (Cramp 1985). They prefer to nest in tall buildings, and Georgian buildings have eaves and bare soffit boards that they can exploit. Modern apartment blocks provide no such nest sites. There are notable Common Swift colonies on buildings in Trinity College in Dublin (Madden *et al.* 1993) and on the Crescent Arts Centre and the former Ormeau Bakery in Belfast (Scott 2004). During recent renovations of the Crescent Arts Centre precautions were taken by the contractor to avoid disturbance of the colony, and Common Swift bricks were incorporated into the new extension of the building (doeni.org. uk). Common Swifts have declined heavily in Galway over the last ten years (Peppiatt, pers. comm.) a fact attributed to the repair and cleaning of old buildings where they once nested.

A Common Swift launches from its nest in a house (Richard T. Mills).

Feral Pigeons scavenge for food in cities (Karl Partridge).

The Feral Pigeon is another typical species of hard urban surfaces. This species is descended from the wild Rock Dove of sea cliffs. They are herbivores and find food in city and town parks where a not inconsiderable part of their food requirements is provided by humans who feed them bread. They prefer to perch on hard surfaces and nest on buildings in sheltered places. They can raise up to four broods of two per year. Numbers have greatly declined in Waterford city since the port activities (which supplied them with spilt grain) declined and the port moved to Belview (Mc Grath 2006). In Galway, Rock Pipits nest on window ledges where Feral Pigeons also perch.

Pigeons in turn provide food for birds of prey – most notably Peregrine. They hunt and breed in urban areas as well as in their more natural cliff habitats. Peregrines also breed on cliffs in Cork city and birds are regularly seen at Cobh (Cork Harbour) around the now disused shipbuilding yard at Rushbrooke.These birds have been observed hunting over central Dublin, over Belfast, Sligo, and at Christ Church Cathedral in Waterford. A pair has famously been recorded nesting in the large letter

'O' of the sign on the Harland and Wolff building in Belfast. In Galway, Peregrines hunt over the city and nest in a quarry by the east side of Lough Corrib. They have been known to drop half-eaten prey on the offices of the Revenue Commissioners, while in Derry they regularly used the roof of St Eugene's Cathedral to pluck the feathers from their prey (Faulkner and Thompson 2011). Madden *et al.* (2009), in their 2002 survey of breeding Peregrine Falcons in Ireland, record breeding in a total of eleven man-made sites i.e. buildings and chimney stacks. Of these, three churches and a power station were in urban areas. The authors feel that use of man-made structures for nesting will increase following the natural colonisation of urban sites by Peregrines.

A more unlikely predator in hard city surfaces is the Barn Owl. The arrival of a soaking-wet Barn Owl in broad daylight into Pearse Street railway station is reported in *Wild Dublin* (Ní Lamhna 2008). Foley *et al.* (2006) give an account of the diet of the Barn Owl in Dublin and base their results on the examination of owl pellets beneath a roost in Dublin 15. Their work shows that wood mice are by far the most important prey species with over 50% of the prey units. House mice, brown rats and pygmy shrews make up the rest. However, Barn Owls are really a very uncommon bird of urban habitats.

One of the most spectacular sights in the bird world is that of dense flocks of Common Starlings wheeling in a winter evening sky before roosting. It has been estimated that 100,000 Common Starlings roost each night between October and February under both the Queen Elizabeth Bridge and the Albert Bridge in Belfast (Scott 2004), although more recently numbers have fallen to between 30,000 and 40,000 (Faulkner and Thompson 2011). These winter flocks are augmented by migrants from frozen Eastern Europe, but cities can hold flocks of native juvenile Common Starlings in summer after they have fledged. A flock of 550 was spotted roosting on the long arm of a crane in Waterford in July 2003 (Mc Grath 2006), while large roosts in the evergreen trees in the grounds of the Berkeley Court hotel in Ballsbridge in Dublin – itself the site of the former Botanic Gardens belonging to Trinity College – caused severe nuisance to the cars parked beneath them. Common Starlings nest – noisily – in roof spaces and probe the grassy areas of parks for food, so city life suits them.

Pied Wagtails also roost in city centres during winter. The night-time winter temperature can be as much as two degrees higher than in surrounding countryside where these birds feed on insects and spiders by day. Dublin had a famous wagtail roost in the plane trees in the main street, O'Connell Street, which reached a maximum of 3,600 in 1950 (Moriarty 1997). They declined after that until there were just 500 by the late 1990s. The street was transformed by the erection of the monument known as the Spire and the old plane trees were replaced with small,

A Peregrine perches on a church gargoyle (Richard T. Mills).

Starlings gather for roosting in a city area (Richard T. Mills).

Pied Wagtails roost in city-centre trees where winter temperatures are several degrees higher (Richard T. Mills).

pleached lime trees. The Pied Wagtails moved their roost and 150 were seen on the trees round the corner in Bachelors Walk in January 2007. There is a winter wagtail roost in Belfast too in a street tree in Bridge Street (Scott 2004). In Galway there are small Pied Wagtail roosts in some of the street trees. There is also a well-known Pied Wagtail roost in Cork city at the north-east end of the Grand Parade. In all about 600 birds (J. Kearney, pers. comm.) foregather in the trees here with many being seen on the street and pavements as dusk approaches. The wagtails temporarily abandoned the site during major renovations of the streetscape in 2009 but returned again in late 2010. A Long-eared Owl was seen quartering the night sky in the mid-1990s directly above the roost when it flew into the beams of a laser show.

Several other species roost in Cork city at night within the relatively unlit, fenced-off, but wooded western end of the Distillery Fields. Here up to 50 Hooded Crows and Magpies noisily foregather at dusk. Night-time singing of European Robins, Blackbirds, Song Thrushes and occasionally Wrens is also known to occur in Cork city and, at least in the case of European Robins, in Dublin as well. In an interesting comparison of the responses of European Robins to playback calls in Dublin and Cardiff, notable differences between the two populations were detected (Thomas *et al.* 2003). Thus, territory-holding European Robins in Dublin and Cardiff responded to playback calls during the day, but only the Cardiff birds responded at night. The authors concluded that this may be a response among Dublin European Robins to the risk of being detected and attacked by Long-eared Owls (Thomas *et al.* 2003). Detailed research into the daily use of feeders by garden birds (Great, Blue and Coal Tits and House Sparrows) in Belfast (Fitzpatrick 1997) showed an early morning, middle of the day and evening peak of attendance, a pattern which may be explained in part by inter-specific competition as well as the risk posed by predators.

European Robins may stay quiet at night to avoid predation by owls (Richard T. Mills).

It has long been known that birds such as Common Swifts, Common Starlings and Feral Pigeons nest on city buildings – but gulls are more recent colonists. Madden and Newton (2004) have revealed that at least 217 pairs of European Herring Gulls and 84 pairs of Lesser Black-backed Gulls were nesting on roofs along the east coast from Dublin City to Howth, Skerries, Balbriggan, Mosney and Drogheda, and also in Belfast (Scott 2004). A population of roof-nesting European Herring Gulls has existed in Dunmore East, Co. Waterford since the late 1970s. There is also a population of at least 20 pairs of European Herring Gulls nesting on roofs in Galway city around Eyre Square and Augustine Street. A Lesser Black-backed Gull has also been spotted nesting there in recent years (Chris Peppiatt, pers. comm.). Lenehan (2009) has been monitoring the European Herring Gulls in the coastal town of Balbriggan, Co. Dublin. The choice of nest site here appears to favour the areas around the chimneys (Table 2).

European Herring Gulls nest on roofs in many coastal towns and cities (Richard T. Mills).

Nest site	1996	2004	Average	Percentage %
Angle of chimney stack and roof	25	36	30.5	59
Between the chimney pots	26	6	16.0	31
On flat roof	5	5	5.0	10
Top of wall	1	0	0.5	1
Total	57	47	52.0	100

Table 15.2. Total number of European Herring Gull nest sites on buildings in Balbriggan (after Lenehan 2009)

The advantages of city nesting by gulls are obvious – plenty of nesting sites (especially chimneys), safe sites from predators and plenty of discarded food. Gulls readily use both domestic houses and commercial buildings. There are even some pairs of European Herring Gulls nesting on Dublin Castle and on Leinster House - the house of the Irish parliament!

Parks and Open Spaces

Even the most densely populated urban area will have much green space in the form of parks and open spaces. Dublin is the greenest city in Europe with 2,579 hectares of green space in the Dublin City Council area alone. A full 45% of Dublin city is green space – 20% parks and 25% gardens (Ní Lamhna 2008). Belfast has over 1,000 hectares of parks and open space and Derry has over 300 hectares. Various habitats occur in urban parks and are classified as five different types by Fossitt (2000). There is much open grassland – either in the form of mowed lawns or playing pitches (Amenity Grassland GA2), or Scattered trees and Parkland (WD5). Parts of larger open spaces can be classified as Artificial Lakes and Ponds (FL8), Riparian Woodland (WN5) and Depositing Lowland Rivers (FW2).

The Phoenix Park is the largest city park in Europe. It covers 707 hectares and is characterised primarily by amenity grassland with scattered stands of trees and artificial lakes and ponds. The size of the park is sufficient to give a rural effect. Wildlife management in the park is a high priority of the Office of Public Works. A survey carried out by Birdwatch Ireland in the Phoenix

Blue Tits are among the most widespread species in public parks (Richard T. Mills).

Park recorded a total of 72 species including 62 species present during the 2008 breeding season. Of these 62 species, 35 were definitely breeding. In winter, 58 of the 72 species were still present. Blue Tit, Great Tit and Magpie were the most widely distributed species and Jackdaw was the most numerous species during both the breeding season and the winter season. Although the park is known to have had breeding Long-eared Owls in the past, none was recorded during this survey. Birds of prey included Sparrowhawk, Common Kestrel and Common Buzzard. Five warbler species and eight finch species, including Brambling, were recorded (Crowe 2008). The recently arrived Great Spotted Woodpecker has also been seen in the Phoenix Park in 2010.

The scattered trees, hedgerows and individual tall trees which occur in suburban gardens are favoured habitat for the Magpie. Kavanagh (1987) concluded that the density of Magpies in Dublin city, at 16.6 pairs per square kilometre, is far in excess of that recorded in any other part of its range anywhere else. Clearly, the conditions where there are sufficient tall trees for them to nest in combined with an abundance of food, particularly when rearing young, have led to this high density and to the survival of enough young each year to establish new territories. Estimates by Hutchinson (1970) in Dublin showed a nest density of only 5.9 nests/km². The numbers have risen by 13% per year since then, giving a figure of 28.6 nests/km² by 1983 (Kavanagh 1987). There has been no diminution of Magpies in more recent times. The results for the Garden Bird Survey coordinated by BirdWatch Ireland in 2008/2009 shows that Magpies have been recorded in 91.6% of Irish gardens (O'Sullivan 2009).

McGrath (2006) also concurs with the theory that Magpies occur in higher densities in cities than in the open countryside or woodlands. He found breeding Magpies in most of the 1km squares in Waterford city and also records flocks of up to 18 together in late summer. They seem to be abundant in the built-up areas of Belfast too although no estimates of density are available for them here (Scott 2004). In Dun Laoghaire, Co. Dublin, Magpies have built nests in telegraph poles where suitable trees sites are already occupied or are not available.

Urban parks with large stands of trees or old woodland with oak often contain populations of Jay. They depend on stores of hoarded acorns to survive the winter and are most visible in autumn as they search for and store acorns. They are recorded from woods near Maypark nursing home in Waterford (McGrath 2006) and from many of the larger parks in Dublin (Ní Lamhna 2008). Scott (2004) reports Jays increasing around Belfast where mature oak trees in parks provide a refuge for them.

Urban parks are often the demesnes of 'big' houses which have come into the possession of the local authorities. Examples include Santry Park, Marlay Park, St Anne's Park, St Enda's Park and Bushy Park in Dublin, Moira Demesne, Lurgan Park, and Sir Thomas and Lady Dixon Park in Belfast. Such areas will always have been a shelter for birds under pressure from increasing urbanisation in the surrounding areas. They contain a variety of habitats such as woodland, grassland parks, and artificial lakes and ponds as well as stretches of old hedgerows, all contributing to high diversity of birds.

Bushy Park in Dublin was studied over a 20-year period and 56 species of birds were recorded here during all seasons in a park of just 40 hectares (Bryan 1997). Thirty-two species of birds were resident all year round. Breeding species include Grey Heron which share a heronry of ten nests in Scots pine. Other waterbirds include Mute Swan, Little Grebe, Mallard, Tufted Duck, Moorhen and Common Coot as well as Common Kingfisher, Dipper and Grey Wagtail on the River Dodder, which forms one boundary of the park. The woodland area provides breeding habitat for Blackbird, European Robin, Song Thrush, Wren, Dunnock, Goldcrest, Long-tailed Tit, Coal Tit, Greenfinch, Chaffinch, Goldfinch and Bullfinch as well as the usual crow species. Sparrowhawks have nested here in a Scots pine until the arrival of the Grey Herons forced them to move to a high beech tree.

A number of regular migrant species have been recorded in summer – Barn Swallow, Common Swift, House Martin and Sand Martin feed over the largest of the lakes, while Blackcap, Chiffchaff and Willow Warbler all breed here. Rare and occasional visitors recorded by Bryan (1997) include Common Kestrel, Linnet, Fieldfare, Waxwing and Brambling, sightings of which depend on the

Little Egret, Grey Heron and Moorhen roost in a Cork city park (Richard T. Mills).

Common Kingfishers are found on all the Dublin city rivers (Richard T. Mills).

Tree Sparrow in a graveyard (Richard T. Mills).

weather conditions pertaining at the time. A total of 56 bird species in just one urban park emphasises the important role such parks play in maintaining biodiversity in otherwise heavily populated urban areas.

In 2006 eight woodland areas in Fingal County were surveyed with a total of 65 bird species (Merne and Roe 2006). Compared with the breeding bird surveys carried out in 1968–72 and 1988–91 some notable increases and decreases were observed. Common Buzzard and Blackcap appear to have increased while Spotted Flycatcher and probably House Sparrow have decreased. Records of Wood Warbler at Howth Castle Demesne and Malahide Demesne were of particular interest as were the occurrences of Common Crossbill and Raven at Portrane Demesne. In 2007 a Great Spotted Woodpecker was recorded at Howth Castle Demesne.

There are few such large parks in Galway city. The grounds of the University have mature trees and urban grassland where Sparrowhawk and Eurasian Treecreeper have both been recorded breeding (C. Peppiatt, pers. comm.). The Biodiversity Action Plan for Dublin City, published in 2008 includes a summary of the range of priority habitats and species of international, national and local importance in the city. Much of this priority habitat is coastal – sand dunes, salt marsh, mud flats and estuary – and so is described elsewhere in this book. Dublin city also has stretches of old hedgerow and of canal. City hedgerows can be very ancient and species-rich (Lyons and Tubridy 2006) and as a result enhance the overall biodiversity of the parks in which they occur. Stretches of the Royal Canal in the city hold Common Kingfisher, while the Grand Canal, in its city stretches, regularly supports 11 different bird species including Great Cormorant, Little Grebe, Common Coot, Moorhen, Tufted Duck, Grey Heron and Mute Swan. Rivers such as the Liffey, Dodder and Tolka have shallower stretches of fast-flowing water, which support Dipper and Grey Wagtail. Common Kingfisher and Grey Heron feed on these rivers too. These habitats are vulnerable to pollution from litter and dumping and breeding birds can suffer from interference and disturbance during the nesting season.

A survey of the graveyards of Dublin city in 2004 (Wilson *et al.* 2004) identified 15 different habitat types which supported a wide variety of animal life including 26 bird species. Some of these, such as Jackdaw and Common Starling, typically nest in buildings and man-made structures. The trees, shrubs and hedgerows there support Wren, Coal Tit, Goldcrest, Greenfinch, Chaffinch , Great Tit and Sparrowhawk. The ubiquitous Rook, Magpie, Blackbird, European Robin and pigeons, unsurprisingly, were the most frequently recorded species.

Waterbirds in Amenity Areas

Amenity grassland, especially that close to the coast, is used by waterbirds to feed when food is scarce in their natural estuarine habitats or when weather and tides there are not suitable.

Oystercatchers

Apart from two studies on Oystercatchers and Brent Geese, the phenomenon of waterbird use of amenity grassland has been a neglected area of study. In the mid-1980s (Quinn and Kirby 1993) studied a flock of up to 400 Oystercatchers, feeding on the playing fields at Belfield in Dublin. Oyster-catchers normally feed on bivalves, particularly cockles and mussels. It is thought that the move inland to feed on worms was linked to the devastation of cockle stocks in England in the early 1960s (Dare 1966). It has also been suggested by the same author that inland feeding by waterbirds is a behaviour exhibited by birds that also breed inland. The Dublin study of Oystercatchers found that weather and tides affected the degree to which the Belfield site was used. Oystercatchers continue to use inland sites around Dublin and may be seen feeding on their own or associating with other waders and gulls on Dublin parks and amenity grasslands. Similar behaviour has been observed in Belfast (Scott 2004).

Brent Geese

Similarly, it has been argued that a single event initiated inland feeding behaviour by Pale-bellied Brent Geese in Ireland. This was severe flooding in the 1970s, which closed off the intertidal areas frequented by the Brent in Wexford. This forced the geese inland in search of new food sources (Merne *et al.* 1999). The increase in the Brent population visiting Dublin has placed resource constraints on the estuarine resources of Dublin Bay and may be a factor forcing the Brent inland in search of alternative feeding sites. Inland feeding effectively extends the ecological range of the geese. Brent Geese are normally found in estuaries where they feed on eelgrass and green algae (*Ulva* and *Enteromorpha* spp). The Dublin Brent are now primarily grass dependent. From November to March, the Brent leave their roost site on the North Bull Island at dawn for grass sites across the city. They return during the day to drink and wash for short periods between feeding bouts. At dusk skeins of geese can be seen arriving back to the safety of the roost site on North Bull Island (Benson 2009).

Numbers frequenting inland sites vary from single figures to over 2000. A record 2,500 Brent Geese were recorded feeding inland on terrestrial grasses on a single site, Red Arches in Baldoyle, during the 2009–2010 season. The number of sites used by Brent Geese in Dublin increased six-fold in the period 1999–2009. There are now 60 known amenity grassland sites in Dublin where they have been recorded (Benson 2009). These sites range from 500m to up to 15km away from the primary Brent roosting site on the North Bull Island. Tymon Park and Greenhills Park are the most distant

Brent Geese graze extensively on amenity grassland as at Fairview, Dublin (John Coveney).

amenity sites used by them. Formerly fertile agricultural lands, these sites in the Tallaght district of west Dublin, have loamy soils, providing nitrogen-rich grazing for the discerning Brent Geese. Some geese from Dublin Bay also commute to Greystones and the North Wicklow Marshes at Kilcoole on a daily basis with up to 800 birds making the 70km round trip.

Other waterbird species in city parks

Apart from Oystercatcher and Brent Goose, the following wader and gull species may also be found in Dublin's parks, golf courses and sports grounds where they feed principally on terrestrial invertebrates: Eurasian Curlew, Black-tailed Godwit, Common Redshank, Great Ringed Plover, European Golden

Gulls and wildfowl at The Lough, Cork city (Richard T. Mills).

Plover, Common Snipe, Black-headed Gull, Common Gull, Lesser-black Backed Gull, Mediterranean Gull. Common Gull and Black-headed Gull are frequently found associating with the Brent Geese on their inland sites (Benson, pers. obs.).

Other birds associated with rivers and water bodies in Dublin's larger public parks are; Little Grebe, Moorhen, Great Cormorant, Grey Heron, Little Egret, Mute Swan, Eurasian Wigeon, Common Teal, Mallard, Northern Shoveler, Common Pochard and Tufted Duck. Vagrants have included Smew (Tymon Park). The Dodder Linear Park, which is characterised by riparian woodland along the river, holds both nesting Dipper and a healthy breeding density of Common Kingfisher, suggesting good ecological quality on this urban river.

Tolka Valley Park is a linear area that runs along an 8km stretch of the River Tolka extending to near the Co. Meath border. An important winter grazing site for Brent Geese, godwits and other waders and gulls, this park is ecologically rich and diverse supporting 55 species of breeding birds (Merne 2007).

There are two well known water bodies in Cork city – namely the Lough and the Atlantic Pond. The Cork Lough is situated on the south side of the city and therefore close (*c.* 2km) to the Kinsale Road landfill, which is now closed. In addition to its wildfowl collection, the Lough is also known internationally as an outstanding location for angling – especially for carp. However, because of the use of lead weights there were some negative impacts of angling on the waterfowl of the Lough, especially the Mute Swan (O'Halloran *et al.* 1988, 1999). This problem appears to have been reduced now through the use of grit (O'Halloran *et al.* 2002; O' Connell *et al.* 2009).

The proximity of the Cork Lough to the Kinsale Road landfill meant that, in the past, this small freshwater lake was an outstanding site to see gulls including some very rare species such as the Laughing Gull, Ring-billed Gull, Kumlien's Gull, Bonaparte's Gull and also the first ever record of Thayer's Gull in the Western Palaearctic (Wilson 1990; Cronin *et al.* 2006). When the landfill was open, gulls used to commute to and from the Lough – presumably to drink fresh water and an analysis by O'Callaghan *et al.* (2001) showed that they stayed for about two and half hours before returning to forage or to depart to their nocturnal roost. Gulls, which at times numbered in excess of 5,000 individuals at the landfill (Buckley 1987; Cummins 1996) have, since its closure, massively reduced in number at the Lough (Murphy 2011). However, the behaviour of other bird species has also been researched at the Cork Lough including the Moorhen (Keane and O' Halloran 1992; Pollock and O'Halloran 1995; Irwin and

Mute Swans, Black-headed Gulls and Feral Pigeons are fed regularly at Bray Harbour, Co. Wicklow (Richard Nairn).

Trees with fruit provide Blackbirds with winter food that improves their survival chances (Richard T. Mills).

O' Halloran 1997). The Atlantic Pond is situated near the Marina and the village of Blackrock, on Cork's south side and its major claim to fame is that a small Little Egret breeding colony is located on the island in the lake (Ronayne 2010).

In Galway city the canal and the Corrib are the freshwater bodies where Dipper and Grey Heron can be seen. Grey Wagtails frequent the rocky parts of the river while the occasional Common Kingfisher is seen, particularly around the new Bridewell. A few pairs of Mute Swan breed along the canal, while a post-breeding flock of 70–150 swans inhabits the area along the Claddagh, at the mouth of the River Corrib. Little Grebe, Moorhen, Common Coot and Mallard also breed along the canal.

In Waterford, freshwater habitat consists of the River Suir, and its tributary the St John's River which drains Kilbarry Bog. These are haunts of Grey Heron which breeds in a heronry on Little Island further south in the Suir. Little Egret have bred successfully on Little Island since 2006 and are now quite commonly seen along the quays and in St John's River (McGrath 2006).

Two of Belfast's parks have significant lakes which support a variety of bird life – particularly in winter. One of them, the Antrim Road waterworks, provides habitat for several hundred Common Coot, Tufted Duck and Common Pochard, with smaller numbers of Little Grebe and Great Cormorant. Regular winter visitors are Great Crested Grebe and Red-breasted Merganser which arrive to fish, as well as occasional Common Goldeneye and Smew (Scott 2004).

Gardens

Suburban gardens are a wonderful habitat for a wide diversity and large numbers of bird species. In the UK, the garden component may support a significant proportion of the national populations of a number of wild bird species (Gregory and Baillie 1998; Cannon *et al.* 2005; Bland *et al.* 2004). They provide a wider diversity of habitats for birds than would otherwise be available in their natural habitat. A good garden for birds will have trees and shrubs for shelter and ground cover under the hedge; it may even have a small pond. There will be a considerable variety of available food ranging from naturally occurring invertebrates to tree-borne fruit and berries, to well-filled and replenished bird feeders and bird tables. There will be an assortment of nest sites including artificial nest boxes. And in well-run gardens there will be an absence of pesticides which reduce the amount of available invertebrate biodiversity and, of course, no predators such as cats. Such a garden may be visited by upwards of 30 different bird species.

In the RSPB's big garden birdwatch in recent years the top three garden birds in Northern Ireland have remained Common Starling, House Sparrow and Chaffinch. Numbers of Goldfinches have increased almost certainly due to artificial feeding (RSPB.org). BirdWatch Ireland has been conducting a garden bird survey over the last 15 winters and they have a wealth of information about bird species and behaviour. Crowe (2005), in an account of the results of the survey from 1994–2004, states that by that stage, data were received from 1,648 gardens, 53% of which were either urban or suburban. Each year they publish a table of the most common species noted, and Table 3 below gives the results for the winter of 2008/2009 (O' Sullivan 2009).

This survey shows that, contrary to the situation in the UK, the occurrence of House Sparrow and Common Starling has remained relatively stable. Sparrowhawk is the most regular bird of prey species and Magpies are very widespread. However, neither species significantly impacts on songbird populations – the greatest threat is from domestic cats (Churcher *et al.* 1987).

Particularly harsh winters such as that of 2008/09 (the coldest in 18 years) and 2009/10 (the coldest since 1947) have had a significant impact both on numbers and on species visiting gardens. An increase in winter migrants from eastern and northern Europe, including Blackcap, Waxwing, Redwing and even Fieldfare, was particularly noticeable in city gardens in January 2010. Common Snipe and Woodcock were both observed on UCC campus during the winter of 2010/11.

Goldfinches have increased due to feeding in gardens (Richie Lort).

In Galway, the newly planted alders along the distribution roads attract lots of Siskins in winter, while the seeds of Japanese Knotweed in a garden near Eyre Square are fed on by flocks of Lesser Redpoll. January 2010 saw flocks of Common Snipe, Woodcock, Blackcap and Fieldfare in city gardens as well as Redwing and just one Waxwing. City gardens with their well-berried shrubs and shelter are an important refuge for these birds during very cold spells when the soil in rural grassland areas is frozen solid.

Table 15.3 Ireland's Top Thirty Garden Birds in winter 2008/2009 (BirdWatch Ireland)			
Species	Percentage of gardens	Species	Percentage of gardens
European Robin	99.9	Woodpigeon	67.2
Blackbird	99.0	Collared Dove	66.8
Blue Tit	98.0	Rook	59.8
Great Tit	95.1	Long-tailed Tit	55.2
Chaffinch	94.5	Blackcap	54.3
Coal Tit	91.9	Siskin	52.6
Magpie	91.6	Pied Wagtail	51.7
Wren	84.1	Hooded Crow	47.1
Goldfinch	83.2	Goldcrest	42.3
Greenfinch	83.1	Mistle Thrush	42.2
House Sparrow	81.9	Bullfinch	32.8
Common Starling	80.9	Lesser Redpoll	29.5
Song Thrush	80.1	Sparrowhawk	28.3
Dunnock	79.0	Feral Pigeon	22.3
Jackdaw	68.8	Redwing	18.8

Waste water treatment works and lagoons

Known politely as waste water treatment works, these municipal installations are a common feature of towns and cities all over the country. In previous centuries, sewage was simply piped to the nearest river, estuary or area of open coast and it was hoped that natural dilution and bacterial action would do the rest. Nowadays, with greatly increased discharges, this is no longer acceptable. Treatment works are highly engineered operations with large holding tanks, usually with a rotating arm, which keeps the mixture agitated, allowing aerobic digestion of the organic matter. The habitat is characterised by warm sewage effluent, attendant small flies and lack of human disturbance. This can make the plants very good for large numbers of winter-roosting Pied Wagtail.

Black-headed Gulls around the outfall from the Ringsend Waste Water Treatment Works, Dublin city (Richard Nairn).

Needless to say, human waste attracts birds, and the most common scavengers around treatment works are the gulls and crows. The major treatment plant at Ringsend in Dublin city is a magnet for large flocks of Black-headed Gulls. At sewage outfalls, the elevated nutrient levels encourage increased growth of aquatic plants and algae, concentrations of fish and filter-feeding bivalves, which in turn attract scavenging waterbirds. Mute Swan will also feed at the outfall pipes as they glean some food remains in the discharges. The large flock of swans that has built up at the mouth of the River Corrib in Galway city was originally feeding in the sewage outfall at the Claddagh. The flock here peaked at around 200 (Whilde 1990).

A survey of 37 sewage works in Britain found a total of 25 breeding wetland bird species associated with the lagoons and surface irrigation (Fuller and Glue 1980). Spring and autumn populations also made use of sewage works during the pre- and post-breeding periods. Most of these were passerines such as Barn Swallow and Common Starling, but Northern Lapwing, Black-headed Gull and Common Swift also commonly occurred in large numbers in the migration periods. There has been no corresponding survey of birds in sewage works in Ireland.

The outfalls of industrial processes are often attractive to foraging birds. A large flock of Mute Swan gathers at the Mill outfall at Millford at the head of Mulroy Bay, Co. Donegal. At the Golden Vale dairy plant at Charleville, Co. Cork, liquid waste water is discharged to a series of man-made lagoons. Some 15 duck species and 21 wader species have been recorded at these lagoons with the majority being passage migrants arriving in the period of autumn migration (Mee 1994). The attraction for birds is the availability of exposed wet mud in a part of the country with very few natural wetlands.

The sugar factory lagoons at Thurles, Co. Tipperary were effluent settlement ponds located on either side of the River Suir. Covering approximately 48 hectares, the lagoons were used in the autumn and winter to store water used for washing sugar beet and they had a high sugar and silt content. As at Charleville, the lagoons attracted a wide range of wildfowl and waders, especially in the autumn migration season (Brennan and Jones 1982).

The Shannon Airport Lagoon was built in the 1940s to protect the newly created airport against flooding from the estuary (Murphy *et al.* 2003). It was used to hold surface water run-off from the airport apron and runways and this was gradually released to the estuary. Originally consisting of tidal mudflats, the lagoon was enclosed and the water became brackish. Now it is largely occupied by reedswamp, with some willow scrub. The lagoon has been carefully monitored by local ornithologists and a wide diversity of bird species recorded here. A long-term ringing programme has shown that the site is especially important for Sedge Warbler on migration to Africa at the end of the breeding season (Murphy *et al.* 2003).

A freshwater lagoon was accidentally created in Belfast Harbour estate during the reclamation process in Belfast Lough. Birds moved in and eventually the site was declared a nature reserve. It is managed by the RSPB and has recorded upwards of 160 species of bird, including nesting Common and Arctic Tern, Wigeon, Common Teal, Black-tailed Godwits, Water Rail, and, in recent years, Little Egret (RSPB 1999).

Quarries

Quarries can be neatly divided into those used for exploiting rock and those dug for sand and gravel. Rock quarries are widespread in the country. Their products have been used especially for road-building and, in limestone districts, for the manufacture of cement. The quarry at Arklow Head has fairly substantial cliffs up to 125m in height with many ledges and crevices that mimic natural cliffs. These artificial cliffs can be exploited by all of the species that use natural crags, including Raven, Jackdaw, Chough, Common Kestrel and Peregrine. A survey of 48 quarries in eastern Ireland found 21 pairs of Peregrine in both active and disused sites (Moore *et al.* 1992). In 1977 some 35 pairs of Peregrine bred in Northern Ireland quarries (Cabot 1999).

Peregrines have been the subject of several national surveys in the 1970s, 1981, 1991 and most recently in 2002 (Madden *et al.* 2009). A principal finding of the 2002 survey was that the overall number

Chalk quarry at Moira, Co. Antrim (Karl Partidge).

of occupied breeding territories on natural cliff sites has been virtually stable since the 1991 survey. However, the survey demonstrated that the trend of nesting in quarries has continued since the early 1990s, and quarry-nesting birds now account for almost a quarter (23.1%) of the national total of (*c.* 450) occupied breeding territories. The rate of increase in quarries has been greatest in the province of Munster.

An unusual example of a bird habitat is the slate quarries of Valentia Island in Co. Kerry. Here there are open cliffs and tunnels that were used to mine the most valuable seams of slate. Chough nest on low shelves in the openings of these tunnels. Ravens prefer a good wide shelf, high on the open quarry face, from where they can survey the surrounding countryside. They usually build a substantial nest of branches and other material and the nest sites can become traditional, if they are undisturbed. In a survey of breeding Ravens in Northern Ireland, between 1980 and 1987, some 25 nest sites (29% of the total) were in quarries (J.H. Wells quoted in Hutchinson 1989). The quarry at Arklow Rock, which is close to the sea, also has several pairs of nesting Northern Fulmar. This seabird species has also nested in one of the old cement quarries north-west of Drogheda, Co. Louth (several kilometres from open sea). Northern Fulmars have nested on both at a quarry and flat roof of a school at Youghal Co. Cork, (P. Smiddy, pers. comm.).

Sand and gravel quarries are concentrated in the regions with the greatest covering of glacial till, such as Wicklow and Kildare and around the shores of Lough Neagh. In active sandpits, the sand faces

Sand Martins nest in temporary quarry faces (Richard T. Mills).

are typically temporary in nature but, even so, they can be used by Sand Martins for creating burrows. The colony may move about from year to year as new sand faces become available. In this way, they mimic the natural sand cliffs that develop on the banks of rivers and, occasionally in sand dunes. As the birds are only present from about March to August each year the colonies are normally deserted for about half the year. Ruttledge (1966) reported a widely scattered survey of Sand Martin in which the largest colonies were of 150 pairs, 6 of over 100 pairs and the average for 24 colonies was about 66 pairs. Sand Martin was one of the species that suffered a population 'crash' in the 1970s due to the droughts in the Sahel region of north Africa. The subsequent working out of many traditional sand pits was probably a constraint on Sand Martin recovery in Ireland (O.J. Merne, pers. comm.). Sand Martins nest in the now disused quarry in the Glen area of Cork city.

Dumps and landfills

While not the most attractive of habitats, dumps and landfills are an all too common feature of the Irish landscape. Up to about the 1970s there were few environmental controls and refuse could be tipped almost anywhere that was not required for farming or forestry. This included river valleys, estuaries, exhausted quarries and even sea cliffs. In the early days, refuse often attracted large numbers of scavenging birds such as corvids, gulls, Common Starlings and Grey Herons. Studies of the Balleally Landfill in Rogerstown estuary, Co. Dublin showed that the European Herring Gulls feeding here were mainly from the large colonies on Lambay Island, off the coast (Macdonald and Goodwillie 1984). This was one of the sites where the problem of avian botulism was identified as affecting

The Kinsale Road dump in Cork city was a magnet for scavenging gulls (Richard T. Mills).

gulls (especially European Herring Gull) at dumps. The birds were eating organic waste in plastic bags. The anoxic conditions in dark, warm, humid environment were ideal for the rapid growth of bacteria that produce the toxin. The 90% decline in the Irish population of European Herring Gull since 1969/70 may be at least partly due to this (Mitchell *et al.* 2004).

More recent monitoring of gull numbers at Balleally Landfill in the winter of 2001/02 showed a dramatic decline in European Herring Gulls compared with the 1980s (Madden and Archer 2005). No gulls at all were present at the landfill at weekends when there were no deliveries of domestic refuse. The overall reduction in gull numbers was in part thought to be due to better management practices such as mimimising the active working area and rapid covering of the dumped material. More enlightened management of landfills includes 'capping' of refuse with topsoil and grassing over which can provide flocks of Brent Geese with winter grazing, e.g. at Rogerstown Estuary, Co. Dublin.

At the Cork municipal refuse dump, gull and corvid attendance was studied in 1984 and 1985. European Herring Gulls were noted to have declined sharply since 1982/83 and Black-headed and Common Gulls had increased correspondingly. Of the corvids, only Rooks occurred consistently and in large numbers here (N.J. Buckley and T.C. Kelly quoted in Hutchinson 1989).

At Dargan Road, Belfast's main landfill site until its closure in 2007, rarer species such as Iceland and Glaucous Gull were regular winter visitors among the resident gulls. (Faulkner and Thompson 2011)

Airports

Airports usually enclose sizeable expanses of open grassland but few trees and shrubs which are, in any case, confined to the boundaries. Hard standing sections including runways, taxiways, aircraft parking areas and aprons are bounded by the grasslands which nowadays are carefully managed according to internationally recommended protocols (Anon 2008). But with the arrival of the jet age all these habitats which are attractive to birds for feeding, loafing and roosting became a problem for aviation safety (Blokpoel 1976; Kelly and Allan 2006); birds collide with moving aircraft and cause what are known as bird strikes and the general threat posed to aviation is known as the bird hazard problem.

The most serious type of bird strike occurs when one or more individuals are sucked into a jet engine – an incident referred to as ingestion. While bird strikes generally may reduce the safety margins of flying, ingestions can, under exceptional circumstances, cause major damage to an aircraft which in turn may on rare occasions result in a 'hull loss' and serious injuries and or loss of life to passengers and crew (for details see Blokpoel 1976; Thorpe 2003, 2005, and 2010). The bird hazard problem is now perhaps becoming more acute as air traffic is increasingly dominated by twin-engined aircraft which are also much less noisy than they were in the past (MacKinnon *et al.* 2001).

It has been known for many years that the mass of the bird, and the flocking tendency of the species, either individually, or especially together, are the major risk factors in terms of the probable scale of damage to an aircraft caused by a bird strike. While the highest possible risk is associated with heavy i.e. >1kg flocking birds like geese (Blokpoel 1976; Dolbeer *et al.* 2000; Dolbeer and Eschen-felder 2003; Cleary *et al.* 2006; Dekker *et al.* 2003) small (i.e. weighing 80–90g) species like Common Starlings have been responsible for at least three hull losses and in excess of 100 human fatalities. Northern Lapwings (120–317g), racing pigeons (450–500g), and Black-headed Gulls (197–325g) are among the species that have also been responsible for major accidents in which people have lost their lives (see Thorpe 2002, 2006 and 2010).

In Ireland, the Common Starling, Northern Lapwing, Black-headed Gull, European Golden Plover, Common Pheasant, Grey Heron and racing pigeons have caused the most serious damage to aircraft. Nowadays airport authorities implement a 'long grass policy' (Bolger and Kelly 2008) and maintain the sward at between 22 and 25 cm. This is a remarkably successful method of deterring the most hazardous bird species from occupying an airfield but it can lead to the presence of breeding Meadow Pipits and Skylarks (e.g. Carty 2010). Although the numbers of the more hazardous bird species on airfields have been considerably reduced, an emerging problem concerns the overflying of active runways by birds commuting across airports (Fennessy *et al.* 2005a, 2005b). However, Rooks – which are highly adapted to open grassland habitats (e.g. Perrins 1985) and other corvid species continue to be daily visitors to airfields, but are relatively rarely struck by aircraft. It appears that Rooks in particular have learned to evade aircraft and this species displays an elaborate array of avoidance manoeuvres when a collision seems likely (Kelly *et al.* 2001).

Rooks are daily visitors which forage on grassland in airports (Karl Partridge).

Harbours and sea walls

Harbours and sea walls are a common feature of the Irish coastline, with hundreds of small piers and slipways built in the nineteenth century (Nairn 2005). Larger harbours and ports have been developed in the twentieth century with modern marinas and breakwaters being a feature of the last few decades.

Black Guillemots commonly nest in crevices in old harbour walls. As crevices appeared in the old stone structure of the North Pier, Bangor, Co. Down so Black Guillemots took advantage of the opportunity and occupied those holes. In the 1970s, the North Pier was renovated and 15 purpose-built holes were part of the refurbishment. The holes, about 1m in depth and with a 30cm square opening, have been used successfully for breeding ever since. In 1985, just seven pairs nested on the North Pier (Greenwood 1998); in 2009 nearly double that number nested on the North Pier. In 1985 just one pair nested in other places in the harbour; in 2009 that had risen to 20 pairs (Greenwood, pers comm). Pipe nesting sites for Black Guillemots have been installed at Giles Quay and Clogher Head (Co. Louth), with some success, and nest boxes are occupied along a sea wall at Portaferry (Co. Down).

The Carlisle Pier in Dun Laoghaire Harbour has been used by nesting Black Guillemots for many years (Madden 1997), as has the Queen's Bridge in the centre of Belfast (Scott 2004).

Harbours and sea walls are good habitats for Rock Pipit (especially as they are often the only hard sites on soft sediment shores), and also as wintering sites for Black Common Redstart. Small flocks of Ruddy Turnstone and Purple Sandpiper often forage on harbour walls, such as the piers at Dun Laoghaire Harbour and Dunmore East, Co. Waterford. Brent Geese feed each winter on spilt grain on the piers in Dublin Port. In Sligo Harbour, the training walls along the shipping channel are important roosting sites for Oystercatcher, Common Redshank and Ruddy Turnstone. The harbour in Dunmore East has an unusual colony of nesting Black-legged Kittiwake. Here the birds use the cliff face at the back of the harbour, with some nests as close as several metres from the traffic below. Birds have even attempted nesting on the lamp standards around the harbour.

Rock pipits are common breeders in harbours and piers (Richie Lort).

Conclusions

Cities and towns can be very rewarding areas in which to look for bird species. In a small and usually quite accessible area, there may be quite a variety of habitats where birds are relatively used to the presence of humans. Gardens can be managed to attract a great variety of birds within easy range of viewing. Some of the associated features of urban areas, such as sewage works, quarries, landfills and harbours, can also support an interesting range of bird species. Familiarity with many of the species encountered should not diminish our appreciation of urban areas as habitat for birds. The biodiversity plans, which each Local Authority is now required to draw up, will, if they are implemented, go a long way to improving urban bird habitats.

Feral Pigeons live in close association with people in cities (Richard Nairn).

16. Habitat Management for Birds

Richard Nairn and Alan Lauder

Introduction

This chapter draws together the main threads of habitat management where this is undertaken specifically for birds in Ireland. It firstly addresses the main principles of habitat management and follows this with an account of management in a variety of habitat types from mountains to the coast. Sound conservation management is a mixture of ecology and practical countryside stewardship. Habitat management is not an exact science. It is a professional practice that needs to be based on the best available evidence and science and but also needs a measure of common sense.

In Ireland, conservation management is still at a relatively formative stage but the lessons learnt in other countries may often be applied here, while some of our habitats and land-use types may require the development of new approaches to manage them for priority birds. Of course, the vast majority of Ireland is not managed for conservation at all, but for other purposes such as agriculture, forestry or recreation and the protection of birds in the wider countryside may be a secondary, but important, consideration.

Whether there is a difference between managing habitats for birds and managing them for general biodiversity depends on the objectives of management. Even where a globally threatened species, such as the Corncrake, is the priority for management, other species and communities, such as the plants and insects of a hay meadow, will benefit from this more sensitive treatment. If a heather moorland is managed to increase cover for Red Grouse, it will also increase the abundance of small birds such as Meadow Pipit, which in turn provide prey for the threatened Hen Harrier. In the case of Special Protection Areas (SPAs), that are classified under the EU Birds Directive, the conservation objectives need to focus on those species for which the site has been designated. However, in practice, most conservation-related management of habitats is a mixture of managing for particular species and managing to maintain communities (Sutherland and Hill 1995). In managing habitats for birds, the needs of other forms of biodiversity should not be overlooked. For example, there is little point in planting a crop for geese to feed on in winter if, by doing this, an area of species-rich grassland is destroyed.

Key factors, such as the quality and quantity of water in a wetland ecosystem, need to be addressed by the conservation manager to ensure that a management plan achieves its objectives. Water levels, soil types and input of nutrients all have a bearing on the availability of food, whether this is plant

Heather moorland can be managed to increase numbers of Red Grouse (Richard Nairn).

material for grazing by geese or invertebrate prey for waders. Invasive non-native species, including plants and animals, can pose serious threats to bird conservation and may need to be controlled before effective conservation can begin. Provision of artificial nest sites is a common approach where the habitat does not naturally have these features.

In the case studies that follow in this chapter, we have tried to blend the knowledge gained from scientific data and practical experience as it relates to habitat management for birds in Ireland.

General principles

Habitat management is defined by Sutherland *et al.* (2004) as the manipulation of habitats to provide suitable conditions for species of interest, or in some cases to reduce the number of species considered pests. Most habitat management involves preventing or reversing vegetation succession. In some cases, it is also used to create suitable vegetation structure, increase food availability, and provide suitable nesting areas. While the broad principles of habitat management are common to many habitat types, each site will have unique characteristics and may require a specific approach to fulfil the site conservation objectives.

Most of the experience in Ireland of habitat management for birds has been in protected areas such as Nature Reserves, National Parks and Special Protection Areas. The exceptions include some areas managed to increase the populations of game birds such as Red Grouse and Grey Partridge.

Availability of suitable nest sites is a limitation for many species where, otherwise, the habitat offers suitable conditions. Anyone who has erected a nest box in their garden knows that it will be readily colonised by a pair of Great or Blue Tits because of the general absence of old trees with cavities in modern gardens. The provision of artificial nest sites can be extended to a great range of species and, while this is only one of their requirements, it can be a key component of habitat management for birds. Examples include nest boxes for Roseate Tern, nesting pipes in harbour walls for Black Guillemot, floating platforms or islands for nesting ducks, hollow bricks for Common Swift, ledges under bridges for Dipper, artificial sandbanks for Common Kingfisher or Sand Martin and nest boxes for Common Kestrel. In all cases, careful location and construction are important to ensure success and the design based on observation of natural nest sites is vital, though many designs are now well established.

Food availability: a food supply that is both abundant and accessible can be a key factor in the suitability of habitats for birds. Vegetation structure can be also key in affecting food availability (see Chapter 3). Many woodland birds rely on a supply of insect larvae being available at exactly the period when young are being fed in the nest. For species such as the waders, high densities of soil invertebrates or intertidal shellfish and worms are usually the main factors that attract them to a site. In the case of inland species, such as Common Snipe, the softness of the substrate is important as they are unable to locate their prey when the ground is hard. Hence they often choose to feed in peat-based soils (Green 1988, Green *et al.* 1990). Chough prefer to probe in short grazed coastal swards but their feeding is

Nest box with a Common Kestrel in residence (John Lusby).

greatly enhanced by the presence of livestock, because dung invertebrates provide a vital food source in winter when other invertebrate prey is hard to find (McCracken and Foster1994; Robertson *et al.* 1995).

For birds of prey and owls, the availability of a supply of mammal, bird or invertebrate prey species is crucial to survival. For example, Barn Owls are thought to have declined with the reduction in numbers of rodents around farmyards, which were a common feature in the past, or through the effects of rodenticide travelling up the food chain from their target. The spread of the bank vole has already been shown to be of benefit to these owls and may well form an important part of the prey of other raptors such as Common Kestrel and Hen Harrier in future (Lusby *et al.* 2009, 2010). Successful reintroduction of extinct species such as the Red Kite is predicated on the availability of suitable prey and foraging opportunities. In the Wicklow reintroduction project, the birds have foraged extensively on tilled land which can at times make a range of invertebrates such as earthworms highly available .

For many species, food shortage at key times becomes a limiting factor, often in winter. This is illustrated by the extinction of the Corn Bunting in Ireland associated with the loss of small-scale arable cropping, especially in the west, the loss of marginal habitats and the increased use of herbicides and pesticides reducing the abundance of their insect prey and therefore reducing breeding productivity (Taylor and O'Halloran 2002). The practice of burning and ploughing in of stubbles in winter, a more common practice in Ireland than elsewhere in Europe, has increased and has undoubtedly reduced populations of granivorous birds such as Yellowhammer. This would equate to the loss of overwinter stubbles, seen elsewhere in Europe, through the conversion from spring-sown to winter-sown cereals. The provision of specific 'wildbird cover crops' or conservation headlands on the edges of arable fields (strips of crop where no weed control is carried out), has been shown to benefit to these species elsewhere (see Chapter 10).

Yellowhammers have suffered through changes in tillage farming (Richard T. Mills).

For geese and swans, winter grazing becomes critical in the early spring period when they must build up body condition for migration and breeding. Methods of increasing the availability of grazing for wildfowl in this key period have been practised at sites such as Wexford Slobs (see Case Study 9). In some habitats food may be abundant but human disturbance can reduce its availability. Fitzpatrick and Bouchez (1998) studied the effects of recreational disturbance on the foraging behaviour of waders on a rocky beach in Northern Ireland. Phalan and Nairn (2007) found flight responses to disturbance at rates of 0.6 to 1.5 events per hour in four key species (Light-bellied Brent Goose, Oystercatcher, Common Common Redshank and Ruddy Turnstone) in Dublin Bay. These species spent between 0.6 and 1.3% of their time in flight as a direct result of human disturbance which is likely to affect their survival during periods of stress.

Management of water quality and quantity are key issues in the successful conservation of wetlands. For some wetland bird species, water quality is the dominant issue. Common Kingfisher and Red-breasted Merganser rely on catching a steady supply of suitable fish species in clear water. If these fish are limited by water quality or if water clarity is affected then the prey will either not survive or be unavailable to catch. Certain waterbirds will use habitats only if the water levels are the correct depth for feeding or roosting. Mute

Water quality affects the fish prey of Common Kingfishers (Richard T. Mills).

swans often feed by upending to reach submerged water plants. If the water is too deep they will be forced to feed elsewhere. Whooper Swans will use open fields for feeding but they roost at night on open water where they are safe from ground predators (see Case Study 4). For diving species such as Tufted Duck or Common Scoter, the depth and clarity of the water are critical for locating their prey. Fresh water is also an attraction for gulls nesting on coastal sites as they need to wash the salt from their plumage regularly. The draw-down of water on wetland edges provides feeding opportunities for waders, and seasonal flooding of grasslands makes seeds available to dabbling ducks. These regimes can be provided by controlling water levels artificially via sluices and the like, particularly where natural conditions have been compromised by previous drainage.

Removal of non-native species can be a key part of habitat management for birds if the introduced species are known to be a limiting factor in the conservation of native species. The invasion of Rhododendron in native broadleaved woodlands is well documented and almost certainly has led to the reduction in diversity of breeding birds through shading of the ground vegetation and consequent absence of nesting sites (Wilson 1977). Its control in such key protected areas as the Killarney National Park has been a priority of habitat management over many decades. In the coastal environment, the introduced hybrid of cord grass has been widely perceived as a threat to waders such as Dunlin that depend of open mudflats for feeding, although there is little evidence to demonstrate any direct impacts (Nairn 1986). A recent review (McCorry *et al.* 2003) suggests that this invasive grass may be less of a problem and, in fact, can have some beneficial effects in estuaries by increasing the cycling of organic matter through the ecosystem to macro-invertebrate populations (Jackson *et al.* 1986). Management may therefore need to be considered on a site-by-site basis.

Introduced mammals such as American mink can have direct negative impacts on ground-nesting birds such as terns, gulls, waders and ducks that breed close to water (Herbert 1997) and seabirds such as Atlantic Puffins and Manx Shearwaters that nest in underground burrows (see Chapter 11). They can be difficult to control in the long-term without continuing effort. Ground predators can, however, be excluded from key nesting areas with the use of carefully planned anti-predator fencing which can produce spectacular results as in the Shannon Callows (Case Study 1).

Introduced bird species may pose a more insidious threat by occupying the habitat of native birds or by competing with them for scarce food resources or even causing genetic issues. For example, the growing population of feral Canada Geese may, in time, cause some problems of competition with wintering Greylag Geese from the Icelandic breeding population that are found in the midland and eastern counties or compete aggressively with other waterbirds for nesting space around wetlands. There is some debate around issues of Common Pheasants, long introduced in Ireland but enhanced by game-shooting interests, competing with farmland birds for winter seed sources, a further pressure on granivorous farmland birds already in difficulty.

Habitat restoration after development or other interference offers the greatest opportunities for managing a site to increase bird diversity. For example, new wetlands can be created in old worked-out quarries, provided that the edges are given a shallow slope to encourage the growth of emergent plants such as common reeds. Tree planting around housing or industrial developments offers the possibility to create a vertical diversity of canopy, shrub and ground layers, thus providing habitat for a range of bird species. On a much larger scale, the restoration of wetlands on some of the cutaway bogs of the Irish midlands offers huge potential for the creation of new habitats for birds. Time is a key ingredient and certain climax habitats such as woodland take much longer to develop.

Sustainability of habitat management: Sustaining the beneficial effects of habitat management for birds requires long-term planning and resourcing. Managing habitats for birds should always be cognisant of the needs of other aspects of biodiversity. Sustainability, in the longer term, should be a guiding principle in many cases. Ideally, if the habitat is appropriate for the local climate, soils and drainage, then it is more likely to sustain itself in the longer term without the need for continual

Mature trees around houses in Cork city (Richard T. Mills).

intervention. This is increasingly important as climate change makes this country less suitable for certain habitats and species.

Climate change is the overarching environmental issue influencing all nature conservation management in the coming decades (see Chapter 17). For all habitat management plans, there is a need to consider whether the measures proposed will have long-term benefits, given the changes in habitats likely to take place in response to climate change. For example, wetlands in the south-east of Ireland are likely to become drier over the next 50 years (Kelly and Stack 2009) so the control of water levels in such places as fens will become critical to their survival. The range of certain breeding bird species is also likely to change in this time period. Some of the breeding birds in this country, such as Red-throated Diver, European Golden Plover and Dunlin, are at the southern limits of their global range. For them to have any survival prospects the habitats they occupy will need to be able to adjust to climate change, by being in the largest possible units and under optimal management. Similarly, some of the non-breeding waterfowl coming to Ireland may naturally change their wintering range in response to climate change. For example, Bewick's Swan, which was formerly quite widespread in Ireland, has been reduced to only a few tens of birds, largely concentrated at the best sites such as Wexford Slobs each winter (see Chapter 13) . The concept of landscape-scale conservation and the use of ecological networks will be an increasingly important tool in our response to climate change

Case studies of habitat management

There are many examples from Ireland of habitat management for birds, which illustrate the general principles above. In selecting case studies we have considered the range of habitat types present in the country and described in the other chapters in this book. For each case study, the authors were asked to provide a succinct account of the objectives and outcomes of the management actions. These are only brief introductions to projects that, in some cases, have been running for decades. Further information can be gained from published work listed in the Bibliography and, in some cases, from the organisations that manage these sites.

Wet grasslands, callows and machair

CASE STUDY 1: Shannon Callows, Co. Offaly

Habitat types: Wet grassland, river callows. *Target bird species:* Corncrake, breeding waders.

The Shannon Callows comprise Ireland's largest area of semi-natural lowland wet grassland and associated wetland habitats and as a result is of high importance for birds and other wildlife with many areas designated as SAC or classified as SPA.

Common Redshank (front) and Northern Lapwing (Richard T. Mills).

Management for Waders

The site once supported one of the three largest concentrations of waders on lowland wet grasslands in Ireland and the UK, including the globally threatened Eurasian Curlew and important populations of the Red-listed Northern Lapwing and Common Redshank (Lynas *et al.* 2007; Lauder and Donaghy 2008) of particular note. One or two pairs of Black-tailed Godwit, one of Ireland's rarest breeding birds, are also believed to nest here.

Between 1987 and 2002 total numbers of breeding waders declined by between 60% and 85% (Tierney et al. 2002). Research funded by NPWS and carried out by BirdWatch Ireland indicated that the declines were likely to have been caused by reduction of habitat quality and high rates of nest and chick losses to predation, probably mostly by foxes (Lynch *et al.* 2007, Prosser *et al.* 2008). The Shannon Callows Breeding Wader Grant Scheme (BWGS), funded by the NPWS and operated by BirdWatch Ireland was introduced in 2005 to improve conditions for breeding. It is an annual voluntary agreement offered to farmers in key areas to protect eggs and chicks from agricultural damage, and to create optimal breeding conditions through habitat improvements such as tree and scrub removal and grazing management. Since its inception, over 200 hectares of land have been entered into the scheme and the number of breeding waders increased from 129 to 149 pairs in 2010. This pilot scheme could be applied more widely through national agri-environment schemes as a tool to restore breeding wader populations in key areas. In order to specifically secure one of the most important breeding wader sites on the Callows, BirdWatch Ireland erected (in 2009), and maintains, an anti-predator fence on Inishee Island. This 4km+ long fence resulted in an immediate and dramatic increase in numbers and productivity of waders on the island.

Management for Corncrakes

Due to the traditional late mowing of hay on the Callows, the area continued to support an important population of Corncrakes long after they had become extinct in many other areas of Ireland. Corncrakes are of global conservation concern and listed on Annex I of the EU Birds Directive. Just over 100 pairs were recorded on the Callows in the early 1990s, when the Corncrake Grant Scheme was introduced. This scheme was funded initially by the RSPB and later by the National Parks and Wildlife Service (NPWS) and operated by, and in partnership with, BirdWatch Ireland. Despite farmers being paid to delay mowing and cut meadows from the centre outwards, numbers of Corncrakes continued to decline by about 5% per year until 2001, probably due to continued small losses of second brood chicks during the mowing season. Without the grant scheme, Corncrakes would almost certainly have become extinct at the site during the 1990s. Research confirmed that improvements to the grant measures could increase productivity of Corncrakes through the introduction of later mowing options and by leaving uncut margins along plot edges (Donaghy 2007) However, from 2002 onwards, a series of severe summer floods during the breeding season greatly exacerbated the decline, and in 2010 just two calling males were recorded. Management options will remain available, in the event of the population recovering or recolonising. The late cut, floristically diverse wet meadows also attract small numbers of breeding Whinchat, Common Quail and Spotted Crake which are all nationally rare and benefit from the management for Corncrakes

Anita Donaghy, BirdWatch Ireland

CASE STUDY 2: Annagh Marsh, Co. Mayo

Annagh Marsh, Co. Mayo (Richard T. Mills).

Habitat types: Machair grassland and marsh. **Target bird species:** Corncrake, breeding waders.

Annagh Marsh is a small marsh system that lies within a larger machair complex on the Mullet Peninsula, Co. Mayo. It is classified as a SPA and designated as a SAC as a result of its importance for Annex I bird species and its priority habitats. Historically, it was the only regular Irish breeding site for Red-necked Phalarope, the most southerly regular nesting of this species in the world. However, because of a deterioration of the habitat, Red-necked Phalaropes became extinct as a breeding species at the site in the early 1990s and other breeding wader species, such as Northern Lapwings started declining in numbers during the 1990s. Restoration and, thereafter, continued suitable management was therefore required to enhance the value of the marsh.

An EU LIFE–Nature sponsored project was approved in 2001 and delivered as a partnership between BirdWatch Ireland and Teagasc, the Irish Agriculture and Food Development Authority. Habitat management work began in September 2002 with the re-creation of open pool areas through the use of machinery to physically clear rank vegetation. This was followed by reintroduction of cattle grazing to the marsh. As a result, each year cattle graze the marsh area during the late summer to autumn period at an annual stocking density of between 0.2 and 0.3 livestock units/ha. This has been sufficient to maintain the marsh habitat mosaic in favourable condition for breeding waders. The benefits of this management have been seen with increases in breeding Northern Lapwing and with a return of breeding Common Redshank after the first three seasons. Despite these increases, research into the breeding ecology of these waders has revealed poor productivity as a result of nest predation by foxes, particularly during the late incubation stage. This has since caused a reverse in the population trend and breeding numbers have declined again in line with national breeding wader populations. With habitat condition still apparently favourable, but the site extent and colony size of waders too small to withstand heavy predation, a future aim is to provide a fox-proof fence to secure successful breeding and a re-establish a wader population at the site. This will be combined with extending the area of suitable chick-rearing habitat within the area enclosed by the fence. With widespread wader declines across the country securing a core site, to be a 'net exporter' of new potential breeders to repopulate other areas, is a high priority.

DAVE SUDDABY, BIRDWATCH IRELAND

Lowland bogs, fens and reedswamps

CASE STUDY 3: BirdWatch Ireland East Coast Nature Reserve, Blackditch, Co. Wicklow

East Coast Nature Reserve with birdwatching hide on left (Richard Nairn).

Habitat types: Fen, wet grassland, wet woodland. *Target bird species:* wetland species.

Birdwatch Ireland's flagship East Coast Nature Reserve is a mixed habitat site and part of the Murrough Wetland, the largest coastal wetland complex on the coast of Co. Wicklow. It is classified as a SPA and designated as a SAC under the Birds and Habitats Directives because of its importance for Annex 1 bird species and the Annex 1 habitat, Calcareous Fen with Saw Sedge. Previously the site was part of a larger, intensively farmed agricultural unit which was managed for livestock. Drainage ditches had been dug to provide suitable dry grazing. A Lodgepole Pine plantation was contributing to the drying out of the land which in turn was adding to the degradation of the fen.

Purchase of the site in 2002 and funding for the first five years of the project was enabled through the EU LIFE–Nature mechanism. Habitat management began in 2004 with the primary focus on gaining control of the hydrology and removal of the Lodgepole Pine plantation and areas of scrub. Following clearance and re-profiling of the ditch banks, three simple sluice gates were installed at key points within the ditch system to re-wet the fen and allow seasonal control of water levels across the site. This has also allowed the creation of areas of seasonal flooding on the coastal grasslands during the winter months. A number of shallow scrapes and pools were excavated to increase the area of open water throughout the year. In addition a grazing regime was established during the early spring to autumn period at an annual stocking density of below 0.5 livestock units per hectare (LSU/ha). The benefits of this management have been a year-on-year increase in the number of wintering waterbird species and the flock size of wintering waterbirds from the low hundreds to an average of over 1,000 over a six-year period, and the first successful breeding of two pairs of Northern Lapwing in 2010. The reserve is now a demonstration site for wetland restoration techniques. The reserve is open to the public with interpretation, provision of sensitive public access and viewing hides.

JERRY WRAY, BIRDWATCH IRELAND

CASE STUDY 4: Kilcolman Wildfowl Refuge, Co. Cork

Whooper Swans arrive at Kilcolman Wildfowl Refuge (Richard T. Mills).

Habitat types: Fen, marsh. *Target bird species:* Whooper Swan, wetland species.

Kilcolman Wildfowl Refuge is a fen located in a glacially eroded limestone hollow, south of the Ballyhoura Mountains in north Cork. It has been a traditional wintering ground for Greater White-fronted Geese and thousands of duck and is also of great botanical importance, harbouring a number of plant species absent or extremely rare (e.g Golden dock) elsewhere in Co. Cork. The reserve was established in 1993, having been run as a private bird refuge for many years before that. The site is now state- and privately owned, having been established by the late Richard Ridgway, and is run today by Margaret Ridgway. The site has a number of active management measures including water level control, drain clearing and grazing management regimes. In the early years a number of islands were constructed to cater for the wintering and nesting needs of ducks. Unfortunately, agricultural drainage outside the refuge caused a general lowering of water levels during winter and drying out of the marsh in spring. This problem was resolved by the installation of a sluice at the southern end of the marsh. This enables the site to maintain the over 100 Whooper Swans that winter annually there. The natural history of the site has been recorded by Ridgway and Hutchinson (1990).

JOHN O'HALLORAN

Upland heath and blanket bog

CASE STUDY 5: Blanket bog restoration on Cuilcagh Mountain

Cuilcagh Mountain viewed from Benbeg, Co. Cavan
(Kieron Gribbon)

Habitat types: Blanket bog. *Target bird species:* Hen Harrier, European Golden Plover.

The upland blanket bog of the Cuilcagh Mountain, which straddles the border between Northern Ireland and the Republic of Ireland, is one of the best preserved and most extensive peatland areas on the island of Ireland. In the late 1980s, this internationally important area of blanket bog started to suffer unsustainable pressure from mechanised peat extraction and associated drainage works. Additional impacts came from overgrazing, uncontrolled burning of surface vegetation and damaging use of all-terrain vehicles. This damage also reduced the bog's ability to retain water, resulting in flooding and abnormally high water levels in the caves downstream. This reduced tourist activity at the Marble Arch Caves, a major attraction in Co. Fermanagh with over 53,000 visitors in 2007.

Fermanagh District Council was concerned that the blanket bog and other linked habitats would be lost and prompted action to restore the area. An EU LIFE-sponsored project to protect the blanket bog in Northern Ireland and Scotland was approved in 1997. In Northern Ireland, the project was a partnership between the Council and the RSPB and has led to the restoration of 28 hectares of cutover blanket bog on Cuilcagh Mountain. The work included filling in and blocking open drainage ditches, modifying the land to form pools and hummocks, and regenerating new pools with *Sphagnum* moss. The ecosystem service provided by the restored peatland will help to maximise the tourism potential of the Marble Arch Caves visitor attraction in the future as well as conserving an important habitat that supports a wealth of wildlife, including the Hen Harrier and European Golden Plover.

JAMES ROBINSON (RSPB NI)

CASE STUDY 6: Slieve Beagh Conservation Management Plan

Sliabh Beagh (RSPB).

Habitat types: Blanket bog.
Target bird species: Greater White-fronted Goose, Merlin, Peregrine, European Golden Plover.

The Slieve Beagh uplands are an extensive area of rolling sandstone uplands, straddling the borders of Co. Fermanagh, Tyrone and Monaghan, with the international border running across the summit approximately north-east to north-west. The Slieve Beagh mountain covers around 3,000 hectares and contains a number of internationally important habitats listed under the EU Habitats Directive, predominantly blanket bog. It has been classified as a SPA under the EU Birds Directive because it supports a nationally important population of Hen Harriers. The sites also supports populations of Greater White-fronted Goose, Merlin, Peregrine, European Golden Plover, and a range of other upland bird species.

The Truagh Development Association, a local community body, established the Slieve Beagh Environment Management Committee in January 2005, as part of a Peace II-funded project, with active participation of the Slieve Beagh Cross-Border Partnership. The need for a conservation management plan for the area was identified in the Bragan Tourism Action Plan, Ecological Survey of Slieve Beagh and the stakeholder survey carried out as part of the Peace II-funded project. The RSPB prepared the plan and published it in 2010. Its key aim is to provide a reference document to support the sustainable environmental management and promotion of the Slieve Beagh uplands, and maintain and enhance the biodiversity and nature conservation value of the area for the benefit of present and future generations. The plan identifies solutions to the management issues at the site that include unregulated burning, unregulated peat extraction, drainage, heather beetle damage and inappropriate development of wind farms. The success of the plan now rests with the conservation agencies and stakeholders that are responsible for the implementation of the actions in the plan.

James Robinson (RSPB NI)

Woodlands

CASE STUDY 7: Crom Estate, Co. Fermanagh.

Blackthorn scrub at Crom Castle, Co. Fermanagh
(Ian Herbert).

Habitat Types: Broadleaved woodland, conifer plantations. ***Target species:*** Garden Warbler.

The National Trust's Crom Estate is at the southern end of Upper Lough Erne in Co. Fermanagh. The estate (833 hectares) contains a large area of woodland and scrub, which covers approximately 200 hectares. Historical and biological records indicate that this woodland has a link with the ancient 'wildwood'. The Estate also has a history of periodic neglect, relating to absentee landlords, that stretches back to the seventeenth century. This has created 'untidy' niche and edge habitat. In addition, woodland is somewhat fragmented, which creates a high 'length to area ratio' margin effect. In some places hedgerows and woodland have invaded the surrounding grassland, with hawthorn, blackthorn and bramble at the leading edge.

The first survey of Garden Warbler on the estate showed that the territories were associated with scrub woodland (sometimes young emergent conifers) containing low bramble and other woody vegetation at either the woodland edge or within canopy gaps (Herbert 1991). Blackcaps were utilising a wider range of woodland habitat – open scrub, canopy gaps *and* closed canopy woodland – as long as bramble or other dense woody vegetation was present under the canopy. The steady loss of woodland and advent of intensive 'tidy' farming would obviously limit the availability of thorn and bramble habitat associated with mature woodland.

Maintaining a stable Garden Warbler population was always part of the nature reserve's Management Plan. General woodland management, which included felling conifers, planting new trees and controlling non-native species created suitable transitional scrub habitat for Garden Warbler and other breeding passerines. Other animals (such as butterflies, hoverflies and dragonflies) and plant life also benefited. In addition, the fallow deer population was reduced by almost 90% and this allowed maximum tree and scrub regeneration over a short period of time. The objective was to maintain the scrub by coppicing one compartment every two years on a 14-year rotation. Three to five native trees were left as standards within each compartment while the conifers were felled *in situ*. The end result was that the Garden Warblers always had sufficient nesting habitat. This project ran for nine years until a change in staff led to its cessation. During this period the number of Garden Warbler territories remained stable until the mid-1990s, peaked during the next few years (when maximum bramble was available) and then went into rapid decline as the canopy closed during the early part of the next decade.

Elsewhere in the estate, 36 hectares of mature spruce forest was felled and planted with native broadleaved trees. The gaps filled with birch, holly and dense bramble, which grew at a faster rate than the planted trees nearby. The result was that suitable Garden Warbler habitat became available after about four years, but once the canopy started to close over the number of birds decreased. At another site the deer population slowed the transition from scrub to closed canopy woodland. It now remains the area with the highest numbers of birds and indicates that woodland grazing can be a way of arresting natural succession and maintaining scrub woodland habitat.

Canopy gaps were created in areas that contained large numbers of mature, semi-mature and sapling sycamore. Within three years of management, the area became a habitat for widely spaced ash, oak and hazel (up to 20m gaps) and filled with almost impenetrable bramble. Four Garden Warblers regularly used this area until natural regeneration refilled the gaps. As a direct result of management the number of Garden Warbler territories in the estate increased from 29 in 1990 to 52 in 1997. However, by 2009, the total number of territories within the entire estate dropped to 24 as the habitat developed into close canopy forest and in other places woodland edge lost its scrub. In addition, deer numbers had increased again and were impacting on scrub development.

The study shows that a period of about ten years appears to be the maximum time available for breeding birds before scrub succeeds to closed canopy woodland. It also indicates that if habitat is manipulated to create a significant area of scrub, either at the woodland edge or in canopy gaps, the Garden Warbler population can be maintained, subject to external factors remaining favourable. with benefits for other scrub or ground-nesting passerines of woodland and woodland edge.

IAN HERBERT

Lowland farmland and raised bog

CASE STUDY 8: Boora Parklands, Co. Offaly

Grey Partridge with chicks at Boora Wetlands, Co. Offaly (Kieran Buckley).

Habitat types: Cutaway Raised bog, farmland. *Target bird species:* Grey Partridge, Northern Lapwing.

The Grey Partridge is a prized game bird and traditional quarry of Irish game shooters, but the end of traditional grassland management and the increasing use of herbicides and pesticides caused a collapse in the national population and effectively ended wild Partridge shooting in Ireland.

The conservation of naturally occurring Partridge in Ireland began at a meeting of Wildlife Rangers in the early 1980s when the issue of their decline was raised. Early research was then followed up with a national population survey in 1994 and in 1996. Funding was then secured from National Parks and

Wildlife Service to undertake detailed research and to employ a gamekeeper to manage predators systematically in the Boora area. This was followed a few years later by the formation of the Irish Grey Partridge Conservation Trust: formed in conjunction with RCSI and the Curlew Trust.

Conservation efforts of the Partridge project were focused on three key aspects; habitat management, reducing predation levels and captive breeding and release of Partridges. Partridge habitat was provided by creating linear strips of tussock-forming grasses for nesting and brood-rearing strips to ensure abundant insect food is available, all formed on shallow peat based soils on cutaway bogs. This landscape provides key ecological requirements: nesting habitat, optimal foraging for young and over winter cover to reduce predation. Predation can limit the restoration of Partridge populations and intensive predator management, mainly systematic corvid and fox control, was carried out across the Boora area to enable rapid population growth.

The Partridge in Boora responded quite well to the conservation measures introduced in the late 1990s and, after the first year, the population had increased by *c.* 30%. The three breeding seasons following this were wet and consequently Partridge productivity fell to an all time low resulting in a critically low and widely dispersed population potentially prone to stochastic events. A decision to augment the population was made, and in 2002 a genetic study on Partridge in Europe was published, based on mitochondrial DNA samples from across Europe (Liukkonen-Anttila *et al.* 2002). Eight Irish feather samples of partridge in Boora, were taken from 1996–98 were included in this study. The results for the European sample analysed divided partridge into two major 'clades' (western and eastern) which differed in the control region by only 3.6% (O'Gorman 2008). The genetic analysis of feather samples from Ireland indicated that Irish birds were of mixed genetic origin. To avoid swamping the Boora population, the number of Partridge released was kept low in order to preserve most of the genetic components of the indigenous population.

In 2002, Partridge were translocated from France to Ireland to test the viability of several captive breeding programmes being run concurrently by gun clubs around the country. However, the only success was at Boora, which underlined the expertise needed to manage such an intricate behavioural process. Two pairs, a French pair and an Irish/French pair were allowed to form naturally: they successfully bred, thus marking the starting basis of the Grey Partridge captive breeding programme in Ireland. In 2005 a translocation of 21 Partridge from Estonia took place for use in the programme. No importations have taken place since 2005.

The combination of management strategies: habitat creation, predator management, and captive breeding have resulted in a significant recovery of the species at Boora. In addition to being of direct conservation benefit the management for partridge has brought spin off benefits to a suite of other farmland bird species of conservation concern, particularly breeding Northern Lapwing which can have high productivity where predators are controlled.

KIERAN BUCKLEY, NPWS

CASE STUDY 9: North Slob, Co. Wexford

Greater White-fronted Geese at Wexford Wildfowl Reserve (Richard Nairn).

Habitat types: Improved agricultural grassland, tillage land. *Target bird species:* Greater White-fronted Goose, Brent Goose, Whooper Swan.

'Greater White-fronted Geese graze grass and grub for roots' is a simple summary of the thinking behind the management of the Wexford Wildfowl Reserve on the North Slob, Co. Wexford. An area of 200 hectares of the North Slob (from a total of 800 hectares) are owned by the NPWS in partnership with BirdWatch Ireland. NPWS staff carry out the day-to-day management under the oversight of a management committee. The site is of prime importance for Greater White-fronted Geese with up to 10,000 birds at peak (more than one third of the world population).

The fields on the reserve are leased to neighbouring farmers from mid-October until early March and they manage the grass by mowing (hay and silage) and by grazing livestock (cattle and sheep). The farmers pay a nominal price per hectare and this allows the NPWS to factor in some crops of beet (up to 8 hectares per year) so the geese can grub as well as graze. The farmers are all next-door neighbours who own important North Slob goose-feeding fields and another part of the deal is that they tolerate geese on that land throughout the winter; they agree not to disturb the birds more than the minimum required for managing their land.

The geese arrive in mid- to late October and many of them, especially family groups with young, gather on cereal stubble fields to glean spilt grain. Others head straight for grass (usually that which has been last-grazed by cattle rather than by sheep, so that it is not too short or compact). Keeping the geese on fields where they are welcome is a priority and shallow pools or 'splashes' have been made in many of the fields so that the geese stay in the reserve fields and walk to their water for bathing and drinking, rather than fly to the North Slob Channel lagoon.

Around the end of December, a harrow is drawn over a part of one of the fodder beet plots so that the geese have easy access to the roots. More and more sections of beet are opened up until the beet is finished in mid-February. Beet is crucial for the geese in hard winters. As the 'spring bite' of grass grows, the geese switch to feeding on grassland. Tillage has increased on parts of the North Slob with the result that the remaining grassland has come under pressure of conversion to arable. In the wet summer of 2008 much of the beet failed due to flooding and supplies had to be bought in and distributed onto cereal stubbles with a muck-spreader. After that wet summer's floods the reserve's grassland was in poor condition and the following winter was a hard one. The resulting grass shortage drove geese to graze on many farms that had never seen geese before, which caused some degree of conflict.

All through each winter the geese are counted, with the numbers of geese in each one of about 120 North Slob fields being noted. These data inform future management. A safe roost seems to be a vital part of the North Slob's attractiveness to geese and every evening the 8,000–10,000 birds stream out over the sea wall to the tidal sandbanks of Wexford Harbour to spend the night. In 2008 the non-reserve fields on the North Slob were classified as a SPA under the EU Birds Directive. Here it is hoped to improve grass supplies for geese on some of the neighbouring farms which should build on the partnerships already working.

DOMINIC BERRIDGE, NPWS

Cliffs, islands and rocky coasts

CASE STUDY 10: Rockabill, Co. Dublin

Roseate Terns have benefited from the use of nesting boxes (Richard T. Mills).

Habitat types: Rocky shore, cliff.
Target bird species: Roseate Tern.

Rockabill sits 7km off the village of Skerries, north of Dublin. It has long been used by seabirds, especially terns, but grew as an important site for Roseate Terns in the late 1980s. The natural nesting habitat of Roseate Terns is usually described as 'under rocks and boulders or under the cover of vegetation'. Thirty-three Roseate Tern nest boxes were deployed in 1989 to increase the number of nest sites, reduce predation by large gulls and to provide shelter from rain and wind. The number of nest boxes deployed has increased to in excess of 650 Roseate Tern nest boxes in 2010. The proportion of the island's tern population using nest boxes has increased from 1.7% in 1989 to 48.6% in 2010.

The objectives to increase the number of nest sites and reduce their vulnerability to gulls was certainly achieved over the first six years of the project (Casey *et al.* 1995). Since then, the key rationale behind nest-box usage has been to increase the capacity of the island to support terns with the added benefit of enabling a portion of the birds to nest away from dense vegetation and in more open areas where inscriptions on leg rings can be 'read' (Newton and Crowe 2000). Since virtually all Roseate Tern chicks are ringed at this colony (and at most others in north-west Europe) ring reading permits the assessment of several key demographic variables including juvenile survival and return rates, age of first breeding, colony fidelity and inter-colony movements, mate fidelity and lifespan (Ratcliffe *et al.* 2008). The protection afforded by nest boxes to both incubating adults and young chicks and is one possible reason why Roseate Tern productivity (average number of chicks fledged per egg-laying pair) is consistently higher than that of open-nesting Common Terns which lay more eggs but raise fewer young. Many mobile, older Common Tern chicks also utilise the nest boxes.

In order to provide space for the growing Roseate Tern population, the current regime has been to clear as much dense vegetation (mostly Tree Mallow but also scurvy grass *Atriplex* and Hottentot Fig) as possible before the terns settle. The slopes are also landscaped into level terraces on which boxes can be deployed at high density. The design of the boxes has been unchanged (30cm x 30cm x 15cm high, with 3cm or 3.5cm sides) though materials have varied. Present structures have been made with plywood whereas early versions were made with wooden walls and a slate roof. Each year the boxes beyond repair are discarded and a new batch is introduced. The latter have been made by the students of Balbriggan Community College using material purchased by the Fingal branch of BirdWatch Ireland. Such local community involvement in the project is one of the many reasons behind the success of the Rockabill Tern Project.

STEPHEN NEWTON, BIRDWATCH IRELAND

Estuaries and Coastal Lagoons

CASE STUDY 11: Belfast Lough

Belfast Lough freshwater lagoon
(Chris Gomersall – rspb-images.com).

Habitat types: Estuary, tidal lagoon. ***Target bird species:*** Wetland birds.

Belfast Lough is the third most important estuary for birds in Northern Ireland, supporting regularly around 19,000 waterbirds during the non-breeding season. It is classified as a SPA, and designated as a Ramsar site and Area of Special Scientific Interest. Within Belfast Lough, the RSPB manages intertidal mud flats, a 13.5-hectare artificial freshwater lagoon, a 8.6-hectare shallow tidal lagoon, and a large area of mixed grassland and limited shallow flooding. The intertidal zone in the lough represents less than 20% of the mudflats present 100 years ago and was under intense pressure for reclamation and development. The freshwater lagoon was created by reclamation and developed, accidentally, into one of the main roosting, loafing and now feeding areas for waterbirds within the lough. Through an innovative EU-funded scheme, habitat improvements and visitor facilities have been provided.

The nature reserves offer a range of conservation opportunities. The intertidal/mudflat zone secures the site against any further reclamation and safeguards feeding areas for the internationally important concentrations of waterbirds. The freshwater lagoon offers a safe roosting/loafing site for waterbirds and breeding site for Common and Arctic Terns and provides a genuine year-round bird spectacle and the opportunity for visitors to view a wide variety of birds at close quarters from superb facilities. The tidal lagoon provides a feeding area for many waterbirds at low water. The unique juxtaposition of these nature reserves to Northern Ireland's major industrial heart provides the opportunity to demonstrate that conservation and industrial development can co-exist.

JAMES ROBINSON, RSPB NI

Artificial nest sites

CASE STUDY 12: Bangor Marina, Bangor, Co. Down

Black Guillemots use nesting pipes in Bangor Marina, Co. Down (Richard Nairn).

Habitat types: Harbour walls. ***Target bird species:*** Black Guillemot.

Black Guillemots have been nesting in the harbour at Bangor for around a century. As crevices appeared in the old stone structure of the North Pier, so Black Guillemots took advantage of the opportunity and occupied those holes. In the 1970s, the North Pier was renovated and 15 purpose-built holes were part of the refurbishment. The holes, about 1m in depth and with a 30cm² opening, have been used successfully for breeding ever since.

Black Guillemots will occupy virtually any nook or cranny for nesting and this habit means that providing artificial nesting sites has been easy. In the 1980s, the harbour at Bangor was developed into a 560-berth marina. There was the opportunity to erect 27 nest boxes on concrete support piles beneath one of the new piers. These boxes were made from two concrete building blocks knocked through from one to the other, to provide a hole with a depth of about 60cm and a cross section of about 20cm. In the following breeding season some of these boxes were used successfully. The marina management were so impressed with the colonisation that they wished to provide some new nesting opportunities for *their* birds in full view of the boat owners. And so in the 1990s, three round plastic tubes were provided; closed at one end and each about 1.3m in length with an approximately 25cm diameter cross section. At least one of those tubes has been used annually ever since. Not only have the Black Guillemots used their purpose-built nesting chambers, but they have nested in a variety of other situations as well, like service ducts beneath the jetties. On one pier in the Belfast Harbour estate, one pair even nested beneath the floor of a large wooden shed used as an office. Another pair nested in an open locker of a sailing boat near to Bangor; the boat owner did not use the boat until the young had fledged successfully. Perhaps he need not have worried as a working tug-boat in Belfast had a pair that successfully fledged young, despite the tug moving around the harbour! The provision of purpose-built nesting chambers has led to successful colonisation in locations where Black Guillemots have previously not nested, like holes in the harbour wall at Glenarm, Co. Antrim and wooden nest boxes on the seawall in Strangford village, Co. Down.

The provision of artificial nesting sites has allowed an increase in the population size at Bangor. In 1985, just seven pairs nested on the North Pier (Greenwood 1998); in 2009 nearly double that number nested on the North Pier. In 1985 just one pair nested in other places in the harbour; in 2009 that had risen to 20 pairs. Although modest, there has been an increase in breeding success, with an average now of about one young fledged per pair in the marina (1.25 young fledged per pair on the North Pier). The accessibility of the holes has allowed comparatively easy retrieval of most young for banding with a consequent rise in recoveries from as far away as Co. Donegal and Rockabill, Co. Dublin. An interesting observation made as a result of easy access to nesting holes is that the timing of egg-laying has advanced in response to warming seawater temperature in the Irish Sea (Greenwood 2007). The provision of easily accessed artificial nesting sites for Black Guillemots has created opportunities to understand more about their everyday lives.

The basic recipe for success is to create a cavity about 1m long, with a cross-section of about 20cm. The cavity can be made from any material as long as it provides a dry nesting opportunity. It should ideally be situated a little out of sight of people. The tunnel can be built into a solid structure like a wall or attached to a wall like a traditional nest box, and the entrance to the nest chamber should always be over water.

JULIAN GREENWOOD, STRANMILLIS COLLEGE, BELFAST

Conclusion

A range of habitat management techniques have been presented for some of the key bird habitats in Ireland and these generally illustrate successful examples. There are many more not mentioned, which range from moorland management for Red Grouse to rafts for nesting terns. The main barriers to successful habitat management for birds in Ireland include the land holding pattern (many small and few large units), lack of political support and limited funding for conservation effort. Voluntary organisations such as the RSPB, Birdwatch Ireland, the Golden Eagle Trust, the Irish Grey Partridge Conservation Trust and the state agencies will no doubt continue to deliver habitat management at reserves and in project areas throughout the country. To be more successful, the barriers to habitat management need to be broken down through the proper application of domestic and international legislation and agreements and partnership working alongside landowners, business and communities

Climate change is becoming an increasingly important factor and adaptation to it will form a major focus in managing habitats for birds in future. To make habitats able to adjust to climate change they need to be managed well and to be as large as possible to withstand change. There are also opportunities for managed realignment on the coast, to adapt to sea-level rise, and restoration of natural floodplains along rivers for flood defence. Such projects can have benefits for habitats, birds and people living in these areas and the implementation of these multi-purpose schemes is likely to be a priority in future.

Acknowledgements

The authors wish to thank those contributors who provided the case studies of habitat management for birds. Dr James Robinson compiled and edited the RSPB Northern Ireland case studies. Ian Herbert is grateful to Stuart Jennings for kind assistance in making National Trust Crom Estate survey records available.

17. Climate Change, Habitats and Birds

Alison Donnelly, James Robinson, John O'Halloran and Richard Nairn

Introduction

The fact that global climate is changing beyond the range of natural variability is now without question. The Intergovernmental Panel on Climate Change (IPCC) in their latest Assessment Report (2007) stated that warming of the climate system is 'unequivocal' and this was 'very likely due to human activity'. The main driver of this anthropogenic rise in temperature has been attributed to an increase in emissions of greenhouse gases (GHGs) primarily from fossil fuel burning and changes in land use. These gases trap heat close to the earth's surface causing a rise in average temperature but also producing many other direct and indirect changes to the climate system (Hurrell and Trenberth 2010). Global average temperature has risen by 0.74 °C over the last century (Parry *et al.* 2007) and the average Irish temperature has risen in line with the global trend by 0.7 °C over the same time period (Figure 17.1). Warming has been greatest in recent decades

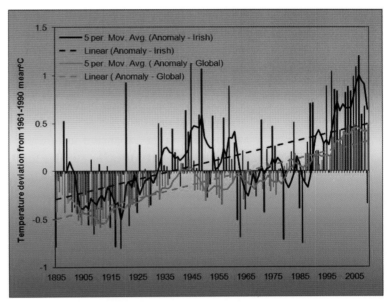

Figure 17.1 Community Climate Change Consortium for Ireland (C4I) project. (Source: Met Éireann.)

and average change in Irish temperature has exceeded the global average. This indicates that climate change is not uniform in space or time. Furthermore, uncertainty remains regarding how climate will change at regional and local levels over the coming decades (Hurrell and Trenberth 2010). Predictions suggest that Ireland may not see as high a rate of warming as other parts of Europe, and this could have important consequences for birds and their habitats (http://ec.europa.eu/environment/water/adaptation/archives.htm). However, one thing is certain, temperatures will continue to rise well into the current century based on even the most conservative emission scenario and must now be considered in many aspects of government planning including conservation strategies.

Other aspects of climate change include a rise in sea level, melting of snow and ice, an increase in the frequency of extreme weather events, such as heatwaves and more intense storms, and changes in precipitation patterns, i.e. amount, intensity, frequency and type of precipitation (Hurrell and Trenberth 2010). All of these components can have an impact on both natural and human systems and will not be considered in depth in this chapter. However, the main aspect of climate change being addressed here is climate warming due to the high level of certainty of how rising temperature effects birdlife. In order to develop appropriate conservation strategies for the future protection of birds and their habitats it is important to establish how climate change is affecting birds at present. Therefore, we will first explore the main impacts of climate change on birds in general and then examine evidence of the impact of warming on birdlife in Ireland. Finally, we will examine the potential consequences of these impacts for the future conservation of birds in Ireland.

Effects of climate change on birds

Defining, detecting and demonstrating how climate change influences birds is a vast topic of research and this chapter can only briefly address the main aspects. However, it is our intention to highlight the importance of this research and to provide a list of references on the subject. Climate change can impact both resident and migratory birds in numerous ways, such as by affecting behaviour, physiology, genetics, ecology (including population dynamics, feeding strategies, migratory patterns) and evolution. In addition, these effects can occur at different stages during the life cycle of a bird but also at different locations along their migration route if they are migratory in nature. Furthermore, these effects are usually species-specific. In addition, climate change may result in mistiming between birds and their food source. As recent studies have shown, climate warming has the potential to disrupt existing synchronies between interdependent species as a result of differential responses of species to increasing temperature (Parmesan and Yohe 2003; Visser and Both 2005; Durant *et al.* 2007; van Asch and Visser 2007; Singer and Parmesan 2010).

Climate change may also have positive effects for some bird species. Just as asynchronous relationships may develop between a species and its food source, equally, weak synchronies may be strengthened or new synchronies forged. In addition, rising temperatures may permit a northward and upward range expansion in bird populations adapted to warmer temperatures, allowing them to exploit new territories if a suitable food source and habitat are available for them to thrive. Earlier arrival at breeding grounds coupled with earlier egg-laying may also lead to greater survival rates and larger population size – if, of course, resources are not limiting.

Climate change effects on bird migration and phenology
In order to address the impact of recent climate change on bird migration and phenology it is essential to have historic records of ornithological data coupled with climate data from the same location. There are many reports of recent warming advancing the timing of spring events such as leaf-unfolding (Peñuelas and Filella 2001; Donnelly *et al.* 2006; Menzel *et al.* 2006), bird migration (Lehikoinen and Sparks 2010; Sparks *et al.* 2005; Donnelly *et al.* 2009) and egg-laying (Crick and Sparks 1999; Both *et al.* 2004; Visser *et al.* 2003; Nielsen and Møller 2006), and appearance of insects (Roy and Sparks 2000; Bale *et al.* 2002; Stefanescu *et al.* 2003; Gordo and Sanz 2005; Gordo and Sanz 2006; Robinet and Roque 2010). All of these studies were based on long-term data sets and the developmental events of the organisms reported were strongly influenced by temperature. The study of the timing of these life-cycle events in plants and animals is called phenology and the developmental events themselves are referred to as phenological events, or phenophases for short.

Phenophases that occur in autumn, such as leaf fall and bird departure are certainly influenced by temperature but the overriding environmental trigger driving the timing of these events is shortening day length. Because phenology, in particular spring phenology, is highly sensitive to temperature it is therefore widely used as an indicator of temperature in climate-change research. Indeed, the IPCC's 4th Assessment Report used the results of a study (Menzel, *et al.* 2006) containing more than 100,000 plant and animal phenological records from 20 European countries, including Ireland, to demon-

European Robin (Karl Partridge).

strate to policy makers that climate change was having a detectable impact on the natural environment.

It is generally accepted that when spring temperature is warm at breeding grounds migrant birds arrive early and when spring temperature is cool they tend to arrive late. This flexibility allows birds and other organisms to adjust to new environmental conditions without altering their genotype and is termed 'phenotypic plasticity'. It enables plants and animals to adjust to seasonal changes in temperature and allows birds and insects to modify their behaviour in response to environmental variation during migration (Hüppop and Hüppop 2003; Vähätalo *et al.* 2004). Migratory birds tend to respond to rising spring temperature by arriving earlier at their breeding grounds (Hüppop and Hüppop 2003; Sparks *et al.* 2005; Donnelly

Early arrival of Barn Swallows in Europe is related to climate change (Richard T. Mills).

et al. 2009; Saino *et al.* 2010; Lehikoinen and Sparks 2010) and by laying their eggs earlier (Both and Visser 2001; Both *et al.* 2006), thus increasing their potential for breeding success.

In order to determine the impact of rising spring temperature on the timing of arrival of a range of sub-Saharan migrant birds to Ireland, Donnelly *et al.* (2009) examined historic (1969–1999) records of first arrival dates of 11 species to the east coast (Table 17.1). They found that 9 out of the 11 birds were arriving earlier at the end of the time period than at the beginning and 7 of these showed a statistically significant trend. Average spring temperature, in March in particular, was negatively correlated with earlier arrival, thus when average temperature was warmer than usual arrival was earlier. Temperature at the wintering ground was also investigated to determine any potential influence on the timing of arrival to Ireland. Mean winter temperature anomalies (oC) for Africa (latitude 6° N to 35° S and longitude 6° W to 42° E) were negatively correlated with arrival dates on the Irish east coast for seven species and positively correlated for the other four species. However, these correlations were not statistically significant.

Table 17.1 Results of partial Mann-Kendall analysis for arrival dates of common summer migrants to Ireland. MK-stat describes the trend. P-value indicates level of statistical significance. Source: Donnelly, *et al.* (2009)

Species	N	MK-Stat	P-value
Common Cuckoo *Cuculus canorus*	23	1.113	0.266
Common Swift *Apus apus*	30	-0.751	0.453
Sand Martin *Riparia riparia*	25	-2.221	0.026
Barn Swallow *Hirundo rustica*	31	-2.792	0.005
House Martin *Delichon urbicum*	19	-3.575	0.000
Whinchat *Saxicola rubetra*	23	-1.787	0.074
Northern Wheatear *Oenanthe oenanthe*	30	-3.005	0.003
Common Grasshopper Warbler *Locustella naevia*	21	-1.913	0.056
Sedge Warbler *Acrocephalus schoenobaenus*	18	1.221	0.222
Common Whitethroat *Sylvia communis*	18	-2.136	0.033
Willow Warbler *Phylloscopus trochilus*	26	-0.332	0.740

Whooper Swans wintering at Kilcolman, Co. Cork have been departing earlier for their Icelandic breeding grounds in response to rising spring temperature. (Richard T. Mills).

The earlier arrival of long-distance birds to Ireland is in agreement with Cotton (2003) who reported earlier arrival of birds in Oxfordshire (UK) over the same time period and for many of the same species. It is notable that the two species (Barn Swallow and House Martin) for which there are significant correlations with spring temperatures are Hirundines. It has been suggested that recent changes in climate may have resulted in selection for earlier and faster migration in these two species (Sparks and Tryjanowski 2007). There have been reports of changing migratory patterns of birds, typically in the form of earlier spring arrival, over the past 30 years at locations throughout Europe but primarily in north-eastern Europe (Sparks *et al.* 2005). In recent reviews, Lehikoinen *et al.* (2004) and Lehikoinen and Sparks (2010) reported a significant earlier arrival for 39% of migratory bird species when examining 983 data sets on first arrival dates of from ten European countries.

Stirnemann *et al.* (in press) examined the timing of arrival and departure of the Icelandic Whooper Swan to their wintering ground at Kilcolman Wildfowl Refuge in Co. Cork over a 38-year period (1971–2008). Arrival at the wintering grounds in Ireland typically occurs between October and December and departure between March and May (O'Halloran *et al.* 1993). The authors reported that there was little change in the timing of arrival over the study period but that the timing of departure in spring advanced significantly. The earlier departure was correlated with an increase in grass growth, the main food source for these birds, which in turn was driven by higher spring temperatures. Similarly, Fox and Walsh (in press) examined departure dates of Greater White-fronted Geese, a winter visitor, from Ireland and Scotland and concluded that these birds were departing earlier in spring as a result of earlier accumulation of reserves. It was suggested that this resulted from an increase in the critical temperature for grass growth over the study period (1973–2007).

There is less variability in the timing of late arriving species when weather is less variable and these species are considered to be under more strict endogenous control (Sparks *et al.* 2005; Lehikoinen and Sparks 2010). Furthermore, not all species respond to rising temperature in the same way. For example, in the Netherlands a study of the Pied Flycatcher did not advance the timing of arrival even though temperature increased significantly over the 20-year period (1980–2000), suggesting that day length in the wintering grounds may be driving migration (Both and Visser 2001). In addition, the Willow Warbler has been shown to arrive later at their breeding grounds in response to increasing temperature (Barrett 2002; Peñuelas *et al.* 2002).

It has been shown that short-distance migrants are able to respond to environmental changes at the breeding grounds relatively quickly whereas long-distance migrants may be constrained in their plastic response as climate at the breeding ground is unlikely to be their cue to begin migration (Visser *et al.* 1998; Cotton 2003; Lehikoinen *et al.* 2004; Jonzén *et al.* 2006; Pulido 2007; Tøttrup, *et al.* 2010; Saino, *et al.* 2010; Lehikoinen and Sparks 2010). However, recent research suggests that teleconnections between large-scale climate systems such as between ENSO (El Niño Southern Oscillation) and the NAO (North Atlantic Oscillation) (Hurrel and Trenberth 2010) may help long-distant migrant birds, such as Barn Swallows, gauge climatic conditions in the breeding grounds if meteorological conditions in Europe (during the breeding season) co-vary with those in Africa (during late winter) and thus phenotypically adjust their migration to optimise arrival time (Saino and Ambrosini 2008).

Climate change effects on the timing of breeding

Earlier arrival at a breeding ground has consequences for the timing of breeding and (where appropriate) the number of broods produced by migratory birds. An increase in the frequency of second broods would require a considerable advance in phenology coupled with an adequate food supply. A significant advance in laying date in response to warming has been reported for a range of bird species at a variety of locations (Dunn and Winkler 2010). Ahola *et al.* (2004) demonstrated that a long-distance migrant, the Pied Flycatcher, could adjust the speed of migration along its route in response to local temperatures. They highlighted the need to examine temperature changes at the appropriate temporal and geographical scales that are driving migration and thus arrival time. Similarly, Both and te Marvelde (2007) compared geographical variation in egg-laying dates of a short-distance (European Common Starling) and a long-distance migrant (Pied Flycatcher) over a 25-year period in Europe. They reported spatial and temporal heterogeneity in annual median egg-laying dates across Europe and suggested this was due to climate warming being more pronounced in some regions than in others. Møller *et al.* (2008) also reported that the impact of climate change on the timing of spring migration might have increased in recent years. Therefore, conditions along the migration routes appear to vary over space and time, with migration and egg-laying dates varying accordingly. As a result, phenological change within a species may differ at different locations.

Evidence of genetic adaptation to climate change

As stated earlier, phenotypic plasticity allows organisms to adapt to environmental change but if the range of environmental conditions exceeds the plastic limits of an organism, genetic adaptation is likely to occur which may help prevent local extinction (Price *et al.* 2003; Gienapp *et al.* 2008). If there is sufficient selective pressure, climate change can contribute to the evolution of new species.

Bearhop *et al.* (2005) reported evidence of speciation through assortative mating in populations of Blackcaps in Europe. In the 1960s, Blackcaps spent their summers in Germany/Austria and wintered in Iberia and northern Africa. However, more and more of these birds have begun to overwinter in Britain and Ireland, attributed at least in part to milder winters, thus leading to a change in migration pattern. This resulted in the birds that spent the winter in Britain and Ireland arriving at their breeding grounds earlier, because critical photoperiods that trigger migration were found to be ten days earlier than in more southern latitudes. In addition, because of the shorter migratory distance, these birds were possibly in better physical condition on arrival. The birds that arrived early tended to mate together and chose the best breeding territories, all of which resulted in greater reproductive success. The later-arriving birds also mated together and, therefore, these two populations paired assortatively. According to Bearhop *et al.* (2005), this temporal separation may result in subpopulations becoming isolated. Consequently, it may be that changes in environmental conditions that result in new migration routes may lead to the evolution of genetically distinct populations or species. It is therefore likely that, for some birds, future warming has the potential to influence speciation. However, according to Sheldon (2010), while this study remains an important

Blackcaps are wintering more frequently in Ireland and can begin breeding earlier as a result of earlier arrival in northern latitudes (Richie Lort).

demonstration of the evolution of a novel migratory pattern, and an underlying genetic change, the relationship to climate remains to be fully established.

Phenotypic plasticity at a populations level is also under selective pressure. The degree of plasticity in the timing of reproduction in birds has been shown to be a heritable trait (Nussey *et al.* 2005; Reed *et al.* 2008). Selection of this heritable component could allow some individuals to track climatic changes better than others and selection of these individuals may enable the population to track food resources beyond points imposed by current plastic limits (Stenseth and Mysterud 2002). As not all species are highly plastic the ability to genetically adapt to changing climatic conditions will inevitably vary.

Great Tits and their caterpillar prey are both breeding earlier in response to climate change. (Richie Lort).

To date many of the evolutionary responses reported for a range of organisms as resulting from climate warming are speculative rather than being strongly supported by empirical data (Nussey *et al.* 2005). This is not to say that evolutionary change, in response to recent warming, has not already occurred or will not occur in future but just that sufficient evidence has not yet been acquired (Sheldon 2010).

Climate-driven mismatches between birds and their host-prey

In order for a population to thrive, birds must synchronise their breeding time with availability of food and this food peak can vary considerably between years depending on local weather conditions. Therefore, it is important to know how the timing and abundance of food supplies changes in response to climate change (Both 2010). In order for the birds to predict the timing of the food peak reliable cues at the time of egg-laying are necessary. However, since organisms respond to climate warming at varying rates there is potential for existing synchronies to become mismatched (Visser and Both 2005; Durant *et al.* 2007; van Asch and Visser 2007). Mismatch occurs when a synchronous partnership is disrupted in time or space resulting in partial or complete trophic decoupling (Stenseth and Mysterud 2002). According to Visser *et al.* (2004) any such decoupling of food web phenology may result in a change in species composition.

On the other hand, there are also reports of inter-dependent species remaining in synchrony with one another, such as Great Tits and their caterpillar prey, both of which advanced at the same rate in response to warming at locations in the UK (Charmantier *et al.* 2008) and Belgium (Matthysen *et al.* 2011). However, for a similar population of tits in the Netherlands, the laying date has advanced less than that of the cater-pillar biomass (Visser *et al.* 1998; Both *et al.* 2009). Thus, the British and Belgian populations improved

Insectivorous birds like Blue Tits need to stay in synchrony with their insect prey so that their chicks hatch when the maximum food resource is available (Richard T. Mills).

their synchrony with their caterpillar food peak whereas the Dutch population showed the opposite (Both 2010). Both (2010) suggested three possible reasons why the Dutch birds responded less than the food peak: (i) caterpillar growth responded more than egg-laying to increased temperature, (ii) to facilitate the production of two broods one must be produced before the peak in food supply and (iii) some genetic component was involved. He further suggested that the differing responses of the Dutch and UK populations may be due to an interaction between climate change and local habitat change over the study period. Blue Tits and Great Tits in Ireland are largely single brooded, thus it is not clear what impact the timing of food availability might have on breeding and productivity. While it is likely that Paridae in Ireland have wider niches and this may provide greater plasticity, the higher over winter survival of adults may have balancing effects.

In order to explore this system even further, Both *et al.* (2009) considered phenological synchrony at four trophic levels: tree–caterpillar–passerine–raptor. The authors reported a decrease in synchrony between all three interactions and attributed this to climate change. They suggested that it could be advantageous for an organism to remain in synchrony with its food source but to form a mismatch with its predator, to avoid being consumed.

Climate change may be contributing to the popluation decline of breeding European Golden Plover (Ian Herbert).

Most studies on climate-warming impacts on avian phenology reported in the literature refer to temperate passerines, but mistiming in other groups may be equally important. Pearce-Higgins *et al.* (2005) reported the potential for a future mismatch to occur between a wading bird, the European Golden Plover, and its main food source, adult tipulids. First clutch hatching is usually synchronised with the emergence of adult tipulids (Pearce-Higgins and Yalden 2004), however, future breeding success may be reduced as chick hatching occurs earlier than the emergence of their prey. More recently, Pearce-Higgins (2010) examined the potential for the reported mismatch to account for a decline in the abundance of European Golden Plover in the Peak District (UK). The authors concluded that the most likely cause of the population decline was a decline in the abundance of cranefly, the main food source of the Plover, linked to desiccation of the larvae caused by relatively high August temperatures in the area. In light of these findings and reports that the breeding population of European Golden Plover across Ireland is in steep decline (Lynas *et al.* 2007), it is possible that the effects of climate warming, as well as other forms of habitat deterioration and loss, may be a contributing factor to this trend.

As regards migratory birds, the timing and speed of migration need to be timed to coincide with the phenology of food sources both at stopover sites and at breeding grounds (for examples, see Visser and Both 2005). But timing and speed of migration decisions are complicated by the fact that climate warming (a) may not occur at the same rate along the migratory route and (b) may not affect the food source's phenology at the same rate as the bird's phenology (Gordo 2007). Therefore, the journey may be disrupted in many different ways at different locations.

In a recent review of climate-driven mismatches between interdependent phenophases in terrestrial and aquatic ecosystems, Donnelly *et al.* (2011) concluded that just as some species may experience a reduction in fitness due, for example, to a mismatch with a vital food source, others must surely be in a position to increase fitness if previously mistimed events become synchronous.

Dunlin (left) and Northern Lapwing are expected to increase in numbers in Ireland in winter (Richard T. Mills).

The northward spread of Little Egret into Ireland is associated with milder winters (Mark Carmody).

Climate change and range shifts

The distribution of an organism is determined by evolution and genetics on one hand and biotic and abiotic factors on the other. One of the main influences on distribution is temperature and for this reason climate warming has the capacity to extend the range of some bird species polewards and towards higher altitudes provided a suitable food source and habitat type are available. But, as stated earlier, species exhibit differential responses to increasing temperature and evidence exists for some species to advance, others to retreat and yet others to remain in their original location (Parmesan and Yohe 2003; Parmesan 2006; Thackeray *et al.* 2010; Singer and Parmesan 2010). According to Brommer and Møller (2010) the composition of an ecosystem will change over time as species will move at different speeds.

Brommer and Møller (2010) examined the shift in range margins of a combined UK and Finnish data set compiled from consecutive atlases of breeding birds from the late 1960s or early 1970s to the late 1980s or early 1990s. They found that insectivorous and terrestrial herbivores, both specialist feeders, showed a rapid change in range margin (northwards) of approximately 4 to 14km/yr respectively whereas birds of prey and generalists showed the lowest range margin shifts of 2 to −0.2km/yr respectively. When considering migration ecology, it was apparent that residents shifted their range least whereas migrants, in particular partial migrants, showed a 6km/yr shift in their range margin. Interestingly, both short- and long-distance migrant range margins moved by approximately the same distance, i.e. 2km/yr. Overall, the authors found mixed evidence of a climate change driven effect underlying the change in breeding bird distributions.

The impact of future increases in temperature on the distribution pattern of a range of wintering waders in Britain revealed both winners and losers. Rehfisch *et al.* (2004) suggests that Northern Lapwing and Dunlin (which are at the north-westerly extreme of their wintering distribution in Britain and Ireland) are expected to increase in population size, especially in southern Britain, but that Oystercatcher, Great Ringed Plover, Common Redshank, Sanderling, Purple Sandpiper, Eurasian Curlew and Ruddy Turnstone are expected to decrease, especially in the west of Britain. The authors emphasis the need to confirm that any apparent decline in population size may be due to redistribution to other wintering grounds rather than an overall population reduction. Conversely, a subsequent study of the waders (Austin and Rehfisch 2005) revealed that in mild winters a smaller proportion of wader populations winter in south-west Britain with a greater proportion remaining in the east where the food source is more plentiful. They suggest that the advantage of wintering in the south-west to avoid cold weather-induced mortality is diminished as mild winters persist. MacLean *et al.* (2008) reviewed counts of waders from *c.* 3,500 sites over 30 years and covering a major portion of western Europe (including Ireland). They were able to demonstrate that the 'weighted centroids' of populations of seven species of wader had undergone substantial shifts of up to 115km, generally in a north-easterly direction.

They went on to propose that, with warming temperatures, hitherto unsuitable sites in north-eastern Europe will host increasingly important wader numbers, but that this may not be matched by declines elsewhere within the study area.

There is also some evidence to suggest that the numbers of Bewick's Swans visiting Britain and Ireland during the winter are smaller when winters are milder and that this may be linked to the large decline in the Irish population since the early 1990s (Robinson *et al.* 2004a). Recent declines in the numbers of Northern Shoveler, Northern Pintail and Red Knot visiting Ireland may also be linked to changes in climate (Lynas *et al.* 2007).

A trend towards the northward shift of species into Ireland has also occurred over recent decades, for example the recent rapid colonisation of the south and east coast of Ireland by the Little Egret (Smiddy and O'Sullivan 1998; Smiddy 2003). The northwards spread of this bird, which is more typically associated with the Mediterranean region, in Europe since the 1970s has been attributed to the absence of severe winters (Voisin 1991). Other birds such as the Mediterranean Gull and more recently the Cattle Egret may also be following this range shift although no published evidence is available to confirm this trend as yet. Likewise, a decline in sightings of species such as the Twite, whose southern range margin extends into the northern part of Ireland, may be as a result of warmer winters but again this cannot be confirmed at present as changes to feeding habitats and nest sites may also be a contributing factor. It is possible that the influence of rising temperatures might be at least partly responsible for other notable changes, particularly the recording of several new nesting bird species in Ireland. For example, Common Reed Warbler resumed nesting in 1980 after a gap of 45 years (Smiddy and O'Mahony 1997). However, whether or not any recorded changes in species distributions in Ireland have been driven by changing climate remains unknown and requires further research.

Based on species climate response models, Huntley *et al.* (2007) have suggested that Ireland has the potential to gain at least 20 new breeding species as temperatures rise by 3 °C. The results of this study also showed that:

- The centre of the potential range of the average species is predicted to shift nearly 550km north-east and will be 80% the size of current range.
- For some species, the potential future range does not overlap with the current range at all. The average overlap is 40%.
- Projected changes for some species found only in Europe, or with only small populations elsewhere, suggest that climate change is likely to increase the risk of extinction.

Of course, the models assume that species and the resources they need will be able to respond at the uniquely rapid rates required. The behaviour of some sedentary species and landscape fragmentation/physical barriers will limit the potential of these species to occupy future suitable range.

By 'retrofitting' these models to known population trends for European birds, it has been demonstrated that those species facing deteriorating climate conditions tend to be declining whereas the populations of those that have improving climatic conditions are increasing (Green *et al.* 2008). Data on long-term population trends of European birds have been used to develop an indicator of the effects of climate change on many species over large areas (Gregory *et al.* 2009). The authors found a significant relationship between interspecific variation in population trend and the change in potential range extent between the late twentieth and late twenty-first centuries, forecasted by climatic envelope models. The indicator also measures divergence in population trend between bird species predicted by climatic envelope models to be favourably affected by climatic change and those adversely affected. The indicator shows a rapid increase in the past 20 years, coinciding with a period of rapid warming.

Red Grouse are dependent on peatlands that may be at risk of drying out due to climate change (Richard T. Mills).

The fish prey of seabirds like Atlantic Puffins may be impacted by climate change (Richard T. Mills).

Other possible effects of climate change on birds

Longer-term changes in the Irish environment could have other significant impacts on birds and their habitats:

Changes in precipitation affecting wetlands: Rainfall is the source of water for Ireland's internationally important freshwater wetlands, which are significant for waterbirds (Crowe 2005a; Nairn 2003). With climate change, it is likely that many wetland ecosystems will experience water stress, with peatlands being amongst the most vulnerable of Irish ecosystems. A recent study showed that areas of optimal climatic conditions for peatlands would be significantly reduced in future as a result of climate change (Jones *et al.* 2006). Although few Irish bird species are completely dependent on peatlands, some breeding species such as Red Grouse, Merlin, Hen Harrier and several wader species use these habitats extensively. Furthermore, Pearce-Higgins (2010) has speculated that abundance of upland bird species may be at risk in future due to a decline in their insect food source as a result of increased summer temperatures causing desiccation of the larvae.

Changes in ocean temperature affecting seabird prey: Sea temperature in the north-east Atlantic is rising and both plankton and fish species have shown northward range extensions since 1980 (Philippart 2007). In the North Sea a decline in the stocks of sand eel has been attributed to the northward movement of their planktonic food and to overfishing. These fish are key prey species for seabirds such as terns, auks and gulls and it is very likely that the alterations in the food web are causing reduction in breeding success in some of these seabird populations (Durant *et al.* 2003; Kitaysky and Golubova 2000). If similar changes occur in the rich feeding areas around Ireland's coast, especially those off the south-west islands, then the consequences for our internationally important breeding seabird populations could be very significant. In estuaries, increasing temperatures are likely to cause intertidal green algae (e.g. *Enteromorpha* spp.) to occur for shorter periods or be absent for most of the summer, as has already happened in more southerly latitudes than Ireland (Hiscock *et al.* 2004). These algae are important food plants for some waterbirds like Light-bellied Brent Goose and Eurasian Wigeon and may already be a factor affecting changes in their feeding habitats in urban areas (Benson 2009). Brown algae (e.g. *Fucus* species) on moderately exposed rocky shores will decline with rising sea and air temperatures (Kendall *et al.* 2004). These seaweeds, and the invertebrate communities that they support, form an important feeding resource for a number of wader species (notably Oystercatcher, Eurasian Curlew, Ruddy Turnstone and Purple Sandpiper (see Chapter 11) and their decline may put extra pressure on the bird populations.

Sea level rise affecting coastal habitats: Sea level rise over the next century is expected to cause an extension of intertidal zones (low-, mid- and high-shore and splash zones) along with their associated invertebrate species in a landward direction (Hiscock *et al.* 2004). Many of Ireland's most important estuaries (e.g. Dublin Bay, Belfast Lough, Cork Harbour) are surrounded by built development while others (Shannon/Fergus Estuary, Lough Foyle, Wexford Harbour) are bounded by sea walls and embankments protecting neighbouring farmland (see Chapter 13 and Crowe 2005). This will certainly cause problems of narrowing of intertidal areas ('coastal squeeze'). This phenomenon can already be observed in north Dublin Bay where the Tolka Estuary has been infilled from the top at Fairview and from the bottom by Dublin Port. The result is that birds leave the estuary to feed and roost as high tide approaches.

The future, adaptation and bird conservation

Developing conservation strategies is a complex and challenging task especially when dealing with a range of species, some of which are migratory, and a consequent array of habitat types which require protection. The challenge is further complicated by the unpredictable nature of future impacts of climate change. Therefore, not only will the wintering and breeding grounds require protection but also indeed the entire migration route will need to be taken into account when developing bird conservation strategies in order to ensure a safe passage for migrants. In addition, it will be necessary to obtain international agreement over large geographical areas to ensure an effective conservation strategy.

Common Redshank roosting on a sea wall. Their prey may decline with a reduction in cover of brown seaweeds as a result of rising sea and air temperatures (John Fox).

Work at the British Trust for Ornithology (BTO), which includes data analysis from sites in Britain and Ireland, is currently documenting climate effects, projecting future scenarios and informing adaptation (Pierce-Higgins *et al.* 2011). If climate change results in significant changes in the distribution and abundance of species, as many models predict, then it may require long-term planning by conservation agencies in order to adapt. This may involve increasing the connectivity of habitats in order for species to track changes in their climate, increasing the size of protected areas, such as Special Protection Areas, to increase the resilience of those populations to climate change, or managing sites to reduce negative climate-change effects. There is much that current research now can do to inform this process. One exciting project being undertaken by the BTO is entitled CHAINSPAN.

Ireland holds a high proportion of the Greenland population of Greater White-fronted Goose in winter (Karl Partridge).

This research programme is using models that are attempting to approximate the likely effects of climate change on the size of populations supported by protected areas that form the Special Protection Area (SPA) network across Europe (Pearce-Higgins *et al.* 2011). For many coastal wetland species, there is good evidence that their distributions are shifting in response to climate change (Austin and Rehfisch 2005, Maclean *et al.* 2008) which may have implications for protected areas. This work by the BTO and RSPB is attempting to model the extent to which such shifts are likely to affect a wider suite of species in order to assess the extent to which any future shifts in the distribution

Semi-natural corridors such as hedgerows are important to allow wildlife species adapt to new climatic conditions (Karl Partridge).

Common Redshank, Dunlin and Northern Lapwing roosting on a frozen shoreline (Richard T. Mills).

of species in response to climate change may affect the proportion of a species population supported by the SPA network. Some questions that arise from this research are: will the status of some SPAs change under climate change scenarios (see Dodd *et al.* 2010 for summary of protected areas and climate change) and what are the implications for the designation process?

In their current analysis, mostly involving the use of Breeding Bird Survey data, they have modelled species abundance in response to projected climate change (Rennick *et al.* in press). This recent analysis has shown that climate change was projected to result in national declines with that in Eurasian Curlew likely to be particularly severe. Are the same factors causing the decline of Eurasian Curlew in Ireland? Perhaps current studies under way by Birdwatch Ireland and University College Cork (Donaghy, Denniston and O'Halloran, unpublished) may unravel the causes and effects.

Observed evidence and predictive models of the responses of birds to climate change in Ireland suggest that action is necessary to enable wildlife to adapt, even though the predicted increase in temperature may be significantly less than elsewhere in Europe. Adaptation measures for birds need to be central to the elements of any adaptation programmes applied by relevant statutory bodies across the island. These measures will be particularly important for species for which Ireland holds a large proportion of the biogeographic population, e.g. the Light-bellied Brent Goose and Greater White-fronted Goose, and for which their future conservation status will rely heavily on action taken on the island.

Given that the changes are occurring against a background of the continuing loss of natural habitats and fragmentation, many bird species may struggle to survive in Ireland. It is clear that the current network of protected areas for birds and other species will be insufficient (e.g. Hickling *et al.* 2006). It will be necessary to make the wider landscape more suitable for species as they shift in response to climatic change. This will require more than just better protection of existing 'hot spots', i.e. within Natura 2000 or the network of protected areas designated under national legislation.

The Irish landscape will need to become more permeable to species that are attempting to respond by adjusting their distributions to new conditions (e.g. Collingham and Huntley 2000). This means that maintaining existing patches of semi-natural habitat in the landscape will be important, and creating new ones will be necessary. The spatial locations of these patches will, of course, determine whether they can act as 'stepping stones' for the suite of species requiring them. Agri-

Extreme weather events such as this storm at Bullock Harbour, Co. Dublin, will become more frequent with climate change (John Coveney).

environment schemes offer an excellent mechanism to provide these patches of habitat in farmed land but new mandatory measures to secure habitat may be required to complement this approach.

Many of our protected areas are based on the presence of rare or threatened species and habitats. Given that Alcamo and Krielman (1996) have identified that more than 40% of the global land area will no longer experience climatic conditions to maintain ecosystems or biomes following climatic change, the species and habitats for which a site was originally protected will, in many cases, not be able to survive there. However, this should not mean we dispense with protected areas because these high-quality natural and semi-natural areas will become important homes to new species and habitats. They will remain important nodes in the overall network of sites if some proportion of global biodiversity is to be conserved as the climate changes. It is, therefore, very important that overdue plans to declare all qualifying sites as protected areas are implemented as a matter of priority.

Selecting new sites that offer a diverse range of physical habitats, even if they currently do not play host to rare or threatened species, offers the best way to sustain a wide diversity of species. In other words, we need to take calculated decisions if we are to maximise our ability to conserve biodiversity in a changing climate; accepting uncertainty requires a refreshed approach to site selection (Hole *et al.* 2009). We must, however, continue to identify and protect less common physical habitats as well.

There is clearly a need to consider new conservation measures to reduce the negative impacts of climate change (Green and Pearce-Higgins 2010; Miller-Rushing *et al.* 2010). To ensure birds in Ireland can adapt to a changing climate, the following general principles should be adopted:

- All existing biodiversity laws, policies and strategies should be implemented across the island to create resilient populations of bird species in healthy habitats;
- The area of land managed for birds and other environmental benefits should be increased, including areas for buffering and linkage outside the protected area network. The management regime for protected sites should build in climate-change resistance for current features and accommodate the requirements of likely new features; and

- Habitat features should be protected and created across the island to make it possible for bird species to permeate the land mass.

In the future, it will be particularly important to investigate which species are most likely to be affected on the island and identify the specific measures required to secure their conservation. There is a growing body of information in the scientific literature that can help conservationists across Ireland to begin this process, but much effort will be required in the future to fill any gaps in our understanding and to implement the adaptation measures required. There is also a growing need to develop practical measures to enable conservation agencies mitigate some of the effects of climate change and to take practical steps in habitat management to protect species of conservation concern. The recent work of Pierce-Higgins (2011) modelling two forms of management – i.e. counteracting management to reduce the severity of effects of climate change and compensatory management to increase populations – provides a possible future framework. This useful study provides a possible way forward for site-based adaptation management to increase the resistance of European Golden Plovers to some degree of future climate change. The model framework developed by Pierce-Higgins for informing climate change adaptation decisions should be developed for other species and habitats not only in Britain but also in Ireland.

Conclusions

We have clearly established that climate change has already affected birdlife in numerous ways. The evidence for a range of impacts is indeed well documented and convincing but when weighing up an impact, i.e. whether it is positive or negative, we must be cognisant of whether we are looking at the issue from a human or wildlife perspective. So, from a bird's point of view, climate change is resulting in changes in the timing of migration and breeding, distribution patterns, synchrony with prey and there is some evidence of a genetic change occurring too. All of these factors result in negative fitness consequences for birdlife and these trends are likely to continue, at least into the near future. There are also some positive aspects to climate warming such as the introduction of species new to Ireland and the potential for earlier arrival and breeding leading to greater breeding success. However, the differential response of bird species to warming further complicates predictions of future impacts on ecosystems as a whole. Therefore, developing suitable conservation strategies will be a challenging task and in doing so, one thing is sure, climate change impacts cannot be ignored.

Acknowledgements

The authors would like to acknowledge the Irish Environmental Protection Agency's (EPA) STRIVE programme, project number 2007-CCRP-2.4, *Climate change impacts on phenology: implications for terrestrial ecosystems*, for supporting this work. In addition, we would like to thank the reviewers for their useful comments and thorough consideration of an earlier draft of this chapter.

18. Bird Habitats
A synthesis and future perspectives

John O'Halloran, Richard Nairn, Pat Smiddy and Olivia Crowe

Throughout this book each chapter describes the major bird habitats in Ireland, reviews the published work and describes the bird communities associated with each. The chapters by their very nature differ in the extent of their description because the studies undertaken in these habitats were somewhat variable, of different duration and carried out at different times. In this chapter we pull together a number of threads woven through each of the others. We provide some synthesis and address the questions set out in the introduction. We will explore to what extent multiple habitats are used by some species, whether we have any knowledge of habitat quality, consider what are the major challenges facing habitats in Ireland, and finally, identify any gaps that might stimulate further research on our birds and their habitats.

In this chapter we summarise knowledge on the occurrence of birds, derived from the checklist

Dipper is one of the habitat specialists completely reliant on rivers (Richie Lort).

of Smiddy (2010a), in the various habitats represented in Ireland, from the data provided in each of the chapters in this book and from Crowe *et al.* (2011b). In Table 18.1 (pp. 260–268) an attempt is made to assign all of the bird species regularly occurring in Ireland to one or more habitats. The table seeks to give a broad summary of the species that one might encounter in each of the habitats. It is clear from the preceding chapters that the bird communities of Irish habitats are a mixture of generalists, or species that occur in a wide range of habitats, and a small number of specialists, or species that have specialised habitat requirements. The status of each species, whether it breeds in Ireland, is a resident or a migrant, is summarised. As a guide, we have identified those species that have a narrow habitat usage at the most critical time of their life history – the breeding season – as those which are associated with one, or a maximum of two, habitats. Thus, for example, while the total number of species known to occur in rivers and canals (Chapter 4, Table 18.1) is 26, there are in fact only six habitat specialists: Dipper, Grey Wagtail, Common Sandpiper, Goosander, Mandarin Duck and Common Kingfisher, based on their reliance on rivers and canals for breeding. The same is true for every habitat: there are many species occurring in them, but only a relatively small number are reliant on only one or two habitats for breeding. It is clear that there are a smaller number of habitat specialist species in Ireland, compared to other countries, and many of the reasons for this were discussed in Chapter 3.

Bird species occurrence and usage of habitats

Over a century ago, Ussher and Warren (1900) noted that 'the most striking contrasts in the bird population of different inland districts are between the species that frequent mountains and bogs on the one hand and those that inhabit the cultivated and wooded parts on the other'. These authors

Redwings become more wide-ranging in severe weather as they search for food (Richie Lort).

believed that 'the greatest amount of dissimilarity in land birds is exhibited by those of the East and those of the West of the island'.

Fuller (1982) noted that species richness (or the number of species present in a given area) varied significantly between habitat types in Britain. For example, woodlands usually support more species of birds than do open heaths or grasslands due to habitat complexity as described in Chapter 3. Flood meadows and salt marshes are richer habitats for wintering birds, both in terms of species number and density of birds, than are uplands. From the foregoing chapters, using the list produced by Smiddy (2010a) and recent studies by Crowe *et al.* (2011) and Crowe (2011b), we are now in a better position to define bird occurrence and habitat usage in Ireland

The assigning of bird species to particular habitat types is not a precise exercise. Some species, such as Barn Swallow, breed primarily in one habitat, such as lowland farmland, but feed very widely in a variety of habitat types. Others, such as the Redwing, may winter mainly in woodland and farmland, but are found more widely in other habitats when severe weather occurs. Some generalist species, such as Rook, and Hooded Crow, may be found in almost all habitats outside the breeding season.

However, taking the occurrences given in Table 18.1, it is possible to total the number of species occurring in each habitat group (Table 18.2). This shows that lowland farmland and estuaries and coastal lagoons are the richest with over 80 species occurring in each, yet in terms of specialists, woodlands, forest and scrub have the highest at 29, similar to that found by Fuller (1982) in Britain. Not surprisingly, given Ireland's importance for seabirds, cliffs, islands and rocky coasts are the second richest habitat as measured by these crude methods.

Table 18.2 Total number of species occurring and breeding in each habitat group. Specialists are defined here as those species in Table 18.1 that typically breed in one or two habitats.

	Rivers and canals	Lakes, reservoirs, turloughs	Wet grasslands	Lowland bogs, fens, reedswamps	Upland heaths, blanket bogs	Woodlands, forest, scrub	Lowland farmland	Cliffs, islands, rocky shores	Beaches and dunes	Estuaries and coastal lagoons	Open sea	Urban habitats
All species	26	55	29	31	29	57	83	50	59	82	35	59
Specialists	6	17	2	4	12	29	21	23	4	5	0	5

Open sea, whilst critical to foraging seabird species, is not identified as a breeding site for obvious reasons. These birds come ashore to nest and are mainly included in the Cliffs, Islands and Rocky Coasts habitat.

There has been a large amount of survey work on birds in Ireland, especially over the last 50 years. We now have evidence to show that wetlands support a relatively high density of birds (Chapters 5 and 6, Mitchell *et al.* 2004, Crowe 2005). Wetlands are largely discrete units that support colonial and flocking species. Their prevalence in the landscape makes Ireland a key location in Europe for the species that are adapted to them. In winter, many coastal estuaries not only support high densities of wetland birds but also support a great diversity of other winter migrants (Chapter 13). During the breeding season, sea cliffs and certain coastal islands support high densities of cliff-, ground- and burrow-nesting seabirds (Chapter 11, Mitchell *et al.* 2004).

By contrast, less is known about the density of birds in dry, or terrestrial, habitats which are considerably more prevalent throughout the island, and which do not form defined or discrete areas such as the wetland habitats described above. Thus, most non-wetland birds are more widely distributed and, with some exceptions, do not form flocks or colonies. These exceptions include Rook, Sand Martin and House Sparrow; Rooks nest in dense colonies in clusters of large trees and up to 100 nests can be found, while Sand Martins nest in steep-sided sandy banks that border rivers and lakes, but also in sand quarries. Several hundred Sand Martin nests may occur in any given colony. A number of species flock later in the breeding season once the young have fledged. Large parties of Rook, Jackdaw, Woodpigeon, Common Starling and Linnet, for example, form single- or mixed-species aggregations. Later still, dense flocks of migrant Common Starlings and thrush species may be found roaming the countryside.

Among these terrestrial habitats, farmland, which occupies more than 60% of the land area of Ireland (Department of Agriculture and Food 2008), hosts the greatest number of bird species, with 21 specialist species (Chapter 10). This includes the typical farmland species (for example, Rook, Common Starling and Common Pheasant), as well as a whole suite of species that are really more typical of different habitat types in other parts of Europe.

Peatlands are the next most widespread habitat in Ireland, covering some 14% of the landscape (Hammond 1981). Irish peatlands offer a variety of bird habitats, including fens, raised bog and blanket bog. They support relatively few species and are dominated by the presence of two species, namely Skylark and Meadow Pipit (Bracken *et al.* 2008). It has been shown that Eurasian Curlew prefers raised bog, while Red Grouse are found almost entirely in blanket bog. Both of these species are of high conservation concern in Ireland (Lynas *et al.* 2007). While raised and blanket bog support similar bird species and assemblages, fens support a higher diversity of species (Chapter 7, Bracken *et al.* 2008).

Atlantic Puffins on Great Saltee. Sea cliffs support very high densities of birds in the breeding season (John Fox).

Rook colonies may number up to 100 nests in areas with good foraging (Karl Partridge).

Spotted Flycatcher is a specialist breeder in woodland (Richie Lort).

The Tree Sparrow is a woodland species that has adapted to nesting close to houses (Richie Lort).

Woodland occupies less than 10% of Ireland's land area (Anon 2007). The fact that Ireland lost its native woodlands thousands of years ago (Hall 2011), has led to a low diversity of woodland bird specialists. True specialists of broadleaved woodland are Blackcap, Spotted Flycatcher and Eurasian Treecreeper (Crowe 2011b, Sweeney *et al.* 2010). Other woodland species not included in these analyses include Jay and, more recently, the Great Spotted Woodpecker, on the basis that they are relatively sparsely distributed and do not occur in a sufficient number of sites for meaningful analyses. A suite of generalist species makes use of the woodland habitat, but many of these same species also occur in a variety of other habitats. These include Wren, European Robin, Blackbird, Song Thrush, Mistle Thrush, Long-tailed Tit, Blue Tit, Great Tit, and Chaffinch. Many of these are also recorded in farmland habitats, especially field margins. Woodlands and tree lines can hold surprisingly high densities of birds when, for example, they are used as winter roost sites by Rooks, Jackdaws and migrant thrushes (Chapter 9).

As towns and cities continue to expand, after substantial growth in the 1980s (Stewart 2005), urban habitats (Chapter 15) cover an increasing proportion of land area in Ireland. There is a suite of species that have become specially adapted to habitats provided in urban and suburban areas, such as buildings and gardens. (Crowe 2011b) identified ten bird species that are especially prevalent in urban habitats. These include a diverse mix of species, such as Collared Dove, Common Swift, Common Starling, House Sparrow and Greenfinch, to name a few. However, parks also offer a diversity of additional habitats which are of significance to birds, especially in busy towns and cities. During a single detailed survey of the birds of Dublin's Phoenix Park in 2007 and 2008 (Crowe 2008, 2011b), a total of 72 species was recorded. These included 62 species during the breeding period and 58 in winter; 35 species were definitely breeding, a further ten were probably breeding, two were possibly breeding, while the remaining 24 species were non-breeders. It is likely that Phoenix Park is atypical of most urban habitats and the additional parkland there probably provides additional habitat types, and hence diversity, compared to other urban areas. BirdWatch Ireland's Garden Bird Survey has shown that Irish gardens support up to 134 species, although approximately 70 species occur regularly. Most gardens support between 15 and 25 species outside the breeding season but that up to 50 species can occur in some exceptional gardens (Crowe 2005). Common Starlings can roost in huge numbers, sometimes in flocks of more than 10,000 birds, in urban areas outside the breeding season. Such commensal species as Feral Pigeons and Mute Swans can occur in high densities where there is a ready food source.

Seasonal influences on bird assemblages are likely to vary between different habitats (Fuller 1982), potentially as a consequence of differences in food availability and predation pressure (Rodriguez *et al.* 2001). For example, broadleaved forests may contain more bird species than coniferous forests in winter, and have distinct bird assemblages (Chapter 9). Native broadleaved woodlands are a seasonal habitat with many deciduous canopy and understorey plant species. Leaves are important feeding areas for some gleaning bird species during the breeding season when invertebrate prey is abundant (Perrins 1979). In contrast, non-native plantations in Ireland are composed primarily of coniferous, evergreen species, and may therefore provide a less variable year-round habitat (Sweeney *et al.* in press). It appears that the overlap in winter species composition between different forest types in Ireland is more pronounced than has been reported in English forests (Donald *et al.* 1997). Similar variation in the seasonal use of habitats is observed in the Hen Harrier, which breeds in the uplands (Chapter 8) and moves to lowland farmland and coastal reedswamps in winter (Chapter 7). In the same way, shorebirds such as Eurasian Curlew, Common Redshank and Northern Lapwing spend their winters mostly on coastal sites, breeding in river valleys, lakeshores and the uplands (Chapters 6 and 8). These patterns in habitat use are not unique to Ireland, but rather represent seasonal use of habitats by birds for different parts of their life history.

Northern Lapwings winter throughout the country but may move to the coast when the ground inland is frozen (Richard T. Mills).

Because the Irish songbird (passerine) fauna is largely composed of generalist species, most species are not restricted to a particular habitat. Many species can therefore exploit a variety of habitats to meet their winter resource requirements, leading to indistinct patterns of bird assemblages, particularly in winter (Figure 18.1).

The birds occurring in the main habitat groups in Ireland are summarised in Table 18.1. This shows strong similarities between the bird species found in lakes, reservoirs and turloughs, and estuaries and coastal lagoons. Many of these species are winter migrants which use wetland habitats for roosting and feeding. Several of these, especially swans and geese, wading bird species

Choughs mix freely with true seabirds on the coastal cliffs (Richard T. Mills).

such as European Golden Plover, Northern Lapwing and Eurasian Curlew, gulls such as Black-headed and Lesser Black-backed also use nearby grasslands for feeding. Some estuarine species, for example Light-bellied Brent Goose and Oystercatcher, have adapted to urban parklands. There are similarities in the habitats used by breeding waterbirds – e.g. Moorhen, Mallard, Mute Swan, Little Grebe – which breed in marginal lake and river habitats and among emergent vegetation. The coastline has a mixture of mainly marine and wetland species. Here seabirds, wildfowl, waders and gulls mix with terrestrial species such as Chough, Stonechat and Twite. The main differences in bird communities are between tall cover habitats (woodland, forest and scrub) and other more open habitats (upland heath, bogs, wet grasslands and farmland) as described for Britain by Fuller (1982).

Passerines and Non-Passerines; Residents and Migrants

Fuller (1982) compared the bird communities of different habitat types in Britain by addressing the relative numbers of passerines and non-passerines. A similar analysis for Ireland (based on Table 18.1) shows that those habitats where passerines outnumber non-passerines are upland heaths and blanket

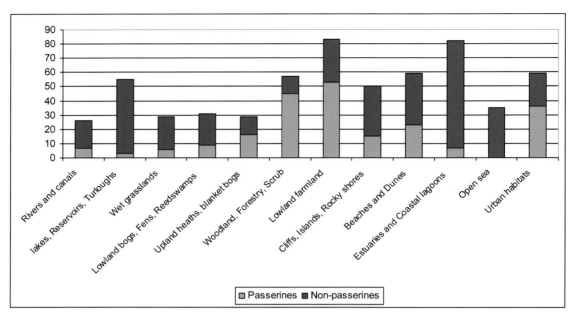

Figure 18.1 Relative numbers of passerine and non-passerine species in each habitat group.

bogs, woodland, forests and scrub, lowland farmland and urban habitats (Figure 18.1). In woodland, forests and scrub, passerines are dominant at 79% of all species. By definition, passerines are perching birds and they naturally occur in areas where trees and shrubs are the predominant vegetation. They are also generally smaller than non-passerines and can thus move more easily through dense vegetation.

A comparison of migrants versus non-migrants in different habitats is somewhat more difficult due to the problems of defining a migrant. Newton (2010) considers migration as a regular return movement of birds each year between separate breeding and wintering areas. While some species are either migratory or non-migratory, others are partial migrants. In the latter group (for example, Mute Swan, Common Snipe or Blackbird) some individuals are resident while others are migrants. True migratory species in Ireland can be divided into three groups. These are summer visitors (e.g. Barn Swallow and Common Tern) that move between tropical and temperate climates, winter visitors (e.g. Light-bellied Brent Goose and Snow Bunting) that visit Ireland from Arctic breeding grounds, and passage migrants (e.g. Eurasian Whimbrel and Firecrest) which neither breed nor winter in Ireland but pass through in spring and/or autumn.

The Eurasian Whimbrels that pass through Ireland in spring and autumn do not breed here (Richard T. Mills).

Table 18.1 (pp. 260-268) shows that the highest proportion of migrant species are found among the waterbirds (including seabirds), that use wetlands, estuaries, beaches, rocky shores and cliffs. Seabirds account for the greatest number of passage migrants, with thousands of individuals passing through the offshore waters around Ireland. The diversity of other species occurring in autumn and/or spring passage is much higher, but generally consists of many fewer individuals, often less than one per species. Fuller (1982) found that resident species in Britain outnumbered migrants in all habitats and that this proportion was relatively uniform across the habitat types. Since Ireland has a lower proportion of migrants to residents in most terrestrial habitats, then we would expect the dominance of resident species in these habitats to be even higher than in Britain. The problem of whether or not to include partial migrants complicates this assessment and makes quantification difficult.

The migratory origin of several species differs between Ireland and Britain, especially among wintering waterbirds (Wernham *et al.* 2002). Definitive conclusions on the migratory origins of some of the wintering waterbirds that occur in Ireland are speculative given the limited marking and re-sighting studies that have taken place in Ireland. However, many wintering bird species here are mainly from the north and west (Iceland/Greenland/Canada), as well as some from the east (Northern Europe/Russian Federation/Siberia). Given its westerly position within Europe, Ireland probably receives a higher proportion of birds migrating from the north and west. It is known that Ireland supports substantial proportions of the eastern high Canadian Arctic population of Light-bellied Brent Goose (almost 100%), Icelandic-breeding Whooper Swan (60%) and Black-tailed Godwit (39%). Ireland is also thought to support the majority of the Icelandic/Faeroes-breeding population of European Golden Plover. It also serves to support passage populations of many wader species, especially those en route to wintering areas further south on the continent or Africa (e.g. Eurasian Whimbrel).

The decline in numbers occurring in Ireland of many of the species that migrate from Northern Europe and further east may be due to the short-stopping of birds in areas closer to their breeding grounds due to climate change (Chapter 17). Certainly there has been a large-scale decline in the total number of Bewick's Swans wintering in Ireland from more than 2,000 during the 1980s to just 84 birds in 2010 (Boland *et al.* 2010b). This rate of decline is much higher than that occurring in Britain and elsewhere within the wintering range of this species (Worden *et al.* 2006). Other species which migrate from the east, and which may be showing a greater rate of decline in Ireland than elsewhere, include Eurasian Wigeon, Common Pochard and Dunlin.

Bewick's Swans are now short-stopping closer to their Arctic breeding grounds and few winter in Ireland (Richard T. Mills).

Differences between Ireland and other parts of Europe

Even the earliest writers noticed that Ireland had fewer species than other European countries. Giraldus Cambrensis, writing about AD 1200, observed that 'some birds that live on the water and build their nests in high places are found here as elsewhere. But other types of birds have been altogether wanting even from the earliest times' (O'Meara 1982).

By the middle of the nineteenth century, Thompson (1849) had already noticed changes in populations of certain bird species in Ireland which he attributed to habitat changes. The kite (probably Red Kite) which had been described as common a century earlier (Smith 1750) was by 1849 'an extremely rare visitant to any part of the island: this species would be affected by the absence of wood'. Thompson also noted that the Bittern 'affected by the draining of the bogs, has almost ceased to breed in Ireland'. He reported that, 'the Eurasian Curlew, European Golden Plover, Northern Lapwing and others, have been driven from many of their breeding grounds by the draining of the bogs'.

Hutchinson (1989) discussed the complete absence as breeding birds from Ireland of Tawny Owl, Green Woodpecker, Great Spotted Woodpecker (now breeding in parts of the east of Ireland, see Chapter 9), Lesser Spotted Woodpecker, Marsh Tit,

The Red Kite was a common breeding bird in Ireland in the early eighteenth century but became extinct shortly afterwards (Richard T. Mills).

Willow Tit and Eurasian Nuthatch and the extreme rarity of other woodland species. He referred to the various theories of island biogeography and the contention of Wilson (1977) that the small size of Irish woods together with the extent of grazing caused the extinction of many woodland birds in Ireland. However, Hutchinson favoured the argument that many of the woodland species found in continental Europe have been excluded by more generalist species which colonised after the last glaciation and occupied the niches which woodpeckers and other specialist species required. In his review of the origins of the avifauna of Ireland, Kelly (2008) concluded that there is a range of possible explanations for the dynamic nature of Irish bird communities. These include glacial refugia for some species, behavioural and island-effect for others and winter climate, which continues to be dominated by heavy rainfall and high average wind velocities.

Lack (1976) found that Ireland supported, as regular members of its avifauna, only some 67% of the land birds breeding in Britain with a further 10% breeding only occasionally. He calculated that only 16 (35%) of the 46 migrant species regularly breeding in Britain also breed in Ireland, while 86 (69%) of the 125 resident species did so. O'Connor (1986) found further evidence that migrancy did not play a major role in promoting invasions by new bird species' colonists. The relative scarcity of migrant species among the land birds of Ireland compared to Britain may be partly explained by the mild oceanic climate of Ireland. This may permit greater survival of resident species and earlier nesting by many compared with Britain and other parts of Europe where a greater seasonality is evident (Hutchinson 1989, Chapter 3).

It is fascinating that many of the species of birds that occur in open landscapes in Irish farmland (Chapter 10) and urban areas (Chapter 15) are truly woodland species in other parts of their range. For example, in Poland, Latvia and many central European countries, Blackbird, Song Thrush and Wren are woodland species and are rarely seen in open grassland and farmland landscapes and in urban areas. However, these species are common and widespread in woodland (Chapter 9), farmland (Chapter 10) and urban areas (Chapter 15) in Ireland. How species can be so plastic in their ecology and show such flexibility is remarkable and would provide a very interesting study on a trans-European level. It is likely that the lower bird species richness and historical loss of woodland habitat has resulted in their distribution in a wider range of Irish habitats. However, Goldcrest and Coal Tit, species commonly associated with coniferous forests throughout Europe, also occur in relatively high abundance in Irish broadleaf woodlands as well as showing a preference for coniferous forests (Chapter 9). The Stock Dove is recognised as a woodland bird in Europe (PECBMS 2009). In Ireland it does nest in woodland but its distribution is largely confined to areas of farmland under tillage, and is coincident

The Goldcrest has a wider habitat niche in Ireland compared to other European countries (Richie Lort).

with that of the Yellowhammer. Crowe (2011) and Crowe et al. (2011b) showed that most common and widespread breeding bird species show preference for farmland habitat with few avoiding it. This plasticity in habitat use is one of the most fascinating aspects of the Irish bird fauna.

The seabird habitats of Britain and Ireland are normally treated as a single biogeographical unit, as the seas that these species inhabit, for the majority of the year, are a continuum around these islands (Mitchell et al. 2004). Ireland has large numbers of breeding seabird species and 23 that we describe as habitat specialists. A small number of species that are found in Britain (e.g. Arctic Skua) do not occur here, but Great Skua is becoming regular in small numbers in the west and north-west (Chapter 11) and is likely to be limited by latitudinal range rather than the absence of suitable habitats. In fact, the habitats for some of the burrow-nesting seabirds (European Storm Petrel, Manx Shearwater, Atlantic Puffin) on islands off south-west Ireland are among the best in the Atlantic Ocean. Similarly, Ireland's position close to the continental shelf edge makes it one of the richest areas of Europe for migratory seabirds (such as Sooty, Great and Cory's Shearwaters, Wilson's and European Storm Petrel)(Chapter 14).

Among the most obvious differences in the Irish avifauna is the fact that the Skylark is mainly a peatland species in Ireland during the breeding season and was once much more widespread (Sharrock 1976), but is a farmland species throughout the rest of Europe. The absence of Skylark from tillage as recorded by Copland *et al.* (in press) is remarkable given the importance of this habitat in other parts of the species' range. Skylarks regularly move onto farmland and away from peatlands outside the breeding season. This may be connected with the heavy grazing pressure on Irish peatlands which may leave little cover and scarce food resources in winter. Studies of Hen Harrier in Britain (Redpath *et al.* 1998) and France (Cormier *et al.* 2008) show that this species prefers to nest in open moorland habitats with tall vegetation and a greater than average cover of heather species. In Ireland, by contrast, the main nesting habitats selected are pre-thicket stages of first rotation and, particularly, second rotation forest plantations, mostly of exotic conifers (Wilson *et al.* 2009). This may also be due to the fact that many Irish peatland habitats (bog and heath) are overgrazed, which could reduce their cover value for nesting, protection from predation and human disturbance as well as lowering prey densities (Wilson *et al.* 2009). The absence of prey species such as field voles in Ireland and the abundance of Meadow Pipit here may also be factors in this difference in habitat selection.

One of the most obvious changes in the last decade in bird communities in Ireland has been an increase in the number of species of birds of prey. The range expansion of the Common Buzzard from the north-east and their increase in numbers (Chapters 9 and 10), the reintroduction of the Golden Eagle, White-tailed Eagle and Red Kite have almost doubled the number of bird of prey species. These changes are also likely to have some very interesting ecological and conservation consequences in the future. It will be fascinating to see how these predator populations influence the prey base and to what extent the arrival (through deliberate or accidental introductions) of new mammal prey (see below) might influence the predator populations themselves.

Differences in ecology between Ireland and other European countries have been shown for almost every species that has been studied in any detail here (Dipper, Stonechat, European Robin, Grey

The Great Skua is now breeding in small numbers in Ireland (John Coveney).

Skylarks regularly move away from peatlands and onto farmland in the winter (Richard T. Mills).

The Common Buzzard has undergone a dramatic range expansion in Ireland over the last two decades (Richard T. Mills).

Wagtail, Song Thrush, Chough, Barn Swallow, Hen Harrier, Barn Owl, Skylark and many others). Some of the differences are quite remarkable, and point to the need for further detailed research on a broad range of species and bird habitats in Ireland. This will help to inform better conservation strategies and provide a deeper understanding of the species, many of which are at the most western distributions of their range.

Habitat quality

In the discussion above of the different habitats, little consideration was given to habitat quality. This is perhaps not too surprising given the limited number of such studies and the focus of research thus far. While birds may use different habitats, the extent to which they use and depend on them for nutrients and energy is a critical consideration for the long-term viability of bird populations. For example, reproductive output and survival of a population is reliant on good breeding success by adults and high-quality breeding habitats. Thus it is possible that a species, although breeding in a habitat, may have low productivity and poor survival. Smiddy and O'Halloran (1991) have shown this for Mute Swans. For example, where they breed in good quality sites, on lakes and ponds, they have good reproductive outputs. In contrast, in poorer habitats such as rivers and estuaries, their reproductive output is low, mostly due to flooding. These latter habitats may lead to so-called ecological traps; where birds use habitats which are suboptimal and invest in breeding with little or no success. To what extent some of the Irish breeding bird fauna are in ecological traps is unknown. This could provide a whole range of research projects in the future, and is critical for our understanding of habitat use, management and conservation.

In contrast to breeding sites, there is some evidence that feeding habitat quality for shorebirds and waterfowl may be about to change, although we recognise they are subject to constant variation. As we have seen in Chapters 5 and 13, and to a lesser extent Chapter 12, many of the bird communities in lakes and estuarine habitats rely on plant material for grazing. Light-bellied Brent Geese or Eurasian Wigeon feed extensively on *Zostera* (eelgrass) or other algae where available and these resources are limited by nutrients either derived from the sediments or from nutrients contained in sewage discharge from urban areas. In the last decade there has been significant investment in sewage waste treatment plants in Ireland, with most major towns and cities seeing significant upgrading in treatment of waste. This treatment is desirable as discharge of raw, or partially treated waste, is not only unsightly,

Brent Geese graze extensively on eelgrass and green seaweeds in estuaries (Richard T. Mills).

but is hazardous and ecologically damaging. Nonetheless, the new treatment plants are more effective at removing waste and will lead to a lower discharge of nutrients and hence will impact on the growth and spread of algae and eelgrass. This can only lead to decline in some birds if they are unable to switch to alternative habitats. It will mean the carrying capacity of the habitat will decline and there will be fewer birds. Whilst there has been no investigation of such changes in bird populations here, Raven and Coulson (2001) have shown, in a study on the River Tyne, a decrease in gull numbers by 37% from 1969/70 to 1994. This decline took place at a time when untreated sewage discharge was reduced by 86% in the study area. It might be argued that the peak in nutrient levels in lakes and estuaries, due to discharges from artificial sources, supported unnatural and unsustainable population levels in certain bird species.

Another change in habitat quality is one that will probably take longer to remedy. This is the growth of coastal algal mats derived from agricultural run-off. Major deterioration in foraging habitat quality in coastal areas of west Cork due to nitrogen release from the catchment have been described by Lewis and Kelly (2001) (Chapter 13). This has lead to rotting algal mats and a reduction in food supply for shorebirds. There are few studies in Ireland linking freshwater bird populations with changes in nutrient levels in the water, although eutrophication is implicated in the decline of Common Scoter on Irish lakes and the changes in wintering duck numbers on Lough Neagh (Chapter 5). However, Abbott *et al.* (2009) have shown a decline in the activity of Daubenton's bats on rivers affected by domestic sewage compared to those without sewage input and this may also be a factor affecting riverine birds in Ireland.

Thus, it is clear that habitats and their quality will change significantly in the next few decades and this will impact on birds, potentially in both positive and negative directions. This will depend on the species and habitats concerned, and further work is required in this area.

One of the most striking changes in habitat quality in suburban and urban areas in the last two decades has been the management of rubbish or landfill sites. Through active management and reduction of the waste mounds, the number of gulls using these sites has declined sharply. While again, this may be desirable from a human safety, public health and aircraft safety point of view, it has resulted in a change in habitat quality of the dumps for gulls and hence a poorer winter survival. Perhaps here too, the massive increase in organic waste in the late twentieth century supported artificially high populations of some scavengers such as European Herring Gull and Rook.

Finally, two changes in the quality of agricultural habitat for winter birds have occurred in recent years. Firstly, the cessation of large-scale beet growing for sugar production (a small acreage is still grown for cattle fodder) since 2006 (Kieran Collins, pers. comm.) has changed the quality of a number of sites and habitats for wintering swans and geese. In the same way the absence of winter stubble due to autumn cereal sowing has reduced (or eliminated) the quality of the habitat for Skylarks and seed-eating finches. In many cases these beet crops have been replaced by maize which, although useful for roosting migrant Barn Swallows (Smiddy 2010b), is of limited or no value to geese and swans. It has recently been suggested that sugar beet may soon be grown again in Ireland for sugar production. Should this be the case it will provide a very useful case study on change of habitat quality for birds. Secondly, land abandonment is likely to be a key driver of future changes in some bird populations. The reduction in grazing caused by land abandonment has become a feature of the Irish landscape in some parts of the west of Ireland in recent years. A study by Kramm *et al.* (2010) has shown that change in habitat quality and biodiversity, including birds, has been significantly influenced by land abandonment. One of the major changes has been the encroachment of scrub leading to losses in species relying on short swards, such as Meadow Pipit and Skylark (Anderson *et al.* unpublished).

Abandonment of farmland leads to changes in bird populations such as the replacement of grassland species with birds of scrub and woodland (John Lusby).

New species arriving either through colonisation or introductions

New bird species, whether originating from introduced or natural colonisation, can potentially have a significant negative impact on habitats and bird communities. Mooney and Cleland (2001) showed that invasive species can alter the evolutionary pathway of native species through competition exclusion, niche displacement, hybridisation, introgression, predation and ultimately extinction. A number of bird species have colonised, recolonised or been introduced to Ireland. In many cases the new species do not behave in Irish habitats as they have in other countries. For example, in the case of the Greater Canada Goose, despite this species being introduced almost 50 years ago to Cork Lough (Chapter 15), the flock, and indeed many other flocks, has not grown exponentially in the same way that it has in other parts of Europe. Why is this the case? Is it the fact that the founder population was too small, and that there are genetic constraints, or is it because the habitats are different? The answers to these questions are unknown. In contrast, the introduced population of Greylag Goose, with similar ecological requirements, has grown in its distribution and numbers across a range of habitats in Ireland. Ruddy Duck numbers have not grown in Ireland either, and perhaps the explanation is similar to that of Canada Geese, but it may also be due to control measures under way in Lough Neagh and Britain which has reduced the source population in Britain (Henderson 2011).

The natural colonisation by Common Reed Warblers seems to be one of greater success. Their arrival as breeders in east Cork, as described by Smiddy and O'Mahony (1997), was followed by an increase in the breeding population at Ballyvergan. More recently, while the numbers have declined somewhat at Ballyvergan, it appears that the species has established a wider distribution across the island of Ireland, ranging at least from Co. Cork along the south coast and up the east coast to Northern Ireland. Has its colonisation and that of other species, such as Little Egret, and more recently Great Spotted Woodpecker, caused any detectable changes in other bird communities or in habitats? There are probably too few studies to date, or the time since their arrival has been too short to detect effects, but these areas will be very interesting research topics in the future.

Perhaps recent arrivals of mammals in the Irish landscape will have a more significant impact on our habitats and their ecology than some of the birds? Some changes have already being detected. The discovery of the Greater White-toothed Shrew in Barn Owl pellets (Tosh *et al.* 2008) provides evidence that our resident birds can and do respond to new prey items appearing in the countryside. The ecological impacts of these have yet to be assessed fully, although some effects have been detected in Barn Owls (Lusby *et al.* unpublished). These records and observations are exciting and important as they may well provide opportunities for Barn Owl populations to recover and perhaps provide a further prey base for the additional birds of prey in the Irish landscape (as mentioned above). The question of the morality and legality of introducing a species deliberately is a different question, if indeed any of the recent mammal introductions are deliberate.

The recent colonisation of Ireland by the Great Spotted Woodpecker may have implications for other birds already present in woodlands (Richard T. Mills).

The question of plant exotics and introductions is much more complicated and few studies have focused on these in relation to birds. The study undertaken by Freeman (1997) on Rhododendron and bird communities at Killarney National Park is one of the few such studies of this kind.

Human impacts and changes

Finally, the impact of human activity on habitats, habitat quality and on bird populations continues to influence bird ecology, distribution and abundance. We live in and share the same habitats as birds. The majority of Ireland's habitats are semi-natural, having had human impact for thousands of years, through land claim, deforestation, drainage, habitat fragmentation, agriculture, urbanisation and so on. Most of these interactions have been described in the preceding chapters. These include climate change (Chapter 17) and building of the urban environment

Forest plantations illustrate the competition for different land uses in the countryside (Richard T. Mills).

and other human structures (Chapter 15). Effects are perhaps more subtle in all other habitats either through growing trees (Chapter 9), grazing on uplands (Chapter 8) or use of rivers and watercourses (Chapter 4), recreation on coastal habitats (Chapters 12 and 13) and leisure and tourism activities throughout the country. The need for greater food production and energy from crops, wind farms and offshore devices may well lead to what is being referred as the *food-energy-environmental trilemma*, i.e. where there are competing demands for food production, energy production and maintenance of environmental quality. Each of these activities has the potential to impact on bird habitats, their quality and extent. Habitat conservation for birds (Chapter 16) is relatively limited in extent but, if applied on a wider scale, could help to counterbalance some of the negative effects. It is only through knowledge and further data collection and research that we can learn more about these interactions and perhaps mitigate negative effects, thus optimising the habitats and countryside for all.

The past generations of researchers and field ornithologists, whose work is described or cited in this book, have contributed to an enormous body of knowledge thus far. The challenges and opportunities that lie ahead are even greater, but ornithologists, birdwatchers and ecologists have always been willing to work and volunteer in contributing to the knowledge of our birds and habitats, and we have no doubt that this will continue in the future. This book hopefully provides a baseline of existing knowledge, and also identifies the gaps in our knowledge in certain areas. A range of exciting opportunities and topics are now awaiting ecologists for further research.

Table 18.1 Habitat preferences of regularly occurring bird species in Ireland. Regularly occurring species are broadly defined as those not in the 'rare' or 'very rare' categories of the Irish Rare Birds Committee (1998), but with the inclusion of a few exceptions, especially those whose status has changed (increased) recently. Rare breeding species (regular or near regular) are included, and are indicated by underlining of the 'B', but occasional breeders are excluded.

R = Resident; M = Migrant; ● = Breeding (B); ▲ = Wintering (W); ◊ = Passage migrant (P)

Species	Occurrence	Rivers and canals	Lakes, reservoirs and turloughs	Wet grasslands	Lowland bogs, fens and reedswamps	Upland heaths and blanket bogs	Woodlands, forest and scrub	Lowland farmland	Cliffs, islands and rocky coasts	Beaches and dunes	Estuaries and coastal lagoons	Open sea	Urban habitats
Mute Swan	R; BW	●▲	●▲	▲	●▲						●▲		●▲
Bewick's Swan	M; W		▲	▲				▲					
Whooper Swan	M; BW	▲	●▲	▲				▲					
Pink-footed Goose	M; W		▲	▲	▲			▲					
Greater White-fronted Goose	M; W		▲	▲	▲	▲		▲					
Greylag Goose	RM; BW		●▲	▲				▲			●▲		
Greater Canada Goose	R; BW	●▲	●▲								●▲		●▲
Barnacle Goose	RM; BW							▲	▲		●▲		
Brent Goose	M; W							▲		▲	▲		▲
Common Shelduck	R; BW								●	●	●▲		
Mandarin Duck	R; BW	●▲											
Eurasian Wigeon	M; BW		●▲	▲							▲		
Gadwall	M; BW		●▲								●▲		
Common Teal	RM; BW	●▲	●▲	●▲	●▲						●▲		
Mallard	R; BW	●▲	●▲	●▲	●▲			●▲			●▲		●▲
Northern Pintail	M; BW		●▲								▲		
Garganey	M; B		●		●						●		
Northern Shoveler	RM; BW		●▲	●							●▲		
Common Pochard	M; BW		●▲								▲		
Tufted Duck	RM; BW	●	●▲	●							●▲		
Greater Scaup	M; W		▲								▲		
Common Eider	R; BW								●▲		▲	▲	
Long-tailed Duck	M; W										▲	▲	

Table 18.1 Habitat preferences of regularly occurring bird species in Ireland. Regularly occurring species are broadly defined as those not in the 'rare' or 'very rare' categories of the Irish Rare Birds Committee (1998), but with the inclusion of a few exceptions, especially those whose status has changed (increased) recently. Rare breeding species (regular or near regular) are included, and are indicated by underlining of the 'B', but occasional breeders are excluded.

R = Resident; M = Migrant; ● = Breeding (B); ▲ = Wintering (W); ◊ = Passage migrant (P)

Species	Occurrence	Rivers and canals	Lakes, reservoirs and turloughs	Wet grasslands	Lowland bogs, fens and reedswamps	Upland heaths and blanket bogs	Woodlands, forest and scrub	Lowland farmland	Cliffs, islands and rocky coasts	Beaches and dunes	Estuaries and coastal lagoons	Open sea	Urban habitats
Common Scoter	M; BW		●									▲	
Velvet Scoter	M; W											▲	
Common Goldeneye	M; W		▲								▲		
Red-breasted Merganser	RM; BW	●	●						●		▲	▲	
Goosander	M; BW	●	●▲								▲		
Ruddy Duck	R; BW		●▲								●▲		
Red Grouse	R; BW				●▲	●▲							
Grey Partridge	R; BW				●▲			●▲					
Common Quail	M; B							●					
Common Pheasant	R; BW						●▲	●▲					
Red-throated Diver	M; BW		●									▲	
Black-throated Diver	M; W											▲	
Great Northern Diver	M; W										▲	▲	
Fulmar	RM; BW								●			▲	
Cory's Shearwater	M; P											◊	
Great Shearwater	M; P											◊	
Sooty Shearwater	M; P											◊	
Manx Shearwater	RM; BW								●			▲	
Balearic Shearwater	M; P											◊	
European Storm Petrel	RM; BW								●			▲	
Leach's Storm Petrel	RM; BW								●			▲	
Northern Gannet	RM; BW								●			▲	
Great Cormorant	R; BW	▲	●▲						●▲		▲	▲	

Table 18.1 Habitat preferences of regularly occurring bird species in Ireland. Regularly occurring species are broadly defined as those not in the 'rare' or 'very rare' categories of the Irish Rare Birds Committee (1998), but with the inclusion of a few exceptions, especially those whose status has changed (increased) recently. Rare breeding species (regular or near regular) are included, and are indicated by underlining of the 'B', but occasional breeders are excluded.

R = Resident; M = Migrant; ● = Breeding (B); ▲ = Wintering (W); ◊ = Passage migrant (P)

Species	Occurrence	Rivers and canals	Lakes, reservoirs and turloughs	Wet grasslands	Lowland bogs, fens and reedswamps	Upland heaths and blanket bogs	Woodlands, forest and scrub	Lowland farmland	Cliffs, islands and rocky coasts	Beaches and dunes	Estuaries and coastal lagoons	Open sea	Urban habitats
Shag	R; BW								●▲			▲	
Little Egret	R; BW	●▲					●			▲	●▲		
Grey Heron	R; BW	●▲	●▲		●▲		●	●		▲	●▲		●▲
Little Grebe	R; BW	●	●▲		●▲						▲		●
Great Crested Grebe	R; BW		●▲		●						▲	▲	
Slavonian Grebe	M; W										▲	▲	
Red Kite	R; BW						●▲	●▲					
White-tailed Eagle	R; BW		●▲			●▲			●▲		▲		
Marsh Harrier	M; P		◊		◊						◊		
Hen Harrier	R; BW		▲		▲	●▲	●▲				▲		
Goshawk	R; BW						●▲						
Sparrowhawk	R; BW						●▲	●▲					●▲
Common Buzzard	R; BW						●▲	●▲	●				
Golden Eagle	R; BW					●▲			●				
Common Kestrel	R; BW					●▲		●▲	●▲	▲			●▲
Merlin	RM; BW					●▲	●	▲	▲	▲	▲		
Peregrine	R; BW					●▲		●▲	●▲	▲	▲		●▲
Water Rail	R; BW	●	●▲		●▲								
Corncrake	M; B			●				●					
Moorhen	R; BW	●▲	●▲	●▲	●▲						●▲		●▲
Common Coot	RM; BW	●	●▲								●▲		●▲
Oystercatcher	RM; BW							▲	●▲	●▲	▲		▲
Great Ringed Plover	RM; BW		●							●▲	▲		

Table 18.1 Habitat preferences of regularly occurring bird species in Ireland. Regularly occurring species are broadly defined as those not in the 'rare' or 'very rare' categories of the Irish Rare Birds Committee (1998), but with the inclusion of a few exceptions, especially those whose status has changed (increased) recently. Rare breeding species (regular or near regular) are included, and are indicated by underlining of the 'B', but occasional breeders are excluded.

R = Resident; M = Migrant; • = Breeding (B); ▲ = Wintering (W); ◊ = Passage migrant (P)

Species	Occurrence	Rivers and canals	Lakes, reservoirs and turloughs	Wet grasslands	Lowland bogs, fens and reedswamps	Upland heaths and blanket bogs	Woodlands, forest and scrub	Lowland farmland	Cliffs, islands and rocky coasts	Beaches and dunes	Estuaries and coastal lagoons	Open sea	Urban habitats
European Golden Plover	RM; BW			▲		•▲		▲			▲		
Grey Plover	M; W									▲	▲		
Northern Lapwing	RM; BW		•▲	•▲	•			•▲			▲		
Red Knot	M; W										▲		
Sanderling	M; W									▲	▲		
Little Stint	M; P									◊	◊		
Pectoral Sandpiper	M; P									◊	◊		
Curlew Sandpiper	M; P		◊							◊	◊		
Purple Sandpiper	M; W								▲	▲			
Dunlin	RM; BW		•	•		•				•▲	▲		
Ruff	M; P		◊								◊		
Jack Snipe	M; W			▲	▲						▲		
Common Snipe	RM; BW		•▲	•▲	•	•		•▲		▲	▲		
Woodcock	RM; BW						•▲	▲					
Black-tailed Godwit	M; BW			•▲				▲			▲		
Bar-tailed Godwit	M; W									▲	▲		
Eurasian Whimbrel	M; P	◊	◊	◊							◊		
Eurasian Curlew	RM; BW		•▲	•	•	•		▲	▲		▲		▲
Common Sandpiper	M; B	•	•										
Green Sandpiper	M; P	◊	◊								◊		
Spotted Redshank	M; P		◊								◊		
Common Greenshank	M; W										▲		
Wood Sandpiper	M; P										◊		

Table 18.1 Habitat preferences of regularly occurring bird species in Ireland. Regularly occurring species are broadly defined as those not in the 'rare' or 'very rare' categories of the Irish Rare Birds Committee (1998), but with the inclusion of a few exceptions, especially those whose status has changed (increased) recently. Rare breeding species (regular or near regular) are included, and are indicated by underlining of the 'B', but occasional breeders are excluded.

R = Resident; M = Migrant; • = Breeding (B); ▲ = Wintering (W); ◊ = Passage migrant (P)

Species	Occurrence	Rivers and canals	Lakes, reservoirs and turloughs	Wet grasslands	Lowland bogs, fens and reedswamps	Upland heaths and blanket bogs	Woodlands, forest and scrub	Lowland farmland	Cliffs, islands and rocky coasts	Beaches and dunes	Estuaries and coastal lagoons	Open sea	Urban habitats
Common Redshank	RM; BW		•▲	•	•					•	▲		▲
Ruddy Turnstone	M; W								▲	▲	▲		
Grey Phalarope	M; P											◊	
Pomarine Skua	M; P											◊	
Arctic Skua	M; P											◊	
Great Skua	M; BP								•			◊	
Sabine's Gull	M; P										◊	◊	
Black-legged Kittiwake	RM; BW								•		▲		
Black-headed Gull	RM; BW		•▲	▲	•			▲	▲	▲	•▲	▲	▲
Little Gull	M; W									▲	▲	▲	
Mediterranean Gull	M; BW									▲	•▲		
Common Gull	RM; BW		•						•	▲	▲		▲
Lesser Black-backed Gull	RM; BW		•					▲	•	▲	▲		•▲
European Herring Gull	R; BW		•						•	▲	▲		•▲
Iceland Gull	M; W									▲	▲		▲
Glaucous Gull	M; W									▲	▲		▲
Great Black-backed Gull	R; BW								•	▲	▲		
Little Tern	M; B									•			
Black Tern	M; P									◊	◊	◊	
Sandwich Tern	M; B		•						•	•			
Common Tern	M; B		•						•	•	•		•
Roseate Tern	M; B								•	•			

Table 18.1 Habitat preferences of regularly occurring bird species in Ireland. Regularly occurring species are broadly defined as those not in the 'rare' or 'very rare' categories of the Irish Rare Birds Committee (1998), but with the inclusion of a few exceptions, especially those whose status has changed (increased) recently. Rare breeding species (regular or near regular) are included, and are indicated by underlining of the 'B', but occasional breeders are excluded.

R = Resident; M = Migrant; • = Breeding (B); ▲ = Wintering (W); ◊ = Passage migrant (P)

Species	Occurrence	Rivers and canals	Lakes, reservoirs and turloughs	Wet grasslands	Lowland bogs, fens and reedswamps	Upland heaths and blanket bogs	Woodlands, forest and scrub	Lowland farmland	Cliffs, islands and rocky coasts	Beaches and dunes	Estuaries and coastal lagoons	Open sea	Urban habitats
Arctic Tern	M; B		•						•	•	•		•
Common Guillemot	RM; BW								•			▲	
Razorbill	RM; BW								•			▲	
Black Guillemot	R; BW								•		▲	▲	•
Little Auk	M; W											▲	
Atlantic Puffin	RM; BW								•			▲	
Rock Dove/Feral Pigeon	R; BW						•▲		•▲				•▲
Stock Dove	R; BW						•▲	•▲					
Woodpigeon	R; BW						•▲	•▲					•▲
Collared Dove	R; BW							•▲					•▲
Turtle Dove	M; P							◊	◊				
Common Cuckoo	M; B					•		•					
Barn Owl	R; BW							•▲					
Long-eared Owl	R; BW						•▲	•▲					
Short-eared Owl	M; <u>B</u>W			▲		•	•		▲	▲	▲		
European Nightjar	M; B					•	•						
Common Swift	M; B												•
Common Kingfisher	R; BW	•▲	▲								▲		
Great Spotted Woodpecker	R; <u>B</u>W						•▲						
Chough	R; BW					•▲			•▲	▲			
Magpie	R; BW						•▲	•▲					•▲
Jay	R; BW						•▲						

Table 18.1 Habitat preferences of regularly occurring bird species in Ireland. Regularly occurring species are broadly defined as those not in the 'rare' or 'very rare' categories of the Irish Rare Birds Committee (1998), but with the inclusion of a few exceptions, especially those whose status has changed (increased) recently. Rare breeding species (regular or near regular) are included, and are indicated by underlining of the 'B', but occasional breeders are excluded.

R = Resident; M = Migrant; ● = Breeding (B); ▲ = Wintering (W); ◊ = Passage migrant (P)

Species	Occurrence	Rivers and canals	Lakes, reservoirs and turloughs	Wet grasslands	Lowland bogs, fens and reedswamps	Upland heaths and blanket bogs	Woodlands, forest and scrub	Lowland farmland	Cliffs, islands and rocky coasts	Beaches and dunes	Estuaries and coastal lagoons	Open sea	Urban habitats
Jackdaw	R; BW						●▲	●▲					●▲
Rook	R; BW						●▲	●▲					●▲
Carrion Crow	R; B̲W							●▲					
Hooded Crow	R; BW			●▲	●▲	●▲		●▲		▲	▲		●▲
Raven	R; BW					●▲		●▲	●▲				
Goldcrest	RM; BW						●▲	●▲		●			●▲
Firecrest	M; P								◊	◊			◊
Blue Tit	R; BW						●▲	●▲					●▲
Great Tit	R; BW						●▲	●▲					●▲
Coal Tit	R; BW						●▲	▲					▲
Skylark	RM; BW				●	●		●▲		●▲			
Sand Martin	M; B	●						●	●	●			
Barn Swallow	M; B							●					●
House Martin	M; B							●	●				●
Long-tailed Tit	R; BW						●▲	●▲					▲
Yellow-browed Warbler	M; P								◊	◊			
Wood Warbler	M; B̲						●						
Chiffchaff	M; BW						●▲	●▲					▲
Willow Warbler	M; B						●	●					
Blackcap	M; BW						●▲	●▲					▲
Garden Warbler	M; B						●						
Lesser Whitethroat	M; B̲						●						
Common Whitethroat	M; B				●	●	●			●			

Table 18.1 Habitat preferences of regularly occurring bird species in Ireland. Regularly occurring species are broadly defined as those not in the 'rare' or 'very rare' categories of the Irish Rare Birds Committee (1998), but with the inclusion of a few exceptions, especially those whose status has changed (increased) recently. Rare breeding species (regular or near regular) are included, and are indicated by underlining of the 'B', but occasional breeders are excluded.

R = Resident; M = Migrant; • = Breeding (B); ▲ = Wintering (W); ◊ = Passage migrant (P)

Species	Occurrence	Rivers and canals	Lakes, reservoirs and turloughs	Wet grasslands	Lowland bogs, fens and reedswamps	Upland heaths and blanket bogs	Woodlands, forest and scrub	Lowland farmland	Cliffs, islands and rocky coasts	Beaches and dunes	Estuaries and coastal lagoons	Open sea	Urban habitats
Common Grasshopper Warbler	M; B			•	•	•	•						
Sedge Warbler	M; B	•		•	•		•						
Common Reed Warbler	M; B				•								
Waxwing	M; W												▲
Eurasian Treecreeper	R; BW						•▲						
Wren	R; BW			•▲		•▲	•▲	•▲		•▲			•▲
Common Starling	RM; BW						▲	•▲	•	▲			•▲
Dipper	R; BW	•▲											
Ring Ouzel	M; B					•							
Blackbird	RM; BW						•▲	•▲					•▲
Fieldfare	M; W					▲	▲	▲					
Song Thrush	RM; BW						•▲	•▲					•▲
Redwing	M; W					▲	▲	▲					▲
Mistle Thrush	R; BW						•▲	•▲					•▲
Spotted Flycatcher	M; B						•	•					
European Robin	R; BW						•▲	•▲					•▲
Black Redstart	M; W								▲	▲			▲
Common Redstart	M; B						•						
Whinchat	M; B			•		•		•					
Stonechat	R; BW					•	•▲	•▲		•▲			
Northern Wheatear	M; B					•			•	•			
Pied Flycatcher	M; B						•						

Table 18.1 Habitat preferences of regularly occurring bird species in Ireland. Regularly occurring species are broadly defined as those not in the 'rare' or 'very rare' categories of the Irish Rare Birds Committee (1998), but with the inclusion of a few exceptions, especially those whose status has changed (increased) recently. Rare breeding species (regular or near regular) are included, and are indicated by underlining of the 'B', but occasional breeders are excluded.

R = Resident; M = Migrant; ● = Breeding (B); ▲ = Wintering (W); ◊ = Passage migrant (P)

Species	Occurrence	Rivers and canals	Lakes, reservoirs and turloughs	Wet grasslands	Lowland bogs, fens and reedswamps	Upland heaths and blanket bogs	Woodlands, forest and scrub	Lowland farmland	Cliffs, islands and rocky coasts	Beaches and dunes	Estuaries and coastal lagoons	Open sea	Urban habitats
Dunnock	R; BW						●▲	●▲		●▲			●▲
House Sparrow	R; BW							●▲					●▲
Tree Sparrow	R; BW							●▲					
Yellow Wagtail	M; <u>B</u>		●	●	●								
Grey Wagtail	R; BW	●▲	●▲					▲					
Pied Wagtail	R; BW	●▲						●▲		▲			●▲
Tree Pipit	M; P						◊	◊					
Meadow Pipit	RM; BW			●		●		●▲		●▲			
Rock Pipit	R; BW								●▲	▲	▲		
Chaffinch	RM; BW						●▲	●▲					●▲
Brambling	M; W						▲	▲					
Greenfinch	R; BW						●▲	●▲					●▲
Goldfinch	R; BW						●▲	●▲					●▲
Siskin	RM; BW						●▲	▲					▲
Linnet	R; BW					●	●▲	●▲		▲			
Twite	R; BW					●▲			●▲	▲	▲		
Lesser Redpoll	R; BW					●	●▲	▲		▲	▲		▲
Common Crossbill	R; BW						●▲						
Bullfinch	R; BW						●▲	●▲					▲
Snow Bunting	M; W					▲				▲	▲		
Yellowhammer	R; BW						●	●▲					
Reed Bunting	R; BW	●		●	●▲		●	●▲		▲	▲		

Appendix 1: Names of Irish Birds

Species names of birds change over time in order to recognise changes in taxonomy. The following list of names follows closely a draft list prepared by BirdWatch Ireland. The order follows Parkin and Knox (2010) and is based broadly on the latest version prepared by the British Ornithologists Union (2010). The BOU is the primary English-language bird taxonomy authority in Europe. In a number of cases, where only one member of a species group has occurred in Ireland, then a simplified name is preferred (with some exceptions such as some wildfowl where escaped species are occasionally recorded). Any BOU international common names that are different from the ones used in this book are given in the last column.

Common Name	Scientific Name	BOU International Name
Mute Swan	*Cygnus olor*	
Bewick's Swan	*Cygnus columbianus*	Tundra Swan
Whooper Swan	*Cygnus cygnus*	
Pink-footed Goose	*Anser brachyrhynchus*	
Greater White-fronted Goose	*Anser albifrons*	
Greylag Goose	*Anser anser*	
Greater Canada Goose	*Branta canadensis*	
Barnacle Goose	*Branta leucopsis*	
Brent Goose	*Branta bernicla*	Brant Goose
Common Shelduck	*Tadorna tadorna*	
Mandarin Duck	*Aix galericulata*	
Eurasian Wigeon	*Anas penelope*	
Gadwall	*Anas strepera*	
Common Teal	*Anas crecca*	Eurasian Teal
Mallard	*Anas platyrhynchos*	
Northern Pintail	*Anas acuta*	
Garganey	*Anas querquedula*	
Northern Shoveler	*Anas clypeata*	
Common Pochard	*Aythya ferina*	
Tufted Duck	*Aythya fuligula*	
Greater Scaup	*Aythya marila*	
Common Eider	*Somateria mollissima*	
Long-tailed Duck	*Clangula hyemalis*	
Common Scoter	*Melanitta nigra*	
Common Goldeneye	*Bucephala clangula*	
Smew	*Mergellus albellus*	
Red-breasted Merganser	*Mergus serrator*	
Goosander	*Mergus merganser*	Common Merganser
Ruddy Duck	*Oxyura jamaicensis*	
White-headed Duck	*Oxyura leucocephala*	
Black Grouse	*Tetrao tetrix*	
Red Grouse	*Lagopus lagopus*	Willow Ptarmigan

Common Name	Scientific Name	BOU International Name
Ptarmigan	*Lagopus mutus*	
Capercaillie	*Tetrao urogallus*	Western Capercaillie
Grey Partridge	*Perdix perdix*	
Common Quail	*Coturnix coturnix*	
Pheasant	*Phasianus colchicus*	Common Pheasant
Red-throated Diver	*Gavia stellata*	Red-throated Loon
Black-throated Diver	*Gavia arctica*	Black-throated Loon
Great Northern Diver	*Gavia immer*	Great Northern Loon
Fulmar	*Fulmarus glacialis*	Northern Fulmar
Cory's Shearwater	*Calonectris diomedea*	
Great Shearwater	*Puffinus gravis*	
Sooty Shearwater	*Puffinus griseus*	
Manx Shearwater	*Puffinus puffinus*	
Balearic Shearwater	*Puffinus mauretanicus*	
Wilson's Storm Petrel	*Oceanites oceanicus*	
European Storm Petrel	*Hydrobates pelagicus*	
Leach's Storm Petrel	*Oceanodroma leucorhoa*	
Madeiran Storm Petrel	*Oceanodroma castro*	
Northern Gannet	*Morus bassanus*	
Great Cormorant	*Phalacrocorax carbo*	
Shag	*Phalacrocorax aristotelis*	European Shag
Great Bittern	*Botaurus stellaris*	
Cattle Egret	*Bubulcus ibis*	
Little Egret	*Egretta garzetta*	
Great Egret	*Ardea alba*	
Grey Heron	*Ardea cinerea*	
Little Grebe	*Tachybaptus ruficollis*	
Great Crested Grebe	*Podiceps cristatus*	
Slavonian Grebe	*Podiceps auritus*	Horned Grebe
Black-necked Grebe	*Podiceps nigricollis*	
Red Kite	*Milvus milvus*	
White-tailed Eagle	*Haliaeetus albicilla*	
Marsh Harrier	*Circus aeruginosus*	Western Marsh Harrier
Hen Harrier	*Circus cyaneus*	Northern Harrier
Goshawk	*Accipiter gentilis*	Northern Goshawk
Sparrowhawk	*Accipiter nisus*	Eurasian Sparrowhawk
Common Buzzard	*Buteo buteo*	
Golden Eagle	*Aquila chrysaetos*	
Osprey	*Pandion haliaetus*	
Common Kestrel	*Falco tinnunculus*	
Merlin	*Falco columbarius*	
Peregrine	*Falco peregrinus*	Peregrine Falcon
Water Rail	*Rallus aquaticus*	
Spotted Crake	*Porzana porzana*	
Corncrake	*Crex crex*	

Common Name	Scientific Name	BOU International Name
Moorhen	*Gallinula chloropus*	
Common Coot	*Fulica atra*	
Common Crane	*Grus grus*	
Oystercatcher	*Haematopus ostralegus*	
Great Ringed Plover	*Charadrius hiaticula*	Common Ringed Plover
Dotterel	*Charadrius morinellus*	
European Golden Plover	*Pluvialis apricaria*	
Grey Plover	*Pluvialus squatarola*	
Northern Lapwing	*Vanellus vanellus*	
Red Knot	*Calidris canutus*	
Sanderling	*Calidris alba*	
Little Stint	*Calidris minuta*	
Pectoral Sandpiper	*Calidris melanotos*	
Curlew Sandpiper	*Calidris ferruginea*	
Purple Sandpiper	*Calidris maritima*	
Dunlin	*Calidris alpina*	
Ruff	*Philomachus pugnax*	
Jack Snipe	*Lymnocryptes minimus*	
Common Snipe	*Gallinago gallinago*	
Woodcock	*Scolopax rusticola*	
Black-tailed Godwit	*Limosa limosa*	
Bar-tailed Godwit	*Limosa lapponica*	
Eurasian Whimbrel	*Numenius phaeopus*	Whimbrel
Eurasian Curlew	*Numenius arquata*	
Common Sandpiper	*Actitis hypoleucos*	
Green Sandpiper	*Tringa ochropus*	
Spotted Redshank	*Tringa erythropus*	
Common Greenshank	*Tringa nebularia*	
Wood Sandpiper	*Tringa glareola*	
Common Redshank	*Tringa totanus*	
Ruddy Turnstone	*Arenaria interpres*	
Red-necked Phalarope	*Phalaropus lobatus*	
Grey Phalarope	*Phalaropus fulicarius*	
Pomarine Skua	*Stercorarius pomarinus*	
Arctic Skua	*Stercorarius parasiticus*	Parasitic Jaeger
Long-tailed Skua	*Stercorarius longicaudus*	Long-tailed Jaeger
Great Skua	*Stercorarius skua*	
Sabine's Gull	*Xema sabini*	
Black-legged Kittiwake	*Rissa tridactyla*	
Bonaparte's Gull	*Chroicocephalus philadelphia*	
Black-headed Gull	*Chroicocephalus ridibundus*	
Little Gull	*Hydrocoloeus minutus*	
Laughing Gull	*Larus atricilla*	
Mediterranean Gull	*Larus melanocephalus*	
Common Gull	*Larus canus*	Mew Gull

Common Name	Scientific Name	BOU International Name
Ring-billed Gull	*Larus delawarensis*	
Lesser Black-backed Gull	*Larus fuscus*	
European Herring Gull	*Larus argentatus*	
Yellow-legged Gull	*Larus michahellis*	
Iceland Gull	*Larus glaucoides*	
Kumlien's Gull	*Larus glaucoides kumlieni*	
Thayer's Gull	*Larus thayeri*	
Glaucous Gull	*Larus hyperboreus*	
Great Black-backed Gull	*Larus marinus*	
Little Tern	*Sternula albifrons*	
Black Tern	*Chlidonias niger*	
Sandwich Tern	*Sterna sandvicensis*	
Common Tern	*Sterna hirundo*	
Roseate Tern	*Sterna dougallii*	
Arctic Tern	*Sterna paradisaea*	
Common Guillemot	*Uria aalge*	Common Murre
Razorbill	*Alca torda*	
Black Guillemot	*Cepphus grylle*	
Little Auk	*Alle alle*	
Atlantic Puffin	*Fratercula arctica*	
Rock Dove/Feral Pigeon	*Columba livia*	Common Pigeon
Stock Dove	*Columba oenas*	
Woodpigeon	*Columba palumbus*	Common Woodpigeon
Collared Dove	*Streptopelia decaocto*	Eurasian Collared Dove
Turtle Dove	*Streptopelia turtur*	European Turtle Dove
Common Cuckoo	*Cuculus canorus*	
Barn Owl	*Tyto alba*	
Snowy Owl	*Bubo scandiacus*	
Tawny Owl	*Strix aluco*	
Long-eared Owl	*Asio otus*	
Short-eared Owl	*Asio flammeus*	
European Nightjar	*Caprimulgus europaeus*	
Common Swift	*Apus apus*	
Common Kingfisher	*Alcedo atthis*	
Green Woodpecker	*Picus viridis*	European Green Woodpecker
Great Spotted Woodpecker	*Dendrocopos major*	
Middle Spotted Woodpecker	*Dendrocopos medius*	
Lesser Spotted Woodpecker	*Dendrocopos minor*	
Chough	*Pyrrhocorax pyrrhocorax*	Red-billed Chough
Magpie	*Pica pica*	Eurasian Magpie
Jay	*Garrulus glandarius*	Eurasian Jay
Jackdaw	*Corvus monedula*	Western Jackdaw
Rook	*Corvus frugilegus*	
Carrion Crow	*Corvus corone*	
Hooded Crow	*Corvus cornix*	

Common Name	Scientific Name	BOU International Name
Raven	*Corvus corax*	Northern Raven
Goldcrest	*Regulus regulus*	
Firecrest	*Regulus ignicapilla*	Common Firecrest
Blue Tit	*Cyanistes caeruleus*	
Great Tit	*Parus major*	
Crested Tit	*Lophophanes cristatus*	
Coal Tit	*Periparus ater*	
Willow Tit	*Peocile montana*	
Marsh Tit	*Peocile palustris*	
Bearded Reedling	*Panurus biarmicus*	
Woodlark	*Lullula arborea*	
Skylark	*Alauda arvensis*	
Sand Martin	*Riparia riparia*	
Barn Swallow	*Hirunda rustica*	
House Martin	*Delichon urbicum*	Common House Martin
Cetti's Warbler	*Cettia cetti*	
Long-tailed Tit	*Aegithalos caudatus*	
Yellow-browed Warbler	*Phylloscopus inornatus*	
Wood Warbler	*Phylloscopus sibilatrix*	
Chiffchaff	*Phylloscopus collybita*	Common Chiffchaff
Willow Warbler	*Phylloscopus trochilus*	
Blackcap	*Sylvia atricapilla*	Eurasian Blackcap
Garden Warbler	*Sylvia borin*	
Lesser Whitethroat	*Sylvia curruca*	
Common Whitethroat	*Sylvia communis*	
Common Grasshopper Warbler	*Locustella naevia*	
Savi's Warbler	*Locustella luscinioides*	
Sedge Warbler	*Acrocephalus schoenobaenus*	
Common Reed Warbler	*Acrocephalus scirpaceus*	Eurasian Reed Warbler
Bohemian Waxwing	*Bombycilla garrulus*	
Nuthatch	*Sitta europaea*	
Treecreeper	*Certhia familiaris*	
Short-toed Treecreeper	*Certhia brachydactyla*	
Wren	*Troglodytes troglodytes*	Winter Wren
Common Starling	*Sturnus vulgaris*	
Dipper	*Cinclus cinclus*	White-throated Dipper
Ring Ouzel	*Turdus torquatus*	
Blackbird	*Turdus merula*	Common Blackbird
Fieldfare	*Turdus pilaris*	
Song Thrush	*Turdus philomelos*	
Redwing	*Turdus iliacus*	
Mistle Thrush	*Turdus viscivorus*	
Spotted Flycatcher	*Muscicapa striata*	
European Robin	*Erithacus rubecula*	
Black Redstart	*Phoenicurus ochruros*	

Common Name	Scientific Name	BOU International Name
Common Redstart	*Phoenicurus phoenicurus*	
Whinchat	*Saxicola rubetra*	
Stonechat	*Saxicola torquatus*	
Northern Wheatear	*Oenanthe oenanthe*	
Pied Flycatcher	*Ficedula hypoleuca*	Eurasian Pied Flycatcher
Dunnock	*Prunella modularis*	
House Sparrow	*Passer domesticus*	
Tree Sparrow	*Passer montanus*	Eurasian Tree Sparrow
Yellow Wagtail	*Motacilla flava*	
Grey Wagtail	*Motacilla cinerea*	
Pied Wagtail	*Motacilla alba*	White Wagtail
Tree Pipit	*Anthus trivialis*	
Meadow Pipit	*Anthus pratensis*	
Rock Pipit	*Anthus petrosus*	Eurasian Rock Pipit
Chaffinch	*Fringilla coelebs*	
Brambling	*Fringilla montifringilla*	
Greenfinch	*Carduelis chloris*	European Greenfinch
Goldfinch	*Carduelis carduelis*	European Goldfinch
Siskin	*Carduelis spinus*	Eurasian Siskin
Linnet	*Carduelis cannabina*	Common Linnet
Twite	*Carduelis flavirostris*	
Lesser Redpoll	*Carduelis cabaret*	
Common Crossbill	*Loxia curvirostra*	Red Crossbill
Bullfinch	*Pyrrhula pyrrhula*	European Bullfinch
Snow Bunting	*Plectrophenax nivalis*	
Yellowhammer	*Emberiza citrinella*	
Reed Bunting	*Emberiza schoeniclus*	Common Reed Bunting
Corn Bunting	*Emberiza calandra*	

Appendix 2: Names of other species of animals and plants

Authorities for names are: mammals (Harris and Yalden 2008); marine fish and invertebrates (Gibson *et al.* 2001); plants (Doogue and Krieger 2010; Johnson 2004; Scannell and Synnott 1987).

Common name	Scientific name
Animals	
American mink	*Neovison vison*
Badger	*Meles meles*
Bank vole	*Myodes glareolus*
Barnacle	*Semibalanus balanoides*
Black Rat	*Rattus rattus*
Brown rat	*Rattus norvegicus*
Cockle	*Cerastoderma edule*
Dab	*Limanda limanda*
Earthworm	*Lumbricus sp.*
Flounder	*Platichthys flesus*
Greater white-toothed shrew	*Crocidura russula*
Herring	*Clupea harengus*
House mouse	*Mus domesticus*
Leatherjackets	*Tipulid larvae*
Mackerel	*Scomber scombrus*
Mountain hare	*Lepus timidus*
Mussel	*Mytilus edulis*
Pine Marten	*Martes martes*
Plaice	*Pleuronectes platessa*
Pygmy shrew	*Sorex minutus*
Rabbit	*Oryctolagus cuniculus*
Red Fox	*Vulpes vulpes*
Sand eel	*Ammodytes tobianus*
Short-tailed field vole	*Microtus agrestis*
Sprat	*Sprattus sprattus*
Stoat	*Mustela ermina*
Wood mouse	*Apodemus sylvaticus*
Zebra mussel	*Dreissena polymorpha*
Plants	
Alder	*Alnus glutinosa*
Annual glasswort	*Salicornia europaea*
Annual seablite	*Suadea maritima*
Ash	*Fraxinus excelsior*

Common name	Scientific name
Bilberry	*Vaccinium myrtillus*
Birch	*Betula pubescens*
Birds-foot trefoil	*Lotus corniculatus*
Bog myrtle	*Myrica gale*
Bracken	*Pteridium aquilinum*
Bramble	*Rubus fruticusus*
Branched bur-reed,	*Sparganium erectum*
Broad-leaved pondweed	*Potamogeton natans*
Brown sedge	*Carex disticha*
Burnet rose	*Rosa spinosissima*
Common glasswort	*Salicornia sp.*
Common reed	*Phragmites australis*
Common scurvygrass	*Cochlearia officinalis*
Common spike rush	*Eleocharis palustris*
Cord grass	*Spartina anglica*
Cotton grass	*Eriophorum angustifolium*
Creeping bent grass	*Agrostis stolonifera*
Creeping buttercup	*Ranunculus repens*
Creeping willow	*Salix repens*
Crowberry	*Empetrum nigrum*
Curled dock	*Rumex crispus*
Dwarf eelgrass	*Zostera noltii*
Floating sweet-grass	*Glyceria fluitans*
Gorse	*Ulex europaeus*
Gutweed	*Enteromorpha sp.*
Hawthorn	*Craetagus monogyna*
Hazel	*Corylus avellana*
Holly	*Ilex aquifolium*
Ivy	*Hedera helix*
Hottentot Fig	*Carpobrotus edulis*
Japanese knotweed	*Fallopia japonica*
Jointed rush	*Juncus articulatus*
Knotgrass	*Polygonum spp.*
Ling heather	*Calluna vulgaris*
Lodgepole pine	*Pinus contorta*
Lyme grass	*Leymus arenarius*
Marine eelgrass	*Zostera marina*
Marram grass	*Ammophila arenaria*
Meadowsweet	*Filipendula ulmaria*
Narrow-leaved eelgrass	*Zostera angustifolia*
Norway spruce	*Picea abies*
Oak	*Quercus sp.*
Orache	*Atriplex sp.*
Pondweed	*Potamogeton sp.*
Purple moor-grass	*Molinia caerulea*

Common name	Scientific name
Ragged robin	*Lychnis flos-cuculi*
Reed sweet-grass	*Glyceria maxima*
Red fescue	*Festuca rubra*
Rowan	*Sorbus aucuparia*
Rye-grass	*Lolium perenne*
Saw Sedge	*Cladium mariscus*
Scots pine	*Pinus sylvestris*
Sea bindweed	*Calystegia soldanella*
Sea buckthorn	*Hippophae rhamnoides*
Sea arrow grass	*Triglochin maritima*
Sea aster	*Aster tripolium*
Sea holly	*Eryngium maritimum*
Sea lettuce	*Ulva lactuca*
Sea milkwort	*Glaux maritima*
Sea plantain	*Plantago maritima*
Sea purslane	*Atriplex portulacoides*
Sea spurge	*Euphorbia paralias*
Sea-spurry	*Spergularia sp.*
Sitka Spruce	*Picea sitchensis*
Smooth meadow grass	*Poa pratensis*
Soft rush	*Juncus effusus*
Stonecrop	*Sedum acre*
Sycamore	*Acer pseudoplatanus*
Thrift	*Armeria maritima*
Tree mallow	*Malva sylvestris*
Water crowfoot	*Ranunculus*
White-beaked sedge	*Carex sp.*
White clover	*Trifolium repens*
Willow	*Salix sp.*
Woodrush	*Luzula sylvatica*
Woolly fringe moss	*Racomitrium lanigunosum.*
Yew	*Taxus baccata*

Bibliography

Aalen, F.H.A., Whelan, K. and Stout, M. (eds.) 1997. *Atlas of the Irish Rural Landscape*. Cork. Cork University Press.

Abbott, I.M., Sleeman, D.P. and Harrison, S. 2009. Bat activity affected by sewage effluent in Irish rivers. *Biological Conservation* 142, 2904–2914.

Agnew, P. and Perry, K.W. 1993. The diet of breeding Dippers in north-west Ireland during the period of incubation. *Irish Birds* 5, 49–54.

Ahola, M., Laaksonen, T., Sippola, K., Eeva, T., Rainio, K. and Lehikoinen, E. 2004. Variation in climate warming along the migration route uncouples arrival and breeding dates. *Global Change Biology* 10, 1610–1617.

Alcamo, J. and Kreilman, E. 1996. Emission scenarios and global climate protection. *Global Environmental Change* 6, 305–334.

Alcorn, S. 2009. *Corncrake Fieldwork in North Donegal 2009*. Unpublished BirdWatch Ireland Report to the National Parks and Wildlife Service, Dublin.

Allen, D. 2010. *An Assessment of the Breeding Waterfowl on Ram's Island, Lough Neagh, Co Antrim 2010*. Unpublished report.

Allen, D., Mellon, C., Enlander, I. and Watson, G. 2004. Lough Neagh diving ducks: recent changes in wintering populations. *Irish Birds* 7, 327–336.

Allen, D., Mellon, C., Mawhinney, K., Looney, D. and Milburne, J. 2005. The status of Red Grouse *Lagopus lagopus* in Northern Ireland 2004. *Irish Birds* 7, 449–460

Allen, D., Mellon C. and Looney, D. 2006. Ruddy Ducks *Oxyura jamaicensis* in Northern Ireland. *Irish Birds* 8, 41–50.

Allen and Mellon Environmental. 2007. *Defining indicative breeding bird assemblages for priority habitats in Northern Ireland*. Environment and Heritage Service Unpublished Report.

Anderson, G. 2009. Providing seeds for farmland birds in winter. Pp. 49–56. In: *The LINNET Project (Lands Invested in Nature – National Eco-Tillage): Establishing Small-Scale Plots for Biodiversity*. National Parks and Wildlife Service.

Anderson, R.M., O'Halloran, J. and Emmerson, M. In preparation. The influence of grazing management on upland habitats and the effects on breeding bird diversity.

Anonymous. 2007. *National forestry inventory – Republic of Ireland*. Wexford. Forest Service.

Anonymous. 1974. *Wetlands Discovered*. Dublin. Forest and Wildlife Service.

Anonymous. 2003. *Northern Ireland Habitat Action Plan. Saline Lagoons*. Final draft, April 2003. Belfast. Northern Ireland Environment Agency.

Anonymous. 2008. Civil Aviation Authority (CAA) Bird Risk Management for Aerodromes. CAP 772.UK

Anonymous. 2010. *DRAFT Offshore Renewable Energy Development Plan (OREDP)*. Department of Communications, Energy and Natural Resources.

Appleyard, I. 1994. *Ring Ouzels of the Yorkshire Dales*. Leeds. Maney & Son.

Armstrong, E.A. 1946. *Birds of the Grey Wind*. London. Lindsay Drummond.

Austin, G.E. and Rehfisch, M.M. 2005. Shifting nonbreeding distributions of migratory fauna in relation to climatic change. *Global Change Biology* 11, 31–38.

Averis, A., Averis, B., Birks, J., Horsfield, D., Thompson, D. and Yeo, M. 2004. *An Illustrated Guide to British Upland Vegetation*. Cambridge. Joint Nature Conservation Committee.

Baer, J. and Newton, S. 2006. Unusual occurrence of summering Red Knot *Calidris canutus* on a small rocky island in the western Irish Sea. *Wader Study Group Bulletin* 111, 24.

Bailey, C. 1982. Waterways Bird Survey on the River Lagan. *Irish Birds* 2, 153–166.

Bale, J.S., Masters, G.J., Hodkinson, I.D., Awmack, C., Bezemer, T.M., Brown, V.K., Butterfield, J., Buse, A., Coulson, J.C., Farrar, J., Good, J.E.G., Harrington, R., Hartley, S., Jones, T.H., Lindroth, R.L., Press, M.C., Symrnioudis, I., Watt, A.D. and Whittaker, J.B. 2002. Herbivory in global climate change research: direct effects of rising temperature on insect herbivores. *Global Change Biology* 8, 1–16.

Bamber, R.M., Gilliland, P.M. and Shardlow, E.A. 2001. *Saline Lagoons: A guide to their management and creation*. Peterborough. English Nature.

Barnes, R.S.K. and Green, J. (eds.) 1972. *The Estuarine Environment*. London. Applied Science Publishers.

Barnes, R.S.K. 1974. *Estuarine Biology*. London. Arnold.

Barrett, R.T. 2002. The phenology of spring bird migration to north Norway. *Bird Study* 49, 270–277.

Barrett, R.T., Camphuysen, K., Anker-Nilssen, T., Chardine, J.W., Furness, R.W., Garthe, S., Hüppop, O., Leopold, M.F., Montevecchi, W.A. and Veit, R.R. 2007. Diet studies of seabirds: a review and recommendations. *ICES Journal of Marine Science: Journal du Conseil* 64, 1675–1691.

Barton, C., Pollock, C., Norriss, D.W., Nagle, T., Oliver, G.A. and Newton, S. 2006. The second national survey of breeding Hen Harriers *Circus cyaneus* in Ireland 2005. *Irish Birds* 8, 1–20.

Bassett, J.A., Curtis, T.G.F. 1985. The nature and occurrence of sand-dune machair in Ireland. *Proceedings of the Royal Irish Academy* 85B, 1–20.

Batten, L.A. 1976. Bird communities of some Killarney woodlands. *Proceedings of the Royal Irish Academy* 76B, 285–313.

Beale, C.M., Burfield, I.J., Sim, I.M.W., Rebecca, G.W., Pearce-Higgins, J.W. and Grant, M.C. 2006. Climate change may account for the decline in British Ring Ouzels *Turdus torquatus*. *Journal of Animal Ecology* 75, 826–835.

Bearhop, S., Fiedler, W., Furness, R.W., Votier, S.C., Waldron, S., Newton, J., Bowen, G.J., Berthold, P. and Farnsworth, K. 2005. Assortative mating as a mechanism for rapid evolution of a migratory divide. *Science* 310, 502–504.

Beatty, I., Berridge, D. and McAdams, D. 1997. Storm Petrels nesting above ground under ling heather *Calluna vulgaris* on Inis Tuaisceart. *Irish Birds* 6, 56.

Beaudoin, J.C. and Cormier, J.P. 1973. La migration des Barges a queue noire, *Limosa limosa* L., dans la region d'Angers (Maine-et-Loire) au printemps 1971. *L'Oiseau et R.F.O.* 43, 16–31.

Begg G.S. and Reid J.B. 1997 Spatial variation in seabird density at a shallow sea tidal mixing front in the Irish Sea. *ICES Journal of Marine Science: Journal du Conseil* 54, 552–565.

Benson, L. 2009. Use of inland feeding sites by Light-bellied Brent Geese in Dublin 2008–2009: a new conservation concern? *Irish Birds* 8, 563–570.

Berg, Å., Nilsson, S.G. and Boström, U. 1992. Predation on artificial wader nests on large and small bogs along a south–north gradient. *Ornis Scandinavica* 23, 13–16.

Berrow, S. 1991. Dipper apparently feeding on road. *Irish Birds* 4, 422.

Berrow, S.D. 1992. The diet of coastal breeding Ravens in Co. Cork. *Irish Birds* 4, 555–558.

Berrow, S.D., Mackie, K.L., O'Sullivan, O., Shepherd, K.B., Mellon, C. and Coveney, J.A. 1993. The second International Chough Survey in Ireland, 1992. *Irish Birds* 5, 1–10.

Bibby, C.J. 1986. Merlins in Wales: site occupancy and breeding in relation to vegetation. *Journal of Applied Ecology* 23, 1–12.

BirdLife International. 2004. *Birds in Europe: Population estimates, trends and conservation status.* Cambridge. BirdLife International.

BirdLife International. 2011. Species factsheet: *Numenius arquata.* (www.birdlife.org/datazone/speciesfactsheet.php?id+3012).

BirdWatch Ireland. 2008. *Summary of Corncrake Fieldwork in Ireland 2008.* Report to National Parks and Wildlife Service. BirdWatch Ireland.

Bland, R.L., Tully, J. and Greenwood, J.J.D. 2004. Birds breeding in British gardens: an underestimated population. *Bird Study* 51, 96–106.

Bleasdale, A. 1998. Overgrazing in the West of Ireland – Assessing Solutions. Pp. 67–78. In: O'Leary, G. and Gormley, F. (eds) *Towards a Conservation Strategy for the Bogs of Ireland.* Dublin. Irish Peatland Conservation Council.

Blokpoel, H 1976. *Bird hazards to Aircraft.* Canada. Clarke Unwin.

Boisseau, S. and Yalden, D.W. 1998. The former status of the Crane *Grus grus* in Britain. *Ibis* 140, 482–500.

Boland, H., Crowe, O. and Walsh, A. 2008. Irish Wetland Bird Survey: results of waterbird monitoring in Ireland in 2006/07. *Irish Birds* 8, 341–350.

Boland, H., Crowe, O. and Walsh, A. 2009 Irish Wetland Bird Survey: results of waterbird monitoring in Ireland in 2007/08. *Irish Birds* 8, 521–532.

Boland, H., Walsh, A. and Crowe, O. 2010a. Irish Wetland Bird Survey: Results of waterbird monitoring in Ireland in 2008/09. *Irish Birds* 9, 55–66.

Boland, H., McIlwaine, J.G., Henderson, G., Hall, C., Walsh, A. and Crowe, O. 2010b. Whooper *Cygnus cygnus* and Bewick's *C. columbianus bewickii* Swans in Ireland: results of the International Swan Census, January 2010. *Irish Birds* 9, 1–10.

Bolger, R and Kelly, T.C 2008. *Wildlife Management Plan.* Dublin Airport Authority

Both, C. 2010. Food availability, mistiming and climatic. Pp. 129–148. In: Møller, A.P., Fiedler, W. and Berthold, P. (eds) *Effects of climate change on birds.* Oxford University Press, London

Both, C. and Visser, M. 2001. Adjustment to climate change is constrained by arrival date in a long-distance migrant bird. *Nature* 411, 296–298.

Both, C., Artemyev, A.V., Blaauw, B., Cowie, R.J., Visser, M.E. 2004. Large-scale geographical variations confirms that climate change causes birds to lay earlier. *Proceedings of the Roayl Society of London Series B – Biological Sciences* 271, 1657–1662.

Both, C., Bouwhius, S., Lessells, C.M. and Visser, M.E. 2006. Climate change and population declines in a long-distance migratory bird. *Nature* 441, 81–83.

Both, C. and te Marvelde, L. 2007. Climate change and timing of avian breeding and migration through Europe. *Climate Research* 35, 93–105.

Both, C., van Asch, M., Bijksma, R.G., van den Burg, A.B. and Visser, M.E. 2009. Climate change and unequal phenological changes across four trophic levels: constraints or adaptations. *Journal of Animal Ecology* 78, 73–83.

Bouchet, P. 2006. The magnitude of marine biodiversity. In: Duarte, C. (ed) The exploration of marine biodiversity: scientific and technological challenges, p 31-62. Fundación BBVA, Bilbao. Available online at http://www.marinebarcoding.org/userfiles/File/bouchetmagnitude.pdf

Bourne, W.R.P. 1966. The Irish seabird situation. *Irish Bird Report* 13, 6–8.

Bourne, W.R.P. 1973a. Cape Clear and seabird studies. Pp. 147–152. In: Sharrock, J.T.R. (ed.) *The Natural History of Cape Clear Island.* Berkhamstead. Poyser.

Bourne, W.R.P. 1973b. Influx of Great Shearwaters in the autumn of 1973. *British Birds* 66, 540.

Bourne, W.R.P. 1986. Late summer seabird distribution off the west coast of Europe. *Irish Birds* 3, 175–186.

Bourke, B.P. 2001. An assessment of potential Golden Eagle habitat in South West Ireland and the modelling of a reintroduced Irish Golden Eagle population. M.Sc. Thesis, Manchester Metropolitan University, UK.

Bourke, D., Hochstrasser, T., Nolan, S. and Schulte, R. 2007. *Historical Grassland Turboveg Database Project, Final Report.* Teagasc, Johnstown Castle, Wexford and School of Biology and Environmental Science, University College, Dublin.

Boyd, H. 1954. The "Wreck" of Leach's Petrels in the Autumn of 1952. *British Birds* 157, 137–163.

Boylan, M. 2011. Aspects of the feeding ecology and breeding biology of the Red-billed Chough (*Pyrrhocorax pyrrhocorax*) in Ireland. Unpublished Ph.D. thesis, University College Cork.

Boyle, P.J. 1977. *Spartina* on Bull Island. Pp. 88–92. In: Jeffrey, D.W. *North Bull Island, Dublin Bay – a modern coastal natural history.* Dublin. Royal Dublin Society.

Blamey, M., Fitter, R. and Fitter, A. 2003. *Wild Flowers of Britain and Ireland.* London. A. & C. Black.

Bracken, F. and Bolger, T. 2006. Effects of set-aside management on birds breeding in lowland Ireland. *Agriculture, Ecosystems & Environment* 117, 178–184.

Bracken, F., McMahon, B.J. and Whelan, J. 2008. An assessment of the breeding bird populations of Irish peatlands. *Bird Study* 55, 169–178.

Brennan, E., McMorrow, T., Warner, P., Roderick, T., Farrell, F. and O'Toole, L. 2008. Boleybrack Mountain Red Grouse Project. *Irish Birds* 8, 445–446.

Brennan, P. and Jones, E. 1982. *Birds of North Munster.* Limerick. Irish Wildbird Conservancy.

Brierley, A.S. and Fernandes, P.G. 2001. Diving depths of northern gannets: acoustic observations of *Sula bassana* from an autonomous underwater vehicle. *The Auk* 118, 529–534.

Briggs, J.D. (ed) 1988. *Montgomery Canal Ecological Survey.* Powys, Wales. Unpublished Survey Report.

Brommer, J.E. and Møller, A.P. 2010. Range margins, climate change and ecology. Pp. 249–274. In: Møller, A.P., Fiedler, W. and Berthold, P. (eds) *Effects of climate change on birds.* London. Oxford University Press.

Brough, T and Bridgman, C.J. 1980. An evaluation of long grass as a bird deterrent on British airfields. *Journal of Applied Ecology* 17, 243–253.

Brown, A.F. and Stillman, R.A. 1993. Bird-habitat associations in the eastern Highlands of Scotland. *Journal of Applied Ecology* 30, 31–42.

Brown, R. 1990. *Strangford Lough: The wildlife of an Irish sea lough.* Belfast. Institute of Irish Studies. Queen's University Belfast.

Brown, R.A. and O'Connor, R.J. 1974. Some observations on the relationships between oystercatchers *Haematopus ostralegus* L. and cockles *Cardium edule* L. in Strangford Lough. *Irish Naturalists' Journal* 18, 73–80.

Bryan, M. 1997. The birds of Bushy Park. *Irish East Coast Bird Report* 1997, 95–106.

BTO. 2011. An Essential early warning system for birds. *BTO News* Magazine, Issue 293, 12.

Buchanan, G.M., Pearce-Higgins, J.W., Wotton, S.R., Grant, M.C. and Whitfield, D.P. 2003. Correlates of the change in Ring Ouzel *Turdus torquatus* abundance in Scotland from 1988–91 to 1999. *Bird Study* 50, 97–105.

Buckley, K., O'Gorman, C., Comerford, P., Swan, V., Flynn, C., Carnus, T., Kavanagh, B. and McMahon, B.J. 2011. The role of habitat creation in the recovery of the Irish grey partridge *Perdix perdix.* In Ó'hUallacháin, D. and Finn, J. (eds.) *Conserving Farmland Biodiversity: Lessons learned & future prospects.* Teagasc, Carlow: Pp 56–57.

Buckley, N.J 1987. *Aspects of the Biology of the Great Black backed Gull (Larus marinus).* Unpublished MSc Thesis. Cork. National University of Ireland.

Buckley, P. 1992. *Bird Communities in the Mulkear Catchment, Counties Limerick and Tipperary.* Dublin. Report to National Parks & Wildlife Service.

Buckley, P. 1993. *The Bird Communities and General Ecology of Rahasane Turlough and the Dunkellin/Lavally River system*. Ph.D. thesis. Galway. National University of Ireland.

Buckley, P. & McCarthy, T.K. 1987. *Bird communities in the Dunkellin/Lavally river system. A pre-drainage survey and environmental impact assessment*. Dublin. Report to Forest & Wildlife Service.

Buckton, S.T. and Ormerod, S.J. 2002. Global patterns of diversity among the specialist birds of riverine landscapes. *Freshwater Biology* 47, 695–709.

Budd, R.G. 1998. St. John's Wood, Co. Roscommon, and the archaeology of Irish woodland. Unpublished report. Department of Archaeology. University College Cork.

Bullock, I.D., Drewett, D.R. and Mickleburgh, S.P. 1983. The Chough in Ireland. *Irish Birds* 2, 257–271.

Burger, A.E. and Simpson, M. 1986. Diving depths of Atlantic puffins and common murres. *The Auk* 103, 828–830.

Byrkjedal, I. and Thompson, D.B.A. 1998. *Tundra Plovers*. London. Poyser.

Cabot, D. 1999. *Ireland: A Natural History*. London. HarperCollins.

Cabot, D. 1963. The breeding birds of the Inishkea Islands, Co Mayo. *Irish Naturalists' Journal* 14, 113–15.

Cabot, D. 1965. The status and distribution of the Chough *Pyrrhocorax pyrrhocorax* (L) in Ireland, 1960–65. *Irish Naturalists' Journal* 15, 95–100.

Cabot, D. 2009. *Wildfowl*. London. HarperCollins.

Cabot, D. and West, A.B. 1983. Studies on the population of Barnacle Geese *Branta leucopsis* wintering on the Inishkea Islands, Co. Mayo. 1. Population dynamics 1961–1983. *Irish Birds* 2, 318–336.

Caffrey, B., Durrant, J. and Watson, D. 2006. *Corncrake Fieldwork in the Shannon Callows 2006*. BirdWatch Ireland Conservation Report No. 06/12.

Calbrade, N.A., Holt, C.A., Austin, G.E., Mellan, H.J., Hearn, R.D., Stroud, D.A., Wotton, S.R. and Musgrove, A.J. 2010. *Waterbirds in the UK 2008/9. The Wetland Bird Survey*. Thetford. BTO/RSPB/JNCC in association with WWT.

Calmé, S., Desrochers, A. and Savard, J.-P.L. 2002. Regional significance of peatlands for avifaunal diversity in southern Québec. *Biological Conservation* 107, 273–281.

Cannon, A.R., Chamberlain, D.E., Toms, M.P., Hatchwell, B.J. and K.J. Gaston 2005. Trends in the use of private gardens in Great Britain 1995–2002. *Journal of Applied Ecology* 42, 659–671.

Carruthers, T.D. 1986. Waterways Bird Survey on the River Flesk, Co. Kerry. *Irish Birds* 3, 229–236.

Carruthers, T.D. and Gosler, A.G. 1994. Distribution of breeding birds in relation to habitat in the Muckross yew wood, Killarney. *Irish Birds* 5, 157–164.

Carruthers, T.D. and Gosler, A.G., 1995. The breeding bird community of the Muckross Yew wood, Killarney. *Irish Birds* 5, 308–318.

Carter, R.W.G. 1988. *Coastal Environments: An introduction to the physical, ecological and cultural systems of coastlines*. London. Academic Press.

Carter, R.W.G. and Orford, J.D. 1982. *Irish Association for Quaternary Studies. Field Guide No. 4. The south and east coasts of Co. Wexford*. Irish Quaternary Association.

Carty, E. 2010. *The birds at Kerry Airport 1990–2009*. Tralee. Kerry Airport.

Casey, S., Moore, N., Ryan, L., Merne, O.J., Coveney, J.A. and del Nevo, A. 1995. The Roseate Tern conservation project on Rockabill, Co. Dublin: a six year review 1989–1994. *Irish Birds* 5, 251–264.

Charmantier, A., McCleery, R.H., Cole, L.R., Perrins, C., Kruuk, L.E.B. and Sheldon, B.C. 2008. Adaptive phenotypic plasticity in response to climate change in a wild bird population. *Science* 322, 800–803.

Cherel, , Y., Phillips, R.A., Hobson, K.A. and McGill, R. 2006. Stable isotope evidence of diverse species-specific and individual wintering strategies in seabirds. *Biology Letters* 2, 301–303.

Cherel, Y., Weimerskirch, H. and Trouvé, C. 2002. Dietary evidence for spatial foraging segregation in sympatric albatrosses (*Diomedea spp.*) rearing chicks at Iles Nuageuses, Kerguelen. *Marine Biology* 141, 1117–1129.

Chivers, L.S. 2007. Courtship feeding and food provisioning of chicks by Common Terns *Sterna hirundo* at Belfast Harbour Lagoon. *Irish Birds* 8, 215–222.

Churcher, P.B. and Lawton, J.H. 1987. Predation by domestic cats in an English village. *Journal of Zoology* 212, 439–455.

Civil Aviation Authority. 1990. *Bird Control on aerodromes*. CAP 384. London. Civil Aviation Authority.

Claassens, A.J.M and O'Gorman, F. 1965. The bank vole *Clethryonomys glareolus* Schreber: a mammal new to Ireland. *Nature* 205, 923-924.

Clarke, R. and Scott, D. 1994. Breeding season diet of the Merlin in County Antrim. *Irish Birds* 5, 205–206.

Cleary, E.T., Dolbeer, R.A. and S.E. Wright 2006. *Wildlife Strikes to Civil Aviation in the United States 1990-2005*. Washington DC.FAA.

Clergeau, P., Jokimaki,J and J-P.L. Savard 2001. Are urban bird communities influenced by the bird diversity of adjacent landscapes? *Journal of Applied Ecology* 38, 1122–1134.

Clifford, M. 2011. *How many Woodpigeons?* Unpublished BSc thesis. Cork. University College, Cork.

COFORD, 2009. *Forestry 2030*. Johnstown Castle, Wexford. Forest Service.

Cole, E.E. and Mitchell, F.J.G. 2003. Human impact on the Irish landscape during the late Holocene inferred from palynological studies at three peatland sites. *The Holocene* 13, 507–515.

Colhoun, K., Austin, G. and Newton, S.F. 2008. Wader populations in non-estuarine coasts in the Republic of Ireland: results of the Non-Estuarine Coastal Waterfowl Survey (Ireland NEWS). Pp. 39–48. In: Burton, N.H.K., Rehfisch, M.M., Stroud, D.A. and Spray, C.J. (eds.) 2008. *The European Non-Estuarine Coastal Waterbird Survey*. International Wader Studies 18. Thetford. International Wader Study Group.

Colhoun, K. and Newton, S.F. 2000. Winter waterbird populations on non-estuarine coasts in the Republic of Ireland: results of the 1997/98 Non-Estuarine Coastal Waterfowl Survey (NEWS). *Irish Birds* 6, 527–542.

Collier, M.P., Banks, A.N., Austin, G.E., Girling, T., Hearn, R.D. and Musgrove, A.J. 2005. *The Wetland Bird Survey 2003/4: Wildfowl and Wader Counts*. Thetford. BTO/WWT/RSPB/JNCC.

Collingham, Y.C. and Huntley, B. 2000. Impacts of habitat fragmentation and patch size upon migration rates. *Ecological Applications* 10, 131–144.

Collins, K.P. 2000. Abundance and habitat associations of Yellowhammers *Emberiza citrinella* breeding in County Tipperary in 1997. *Irish Birds* 6, 431–432.

Collins, K.P. 2008. Little Ringed Plover *Charadrius dubius* breeding in County Tipperary in 2008. *Irish Birds* 8, 435–436.

Collins, R. 1991. Breeding performance of an Irish mute swan *Cygnus olor* population. Proceedings of 3rd International Swan Symposium. *Wildfowl* Supplement 1, 144–150.

Conder, P. 1989. *The Wheatear*. London. Helm.

Connolly, J. and Holden, N. 2008. Updating maps of peat soil extent in Ireland: a GIS rules-based mapping approach. Pp. 674–676. In: Feehan, J. (ed.) *13th International Peat Congress*. Tullamore. International Peat Society.

Connolly, J., Holden, N.M. and Ward, S.M. 2007. Mapping peatlands in Ireland using a rule-based methodology and digital data. *Soil Science Society of America Journal* 71, 492–499.

Connor, D.W., Brazier, D.P., Hill, T.O. and Northen, K.O. 1997. *Marine Nature Conservation Review: marine biotope classification for Britain and Ireland*. Volume 1. Littoral biotopes. Joint Nature Conservation Committee Report, No. 229.

Coombes, R.H. 2009. Woodpeckers move in. *Wings* Magazine 55, Winter 2009.

Coombes, R.H., Crowe, O., Lauder, A., Lysaght, L., O'Brien, C., O'Halloran, J., O'Sullivan, O., Tierney, T.D., Walsh, A.J. and Wilson, H.J. 2009. *Countryside Bird Survey Report 1998–2007 (Report No. 3)*. Wicklow. BirdWatch Ireland.

Cooney, T. 1998. Ringed Plovers *Charadrius hiaticula* nesting on cut-away peat in County Offaly. *Irish Birds* 6, 283–284.

Cooper, A. and McCann, T. 2002. *Habitat Change in the Northern Ireland Countryside*. Coleraine. University of Ulster.

Cooper, A. McCann, T. and Rogers, D. 2009. *Northern Ireland Countryside Survey 2007: Broad Habitat Change 1998–2007*. Northern Ireland Environment Agency Research and Development Series No. 09/06 (see also www.science.ulster.ac.uk/nics).

Copland, A.S. 2002. Delivering Corncrake *Crex crex* conservation in Ireland: past, present and future. *Irish Birds* 7, 33–42.

Copland, A.S. 2009. Bird Populations of Lowland Irish Farmland (with special reference to agri-environment measures). Unpublished Ph.D. thesis to University College, Cork.

Copland, A.S. and Buckley, K. 2010. Back from the brink: Grey Partridge rescued from oblivion. *Wings* 59, 17–19.

Copland, A.S. and O'Halloran, J. 2010a. Simple and rapid biodiversity assessments (SARBAS): An evaluation method of Ireland's Agri-Environment Scheme. *Aspects of Applied Biology* 100, 385–390.

Copland, A.S. and O'Halloran, J. 2010b. Agri-environment impacts and opportunities for summer bird communities on lowland Irish farmland. *Aspects of Applied Biology* 100, 77–87.

Copland, A.S., Crowe, O., O'Halloran, J. and Lauder, A.W. 2011. Conserving Ireland's farmland birds: performance and prospects of Ireland's agri-environment schemes. Pp. 56–57. In: Ó'hUallacháin, D. and Finn, J. (eds) *Conserving Farmland Biodiversity: Lessons learned & future prospects*. Carlow. Teagasc.

Copland, A.S., Crowe, O., Wilson, M. and O'Halloran, J. In review. Habitat associations of Sky Lark *Alauda arvensis* breeding on Irish farmland and implications for agri-environment planning.

Cormier, J.P., Fustec, J., Pithon, J. and Choisy, P. 2008. Selection of nesting habitat by Montagu's Harriers *Circus pygargus* and Hen Harriers *Circus cyaneus* in managed heaths. *Bird Study* 55, 86–93.

Cotton, P.A. 2003. Avian migration phenology and global climate change. *Proceedings of the National Academy of Science, USA* 100, 12219–12222.

Coulson, J.C. 2002. Colonial breeding in seabirds. Pp. 87–113. In: Schreiber, E.A. and Burger, J. (eds.) *Biology of marine birds*. London. CRC Press.

Cox, R.B., Eddleston, C.R. and Newton, S.F. 2002. *Upland Bird Survey Report 2002*. Newcastle. BirdWatch Ireland. Unpublished Report for National Parks & Wildlife Service.

Coxon, C.E. 1986. A study of the hydrology and geomorphology of turloughs. Ph.D. Thesis, Department of Geography, Trinity College, Dublin.

Craik, J.C.A. 1995. Effects of North American Mink on the breeding success of terns and smaller gulls in west Scotland. *Seabird* 17, 3–11.

Cramp, S. (ed.) 1988. *The Birds of the Western Palaearctic*. Volume V. Tyrant Flycatchers to Thrushes. Oxford. Oxford University Press.

Cramp, S. (ed.) 1985. *The Birds of the Western Palaearctic*. Volume IV. Terns to Woodpeckers. Oxford. Oxford University Press.

Cramp, S., Bourne, W.R.P. and Saunders, D. 1974. *The Seabirds of Britain and Ireland*, London. Collins.

Cramp, S. and Simmons, K.E.L. (eds.) 1977. *The Birds of the Western Palearctic*. Volume I. Ostrich to Ducks. Oxford. Oxford University Press.

Cramp, S. and Simmons, K.E.L. (eds.) 1980. *The Birds of the Western Palearctic*. Volume II. Hawks to Bustards. Oxford. Oxford University Press.

Cramp, S. and Simmons, K.E.L. (eds.) 1983. *The Birds of the Western Palearctic*. Volume III. Waders to Gulls. Oxford. Oxford University Press.

Cramp, S. and Perrins, C.M. (eds.) 1994. *The Birds of the Western Palaearctic*. Volume VIII. Crows to Finches. Oxford. Oxford University Press.

Creme, G.A., Walsh, P.M., O'Callaghan, M. and Kelly, T.C. 1997. The changing status of the lesser black-backed gull *Larus fuscus* in Ireland. *Biology and Environment: Proceedings of the Royal Irish Academy* 97B, 149–156.

Crick, H.Q.P. 1992. A bird-habitat coding system for use in Britain and Ireland incorporating aspects of land-management and human activity. *Bird Study* 39, 1–12.

Crick, H.Q.P. and Ratcliffe, D.A. 1995. The Peregrine *Falco peregrinus* population of the United Kingdom in 1991. *Bird Study* 42, 1–19.

Crick, H.Q.P. and Sparks, T.H. 1999. Climate change related to egg-laying trends. *Nature* 399, 423–424.

Cromie, J. 2002. Breeding status of Red-throated Diver *Gavia stellata* in Ireland. *Irish Birds* 7, 13–20.

Cronin, C., Barton, C., Hussey, H and Carmody M. 2006. *Cork Bird Report 1996–2004*. Cork.

Cronin, M. and Mackey, M. 2002. *Cetaceans and seabirds in waters over the Hatton-Rockall region*. Cruise report to the Geological Survey of Ireland May 2002. Cork. Coastal and Marine Resources Centre.

Cross, J.R. 1981. The establishment of *Rhododendron ponticum* in the Killarney oakwoods, S. W. Ireland. *Journal of Ecology* 69, 807–824.

Cross, J.R. 1998. An outline and map of the potential natural vegetation of Ireland. *Applied Vegetation Science* 1, 241–252.

Crowe, O. 2005a. *Ireland's Wetlands and their Waterbirds: Status and distribution*. Newcastle. BirdWatch Ireland.

Crowe, O. 2005b. The Garden Bird Survey: Monitoring birds of Irish gardens during winters between 1994/95 and 2003/04. *Irish Birds* 7, 475–482.

Crowe, O. 2008. *The Birds of the Phoenix Park, Co. Dublin: Results of a survey in Summer 2007 and Winter 2007/2008*. Dublin. Report by BirdWatch Ireland to the Office of Public Works.

Crowe, O. 2011a. The birds of the Phoenix Park, County Dublin: results of a survey in summer 2007 and winter 2007/08. *Irish Birds* 9.

Crowe, O. 2011b. Recent patterns and trends in terrestrial bird populations in Ireland: their value in supporting bird conservation. Unpublished Ph.D. thesis, University College Cork.

Crowe, O., Austin, G.E., Colhoun, K, Cranswick, P.A., Kershaw, M. and Musgrove, A.J. 2008a. Estimates and trends of waterbird numbers wintering in Ireland, 1994/95 to 2003/04. *Bird Study* 55, 66–77.

Crowe, O., Webb, G., Collins, E. and Smiddy, P. 2008b. *Assessment of the distribution and abundance of Kingfisher* Alcedo atthis *and other riparian birds on two SAC river systems in Ireland*. Dublin. Unpublished report to National Parks and Wildlife Service.

Crowe, O., Cummins, S., Gilligan, N., Smiddy, P. and Tierney, T.D. 2010. An assessment of the current distribution and status of the Kingfisher *Alcedo atthis* in Ireland. *Irish Birds* 9, 41–54.

Crowe, O., Copland, A., Wilson, M. and O'Halloran, J. (2011a). Status of key habitat indicators in Ireland using common and widespread birds.

Crushell, P. 2000. *Irish Fen Inventory – A Review of the Status of Fens in Ireland*. Dublin. Irish Peatland Conservation Council.

Crushell P. 2002. *SACs in Ireland – NGO Review. An Taisce – The National Trust, Birdwatch Ireland, CoastWatch Ireland, Irish Peatland Conservation Council and the Irish Wildlife Trust*. Dublin. Irish Peatland Conservation Council.

Culbert, R.W. and Furphy, J.S. 1978. The Ruddy Duck in Lough Neagh, Co. Armagh. *Irish Birds* 1, 234–236.

Cullen, C. and Smiddy, P. 2008. Spring and summer use of a reedbed by Barn Swallows (*Hirundo rustica*) and Sand Martins (*Riparia riparia*) in Co. Cork. *Irish Naturalists' Journal* 29, 126–128.

Cummins, S. 1996. *The gull (Laridae) community of a landfill*. Unpublished BSc thesis, Cork. University College Cork.

Cummins, S., Bleasdale, A., Douglas, C., Newton, S., O'Halloran, J. and Wilson, J.W. 2010. *The status of Red Grouse in Ireland and the effects of land use, habitat and habitat quality on their distribution*. Irish Wildlife Manuals No. 50, Dublin. National Parks and Wildlife Service, Department of the Environment, Heritage and Local Government.

Cummins, S., Corbishley, H. and Newton, S.F. 2003. *Upland Bird Survey Report 2003*. BirdWatch Ireland. Unpublished Report for National Parks & Wildlife Service.

Cummins, S.T. and O'Halloran, J. 2002. An assessment of the diet of nestling Stonechats *Saxicola torquata* using compositional analysis. *Bird Study* 49, 139–145.

Cummins, S.T. and O'Halloran, J. 2003. The breeding biology of the Stonechat *Saxicola torquata* in southwest Ireland. *Irish Birds* 7, 177–186.

Cummins, S., Swann, M. and Newton, S.F. 2004. *Upland Bird Survey Report 2004*. BirdWatch Ireland Unpublished Report for National Parks & Wildlife Service.

Curtis, T.G.F. 1991a. A site inventory of the sandy coasts of Ireland. Pp. 6–17. In: Quigley, M.B. (ed) *A Guide to the Sand Dunes of Ireland*. Galway. European Union for Dune Conservation and Coastal Management.

Curtis, T.G.F. 1991b. The flora and vegetation of sand dunes in Ireland. Pp. 42–66. In: Quigley, M.B. (ed) *A Guide to the Sand Dunes of Ireland*. Galway. European Union for Dune Conservation and Coastal Management.

Curtis, T.G.F. and Sheehy Skeffington, M.J. 1998. The salt marshes of Ireland: an inventory and account of their geographical variation. *Biology and Environment: Proceedings of the Royal Irish Academy* 98B, 87–104.

DAFRD (Department of Agriculture, Food and Rural Development). 2000. *Agri-Environmental Specifications For REPS 2000*. DAFRD, Johnstown Castle, Co. Wexford.

D'Arcy, G. 1999. *Ireland's Lost Birds*. Dublin. Four Courts Press.

Dare P.J. 1966. The breeding and wintering populations of the Oystercatcher (*Haematopus ostralegus* L.) in the British Isles. *Fishery Investigations, London*, Series 2, No. 9.

Daunt, F., Benvenuti, S., Harris, M., Dall'Antonia, L., Elston, D. and Wanless, S. 2002. Foraging strategies of the black-legged kittiwake *Rissa tridactyla* at a North Sea colony: evidence for a maximum foraging range. *Marine Ecology Progress Series* 245, 239–247.

Davenport, J., O'Halloran, J. and Smiddy, P. 2004. Plumage temperatures of Dippers Cinclus cinclus on the roost and in the hand: implications for handling small passerines. *Ringing and Migration*. 22, 65–69.

Davenport, J., O'Halloran, J., Hannah, F., McLaughlin, O. and Smiddy, P. 2009. Comparison of plumages of White-throated Dipper *Cinclus cinclus* and Blackbird *Turdus merula*. *Waterbirds* 32, 169–178.

Davies, N.B. 2000. *Cuckoos, Cowbirds and other cheats*. London. Poyser.

Dawson, P.A.C. 2005. Hen Harrier *Circus cyaneus* utilisation of a limestone fen in north County Cork. *Irish Birds* 7, 503–510.

De Buitléar, E. (ed.) 1985. *Irish Rivers*. Dublin. Country House.

DEFRA (Department for Environment, Food and Rural Affairs). 2008. *June Survey of Agriculture and Horticulture (Land Use and Livestock on Agricultural Holdings at 1 June 2008): UK – Provisional Results*. Department for Environment, Food and Rural Affairs, York, England.

Dekker, A., van Gasteren, H and Shamoun Barranes, J 2003. Eurbase. Progress report and first impressions of bird species. *Proceedings of the International Bird Strike Committee* 26, 225–238.

De Laet, J., Peach, W.J. and J. Summers-Smith 2011. Protocol for censusing urban sparrows. *British Birds* 104, 255–260.

Department of Agriculture and Food. 2007. *Compendium of Irish Agricultural Statistics 2007*. Dublin. Department of Agriculture and Food.

Department of Agriculture and Food. 2008. *Compendium of Irish Agricultural Statistics 2008*. Dublin. Department of Agriculture and Food.

DG AGRI. 2009. *Agriculture in the European Union: Statistical and Economic Information 2008*. Brussels. European Union Directorate-General for Agriculture and Rural Development.

Delany S. 2003. How many of the world's wader species are declining and where are the globally threatened species? (abstract) *Wader Study Group Bulletin* 101/102, 13.

Delany, S. and Gittings, T. 1996. *Survey of Common Scoters at known Irish breeding sites, May 1996*. Unpublished Report. Dublin. BirdWatch Ireland.

Delany, S., Scott, D., Dodman, T. and Stroud, D. 2009. *An Atlas of Wader populations in Africa and Western Eurasia*. Wageningen, The Netherlands. Wetlands International.

D'Elbée, J. and Hémery, G. 1998. Diet and foraging behaviour of the British Storm Petrel *Hydrobates pelagicus* in the Bay of Biscay during summer. *Ardea* 86, 1–10.

Dempsey, E. and O'Clery, M. 2007. *Finding Birds in Ireland: the complete guide*. Dublin. Gill & Macmillan.

Desrochers, A. and van Duinan, G-J. 2006. Peatland Fauna. Pp. 67–100. In: Wieder, R.K. and Vitt, D.H. (eds.) *Boreal Peatland Systems*. Berlin. Springer-Verlag.

Desrochers, A., Rochefort, L. and Savard, J.-P.L. 1998. Avian recolonisation of eastern Canadian bogs after peat mining. *Canadian Journal of Zoology* 76, 989–997.

Devlin, T.R.E. 1966. Atlantic Sea-watch: Auk movements in the spring of 1965. *Sea-Bird Bulletin* 2, 24–25.

Dobinson, H.M. and Richards, A.J. 1964. The effects of the severe winter of 1962/63. *British Birds* 57, 373–434.

Dodd, A., Hardiman, A, Jennings, K. and Williams, G. 2010. Protected areas and climate change; reflections from a practitioner's perspective. *Utrect Law Review* 6, 141–150.

Dolbeer, R.A and Eschenfelder, P 2003. Amplified bird strike risks related to population increases of large birds in North America. *Proceedings of the International Bird Strike Committee* 26, 49–67.

Dolbeer, R.A, Wright, S.E. and E.C. Cleary 2000. Ranking the Hazard level of Wildlife species to aviation. *Wildlife Society Bulletin* 28, 372–378.

Donaghy, A. 2007. Management of habitats on the Shannon Callows with special reference to their suitability for corncrake *Crex crex*. Unpublished Ph.D. thesis, University College Cork.

Donaghy, A. and Murphy, J. 2000. *Birds of Irish Farmland: Conservation management guidelines*. Royal Society for the Protection of Birds, Sandy, Beds.

Donald, P.F., Haycock, D. and Fuller, R.J. 1997. Winter bird communities in forest plantations in western England and their response to vegetation, growth stage and grazing. *Bird Study* 44, 206–219.

Donnelly, A., Salamin, N. and Jones, M.B. 2006. Changes in tree phenology: an indicator of spring warming in Ireland? *Biology and Environment; Proceedings of the Royal Irish Academy* 106, 47–55.

Donnelly, A., Cooney, T., Jennings, E., Buscardo, E. and Jones, M.B. 2009. Response of birds to climatic variability; evidence from the western fringe of Europe. *International Journal of Biometeorology* 53, 211–220.

Donnelly, A., Caffarra, A., Diskin, E., Kelleher, C.T., O'Neill, B.F., Pletsers, A., Proctor, H., Stirnemann, R., Jones, M.B., O'Halloran, J., Peñuelas, J., Hodkinson, T. R. and Sparks, T. Submitted. Phenotypic plasticity and evolutionary adaptation in response to climatic change. *Functional Ecology*.

Donnelly, A., Caffarra, A. and O'Neill, B.F. In press. A review of climate–driven mismatches between interdependent phenophases in terrestrial and aquatic ecosystems. *International Journal of Biometeorology* DOI, 10.1007/s00484-011-0426-5.

Douglas, C., Valverder, F.F. and Ryan, J. 2008. Peatland habitat conservation in Ireland. Pp. 681–685. In: Farrell, C.A. and Feehan, J. (eds.) 13th International Peat Congress: After-Wise Use: The future of Peatlands 1. International Peat Society, Tullamore, Co. Offaly, Ireland.

Dromey, M., Johnston, B. and Nairn, R. 1991. Ecological Survey of the Royal Canal. Volumes 1–3. Dublin. Office of Public Works.

Dunn, P.O. and Winkler, D.W. 2010. Effects of climate change on timing of breeding and reproductive success in birds. Pp. 113–128. In: Møller, A.P., Fiedler, W. and Berthold, P. (eds) Effects of climate change on birds. London. Oxford University Press.

Durant, J.M., Anker-Nilssen, T. and Stenseth, N.C. 2003. Trophic interactions under climate fluctuations: the Atlantic puffin as an example. Proceedings of the Royal Society of London B 270, 1461-1466.

Durant, J.M., Hjermann, D.Ø., Ottersen, G. and Stenseth, N.C. 2007. Climate and the match or mismatch between predator requirements and resource availability. Climate Research 33, 271–283.

EEA. 2006. Corine Land Cover 2000 – Mapping a decade of change. Wexford. European Environment Agency.

EEA/EPA. 2009. CORINE Land Cover – Ireland. Land Cover Update for 2006. Final Report. Wexford. European Environment Agency/Environmental Protection Agency.

Egevang, C., Stenhouse, I., Phillips, R., Petersen, A., Fox, J. and Silk, J. 2010. Tracking of Arctic terns Sterna paradisaea reveals longest animal migration. Proceedings of the National Academy of Sciences 107, 2078.

Elkins, N. 2004. Weather and Bird Behaviour. Calton. Poyser.

Elkins, N. and Yésou, P. 1998. Sabine's Gulls in western France and southern Britain. British Birds 91, 386–397.

Elton, C.S. 1933. The Ecology of Animals. London. Methuen.

Elton, C.S. 1966. The Pattern of Animal Communities. London. Chapman and Hall.

Elton, C.S. and Miller, R.S. 1954. The ecological survey of animal communities with a practical system of classifying habitats by structural characters. Journal of Ecology 42, 460–496.

Eltringham, S.K. 1971. Life in Mud and Sand. London. English University Press.

Enstipp, M.R., Daunt, F., Wanless, S. Humphreys, E.M., Hamer, K.C., Benvenuti, S. and Gremillet, D. 2006. Foraging energetics of North Sea birds confronted with fluctuating prey availability. In: Boyd, I.L., Wanless, S. and Camphuysen, C.J. (eds) Top predators in marine ecosystems: their role in monitoring and management. Cambridge. Cambridge University Press.

Enticott J.W., 1999. Britain and Ireland's first 'Soft-Plumaged Petrel' – An Historical and Personal Perspective. British Birds 92, 504–518.

EPA. 2004. Ireland's Environment 2004. Wexford. Environmental Protection Agency.

European Commission 2007 An Interpretation Manual of European Union Habitats. Brussels. European Commission.

Evans, D.M. 2000. The Ecology and Spatial Dynamics of Wintering Waterfowl on Lough Neagh. Unpublished Ph.D. thesis, University of Ulster, Coleraine.

Fahy, E., Goodwillie, R., Rochford, J. and Kelly, D. 1975. Eutrophication of a partially enclosed estuarine mudflat. Marine Pollution Bulletin 6, 29–31.

Farwig, N., Sajita, N. and Böhning-Gaese, K. 2008. Conservation value of forest plantations for bird communities in western Kenya. Forest Ecology and Management 255, 3885–3892.

Faulkner, J. and Thompson, R. 2011. The Natural History of Ulster. Holywood. National Museums Northern Ireland.

Feehan, J. and O'Donovan, G. 1996. The Bogs of Ireland – An Introduction to the Natural, Cultural and Industrial Heritage of Irish Peatlands. Dublin. Environmental Institute, University College Dublin.

Ferguson, A. 1967. The breeding of the common scoter on Lower Lough Erne, Co. Fermanagh. Irish Bird Report 15, 8–11.

Ferguson-Lees, J. and Christie, D.A. 2001. Raptors of the World. London. Christopher Helm.

Fennessy, G.J. 2001. Aspects of the ecology of the Robin, Eritracus rubecula L. Unpublished Ph.D. thesis, University College, Cork.

Fennessy, G.J. and Kelly, T.C. 2006. Breeding densities of Robin Erithacus rubecula in different habitats: the importance of hedgerow structure. Bird Study 53, 97–104.

Fennessy, G., Kelly, T.C., Bolger, R., Sheehy, S. and O'Callaghan, M.J.A. 2005a Ground versus air-seasonal changes in the use of birds of an Irish airport. Proceedings of International Bird Strike Committee 27, 1–6.

Fennessy, G., Sheehy, S., Kelly, T.C., O' Callaghan, M.J.A. and Bolger, R. 2005b Over-flying of birds at an airport: developing a methodology. Proceedings of International Bird Strike Committee 27, 353–360.

Finney, K., Copeland, A., Baylis, J. and Power, E. 2006. The NPWS Shannon Callows Breeding Wader Project 2006. Report to NPWS. BirdWatch Ireland.

Finney, K. and Warnock, N. 2009. Shannon Callows Breeding Wader Management Project. Final Report to NPWS, Nov 2009. BirdWatch Ireland.

Finney, K. and Warnock, N. 2010. Shannon Callows Breeding Wader Management Project. Final Report October 2010 to NPWS. BirdWatch Ireland.

Fisher, J. 1952. The Fulmar. London. Collins New Naturalist.

Fitzpatrick, S. 1997. Temporal patterns of feeder use by garden birds in Belfast. Irish Birds 6, 35–44.

Fitzpatrick, S. and Bouchez, B. 1998. Effects of recreational disturbance on the foraging behaviour of waders on a rocky beach. Bird Study 45, 157–171.

Flynn, M. 2002. An investigation of the Relationship between Avian Biodiversity and Hedgerow Management as predicted under the Rural Environment Protection Scheme (REPS). Unpublished Ph.D. thesis, RCSI/NUI, Dublin.

Foley, M., Kelly, T.C. and Sleeman, D.P. 2006. The diet of the Barn Owl Tyto alba in Dublin. Irish Birds 8, 145–147.

Ford, R.G., Ainley, D.G., Brown, E.D., Suryan, R.M. and Irons, D.B. 2007. A spatially explicit optimal foraging model of Black-legged Kittiwake behaviour based on prey density, travel distances, and colony size. Ecological Modelling 204, 335–348.

Forero, M.G., Bortolotti, G.R., Hobson, K.A., Donazar, J.A., Bertelloti, M. and Blanco, G. 2004. High trophic overlap within the seabird community of Argentinean Patagonia: a multiscale approach. Journal of Animal Ecology 73, 789–801.

Forest Service. 2000a. Code of Best Forest Practice. Johnstown Castle, Wexford. Forest Service.

Forest Service. 2000b. Forest Biodiversity Guidelines. Johnstown Castle, Wexford. Forest Service.

Forest Service. 2004. Forestry Schemes Manual. Johnstown Castle, Wexford. Forest Service.

Foss, P. 2007. Study of the extent and conservation status of springs, fens and flushes in Ireland 2007. Dublin. Department of the Environment, Heritage and Local Government.

Foss, P.J., O'Connell, C.A. and Crushell, P.H. 2001. Bogs and Fens of Ireland Conservation Plan 2005. Dublin. Irish Peatland Conservation Council.

Fossitt, J.A. 2000. A Guide to Habitats in Ireland. Kilkenny. Heritage Council.

Foster, S., Boland, H., Colhoun, K., Etheridge, B. and Summers, R. 2010. Flock composition of Purple Sandpipers Calidris maritima in the west of Ireland. Irish Birds 9, 31–34.

Fox, A.D. 2003. The Greenland White-fronted Goose Anser albifrons flavirostris. The annual cycle of a migratory herbivore on the European continental fringe. Doctorate dissertation (D.Sc.). Denmark. National Environmental Research Institute.

Fox, A.D., Bell, M.C., Brown, R.A., Mackie, P. and Madsen, J. 1994a. An analysis of the abundance and distribution of Brent Geese and Wigeon at Strangford Lough, 1965/6–1988/9. *Irish Birds* 5, 139–150.

Fox, A.D., Norriss, D.W., Stroud, D.A. and Wilson, H.J. 1994b. *Greenland White-fronted Geese in Ireland and Britain 1982/83 – 1993/94: the first twelve years of international conservation monitoring. Greenland White-fronted Goose Study Research Report No. 8.* Dublin. Greenland White-fronted Goose Study and the NPWS/OPW.

Fox, A.D., Stroud, D., Walsh, A., Wilson, J., Norriss, D. and Francis, I. 2006. The rise and fall of the Greenland White-fronted Goose: a case study in international conservation. *British Birds* 99, 242–261.

Fox, A.D. and Walsh, A. (In press). Warming winter effects, fat store accumulation and timing of spring departure of Greenland White-fronted Geese *Anser albifrons flavirostris* from their winter quarters. *Hydrobologia.*

Freeman, K. 1997. Woodland bird communities in Killarney National Park, with special reference to the influence of *Rhododendron ponticum* and its clearance. *Irish Birds* 6, 128.

Freshwater Ecology Group, Trinity College Dublin and Compass Informatics. 2007. *Conservation Assessments of Freshwater Lake Habitats in the Republic of Ireland.* Draft Report for National Parks and Wildlife Service.

Fuller, R.J. 1982. *Bird Habitats in Britain.* Calton. Poyser.

Fuller, R.J. 1995. *Bird life of woodland and forest.* Cambridge. Cambridge University Press.

Fuller, R.J. 2012. *Birds and Habitat: Relationships in a changing climate.* Cambridge. Cambridge University Press.

Fuller, R.J. and Browne, S. 2003. Effects of plantation structure and management on birds. Pp. 93–99. In: Humphrey, J., Ferris R. and Quine, C. (Eds), *Biodiversity in Britain's Planted Forests.* Results from the Forestry Commission's Biodiversity Assessment Project. Edinburgh. Forestry Commission.

Fuller, R.J., Gaston, K.J. and Quine, C.P. 2007. Living on the edge: British and Irish woodland birds in a European context. *Ibis* 149, 53–63.

Fuller, R.J. and Glue, D.E. 1978. Seasonal activity of birds at a sewage-works. *British Birds* 71, 235–244.

Fuller, R.J. and Glue, D.E. 1980. Sewage works as bird habitats in Britain. *Biological Conservation* 17, 165–181.

Fuller, R.J. and Gough, S.J. 1999. Changes in sheep numbers in Britain: implications for bird populations. *Biological Conservation* 91, 73–89.

Fuller, R.J. and Jackson, D.B. 1999. Changes in populations of breeding waders on the machair of North Uist, Scotland, 1983–1998. *Wader Study Group Bulletin* 90, 47–55.

Fuller, R.J., Reed, T.M., Buxton, N.E., Webb, A., Williams, T.D. and Pienkowski, M.W. 1986. Populations of breeding waders Charadrii and their habitats on the crafting islands of the Outer Hebrides, Scotland. *Biological Conservation* 37, 33–361.

Fuller R.J. and Youngman R.E. 1979. The utilisation of farmland by Golden Plovers wintering in Southern England. *Bird Study* 26, 37–46.

Furness, R.W. 2003. Impacts of fisheries on seabird communities. *Scientia Marina* 67, 33–45.

Furness, R.W. and Birkhead, T.R. 1984. Seabird colony distributions suggest competition for food supplies during the breeding season. *Nature* 311, 655–656.

Furphy, J.S. 1977. Census of Great Crested Grebes, Northern Ireland, Summer 1975. *Irish Birds* 1, 56–58.

Galbraith, H. and Tyler, S.J. 1982. Movements and mortality of the Dipper as shown by ringing recoveries. *Ringing and Migration* 4, 9–14.

Galbraith, H., Murray, S., Duncan, K., Smith, R., Whitfield, D.P. and Thompson, D.B.A. 1993. Diet and habitat use of the Dotterel *Charadrius morinellus* in Scotland. *Ibis* 135, 148–155.

Gallagher, C. 2009. *Corncrake Fieldwork in the Shannon Callows 2009.* Unpublished BirdWatch Ireland Report to the National Parks and Wildlife Service, Dublin.

Galen, C. 1990. Limits to the distributions of alpine tundra plants: herbivores and the Alpine Skypilot, *Polemonium viscocsum. Oikos* 59, 355–358.

Gamero, A., McNaghten, L. and Suddaby, D. 2008. *Research of breeding Dunlin ecology associated with machair and upland NATURA 2000 sites in N.W. Mayo.* BirdWatch Ireland. Unpublished report to National Parks and Wildlife Service, Dublin.

Game and Wildlife Conservation Trust Review. 2008. Review of 2007. Issue 39, 1–96.

Garthe, S., Benvenuti, S. and Montevecchi, W.A. 2000. Pursuit plunging by northern gannets (*Sula bassana*) 'feeding on capelin (*Mallotus villosus*)'. *Proceedings of the Royal Society of London Series B: Biological Sciences* 267, 1717–1722.

Garthe S., Montevecchi, W.A. and Davoren, G.K. 2007. Flight destinations and foraging behaviour of northern gannets (*Sula bassana*) preying on a small forage fish in a low-Arctic ecosystem. Deep Sea Research Part II: *Topical Studies in Oceanography* 54, 311–320.

Gaynor, K. 2006. The vegetation of Irish machair. *Biology and Environment: Proceedings of the Royal Irish Academy* 106B, 311–321.

Gibbons, D.W., Reid, J.B. and Chapman, R.A. 1993. *The New Atlas of Breeding Birds in Britain and Ireland: 1988 – 1991.* London. Poyser.

Gibbs, A., Nisbet, I.C.T. and Redman, P.S. 1954. Birds of north Donegal in Autumn, 1953. *British Birds* 157, 217–228.

Gibson, C.E. and Jordan, C. 2002. A new synoptic survey of Northern Ireland lakes: sampling from the air. *Freshwater Forum* 19, 11–20.

Gienapp, P., Teplitsky, C., Alho, J.S., Mills, A.J. and Merilä, J. 2008. Climate change and evolution: disentangling environmental and genetic responses. *Molecular Ecology* 17, 167–178.

Gilbert, J. and Ausden, M. 2009. *RSPB Reserves 2009.* Sandy. RSPB.

Gilg, O., Hanski, I. and Sittler, B. 2003. Cyclic dynamics in a simple vertebrate predator-prey community. *Science* 302, 866–868.

Gill, R.M.A., Fuller, R.J. 2007. The effects of deer browsing on woodland structure and songbirds in lowland Britain. *Ibis* 149, 119–127.

Gillings, S., Wilson, A.M., Conway, G.J., Vickery, J.A. and Fuller, R.J. 2008. Distribution and abundance of birds and their habitats within the lowland farmland of Britain in winter. *Bird Study* 55, 8–22.

Good, J.A. and Butler, F.T. 1998. Coastal lagoon shores as a habitat for Staphylinidae and Carabidae (Coleoptera) in Ireland. *Bulletin of the Irish Biogeographical Society* 21, 22–65.

Gordo, O. and Sanz, J.J. 2005. Phenology and climate change: a long-term study in a Mediterrranean locality. *Oecologia* 146, 484–495.

Gordo, O. and Sanz J.J. 2006. Temporal trends in phenology of the honey bee *Apis mellifera* (L.) and the small white *Pieris rapae* (L.) in the Iberian Peninsula (1952–2004). *Ecology and Entomology* 31, 261–268.

Gordo, O. 2007. Why are bird migration dates shifting? A review of weather and climate effects on avian migratory phenology. *Climate Research* 35, 37–58.

Gordon, T. 2009. *Corncrake Fieldwork in Mayo and West Connaught 2009.* Unpublished BirdWatch Ireland Report to the National Parks and Wildlife Service, Dublin.

Gosler, A.G. and Carruthers, T.D. 1994. Bill size and niche breadth in the Irish Coal Tit *Parus ater hibernicus. Journal of Avian Biology* 25, 171–177.

Grant, J.D. 1982. *A study of the winter feeding ecology of common wading birds of the North Bull Island, Dublin Bay.* B.Sc. thesis, University College, Dublin.

Grant, M.C., Orsman, C., Easton, J., Lodge, C., Smith, M., Thompson, G., Rodwell, S. and Moore, N. 1999. Breeding success and causes of breeding failure of Curlew *Numenius arquata* in Northern Ireland. *Journal of Applied Ecology* 36, 59–74.

Gray, N., Thomas, G., Trewby, M. and Newton, S.F, 2003. The status and distribution of Choughs *Pyrrhocorax pyrrhocorax* in the Republic of Ireland 2002/2003. *Irish Birds* 7, 147–156.

Green, R.E. 1986. *The management of lowland wet grassland for breeding waders*. Unpublished report. Sandy. RSPB.

Green, R.E. 1988. Effects of environmental factors on the timing and success of breeding of Common Snipe *Gallinago gallinago* (Aves: Scolopacidae) in Northern Ireland. *Journal of Applied Ecology* 25, 79–93.

Green, R.E., Collingham, Y.C., Willis, S.G., Gregory, R.D., Smith, K.W. and Huntley, B. 2008. Performance of climate envelope models in retrodicting recent changes in bird population size from observed climate change. *Biology Letters* doi:10.1098/rsbl.2008.0052.

Green, R.E., Hirons, G.J.M. and Cresswell, B.H. 1990. Foraging habitats of female Common Snipe *Gallinago gallinago* during the incubation period. *Journal of Applied Ecology* 27, 325–335.

Green, R.E. and Pearce-Higgins, J. 2010. Species management in the face of a changing climate. Pp. 517–536. *Species Management: Challenges and Solutions for the 21st Century*. Edinburgh. HMSO.

Green, M., Knight, A., Cartmel, S. and Thomas, D. 1988. The status of wintering waders on the non-estuarine west coast of Ireland. *Irish Birds* 3, 569–574.

Green, T. 1965. Cape Clear Bird Observatory. *Sea-Bird Bulletin* 1, 27–28.

Greenwood, J.G. 1998. Breeding biology of Black Guillemots *Cepphus grylle* at Bangor, Co. Down. *Irish Birds* 6, 191–200.

Greenwood, J.G. 2007. Earlier laying by Black Guillemots *Cepphus grylle* in Northern Ireland in response to increasing sea-surface temperature. *Bird Study* 54, 378–379.

Greenwood, J. 2010. Black Guillemots at Bangor, Co. Down: a 25-year study. *British Wildlife* 21, 153–158.

Gregory, R.D. and Baillie, S.R. 1998. Large-scale habitat use of some declining British birds *Journal of Applied Ecology* 35, 785–799.

Gregory, R.D., van Strien, A., Vorisek, P., Gmelig Meyling, A.W., Noble, D.G., Foppen, R.P.B. and Gibbons, D.W. 2005. Developing indicators for European birds. *Philosophical Transactions of the Royal Society* 360B, 269–288.

Gregory, R.D., Willis, S.G., Jiguet, F., Voříšek, P., Klvaňová, A., van Strien, A., Huntley, B., Collingham, Y.C., Couvet, D. and Green, R.E. 2009. An Indicator of the Impact of Climatic Change on European Bird Populations. *PLoS ONE* 4e4678. doi:10.1371/journal.pone.0004678.

Greig-Smith, P.W. 1984. Seasonal changes in the use of nesting cover by Stonechats *Saxicola torquauta. Ornis Scandinavica* 15, 11–15.

Grémillet, D., Kuntz, G., Delbart, F., Mellet, M., Kato, A., Robin, J.P., Chaillon, P.E., Gendner, J.P., Lorentsen, S.H. and Le Maho, Y. 2004. Linking the foraging performance of a marine predator to local prey abundance. *Functional Ecology* 18, 793–801.

Grémillet, D., Wilson, R.P., Storch, S. and Gary, Y. 1999. Three-dimensional space utilization by a marine predator. *Marine Ecology Progress Series* 183, 263–273.

Gretton, A. & Mellon, C. 1986. *Fermanagh Breeding Wader Survey – Team 2 Report.* (Unpublished). Sandy. Research Department, RSPB.

Guilford, T., Meade, J., Freeman, R., Biro, D., Evans, T., Bonadonna, F., Boyle, D., Roberts, S. and Perrins, C. 2008. GPS tracking of the foraging movements of Manx Shearwaters *Puffinus puffinus* breeding on Skomer Island, Wales. *Ibis* 150, 462–473.

Guilford, T., Meade, J., Willis, J., Phillips, R.A., Boyle, D., Roberts, S., Collett, M., Freeman, R. and Perrins, C.M. 2009. Migration and stopover in a small pelagic seabird, the Manx shearwater *Puffinus puffinus*: insights from machine learning. *Proceedings of the Royal Society B: Biological Sciences* 276, 1215–1223.

Hagemeijer, E.J.M. and Blair, M.J. 1997. *The EBCC Atlas of European Breeding Birds: Their Distribution and Abundance*. London. Poyser.

Hakala, A. 1971. A quantitative study of the bird fauna of some open peatlands in Finland. *Ornis Fennica* 63, 97–111.

Hall, V. 2011. *The Making of Ireland's Landscape since the Ice Age*. Cork. The Collins Press.

Hamer, K.C., Phillips, R.A., Hill, J.K. and Wanless, S. 2001. Contrasting foraging strategies of gannets *Morus bassanus* at two North Atlantic colonies: foraging trip duration and foraging area fidelity. *Marine Ecology Progress Series* 224, 283–290.

Hamer, K.C., Thompson, D.R. and Gray, C.M. 1997. Spatial variation in the feeding ecology, foraging ranges, and breeding energetics of northern fulmars in the north-east Atlantic Ocean. *ICES Journal of Marine Science* 54, 645–653.

Hammond, M.E.R. and Cooper, A. 2002. *Spartina anglica* eradication and intertidal recovery in Northern Ireland estuaries. Pp. 124–131. In: Veitch, D. & Clout. M. (eds.) *Turning the Tide: the Eradication of Invasive Species*. IUCN (International Union for Conservation of Nature).

Hammond, R.F. 1981. *The peatlands of Ireland*. Soil Survey Bulletin No. 35. Dublin. An Foras Talúntais.

Hannon, C., Berrow, S.D. and Newton, S.F. 1997. The status and distribution of breeding Sandwich *Sterna sandvicensis*, Roseate *S. dougallii*, Common *S. hirundo*, Arctic *S. paradisaea* and Little Terns *S. albifrons* in Ireland in 1995. *Irish Birds* 6, 1–22.

Harris, M., Daunt, F., Newell, M., Phillips, R. and Wanless, S. 2010. Wintering areas of adult Atlantic puffins *Fratercula arctica* from a North Sea colony as revealed by geolocation technology. *Marine Biology* 157, 827–836.

Harris, S. and Yalden, D.W. 2008. *Mammals of the British Isles*. London. The Mammal Society.

Harrison C.J.O. & Castell P. 1998. *Collins Field Guide; Bird Nests, Eggs & Nestlings of Britain and Europe*. London. HarperCollins.

Hatch, P. and Healy, B. 1998. Aquatic vegetation of Irish coastal lagoons. *Bulletin of the Irish Biogeographical Society* 21, 2–21.

Haworth, P.F. 1985. *A survey of upland breeding birds in West Galway, Eire*. Report to the World Wildlife Fund. Project 147/84.

Haworth, P.F. 1987. *Survey of West Galway*. Report to the World Wildlife Fund. Project 26/86.

Haworth, P.F. and Thompson, D.B.A. 1990. Factors associated with the breeding distribution of upland birds in the south Pennines, England. *Journal of Applied Ecology* 27, 562–577.

Hayhow, B. 2008. Shorebird use of an intertidal and terrestrial habitat matrix during winter: analysis of relative profitability of foraging habitats. *Irish Birds* 8, 458.

Hayhow, B. 2009. The importance of inland callows for wintering and migrating black-tailed godwits *Limosa limosa*. In: Heery, S. 1996. *Birds in Central Ireland – fourth mid Shannon Bird Report*. BirdWatch Ireland.

Hayward, P.J. 1967. Atlantic Sea-watch: Kittiwake movements in 1965. *Sea-Bird Bulletin* 3, 58–63.

Hayward, P., Nelson-Smith, T. and Shields, C. 1996. *Seashore of Britain and Northern Europe*. London, Collins Pocket Guide.

Healy, B. 2003. Coastal lagoons. Pp. 51–78. In: Otte, M.L. (ed.) *Wetlands of Ireland: Distribution, ecology, uses and economic value*. Dublin. University College Dublin Press.

Healy, B. and Oliver, G.A. 1998. Irish coastal lagoons: summary of a survey. *Bulletin of the Irish Biogeographical Society* 21, 116–150.

Healy, E., Moriarty, C. and O'Flaherty, G. (eds.) 1988. *The Book of the Liffey from Source to Sea*. Dublin. Wolfhound Press.

Heery, S. 1993. *The Shannon Floodlands. A Natural History*. Kinvara. Tir Eolas.

Heery, S. 1998. *Lough Boora Parklands – Habitat survey and conservation*. Boora. Report prepared for Bord na Móna.

Heery, S. (ed) 1996, 2000, 2005, & 2009. *Birds in Central Ireland – first, second, third and fourth mid Shannon Bird Reports*. BirdWatch Ireland.

Heery S. 2003. Callows and floodplains. Pp. 109–123. In: Otte, M.L. (ed.) *Wetlands of Ireland: distribution, ecology, uses and economic value*. Dublin. University College Dublin Press.

Heery, S. and Madden, B. 1997. A summer concentration of Little Grebes *Tachybaptus ruficollis* in south County Galway. *Irish Birds* 6, 53–54.

Heffernan, M.L. and Hunt, J. 2004. A pre-breeding census of the Common Scoter *Melanitta nigra* on Loughs Conn and Cullin, County Mayo in 2004. *Irish Birds* 7, 435–437.

Heldbjerg, H. and Fox, T. 2008. Long-term population declines in Danish trans-Saharan migrant birds. *Bird Study* 55, 267–279.

Henderson, I.G. 2011. Ruddy Duck eradication in the UK. P. 154. *Programme and abstracts. 8th Conference of the European Ornithologists' Union*. 27–30 August 2011, Riga.

Henderson, I.G., Cooper, J., Fuller, R.J. and Vickery, J. 2000. The relative abundance of birds on set-aside and neighbouring fields in summer. *Journal of Applied Ecology* 37: 335-347.

Henderson, I.G., Wilson, A.W., Steele, D. and Vickery, J.A. 2002. Population estimates, trends and habitat associations of breeding Lapwing *Vanellus vanellus*, Curlew *Numenius arquata* and Snipe *Gallinago gallinago* in Northern Ireland in 1999. *Bird Study* 49, 17–25.

Herbert, I.J. 1991. The status and habitat of the Garden Warbler at Crom Estate, Co. Fermanagh, and a review of its status in Ireland. *Irish Birds* 4, 369–376.

Herbert, I.J. 1997. The role of landscape structure in limiting breeding success in a declining lapwing *Vanellus vanellus* population. Pp. 159–166. In: *Species Dispersal and Land Use Processes*. (ed.) Cooper, A. and Power, J. Coleraine. University of Ulster.

Herbert, I.J., Heery, S. & Meredith, C.R.M. 1990. Distribution of breeding waders in relation to habitat features on the River Shannon callows at Shannon-harbour, Ireland, 1987–89. *Irish Birds* 4, 203–216.

Hewson, C.M., Amar, A., Lindsell, J.A., Thewlis, R.M., Butler, S., Smith, K. and Fuller, R.J. 2007. Recent changes in bird populations in British broadleaved woodland. *Ibis* 149, 14–28.

Hewson, C.M. and Noble, D.G. 2009. Population trends of breeding birds in British woodlands over a 32-year period: relationships with food, habitat use and migratory behaviour. *Ibis* 151, 464–486.

Hickling, R., Roy, D.B., Hill, J.K., Fox, R. and Thomas, C.D. 2006. The distributions of a wide range of taxonomic groups are expanding polewards. *Global Change Biology* 12, 450–455.

Hilgerloh, G., O'Halloran, J., Kelly, T.C. and Burnell, G.M. 2001. A preliminary study on the effects of oyster culture structures on birds in a sheltered Irish estuary *Hydrobiologia* 465, 175–180.

Hillis, J.P. 1971. Sea-birds scavenging at trawlers in Irish waters. *Irish Naturalist's Journal* 17, 129–132.

Hillis, J.P. 2003. Rare Irish breeding Birds, 1992–2001. *Irish Birds* 7, 157–172.

Hillis, J.P. 2004. First Annual Report of the Irish Rare Breeding Birds Panel, 2002. *Irish Birds* 7, 375–384.

Hillis, J.P. 2007. Rare breeding birds in Ireland 2005 and 2006. *Irish Birds* 8, 249–262.

Hillis, J.P. 2008. Rare Irish Breeding Birds, 2007. The Annual Report of the Irish Rare Breeding Birds Panel (IRBBP). *Irish Birds* 8, 365–372

Hillis, J.P. 2010. Rare Irish Breeding Birds, 2009. The Annual Report of the Irish Rare Breeding Birds Panel (IRBBP). *Irish Birds* 9, 67–76.

Hillis, J.P. and Cotton, D.C.F. 1989. Black-necked grebes breeding in Ireland. *Irish Birds* 4, 72.

Hiscock, K., Southward, A., Tittley, I.A.N. and Hawkins, S. 2004. Effects of changing temperature on benthic marine life in Britain and Ireland. *Aquatic Conservation* 14, 333–362.

Hobson, K.A., Fisk, A., Karnovsky, N., Holst, M., Gagnon, J-M. and Fortier, M. 2002. A stable isotope (δ13C, δ15N) model for the North Water food web: implications for evaluating trophodynamics and the flow of energy and contaminants. Deep Sea Research Part II. *Topical Studies in Oceanography* 49, 5131–5150.

Hole, D.G., Willis, S.G., Pain, D.J., Fishpool, L.D., Butchart, S.H.M., Collingham, Y.C., Rahbek, C. and Huntley, B. 2009. Projected impacts of climate change on a continent-wide protected areas network. *Ecology Letters* 12, 420–431.

Holloway, S. 1996. *The Historical Atlas of Breeding Birds in Britain and Ireland 1875–1900*. London. Poyser.

Hooijer, A. 1996. Floodplain hydrology. An ecologically oriented study of the Shannon Callows, Ireland. Ph.D. Thesis Vrije Universiteit Amsterdam.

Hounsome, M.V. 1968. The Atlantic Sea-Watch 1965 – The Gannet. *Sea-Bird Bulletin* 4, 7–26.

Hourlay, F., Libois, R., D'Amico, F., Sarà, M., O'Halloran, J. and Michaux, J.R. 2008. Evidence of a highly complex phylogeographic structure on a specialist river bird species, the Dipper (*Cinclus cinclus*). *Molecular Phylogenetics and Evolution* 49, 435–444.

Houston, J.A., Edmondson, S.E. and Rooney, P.J. 2001. *Coastal Dune Management: Shared experience of European Conservation Practice*. Liverpool. Liverpool University Press.

Hudson, A.V. 1982. Great Black-backed Gulls on Great Saltee Island, 1980. *Irish Birds* 2, 167–175.

Hudson, J., Tierney, T.D. and Casey, C. 2002. Breeding waders on cutaway bog in County Offaly, 2002. *Irish Birds* 7, 61–64.

Hudson, P.J. and Newborn, D. 1995. *A Manual of Red Grouse and Moorland Management*. Fordingbridge. Game Conservancy Trust.

Hughes, B., Robinson, J.A., Green, A.J., Li, Z.W.D. and Mundkur, T. (eds.) 2006. *International Single Species Action Plan for the Conservation of the White-headed Duck* Oxyura leucocephala. Bonn, Germany. CMS Technical Series No. 13 & AEWA Technical Series No.8.

Hulsman, J. Reddy, N. and Newton, S.F. 2007. *Rockabill Tern Report 2007*. Newtown. BirdWatch Ireland.

Humphreys, G.R. 1978. Ireland's former premier breeding haunt of aquatic birds. *Irish Birds* 1, 171–187.

Hunt, J. and Heffernan, M. L. 2006. Check date. *A survey of the Lough Mask breeding gull population*. Unpublished report to The Heritage Council and NPWS.

Hunt, J. and Heffernan, M. L. 2007a. *A survey of breeding gulls and terns on Lough Corrib, Cos. Galway and Mayo*. Unpublished report to The Heritage Council.

Hunt, J. and Heffernan, M.L. 2007b. *Mink trapping at Lough Mask 2007 to protect breeding gulls*. Unpublished report to The Heritage Council.

Hunt, G. and Kiely, A. 2002. Yellowhammer Emberiza citronella *Survey of West Limerick 2000*. Unpublished Report to the Heritage Council, Kilkenny.

Huntley, B., Green, R.E., Collingham, Y.C. and Willis, S.G. 2007. *A climatic atlas of European breeding birds*. Barcelona. Durham University, The RSPB and Lynx Ediciones.

Hüppop, O., Dierschke, J., Exo, K.M., Fredrich, E. and Hill, R. 2006. Bird migration studies and potential collision risk with offshore wind turbines. *Ibis* 148, 90–109.

Hüppop, O. and Hüppop, K. 2003. North Atlantic Oscillation and timing of spring migration in birds. *Proceedings of the Royal Society of London. B: Biological Sciences* 270, 233–240.

Hurley, J. 1997. *Water levels at Lady's Island Lake, 1984–1996*. Kilmore Quay. SWC Promotions.

Hurley, J. 1998. *Water levels at Lady's Island Lake, 1997*. Kilmore Quay. SWC Promotions.

Hurrell, J.W. and Trenberth, K.E. 2010. Climate change. Pp. 9–38. In: Møller, A.P., Fiedler, W. and Berthold, P. (eds) *Effects of climate change on birds*. Oxford. Oxford University Press.

Hutchinson, C.D. 1970. Magpies in Dublin City. *Dublin and North Wicklow Bird Report* 2, 22–23.

Hutchinson, C.D. 1979. *Ireland's Wetlands and their Birds*. Dublin. Irish Wildbird Conservancy.

Hutchinson, C.D. 1994. *Where to Watch Birds in Ireland*. Dublin. Gill and Macmillan.

Hutchinson, C.D. 1989. *Birds in Ireland*. Calton. Poyser.

Hutchinson, C.D. and O'Halloran, J. 1994. The ecology of Black-tailed Godwits at an Irish south coast estuary. *Irish Birds* 5, 165–172.

Hutchinson, C.D., O'Halloran, J. and O'Sullivan, W. 1998. Birds and mammals. Pp. 213–247. In: Giller, P.S. (ed.). *Studies in Irish Limnology*. Dublin. Marine Institute.

Huvendiek, B. 1996. Studies of dispersion patterns and habitat relationship of breeding bird species on raised bogs of the Atlantic type in Central Ireland – Impact of natural woodland. Ph.D. Thesis, Braunschweig, Germany. Zoological Institute Technical University of Braunschweig.

IRBC. 1998. *Checklist of the Birds of Ireland*. BirdWatch Ireland, Dublin.

Inger, R., Bearhop, S., Robinson, J.A. and Ruxton, G. 2006a. Prey choice affects the trade-off between predation and starvation in an avian herbivore. *Animal Behaviour* 71, 1335–1341.

Inger, R., Ruxton, G.D., Newton, J., Colhoun, K., Mackie, K., Robinson, J.A., Bearhop, S. 2006b. Using daily ration models and stable isotope analysis to predict biomass depletion by herbivores. *Journal of Applied Ecology* 43, 1022–1030.

Inger, R., Ruxton, G.D., Newton, J., Colhoun, K., Robinson, J.A., Jackson, A.L., Bearhop, S. 2006c. Temporal and intrapopulation variation in prey choice of wintering geese determined by stable isotope analysis. *Journal of Animal Ecology* 75, 1190–1200.

Iremonger, S., O'Halloran, J., Kelly, D., Wilson, M., Smith, G., Gittings, T., Giller, P.S., Mitchell, F., Oxbrough, A., Coote, L., French, L., O' Donoghue, S., McKee, A., Pithon, J., O'Sullivan, A., Neville, P., O'Donnell, V., Cummins, V., Kelly, T. and Dowding, P., 2006. *Biodiversity in Irish plantation forests*. BioForest Project Final Synthesis Report made to the EPA and COFORD.

Irish Rare Birds Committee. 1998. *Checklist of the Birds of Ireland*. Dublin. Irish Wildbird Conservancy.

Irish Raptor Study Group. 2006. *Birds of Prey and Owls in Ireland*. Irish Raptor Study Group.

Irwin, S. 2009. A novel approach to forest biodiversity assessment. *Science Spin*, 37, 15.

Irwin, S. and O'Halloran, J. (1997). The wintering behaviour of Coot *Fulica atra* at Cork Lough, south-west Ireland. *Biology and Environment: Proceedings of the Royal Irish Academy*. 97B, 157–162.

Irwin, S., Wilson, M., Kelly, T.C., O'Donoghue, B., O'Mahony, B., Oliver, G., Cullen, C., O'Donoghue, T. and O'Halloran, J. 2008. Aspects of the breeding biology of Hen Harriers *Circus cyaneus* in Ireland. *Irish Birds* 8, 331–334.

Jackson, D.B., Fuller, R.J. and Campbell, S.T. 2004. Long-term changes among breeding shorebirds in the Outer Hebrides, Scotland, in relation to introduced hedgehogs *(Erinaceus europaeus)*. *Biological Conservation* 17, 151–166.

Jackson, D.B. and Green, R.E. 2000. The importance of the introduced hedgehog *(Erinaceus europaeus)* as a predator of the eggs of waders Charadrii on the machair of South Uist, Scotland. *Biological Conservation* 93, 333–348.

Jackson, D., Harkness, D.D., Mason, C.F. and Long, S.P. 1986. *Spartina anglica* as a carbon source for saltmarsh invertebrates: a study using 13c values. *Oikos* 46, 163–170.

Jeffrey, D.W. (ed) 1977. *North Bull Island, Dublin Bay – a modern coastal natural history*. Dublin. Royal Dublin Society.

Jeffrey, D.W., Madden, B., Rafferty, B., Dwyer, R., Wilson, J. and Arnott, N. 1992. *Dublin Bay water quality management plan*. Technical report 7. Algal Growths and Foreshore Quality. Dublin. Environmental Research Unit.

Johnston, B. and Dromey, M. Undated. *Nature on Irish Canals*. Dublin. The Stationery Office.

Johnson, G.C. 2008. Granivorous passerines across an agricultural gradient in winter: from habitat use to community structure. Unpublished Ph.D. thesis to the University of Dublin, Trinity College.

Johnson, O. 2004. *Collins Tree Guide*. London. Harper Collins.

Joint Nature Conservation Committee. 1993. *Handbook for Phase 1 Habitat Survey: a technique for environmental audit*. Peterborough. Joint Nature Conservation Committee.

Joint Nature Conservation Committee. 1999. *The Birds Directive. Selection Guidelines for Special Protection Areas*. Peterborough. Joint Nature Conservation Committee.

Jones, E. 1979. Breeding of the Short-eared Owl in south-west Ireland. *Irish Birds* 1, 377–380.

Jones, J.H. and Tasker, M.L. 1982. *Seabird movement at coastal sites around Great Britain and Ireland 1978–1980*. Aberdeen. Nature Conservancy Council and Seabird Group.

Jones, M.B., Donnelly, A and Albanito, F. 2006. Responses of Irish vegetation to future climate change. *Biology and Environment: Proceedings of the Royal Irish Academy* 106B, 323–334.

Jones, R. 1996. A study of Ring Ouzels breeding on Dartmoor. *Devon Birds* 49, 54–60.

Jonzén, N., Lindén, A., Ergon, T., Knudsen, E., Vik, J.O., Rubolini, D., Piacentini, D., Brinch, C., Spina, F., Karlsson, L., Stevander, M., Ansersson, A., Waldenström, J., Lehikoinen, A., Edvardsen, E., Solvang, R. and Strenseth, N.C. 2006. Rapid advance of spring arrival dates in long-distance migratory birds. *Science* 312, 1959–1961.

Joyce, P.M. and O'Carroll, N. 2002. *Sitka spruce in Ireland*. Dublin. COFORD.

Kaiser, M., Galanidi, M., Showler, D., Elliott, A., Caldow, R., Rees, E., Stillman, R. and Sutherland, W. 2006. Distribution and behaviour of Common Scoter *Melanitta nigra* relative to prey resources and environmental parameters. *Ibis* 148,110–128.

Kavanagh, B.P. 1987. The breeding density of the Magpie in Dublin city. *Irish Birds* 3, 387–394.

Kavanagh, B. 1990a. Bird communities of two short rotation forestry plantations on cutover peatland. *Irish Birds* 4, 169–180.

Kavanagh, B. 1990b. *Baseline ecological survey of Turraun Cutaway Bog, Co. Offaly*. Dublin. Report prepared for Bord Na Móna. Biology Division, Royal College of Surgeons.

Kavanagh, B. 1998. Cutaway boglands: a new landscape for birdlife. Pp. 34–40. In: Anon. *The Future Use of Cutaway Bogs. Proceedings from the first comprehensive conference on cutaway bog rehabilitation*. Ferbane. Brosna Press.

Kavanagh, B. and Fattebert, K. 2009. The Role of Habitat Management in the Conservation of the Nationally Endangered Grey Partridge *Perdix perdix* in Ireland. Pp. 61–69. In: *The LINNET Project (Lands Invested in Nature – National Eco-Tillage): Establishing Small-Scale Plots for Biodiversity*. Dublin. National Parks and Wildlife Service.

Keane, E.M. and O'Halloran, J. 1992. The behaviour of a wintering flock of Mute swans *Cygnus olor* in southern Ireland. *Wildfowl* 43, 12–19.

Kelcey, J.G. and Rheinweld, G. (eds.) 2005. *Birds in European Cities*. St Katharinen. Ginster Verlag.

Keleman, J. 2009. The LINNET Project. Pp. 1–11. In: *The LINNET Project (Lands Invested in Nature – National Eco-Tillage): Establishing Small-Scale Plots for Biodiversity*. Dublin. National Parks and Wildlife Service.

Kelleher, K.M. 2006. The ecology of the Song Thrush *Turdus philomelos* in Ireland. Unpublished Ph.D. thesis to University College, Cork.

Kelleher, K. and O'Halloran, J. 2006. The breeding biology of the Song Thrush, *Turdus philomelus*, in an island population. *Bird Study* 53, 142–155.

Kelleher, K. and O'Halloran, J. 2007. Influence of nesting habitat on breeding Song Thrush *Turdus philomelos*. *Bird Study* 54, 221–229.

Kelly, B. and Stack, M. (eds.) 2009. *Climate Change, Heritage and Tourism: implications for Ireland's coast and inland waterways.* Kilkenny. Heritage Council and Failte Ireland.

Kelly, P. 1984. 'Ireland' Pp. 48–83. In: Baldock, D. (ed.) *Wetland Drainage in Europe; the effects of Agricultural Policy in four EEC countries.* Institute for European Environmental Policy & International Institute for Environment and Development.

Kelly, T.C. 2008. The origin of the avifauna of Ireland. Pp. 97–107. In: Davenport, J.L. and Sleeman, D.P. (eds.). Mind the gap: postglacial colonization of Ireland. *Irish Naturalists' Journal* Special Supplement. Belfast.

Kelly, T. C and Allan, J 2006. Ecological effects of aviation. In: Davenport, J and Davenport, J.L (eds.) *The ecology of Transportation: Managing Mobility for the Environment.* Pp 5–24. New York. Springer.

Kelly, T.C., Bolger, R., Fennessy, G., Sheehy, S. and.O' Callaghan M.J.A. 2005. The Rabbit (*Oryctolagus cuniculus*): An emerging problem at airports. *Proceedings of the International Bird Strike Committee* 27, 214.

Kelly, T.C., Murphy, J. and Bolger, R. 2000. Okologische Storungen und Vogelschlagbekampfung. *Vogel und Luftverkehr* 20, 21–25.

Kelly, T.C., O' Callaghan, M.J.A and R. Bolger 2001. *The Avoidance Behaviour Shown by the Rook (Corvus frugilegus) to Commercial Aircraft.* In: Pelz, H.-J., Cowan, D.P and Feare, C.J (eds.)(2001) *Advances in Vertebrate Pest Management.* Pages 291–300. Furth. *Filander Verl., (Zoological Library)* Vol 2.

Kendall, M.A., Burrows, M.T., Southward, A.J. and Hawkins, S.J. 2004. Predicting the effects of marine climate change on the invertebrate prey of the birds of rocky shores. *Ibis* 146, 40–47.

Kennedy, P.G., Ruttledge, R.F. and Scroope, C.F. 1954. *The Birds of Ireland.* London and Edinburgh. Oliver and Boyd.

Kennedy, S.J.A. and Greer, J.E. 1988. Predation by Cormorants *Phalacrocorax carbo* L. on the salmonid populations of an Irish river. *Aquaculture and Fish Management* 19, 159–170.

Keogh, N.T., Macey, C., McAvoy, S., McGuirk J. and Newton S.F. 2010. *Kilcoole Little Tern Report 2010.* BirdWatch Ireland Seabird Conservation Report 10/S2.

Kirby, J., Cartmel, S. and Green, M. 1991. Distribution and habitat preferences of waders wintering on the non-estuarine west coast of Ireland. *Irish Birds* 4, 317–334.

Kitaysky, A.S and Golubova, E.G. 2000. Climate change causes contrasting trends in reproductive performance of planktivorous and piscivorous alcids. *Journal of Animal Ecology* 69, 248–262.

Kleijn, D and Sutherland, W.J. 2003. How effective are European agri-environment schemes in conserving and promoting biodiversity? *Journal of Applied Ecology* 40, 947–969.

König, C., Weick, F. and Becking, J-H. 1999. *Owls: A Guide to the Owls of the World.* Sussex. Pica Press.

Kramm, N., Anderson, R., O'Rourke, E., Emmerson, M., O'Halloran, J. and Chisholm, N. 2010. *Farming the Iveragh Uplands: a tale of humans and nature.* Cork. University College Cork.

Lack, D. 1976. *Island biology illustrated by the land birds of Jamaica.* Oxford. Blackwell Scientific Publications.

Lack, P. 1986. *The Atlas of Wintering Birds in Britain and Ireland.* Tring. British Trust for Ornithology and Irish Wildbird Conservancy.

Lance, A.N. 1972. *Red Grouse in Ireland: a summary of research up to 1972.* Dublin. An Forás Talúntais.

Langston, R.H.W. 2010. *Offshore wind farms and birds: Round 3 zones, extensions to Round 1 & Round 2 sites & Scottish Territorial Waters.* RSPB Research Report No. 39. Sandy, Bedfordshire. The Royal Society for the Protection of Birds.

Lappalainen, E. 1996. *Global peat resources.* Saarijärvi, Finland. International Peat Society.

Larsen, J.K. and Guillemette, M. 2007. Effects of wind turbines on flight behaviour of wintering common eiders: implications for habitat use and collision risk. *Journal of Applied Ecology* 44, 516–522.

Lauder, C. 2010. Conservation news. *Wings* No 56, Spring 2010, 12.

Lauder, C. and Donaghy, A. 2008. *Breeding Waders in Ireland 2008: A review and recommendations for future actions.* Report to the National Parks and Wildlife Service. Newtown. BirdWatch Ireland.

Lauga, B., Cagnon, C., D'Amico, F., Karama, S. and Mouchès, C. 2005. Phylogeography of the White-throated Dipper *Cinclus cinclus* in Europe. *Journal of Ornithology* 146, 257–262.

Lehikoinen, E., Sparks, T. H. and Zalakevicius, M. 2004. Arrival and departure dates. Pp. 1–31. In: Møller, A.P., Fiedler, W. and Berthold, P. (eds) *Birds and climate change. Advances in Ecological Research 35.* Place of publication. Academic Press.

Lehikoinen, E. and Sparks, T.H. 2010. Changes in migration. Pp. 89–128. In: Møller, A.P., Fiedler, W. and Berthold, P. (eds) *Effects of climate change on birds.* London. Oxford University Press.

Lenehan, L. 2009. Herring Gulls nesting on buildings at Balbriggan, Co. Dublin. *Irish East Coast Bird Report 2003,* 101–102.

Lewis, L.J., Davenport, J. and Kelly, T.C. 2003. Responses of benthic invertebrates and their avian predators to the experimental removal of macroalgal mats. *Journal Marine Biological Association UK* 83, 31–36.

Lewis, L.J. and Kelly, T.C. 2001. A short-term study of the effects of algal mats on the distribution and behavioural ecology of estuarine birds. *Bird Study* 48, 354–360.

Lewis, S., Benvenuti, S., Dall–Antonia, L., Griffiths, R., Money, L., Sherratt, T.N., Wanless, S. and Hamer, K.C. 2002. Sex-specific foraging behaviour in a monomorphic seabird. *Proceedings of the Royal Society of London Series B: Biological Sciences* 269, 1687–1693.

Liukkonen-Anttila, T., Uimaniemi, M. and Lumme, J. 2002. Mitochondrial DNA variation and the phylogeography of the grey partridge (*Perdix perdix*) in Europe: from Pleistocene history to present day populations. *Journal of Evolutionary Biology* 15, 971–982.

Lloyd, C. 1981. *Birdwatching on Estuaries, Coast and Sea.* London. Severn House Naturalist's Library.

Lovatt, J.K. 1988. Great Crested Grebe census in County Cavan, summers 1986–1988. *Irish Birds* 3, 575–580.

Lovatt, J.K. 1997. Occurrence of the Garden Warbler *Sylvia borin* around Lough Ree and County Cavan, 1995–1997. *Irish Birds* 6, 58–60.

Lusby, J., Watson, D. and Copland, A. 2009. *Barn Owl Research Project; 2009 Report.* Unpublished report by BirdWatch Ireland.

Lusby, J. and Watson, D. 2009. *The ecology of the Kestrel Falco tinnunculus in Ireland; The Kestrel Research Project.* BirdWatch Ireland unpublished report to the Heritage Council.

Lusby, J., Watson, D., Nagle, T. and O'Halloran, J. 2010. *The ecology and conservation of the Barn Owl Tyto alba in County Cork; Cork Barn Owl Research Project, 2010 Report.* Unpublished report to BirdWatch Ireland.

Lynas, P., Newton, S.F. and Robinson, J.A. 2007. The status of birds in Ireland: an analysis of conservation concern 2008–2013. *Irish Birds* 8, 149–166.

Lynch, Á., Denniston, H., Finney, K. and Copland, A. 2007. *Shannon Callows Breeding Wader Project: Final Report 2007.* Unpublished report to BirdWatch Ireland, Co. Wicklow, and the National Parks and Wildlife Service, Dublin.

Lyons, M. and Tubridy, M. 2006. *A survey of ancient and species rich hedgerows in Dublin City.* The Heritage Council.

Lysaght, L. 1989. Breeding bird populations of farmland in mid-west Ireland in 1987. *Bird Study* 36, 91–98.

MacArthur, R.H. and Wilson, E.O. 1967. *The theory of Island Biogeography.* Princeton, NJ. Princeton University Press.

Macdonald, M.A. and Bolton, M. 2008. Predation on wader nests in Europe. *Ibis* 150 (Supplement1), 54–73.

Macdonald, R.A. 1987. The breeding population and distribution of the Cormorant in Ireland. *Irish Birds* 3, 405–416.

Macdonald, R.A. 1988. The Cormorant *Phalacrocorax carbo* in relation to salmon fisheries. (abstract) *Ibis* 130, 590.

Macdonald, R. and Goodwillie, R. 1984. *Gull Management in the Dublin area.* Dublin. An Foras Forbartha.

Mackey, M., Ó Cadhla, O., Kelly, T.C., Aguilar de Soto, N. and Connolly, N. 2004. *Cetaceans and seabirds of Ireland's Atlantic margin.* Volume I. Seabird distribution, density & abundance. Cork. Coastal and Marine Resources Centre & Department of Zoology, Ecology and Plant Science.

Mackinnon, B, Sowdon, R and Dudley, S. (Eds.) 2001. *Sharing the skies – An Aviation Industry Guide to the Management of Wildlife Hazards.* Ottawa. Transport Canada.

Maclean, I.M.D., Austin, G.E., Rehfisch, M.M., Blew, J., Crowe, O., Delany, S., Devos, K., Deceuninck, B., Günther, K., Laursen, K., van Roomen, M. and Wahl, J. 2008. Climate change causes rapid changes in the distribution and site abundance of birds in winter. *Global Change Biology* 14, 2489–2500.

Maclean, I.M.D., Burton, N.H.K. & Austin, G.E 2007. *Declines in over-wintering diving ducks at Lough Neagh and Lough Beg: comparisons of within site, regional, national and European trends.* BTO Research report 432. Thetford. BTO.

MacLochlainn, C. 1984. Breeding and wintering bird communities of Glenveagh National Park, Co. Donegal. *Irish Birds* 2, 482–500.

MacLochlainn, C. 2002. *Special Protection Areas for Birds in Ireland.* Dublin. Dúchas, The Heritage Service.

Madden, B. 1987a. The birds of Mongan Bog, Co. Offaly. *Irish Birds* 3, 441–448.

Madden, B. 1987b. The fauna of bogs. Pp. 23–27. In: O'Connell, C. (ed.). *The IPCC Guide to Irish Peatlands.* Dublin. Irish Peatland Conservation Council.

Madden, B. 1987c. The fauna of fens. Pp. 28–30. In: O'Connell, C. (ed.) *The IPCC Guide to Irish Peatlands.* Dublin. Irish Peatland Conservation Council.

Madden, B. 1997. Black Guillemots breeding at Dun Laoghaire, Co. Dublin. *Irish East Coast Bird Report 1996,* 83–84.

Madden, B. and Archer, E. 2005. Scavenging gulls at Balleally Landfill, Lusk, County Dublin. Long-term population trends. *Irish Birds* 7, 511–516.

Madden, B., Cooney, T., O'Donoghue, A. and Merne, O.J. 1998. Breeding waders of machair systems in Ireland in 1996. *Irish Birds* 6, 177–190.

Madden, B. and Heery, S. 1997. Wintering waterfowl in South Galway area. In: Southern Water Global and Jennings O'Donovan & Partners (eds). *An investigation into the flooding problems in the Gort–Ardrahan area, south Galway.* Ecology Baseline Vol 1. Dublin. Office of Public Works.

Madden, B., Hunt, J. and Norriss, D. 2009. The 2002 survey of the Peregrine *Falco peregrinus* breeding population in the Republic of Ireland. *Irish Birds* 8, 543–548.

Madden, B., Merne, O., McNally, J., Newton, S.F. and Murphy, D. 2004. Wintering waterbirds of Lambay, County Dublin. *Irish Birds* 7, 337–346.

Madden, B., Merne, O.J. and Newton, S.F. 2001. East Coast Black Guillemot Survey 1998. *Irish East Coast Bird Report* 1999, 82–86.

Madden, B., Mitchell, L.S. and Cooney, 1993. *Birds of Trinity College Dublin.* Trinity College Dublin Press. Dublin.

Madden. B. and Newton, S.F. 2004. Herring Gull *Larus argentatus.* Pp. 242–262. In Mitchell, P.I., Newton, S.F., Ratcliffe, N. and Dunn, E. (eds) *Seabird Populations of Britain and Ireland.* London, Poyser.

Magee, J.D. 1965. The breeding distribution of the Stonechat in Britain and the causes of its decline. *Bird Study* 12, 83–89.

Maguire, C.M. and Gibson, C.E. 2005. Ecological changes in Lough Erne: influence of catchment changes and species invasions. *Freshwater Forum* 24, 38–58.

Mainwaring, M.C. and Hartley, I.R., 2008. Covering nest boxes with wire mesh reduces Great Spotted Woodpecker *Dendrocopos major* predation of blue tit *Cyanistes caeruleus* nestlings, Lancashire, England. *Conservation Evidence* 5, 45–46.

Malone, S. and O'Connell, C. 2009. *Ireland's Peatland Conservation Action Plan 2020 – Halting the loss of peatland biodiversity.* Lullymore. Irish Peatland Conservation Council.

Marchant, J.H., Hudson, R., Carter, S.P. and Whittington, P. 1990. *Population Trends in British Breeding Birds.* Tring. British Trust for Ornithology.

Marchant, J.H. and Hyde, P.A. 1980. Aspects of the distribution of riparian birds on waterways in Britain and Ireland. *Bird Study* 27, 183–202.

Marzluff, J.M., Bowman, R. and Donnelly R. (eds.) 2001. *Avian Ecology and Conservation in an Urbanising World.* Massachusetts. Kluwer Academic Boston.

Masden, E.A., Haydon, D.T., Fox, A.D. and Furness, R.W. 2010. Barriers to movement: Modelling energetic costs of avoiding marine wind farms amongst breeding seabirds. *Marine Pollution Bulletin* 60, 1085–1091.

Mathers, R. 1993. Feral Mandarin Duck population breeding in County Down. *Irish Birds* 5, 76.

Mathers, R.G. and Montgomery, W.I. 1997. Quality of food consumed by overwintering Pale-bellied Brent Geese *Branta bernicla hrota* and Wigeon *Anas penelope. Biology and Environment: Proceedings of the Royal Irish Academy* 97B: 81–90.

Mathers, R.G., Montgomery, W.I., Portig, A.A. and Stone, R. 1998. Winter habitat use by Brent Geese *Branta bernicla* and Wigeon *Anas penelope* on Strangford Lough, Co. Down. *Irish Birds* 6, 257–268.

Matthysen, E., Adriaensen, F. and Dhondt, A.A. 2011. Multiple responses to increasing spring temperatures in the breeding cycle of blue and Great Tits (*Cyanistes caeruleus, Parus major*). *Global Change Biology* 17, 1–6.

Mawhinney, K. 2009. Giant Bird Tables. Pp. 57–60. In: *The LINNET Project (Lands Invested in Nature – National Eco-Tillage): Establishing Small-Scale Plots for Biodiversity.* National Parks and Wildlife Service.

Mayes E. 1991. The winter ecology of Greenland White-fronted Geese *Anser albifrons flavirostris* on semi-natural grassland and intensive farmland. *Ardea* 79, 295–304.

Mayes, E., Partridge, K. and Shannon, J. 2009. Greenland White-fronted Geese *Anser albifrons flavirostris*: the brief recorded history of the Caledon flock. *Irish Birds* 8, 497–506.

Mayes E. and Stowe T.J. 1989. The status and distribution of Corncrakes in Ireland in 1988. *Irish Birds* 4, 1–12.

McCarthy, T.K. 1986. Biogeographical aspects of Ireland's invertebrate fauna. Pp. 68–71. In: Sleeman, D.P., Devoy, R.J. and Woodman, P.C. (eds.) *Occasional Publications of Irish Biogeographical Society* No 1.

McCorry, M.J., Curtis, T.G.F. and Otte, M.L. 2003. *Spartina* in Ireland. Pp. 44–50. In: Otte, M.L. (ed.) *Wetlands of Ireland: distribution, ecology, uses and economic value.* Dublin. University College Dublin Press.

McCracken, D.I. and Foster, G.N. 1994. Invertebrates, cow dung and the availability of potential food for the Chough *Pyrrhocorax pyrrhocorax* L. on pastures in North-West Islay. *Environmental Conservation* 21, 262–266.

McCracken, E. 1971. *The Irish Woods since Tudor Times: Distribution and Exploitation.* Newton Abbot. David and Charles.

MCPFE. 2007. *State of Europe's forests 2007.* Oslo. Forest Europe. Available on-line: http://www.mcpfe.org/filestore/mcpfe/Publications/pdf/state_of_europes_forests_2007.pdf.

McElheron, A. 2005. *Merlins of the Wicklow Mountains.* Dublin. Currach Press.

McElwaine, J.G. 1991. Wintering waterfowl on County Down lakes, 1986/87–1990/91. *Irish Birds* 4, 335–368.

McGrath, D. 2001. *A Guide to Tramore Bay, Dunes and Backstrand.* Waterford. Privately published.

McGrath, D. 2004. Integrated Kittiwake *Rissa tridactyla* monitoring at Dunmore East, County Waterford, 1987–2002. *Irish Birds* 7, 351–360.

McGrath, D. 2006. *A Guide to Wildlife in Waterford City*. Waterford. Privately Published.

McGreal, E. 2007. The breeding status of the raven *Corvus corax* in Southwest Mayo. *Irish Birds* 8, 237–242.

McKenna, J., MacLeod, M., Power, J. and Cooper, A. 2000. *Rural Beach Management: A good practice guide*. Lifford. Donegal County Council.

McLoughlin, D. 2009. The Ecology of Twite Carduelis flavirostris in Ireland. Unpublished Ph.D. thesis, Institute of Technology, Sligo.

McLoughlin, D. and Cotton, D. 2008. The status of Twite *Carduelis flavirostris* in Ireland 2008. *Irish Birds* 8, 323–330.

McMahon, B.J. 2005. Avian Biodiversity in Farmland. Unpublished Ph.D. thesis, University College, Dublin.

McMahon, B.J. 2007. Irish agriculture and farmland birds, research to date and future priorities. *Irish Birds* 8, 195–206.

McMahon, B.J., Helden, A., Anderson, A., Sheridan, H., Kinsella, A. and Purvis, G. 2010. Interactiosn between livestock systems and biodiversity in South-East Ireland. *Agriculture, Ecosystems and Environment* 139, 232–238.

McMahon, B.J., Purvis, G. and Whelan, J. 2008. The influence of habitat heterogeneity on bird diversity in Irish farmland. *Biology and Environment: Proceedings of the Royal Irish Academy* 108B, 1–8.

McMahon, B.J. and Whelan, J. 2005. Grassland and avian biodiversity within Irish agriculture. P. 654. In: O'Mara, F., Wilkins, R.J., 't Mannetje, L., Lovett, D.K., Rodgers, P.A.M. and Boland, T. (eds.) *XX International Grassland Congress*. University College Dublin. Wageningen Academic Publishers.

McMahon, B.J., Whelan, J., Bracken, F. and Kavanagh, B. 2003. The impact of farming on over-wintering bird populations. *Tearmann* 3, 67–76.

Mee, A. 1997. *Status and breeding ecology of Golden Plover Pluvialis apricaria in the Moorfoot Hills in 1997*. Unpublished report. Edinburgh. Scottish Natural Heritage.

Mee, T. 1994. Charleville Lagoons: a site guide. In: *Birds of Clare and Limerick 1982–1991*. Limerick. Irish Wildbird Conservancy.

Meehan, C., Stronach, B.W.H., Huxley, C. and Stronach, N. 2009. A review of changes in duck populations on Lough Carra, County Mayo, 1967–2006. *Irish Birds* 8, 507–520.

Menzel, A., Sparks, T. H., Estrella, N., Koch, E., Aasa, A., Ahas, R., Alm-Kübler, K., Bissolli, P., Braslavská, O., Briede, A., Chmielewski, F. M., Crepinsek, Z., Curnel, Y., Dahl, Å., Defila, C., Donnelly, A., Filella, Y., Jatczak, K., Måge, F., Mestre, A., Nordli, Ø., Peñuelas, J., Pirinen, P., Remisová, V., Scheifinger, H., Striz, M., Susnik, A., Wielgolaski, F.-E., van Vliet, A., Zach, S. and Zust, A. 2006. European phenological response to climate change matches the warming pattern. *Global Change Biology* 12, 1–8.

Merne, O.J. 1974. *The Birds of Wexford*. Dublin. Bord Failte/South-East Tourism.

Merne, O.J. 1975. The spring departure of Greenland White-fronted Geese from Ireland. *Irish Bird Report* 1974, 62–71.

Merne, O.J. 1977. The changing status and distribution of the Bewick's Swan in Ireland. *Irish Birds* 1, 3–15.

Merne, O. J. 1980 *Ornithological study of Carnsore Point area, Co. Wexford*. Unpublished report. Dublin. Forest and Wildlife Service.

Merne, O.J. 1985. The infauna of the Shannon and Fergus estuarine mudflats as a food resource for shorebirds. M.Sc. thesis, Environmental Sciences Unit, Trinity College, Dublin.

Merne, O. J. 1991. Birds of Irish Dunes. Pp. 72–76. In: Quigley, M.B. (ed) *A Guide to the Sand Dunes of Ireland*. Galway. European Union for Dune Conservation and Coastal Management.

Merne, O.J. 1993. Tree nesting Shags at Lambay Island, County Dublin. *Irish East Coast Bird Report* 1992, 70.

Merne O.J. 2004. Common *Sterna hirundo* and Arctic Terns *S. paradisaea* breeding in Dublin Port, County Dublin, 1995–2003. *Irish Birds* 7, 369–374.

Merne, O.J. 2005. Coastal wetland birds and the EU Birds Directive. Pp. 36–42. In: Wilson, J.G. (ed). *The Intertidal Ecosystem: The value of Ireland's Shores*. Dublin. Royal Irish Academy.

Merne, O. 2007. *Study of the Breeding Birds of the Tolka River Valley Park in Fingal County*. Swords. Fingal County Council.

Merne, O.J. 2010. Terns roosting in Dublin Bay, autumn 2010. *Irish Birds* 9, 126–128.

Merne, O.J., Boertmann, D., Boyd, H., Mitchell, C., Ó Briain, M., Reed, A. and Sigfusson, A. 1999. Light-bellied Brent Goose *Branta bernicla hrota* – Canada. Pp. 298–311. In: Madsen, J., Cracknell, G., Fox, T. (eds). *Goose populations of the Western Palearctic – a review of status and distribution*. Denmark. Wetlands International Publication No. 48. National Environmental Research Institute.

Merne, O.J., Madden, B., Archer, E. and Porter, B. 2008. Autumn roosting terns in south Dublin Bay. *Irish Birds* 8, 335–340.

Merne, O.J., Madden, B., Archer, E. Porter, B. and Holohan, S. 2009. Abundance of non-breeding gulls in Dublin Bay, 2006–2007. *Irish Birds* 8, 549–562.

Merne, O.J. and Madden, B. 1999. Breeding seabirds of Lambay, Co. Dublin. *Irish Birds* 6, 345–358.

Merne, O.J. and Madden, B. 2000. Breeding seabirds of Ireland's Eye, Co. Dublin. *Irish Birds* 6, 495–506.

Merne, O.J. and Roe, J. 2006. *Ecological Study of the Countryside Habitats in County Fingal Phase III – Woodland Birds*. Swords. Fingal County Council.

Merne, O.J. and Walsh, A. 1994. Barnacle Geese in Ireland, spring 1993 and 1994. *Irish Birds* 5, 151–156.

Michener, R.H. and Schell, D.M. 1994. Stable isotope ratios as tracers in marine aquatic food webs. Pp. 138–158. In: Lajtha, K., Michener, R.H. (eds.) *Stable isotopes in ecology and environmental science*. Oxford. Blackwell.

Miller-Rushing, A.J., Primack, R.B. and Sekercioglu, C.H. 2010. Conservation consequences of climate change for birds. Pp. 295–309. In: Møller, A.P., Fiedler, W. and Berthold, P. (eds) *Effects of climate change on birds*. London. Oxford University Press.

Mitchell, F. 2006. Where did Ireland's trees come from? *Biology & Environment: Proceedings of the Royal Irish Academy* 106, 251–259.

Mitchell, F.J.G. 1990. The history and vegetation dynamics of a Yew wood (*Taxus baccata* L.) in S.W. Ireland. *New Phytologist* 115, 573–577.

Mitchell, P.I. and Newton, S.F. 2004. European Storm-petrel *Hydrobates pelagicus*. Pp. 81–100. In: Mitchell, P.I., Newton, S.F., Ratcliffe, N. and Dunn, E. (eds.) *Seabird Populations of Britain and Ireland*. London, Poyser.

Mitchell, P.I., Newton, S.F., Ratcliffe, N. and Dunn, T.E. 2004. *Seabird Populations of Britain and Ireland*. Results of the Seabird 2000 census (1998–2002). London. Poyser.

Moles, R.T. and Breen, J. (1995) Long-term change within lowland farmland bird communities in relation to field boundary attributes. *and Environment: Proceedings of the Royal Irish Academy* 95B, 203–215.

Mollan, C. (ed.). 1993. *Water of Life*. Seminar Proceedings 5. Dublin. Royal Dublin Society.

Møller, A. P., Rubolini, D. and Lehikoinen, E. 2008. Populations of migratory bird species that did not show a phenological response to climate change are declining. *Proceedings of the National Academy of Sciences, USA* 105, 16195–16200.

Monaghan, P., Walton, P., Wanless, S., Uttley, J.D. and Burns, M.D. 1994 Effects of prey abundance on the foraging behaviour, diving efficiency and time allocation of breeding Guillemots *Uria aalge*. *Ibis* 136, 214–222.

Mooney, H.A. and Cleland, E.E. 2001. The evolutionary impact of invasive species. *Proceeding of the National Academy of Sciences* 98, 5446–5451.

Moore, C.C. 1975. An analysis of large scale autumn passage in the northwest Irish Sea. *Irish Bird Report* 22, 40–52.

Moore, D.J., Wilson, F.R.J. and Curtis, T.G.F. (In press). The shingle beaches of Ireland: An inventory, their geographical variation and an assessment of their conservation significance.

Moore, J.J., O'Reilly, H. 1977. Saltmarsh: vegetation pattern and trends. Pp. 83–87. In: Jeffrey, D.W. (ed) *North Bull Island, Dublin Bay – a modern coastal natural history*. Dublin. Royal Dublin Society.

Moore, N., Kelly, P. and Lang, F. 1992. Quarry-nesting by peregrine falcons in Ireland. *Irish Birds* 4, 519–524.

Moore, N.P., Kelly, P.F., Lang, F.A., Lynch, J.M. and Langton, S.D. 1997. The Peregrine *Falco peregrinus* in quarries: current status and factors influencing occupancy in the Republic of Ireland. *Bird Study* 44, 176–181.

Moriarty, C. 1991. *Down the Dodder*. Dublin. Wolfhound Press.

Moriarty, C. 1997. *Exploring Dublin: Wildlife, Parks and Waterways*. Dublin. Wolfhound Press.

Moriarty, C. (ed.). 1998. *Studies of Irish Rivers and Lakes*. Dublin. Marine Institute.

Morrison, P. 1989. *Bird Habitats of Great Britain and Ireland*. London. Michael Joseph.

Moser, M.E. and Prys-Jones, R.P. 1988. Population estimates, distribution patterns and site evaluations for waders wintering on the coast of Northern Ireland. *Irish Birds* 3, 551–568.

Murphy, J.N., Cooney, A., Rattigan, J. and Lynch, T. 2003. *The Shannon Estuary Lagoon: A unique Irish habitat*. Newmarket on Fergus. BirdWatch Ireland.

Murphy, G. 2011. *An investigation into the influence of waterfowl and recreational uses on water quality and amenity value in Cork Lough*. Unpublished MSc thesis. Cork. University College, Cork.

Murphy, S., Lewis, L.J. and Kelly, T.C. 2006. The spatial ecology of wildfowl in Courtmacsherry Bay, southern Ireland, with particular reference to Shelduck *Tadorna tadorna*. *Irish Birds* 8, 51–58.

Murray, T. and O'Halloran, J. 2003. Population estimate for Red Grouse in the Owenduff–Nephin Special Protection Area, Co. Mayo. *Irish Birds* 7, 187–192.

Nagle, T. 2004. The status of birds of prey and owls in County Cork. *Cork Bird Report 1996–2004*, 285–308.

Nagle, T. 2007. The loss of Barn Owl *Tyto alba* breeding and roost sites in County Cork: a contributory factor in the species decline. *Irish Birds* 8, 314–315.

Nairn, R.G.W. 1986. *Spartina anglica* in Ireland and its potential impact on wildfowl and waders – a review. *Irish Birds* 3, 215–228.

Nairn, R.G.W. 2003. Birds of Irish wetlands: a literature review. Pp. 197–201. In: Otte, M.L. (ed.). *Wetlands of Ireland*. Dublin. University College Dublin Press.

Nairn, R.G.W. 2005a. Use of a high tide roost by waders during engineering work in Galway Bay, Ireland. *Irish Birds* 7, 489–496.

Nairn, R.G.W. 2005b. *Ireland's Coastline: Exploring its Nature & Heritage*. Cork. Collins Press.

Nairn, R.G.W. and Farrelly, P. 1991. Breeding bird communities of broad-leaved woodland in the Glen of the Downs, Co. Wicklow. *Irish Birds* 4, 377–392.

Nairn, R.G.W., Hamilton, C. and Herbert, I.J. (In press). Habituation by water birds to onshore windfarms in Ireland.

Nairn, R.G.W., Herbert I.J. and Heery S. 1988. Breeding waders and other wet grassland birds of the River Shannon Callows, Ireland. *Irish Birds* 3, 521–537.

Nairn, R.G.W., Madden, B. and Partridge, J.K. 2004. Redshank *Tringa totanus* breeding on bogs in Ireland. *Irish Birds* 7, 347–350.

Nairn, R.G.W and Robinson, J.A. 2003. *All-Ireland review of intertidal Eel-grass (Zostera) beds*. Unpublished report to the Heritage Council. Wicklow. NATURA Consultants.

Nairn, R.G.W. and Sheppard, J.R. 1985. Breeding waders of sand dune machair in north-west Ireland. *Irish Birds* 3, 53–70.

Nairn, R.G.W., ten Cate, W.E. and Sharkey, N. 2000. Long-term monitoring of wintering waterbirds in Inner Galway Bay, 1980/81 to 1999/2000. *Irish Birds* 6, 453–468.

Nairn, R.G.W. and Whatmough, J.A. 1978. Breeding bird communities of a sand dune system in north-east Ireland. *Irish Birds* 1, 160–170.

Neilson, B. and Costello, M.J. 1999. The relative lengths of intertidal substrata around the coastline of Ireland as determined by digital methods in a Geographical Information System. *Estuarine and Coastal Shelf Sciences* 49, 501–508.

Newell, R.G. 1968. Influx of Great Shearwaters in autumn 1965. *British Birds* 61, 145–159.

Newton, I., 1994. The role of nest sites in limiting the numbers of hole-nesting birds: A review. *Biological Conservation* 70, 265–276.

Newton, I., 1998. *Population Limitation in Birds*. London. Academic Press.

Newton, I. 2010. *Bird Migration*. New Naturalist Library. London. Collins.

Newton, I. 2004a. The recent declines of farmland bird populations in Britain: an appraisal of causal factors and conservation actions. *Ibis* 146, 579–600.

Newton, S.F. 2004b. Roseate Tern *Sterna dougallii*. Pp. 302–314. In: Mitchell, P.I., Newton, S.F., Ratcliffe, N. and Dunn, E. (eds) *Seabird Populations of Britain and Ireland*. London. Poyser.

Newton, S.F. and Crowe, O. 1999. *Kish Bank – a preliminary assessment of its ornithological importance*. Dublin. BirdWatch Ireland Conservation Report 99/8.

Newton, S.F. and Crowe, O. 2000. *Roseate Terns – The Natural Connection. A conservation / research project linking Ireland and Wales*. Maritime Ireland / Wales INTERREG Report No. 2.

Newton, S.F., Donaghy, A., Allen, D. and Gibbons, D. 1999. Birds of Conservation Concern in Ireland. *Irish Birds* 6, 333–344.

Newton, S.F., Moralee, A. and Cabot, D. 2002 Great Skua *Catharacta skua* breeding in Ireland. *Irish Birds* 7, 129.

Newton, S.F., Thompson, K. and Mitchell, P.I. 2004. Manx Shearwater *Puffinus puffinus*. Pp. 63–80. In: Mitchell, P.I., Newton, S.F., Ratcliffe, N. and Dunn, E. (eds) *Seabird Populations of Britain and Ireland*. London, Poyser.

NIBA. 1998–2006. *Northern Ireland Bird Reports 1981–2004*. Northern Ireland Birdwatchers' Association, Belfast.

NIBR. 2008. *Northern Ireland Bird Report*. Volume 17. Belfast. Northern Ireland Birdwatchers' Association.

NIBA 2009. Northern Ireland Bird Report Volume 153. Northern Ireland Birdwatchers' Association.

Ní Dhubháin, A. 2003. *Continuous Cover Forestry: COFORD connects, silviculture and forest management*. No. 8. Dublin. COFORD.

NIEA. 2005. *Northern Ireland Habitat Action Plan*. Eutrophic Standing Waters. Belfast. Northern Ireland Environment Agency.

Nielsen, J.T. and Møller, A.P. 2006. Effects of brood abundance, density and climate change on reproduction in the sparrowhawk *Accipiter nisus*. *Oecologia* 149, 505–518.

Ni Lamhna, E. 2008. *Wild Dublin: Exploring Nature in the City*. Dublin. O'Brien Press.

Ni Shuilleabhain, A. 2000. Association between spatial distribution of waterfowl on Lough Leane, Co. Kerry, Ireland and limnological characteristics of the lake. *Irish Birds* 6, 469–484.

Norriss, D.W. 1991. The status of the Buzzard as a breeding species in the Republic of Ireland, 1977–1991. *Irish Birds* 4, 291–299.

Norriss, D.W. 1995. The 1991 survey and weather impacts on the Peregrine *Falco peregrinus* breeding population in the Republic of Ireland. *Bird Study* 42, 20–30.

Norriss, D.W., Haran, B., Hennigan, A., McElheron, D.J., McLaughlin, D.J., Swan, V. and Walsh, A. 2010. Breeding biology of Merlins *Falco columbarious* in Ireland, 1986–1992. *Irish Birds* 9, 23–30.

Norriss, D.W., Marsh, J., McMahon, D. and Oliver, G.A. 2002. A national survey of breeding Hen Harriers *Circus cyaneus* in Ireland 1998–2000. *Irish Birds* 7, 1–12.

Norriss, D.W. and Walsh, A. 2008. Monitoring of Greenland White-fronted Geese *Anser albifons flavirostris* in Ireland. *Irish Birds* 8, 473.

NPWS. 2004. *Lough Corrib SPA and Lough Mask SPA Site Synopses*. Dublin. National Parks and Wildlife Service.

NPWS. 2005. *Poulaphouca Reservoir SPA Site Synopsis*. Dublin. National Parks and Wildlife Service.

NPWS. 2008. *The Status of EU-protected Habitats and Species in Ireland*. Dublin. National Parks and Wildlife Service.

Nussey, D.H., Postma, E., Gienapp, P. and Visser, M.E. 2005. Selection on heritable phenotypic plasticity in a wild bird population. *Science* 310, 304–306.

Ó Briain, M. 1991. Use of a *Zostera* bed in Dublin Bay by Light-bellied Brent Geese, 1981/82 to 1990/91. *Irish Birds* 4, 299–316.

Ó Briain, M. 2011. EU Guidelines on Wind Energy and Nature Conservation. P. 43. In: May, R. and Bevanger, K. (eds.) *Proceedings on Conference on Wind Energy and Wildlife impacts, 2–5 May 2011*. Trondheim, Norway.

Ó Briain, M. and Farrelly, P. 1990. Breeding biology of the Little Tern at Newcastle, Co. Wicklow and the impact of conservation action 1985–1990. *Irish Birds* 4, 149–168.

Ó Briain, M. and Healy, B. 1991. Winter distribution of Light-bellied Brent Geese *Branta bernicla hrota* in Ireland. *Ardea* 79, 271–326.

O'Callaghan, M.J.A., Meade, J. and Kelly, T.C. 2001 *A Method for Calculating the Duration of Stay of Gulls at an Amenity Lake Near a Landfill*. Pp. 283–290 in Pelz, H.-J., Cowan, D.P and Feare, C.J (eds) (2001) *Advances in Vertebrate Pest Management*. Furth. Filander Verl., (Zoological Library).

O'Carroll, N. 1984. *The forests of Ireland. History, distribution and silviculture*. Dublin. Turoe Press.

O'Connell, C. and Foss, P. 1999. *A survey of cutover and cutaway bog habitats of the Irish midlands*. Dublin. Irish Peatland Conservation Council.

O'Connell, M.M. Smiddy, P. and O'Halloran, J. 2009. Blood lead levels in Mute Swans over two decades. *Proceedings of Royal Irish Academy: Biology and Environment* 109B, 53–60.

O'Connor, R.J. 1986. Biological characteristics of invaders among bird species in Britain. *Philosophical Transactions of the Royal Society of London. Series B, Biological Sciences* 314, 583–598.

O'Donoghue, P. and O'Halloran, J. 1994. The behaviour of a wintering flock of Whooper Swans (*Cygnus cygnus*) in southern Ireland. *Biology and Environment: Proceedings of the Royal Irish Academy* 94B, 109–118.

O'Flynn, W.J. 1983. Population changes of the Hen Harrier in Ireland. *Irish Birds* 2, 337–343.

O'Gorman, E.C. 2001. Home range and habitat use of the endangered grey partridge (*Perdix perdix*) in the Irish midlands. Ph.D. thesis, Trinity College, Dublin.

O'Halloran, J., Irwin, S., Harrison, S., Smiddy, P. and O'Mahony, B. 2003. Mercury and organochlorine content of Dipper *Cinclus cinclus* eggs in south-west Ireland: trends during 1990–1999. *Environmental Pollution* 123, 85–93.

O'Halloran, J., Kelly, T.C., Irwin, S. and Newton S.F. 2008. Current Ornithological Research in Ireland: fifth ornithological research conference, UCC November 2008. *Irish Birds* 8, 441–488.

O'Halloran, J., Myers, A.A. and Duggan, P.F. 1988. Lead poisoning in swans and sources of contamination in Ireland. *Journal of Zoology (London)* 216, 211–223.

O'Halloran, J., Myers, A. A. and Duggan, P. F. 1989. Some sub-lethal effects of lead on Mute swans, *Cygnus olor*. *Journal of Zoology (London)* 218, 627–632.

O'Halloran, J., Ormerod, S.J., Smiddy, P. and O'Mahony, B. 1993. Organochlorine and mercury content of Dipper eggs in south-west Ireland. *Biology and Environment: Proceedings of the Royal Irish Academy* 93B, 25–31.

O'Halloran, J., Ridgeway, M. and Hutchinson, C.D. 1993. A whooper swan *Cygnus cygnus* population wintering at Kilcolman wildfowl refuge, Co. Cork, Ireland: trends over 20 years. *Wildfowl* 44, 1–6.

O'Halloran, J., Smiddy, P., O'Mahony, B., Taylor, A.J. and O'Donoghue, P.D. 1999. Aspects of the population biology of the Dipper in south west Ireland. *Irish Birds* 6, 359–364.

O'Halloran, J., Smiddy, P. and O'Mahony, B. 2000. Movements of Dippers *Cinclus cinclus* in southwest Ireland. *Ringing & Migration* 20, 147–151.

O'Halloran, J., Smiddy, P., Quishi, X., O'Leary, R. and Hayes, C. 2002. Trends in Mute Swan blood lead levels: evidence of grit reducing lead poisoning. *Waterbirds* 25, 363 367.

O'Halloran, J., Walsh, P.M., Giller, P.S., Kelly, T.C. and Duffy, B.L. 1998. An assessment of avian biodiversity and opportunities for enhancement in Ireland's forests: overview and preliminary results. *Irish Forestry* 55, 2–14.

O'Higgins, T.G. and Wilson, J.G. 2005. Impact of the river Liffey discharge on nutrient and chlorophyll concentrations in the Liffey estuary and Dublin Bay (Irish Sea). *Estuarine, Coastal and Shelf Science* 64, 323–334.

Ó hUallacháin, D. and Dunne, J. 2007. The winter diet of Pheasants *Phasianus colchicus*: a comparison of estate-reared and wild birds. *Irish Birds* 8, 189–194.

O'Keeffe, P. and Simington, T. 1991. *Irish Stone Bridges: history and heritage*. Dublin. Irish Academic Press.

Oliver, G. and Healy, B. 1998. Records of aquatic fauna from coastal lagoons in Ireland. *Bulletin of the Irish Biogeographical Society* 21, 66–115.

Ollason, J., Bryant. A., Davis, P., Scott, B. and Tasker, M. 1997 Predicted seabird distributions in the North Sea: the consequences of being hungry. *ICES Journal of Marine Science: Journal du Conseil* 54, 507.

O'Meara, J. (ed.). 1982. *Giraldus Cambrensis (Gerald of Wales). The History and Topography of Ireland (Topographia Hibernia)*. Portlaoise. Dolmen Press.

Orford, J.D. and Carter, R.W.G. 1982. Geomorphological changes on the barrier coasts of South Wexford. *Irish Geography* 15, 70–84.

Ormerod, S.J. and Perry, K.W. 1985. The diet of breeding Dippers and their nestlings in north-west Ireland. *Irish Birds* 3, 90–95.

O'Sullivan, A. 1973. Discussion. P. 19. In: O'Gorman, F. and Wymes, E. (eds) *The Future of Irish Wildlife – A Blueprint for Development*. Dublin. An Foras Talúntas.

O'Sullivan, A.M. 1982. The lowland grasslands of Ireland. Pp. 131–142. In: White, J. (ed) *Studies on Irish Vegetation*. Dublin. Royal Dublin Society.

O'Sullivan, B., Keady, S., Keane, E., Irwin, S. and O'Halloran, J. 2010. Data mining for biodiversity prediction in forests. *Frontiers in Artificial Intelligence and Applications* 215, 289–294.

O Sullivan, O. 2009. Garden Bird Survey in *Wings* Nov. 2009. Birdwatch Ireland.

Owen, M., Atkinson-Willes, G.L. and Salmon, D.G. 1986. *Wildfowl in Great Britain*. 2nd Edition. Cambridge. Cambridge University Press.

Parkin, D.T. and Knox, A.G. 2010. *The Status of Birds in Britain and Ireland*. London. Christopher Helm.

Parmesan, C. 2006. Ecological and evolutionary responses to recent climate change. *Annual Review of Ecology, Evolution and Systematics* 37, 637–669.

Parmesan, C. and Yohe, G. 2003. A globally coherent fingerprint of climate change impacts across natural systems. *Nature* 421, 37–42.

Parr, S.J. 1994. Changes in the population size and nest sites of Merlins *Falco columbarius* in Wales between 1970 and 1991. *Bird Study* 41, 42–47.

Parry, M.L., O.F. Canziani, J.P. Palutikof, P.J. van der Linden, C.E. Hanson, Eds, 2007. *Climate Change 2007: Impacts, Adaptation and Vulnerability. Contribution of Working Group II to the Fourth Assessment Report of the Intergovernmental Panel on Climate Change*. Cambridge. Cambridge University Press.

Partridge J.K. 1988a. *Northern Ireland Breeding Wader Survey. Final Report 1987*. Sandy. RSPB.

Partridge, J.K. 1988b. *Northern Ireland Breeding Wader Survey, Final Report.* Sandy. RSPB.

Partridge, J.K. 1988c. *The Lough Erne decline in an all-Ireland context.* Unpublished report to DoE(NI), Sandy. RSPB.

Partridge J.K. and Smith K.W. 1992. Breeding wader populations in Northern Ireland, 1985–87. *Irish Birds* 4, 497–518.

Pearce-Higgins, J.W. 2010. Using diet to assess the sensitivity of northern and upland birds to climate change. *Climate Research* 45, 119–130.

Pearce-Higgins, J.W. 2011. Modelling conservation management options for a southern range-margin population of Golden Plover *Pluvialis apricaria* vulnerable to climate change. *Ibis* 153, 345–356.

Pearce-Higgins, J.W. and Gill, J.A. 2010. Unravelling the mechanisms linking climate change, agriculture and avian population declines. *Ibis* 152, 439–442.

Pearce-Higgins, J.W. and Grant, M.C. 2006. Relationships between bird abundance and the composition and structure of moorland vegetation. *Bird Study* 53, 112–125.

Pearce-Higgins, J.W., Stephen, L., Langston, R.H.W. and Bright, J.A. 2008. Assessing the cumulative impacts of wind farms on peatland birds: a case study of Golden Plover *Pluvialis apricaria* in Scotland. *Mires and Peat* 4, Article 01, 1–13.

Pearce-Higgins, J.W., Stephen, L., Langston, R.H.W., Bainbridge, I.P. and Bullman, R. 2009. The distribution of breeding birds around upland wind farms. *Journal of Applied Ecology* 46, 1323–1331.

Pearce-Higgins, J.W. and Yalden, D.W. 2004. Habitat selection, diet, arthropod availability and growth of a moorland wader: the ecology of European Golden Plover *Pluvialis apricaria* chicks. *Ibis* 146, 335–346.

Pearce-Higgins, J.W., Yalden, D.W. and Whittingham, M.J. 2005. Warmer springs advance the breeding phenology of golden plover *Pluvialis apricaria* and their prey (Tipulidae). *Oecologia* 143, 470–476.

PECBMS. 2009. *State of Europe's Common Birds, 2008.* Prague. CSO/RSPB.

Penk, M., Brophy, J. and Nash, R. 2009. Implications for the natural heritage of Ireland's coast and inland waterways. Pp. ??–??. In: Kelly, B. and Stack, M. (eds.) *Climate Change, Heritage and Tourism: Implications for Ireland's coast and inland waterways.* Kilkenny. Heritage Council, Failte Ireland.

Peñuelas, J. and Filella, I. 2001. Responses to a warming world. *Science* 294, 793–795.

Peñuelas, J., Filella, I. and Comas, P. 2002. Changed plant and animal life cycles from 1952–2000 in the Mediterranean region. *Global Change Biology* 8, 531–544.

Perrin, P.M., O'Hanrahan, B., Roche, J.R. and Barron, S.J. 2009. *Scoping Study and Pilot Survey for a National Survey and Conservation Assessment of Upland Vegetation and Habitats in Ireland.* Unpublished report to National Parks and Wildlife Service, Department of Environment, Heritage and Local Government, Dublin.

Perrins, C.M. 1979. *British Tits.* London. Collins.

Perrins, C.M 1985. *The effect of Man on the British avifauna*: pages 5 to 29 in Bunning, L.J (Ed.) Proceedings of the Birds and Man Symposium. Witwatersrand Bird Club. Johannesburg.

Perry, K.W. 1983. Population changes of Dippers in north-west Ireland. *Irish Birds* 2, 272–277.

Perry, K.W. 1986. *The Irish Dipper.* Belfast. Privately published.

Perry, K.W. 2000. The ecology and conservation of great crested grebe *Podiceps cristatus* at Lough Neagh, Northern Ireland. Unpublished Ph.D. thesis. University of Ulster, Coleraine.

Perry, K.W. 2006. Whimbrel *Numenius phaeopus* – a new breeding species for Ireland? Observations from Connaught in May–June 2005. *Irish Birds* 8, 142–145.

Perry, K.W. and Agnew, P. 1993. Breeding Dipper populations in north-west Ireland, 1972–1992. *Irish Birds* 5, 45–48.

Perry, K.W., Antoniazza, M. and Day, K.R. 1998a. Abundance and habitat use by breeding Great Crested Grebes *Podiceps cristatus* at Lough Neagh (Northern Ireland) and at Lake Neuchâtel (Switzerland). *Irish Birds* 6, 269–276.

Perry, K.W. and Speer, A. 2003. A review of the breeding productivity of Sandwich Terns in 2003 in northern Co. Donegal: the 18th annual report on breeding performance at tern colonies in Mulroy Bay and Lough Swilly. Report to *Dúchas*, The Heritage Service.

Perry, K.W. and Speer, A. 2004. A review of habitat management and breeding productivity of Sandwich Terns in northern Co. Donegal: the 19th annual report on breeding performance at tern colonies in Mulroy Bay and Lough Swilly. Report to National Parks and Wildlife.

Perry, K.W., Wells, J.H. and Smiddy, P. 1998b. Recent increases in range and abundance of Ruddy Ducks *Oxyura jamaicensis* in Ireland, 1995–98. *Irish Birds* 6, 217–222.

Pettitt, G. 1965. The Atlantic Sea-watch. *Sea-Bird Bulletin* 1, 28–31.

Phalan, B. and Nairn, R.G.W. 2007. Disturbance to waterbirds in South Dublin Bay. *Irish Birds* 8, 223–230.

Philippart, C.J.M. (ed) 2007. *Impacts of climate change on the European marine and coastal environment: ecosystems approach.* ESF Marine Board Position Paper. Strasbourg. European Science Foundation, Marine Board.

Phillips, J.H. 1965. Movements of Atlantic Seabirds at Erris Head in the autumn. *Sea-Bird Bulletin* 1, 26–27.

Piatt, J.F. and Nettleship, D.N. 1985. Diving depths of four alcids. *The Auk* 102, 293–297.

Pierce, S. and Roe, J. 2006. Merlins *Falco columbarius* hunting at a small marine island. *Irish Birds* 8, 79–84.

Pierce S. & Wilson J. 1980. Spring migration of Whimbrels over Cork Harbour. *Irish Birds* 1, 514–516.

Pitkin, P.H. 1977. *Distribution and biology of algae.* Pp. 32–37. In: Jeffrey, D.W. *North Bull Island, Dublin Bay – a modern coastal natural history.* Dublin. Royal Dublin Society.

Pithon, J.A., Moles, R. and O'Halloran, J. 2005. The influence of coniferous afforestation on lowland farmland bird communities in Ireland: different seasons and landscape contexts. *Landscape and Urban Planning* 71, 91–103.

PLANFORBIO programme, 2007–2012. Check full reference.

Pohler, T. 1996. Studies of dispersion patterns and habitat relationship of breeding bird species on raised bogs of the Atlantic type in Central Ireland – Impact of drainage measures. Ph.D. Thesis. Braunschweig, Germany. Zoological Institute Technical University of Braunschweig.

Pollock, C.M. 1994. Observations on the distribution of seabirds off south-west Ireland. *Irish Birds* 5: 173–182.

Pollock C.M. and Barton, C. 2008. A Gap Analysis of Irish Waters using the European Seabirds at Sea (ESAS) database. *Irish Wildlife Manuals Report to the National Parks and Wildlife Service.*

Pollock, C.M. and O'Halloran, J. 1995. The winter behaviour of the Moorhen *Gallinula chloropus* L., (Gruiformes: Rallidae) at Cork Lough. *Biology and Environment: Proceedings of the Royal Irish Academy.* 95, 59–64.

Pollock C.M., Reid, J.B., Webb, A. and Tasker M.L. 1997. *The distribution of seabirds and cetaceans in the waters around Ireland.* Aberdeen. Joint Nature Conservation Committee. Report No 267.

Prater, A.J. 1981. *Estuary Birds of Britain and Ireland.* Calton. Poyser.

Preston, K. 1976. Census of Great Crested Grebes, Summer 1975. *Irish Bird Report* 1975, 38–43.

Preston, K. 1979. Twenty-sixth Irish Bird Report, 1978. *Irish Birds* 1, 413–449.

Price, R. and Robinson, J.A. 2008. The persecution of kites and other species in 18th century Co. Antrim. *Irish Naturalists' Journal* 29, 1–6.

Price, T.D., Qvarnstrom, A. and Irwin, D.E. 2003. The role of phenotypic plasticity in driving genetic evolution. *Proceedings of the Royal Society of London, B: Biological Sciences* 270, 1433–1440.

Pritchard, D.E. 1982. The feeding distribution of shorebirds at Strangford Lough and possible impact of a barrage. *Irish Birds* 2, 176–188.

Prosser C., Fernandez D. and Denniston H. 2008. *Shannon Callows Breeding Wader Research Project – Interim Report.* Unpublished report BWI/NPWS.

Pulido, F. 2007. Phenotypic changes in spring arrival: evolution, phenotypic plasticity, effects of weather and condition. *Climate Research* 35, 5–23.

Quigley, M. (ed) 1991. *A Guide to the Sand Dunes of Ireland*. Galway. European Union for Dune Conservation and Coastal Management.

Quinn, A.C.M. 1977. *Sand dunes: Formation, erosion and management.* Dublin. An Foras Forbartha.

Quinn, J.L. and Kirby, J.S. 1993. Oystercatchers feeding on grasslands and sand flats in Dublin Bay. *Irish Birds* 5, 35–44.

Rackham, O. 1995. Looking for ancient woodland in Ireland. Pp. 1–12. In: Pilcher, J.R., Mac an tSoir, S. (Eds), *Wood's, trees and forests in Ireland*. Dublin. Royal Irish Academy.

Raine, R., O'Mahony, J., McMahon, T. and Roden, C. 1990. Hydrography and phytoplankton of waters off south-west Ireland. *Estuarine, Coastal and Shelf Science* 30, 579–592.

Ranwell, D.S. 1972. *Ecology of Salt-marshes and Sand-dunes*. London. Chapman & Hall.

Ranwell, D.S. and Boar, R. 1986. *Coast Dune Management Guide*. Huntingdon. Institute of Terrestrial Ecology.

Ratcliffe, N., Newton, S.F., Morrison, P., Merne, O., Cadwallender, T. and Frederiksen, M. 2008. Adult survival and breeding dispersal of Roseate Terns within the northwest metapopulation. *Waterbirds* 31, 320–329.

Ratcliffe, N. Nisbet, I. and Newton, S. 2004. *Sterna dougallii* Roseate Tern. *BWP Update* 6 (1–2), 77–90.

Raven, S.J. and Coulson, J.C. 2001. Effects of cleaning a tidal river of sewage on gull numbers: a before-and-after study of the River Tyne, northeast England. *Bird Study* 48, 48–58.

Rebecca, G.W. and Bainbridge, I.P. 1998. The breeding status of the Merlin *Falco columbarius* in Britain in 1993–94. *Bird Study* 45, 172–187.

Redpath, S., Madders, M., Donnelly, E., Anderson, B., Thirgood, S., Martin, A. and McLeod, D. 1998. Nest site selection by Hen Harriers in Scotland. *Bird Study* 45, 51–61.

Redpath, S.M. and Thirgood, S.J. 1997. *Birds of Prey and Red Grouse*. London. Stationery Office.

Redpath, S. and Thirgood, S. 1999. Numerical and functional responses in generalist predators: Hen Harriers and Peregrines on Scottish grouse moors. *Journal of Animal Ecology* 68, 879–892.

Redpath, S., Thirgood, S. and Clarke, R. 2002. Field Vole *Microtus agrestis* abundance and Hen Harrier *Circus cyaneus* diet and breeding in Scotland. *Ibis* 144, E33–E38.

Reed, T.E., Kruuk, L.E., Wanless, S., Frederiksen, M., Cunningham, E.J. and Harris, M.P. 2008. Reproductive senescence in a long-lived seabird: rates of decline in late-life performance are associated with varying costs of early reproduction. *The American Naturalist* 171, 89–101.

Reed, T.M., Barret, C., Barret, J., Hayhow, S. and Minshull, B. 1985. Diurnal variability in the detection of waders on their breeding grounds. *Bird Study* 32, 71–74.

Rehfisch, M.M., Austin, G.E., Freeman, S.N, Armitage, M.J.S. and Burton, N.H.K. 2004. The possible impact of climate change on the future distributions and numbers of waders on Britain's non-estuarine coast. *Ibis* 146 (Supplement1), 70–81.

Reid, J.M., Cresswell, W., Holt, S., Mellanby, R.J., Whitfield, D.P. and Ruxton, G.D. 2002. Nest scrape design and clutch heat loss in Pectoral Sandpipers (*Calidris melanotos*). *Functional Ecology* 16, 305–312.

Rennick, A.R., Massimino, D., Newson, S.E., Chamberalin, D.E., Pearce-Higgins, J.W. and Johnson, A. (In press) Modelling changes in species abundance in response to projected climate change. *Biodiversity Research*.

Renou-Wilson, F., Bolger, T., Convery, F., Curry, J., Wilson, D., Ward, S. and Müller, C. 2010. *BOGLAND – a protocol for the sustainable management of peatlands in Ireland*. Strive EPA report 2004-CD-P1-M2. Johnstown Castle, Wexford. Environmental Protection Agency.

Reynolds, J. (ed.). 1996. *The Conservation of Aquatic Systems*. Dublin. Royal Irish Academy.

Reynolds, J. (ed.). 1998. *Ireland's Freshwaters*. Dublin. Marine Institute.

Richie, W. 2001. Coastal dunes: resultant dynamic position as a conservational managerial objective. Pp. 1–16. In: Houston, J.A., Edmondson, S.E. and Rooney, P.J. (eds.) 2001. *Coastal Dune Management: Shared experience of European Conservation Practice*. Liverpool. Liverpool University Press.

Riddiford, N. and Findlay, P. 1981. *Seasonal movements of summer migrants*. BTO Guide No. 18. Tring. British Trust for Ornithology.

Ridgway, M. and Hutchinson, C. (eds.). 1990. *The Natural History of Kilcolman*. Kilcolman. Privately published.

Risely, K., Noble, D.G. and Baillie, S.R. 2009. *The Breeding Bird Survey 2008*. Thetford. British Trust for Ornithology.

Robertson, A., Jarvis, A.M. and Day, K.R. 1995. Habitat selection and foraging behaviour of Chough *Pyrrhocorax pyrrhocorax* in Co. Donegal. *Biology and Environment: Proceedings of the Royal Irish Academy* 95B, 69–74.

Robinet, C. and Roques, A. 2010. Direct impacts of recent climate warming on insect populations. *Integrative Zoology* 5, 132–142.

Robinson, J.A., Colhoun, K., McElwaine, J.G. and Rees, E.C. 2004a. *Bewick's Swan Cygnus columbianus bewickii (Northwest Europe population) in Britain and Ireland 1960/61–1999/2000*. Waterbird Review Series, The Wildfowl & Wetlands Trust/Joint Nature Conservation Committee.

Robinson, J.A., Colhoun, K., Gudmundsson, G.A.,Boertmann, D., Merne, O.J., O'Briain, M., Portig, A.A., Mackie, K., Boyd, H. 2004b. *Light-bellied Brent Goose Branta bernicla hrota (East Canadian High Arctic population) in Canada, Ireland, Iceland, Greenland, France, the Channel Islands, Britain and Spain 1960/61 – 1999/2000*. Slimbridge. WWT/JNCC Waterbird Review Series.

Robinson, J.A., Gudmundsson, G.A., Clausen, P. 2006. Flyways of the East Canadian High Arctic Light-bellied Brent Goose *Branta bernicla hrota*: results of a satellite telemetry study. P. 519. In: Boere, G.C., Galbraith, C.A. and Stroud, D.A. (eds.) Edinburgh. The Stationery Office.

Robinson, R.A. 2005. *Birdfacts: species profiles of birds occurring in Britain and Ireland*. Thetford. British Trust for Ornithology.

Rochford, J.M. 1988. *Breeding bird communities of the Clonmacnoise Heritage Zone Study 1987*. Unpublished Report to the Clonmacnoise Heritage Zone Study.

Rodriguez, A., Andren, H. and Jansson, G. 2001. Habitat-mediated predation risk and decision making of small birds at forest edges. *Oikos* 95, 383–396.

Rodwell, J.S. (ed) 1991–2000. *British Plant Communities*. Volumes 1–5. Cambridge. Cambridge University Press.

Ronayne, S. 2010. *Aspects of the breeding ecology of the Little Egret (Egretta garzetta) in South-Eastern Ireland*. Unpublished M. Sc. thesis. University College Cork.

Roos, S., Humphreys, L., Wernham, C. and Burton, N. 2010. *Informing appropriate assessment of the Pentland Firth strategic area leasing round. Ornithology scoping report*. Thetford. British Trust for Ornithology.

Rosenzweig, M.L. 1995. *Species diversity in space and time*. Cambridge. Cambridge University Press.

Round, P.D. and Moss, M. 1984. The waterbird populations of three Welsh rivers. *Bird Study* 31, 61–68.

Rowe, E. 2005. *Avian diversity along an Urban – Rural gradient.* Unpublished BSc thesis. Cork. University College, Cork.

Roy, D.B. and Sparks, T.H. 2000. Phenology of British butterflies and climate change. *Global Change Biology* 6, 407–416.

Roycroft, D., Cronin, M., Mackey, M., Ingram, S. and Ó Cadhla, O. 2006. Risk assessment for marine mammal and seabird populations in south-western Irish waters (R.A.M.S.S.I.). Cork. Coastal and Marine Resources Centre, University College Cork.

Roycroft, D., Kelly, T.C. and Lewis, L.J. 2004a. Birds, seals and the suspension culture of mussels in Bantry Bay, a non-seaduck area in Southwest Ireland. *Estuarine Coastal Shelf Science* 61, 703–712.

Roycroft, D., Kelly, T.C. and Lewis, L.J. 2004b. Behavioural interactions of seabirds with suspended mussel longlines. *Aquaculture International* 15, 25–36.

Roycroft, D., Kelly, T.C. and Lewis, L.J. 2007. Behavioural interactions of seabirds with suspended mussel longlines. *Aquaculture International* 15, 25–36.

Roycroft, D. and Sleeman, D.P. 2008. Further observations on birds in Irish farmyards in winter. *Irish Birds* 8, 433–434.

Ruddock, M., Dunlop, B.J., O'Toole, L., Mee, A. and Nagle, T. 2011. *Republic of Ireland Hen Harrier survey 2010.* Unpublished report by the Irish Raptor Study Group and the Golden Eagle Trust Ltd for the Department of Environment, Heritage and Local Government.

Ruttledge, R.F. 1966. *Ireland's Birds.* London. Witherby.

Ruttledge, R.F. 1968. The kingfisher population. *Irish Bird Report* 15, 11–14.

Ruttledge, R.F. 1983. The breeding range of the blackcap in western Ireland. *Irish Birds* 2, 294–302.

Ruttledge, R.F. 1987. The breeding distribution of the Common Scoter in Ireland. *Irish Birds* 3, 417–426.

Ruttledge, R.F. 1989. *Birds in Counties Galway and Mayo.* Dublin. Irish Wildbird Conservancy.

Ruttledge, R.F. and Ogilvie, M.A. 1979. The past and current status of the Greenland White-fronted Goose in Ireland and Britain. *Irish Birds* 1, 293–363.

Ryall, C. and Briggs, K. 2006. Some factors affecting foraging and habitat of Ring Ouzels *Turdus torquatus* wintering in the Atlas Mountains of Morocco. *Bulletin of the African Bird Club* 13, 17–31.

Ryan, T.D. 1986. Agricultural drainage practices in Ireland. *Environmental, Geological and Water Science* 9, 31–40.

Saino, N. and Ambrosini, R. 2008. Climatic connectivity between Africa and Europe may serve as a basis for phenotypic adjustment of migration schedules of trans-Saharan migratory birds. *Global Change Biology* 14, 250–263.

Saino, N., Ambrosini, R., Rubolini, D., von Hardenberg, J., Provenzale, A., Hüppop, K., Hüppop, O., Lehikoinen, A., Lehikoinen, E., Rainio, K., Romano, M. and Soklolov, L. 2010. Climate warming, ecological mismatch at arrival and population decline in migratory birds. *Proceedings of the Royal Society* 10B, 1–8.

Scannell, M.J.P. and Synnott, D.M. *Census Catalogue of the Flora of Ireland.* Dublin. Stationery Office.

Scott, D. 1999. Short-eared Owl *Asio flammeus* breeding in Northern Ireland in 1997. *Northern Ireland Bird Report* 1997, 108–110.

Scott, D. 2000. Marking a decade of tree nesting by Hen Harriers *Circus cyaneus* in Ireland, 1991–2000. *Irish Birds* 6, 596–599.

Scott, D., Scott, L. and McHaffie, P. 2009. Unexpected breeding of the Marsh Harrier *Circus aeruginosus* in County Down, during 2009. *Irish Birds* 8, 625–627.

Scott, D., Wetch, D., van der Wal, R. and Elston, D.A. 2007. Response of the moss *Racomitrium lanuginosum* to changes in sheep grazing and snow-lie due to a snow fence. *Applied Vegetation Science* 10, 229–238.

Scott, R. 2004. *Wild Belfast: On safari in the city.* Belfast. Blackstaff Press.

Scott, R. 2011. Living alongside people: Urban and industrial habitats. In: Faulkner, J. and Thompson, R. (eds.) *The Natural History of Ulster.* Holywood. National Museums Northern Ireland.

Sealy, S.G., O'Halloran, J. and Smiddy, P. 1996. Cuckoo hosts in Ireland. *Irish Birds* 5, 381–390.

Sergeant, D.W. 1952. Little Auks in Britain, 1948 to 1951. *British Birds* 45: 122–133.

Shaffer, S.A., Tremblay, Y., Weimerskirch, H., Scott, D., Thompson, D.R., Sagar, P.M., Moller, H., Taylor, G.A., Foley, D.G. and Block, B.A. 2006. Migratory shearwaters integrate oceanic resources across the Pacific Ocean in an endless summer. *Proceedings of the National Academy of Sciences* 103, 127–99.

Sharrock, J.T.R. 1969. Grey Wagtail passage and population fluctuations in 1956–67. *Bird Study* 16, 17–34.

Sharrock J.T.R. 1973. Sea-watching. Pp. 141–146. In: Sharrock, J.T.R. (ed.) *The Natural History of Cape Clear Island.* Berkhamstead. Poyser.

Sharrock, J.T.R. 1976. *The Atlas of Breeding Birds in Britain and Ireland.* Berkhamsted. Poyser.

Shawyer, C.R. 1998. *The Barn Owl.* Wheathampstead. Arlequin Press.

Shealer, D.A. 2002. Foraging behaviour and food of seabirds. Pp. 137–177. In: Schreiber, E.A., Burger, J. (eds.) *Biology of Marine Birds.* London, CRC Press.

Sheldon, B.C. 2010. Genetic perspectives on the evolutionary consequences of climate change in birds. Pp. 149–168. In: Møller, A.P., Fiedler, W. and Berthold, P. (eds) *Effects of climate change on birds.* London. Oxford University Press.

Sheppard, J.R. 1978. The Breeding of the Goosander in Ireland 1978. *Irish Birds* 1, 224–228.

Sheppard, R. 1993. *Ireland's Wetland Wealth – the birdlife of the estuaries, lakes, coasts, rivers, bogs and turloughs of Ireland.* Dublin. Irish Wildbird Conservancy.

Sim, I.M.W., Burfield, I.J., Grant, M.C., Pearce-Higgins, J.W. and Brooke, M. de L. 2007a. The role of habitat composition in determining breeding site occupancy in a declining Ring Ouzel *Turdus torquatus* population. *Ibis* 149, 374–385.

Sim, I.M.W., Dillon, I.A., Eaton, M.A., Etheridge, B., Lindley, P., Riley, H., Saunders, R., Sharpe, C. and Tickner, M. 2007b. Status of the Hen Harrier *Circus cyaneus* in the UK and Isle of Man in 2004, and a comparison with the 1988/89 and 1998 surveys. *Bird Study* 54, 256–267.

Sim, I.M.W., Rollie, C., Arthur, D., Benn, S., Booker, H., Fairbrother, V., Green, M., Hutchinson, K., Ludwig, S., Nicoll, M., Poxton, I.,Rebecca, G., Smith, L., Stanbury, A. and Wilson, P. 2010. The decline of the Ring Ouzel in Britain. *British Birds* 103, 229–239.

Simberloff, D., 2009. The role of propagule pressure in biological invasions. *Annual Review of Ecology, Evolution and Systematics* 40, 81–102.

Singer, M.C. and Parmesan, C. 2010. Phenological asynchrony between herbivorous insects and their hosts: signal of climate change or pre-existing adaptive strategy? *Philosophical transactions of the Royal Society of London, Series B Biological Sciences* 365, 3161–3176.

Sirami, C., Brotons, L., Burfield, I., Fonderflick, J. and Martin, J.-L. 2008. Is land abandonment having an impact on biodiversity? A meta-analytical approach to bird distribution changes in the north-western Mediterranean. *Biological Conservation* 141, 450–459.

Sleeman, D.P., Roycroft, D. and Buckley, D.J. 2006. Birds observed in winter cattle housing in County Cork. *Irish Birds* 8, 141.

Smiddy, P. 1977. The feeding and roosting of ducks and waders at Ballymacoda, Co. Cork. *Cork Bird Report* 1976, 38–41.

Smiddy, P. 1992. The waterfowl of Ballymacoda, Co. Cork. *Irish Birds* 4, 525–548.

Smiddy, P. 1996. Badgers preying on nestling birds. *Irish Naturalists' Journal* 25, 224–225.

Smiddy, P. 1998. Cormorant *Phalacrocorax carbo* breeding numbers in Waterford, east Cork and mid Cork. *Irish Birds* 6, 213–216.

Smiddy, P. 2000. Short-eared Owls *Asio flammeus* hunting from perch and predating nest of Meadow Pipit *Anthus pratensis*. *Irish Birds* 6, 596.

Smiddy, P. 2001. *The Wildlife Wonders of Youghal*. Youghal. Ballyvergan Marsh Committee.

Smiddy, P. 2002. Breeding of the Little Egret *Egretta garzetta* in Ireland, 1997–2001. *Irish Birds* 7, 57–60.

Smiddy, P. 2003. Storm Petrels *Hydrobates pelagicus* nesting under Ling Heather *Calluna vulgaris*: a clarification. *Irish Birds* 7, 267.

Smiddy, P. 2005. Breeding waterfowl at Ballycotton, County Cork, 1960–2004. *Irish Birds* 7, 497–502.

Smiddy, P. 2008. The site characteristics and use of nests of the Barn Swallow (*Hirundo rustica* L.). *Irish Naturalists' Journal* 29, 107–110.

Smiddy, P. 2010a. A systematic list of Irish Birds. *Irish Birds* 9, 130–134.

Smiddy, P. 2010b. Roosting by Barn Swallows (*Hirundo rustica*) and Sand Martins (*Riparia riparia*) in fields of Maize (*Zea mays*) in Co. Cork. *Irish Naturalists' Journal* 31, 128–130.

Smiddy, P., Cullen, C. and O'Halloran, J. 2007a. Autumn use of a reedbed by Barn Swallows *Hirundo rustica* and Sand Martins *Riparia riparia* in County Cork. *Irish Birds* 8, 243–248.

Smiddy, P., Cullen, C. and O'Halloran, J. 2007b. Time of roosting of Barn Swallows *Hirundo rustica* at an Irish reedbed during autumn migration. *Ringing & Migration* 23, 228–230.

Smiddy, P. and O'Halloran, J. 1991. The breeding biology of Mute Swans *Cygnus olor* in southeast Cork, Ireland. *Wildfowl* 42, 12–16.

Smiddy, P. and O'Halloran, J. 1998. Breeding biology of the Grey Wagtail *Motacilla cinerea* in southwest Ireland. *Bird Study* 45, 331–336.

Smiddy, P. and O'Halloran, J. 2004. The ecology of river bridges: their use by birds and mammals. Pp. 83–97. In: Davenport, J. and Davenport, J.L. (eds.). *The Effects of Human Transport on Ecosystems: cars and planes, boats and trains*. Dublin. Royal Irish Academy.

Smiddy, P. and O'Halloran, J. 2006a. The waterfowl of Ballycotton, County Cork: population change over 35 years, 1970/71 to 2004/05. *Irish Birds* 8, 65–78.

Smiddy, P. and O'Halloran, J. 2006b. Ballycotton: habitat change and loss of wetland avian biodiversity, 1970–2004. *Cork Bird Report* 1996–2004, 309–318.

Smiddy, P. and O'Halloran, J. 2008. The distribution of waterfowl at Ballycotton, County Cork in relation to habitat and habitat change. *Irish Birds* 8, 351–358.

Smiddy, P. and O'Halloran, J. 2010. Breeding biology of Barn Swallows *Hirundo rustica* in Counties Cork and Waterford, Ireland. *Bird Study* 57, 256–260.

Smiddy, P., O'Halloran, J. and O'Mahony, B. 2000. The birds and mammals of Beginish and Youngs Island (Blaskets), Co. Kerry (1988–2001). *Irish Birds* 6, 593–596.

Smiddy, P., O'Halloran, J., O'Mahony, B. and Taylor, A.J. 1995. The breeding biology of the Dipper *Cinclus cinclus* in south-west Ireland. *Bird Study* 42, 76–81.

Smiddy, P. and O'Mahony, B. 1997. The status of the Reed Warbler *Acrocephalus scirpaceus* in Ireland. *Irish Birds* 6, 23–28.

Smiddy, P. and O'Sullivan, O. 1998. The status of Little Egret *Egretta garzetta* in Ireland. *Irish Birds* 6, 201–206.

Smith, A.A., Redpath, S.M., Campbell, S.T. and Thirgood, S.T. 2001. Meadow pipits, Red Grouse and the habitat characteristics of managed grouse moors. *Journal of Applied Ecology* 38, 390–400.

Smith, C. 1750. *The Antient and Present State of the County and City of Cork*. Dublin. Privately published.

Sparks, T.H., Bairlein, F., Bojarinova, J.G., Huppop, O., Lehikoinen, E.A., Rainio, K., Sokolov, L.V. and Walker, D. 2005. Examining the total arrival distribution of migratory birds. *Global Change Biology* 11, 22–30.

Sparks, T.H. and Tryjanowski, P. 2007. Patterns of spring arrival dates differ in two hirundines. *Climate Research*, 35, 159–164.

Speer, A. 2011. Nature Conservation. Pp 138-148. In: Cooper, A. (ed.) *Lough Swilly: A living landscape*. Dublin. Four Courts Press.

Stanbury A., O'Brien M. and Donaghy A. 2000. Trends in breeding wader populations in key areas within Northern Ireland between 1986 and 2000. *Irish Birds* 6, 513–526.

Steer, M. (ed.) 1991. *Irish Rivers: biology and management*. Dublin. Royal Irish Academy.

Stefanescu, C., Peñuelas, J. and Filella, I. 2003. Effects of climatic change on the phenology of butterflies in the northwest Mediterranean Basin. *Global Change Biology* 9, 1494–1506.

Stenseth, N.C. and Mysterud, A. 2002. Climate, changing phenology, and other life history traits: Non-linearity and match-mismatch to the environment. *Proceedings of the National Academy of Sciences, USA* 99, 13379–13381.

Stewart, D. 2005. Smart growth in Ireland: from rhetoric to reality. *Progress in Urban Studies* 1, 21–30.

Stillman, R.A. and Brown, A.F. 1994. Population sizes and habitat associations of upland breeding birds in the South Pennines, England. *Biological Conservation* 69, 307–314.

Stirnemann, R.L., O'Halloran, J., Ridgway, M. and Donnelly, A. (in press) Can wintering conditions determine the phenology of whooper swan (*Cygnus cygnus*)? *Ibis*.

Stoate, C., Szczur, J. and Aebischer, N.J. 2009. Winter use of wild bird cover crops by passerines on farmland in northeast England. *Bird Study* 43, 320–332.

Stone, C.J., Webb, A. and Tasker, M.L. 1995. The distribution of auks and Procellariformes in north-west European waters in relation to depth of sea. *Bird Study* 42, 50–56.

Stroud, D.A., Chambers, D., Cook, S., Buxton, N., Fraser, B., Clement, P., Lewis, P., McLean, I., Baker, H., Whitehead, S. 2001. *The UK SPA network: its scope and content. Volume 3: Site accounts*. Peterborough. JNCC.

Stroud, D.A., Reed, T.M., Pienkowski, M.W. and Lindsay, R.A. 1987. *Birds, bogs and forestry: The peatlands of Caithness and Sutherland*. Peterborough. Nature Conservancy Council.

Suddaby, D., Gamero, A., McNaghten, L., Thompson, L. and Newton, S.F. 2008. Research of breeding Dunlin *Calidris alpina* ecology associated with machair and upland NATURA 2000 sites in NW Mayo. *Irish Birds* 8, 483–484.

Suddaby, D., Nelson, T. and Veldman, J. 2009. Resurvey and comparative changes of breeding wader populations of Irish machair and associated wet grasslands in 2009. *Irish Birds* 8, 533–542.

Suddaby, D., Nelson, T. and Veldman, J. 2010. *Resurvey of breeding wader populations of Machair and associated wet grasslands in north-west Ireland*. Irish Wildlife Manuals, No. 44. Dublin. National Parks and Wildlife Service, Department of the Environment, Heritage and Local Government.

Sutherland, W.J. and Hill, D.A. 1995. *Managing Habitats for Conservation*. Cambridge. Cambridge University Press.

Sutherland, W.J., Newton, I. and Green, R.E. 2004. *Bird Ecology and Conservation: a handbook of techniques*. Oxford. Oxford University Press.

Sweeney, O.F.McD., Wilson, M.W., Irwin, S., Kelly, T.C. and O'Halloran, J. 2010a. Are bird density, species richness and community structure similar between native woodlands and non-native plantations in an area with a generalist bird fauna? *Biodiversity & Conservation* 19, 2329–2342.

Sweeney, O.F.McD., Wilson, M.W., Irwin, S., Kelly, T.C. and O'Halloran, J. 2010b. Breeding bird communities of second rotation plantations at different stages of the forest cycle. *Bird Study*, 57, 301–314.

Sweeney, O.F.McD., Martin, R.D., Irwin, S., Kelly, T.C., O'Halloran, J., Wilson, M.W. and McEvoy, P.M. 2010c. A lack of large-diameter logs and snags characterises dead wood patterns in Irish forests. *Forest Ecology and Management* 259, 2056–2064.

Sweeney, O.F.M., Wilson, M.W., Irwin, S., Kelly, T.C. and O'Halloran, J. in press. Vegetation and structural factors influencing winter bird density and diversity in Irish forests, and comparisons with breeding season patterns. *Bird Study*.

Tansley, A.G. 1949. *The British Islands and their Vegetation*. Volumes 1 and 2. Cambridge. Cambridge University Press.

Tasker, M.L. 2000. The UK and Ireland seabird monitoring programme – a history and introduction. *Atlantic Seabirds* 2, 97–102.

Taylor, A.J. and O'Halloran, J. 1997. The diet of the Dipper *Cinclus cinclus* as represented by faecal and regurgitated pellets: a comparison. *Bird Study* 44, 338–347.

Taylor, A.J. and O'Halloran, J. 1999. The decline of the Corn Bunting (*Miliaria calandra*) in the Republic of Ireland, with reference to other seed eating birds. Kilkenny. The Heritage Council.

Taylor, A.J. and O'Halloran, J. 2001. Diet of Dippers *Cinclus cinclus* during an early winter spate and the possible implications for Dipper populations subjected to climate change. *Bird Study* 48, 173–179.

Taylor, A.J. and O'Halloran, J. 2002. The decline of the Corn Bunting, *Miliaria calandra*, in the Republic of Ireland. *Biology and Environment: Proceedings of the Royal Irish Academy* 102B, 165–175.

Taylor, I.R. 1994. *Barn Owls: Predator – Prey Relationships and Conservation*. Cambridge. Cambridge University Press.

Teunissen, W., Schekkerman, H., Willems, F. & Majoor, F. 2008. Identifying predators of eggs and chicks of Lapwing *Vanellus vanellus* and Black-tailed Godwit *Limosa limosa* in the Netherlands and the importance of predation on wader reproductive output. *Ibis* 150 (Supplement 1), 74–85.

Thackeray, S.J., Sparks, T.H., Frederiksen, M., Burthe, S., Bacon, P.J., Bell, J.R., Botham, M.S., Brereton, T.M., Bright, P.W., Caravalho, L., Clutton-Brock, T., Dawson, A., Edwards, M., Elliott, J.M., Harrington, R., Johns, D., Jones, I.D., Jones, J.T., Leech, D.I., Roy, D.B., Scott, W.A., Smith, M., Smithers, R.J., Winfield, I.J. and Wanless, S. 2010. Trophic level asynchrony in rates of phenological change for marine, freshwater and terrestrial ecosystems. *Global Change Biology* 16, 3304–3313.

Thomas, G.J. 1980. The ecology of breeding waterfowl at the Ouse Washes, England. *Wildfowl* 31, 73–88.

Thomas, G.J. 1982. Autumn and winter feeding ecology of waterfowl at the Ouse Washes, England. *Journal of Zoology* 197, 131–172.

Thomas, R.J., Drewitt, J.A., Kelly, D.J., Marples, N.M and Semple, S. 2003. Nocturnal playbacks reveal hidden differences in singing behaviour between populations of the Robin *Erithacus rubecula*: birds subjected to playbacks of conspecific song strongly by day in both Wales and Ireland and strongly at night only in Wales. *Bird Study* 50, 84–87.

Thompson, D.B.A. and Brown, A. 1992. Diversity in montane Britain: habitat variation, vegetation diversity and some objectives for conservation. *Biodiversity and Conservation* 1, 179–208.

Thompson, D.B.A. and Whitfield, D.P. 1993. Research Progress Report. *Scottish Birds* 17, 1–8.

Thompson, W. 1849–1850. *Natural History of Ireland*. Reeves. London.

Thorpe, J. 2003. Fatalities and Destroyed Civil Aircraft due to Bird Strikes 1912–2002. *Proceedings of International Bird Strike Committee* 26, 87–115.

Thorpe, J. 2005 Fatalities and Destroyed Civil Aircraft due to Bird Strikes 2002–2004 *Proceedings of International Bird Strike Committee* 27, 65–94.

Thorpe, J. 2010. Update on fatalities and destroyed civil aircraft due to bird strikes with appendix for 2008 and 2009. *Proceedings of International Bird Strike Committee* 29, in press.

Thorup. O. 2006. *Breeding Waders in Europe 2000*. International Wader Studies, Vol. 14. UK. International Wader Study Group.

Tickner, M. 1990. *A vegetation and breeding bird survey of Lower Lough Erne islands*. Unpublished Report, Reserves Ecology Department. Sandy. RSPB.

Tierney, T.D., Dunne, J. and Callanan, T. 2000. The Common Scoter *Melanitta nigra nigra* breeding in Ireland, range expansion or site relocation. *Irish Birds* 6, 447–452.

Tierney, T.D., Hudson, J. and Casey, C. 2002. Survey of breeding waders on the River Shannon Callows, 2002. *Irish Birds* 7, 21–32.

Tosh, D., Lusby, J., Montgomery, W. and O'Halloran, J. 2008. First record of Greater White-toothed Shrew *Crocidura russula* in Ireland. *Mammal Review* 38, 321–326.

Tøttrup, A.P., Rainio, K., Coppack, T., Lehikoinen, E., Rahbek, C. and Thorup, K. 2010. Local temperature fine-tunes the timing of spring migration in birds. *Integrative and Comparative Biology* 50/3, 293–304.

Trewby, M., Gray, N., Cummins, S., Thomas, G. and Newton, S. 2006. *The status and ecology of the Chough* Pyrrhocorax pyrrhocorax *in the Republic of Ireland, 2002-2005*. BirdWatch Ireland Final Report to the National Parks and Wildlife Service.

Trewby, M., Thomas, G. and Newton, S. 2004a. *The distribution and feeding ecology of the Chough in south-west Cork. September 2003 to August 2004*. BirdWatch Ireland Report.

Trewby, M., Thomas, G. and Newton, S. 2004b. The distribution and feeding ecology of the chough in Kerry. September 2003 to August 2004. BirdWatch Ireland Report.

Troake P. & Suddaby D. 2008. Monitoring and measuring breeding parameters of Lapwing and other waders at selected NATURA 2000 sites in N.W. Mayo. Report by BirdWatch Ireland.

Tubridy, M. 1987. *The Heritage of Clonmacnoise*. Environmental Sciences Unit in association with County Offaly Vocational Education Committee.

Tucker, G.M. and Evans, M.I. 1997. *Habitats for Birds in Europe: a conservation strategy for the wider environment*. BirdLife Conservation Series No. 6. Cambridge. BirdLife International.

Tucker, G.M. and Heath, M.F. 1994. *Birds in Europe: Their conservation status*. BirdLife Conservation Series No. 3. Cambridge. BirdLife International.

Tucker, G. 2004. The burning of uplands and its effect on wildlife. *British Wildlife* 15, 251–257.

Turner, A.K. 2006. *The Barn Swallow*. London. Poyser.

Twomey, F. and McGettigan, T. 2009. *Lovely flows the Lee*. Dublin. Woodpark Publications.

Tyler, S.J. 1979. Mortality and movements of Grey Wagtails. *Ringing & Migration* 2, 122–131.

Tyler, S.J. and Ormerod, S.J. 1994. *The Dippers*. London. Poyser.

Underhill, M.C., Gittings, T., Callaghan, D.A., Hughes B., Kirby, J.S. and Delany, S. 1998. Status and distribution of breeding Common Scoters *Melanitta nigra nigra* in Britain and Ireland 1995. *Bird Study* 45, 146–156.

Ussher, R.J. 1905. Common Scoter breeding in Ireland. *Irish Naturalist* 14: .

Ussher, R.J., More, A.G. 1894. Report on the breeding-range of birds in Ireland. *Proceedings of the Royal Irish Academy* (1889–1901) 3, 401–414.

Ussher, R.J. and Warren, R. 1900. *Birds of Ireland*. London. Gurney and Jackson.

Vähätalo, A.V., Rainio, K., Lehikoinen, A. and Lehikoinen, E. 2004. Spring arrival of birds depends on the North Atlantic Oscillation. *Journal of Avian Biology* 35, 210–216.

Väisänen, R.A. and Järvinen, O. 1977. Structure and fluctuation of the breeding bird fauna of a north Finnish peatland area. *Ornis Fennica* 54, 143–153.

Van Asch, M. and Visser, M.E. 2007. Phenology of forest caterpillars and their host trees: the importance of synchrony. *Annual Review of Entomology* 52, 37–55.

Van Bushkirk, J. and Willi, Y. 2004. Enhancement of farmland biodiversity within set-aside land. *Conservation Biology* 18, 987–994.

Village, A. 1990. *The Kestrel*. Calton. Poyser.

Visser, M.E., Adriaensen, F., van Balen, J.H., Blondel, J., Dhondt, A.A., van Dongen, S., du Feu, C., Ivankina, E.V., Kerimov, A.B., de Laet, J., Matthysen, E., McClerry, R., Orell, M. and Thomson, D.L. 2003. Variable responses to large-scale climate change in European *Parus* populations. *Proceedings of the Royal Society of London Series B – Biological Sciences* 270, 367–372.

Visser, M.E. and Both, C. 2005. Shifts in phenology due to global climate change: The need for a yardstick. *Proceedings of the Royal Society of London Series B – Biological Sciences* 272, 2561–9.

Visser, M.E., Both, C. and Lambrechts, M.M. 2004. Global climate change leads to mistimed avian reproduction. *Advances in Ecological Research* 35, 89–110.

Visser, M.E., van Noordwij, A. J., Tinbergen, J. M. and Lessells, C.M. 1998. Warmer springs lead to mistimed reproduction in great tits (*Parus major*). *Proceedings of the Royal Society of London, B: Biological Sciences* 265, 1867–1870.

Voisin, C. 1991. *The Herons of Europe*. London. Poyser.

von dem Bussche, J., Spaar, R., Schmid, H. and Schroder,B. 2008. Modelling the recent and future spatial distribution of the Ring Ouzel (*Turdus torquatus*) and Blackbird (*T. merula*) in Switzerland. *Journal of Ornithology* 149, 529–544.

Votier. S., Bearhop, S., Witt, M., Inger, R., Thompson, D. and Newton, J. 2010. Individual responses of seabirds to commercial fisheries revealed using GPS tracking, stable isotopes and vessel monitoring systems. *Journal of Applied Ecology* 47: 487–497.

Walsh, A.J. and Crowe, O. 2008. Barnacle Geese *Branta leucopsis* in Ireland, spring 2008. *Irish Birds* 8, 430–432.

Walsh, P.M., O'Halloran, J., Kelly, T.C. and Giller, P.S. 2000. Assessing and optimizing the influences of plantation forestry on bird diversity in Ireland. *Irish Forestry* 57, 2–10.

Wanless, S., Harris, M.P. and Morris, J.A. 1991. Foraging range and feeding locations of shags *Phalacrocorax aristotelis* during chick rearing. *Ibis* 133, 30–36.

Watson, A. 1957. The behaviour, breeding, and food ecology of the Snowy Owl *Nyctea Scandica*. *Ibis* 99, 419–462.

Watson, A. and O'Hare, P.J. 1979a. Bird and mammal numbers on untreated and experimentally treated Irish bog. *Oikos* 33, 97–105.

Watson, A. and O'Hare, P.J. 1979b. Red Grouse populations on experimentally treated and untreated Irish Bog. *Journal of Applied Ecology* 16, 452–533.

Watson, A and O'Hare, P.J. 1980. Dead sheep and scavenging birds and mammals on Mayo bog. *Irish Birds* 1, 487–491.

Watson, P.S. 1978. Seabirds at commercial trawlers in the west Irish Sea. *Ibis* 120, 107.

Watson, P.S. 1981. Seabird observations from commercial trawlers in the Irish Sea 1968–1975. *British Birds* 74, 82–90.

Watson, P.S. 1984. *Blackwater Habitat and Bird Surveys*. Belfast. Royal Society for the Protection of Birds & Ulster Trust for Nature Conservation.

Wells, J. 2007. The *Northern Ireland Peregrine population 1977–2007*. P. 57. In: Abstracts of the Peregrine conference, Poland, 2007.

Wernham, C.V., Toms, M.P., Marchant, J.H., Clark, J.A., Siriwardena, G.M. and Baillie, S.R. (eds.) 2002. *The Migration Atlas: movements of the birds of Britain and Ireland*. London. Poyser.

Wesołowski, T. and Fuller, R.J. in press. Spatial variation and temporal shifts in habitat use by birds at the European scale. In: Fuller, R.J. (ed). *Birds and Habitat: Relationships in Changing Landscapes*. Cambridge. Cambridge University Press.

Wetlands International. 2006. *Waterbird Population Estimates*. Fourth Edition. Wageningen, The Netherlands.

Wheater, C.P. 1999. *Urban Habitats*. London. Routledge.

Whilde, A. 1978. A Survey of gulls breeding inland in the West of Ireland in 1977 and 1978 and a review of the inland breeding habit in Ireland and Britain. *Irish Birds* 1, 134–159.

Whilde, A. 1985. The 1984 All Ireland Tern Survey. *Irish Birds* 3, 1–32.

Whilde, A. 1993. *Irish Red Data Book 2: Vertebrates*. Belfast. HMSO.

Whilde, A., Cotton, D.C.F. and Sheppard, J.R. 1993. A repeat survey of gulls breeding inland in Counties Donegal, Sligo, Mayo and Galway, with recent counts from Leitrim and Fermanagh. *Irish Birds* 5, 67–72.

Whilde T. 1990. *Birds of Galway*. Galway Branch, Irish Wildbird Conservancy.

Whiteside, L., McDevitt, A-M, Colhoun, K., Bolton, M. and Robinson, J. 2008. *Lapwing Recovery Project Northern Ireland, Progress Report 2006–08*. Belfast. RSPB, Northern Ireland Office.

Whitfield, D.P. 2002. Status of breeding Dotterel *Charadrius morinellus* in Britain in 1999. *Bird Study* 49, 237–349.

Whittingham, M.J., Percival, S.M. and Brown, A.F. 2001. Habitat selection by Golden Plover *Pluvialis apricaria* chicks. *Basic and Applied Ecology* 2, 177–191.

Wikelski, M., Spinney, L., Schelsky, W., Scheuerlein, A. and Gwinner, E. 2003. Slow pace of life in tropical sedentary birds: a common-garden experiment on four Stonechat populations from different latitudes. *Proceedings of the Royal Society of London* 270, 2383–2388.

Wilcock, D.N. 1997. Rivers, drainage basins and soils. Pp. 85–98. In: Cruickshank, J.G. (ed.) *Soil and Environment: Northern Ireland*. Belfast. Agricultural & Environmental Science Division, DANI and Agricultural & Environmental Science Department, Queens University.

Williams, B., Walls, S., Walsh, M. and Bleasdale, A. 2009. Proposing an efficient indicator of grazer distribution on heterogeneous hill vegetation. *Applied Ecology and Environmental Research* 7, 341–358.

Williams, G., Newson, M. and Browne, D. 1988. Land drainage and birds in Northern Ireland. *RSPB Conservation Review* 2, 72–77.

Wilson, A.M., Ausden, M. and Milsom, T.P. 2004. Changes in breeding wader populations on lowland wet grasslands in England and Wales: causes and potential solutions. *Ibis* 146 (Supplement 2), 32–40.

Wilson, A.M., Vickery, J.A. Brown, A., Langston, R.H.W., Smallshire, D., Wotton, S. and Vanhinsbergh, D. 2005. Changes in the numbers of breeding waders on lowland wet grasslands in England and Wales between 1982 and 2002. *Bird Study* 52, 55–69.

Wilson, F. Goodbody, R. and Nairn, R. 2004. *Dublin City Graveyards Study*. A report for Dublin City Council.

Wilson, H.J. 1977. Some breeding bird communities of sessile oak woodlands in Ireland. *Polish Ecological Studies* 3, 245–256.

Wilson, H.J. 1990. Birds of raised bogs. Pp. 29–36. In: Cross, J.R. (ed.) *The raised bogs of Ireland*. Dublin. Unpublished report to the Minister of State of the Department of Finance.

Wilson, J. 2002. *The Birds of Irish Bog*. IPCC Information Sheet. Vol. 2006. Irish Peatland Conservation Council. (Website: www.ipcc.ie/infobogbirdsfs.html accessed 28/2/2010).

Wilson, J., O'Mahony, B., Smiddy, P. 2000. Common Terns *Sterna hirundo* nesting in Cork Harbour. *Irish Birds* 6, 597–599.

Wilson, J.D., Taylor, R. and Muirhead, L.B. 1996. Field use by farmland birds in winter: an analysis of field type preferences using resampling methods. *Bird Study* 43, 320–33.

Wilson, Jr., W.H., Zierzow, R.E. and Savage, A.R. 1998. Habitat selection by peatland birds in a central Maine bog: The effects of scale and year. *Journal of Field Ornithology* 69, 540–548.

Wilson, J.G. 1982. The littoral fauna of Dublin Bay. *Irish Fisheries Investigations Series B (Marine)* No 26, 1–19.

Wilson, J.G. and Emblow, C. 2002. Biodiversity of macrofauna on sandy and muddy shores. Pp. 5–14. In: Nunn, J.D. (ed.) *Marine biodiversity in Ireland and adjacent waters*. Belfast. Ulster Museum.

Wilson, M.W., Gittings, T., Kelly, T.C., O'Halloran, J. 2010. The importance of non-crop vegetation for bird diversity in Sitka spruce plantations in Ireland. *Bird Study* 57, 116–120.

Wilson, M.W., Irwin, S., Norriss, D.W., Newton, S.F., Collins, K., Kelly, T.C. and O'Halloran, J. 2009. The importance of pre-thicket conifer plantations for nesting Hen Harriers *Circus cyaneus* in Ireland. *Ibis* 151, 332–343.

Wilson, M.W., Pithon, J., Gittings, T., Kelly, T.C., Giller, P.S. and O'Halloran, J. 2006. The effects of growth stage and tree species composition on breeding bird assemblages of plantation forests. *Bird Study* 53, 225–236.

Winfield, D.K, Davidson, R.D. and Winfield, I.J. 1989. Long term trends (1965–1988) in the numbers of waterfowl overwintering on Lough Neagh and Lough Beg, Northern Ireland. *Irish Birds* 4, 19–42.

Woodland Trust, The. 2007. *Back on the Map: An inventory of ancient and long-established woodland for Northern Ireland*. Preliminary report. Bangor. The Woodland Trust.

Worden, J.P., Cranswick, A., Crowe, O., McElwaine, G. and Rees. E.C. 2006. Numbers and distribution of Bewick's Swan *Cygnus columbianus bewickii* wintering in Britain and Ireland: results of international censuses, January 1995, 2000 and 2005. *Wildfowl* 50, 3–22.

Wotton, S.R., Langston, R.H.W. and Gregory, R.D. 2002. The breeding status of the Ring Ouzel *Turdus torquatus* in the UK in 1999. *Bird Study* 49, 26–34.

Yalden, D.W. and Carthy, R.I. 2004. The archaeological records of birds in Britain and Ireland compared: extinctions or failures to arrive? *Environmental Archaeology* 9, 123–126.

Index

Pictures are indicated by page numbers in bold.

Abbeyshrule (Co Longford) 43
Africa 6, 102, 142, 168, 180, 188, 237, 253
alder 74, 87, 106
All Saint's Bog (Co Offaly) 76
Altan Lough (Co Donegal) **57**
America see North America; South America
American mink 28, 35, 36, 38, 48–9, 50, 54, 66, **146**, 146–7, 216
Annagh Marsh (Co Mayo) **219**, 219–20
annual glasswort 176
annual seablite 176
Antrim Road waterworks (Belfast) 206
Aran Islands (Co Galway) 143, 148, 153
Arctic Skua 141, 191, 254
Arctic Tern 51, 148, 150, 151, 155, 157, 175, 176, **179**, 179, **182**, 182, 191, 209, 230
Arklow Head (Co Wicklow) 209
Arrow, Lough (Co Sligo) 48
ash 11–12, 21, 106, 225
Atlantic Pond (Cork) 205, 206
Atlantic Puffin 138, 143, 146, **147**, 147, 150–51, 182, 185, 186, 187, 188, 189, **190**, 190–91, 216, **242**, **249**, 255
Atlas Mountains 102
Auk see Common Guillemot, Black Guillemot, Little Auk, Razorbill
Austria 237

badger 28, 101
Balbriggan (Co Dublin) 200
Baldoyle (Co Dublin) 204
Baldoyle Bay (Co Dublin) 159, 178
Balearic Shearwater 190, 193
Balleally Landfill (Co Dublin) 210
Ballinacor (Co Wicklow) **105**
Ballycotton (Co Cork) 82, 83, 85, 153
Ballyhoura Mountains (Co Cork/Limerick) 85, 96, 221
Ballylee, Lough (Co Galway) 56
Ballymacoda (Co Cork) 162, 167
Ballynacarrigy (Co Longford) 43
Ballyness Bay (Co Donegal) 156
Ballysadare Bay (Co Sligo) 171
Ballyvergan Marsh (Co Cork) 83, 85–7, 258
Baltray (Co Louth) 154
Banduff (Co Sligo) **127**
Bangor, (Co Down) **22**, 22, **148**, 212, **230**, 230–31
bank vole 96, 215
Bann Estuary (Co Derry) 171
Bannow Bay (Co Wexford) 156, 167, 178
Bantry Bay (Co Cork) 22
Barn Owl 124, 125, **135**, 135–6, 199, 215, 256, 258

Barn Swallow 22, 85, **86**, 86, 126, 128, 133, 134, **136**, 180, 208, **235**, 235, 236, 248, 252, 256, 257
barnacle 149
Barnacle Goose 149–50, **150**, 159, 165
Barrow, River 25, 29
Bar-tailed Godwit **16**, 17, 56, 156, **158**, 167, 168, 172, 177
bat see Daubenton's bat
Beara Peninsula (Co Cork) 102
Bearded Reedling 84
Beg, Lough 48, 52–3, 64, 66, 68
Beginish (Co Kerry) 147
Belfast 197, 198–9, 200, 201, 202, 204, 206, 212
Belfast Harbour 151, 209
Belfast Lough 167, 171, 175, 178, **229**, 229–30, 243
Belfield (Dublin) 21–2, 204
Belgium 238–9
Bellacorick flush (Co Mayo) 79–80
Benbulben (Co Sligo) **124**
Benwisken (Co Sligo) 100
Berney Marshes (Norfolk) 72
Bewick's Swan 5, 53, 70–71, **128**, 217, 241, **253**
Białowieża forest (Poland) 23
bilberry 90, 102
birch 74, 80, 106, 224
bird's-foot trefoil 159
Bittern see Great Bittern
Black Grouse 109
Black Guillemot **22**, 22, 142, **148**, 148, 151, 175, 187, 212, 214, **230**, 230–31
black rat 147
Black Redstart 212
Black Tern 157
Black-backed Gull see Great Black-backed Gull; Lesser Black-backed Gull
Blackbird 19, 32–3, 43, 77, 80, 81, 87, 110, 121, 128, 130, 132, 133, 134, 161, 162, 200, 202, **206**, 207, 250, 252, 254
Blackcap 40, 108, 111, 121, 202, 203, 207, 224, **237**, 237, 250
Black-headed Gull 21, **23**, 39, 49, 50–51, **51**, 57, 78, 88, 130, 143, **155**, 155, 156, 179, 205, **206**, **208**, 208, 211, 251
Black-legged Kittiwake 50, 143, 144, **145**, 145, 147, **151**, 151, 182, **185**, 185, 187, 188, 190, 191, 195, 212
Black-necked Grebe 57, 83
Blackrock Lighthouse (Co Mayo) 183
Black-tailed Godwit 2, 15, 17, 22, 38, 56, 65, **69**, 69–70, 167, **168**, 168, 172, 175, **180**, 180, 205, 209, 218, 253
blackthorn 161, **224**, 224

Black-throated Diver 191
Blackwater Callows (Co Waterford/Cork) **61**, 62, 69
Blackwater Cutaway Bog (Co Offaly) 81
Blackwater, River (Munster) 24, 28, 29, 30, 31, 32, 35, 36–7, 38, 39, 40
Blackwater, River (Northern Ireland) 28, 29, 30, 32, 35, 36
Blasket Islands (Co Kerry) 138, 147, 150, 187
Bloody Foreland (Co Donegal) 153
blue mussel 149
Blue Tit 2, 20, 22, 110, 117, 119, 121, 130, 134, 200, **201**, 201, 207, 214, **238**, 239, 250
Bluestack Mountains (Co Donegal) 101
bog cotton **73**
bog myrtle 97
Bohemian Waxwing 15, 202, 207
Bonaparte's Gull 157, 205
Boora (Co Offaly) 132, 225–6
Boyne Estuary (Co Louth/Meath) 167, 171, 177
Boyne, River 24, 28–9, 30, 31, 32, 35, 36–7, 39, 40
bracken 97, 99, 140, 159, 160
bramble 97, 106, 140, 161, 224–5
Brambling 201, 202
branched bur-reed 66
Brandon Creek (Co Kerry) 141
Brandon Head (Co Kerry) 191, 192, 193
Bray Harbour (Co Wicklow) **206**
Bray Head (Co Wicklow) 146, 148
Bray Head (Valentia Island) 141
Brent Goose 21, **126**, 126, **158**, 159, 167, 168, 172, **173**, 173–4, **177**, 177, 179, 180, **204**, 204–5, 210, 212, 215, 242, 244, 251, 252, 253, **256**, **256**
Bride, River (Co Cork) 39
Bridges of Ross (Co Clare) 151, **183**, 191, 193
Brierfield Turlough (Co Roscommon) 57
Britain 41–2, 49, 52, 71, 82, 84, 88, 91, 92, 95, 97, 98–9, 108, 109, 136, 142, 151, 153, 168, 207, 208, 237, 238–9, 240–41, 248, 252–3, 254, 255, 258; see also England; Scotland; Wales
Brittas Bay (Co Wicklow) 156
broad-leaved pondweed 58
Broadmeadow Estuary (Co Dublin) 167
brown rat 147, 199
brown sedge 69
Bull Rock (Co Cork) 145
Bullfinch 121, 135, 202, 207
Bullock Harbour (Co Dublin) **245**
bulrush 83
Bunduff Lough (Co Sligo) 44
Bunting see Corn Bunting; Reed Bunting; Snow Bunting

burnet rose 159, 160
Burren (Co Clare) **106**, 107
Bush, River (Co Antrim) 38
Bushy Park (Dublin) 202–3
buttercup see creeping buttercup
Buzzard see Common Buzzard

caddis fly **34**, 34
Canada 168, 180, 192, 253
Canada Goose see Greater Canada Goose
Cape Clear see Clear Island (Co Cork)
Capercaillie 109
Carlingford Lough (Co Louth/Down) 167, 171, 175
Carnsore Point (Co Wexford) 153, 160, 161
Carrowbehy Bog (Co Roscommon) 75, 77
Castlemaine Harbour (Co Kerry) 156, 171, 173, 178
cattle 94, 100, 219–20, 227
Cattle Egret 241
Cetti's Warbler 84, 120
Chaffinch 16, 43, 80, 81, 111, **113**, 113, 121, 128, 129, 130, 132, 135, 137, 160, 161, 202, 204, 206, 207, 250
Charleville (Co Cork) 208
Charleville Castle (Co Offaly) **11**
Chiffchaff 2, 40, 80, 87, 111, 121, 202
Chough 94, 101, **102**, 102, 124, 125, 127, 135, 139, 140–41, **141**, 151, 153, 162, 164, 209, 214–15, **251**, 251, 256
Clara Bog (Co Offaly) 75, 76–8
Clare Island (Co Mayo) 143, 145
Clare River (Co Galway) 29
Clear Island (Co Cork) 30, 69, 183, 191, 193
Clew Bay (Co Mayo) 153
Clifden (Co Galway) 170
Cliffs of Moher (Co Clare) 138
Clogher Head (Co Louth) 212
Clonmacnoise (Co Offaly) **60**, 66
Clonmel (Co Tipperary) 26
Clonsast Bog (Co Offaly) 81
clover see white clover
Coal Tit **11**, 11, 20, 21, **107**, 108, 111, 113–14, 117, 121, 130, 134, 200, 202, 204, 207, 254
Cobh (Co Cork) 198
cockle 158
Collared Dove 134, 207, 250
Comeragh Mountains (Co Waterford) 101
Common Buzzard 22, **114**, 114, 137, 141, 201, 203, **255**, 255
Common Coot 36, 38, 40, 41, 46, 53, 54, 83, 202, 203, 206
Common Crane 82
Common Crossbill 21, 108, 114, 203
Common Cuckoo 85, 88, 121, 235
Common Eider 149, 155, 178
common glasswort 175, 176
Common Goldeneye 52, 53, 54, 80, 178, 206
Common Grasshopper Warbler 40, 66, 67, 76, 79, 80, 84, 88, **89**, 89, 112, 121, 235
Common Greenshank 56
Common Guillemot 144, 145, 146, 147, 187, 188, 189, **194**
Common Gull 21, 50, 57, 147, 155, 156, 205, 211

Common Kestrel 75, 76, 77, 80, 85, 108, 134, 135, 136, **141**, 141, 155, 162, 201, 202, 209, **214**, 214, 215
Common Kingfisher 27–9, **28**, 36, 37, 40, 41, 43, 202, **203**, 203, 205, 206, 214, **215**, 215, 247
Common Pheasant 122, **128**, 128, 129, 130, 131, 134, 211, 216, 249
Common Pochard 38, 47, **52**, 52, 53, 55, 57, 65, 66, 80, 83, 205, 206, 253
Common Quail 66, 219
Common Redshank 15, **16**, **17**, 17, 38–9, **56**, 56, 57, 60, 63, **64**, 64, 66, 71, 76, 77, 78, 80, 81, 88, 89, 149, 155, 156, 164, 167, **168**, 168, 172, 175, 176, 177, 205, 212, 215, **218**, 218, 220, 240, **243**, **244**, 251
Common Redstart 19, 23, 108, 109, 110, 212
common reed 74, 83, 216
Common Reed Warbler 39, 83–4, 85, 88, 89, 241, 258
common saltmarsh grass 175, 177
Common Sandpiper 36, **39**, 39, 41, 51, 57, 81, 247
Common Scoter 48, 48, 59, 178, 216, 257
common scurvygrass 176
Common Shelduck 2, 48, 161–2, 167, **172**, 172
Common Snipe 38–9, 40, 56, 60, 63, **64**, 64–5, 66, 69, 71, 75, 76–8, 79, 80, 81, **88**, 88, 89, 92, 94, 126, 129, 130, 131, 163, 164, 205, 207, 214, 252
common spike rush 66, 69
Common Starling 21, 22, 80, 86–7, **87**, 89, 126, 130, 131, 133, 135, 137, **199**, 199, 200, 203, 206, 207, 208, 210, 211, 236, 249, 250
Common Swift 23, 134, **198**, 198, 200, 202, 208, 214, 235, 250
Common Teal 37, 47, 54, 55, 56, 57, 65, 66, 69, 80, 88, 168, 172, 177, 205, 209
Common Tern 50–51, **51**, **148**, 148, 150, 151, 154, 155, 157, **174**, 175, 176, 179, 187, 188, 209, 229, 230, 252
Common Whitethroat 19, 40, 80, 112, 122, 235
Conn, Lough (Co Mayo) 48, 66
Coole/Garryland turlough complex (Co Galway) 56
Coot see Common Coot
Copeland Islands (Co Down) 142
cord grass 176, 216
Cork city **196**, 197, 198, 200, **202**, 205–6, 210, **217**
Cork Harbour 68, 69, 167, 171, 175, 178, 243
Cork Lough **205**, 205–6, 258
Cormorant see Great Cormorant
Corn Bunting 124, 137, 215
Corncrake **2**, 2, 4, 18, 61, 62, 65, 66, 67, 71, 124, **125**, 125, 127, 137, 178, 213, 218–19
Corrib, Lough (Co Galway) 45, 48, 50, 51, **52**, 52, 53, 59, 62, 66
Corrib, River (Co Galway) 24, 206, 208
Cory's Shearwater **190**, 190, 193, 255
cotton grass 78, 126
Coy, Lough (Co Galway) 56
Crake see Spotted Crake
Crane see Common Crane
creeping bent grass 69, 70

creeping buttercup 70
creeping willow 160
Crested Tit 109, 120
Crom Estate (Co Fermanagh) 224–5
Crossbill see Common Crossbill
cross-leaved heath 90
Crow see Hooded Crow
crowberry 90
Cruninish Island (Lough Erne) 62
Cuckoo see Common Cuckoo
Cuilcagh Mountain (Co Leitrim) **222**, 222
Cull and Killag (Co Wexford) 167
Cullin, Lough (Co Mayo) 48
curled dock 66, 69
Curlew Sandpiper 56
Curlew see Eurasian Curlew
Cutra, Lough (Co Galway) 50

dab 172
Dalkey (Co Dublin) 148
Dargan Road Landfill (Belfast) 211
Daubenton's bat 257
Deenish Island (Co Kerry) 147, 150
deer sedge 126
deer see fallow deer
Derg, Lough (Co Donegal) 50
Derg, Lough (Shannon) 45, 47, 50, 52, 54, 64, 66
Dernish Island (Lough Erne) 62
Derravaragh, Lough (Co Westmeath) 52
Derry 197, 199, 201
Derrynane (Co Kerry) 156
Derryveagh Mountains (Co Donegal) 101, 103
Dingle Peninsula (Co Kerry) 102, 170
Dipper 2, 17, 22, 27, 31–5, **31**, **32**, **34**, 36, 40, 41, 43, 202, 203, 205, 206, 214, **247**, 247, 255
Diver see Black-throated Diver; Great Northern Diver; Red-throated Diver
dock see curled dock; golden dock
Dodder Linear Park (Dublin) 205
Dodder, River (Co Dublin) **31**, 202, 203
Donegal Bay 156
Donnell, Lough (Co Clare) 170
Doolough Turlough (Co Galway) 56
Dotterel 92, 93
Dove see Collared Dove; Rock Dove; Stock Dove
Drogheda (Co Louth) 200, 210
Dromore Wood (Co Clare) 106
Drumcliff Bay (Co Sligo) 171
Dublin 196, 197, 198, 199–200, 201–5, 250
Dublin Bay 156–8, 159, **166**, 167, 171, 175, 205, 215, 243
Dublin Port 151, **174**, 175, 212, 243
Duck see Mandarin Duck; Ruddy Duck; Tufted Duck; White-headed Duck
Dun Laoghaire (Co Dublin) 202, 212
Dundalk Bay (Co Louth) 156, 167, 171, 177, 178
Dundrum Bay (Co Down) 153, 156, 171
Dungarvan (Co Waterford) 153, **158**, 158
Dungarvan Harbour (Co Waterford) 156, 167
Dunkellin River (Co Galway) 29, 31, 35, 36, 56, 75, 77, 78
Dunlin 15, **16**, 17, 38, 56, 57, 63, 65, 92, **94**, 94, **148**, 148, **153**, 155, 156, 157, **158**, 158, 163, **164**, 164, 168, 172, **174**, 175, 187, 216, 217,

240, 240, **244**, 253
Dunloy Bog (Co Antrim) 75
Dunmore East (Co Waterford) 142, **151**, 151, 200, 212
Dunnock 19, 80, 81, 121, 130, 132, 133, 134, 161, 202, 207
Duvillaun Beg (Co Mayo) 155, 165
dwarf eelgrass 173

Eagle *see* Golden Eagle; White-tailed Eagle
earthworm 21, 69, 215
East Coast Nature Reserve (Co Wicklow) **220**, 220–21
eel *see* sand eel
eelgrass *see* dwarf eelgrass; marine eelgrass; narrow-leaved eelgrass
Egret *see* Cattle Egret; Little Egret
Eider *see* Common Eider
elder 144
England 4, 5, 29, 30, 39–40, 42, 49, 50, 65, 69, 72, 93, 99, 100, 150, 196; *see also* Britain
Erne, Lough (Lower) 45, 46, 48, 50, 51, 54, 59, **62**, 62, 63–4, 65, 72
Erne, Lough (Upper) 45, **46**, 47, 52, 53, 54, 62, 63, 64, 65, 68
Erriff Valley (Co Mayo) **3**
Estonia 226
Eurasian Curlew 2, **4**, 4, 15, **16**, 38–9, 56, 60, 63–4, 66, 69, 71, 75, 76–8, 79, 80, 81, 88, 89, 92, 94–5, 149, 155, 156, 168, 172, 175, 205, 218, 240, 242, 244, 249, 251, 253
Eurasian Nuthatch 4, 108, 109, 120, 254
Eurasian Treecreeper 2, **19**, 19, 20, 117, 122, 203, 250
Eurasian Whimbrel 54, 56, **68**, 68, 70, 88, 100, 149, 187, **252**, 252, 253
Eurasian Wigeon 5, 37, 54, **55**, 55, 56, 69, 70, 80, 172, **173**, 173, 174, 177, **180**, 205, 209, 242, 253, 256
European Golden Plover 2, **14**, 38, **54**, 54, 55, 56, 69, 75, 77, 88, 89, 92, **93**, 94, 129, 130, 149, 155, 167, 168, **169**, 172, 175, 177, 205, 211, 217, 222, 223, **239**, 239, 246, 251, 253
European Herring Gull 13, 21, 50, 144, 146, 155, 156, 176, **200**, 200–201, 210, 211, 257
European Robin **16**, 16, 19, 43, 77, 80, 81, 110, 113, 122, 125, 130, 132, 133, 134, 137, 161, **200**, 200, 202, 204, 207, **234**, 250, 255
European Storm Petrel 143, 147, **150**, 150–51, 155, 165, **181**, **188**, 188, 255

Faeroe Islands 150, 151, 168, 253
Fair Head (Co Cork) 141
fallow deer 224, 225
Fanore (Co Clare) 156
Fennoscandinavia *see* Scandinavia
Feral Pigeon 137, 140, 142, **198**, 198, 200, 204, **206**, 207, **212**, 250; *see also* Rock Dove
Fergus Estuary 167, 171, 177, 178, 243
Fermoy (Co Cork) 26
fescue *see* red fescue
Fieldfare 15, 40, 87, 130, 134, **159**, 162, 202, 207
fig *see* hottentot fig
Finland 88, 102, 240

Finn Lough (Co Offaly) 75
Firecrest 109, 120, 252
Flesk, River (Co Kerry) 29, 31, 32, 35, 36, 38, 39
floating sweet grass 69
flounder 172
Flycatcher *see* Pied Flycatcher; Spotted Flycatcher
Fortwilliam Turlough (Co Longford) 56
fox *see* red fox
Foxford (Co Mayo) 62
Foyle, Lough (Co Donegal/Derry) 127, 156, 159, 167, 171, 173, 177, 178, 243
France 49, 150, 226, 255
frog **84**
Fulmar 101, **143**, 143, 144, 182, **185**, 187, 188, **189**, 189, 190, **195**, 195, 209–10
Funshinagh, Lough (Co Roscommon) 57, 83

Gadwall **47**, 47, 57, 65, 66, 69, 80, 83, 179
Galley Head (Co Cork) 151, 191
Galway 197, 198, 199, 200, 203, 206, 207, 208
Galway Bay 156, 167, 171
Gannet *see* Northern Gannet
Garden Warbler 4, 108, 112, 224–5
Garganey 57, 70, 180
Germany 237
Giles Quay (Co Louth) 212
Gill, Lough (Co Kerry) 170
Gill, Lough (Co Sligo) **51**
glasswort *see* annual glasswort; common glasswort
Glaucous Gull 157, 211
Glen Head (Co Donegal) 141
Glenade (Co Leitrim) **103**
Glenamaddy (Co Mayo) 57
Glenarm (Co Antrim) 231
Glencolumbkille Peninsula (Co Donegal) 103, 142
Glendalough (Co Wicklow) **58**, 58
Glenveagh National Park (Co Donegal) 100, **111**, 116
Glenwhirry (Co Antrim) 64
Gobbins Cliffs (Co Antrim) 142
Godwit *see* Bar-tailed Godwit; Black-tailed Godwit
Goldcrest 21, 111, 113, 114, 117, **118**, 121, 134, 202, 204, 207, **254**, 254
golden dock 221
Golden Eagle 95, 101, 141, 255
Golden Plover *see* European Golden Plover
Goldeneye *see* Common Goldeneye
Goldfinch 76, 79, 80, 88, 130, 135, 177, 202, 206, **207**, 207
Goosander 38, 58, 247
Goose *see* Barnacle Goose; Brent Goose; Greater Canada Goose; Greater White-fronted Goose; Greylag Goose; Pink-footed Goose
gorse 96, 97, 106, 159, 161
Goshawk 108
Grand Canal **25**, 25, 203
Grasshopper Warbler *see* Common Grasshopper Warbler
Great Bittern 81–2, 89, 253
Great Black-backed Gull 50, 143, 144, 146, 155,

156, **185**, 187, 189
Great Blasket *see* Blasket Islands (Co Kerry)
Great Cormorant 38, **49**, 49–50, 54, **144**, 145, **146**, 146, 151, 155, 172, 173, **187**, 187, 188, 195, 203, 205, 206
Great Crested Grebe 46, **47**, 80, 82–3, **83**, 89, 178, 206
Great Northern Diver 22, 167, **187**, 187, 191–2
Great Ringed Plover **16**, 51, 81, **153**, 153–4, 155, 156, 157, 160, 163, 164, 168, 175, 176, 205, 240
Great Saltee (Co Wexford) **139**, 144, 145, 146, 147, 189, **249**
Great Shearwater 183, **190**, 190, 191, 193, 255
Great Skellig (Co Kerry) *see* Skellig Michael (Co Kerry)
Great Skua 143, 147, 150, 190, 191, 254, **255**
Great Spotted Woodpecker 5, 23, 109, **119**, 119–20, 201, 203, 250, 253, **258**, 258
Great Tit 2, 77, 110, 117, 119, 121, 134, 200, 201, 204, 207, 214, **238**, 238–9, 250
Greater Canada Goose 216, 258
Greater Scaup **52**, 52–3, 178
Greater White-fronted Goose 37, 55, 56, 58, 59, 69, 70, 78, **100**, 100, 126–7, 159, 167, 168, 170, 177, 221, 223, **227**, 227–8, 236, **243**, 244
greater white-toothed shrew 258
Grebe *see* Black-necked Grebe; Great Crested Grebe; Little Grebe
Green Sandpiper 39
Green Woodpecker 253
Greenfinch 76, 79, 80, 88, 121, 130, 135, 137, 177, 202, 204, 207, 250
Greenhills Park (Dublin) 204–5
Greenland 6, 150, 168, 180, 191, 192, 252
Greenshank *see* Common Greenshank
Grey Heron 38, **68**, 80, 83, **84**, 172, **178**, 178, **202**, 202, 203, 205, 206, 210, 211
Grey Partridge 80, 81, **82**, 89, 124, 132, 214, **225**, 225–6
Grey Phalarope 141, 193
Grey Plover 149
Grey Wagtail 22, 27, 29–31, **30**, 36, 40, 41, **42**, 42, 43, 130, 133, 134, 137, 202, 203, 206, 247, 255–6
Greylag Goose 37, 58, 127, 167, 177, 216, 258
Greystones (Co Wicklow) 205
Grouse *see* Black Grouse; Red Grouse; Willow Grouse
Guillemot *see* Black Guillemot; Common Guillemot
Gull *see* Black-headed Gull; Bonaparte's Gull; Common Gull; European Herring Gull; Glaucous Gull; Great Black-backed Gull; Iceland Gull; Laughing Gull; Lesser Black-backed Gull; Mediterranean Gull; Ring-billed Gull; Sabine's Gull; Thayer's Gull; Yellow-legged Gull
gutweed 174
Gweebarra Bay (Co Donegal) 156

haddock 185
hake 185
Hare Island (Lough Erne) **62**, 62

hare *see* mountain hare
Harrier *see* Hen Harrier; Marsh Harrier
hawthorn 117, 159, 161, 224
hazel 11–12, **106**, 106, 107, 225
heath *see* cross-leaved heath
heather 91, 95, 97, 102, 103, 140, 213; *see also* ling heather
heather-fern 95
hedgehog 155
Hen Harrier 80, 85, **86**, 92, 95, **96**, 96–7, 99, **114**, 115, 177, 213, 215, 222, 223, 242, 251, 255, 256
Heron *see* Grey Heron
herring 172, 185
Herring Gull *see* European Herring Gull
High Island (Co Galway) 147
holly 106, 224
Hooded Crow 7, 21, 71, 76, 77, 95, 126, 130, 135, 141, 146, 155, 200, 207, 248
Horse Island (Lough Erne) 62
hottentot fig 229
House Martin 133, 134, **142**, 142, 202, 235, 236
house mouse 199
House Sparrow 131, 132, 133, 135, 137, 200, 203, 206, 207, 249, 250
Howth (Co Dublin) 200
Howth Castle Demesne (Co Dublin) 203
Howth Deer Park (Co Dublin) **116**

Iceland 52, 54, 150, 168, 180, 253
Iceland Gull 157, 211
Inch Lough (Co Donegal) **179**, 179
Inch Strand (Co Kerry) 158, 161
Inishbofin (Co Galway) 140, 141, 142, 144
Inishglora (Co Mayo) 147, 155
Inishkea Islands (Co Mayo) 62–3, 140, 149–50, 164–5
Inishkeeragh (Co Mayo) 155
Inishmore (Aran Islands) 153
Inishmurray (Co Sligo) 147
Inishshark (Co Galway) 140, 141
Inishtearaght (Co Kerry) 140
Inishtrahull (Co Donegal) 140, 183
Inniscarra Reservoir (Co Cork) 52, **59**, 59
Ireland's Eye (Co Dublin) 145, 146
Iron, Lough (Co Westmeath) 53
Islandmagee (Co Antrim) 142
Iveragh Peninsula (Co Kerry) 102
ivy 142

Jack Snipe 69
Jackdaw 21, 80, **126**, 126, 128, 130, 133, 134, 137, 141, 201, 203, 207, 209, 249, 250
Japanese knotweed 207
Jay 19, 108, 121, 202, 250
jointed rush 70

Kebble Fen (Rathlin Island) 80
Kestrel *see* Common Kestrel
Kilcolman Wildfowl Refuge (Co Cork) 85, 221, **236**, 236
Kilcoole (Co Wicklow) 154, 178, 205
Kilcummin Head (Co Mayo) 151, 191, 193
Kilkenny 197

Killag *see* Cull and Killag (Co Wexford)
Killala Bay (Co Mayo/Sligo) 171
Killarney (Co Kerry) 36, 106
Killarney National Park (Co Kerry) 116, 216, 259
Killucan (Co Westmeath) 42
Killybegs (Co Donegal) 157
Kiltullagh Lough (Co Galway) 52
Kingfisher *see* Common Kingfisher
Kinsale Road Landfill (Cork) 205, **210**, 211
Kite *see* Red Kite
Kittiwake *see* Black-legged Kittiwake
Knot *see* Red Knot
knotgrass 66

Lady's Island Lake (Co Wexford) **170**, 170, 176, **179**, 179
Lagan Canal (Co Antrim) 25
Lagan, River (Co Antrim/Down) 24, 29, 30, 31, **35**, 35–6, 37–8, 39, 40
Lambay Island (Co Dublin) 142, 144, 145–6, 147, 149, 210
Lapwing *see* Northern Lapwing
Larne Lough (Co Antrim) 151, 171, 178
Latvia 254
Laughing Gull 157, 205
Laune, River (Co Kerry) 36, 37–8
Lavally River (Co Galway) 29, 31, 35, 36, 75, 77, 78
Leach's Storm Petrel 141, 147, 150, 183, 190, 193
Leane, Lough (Co Kerry) 45
leatherjackets 93
Lee, River (Co Cork) 24, 26
Lesser Black-backed Gull 50, 58, 78, 146, 156, 180, 187, 188, **189**, 189, 192, 200, 205, 251
Lesser Redpoll 40, 77, 87, 88, 111, **112**, 117, 121, 130, 135, 207
Lesser Spotted Woodpecker 109, 120, 253
Lesser Whitethroat 120
Lettermacaward (Co Donegal) 156
Licky, River (Co Waterford) 28
Liffey, River 24, **25**, 203
Light-bellied Brent Goose *see* Brent Goose
Limerick 197
ling heather **90**, 90, 140, 147
Linnet 19, 76, 77, 80, 111–12, 115, 121, 129, 130, **131**, 132, 135, 160, 161, 177, 202, 249
Little Auk 183
Little Brosna Callows (Co Offaly) 55, 62, 69, 70
Little Brosna River (Co Offaly/Tipperary) 68
Little Egret **5**, 5, 38, 56, 114, **176**, 178, **202**, 205, 206, 209, **240**, 241, 258
Little Grebe 35, 36, 38, 40, 46, 57, 80, 81, 202, 203, 205, 206, 251
Little Island (Waterford) 206
Little Ringed Plover 51
Little Skellig (Co Kerry) 145, 147, 151
Little Tern 143, 148, 153, **154**, 154–5, 156, 157, 165, 179
lodgepole pine 220
Long-eared Owl 114, 162, 200, 201
Long-tailed Skua 191, 192, 193
Long-tailed Tit 33, 87, **116**, 117, 121, 202, 207, 250

Loop Head (Co Clare) **138**
Loughros Bay (Co Donegal) 156
lugworm **4**, 15, 17
Lurgan Park (Belfast) 202
Lurgan Park Lake (Armagh) 49
lyme grass 160

MacGillycuddy's Reeks (Co Kerry) 102, 103
mackerel 172, 185
Madeiran Storm Petrel 183
Maghara (Co Donegal) **24**
Magpie 130, 131, 134, 200, 201–2, 204, 207
Maigue, River (Co Limerick) 28, 29, 31, 35, 36
Malahide Bay (Co Dublin) 159, 160, 173, 176
Malahide Demesne (Co Dublin) 203
Malin Head (Co Donegal) 183
Mallard 37, 40, **41**, 42, 43, 47, 49, 54, 57, **65**, 65–6, 75, 77, 79, 83, 88, 172, 202, 205, 206, 251
Mandarin Duck **37**, 38, 247
Manx Shearwater 141, 146, 147, 150–51, 182, **183**, **187**, 187, 188, 189, 190, 216, 255
marine eelgrass 173
Marlay Park (Dublin) 202
marram grass 159
Marsh Harrier 54, 82, 89
Marsh Tit 108, 109, 120, 253
Martin *see* House Martin; Sand Martin
Mask, Lough (Co Mayo) 46, 50, 66
mayfly 34
Maynooth (Co Kildare) 42
meadow grass *see* smooth meadow grass
Meadow Pipit 18, 22, 62, 66, **74**, 75, 76–8, 79, 80, 88, 96, **98**, 98–9, 101, 111, 117, 122, 129, 130, 131, 132, 134, 160, 161, 164, 176, 211, 213, 249, 255, 257
meadow sweet 74
Mediterranean Gull **5**, 143, 156, 179, 205, 241
Merganser *see* Red-breasted Merganser
Merlin **75**, 75, 81, 85, **95**, 95–6, 134, 177, 223, 242
Merrion Strand (Dublin Bay) 157, 159, 173
Middle Spotted Woodpecker 120
Millford (Co Donegal) 208
mink *see* American mink
Mistle Thrush 122, 129, 130, **133**, 133, 134, 207, 250
Moira (Co Antrim) **209**
Moira Demesne (Belfast) 202
Mongan Bog (Co Offaly) 76, 77, 80
moor-grass *see* purple moor-grass
Moorhen **35**, 35, 36, 38, 40, 42, 43, **46**, 46, 65, 66, 76, 79, 80, 83, 87, **88**, 88, **202**, 202, 203, 205, 206, 251
moss *see* woolly fringe moss
Mossvale (Co Down) 183
mountain hare 101
Mourne Mountains (Co Down) **136**
mouse *see* house mouse; wood mouse
Moy, River (Co Sligo/Mayo) 29, 31, 35, 36, 39, 62
Muckross Wood (Co Kerry) 106
Mulkear River (Co Limerick/Tipperary) 29, 31, 35, 36

Mullaghanish (Co Cork) **107**
Mullaghareirk Mountains (Co Kerry/Limerick/
  Cork) 96
Mullet (Co Mayo) 156
Mullingar (Co Westmeath) 42
Murlough (Co Down) 160, 161
Murrough (Co Wicklow) 153, 154–5, 220–21
mussel 22, 143, 149, 169, 178; *see also* blue
  mussel; zebra mussel
Mute Swan 36, **37**, 37, 40, 41–2, **42**, 43, **48**, 48,
  69, 76, 79, 80, 83, **84**, 167, 168, 179, **180**, 202,
  203, 205, **206**, 206, 208, 215–16, 250, 251,
  252, 256
Mutton Island (Co Galway) 153, 156

Nagles Mountains (Co Cork) 96
narrow-leaved eelgrass 173
Neagh, Lough 44, 45, 46, 47, 48, 49, 50, 51, 52–3,
  54, 58, 59, 64, 65, 66, 68, 82–3, 257, 258
Nephin Beg Mountains (Co Mayo) 101
Nephin More (Co Mayo) 93
Netherlands 49, 236, 238–9
Nethertown (Co Wexford) 158
Newcastle (Co Down) 38
Newport (Co Mayo) 38
Newry Canal 25
Nore, River 28, 29
North America 88
North Bull Island (Dublin Bay) 158, 159, 161,
  177, 177, 178, 204
Northern Diver *see* Great Northern Diver
Northern Gannet **145**, 145–6, 151, 182, **184**,
  185, **186**, 186, 187, 188, 189, 190, 195
Northern Lapwing **2**, 21, 38–9, 54, 56, 57, 60, 62,
  63, 63, 66, 69, 71, 75, 77, 80, 81, 88, 89, 124,
  128, 129, 130, 132, 149, 155, **163**, 163, 164,
  168, 172, 175, 208, 211, **218**, 218, 219–20,
  221, 226, **240**, 240, **244**, **251**, 251, 253
Northern Pintail 37, 55, 56, 57, 69, 80, 180, 241
Northern Shoveler 37, 47, 54, 56, 57, 65, 66, 69,
  80, 83, 205, 241
Northern Wheatear 91, **98**, 99, 142, 164, 235
Norway spruce 114
Nuthatch *see* Eurasian Nuthatch

oak **11**, 11–12, **105**, 106, **110**, 225
Old Head of Kinsale (Co Cork) 191
Osprey 54
Oughter, Lough (Co Cavan) 45, 53
Ourna, Lough (Co Tipperary) 47
Ouse Washes (England) 69
Outer Ards (Co Down) 167
Ouzel *see* Ring Ouzel
Owel, Lough (Co Westmeath) 52
Owenduff-Nephin SPA (Co Mayo) 99
Owenmore River (Co Mayo) 29, 31, 35, 36,
  39, 78
Owenreagh Windfarm (Co Tyrone) **104**
Owl *see* Barn Owl; Long-eared Owl; Short-eared
  Owl; Snowy Owl; Tawny Owl
Ox Mountains (Co Mayo) 101
oyster *see* Pacific oyster
Oystercatcher **15**, 15, **16**, 21–2, 51, 139, 149, **154**,
  154, 155, 156, **158**, 158, 163, 164, 167, 168,

172, 174, 175, 176, 187, 204, 212, 215, 240,
  242, 251

Pacific oyster 22
Partridge *see* Grey Partridge
perch 38
Peregrine 22, 56, 75, 77, 85, 91, 95, **101**, 101, 135,
  136–7, 141, 155, 160, 177, 198–9, **199**, 209,
  223
Pettigo Bog SPA (Co Donegal) 116
Phalarope *see* Grey Phalarope; Red-necked
  Phalarope
Pheasant *see* Common Pheasant
Phoenix Park (Dublin) 201, 250
Pied Flycatcher 109, 110, 236, 237
Pied Wagtail 39, 40, 86, 129, 130, 133, 134, **137**,
  137, **199**, 199–200, 207
Pigeon *see* Feral Pigeon; Woodpigeon
pine marten 146
pine *see* lodgepole pine; Scots pine
Pink-footed Goose 56
Pintail *see* Northern Pintail
Pipit *see* Meadow Pipit; Rock Pipit; Tree Pipit
plaice 172
Plover *see* European Golden Plover; Great
  Ringed Plover; Grey Plover; Little Ringed
  Plover
Pochard *see* Common Pochard
Poland 23, 254
Pollardstown Fen (Co Kildare) 79–80
Pomarine Skua 191, **192**, 192, 193
pondweed 66; *see also* broad-leaved pondweed
Portaferry (Co Down) 212
Portmarnock (Co Dublin) 156
Portmore Lough (Co Antrim) 50, **71**, 72, 84
Portrane Demesne (Co Dublin) 203
Portugal 168
Poulaphouca Reservoir (Co Kildare/Wicklow)
  58
Ptarmigan 92
Puffin Island (Co Kerry) 142, 145, 146, 147,
  150, 189
Puffin *see* Atlantic Puffin
purple moor-grass 90, 97
Purple Sandpiper 139, **149**, 149, 158, 212, 240,
  242
pygmy shrew 199

Quail *see* Common Quail
Quilty (Co Clare) **155**, **158**, 158

rabbit 22, 99, 101, 147, 150
ragged robbin 74
ragworm 15, 17
Rahasane Turlough (Co Galway) 56
Raheenmore Bog (Co Offaly) 76
Rail *see* Water Rail
Ram's Island (Lough Neagh) 47
rat *see* black rat; brown rat
Rathlin Island (Co Antrim) 80, 142
Raven 22, 77, 91, 101–2, **102**, 141–2, 203, 209
Raven Point (Co Wexford) 158, 159, 161
Ravernet, River (Co Antrim) 38
Razorbill **vi**, **139**, 144, 145, 147, 151, 187, 188,

189
Rea, Lough (Co Galway) 54
red fescue 150, 176
red fox 62, 71, 95, 101, 146, 155, 218, 220, 226
Red Grouse 75, 76, 77, 79, 89, 92, 94, **99**, 99–100,
  101, 103, 213, 214, 231, **242**, 242, 249
Red Kite 215, **253**, 253, 255
Red Knot **16**, 149, 167, 168, 172, 177, 241
Red-breasted Merganser 38, 48, 49, 57, 178, 206,
  215
Redcross (Co Wicklow) **132**
Red-necked Phalarope 57, 219
Redpoll *see* Lesser Redpoll
Redshank *see* Common Redshank; Spotted
  Redshank
Redstart *see* Black Redstart; Common Redstart
Red-throated Diver 57–8, **58**, 59, 187, 191, 217
Redwing 15, 40, 87, 117, 130, 162, 207, **248**, 248
Ree, Lough (Co Westmeath/Longford/
  Roscommon) 45, 48, 52, 64, 66
Reed Bunting 19, **36**, 36, 40, 66, **67**, 67, 76, 77,
  78, 79, 80, **81**, 81, 85, 87, 88, 89, 111, 117, 122,
  132, 135, 160, 161
reed *see* common reed
Reed Warbler *see* Common Reed Warbler
rhododendron **116**, 116, 216, 259
Ring Ouzel 91, 99, 101, 102–3, 104, 142
Ring-billed Gull 205
Ringed Plover *see* Great Ringed Plover; Little
  Ringed Plover
Ringsend Waste Water Treatment Works
  (Dublin) **208**, 208
roach 38
Robin *see* European Robin
Rock Dove 140
Rock Island (Co Galway) 148
Rock Pipit 139, **140**, 140, 198, **212**, 212
Rockabill (Co Dublin) 22, 142, 148, 149, 151,
  228–9, 231
Rogerstown Estuary (Co Dublin) 159, 167
Rook 21, 76, 77, 79, **126**, 126, 128, 129, 130, 133,
  134, 137, 155, 204, 207, **211**, 211, 248, **249**,
  249, 250, 257
rose *see* burnet rose
Roseate Tern 148, 150, 151, 157, 176, 179, 214,
  228, 228–9
Rosses Point (Co Sligo) 158, 159
Rostaff Turlough (Co Mayo) 56
rowan 106, 117
Royal Canal 25, 41–3, 203
Ruddy Duck 49, 83, 258
Ruddy Turnstone 56, 139, 149, **153**, **155**, 155,
  156, 158, 187, 212, 215, 240, 242
Ruff 38, 56, 70
rush *see* common spike rush; jointed rush; sea
  rush; soft rush
Russia 54, 168, 180, 253
rye-grass 70, 126, 131

Sabine's Gull 157, 192, 193
sallow 87
salmon 38
saltmarsh grass *see* common saltmarsh grass
sand eel **vi**, 155, 172, 185

Sand Martin **36**, 37, 39, 41, 85, 86, 134, 180, 202, **210**, 210, 214, 235, 249
Sanderling **6**, 6, 149, **151**, 155, **157**, 157, 158, 240
Sandpiper *see* Common Sandpiper; Curlew Sandpiper; Green Sandpiper; Purple Sandpiper
Sandwich Tern 51, 143, 148, 150, 154, 155, 157, 170, 179
Sandymount Strand (Dublin Bay) 21, 157
Santry Park (Dublin) 202
Savi's Warbler 84
saw sedge 75, 220
Scandinavia 88, 102, 168, 180
Scannive, Lough (Co Galway) 50
Scariff Island (Co Kerry) 147, 150
Scaup *see* Greater Scaup
Scoter *see* Common Scoter
Scotland 4, 30, 48, 93–4, 99, 100, 101, 103, 119, 140, 150, 151, 153, 158, 163, 164, 168, 190, 236; *see also* Britain
Scots pine 202
Scragh Bog (Co Westmeath) **78**, 78–80
scurvygrass *see* common scurvygrass
sea arrow grass 176
sea aster 176
sea bindweed 159
sea buckthorn 159–60, 161, 162, 165
sea holly 159
sea lavender 175
sea lettuce 174
sea milkwort 176
sea plantain 176
sea purslane 176
sea rush 176
sea spurge 159
seablite *see* annual seablite
sea-spurry 176
sedge *see* brown sedge; deer sedge; saw sedge; white-beaked sedge
Sedge Warbler 19, **39**, 39–40, 43, 66, **67**, 67, 76, 77, 79, 80, 81, 82, 83, **85**, 85, 88, 89, 112, 122, 209, 235
Shag 22, **144**, 144, 151, 187, 188
Shannon Airport Lagoon (Co Clare) 208–9
Shannon Callows 62, 63, 64–5, 66, 67, 68–9, 71–2, 127, 163, 216, 218–19
Shannon Estuary 167, 171, 173, 178, 243
Shannon, River 24, 27, 64
Sharavogue Bog (Co Offaly) 75, 77
Shearwater *see* Balearic Shearwater; Cory's Shearwater; Great Shearwater; Manx Shearwater; Sooty Shearwater
sheep 91, 93–4, 99, 100, 101, 102, 227
Sheephaven Bay (Co Donegal) 156
Shelduck *see* Common Shelduck
Shenick Island (Co Dublin) 143
Sheskinmore (Co Donegal) 161
Shimna River (Co Down) 38
Short-eared Owl 22, 85, 95, **97**, 97, **162**, 162, 177
Short-toed Treecreeper 120
Shoveler *see* Northern Shoveler
shrew *see* greater white-toothed shrew; pygmy shrew
Silent Valley Reservoir (Co Down) 59

Sir Thomas and Lady Dixon Park (Belfast) 202
Siskin 40, 80, 108, 114, 122, 207
Sitka spruce 21, 107, 113, 114, 117
Skellig Michael (Co Kerry) 138, 140, 143, 145, **147**, 147, 150, 189, 190
Skerries (Co Dublin) 200
Skua *see* Arctic Skua; Great Skua; Long-tailed Skua; Pomarine Skua
Skylark 18, 21, 22, 66, 75, 76–8, **78**, 79, 80, 88, 89, 92, 96, 98, 122, 124, 129, 130, 131, 132, **160**, 160, 161, 164, 176, 211, 249, **255**, 255, 256, 257
Slaney, River (Co Wicklow/Carlow/Wexford) 24
Slea Head (Co Kerry) 141
Slieve Aughty Mountains (Co Clare) 96
Slieve Beagh (Co Fermanagh/Monaghan/Tyrone) 58, 96, **223**, 223
Slieve Fyagh plateau (Co Mayo) 94
Slieve League (Co Donegal) 138, 142
Slieve Mish Mountains (Co Kerry) 93
Slieve Tooey (Co Donegal) **102**, 141, 142
Sligo Bay 156, 159, 171, 173, 212
Sligo town 198
slug 126
Slyne Head (Co Galway) 148
Smew 205, 206
smooth meadow grass 150
Snipe *see* Common Snipe; Jack Snipe
Snow Bunting 92, 94, 177, 252
Snowy Owl 100
soft rush 142
Song Thrush 2, 19, 77, 87, 122, 125, 130, 133, 134, 162, 200, 202, 207, 250, 254, 256
Sooty Shearwater 183, 186, 190, **191**, 191, 255
South Africa 188
South America 188
Southern Roscommon Lakes 52, 54
Spain 49, 102, 168
Sparrow *see* House Sparrow; Tree Sparrow
Sparrowhawk 80, 85, **108**, 108, 122, 162, 177, 201, 202, 203, 204, 207
spike rush *see* common spike rush
Spotted Crake 83, 219
Spotted Flycatcher 111, 134, 203, **250**, 250
Spotted Redshank 56
sprat 155, 172, 185
spruce *see* Norway spruce; Sitka Spruce
St Anne's Park (Dublin) 202
St Enda's Park (Dublin) 202
St John's River (Waterford) 206
St John's Wood (Co Roscommon) 106
St Patrick's Island (Co Dublin) 146
Stacks Mountains (Co Kerry) 96
Stags of Broadhaven (Co Mayo) 147, 190
Starling *see* Common Starling
stoat 146, 155
Stock Dove 132, 134, 142, 254
Stonechat 19, 21, 66, 76, 77, 79, 80, **97**, 97–8, 111, 112, 122, 134, 160, 161, 251, 255
stonecrop 159
Storm Petrel *see* European Storm Petrel; Leach's Storm Petrel; Madeiran Storm Petrel; Wilson's Storm Petrel
Strangford Lough (Co Down) 153, 154, 158,

167, 170, 171, 173, 175, 177, 178–9
Strangford village (Co Down) 231
Streedagh (Co Sligo) 158
Suck, River 69
Suir, River 24, 206
Swallow *see* Barn Swallow
Swan *see* Bewick's Swan; Mute Swan; Whooper Swan
sweet grass *see* floating sweet grass
Swift *see* Common Swift
Swilly, Lough (Co Donegal) 127, 167, 170, **171**, 173, 178
Sybil Point (Co Kerry) 141
sycamore 159, 161, 225

Tacumshin Lake (Co Wexford) 167, 170, 176, 179, 180
Tarnbrook Fell (Lancashire) 50
Tawny Owl 4, 253
Teal *see* Common Teal
Termon North (Co Galway) 57
Termoncarragh Lake (Co Mayo) 165
Tern Island (Wexford Harbour) 160
Tern *see* Arctic Tern; Black Tern; Common Tern; Little Tern; Roseate Tern; Sandwich Tern
Thayer's Gull 205
thrift 140
Thrush *see* Mistle Thrush; Song Thrush
Thulla (Co Dublin) 146
Thurles (Co Tipperary) 208
Timoleague (Co Cork) **176**
Tit *see* Blue Tit; Coal Tit; Crested Tit; Great Tit; Long-tailed Tit; Marsh Tit; Willow Tit
Tolka Valley Park (Co Dublin) 205
Tolka, River 203
Tollymore Forest Park (Co Down) 38
Tomnafinnogue (Co Wicklow) 106
Tory Island (Co Donegal) 140
Tralee Bay (Co Kerry) 156, 167, 171, 173, 178
Tramore (Co Waterford) 156, 160, 161
Tramore Bay (Co Waterford) 156, 159
Trawbreaga Bay (Co Donegal) **159**
tree mallow 229
Tree Pipit 120
Tree Sparrow 40, **203**, **250**
Treecreeper *see* Eurasian Treecreeper; Short-toed Treecreeper
Tufted Duck 36, 37, 40, 41, 47, **49**, 49, 52, 53, 54, 55, 56, 57, 59, 65, **66**, 66, 80, 81, 202, 203, 205, 206, 216
Turloughcor (Co Mayo) 57
Turnstone *see* Ruddy Turnstone
Turraun Cutaway Bog (Co Offaly) 80–81
Twite 97, 125, 177, 241, 251
Tymon Park (Dublin) 204–5

Ulster Canal 25
United Kingdom *see* Britain

Valentia Island (Co Kerry) 141, 209
Vee, the (Co Waterford) 116
vole *see* bank vole

Wagtail *see* Grey Wagtail; Pied Wagtail

Wales 4, 29, 30, 32, 39, 40, 42, 49, 65, 93, 119, 142, 147, 150, 151, 196; *see also* Britain
Warbler *see* Cetti's Warbler; Common Grasshopper Warbler; Common Reed Warbler; Garden Warbler; Savi's Warbler; Sedge Warbler; Willow Warbler; Wood Warbler
water crowfoot 42
Water Rail 38, 40, 66, 80, 82, **83**, 83, 87, 88, 209
Waterford City 197, 198, 199, 202, 206
Waterford Harbour 171
Waxwing *see* Bohemian Waxwing
Wexford Harbour 156, 159, 160, 167, 171, 228, 243
Wexford Slobs 100, 167, 170, 215, 217, 227–8
Wexford Wildfowl Reserve **126**, 126, **227**, 227
Wheatear *see* Northern Wheatear
Whiddy Island (Co Cork) 22
Whimbrel *see* Eurasian Whimbrel
Whinchat **21**, 21, 66, 80, 99, 219, 235
white clover 70, 131, 150
White Park Bay (Co Antrim) 156
white-beaked sedge 78
White-fronted Goose *see* Greater White-fronted Goose
White-headed Duck 49
White-tailed Eagle 104, 141, 255

Whitethroat *see* Common Whitethroat; Lesser Whitethroat
white-toothed shrew *see* greater white-toothed shrew
whiting 185
Whooper Swan 18, 37, 48, **53**, 55, 56, 58, **61**, 69, **70**, 70–71, 80, 126–7, 167, 168, 170, 172, 177, 179, 216, **221**, 221, **236**, 236, 253
Wicklow Head 148
Wicklow Mountains 101
Wicklow town **23**
Wigeon *see* Eurasian Wigeon
willow 74, 80, 81, 97, 106, 117; *see also* creeping willow
Willow Grouse 103
Willow Ptarmigan *see* Red Grouse
Willow Tit 108, 109, 120, 254
Willow Warbler 40, 43, 66, 76, 77, 79, 80, 81, 88, 112, **119**, 122, 134, **161**, 161, 202, 235, 236
Wilson's Storm Petrel 183, 191, 255
wood mouse 199
Wood Sandpiper 88
Wood Warbler 19, 108, 109, 110, 203
Woodcock **109**, 207
Woodlark 120
Woodpecker *see* Great Spotted Woodpecker;

Green Woodpecker; Lesser Spotted Woodpecker; Middle Spotted Woodpecker
Woodpigeon 76, 79, 80, 101, 117, 122, 130, **131**, 131, 134, 207, 249
woodrush 103
woolly fringe moss 93
Wren 2, 16, 19, 22, 33, 43, 67, 75, 76, 77, 79, 80, 81, 88, **111**, 111, 116, 122, 132, 133, 134, 139, 140, 160, 161, 200, 202, 204, 207, 250, 254

Yellowhammer 124, 128, **129**, 129, 130, 132, 133, 135, 137, **215**, 215, 254
Yellow-legged Gull 157
yew 106, 108, 113–14
Youghal (Co Cork) 210
Youghal Harbour (Co Cork) 156, 171

zebra mussel 54